By Julia Sweig

Lady Bird Johnson: Hiding in Plain Sight

Cuba: What Everyone Needs to Know

Friendly Fire: Losing Friends and Making Enemies in the Anti-American Century

Inside the Cuban Revolution: Fidel Castro and the Urban Underground

Lady Bird Johnson
Hiding in Plain Sight

Lady Bird Johnson
Hiding in Plain Sight

Julia Sweig

Random House | New York

Published in the United States by Random House,
an imprint and division of Penguin Random House LLC, New York.

RANDOM HOUSE and the HOUSE colophon are registered trademarks of
Penguin Random House LLC.

Library of Congress Cataloging-in-Publication Data
Names: Sweig, Julia, author.
Title: Lady Bird Johnson: Hiding in plain sight / Julia Sweig.
Description: First edition. | New York: Random House, [2020] | Includes
bibliographical references and index.
Identifiers: LCCN 2020001666 (print) | LCCN 2020001667 (ebook) |
ISBN 9780812995909 (hardback) | ISBN 9780812995916 (Ebook)
Subjects: LCSH: Johnson, Lady Bird, 1912–2007. | Presidents'
spouses—United States—Biography. | Johnson, Lyndon B. (Lyndon Baines),
1908–1973. | Presidents—United States—Election—1964. | United
States—Politics and government—1963–1969.
Classification: LCC E848.J64 S94 2020 (print) | LCC E848.J64 (ebook) |
DDC 973.923092 [B]—dc23
LC record available at https://lccn.loc.gov/2020001666
LC ebook record available at https://lccn.loc.gov/2020001667

Printed in the United States of America on acid-free paper

randomhousebooks.com

2 4 6 8 9 7 5 3 1

First Edition

Book design by Virginia Norey

To my parents, Carol Sweig and James Lawry

As ever, for Reed, Isabel, and Alexander Thompson

Contents

Lady Bird Johnson's White House Diary

Eight days after the assassination of John Fitzgerald Kennedy, and a week before she moved into the White House, Lady Bird Johnson taped the first of over 850 diary entries narrated during her White House years. The first recording describes in vivid detail her experience of November 22, 1963, "that fateful and dreadful" day in Dallas. Her final entry, dated January 31, 1969, recorded from the LBJ Ranch, recounts the prosaic terms of her adjustment to private life. In 1970, Holt Rinehart published the nearly eight-hundred-page *A White House Diary* to mixed reviews. The redacted selection of her diary represented just a fraction of the 1,750,000 words she recorded during the 1,886 days of Lyndon Baines Johnson's presidency.

Six years after her death in 2007, the LBJ Presidential Library began the public release of the diary recordings and transcripts, in almost entirely unredacted form. Listening to and reading the contemporaneous accounts of her White House years, one finds in Lady Bird Johnson a prodigiously disciplined participant, actor, and witness to and student of history. Hidden within the sheer scale and, at times, overwhelming detail of the diary are golden nuggets of insight about her husband and herself, the marriage they created, and the ambitions animating the presidency they together crafted. Similarly rewarding and surprising are the elegant word pictures from her nature writing, her character studies of the men and women who entered and exited their world, and the riveting details of her experiences during the White House years. Like the correspondence between Abigail and John Adams, her diary is indispensable for understanding Lady Bird and Lyndon Johnson, and yet the diary's daunting scope, combined with the massive documentation from her husband's life and presidency, seems to have relegated Lady Bird and her diary if not to oblivion, then to the role of a diminished supporting actor in the sweeping narrative dominated by her husband.

Perhaps this was by design. In college, she studied journalism and history, and throughout her career as a political wife, those two skills served her well as she crafted the public record of what she called "our presidency," Lyndon Johnson's legacy and her own. She was in full command of her sources, drawing from her and her husband's daily diaries, newspaper clippings, and the voluminous documents compiled each day by her staff. Hers is a perspective not merely of a dutiful political spouse but of a fully engaged participant in many of the deepest workings of the presidency.

When Mrs. Johnson recorded the first entry in the ten days following the assassination, before she moved into the White House, she "did this primarily as a form of therapy—to help me over the shock and horror of the experience of President Kennedy's assassination," as she wrote the Warren Commission, not intending at the time she recorded it "that the tape be used."[1] But she decided that it reflected her best, most accurate recollection of the day, and thus submitted the seven-page transcript of the recording as her formal testimony in July 1964. Whether on her light-blue velvet couch in her private sitting room looking out over the magnolia tree Andrew Jackson had planted in his wife Rachel's memory, to the Washington Monument in the distance, or at her desk looking into the Rose Garden and Lyndon's office, in hotels or at the Ranch, she recorded hundreds of entries in her diary, a practice she maintained beginning with the first entry, just a few days after November 22, 1963.

* * *

It didn't take long for the exercise to become much more than a form of therapy. In the introduction to the 1970 edition of her diary, she asked and answered the question "Why did I record it?"

> I think for the following reasons: I realized shortly after November 22, that—amazed and timorously—I stood in a unique position, as wife of the President of the United States. Nobody else would live through the next months in quite the way I would and see the events unroll from this vantage point. And this certain portion of time I wanted to preserve as it happened. I wanted to remember it, and I wanted my children and grandchildren to see it through my eyes. The second reason is a difficult one to describe—it has something to do with discipline. I wanted to see if I could keep up this arduous task. In a way, I made myself a dare. And somehow if you make yourself record what went on in the day, it makes you more organized, it makes you remember things better. My third reason for recording this diary was that I like writing—fearful labor though I sometimes find it—I like words. As time passed[,] there began to emerge a fourth reason, dimly felt, something like this—I wanted to share life in this house, in these times. It was too great a thing to have alone.[2]

In his review of the edited collection, the *New York Times* book critic Christopher Lehmann-Haupt described the "huge pile of motionless material" as "personal but curiously unrevealing."[3] The diary can at times be anodyne, and yes, eye-glazing in its detail about whom Lady Bird seated where at which state dinner and the like. This is where the dutiful scribe seems to appreciate a reality that may be opaque for most readers: the way that seating arrangements at White House state dinners represent the ultimate exercise of power and prerogative. Lady Bird was adept at advancing both, even if her account can at times appear reticent. However "motionless" one reviewer may have found the diary, he surmised nevertheless that Lady Bird Johnson was "shrewd, able, and extremely likeable." How, then, is it possible for several thousand hours of recordings to be nevertheless "unrevealing"? Here, like so many of her and LBJ's biographers, Lehmann-Haupt fell for Lady Bird's very female gift, and one in dramatic contrast to her husband's tendency to overshare, at revealing her experience without revealing herself.

I have become very familiar with that talent, after having read every word of every transcript and listened to countless hours of her voice. In this act of self-representation, this record of her devotion to the policies, pageantry, and effort in easing the anguish of Lyndon's presidency, and in her openness about the emotional and physical toll it took on both of them, I think she actually revealed both her experience and herself. In making her choices about what to include and what to exclude in what she recorded, I see Lady Bird Johnson not dissembling but, rather, deliberately pointing us toward a more three-dimensional picture of a woman at the height of her power. She was someone whose public persona could often feel infuriatingly two-dimensional if one relied on the stiff portrayals of staged White House photographs, rapt hagiographies, and gendered histories of the Johnson presidency. Like her White House years themselves, during which she served her husband and his presidency while forging for herself an ambitious agenda of public service, the diary allowed the First Lady to straddle the space between telling her own through-her-eyes story and offering almost intimate access into her agency in the comingled enterprise that propelled the Johnsons through their accomplishments and failures. Their partnership shaped a presidency, for better and for worse. And it was a presidency that grappled with issues of equity, of justice, of wars within and without—issues the Johnsons brought to the fore during their five years, one month, and twenty-nine days in the White House.

Prologue

The Huntland Strategy Memo

In the spring of 1964, mounting political pressures compelled Lady Bird Johnson to trade the tensions of the White House for a few days of relative solitude away from Washington. Usually she could satisfy her need for a spell in nature by hiking in the West Texas Hill Country. But this time she fled to Huntland, a borrowed estate of occasional presidential respite in the rolling horse country of Middleburg, Virginia, about an hour's drive from the White House.

It was May 13, 1964. The two days spanning Lady Bird's arrival at her Virginia retreat and her return to Lyndon in Washington, D.C., marked a defining moment in their relationship, in their marriage, and in the Johnson presidency. They had been in the White House for just over five months. Lyndon had announced his War on Poverty but hadn't yet given his Great Society speech. He had begun the political battle in Congress to pass the Civil Rights Act, but opposition from the South, from Republicans, and from within his own party was fierce, and mounting violence against civil rights activists was lethal. That day, before a roaring crowd of eighteen thousand at Madison Square Garden, Arizona's rock-jawed senator, Barry Goldwater, the leading Republican contender for the presidency, described LBJ as a "cheerleader for a frightful game of violence, destruction and obedience" for his embrace of civil rights; Goldwater demanded "facts about how far we're willing to go to appease Communists" in Vietnam, Cuba, and the Soviet Union.[1] At the same time, Secretary of Defense Robert McNamara was making his fifth visit to Vietnam in nearly as many months, to assess whether the American ally in South

Vietnam's capital, Saigon, had the political and military wherewithal to stave off an increasingly virulent insurgency backed by the Communist nationalists in Hanoi. Rattled by what he found, McNamara was scheduled to brief the president and make his recommendations for a qualitative and quantitative jump in American military assistance the next morning, May 14.[2]

Lyndon hated Lady Bird's absences. But he understood that they were essential to her ability to sustain the energy required to be married to him. Lady Bird found solace in the countryside. "Virginia in mid-May is balm for any trouble. No *Silent Spring* here," she recorded. "The green arch of fresh spring leaves" over a country road and the vista of the Blue Ridge Mountains in the distance would help her flush from her system the political toxins of a federal city gearing up for a presidential campaign. The First Lady had invited two of the president's doctors to Huntland for dinner, to discuss Lyndon's health, mental and physical, and its bearing on his state of mind about running for his own term in office.

She could see that LBJ already felt trapped. She had watched him as he watched himself struggling but failing to reject the logic of escalation presented to him by his civilian deputies and his military brass that spring. He was unable to visualize a path out of Vietnam that would not appear to members of both parties like capitulation to communism. A targeted air war, better planes, more money, more training, more advisers—before he had even heard these recommendations from McNamara's report about Saigon's weakness and the powerful show of force from Hanoi, LBJ knew there would be no such thing as a limited war. Between the image of a deeply flawed and corrupt ally in South Vietnam barely clinging to power and the pressure from his political adversaries to step up the heat, Lyndon could already see Vietnam threatening to eclipse his ambitions for a presidency focused on repairing the cleavages of racial and economic inequality in his own country.

So, when he picked up the phone to say good night to Lady Bird before his briefings on Vietnam the next morning and Bird's meeting with his doctors, LBJ was looking ahead to the general election with the very familiar emotion that accompanied him on the eve of major decisions, this time over whether to stand for election in November: pure, unmitigated dread. Lady Bird was familiar with his dread, with the tone in his voice when he experienced it, with his need to ruminate, to explore all scenarios. That evening was no different. On the phone, they talked and talked, and Lady Bird assured him that he must run, and she explained why. But Lyndon needed to see the case spelled out in black and white, and by a person of unimpeachable trust. To him, Lady Bird possessed such standing, and he asked her to write a memo setting forth the pros and cons, as she saw them, of running in the 1964 presidential election. Lady Bird read a bit and went to sleep.

Bird's dinner with her husband's physicians was set for the next evening. She wanted to be in on the discussion about the findings by Lyndon's cardiologist and personal physician without having to sit through a White House meeting as opinions about the president's fitness were bandied about. She especially wanted to preempt Lyndon's likely attempt to elicit some sort of cautionary doctor's note, using his health as an excuse not to run.[3] With LBJ's doctors all to herself in Virginia, after dinner the First Lady guided the conversation to the "psychological aspects" of "Lyndon's problems"—by which she meant that however miserable the president felt at the moment, "inaction, idleness, lack of command, would be a harder role for him than the long hours and heavy responsibility he now shoulders."[4] The two doctors concurred and agreed to call Lady Bird the next day after examining Lyndon. It was not the first and would not be the last instance when the First Lady sought out LBJ's doctors to probe their views about her husband's readiness to run. But as much as they seemed to understand the internal dynamics animating the president, what they could not see, and what she did not share, was her own doubt about the threat of Vietnam. "I don't know, though, that either one really understands the depth of his pain, when and if he faces up to the possibility of sending many thousands American boys to Viet Nam."[5] The conflict in Southeast Asia had already filtered into Lady Bird's diary, and this reference indicates how the realities of the war had become both a symbol and the emotional fact of his, and their, vision of his presidency.

When she sat down to write her memo for Lyndon with her analysis of his options, Lady Bird marshaled all her gifts as a media-savvy wife, confidante, career and business partner, and political adviser. And she did so as perhaps the only person with full knowledge of her husband's greatest strengths, weaknesses, ambition, and ambivalence—and, crucially, with his complete trust. As important, she was able to distill what each of them needed as individuals and for the well-being of their marriage as it entered its fourth decade. In essence, Lady Bird Johnson's Huntland strategy memo allowed her husband to choose the degree of pain he felt he could endure based on the choices she set forth. She started off by providing him with a draft announcement of his resignation, one she later dictated into her recorder with the tone and authority of a newscast—a shrewd starting point, because the statement forced her husband to digest at the outset the potent emotional impact of taking such a radical step. Her voice clipped and authoritative, she read:

> I wish now to announce that I will not be a candidate for re-election. I wish to spend the rest of my life in my home state, in peace with my family, for whom the rigors of my duties have left me too little time for companionship. This decision is made easier by the fact that I can feel my conduct of the Presidency, which came in such a tragic hour of national rending, has not been without some solid accomplishment, thanks to the Grace of God, and the sturdy cooperation of the American people.

She sighed into the recorder and quickly added, "I hope he won't use it. That's that!"[6] She then outlined the president's options as he looked forward to the 1964 election, as well as her perception of their consequences. First, she set forth the likely outcomes should he decline to run in November:

I. If you do get out we will most probably return to the ranch to live.

1. In the course of the next few months—or until we are forgotten—we will be criticized and our motives questioned—"what skeleton in the closet"—what fear of what disclosure—caused you to make this decision? etc. etc.

   That will be painful.

2. There will be a wave of feeling, national this time and not largely state wide—of "you let us down"—even bitter, disappointment—similar to the wave of feeling after you accepted the Vice Presidency job with Kennedy.

   This will be more painful.

3. You may live longer, and certainly you will have more time for the Hill Country you love and for me and Lynda and Lucy. And that we'll all love!

   But Lynda and Lucy will in a year or so cease to be permanent residents of our life—only available for occasional companionship.

4. You will have various ranch lands, small banking interests, and presumably the TV to use up your talents and your hours.

They are chicken feed compared to what you are used to.

That may be relaxing—for a while. I think it is not enough for you at 56. And I dread seeing you semi-idle, frustrated looking back at what you left.

I dread seeing you look at Mr X running the country and thinking you could have done it better.

You may look around for a scape-goat. I do not want to be it.

You may drink too much for lack of a higher calling.[7]

And over the phone with Lyndon and in her diary, she posited the excruciating question: Having walked away from a run at becoming president of the United States as a result of an electoral mandate rather than an assassination, would living longer even be worth it? Only the intimacy of the many decades of marriage and political partnership could safely allow for such an unvarnished expression of the truth.

Setting forth what to anticipate should he run for the presidency and emerge the victor, the second part of the memo contained her answer:

> II. If you do *not* get out you will most probably be elected President.
>
> 1. In the course of the campaign and in the ensuing years, you—and I—and the children—will certainly get criticized and cut up for things that we have done, or maybe partly-in-a-way have done, and for others that we never did at all.
>
> That will be painful.
>
> 2. You are bound to make some bad decisions, be unable to achieve some high vaulting ambitions, be disappointed at the inadequacies of helpers—or perhaps on your own.
>
> That will be painful even more.
>
> 3. You may die earlier than you would otherwise. Nobody can tell that—as the last 6 months show maybe Dr. Cain & Dr. Hurst can be helpful in advising here.
>
> My Conclusion
>
> Stay in.
>
> Realize it's going to be rough—but remember we worry much in advance about troubles that never happen!
> Pace yourself, within the limits of your personality.
> If you lose in November—it's all settled anyway![8]

Then Lady Bird gave her husband a point in time after which he might safely unburden himself and embark upon his post-presidential years with a feeling of satisfaction, rather than regret over roads not taken. "If you win," she concluded, "let's do the best we can for three years and three or four months." Why such specificity? "And then, the Lord letting us live that long, announce in Feb. or Mar., 1968 that you are not a candidate for re-election."[9] Without knowing exactly how Vietnam or Martin Luther King or Eugene McCarthy or Bobby Kennedy or urban riots or massive protests would rock LBJ's presidency, barely six months out from JFK's assassination, Lady Bird Johnson projected that by February or March 1968, Lyndon Johnson might well walk away from the American presidency.

With Lyndon turning a "mellow 60" by the end of that term, she wrote, "I believe the juices of life will be stilled enough to let you come home in relative peace and acceptance. (We may even have grand-children!)." She signed what was both a strategy memo and a love letter "Your Loving Wife."[10] She gave the memo, sealed in an envelope marked "Personal, please," to the doctors and sent them back to Washington with instructions to deliver it to Lyndon.[11] And of course, it was personal. But in its structure, argument, and conclusion, it was also far more than a private note from one spouse to the other. It stands out as a political strategy document that would set the course for the arc of the Johnson presidency.

There was nothing about the president's day—a staff meeting, a Vietnam briefing, a congressional lunch, a congressional funeral, and a late-night appearance at a party for Justice William Douglas, all on barely four hours' sleep—that had altered his frame of mind about the future when a "lonesome-sounding Lyndon" called Bird after midnight the next day. Theirs "was a sad-happy talk," Lady Bird recorded, about her own troubles and "about his restive desires to seek a way out of the burdens he carries."[12] We don't know exactly when Lyndon read the content of the sealed envelope. Nonetheless, over the course of the spring and summer of 1964, neither the ambition of the Great Society, the passage of the Civil Rights Act, nor his wife's arguments in favor immediately helped clarify his decision to run in the fall of that year. That would require Lady Bird to do battle with yet another round of dread and paralysis a few months later.

But the strategy outlined in the Huntland options memo did make a lasting, indelible impression. Three years, ten months, and eighteen days later, on March 31, 1968, Lyndon Johnson concluded a televised address billed as a major statement on Vietnam with the surprise announcement that he would not run for a second term of office.[13] Save for a few staffers, whom he and Lady Bird had sworn to secrecy to help them wordsmith his statement, LBJ's decision to stay out of the 1968 race shocked his own White House, the national press corps, his many political adversaries of both parties, and Americans across the country. Only Lyndon and Lady Bird knew that in arguing the case for him to stay and run in the 1964 election, the woman born Claudia Alta Taylor had also given him, given *them*, the very time line and exit strategy that, from the "depth of his pain," Lyndon Baines Johnson would ultimately follow.

Very quickly, the explanations for his decision congealed around the most apparent factors that by March 1968 had so severely weakened his presidency: Vietnam, where bombing and body bags had riven the body politic and thwarted LBJ's ambitions for domestic renewal; Eugene McCarthy, whose loss by just eight points to the sitting president earlier that month in the New Hampshire primary had nevertheless signaled a precarious path to the nomination for Johnson; and Bobby Kennedy, whose entrance into the race a few days after McCarthy's strong showing had in any case been anticipated by the Johnsons for years. The immense historiography of the richly documented Johnson presidency largely repeats these explanations, albeit with more nuance, detail, or emphasis.

Yet, what almost all historians and journalists miss in writing about Lyndon Johnson and, in this instance, his decision to stand for only one term, is the weight of Lady Bird's influence within their marriage and on LBJ's presidency, and not only on his decision to run. Only a handful refer to or quote her 1964 Huntland options memo at any length, or the fact that LBJ asked her to write it at all.[14] Fewer still connect its content and time line to his March 31, 1968, announcement or to her more widely recognized role in jolting him out of his paralysis on the eve of the 1964 Democratic National Convention in Atlantic City. But her exclusion is not for lack of evidence. In 1970, Lady Bird Johnson published just snippets of the Huntland memo in a redacted, abridged selection of her White

House diary. Throughout that 783-page volume, a fraction of the full transcripts, Bird offers an ample, albeit incomplete, opening into her advisory role throughout her husband's presidency and into her role in thinking through—indeed, managing—what she described as "Lyndon's dilemma" from 1964 until the day in 1968 when he surprised the country with his decision not to run. And between 2013 and 2017, the LBJ Presidential Library completed the release to the public of the full, unedited transcripts of her diary, along with all 123 hours of their original voice recordings.

But there is one author who does credit Lady Bird Johnson for her role during this crucial moment in the Johnson presidency: LBJ himself. In his 1971 memoir, published two years before his death, the former president gave readers a far fuller view into this moment than had Lady Bird herself, reproducing the seven-page Huntland memo in its entirety. LBJ wrote that during the spring of 1964, he had shared his anxiety and doubts over running that autumn with his usual confidants in Texas; his mentor Senator Richard Russell; his closest White House aide, Walter Jenkins; and "of course, Lady Bird." Of course. "She and I went over it many times, from every view point. That spring of 1964 I asked her to summarize and put down on paper the pros and cons and her own conclusions. This was the memo she gave me on May 14, written by hand on several sheets torn from a stenographer's notebook."[15]

But despite his choice a half century ago to reproduce the entire memo, what to LBJ was an observable fact of his story, the centrality of his wife's role in his career, was to most of his biographers far from apparent—or, if apparent, generally treated as peripheral to the many other dimensions (power, war, peace, protest, policies, politics, the press, and the men who helped LBJ or got in his way) that we associate with the drama and tension of the LBJ presidency.

Perhaps because just two years after he left Washington a broken and tragic man, a memoir written by Lyndon Johnson could be digested only with a considerable degree of skepticism. And since? A photocopy of the memo has been sitting at the LBJ Presidential Library in a folder entitled "Mrs. Johnson 1964 Campaign (letters to LBJ)" since 1971, along with a rich trove of material detailing her own prodigious tenure in the White House well beyond the role of Lyndon's personal confidante. Since the day she walked into the Executive Mansion, Lady Bird Johnson made an array of conscious choices intended to document and shape the Lyndon Johnson legacy. In the decades following LBJ's death, she gave many interviews to that end—some about Lyndon, some about her own work during the White House years. In 1997, after she authorized the director of the LBJ Library to release the White House tapes, she severed her involvement with one biographer, writing her that "Your conclusion about me may well come at Lyndon's expense," not only for the biographer's focus on LBJ's infidelities she implied, but for failing to recognize that "There is no way to separate us and our role in each other's lives."[16]

How have so many observers missed this essential truth? It might be understood by how Lady Bird made conscious and unconscious decisions to conceal her own power while deliberately leaving behind vast documentary evidence to reveal it. Perhaps it has just been impossible to consider the disarmingly modern nature of Lady Bird and Lyndon's partnership, easier to accept certain gendered, clichéd assumptions, dressed as their relationship was, by instinct and design, in so many midcentury, southern, Texan accents. Or perhaps the story of LBJ is itself so enormous, and the source material so vast, that the question of Lady Bird's role and influence has very seldom been asked—or, if asked, rarely answered. Hiding in plain sight for so many years, the Huntland strategy memo, like her White House diary, tells a surprising story, one that Lady Bird Johnson purposely left behind for future historians to write.[17] When that story is pieced together, Claudia Taylor Johnson emerges with dimensions and complexity matched only by her husband, the thirty-sixth president of the United States.

Act I

August 1960–January 1965

Chapter 1

The Surrogate

Neither the fanatics nor the faint-hearted are needed. And our duty as a party is not to our party alone, but to the nation, and indeed to all mankind. Our duty is not merely the preservation of political power but the preservation of peace and freedom.

So let us not be petty when our cause is so great, let us not quarrel amongst ourselves when our nation's future is at stake.

—John F. Kennedy, speech to have been delivered in Austin, Texas, November 24, 1963

When he came to the White House, suddenly everyone saw what the New Frontier was going to mean.

It meant a poet at the Inauguration; it meant swooping around Washington, dropping in on delighted and flustered old friends; it meant going to the airport in zero weather without an overcoat; it meant a rocking chair and having the Hickory Hill seminar at the White House when Bobby and Ethel were out of town; it meant fun at presidential press conferences.

It meant dash, glamour, glitter, charm. It meant a new era of enlightenment and verve; it meant Nobel Prize winners dancing in the lobby; it meant authors and actors and poets and Shakespeare in the East Room.

—Mary McGrory, *The Evening Star*, November 24, 1963

Claudia Taylor Johnson drew her initial impression of Jacqueline Bouvier Kennedy not from a luncheon for spouses or an evening social event in Washington, but rather, from Jack and Jackie's 1953 *Life* magazine wedding pictures. Jackie, she thought, was "absolutely the essence of romance and beauty."[1] When the newlywed Kennedys moved to Washington, real life, as it turned out, was even more remarkable than the photos. As a freshman senator's wife, Jackie was "a bird of beautiful plumage" who "couldn't have been more gracious." By comparison, Bird felt, she and the other Senate wives were "little gray wrens."[2] When the Kennedys married and Jack began his first term in the Senate, the Johnsons had already been in that chamber for four years. In the Washington, D.C., of the 1950s, the Johnsons and the Kennedys were not personally close. They didn't run in the same social circles. In fact, by the 1956 Democratic convention, Jack and Lyndon had become quasi-overt rivals. Elected Senate majority leader in 1955 and approaching the peak of his power in Congress, LBJ conveyed his standing to Lady Bird, who ruled the roost of Senate wives. Despite the differences between their husbands, Bird graciously inducted Jackie into the carefully choreographed courtlike world of Washington spouses, hosting her at their brick Colonial on 30th Place, Northwest, and otherwise brushing up against her youth and glamour throughout the decade. Finding Jackie impossibly young, Lady Bird worked to put her at ease at these spouse gatherings; Jackie liked Lady Bird and made a point of connecting with the Johnsons' elder daughter, Lynda, just eleven when they first met. But Washington was not entirely new to Jackie: At fourteen, she'd moved with her mother and her mother's new husband to an estate in Virginia's hunt country. She briefly attended the private girls' school Holton-Arms, and she finished her undergraduate degree at George Washington University before marrying Jack.

An accomplished equestrian, Jackie summered in the Hamptons and Newport; had studied at Miss Porter's School, Vassar, and the Sorbonne; and spoke French and Spanish. Lady Bird had studied French, briefly, and her Spanish was still limited to what she had picked up during her childhood in Texas. Jackie was twenty-three years old, Bird's age when Lyndon had already served for two years in the House. While Bird worked assiduously to grease the wheels of Lyndon's political office with endless socializing, charity events, and travel back and forth to and across Texas, Jackie struck Bird as being uninterested in the tedium of the game, content to spend her early years married to Jack as a society photographer for the *Washington Times-Herald,* taking a course in American history at Georgetown, or repairing to Hickory Hill, the country house in McLean, Virginia, that the newlyweds had purchased and later gave to Bobby and Ethel. Even if outward the cultural signs of their differences were rife, inward, the parallels between Lady Bird and Jackie ran deep. Each had made her mark in Washington as the young, newlywed wife of a young, ambitious husband. Both soon had to contend with their husbands' infidelities and the humiliation of knowing that their own political and social circles knew of and, indeed, often facilitated the behavior. Miscarriage after miscarriage plagued their quest for offspring. And by 1960, both had husbands for whom serious illness made the prospect of death loom large—Addison's disease dogged JFK throughout his adult life; depression, heart disease, and other itinerant maladies afflicted Lyndon. Both their husbands smoked and drank too much. Yet, it was not until the 1960 campaign that Jackie and Lady Bird had real occasion to fully evaluate each other. By pairing their husbands on a surprise presidential ticket, the party convention that summer in Los Angeles forced upon the two women a rapid, at times uncomfortable bond, but one that eventually grew into a lifelong empathy and unexpected intimacy.

* * *

Neither Lyndon nor Lady Bird went to the 1960 Los Angeles convention with the ambition of landing the vice-presidential slot. Having turned down Joe Kennedy's earlier offer to finance an LBJ-JFK ticket in 1956, Lyndon had instead delivered the Texas delegation for JFK's own failed bid for the vice presidency during the Democratic National Convention in Chicago that year—former Illinois governor Adlai Stevenson was the presidential nominee—on the surface a magnanimous gesture, but one unambiguously intended to telegraph to the young senator and his family that LBJ had the power to act as kingmaker within the party. But by the end of the decade, Joe, Jack, and Bobby made their play to build a national profile and organization to elect Jack to the White House. By 1960, much to the Kennedy clan's distaste, they needed LBJ, for his regional roots and political chops. In assessing his own prospects for a presidential run, Johnson remained clear-eyed that while as majority leader he could organize massive support in the U.S. Senate, his leverage in Congress would not automatically translate into the national stature necessary for a successful presidential run. After working as a congressional staffer and then running a New Deal youth employment program in Austin, he won his first House seat in a special election in 1937 with ten thousand dollars in financing from Lady Bird's inheritance. He went on to win it handily, and mostly unopposed, in 1938, 1940, 1942, 1944, and 1946. He lost a bid for the Senate in 1941, and in 1948 he authorized a fraudulent voting operation to secure victory against a primary opponent, winning by just 87 votes, before winning in the general election that year.[3]

Ambivalence, the prospect of loss, the suggestion of illegitimacy—these were constant themes in Lyndon Johnson's political career. From Lady Bird's perspective when it came to national office, her husband had been "deeply uncertain about his ability, his health, his being a southerner, whether that was a good thing for him to do."[4] Yet, by the end of 1959, Lyndon, she recalled, had about "sucked the orange dry" from his tenure as Senate majority leader.[5] "We were reaching a point of no return, a certain defining of pathways" leading toward a presidential bid for Lyndon.[6] Despite his mentor Congressman Sam Rayburn and his longtime aide, future Texas governor John Connally, pushing LBJ to publicize his campaign for the top of the ticket more aggressively, Lady Bird's husband had instead run an undeclared, ambivalent campaign in 1960. Bird had been at her dying father's bedside in a hospital in Marshall, Texas, a trip she would make five times that year, when what she knew to be a halfhearted Lyndon finally announced his candidacy just three days before the kickoff of the 1960 convention in Los Angeles. By then, Bobby Kennedy's national strategy for his brother's campaign enabled JFK to trounce LBJ by more than double in the first delegate ballot. The night after the bruising defeat, Lady Bird and Lyndon treated themselves to "the best night's sleep we'd both had in a long time."[7] But the defeat was a humiliation, and only the first.

But by 1960, she had become a reliable part of his political operation. At the convention, she established a permanent presence in the Johnson suite on the seventh floor of the Biltmore Hotel, fielding interviews with the female press corps and accompanying Lyndon through the wrenching drama that resulted in their accepting the vice-presidential slot on the ticket. After dominating the Senate and wielding legislative and political power as majority leader far greater than his predecessors', "to assume a new role as number two man" didn't suit Lyndon, Bird thought. "The people of the state of Texas would think we'd deserted them, that we'd walked out on them. They would be hurt and angry. So I really didn't want him to" accept the offer from Kennedy.[8] In what would be one of many counseling sessions to come, Bird laid out for her husband the argument against accepting the vice-presidential slot. Turning down Kennedy's unsolicited and unwanted offer would leave Lyndon possibly more politically neutered than remaining in the Senate—a rubber-stamp majority leader rather than a powerful policy mastermind. Yet, accepting the offer might provide a convenient route for the Kennedys to bring Lyndon under their direct control. Jackie agreed. She later told one historian that Jack had to "have Lyndon as his running mate—to annul him as Majority Leader because here this man with this enormous ego [who] would have been just enraged and blocking Jack in every way."[9] But Bird also told LBJ, as she would with all major career decisions, that this was "his life, his job, his career." She "wouldn't dare try to persuade him" otherwise—at least not while he was climbing to the top.[10] Holed up in the Biltmore suite during the convention, Bird participated in the marathon consultations with Lyndon and his advisers. Within a span of a little more than twenty-four hours, her perfectly attuned analysis of the downside for Lyndon of accepting the vice presidency ultimately yielded to the logic and momentum of the moment. While she "had no hunger for the job" of the presidency and wanted to "stand and object," on July 15, 1960, she stood beside her husband as he told a throng of reporters that he would accept the number two spot.[11] Later that day, when she saw DNC chair Scoop Jackson appear on television to announce LBJ's selection as VP, Lady Bird burst out crying. It was an act, according to Nancy

Dickerson, the only female network journalist covering the convention, "unheard of for this disciplined and controlled woman."[12]

* * *

Sharing their physical space—that's how it all started. After a brief and difficult return to Texas following the convention, the Johnsons flew to Cape Cod to plan the fall 1960 campaign against the Nixon-Lodge ticket. Now it was Jackie's turn to put Lady Bird at ease. The night the Johnsons arrived, the Kennedys cleared out their bedroom closets and drawers, leaving "no trace of anybody's toothbrush anywhere," and slept in a single bed in a tiny guest room, so that the Johnsons wouldn't know they were sleeping in the Kennedy's bedroom or otherwise feel they had imposed upon them. With the Johnsons' arrival at eleven P.M., lobster, Bird's favorite, was offered though declined: too late in the evening for such a rich meal.[13]

Chatting before they went to sleep, Jackie learned that rather than "resting up since that madhouse" in Los Angeles, Mrs. Johnson had spent the interregnum back at the Ranch writing thank-you notes to every single Texas friend and constituent who had cheered them on.[14] Bird, of course, left out the fact that the mood on the return trip from the convention to the Ranch had felt "like a wake."[15] Six months pregnant at the time, Jackie had not attended the convention, and Bird found her unsettled by exactly how she might help Jack with the presidential campaign. Surveying the Hyannis home filled with Cape Cod curios, images of sailboats, and fashionable floral drapes, Bird tried to comfort the very private Jackie, suggesting she help her husband's campaign by inviting journalists to see the house and talk about something that seldom interested Bird: home décor. With this suggestion, Bird, now a seasoned campaigner, gave Jackie a way to manage her delicate pregnancy after two miscarriages and feel politically useful to her husband. She also gave her a platform and context for projecting her public image.[16]

Unlike Lyndon, Lady Bird didn't feel uncomfortably subordinate to the new and very young spouse of the "next gen" presidential candidate. She felt free to give advice—freed by her own political experience and also by the vast distance between their two worlds, she the country girl, and Jackie the savvy, cosmopolitan, multilingual Francophile. Bird, though, was also "the daughter of the biggest man in our village, in our county in East Texas."[17] Status in East Texas, Bird understood, was not so different from status on a national scale, and it gave her the confidence to comport herself, just a year shy of fifty, as the thirty-one-year-old Jackie's equal, if not equivalent. She also felt capable of understanding the dynastic ways of the Kennedy family. She was particularly impressed by how Rose Kennedy, the matriarch of the clan, asserted "her own particular sort of indomitable strength" even as Joe Kennedy, JFK's father and political counsel, "appeared to me then and always . . . as being a pretty strong dominant autocrat." Indeed, Bird (correctly) credited Joe with having pressed Jack to choose Lyndon over Adlai Stevenson or Stu Symington in order to beat Nixon in the South.[18] Yet, the move to the diminished vice-presidential slot on the 1960 Democratic ticket still felt "like trying to swallow a nettle: hurt, sticky, spiny," to the maybe-Second-Lady-to-be. But in Hyannis, on the first of many trips to New England, Bird swallowed the nettle, if not the lobster, and prepared herself for a rapid pivot onto the campaign trail.[19]

The next day, the two campaign teams met in the Hyannis compound's equivalent of the big house, Rose and Joe Kennedy's larger home, first privately and then for a press gaggle. The main house was the focal point of a sprawling six-acre estate on Nantucket Sound. Television clips from the press briefing highlight the awkward pairing between Boston and Austin. In one video, Lyndon and Jack position themselves at one end of the living room. Before the press exchange starts, Lyndon takes off his ten-gallon hat and casually plops it on top of a floor lamp in the corner. Jackie bristled at Lyndon's gruff manner. And she was equally taken aback by the working relationship she observed between him and Lady Bird. Although Jackie came to speak admiringly about Lady Bird's capacity to stay plugged into Lyndon's conversations while sitting across the room from him—even as she conducted her own with Jackie and Jack's sisters—as a still-grieving widow interviewed by Arthur Schlesinger, Jr., she offered far more unvarnished observations of that first Kennedy-

Johnson campaign gathering. Whenever Lyndon spoke, Jackie told Schlesinger just months after the assassination, "Lady Bird would get out a little notebook—I've never seen a husband and a wife so—sort of like a trained hunting dog." For much of their professional partnership, Lady Bird had used small spiral notebooks to keep detailed shorthand records of the who and what of their political life.[20] But Jackie's derision at, and discomfort with, the Johnsons' meticulously comingled enterprise was palpable. "I mean she had every name, phone number—it was"—Jackie audibly shuddered—"sort of a funny kind of way of operating."[21] Alien to Jackie and mistaken as a sign of Lady Bird's subordination to Lyndon—not even a paid secretary, but a captive dog—the spiral notebooks, Jackie failed to see, represented the meticulously gathered and assembled brick and mortar of the political network the Johnsons had built together over almost three decades.

* * *

After the weekend in Hyannis, the Kennedy-Johnson ticket moved into high gear. In an unusually modern move for a midcentury presidential campaign, the Johnsons hired someone to plan Lady Bird's campaign strategy and schedule. Among Bird's Washington coterie, Liz Carpenter ranked first among all equals. Born in Salado, Texas, on September 1, 1920, Mary Elizabeth Sutherland was the third of five children born to a successful rancher who later went into the road construction business. A sixth-generation Texan, Liz claimed that one of her ancestors wrote the Texas Declaration of Independence and another died at the Alamo. When she was a teenager, her family moved to Austin, where she became the editor of her high school newspaper. She went on to study journalism at the University of Texas at Austin, where she worked for the university's newspaper, the *Daily Texan,* and served as the first female vice president of the student body.[22] At twenty-two, Liz took a trip to the nation's capital as a college graduation present, but decided to stay and work for Esther Van Wagoner Tufty ("the Duchess"), a newspaperwoman who ran the Washington news bureau for twenty-six Michigan papers.[23]

One of the first things Liz did was call on her congressman. But it was June 1942, and Congressman Lyndon Baines Johnson was somewhere in the Pacific. It was Lady Bird Johnson, therefore—without children, still relatively new to Washington, and running Lyndon's congressional office—who greeted Liz. The encounter between the two journalism majors from Texas began a political collaboration and personal friendship that would ultimately help shape a presidency.[24] Two years after she met Lady Bird, Liz married Leslie "Les" Carpenter, her high school sweetheart and a fellow journalism student at UT. The Johnsons attended their wedding at the National Cathedral. Liz soon took a job as a UPI reporter, focusing mainly on the Hill—"I was there in the glory days with Sam Rayburn as speaker and LBJ as majority leader."[25] Liz and Les soon started their own news service, and became core members of the Texans-in-Washington social circle, anchored by Lady Bird and Lyndon. In 1954, a time when women were still banned from the male-only National Press Club, Carpenter became president of the National Women's Press Club.[26] In 1960, Lady Bird called her and asked her to join the Johnson campaign staff; she was detailed to Lady Bird as her press secretary.[27]

Carpenter's strategy for Lady Bird, as with Lyndon, was to help introduce the Kennedys to the South. Bird traveled to twenty-five states in September and October—eleven of them on her own. She delivered a total of sixty-five speeches lauded as "sheer magic" by an adoring press.[28] She made sixteen joint appearances with the Kennedy women—Rose, Eunice Shriver, Patricia Lawford, and Ethel—to test the Kennedy brand in "the Bible belt" and in Texas, including Houston, Dallas, Wichita Falls, Midland-Odessa, El Paso, and Stonewall, site of the LBJ Ranch. Despite spraining her ankle on the way to one event, Lady Bird fought through the pain to greet nearly five thousand people at the Shamrock Hotel in Houston. During these solo trips, she would regularly update Lyndon over the phone, where "she gave it to him in about 5 minutes"—"it" being a thorough report on factions, numbers of people at each stop, and crowd quality.[29] In addition to campaigning on her own, throughout the 1960 campaign Lady Bird joined LBJ on 150 of his own campaign stops.[30]

By Liz's rough estimate, Bird shook one hundred thousand hands in a span of just three months. Once Lyndon became vice president, he brought Liz on as his executive assistant.

Perhaps it was because most of the traveling and local press corps covering Lady Bird were themselves women. Or because Liz, a professional journalist and former head of the National Women's Press Club, was Bird's strategist, manager, and press liaison. But despite a cultural bias toward clothing, hair, and homemaking, the press focused on Lady Bird's tenacity in sticking to substance. Indeed, Bird turned the tendency to trivialize women into a political plus. Bess Furman reported for *The New York Times* that when Bird held a press conference to announce a Texas tour with the Kennedy women, "a male voice asked" her to opine on Jackie's hairdo. Lady Bird replied, "I think it's more important what's inside the head than what's outside."[31] At appearances in New York City, Baltimore, and Atlanta, when asked about her clothing, she embraced the contrast with Jackie, describing her own style as "unremarkable," "No Paris, alas . . . ," adding, "the sooner we quit talking about clothes[,] the better."[32] Patricia Jansen Doyle of *The Kansas City Star* noted that as "a mother, political leader's wife, and shrewd businesswoman, [she] mixes a light-hearted wit with serious depth of thought."[33] Indeed, Lady Bird used her platform to talk about the "staggering" costs of healthcare and the value of the women's vote to the Democratic Party. On JFK's religion, she predicted that the puritans concerned about a Catholic in the White House would ultimately be a "wind blowing itself out."[34] Even as the female press corps cheered Bird's substance and stamina, they dutifully reported on her "nice legs" and her "trim figure of five feet four ½ inches, 114 pounds."[35] The home she created for Lyndon was an "island of peace," Bird drawled, and she hoped the public might better "judge the whole man" by getting to know his choice of spouse.[36] At a campaign stop in New York City, Lady Bird gave a "very engaging performance," arguing that a candidate's wife "belongs in the heat of battle"—this from the woman who, not three months before, could barely stomach the thought of the vice presidency.[37]

Lady Bird's talents on the campaign trail were not surprising—Lyndon had a knack for choosing tenacious, hardworking, often brilliant, low-ego individuals to staff his inner circle. By 1960, many of his closest aides, including Walter Jenkins and John Connally, had already worked for him for several decades. Lyndon was highly intuitive about people and could size up their strengths and weaknesses in a flash. When Lady Bird was just twenty-two, Lyndon quickly thought her to be the "smartest and most deliberate little girl in all the world."[38] A mutual friend in Austin had introduced them on August 31, 1934. The next day, the two met for breakfast at Austin's Driskill Hotel, and spent the day driving around, talking. Bird was aghast when Lyndon proposed to her at the end of the date—but also enticed. A week later, Johnson brought her to meet his parents in San Marcos and his boss, Congressman Richard Kleberg, whose family owned the gigantic King Ranch. Before heading back to Washington, he appeared at the Brick House in Karnack to meet T. J. Taylor, Lady Bird's father, who quickly caught something different in Lyndon from Bird's other suitors.

Over the next ten weeks, through an almost daily correspondence, sometimes punctuated by very expensive "person-to-person" phone calls Lyndon placed from Washington to Karnack, Lady Bird and Lyndon found each other's match. As hard as Lyndon pushed Bird for an answer to his proposal, she pushed back, leery of the rush act, though steadily seduced by the books he sent her, the life in Washington she imagined herself joining, and his passion and ambition. She wanted to know everything about his work, law school, and future job prospects. He wanted total assurance that she loved him. She believed that she did, and told him as much.

Pretty but not beautiful, the awkward girl who would become an excellent student of character was stunned to find in Lyndon someone who studied her. To be appreciated for the intelligent, well-read person she had become, and by a man with such personal and physical charisma, was intoxicating. And in the ten weeks of their courtship, Bird came to see Lyndon as the ticket to a life she could not possibly engineer on her own. She also understood from the very beginning that becoming part of Lyndon's blizzard of activity, need, desire, insecurity, ambition, potency, anxiety, and intelligence would involve significant uncertainty and risk—but also reward.

After hinting at a visit around Thanksgiving, Lyndon surprised Bird at the Brick House in the middle of November: he had quit law school to drive the twelve hundred miles from Washington to Karnack, and wanted an answer, now or never. This time, Bird accepted his proposal. Her remarried father, who felt but seldom overtly showed genuine affection for his daughter, supported Lyndon's proposal and Bird's decision. There was no doubt in Lyndon's mind that the wisest choice of his entire adult life was to insist that she marry him. For, as he wrote, she "contributed to [his] peace of mind—to stimulating in it bigger and better things."[39] Lady Bird possessed the "alfootness [*sic*], independence and indifference" to help him retain "a semblence [*sic*] of sanity when presented with" foolhardy thoughts—precisely the qualities Lyndon knew he needed in order to take his place in Washington, D.C.[40]

But what of Lady Bird's choice? Early on, Lady Bird worried about the pace of Lyndon's Washington lifestyle. "And whenever do you play, Lyndon?" she teased in one of their early courtship letters.[41] And she did not take well to the thought of a life in politics. Worried about why one of his letters was so delayed in its arrival, she fretted, "I am *afraid* its politics—Oh, I know I haven't any business—not any 'proprietary interest'—but I would hate for you to go into politics."[42] Commuting between various tiny apartments in Washington and their Thermocrete home on San Pedro Street in Austin; caring for Lyndon's mother, sister, and brother; starting a business; running his office during World War II; developing an extensive network of women friends from their political circles; trying to become pregnant—Bird largely stayed off the campaign trail until Lyndon's 1948 Senate campaign. Prior to that point, she described her involvement as one of only a "highly interested observer." But she fully absorbed the exhausting work of building what she called "our political machine."[43] She had memorized the name of every county and county seat head in the district, and could rattle off the names of the barbers, ministers, blacksmiths, journalists, teachers, and boyhood and family friends whom Lyndon had tapped to help him win.

By the fall of 1960, in showcasing Lyndon's excellent, evergreen choice, Lady Bird often appeared sitting between two enormous photographs, one of JFK and one of LBJ. While she was very much her husband's advocate and surrogate, when barraged with questions about Jackie, the wren protected the dove, respectful of the latter's choice to sit out the campaign during her third trimester. Yet, Lady Bird was more than Jackie's surrogate; she was becoming a formidable politician in her own right, an unanticipated, unexpected consequence of JFK's surprising, complicating selection of LBJ for his vice president.

* * *

In a career punctuated by the emotional charge and adrenaline rush of electoral and legislative highs and lows, LBJ's transition from the Senate to the vice presidency marked "one of the most dramatic moments in [their] lives."[44] As Lady Bird told LBJ aide Bill Moyers, "I was so happy being the wife of the senator from Texas," and, according to Nancy Dickerson, who spent considerable time covering Lyndon and socializing with and covering the Johnsons during his Senate years, "that's all she wanted."[45] But the shift to the executive branch was not without its benefits: If the 1960 campaign began to open up the country to Lady Bird (its cultural, political, and geographic diversity especially), the vice presidency opened up the world. With her fourteen- and sixteen-year-old daughters at home attending Alice Deal Junior High School and the National Cathedral School, respectively, Bird and Lyndon logged 120,000 miles visiting thirty-three countries together in Africa, Asia, the Middle East, Central Asia, and Europe. Grinding poverty in Senegal, the lack of electricity in Pakistan, and the need to harness water resources in Iran resonated with what Bird had witnessed in the still-underdeveloped corners of her own country and in Lyndon's Texas Hill Country.[46] Often with a separate itinerary from Lyndon's on the ground, Bird frequently departed from standard embassy programs developed for the wives of visiting American officials. Although she gave and received gifts and took in the sights as was expected of someone in her post, she also made it a point to meet women professionals in the Middle East and Asia. By shining the light of her interest on them, she offered them a platform to advance their standing in their own societies. She did this without any sort of label or explicit political agenda, but the message and intent were clear.

Abroad, there was only so much control over international itineraries planned by American embassy staff wed to their Rolodexes. But at home, the vice presidency marked for Lady Bird a deepening confidence to empower her own staff to find ways to display the standing and status of professional American women. In the ornate dining room of the Elms, the Johnsons' home in the Washington neighborhood of Spring Valley, she began to host what she termed "Doers Luncheons," highlighting professional women: Indira Gandhi of India and Empress Farah of Iran, a scientist in the space program, a political scientist and strategist for the Democratic Party in the state of Maryland, a judge, a PhD active in promoting better regulation of food and drugs, a philanthropist advocating for federal dollars for medical research—Lady Bird infused her ceremonial and political duties with a professional, activist message about the importance of women in the workplace. Behind her guarded and, to some observers, even subservient public persona stood an advocate for women. Women, Lady Bird firmly believed, could have it all, meaningful careers and a rewarding personal life, if they worked within the era's constraints to push the boundaries forward. And those boundaries were being debated all around her.[47]

Although most of the international trips Lady Bird made were not in Jackie's stead, stateside during the two years and ten months of Lyndon's vice presidency, the pattern that had begun in the 1960 campaign continued, with Jackie and her staff prevailing upon Bird and hers to stand in for the First Lady in countless East Wing public duties. Much to her surprise, Bird relished the job. Lyndon's depression over his loss of standing and status—the vice presidency "was somewhat limiting to the capacities of Lyndon," his wife archly observed—was the only part of those years Lady Bird regretted.[48] And she felt that even in his misery, Lyndon "took wry pleasure in seeing what fun" she was having.[49]

* * *

Unifying the split within the Texas Democratic Party and raising money for the 1964 presidential campaign drew JFK down to Texas in November 1963 for his first extended appearance there since the 1960 campaign.[50] Lyndon, who had lost conservative allies in Texas by jumping on the Kennedy ticket, told *Evening Star* columnist Mary McGrory, "I'm a Communist in Texas . . . and a Dixiecrat in Washington."[51] Though the Johnsons had delivered the state's 24 electoral votes in the 1960 election, the West Wing begrudged Lyndon's inability to manage the potentially divisive intraparty tensions between LBJ's longtime ally, friend, and confidant, the recently elected, more politically conservative Texas governor, John Connally, and the more liberal senator Ralph Yarborough.[52] Although JFK reassured LBJ from time to time, rumors swirled throughout 1963 that Jack intended to drop him from the 1964 ticket. Even as they put plans in place in anticipation of Lyndon's coming off the ticket, Lady Bird and LBJ, who had so many times in the past used an extended visit to the Ranch to cultivate allies and manage adversaries, saw hosting Jack and Jackie as a chance to solidify LBJ's standing both with the president and as a national figure in the next presidential election. Although Kennedy's campaign team largely sidelined the Johnsons in planning the two-day, four-city Texas tour, the itinerary had Jack and Jackie arriving at the Ranch after a fundraising dinner in Austin.

Now, three years after the Hyannis gathering, the Johnsons turned their home upside down for the Kennedys. Jackie joined President Kennedy on the Texas tour—her Spanish went over well in Houston and San Antonio—and her presence added to the glamour and glow. Her participation in the trip, however, was unexpected. Not three months before, the First Lady had gone into preterm labor to deliver Patrick Bouvier Kennedy by caesarean section. He was born with a lung affliction that blocked oxygen from his bloodstream. While Jackie underwent two blood transfusions in one hospital in Boston, pediatric surgeons in another placed the tiny infant into an enormous steel hyperbaric chamber to infuse the baby's lungs with oxygen. Patrick lived for only thirty-nine hours. The president held him as he died.[53] The trip to Texas was to be Jackie's first to the state, and among the first public duties the still-grieving First Lady could muster the energy to join.

Lady Bird spent the week preparing for the First Couple's visit to the Ranch. She deployed Liz Carpenter and their aide Bess Abell, the daughter of Kentucky senator Earle Clements, and sent her household staff Helen and Gene Williams from Washington to help with the details: a horsehair mattress and special bed board would be installed to accommodate the president's chronic back pain—Jack in Lyndon's bedroom, Jackie in a smaller room of her own, one stocked by Lady Bird with special perfume and soap; Lyndon would move in with Bird. The Johnsons borrowed eight different horses to have on hand in case Jackie wanted to go riding, and sent for Lady Bird's Tennessee walking horse to be driven in from the Volunteer State. There was something again forced, yet strangely informal and intimate, about these two very different couples playing musical bedrooms in their family homes. Bess taught the staff to pour champagne on the rocks, Jackie's custom. She attempted a degree of damage control as the Signal Corps ripped holes in the walls to install new phone lines. And she made final arrangements for the next day's barbecue along the banks of the Pedernales River: twenty pecan pies, eighteen loaves of bread, a horseman with a lasso, and a sheepdog act awaited the president and First Lady.[54]

Chapter 2

"Shame for Texas"

Then almost at the edge of town, on our way to the Trade Mart where we were going to have the luncheon, we were rounding a curve, going down a hill, and suddenly there was a sharp loud report—a shot. It seemed to me to come from a building right above my shoulder. Then a moment and then two more shots in rapid succession. There had been such a gala air that I thought it must be firecrackers or some sort of celebration. Then the Secret Service men were suddenly down in the lead car. I heard over the radio system, "Let's get out of here," and our Secret Service man who was with us (Rufe Youngblood, I believe it was) vaulted over the front seat on top of Lyndon, threw him to the floor, and said, "Get down."

—Lady Bird Johnson, White House diary, November 22, 1963

Instead, the unimaginable. November 22, 1963, the day in Dallas that, as Bird described it in her first diary entry, "all began so beautifully," had ended with a flight back to Washington with Lady Bird, the surrogate, now the new First Lady, Lyndon the president, Jack in a coffin, and Jackie a widow. Mrs. Johnson had learned as a journalism student about the use of short sentences to punctuate and give a feeling of drama. Recording her diary eight days after the assassination, she brought that talent to bear in describing one of the most gruesome moments in American history:

> We all sat around the plane. The casket was in the hall. I went in the small private room to see Mrs. Kennedy, and though it was a very hard thing to do, she made it as easy as possible. She said things like,

> "Oh, Lady Bird, we've liked you two so much. . . . Oh, what if I had not been there. I'm so glad I was there." I looked at her. Mrs. Kennedy's dress was stained with blood. One leg was almost entirely covered with it and her right glove was caked, it was caked with blood—her husband's blood. Somehow that was one of the most poignant sights—exquisitely dressed, and caked in blood.

Bird suggested a change of clothes, but Jackie's own sense of drama told her to stay in the bloody pink suit in order for "them to see what they have done to Jack." Bird didn't stay long with Jackie, but she recorded, before leaving her in the president's cabin on Air Force One to return to the main cabin, "I tried to express something of how we felt. I said, 'Oh, Mrs. Kennedy, you know we never even wanted to be Vice President and now, dear God, it's come to this.'"[1] An understatement. After Lyndon backed JFK for the vice presidency in 1956, Jack had regifted the prospect of the post to Lyndon in 1960—a gift that had turned out to be far more consequential than they could ever have expected.

For the Johnsons, the assassination of JFK was another moment in public and private life punctuated and propelled for almost thirty years by death—of politicians whose open seats Lyndon ran for and won; of Lady Bird's brother and her father in the middle of two of Lyndon's campaigns; of Lyndon's mother, the formidable Rebekah Baines Johnson; and of their political father, Sam Rayburn. But with the assassination of John Fitzgerald Kennedy, though the Johnsons gained the presidency, they were left with a profound and pervasive feeling of loss. Kennedy's death brought Bird a deep "sense of shame over the violence and hatred that has gripped our land."[2] The gruesome events of November 22, 1963, had only hardened her desire to repair the breach. "Shame for America! Shame for Texas!"[3] She knew that Dallas was different—more extreme, less tolerant, than the southwest of Austin or the Hill Country of Lyndon's birth and their home.[4] During the 1960 campaign, she had experienced the virulence of the Dallas coiffed set at a campaign event, where the "Mink Coat Mob" spat at and taunted her and Lyndon, yelling, "LBJ, the Texas traitor!," "Let's ground Lady Bird!," and "LBJ—counterfeit Confederate."[5] But she also knew that most Americans wouldn't bother to distinguish one part of the state from another. They just knew that Texas was different, and now Texas was responsible for the assassination of the most wildly popular president since FDR. To add to the insult, a Texan long derided as culturally inferior and suspected as brazenly hungry for power would become commander in chief. As Bird said, they had "never even wanted" what everyone in Washington regarded as the worst job in American politics, and by inheriting, not winning, the presidency, Lady Bird and Lyndon feared they had lost for good their chance at a legitimate run for the White House.

In Washington and Austin, the Secret Service deployed quickly to gather Luci from Spanish class at the National Cathedral School and Lynda from her dorm at the University of Texas.[6] As of 2:38 P.M. Central Time that Friday, November 22, 1963—less than two hours after JFK was declared dead—their parents were now the president and First Lady of the United States of America.

When Air Force One landed at Andrews Air Force Base, Bobby Kennedy stormed past the Johnsons to find Jackie, and the two in-laws stood as Jack's coffin was lowered off the plane. After brief remarks, Lyndon and Lady Bird found Jackie and said goodbye to her. They took the short helicopter ride to the White House, where Lyndon repaired to the Old Executive Office Building and Lady Bird and Liz headed by car to the Elms. Together, the two women had helped Jack win Texas, but now their Lone Star State had made him a martyr. "It's a terrible thing to say," Liz acknowledged, "but the salvation of Texas is that the governor was hit." "Don't think I haven't thought of that," the new First Lady replied. "I only wish it could have been me."[7]

The next day was gray and overcast. Lady Bird left Luci at home with their beagles, Him and Her, to join Lyndon in the Old Executive Office Building, and together they walked across West Executive Avenue to the White House, where President Kennedy's body lay in state. They met members of the Kennedy clan in the Green Room, the small state parlor generally used for teatime or cocktail hour. From there, the Johnsons followed the Kennedys into the East Room. Bird described the East Room as adorned with a hybrid of American military and Catholic symbols—the chandelier draped in black crepe, "a catafalque in the center and on it the casket, draped with the American flag, and at each corner a large candle and a very rigid military man, representing each one of the [armed] services"—to observe the death of a commander in chief.[8] Catholic mourning ritual on semipublic display in the White House was surely not what Lady Bird and Lyndon contemplated when they both cautioned their fellow Texans against anti-Catholic bias during the 1960 campaign.

Sunday, November 24, "a bright clear day, of sparkling sun," was for Lady Bird Johnson "the day I will never forget," the day President Kennedy's body lay in state in the rotunda of the Capitol Building.[9] After church services at St. Mark's on Capitol Hill, the Johnsons joined the Kennedy family again in the Green Room. Eunice Shriver, whom Bird had campaigned alongside three years earlier, told her that Lee Harvey Oswald, Kennedy's assassin, had been killed. Jackie then arrived, holding the hands of John Jr. and Caroline, both dressed "in two darling blue coats." Bird scrutinized every detail, her account of the scene moving, in just a breath, from Oswald's death to the children's attire. One detail made her very uncomfortable: White House protocol staff informed the Johnsons that they would ride to the Capitol in the same limousine as Jackie and Bobby. The sharing of confined spaces—this was something the Kennedys and Johnsons had some practice in, most recently two days earlier, during the overheated, too-long wait for LBJ's swearing in and then their return to Washington aboard Air Force One. Cognizant of so much pain, Jackie's and the children's, and Bobby's distrust and anger, Lady Bird and Lyndon both would have preferred a separate limousine, to further absorb their fate alone and to give Jack's widow, brother, and children a measure of privacy.[10]

But they all rode together—Lyndon and Jackie in the backseat, Bobby and Lady Bird on the jump seats, Caroline next to Jackie, and John-John jumping back and forth between his uncle's lap and his mother's seat. As the two families left the White House gates, Bird suppressed tears seeing "that sea of faces, stretching away on every side, silent." Hers would have been a cry, she thought, that channeled the collective trauma on those faces, but the strength and dignity of Jackie and the Kennedy family and "the continuity of strength" the moment required from all of them made it "impossible to permit the catharsis of tears." In front of the shared limousine, "Black Jack," the riderless black horse, boots set in their stirrups but facing backward, symbolizing the fallen warrior, led the procession up Pennsylvania Avenue. Mrs. Johnson's recording of the day captures the images and sounds and silences of the moment—flags at half-mast, six white horses and the flag-draped caisson, muffled drums. "But most of all was the sea of faces all around us and that curious sense of silence, broken only by an occasional sob."[11]

The drive to the Capitol felt interminable. While "the absolutely peripatetic" three-year-old John-John flitted about the limousine, Bobby Kennedy wore "a grave, white, sorrowful face, and there was a flinching of the jaw at that moment that almost made—well, it made your soul flinch for him."[12] Wearing a black coat on loan from Nancy Dickerson, Lady Bird, along with Lyndon, followed the Kennedys as they entered the rotunda, where an honor guard stood around JFK's flag-draped coffin. Bird watched as Lyndon laid a wreath at the foot of the casket. When the funeral procession was over, Bird, relieved to be at least departing the Capitol in a separate limousine from the Kennedys, fixed her attention, like the rest of the country, on Jackie, but also cast an indirect spotlight on how the very difference between the two women would help Mrs. Johnson craft her own public identity.

> To me, one of the saddest things in the whole tragedy was that Mrs. Kennedy achieved, on this desperate day, something that she had never quite achieved in the years she'd been in the White House—that is—a state of love, a state of rapport between her and the people of this country. I mean the sort of people who write their Congressman on tablet paper with a pencil. Her behavior from the moment of the shot until I said goodbye to her the other day is, to me, one of the most memorable things of all. Maybe it's a combination of great breeding, great discipline, [and] great character. I only know it's great.

Meditating on their relationship, Lady Bird felt "something of a gulf" open up between herself and the Kennedys.[13] But her instinct was to bridge it.

With her own eye for public theater and mythmaking, Bird was onto something, and she instinctively appreciated how, in the aftermath of the president's death, achieving greatness for John Fitzgerald Kennedy emerged as Jackie's overriding aspiration and ultimately became her most significant accomplishment. In planning every detail of public mourning—echoing President Lincoln's funeral, personally vetting the invitation list, hand-designing the invitations to the Mass at the Cathedral of St. Matthew, choosing a burial site at Arlington National Cemetery over a local plot in Boston, the way she sited and adorned his grave, and her inclusion of her children in the most public of rituals—Jacqueline Bouvier Kennedy solidified the exquisite balance between democracy and monarchy that she and Jack had cultivated so expertly during their one thousand days in office. With all this, she ensured the enduring image of the Kennedy White House as the modern era's "there-will-never-be-another" Camelot. "Everything she has done," wrote Mary McGrory, "seems to be a conscious effort to give to his death the grandeur that the savagery in Dallas was calculated to rob it of." Bringing "meaning to tragic chaos," Jacqueline Kennedy "has borne herself with the valor of a queen in a Greek tragedy."[14] There was no chance Lady Bird could fill such shoes, and that awareness felt oddly liberating.

Still, comparisons between two such different presidential couples were inevitable and irresistible. One couple was glamorous, the other pedestrian; one was cultured, the other not so much. One throbbed with youth, and the other was sedate in middle age. The Harvard Brahmin life and education that bespoke intellectual sophistication was set off against the bare-knuckle hillbilly instincts from Texas. To the world, Kennedy's deployment of power was optimistic and enlightened, as opposed to the perception of Johnson's cynical and likely racist backroom manipulations, LBJ's leadership of the 1957 civil rights bill notwithstanding. While Jackie dressed in couture, Lady Bird marked a return to a Mamie Eisenhower off-the-rack simplicity. All these truisms do what they always do: simplify and obscure, but also suggest some core truth.

Abbreviated as it was, Jack and Jackie Kennedy's presidency, in dramatic contrast to the square Republican stoicism of Ike and Mamie's sexless White House, was indeed completely different from what the Johnsons would and could deliver. In temperament and public persona, Jack and Jackie were radically different from Lyndon and Lady Bird. For all that Lady Bird and Jackie may have shared as the wives of presidents, Jackie despised politics. "She breathes all the political gases that flow around us but she never seems to inhale them," Jack said in 1959.[15] Politics for Lady Bird, in contrast, had, by 1948, Lyndon's first Senate campaign, become her daily infusion of oxygen, her second skin. And yet Jackie—the reluctant public figure, the First Lady determined to ensure her children's privacy, who avoided most of the traditional ceremonial duties of the position, who frequently fled Pennsylvania Avenue to yacht and to hunt and to escape the humiliations of Jack's profligate liaisons—still managed to make herself an asset to the president on the global stage and to make her own mark on the White House and on the country at large.

When Jackie moved into the White House, she found the interior had not been updated since 1948. There was no sense of design gravitas suited to the building's historic status and national stature. Jackie bristled at the feeling of "interior remoteness" in the private quarters and at the second-rate nature of the décor in the public spaces, which looked more like an afterthought than intentional.[16] Under her watch, a Congress that passed almost none of her husband's legislation did pass a bill designating the White House with permanent museum status under the auspices of the Smithsonian and created a permanent curator for the Executive Mansion. Jackie organized the White House Fine Arts Committee, comprising the country's preeminent antiquarian experts and doyennes of taste, who helped raise funds and find the right materials to restore each room of the White House with period furniture, finishes, paintings, china, and other amenities.

Jackie organized the production of the first ever White House guidebook, the sales of which helped offset the cost of the redecoration. She established a separate library committee to get rid of the volumes of Agatha Christie preferred by the Trumans and line the shelves instead with volumes of greater historic resonance. She invited the prolific horticulturalist of Virginia's hunt country, the aristocrat Bunny Mellon, to help her redesign and replant the foliage on the White House grounds. Jackie conducted the first nationally televised tour of "the people's home" and won an Emmy for the gesture.[17] (Lady Bird was deployed to Hollywood to accept the award on Mrs. Kennedy's behalf.) She built a stage for performances in the East Room and brought in opera, Shakespeare, ballet, and the greatest musicians of the times. She ended the well-worn practice of segregating the sexes for White House after-dinner activities. She invited statesmen, scientists, poets, and playwrights; organized concerts for children; and promoted the very French idea that the nation's capital needed a national cultural center. She stopped the destruction of the historic buildings around Lafayette Square, across from the White House, and initiated the restoration and redecoration of Blair House, the presidential guesthouse.[18]

On solo trips to India, Pakistan, and Mexico, Jackie dazzled her hosts with her diplomacy and personal touch. And on joint trips with Jack to Europe, she upstaged the president of the United States, dazzling royals, prime ministers, and publics with her international, cosmopolitan palette of language, poise, and sartorial panache. In the transcripts of her 1964 interviews with Arthur Schlesinger, Jr., Jackie comes off keenly aware of the inside politics of various international crises her husband and brother-in-law managed the country through, speaking in considerable detail about the Bay of Pigs, the Cuban Missile Crisis, the Berlin Crisis, and the Nuclear Test Ban Treaty. Yet, however much geopolitical detail Jack may have shared with Jackie, however enriching the intellectual and cultural life of their White House became, and however devoted to raising healthy young children (and enduring a very public infant death), the personal complexities of being married to Jack Kennedy and Jackie's distaste for the public tedium of a First Lady's ceremonial duties give the enduring impression of a woman who felt profound ambivalence toward her station—unlike her successor.

On Monday, November 25 (John-John's birthday), the nation, Jackie, and the Kennedy family laid JFK to rest at Arlington National Cemetery. The journey from the Capitol Building to the cemetery was set to begin at 10:30 A.M. Nearly one million people lined the route. At the White House, the first stop of the burial procession, Jackie and the Kennedy brothers, Ted and Bobby, exited their car and walked the six blocks north to the Cathedral of St. Matthew for Mass. The Johnsons, including Luci and Lynda Bird, followed closely behind. Following Mass, the mourners made their way to the cemetery. And at 3:34 P.M. Eastern Standard Time, JFK's remains were lowered into the ground in a three-thousand-pound copper triune burial vault, making him just one of two presidents—the other was William Howard Taft—to be buried at Arlington. Foreign dignitaries, including French president Charles de Gaulle, German chancellor Ludwig Erhard, and Prince Philip of the United Kingdom, made the trip in order to pay their respects. Air Force One flew past and dipped its wing as a final tribute to the fallen president. Now it was up to the Johnsons to provide solace to a mourning nation—and up to Lyndon to find a way to signal continuity not just in the constitutional chain of command his assumption of the presidency represented, but also in the substance he would bring to the office.

* * *

The practicalities of moving households and the organizational details required to do so provided focus and even some comfort to Lady Bird. But no amount of to-do lists could distract from the horrific circumstances that had brought her to this moment. And so, the scene at the White House (tea with Jackie, an overview of the staff, and a room-by-room tour of the private quarters), when she went there for a few hours on the day after Jack's burial, in preparation for the move, in Lady Bird's telling, is punctuated by contrasts. Her detailed, unrestrained descriptions of the drawings, paintings, and fabric choices ("like exquisite little gay confections," in Caroline and John-John's rooms) clash with the stark and sudden encounter, in the Yellow Oval Room, with the boots worn by Black Jack, the horse in President Kennedy's funeral procession, and Jackie's reference to Jack in the present tense, as if he were still alive.[19]

There was no hard-and-fast requirement for Jackie to personally give the new First Lady a tour of the home she would soon vacate: the chief White House usher, J. B. West, had already visited Lady Bird the morning after the funeral, showing her the layout and dimensions of the rooms in the private quarters. How remarkable, then, that with her husband's assassination, the freshness of his bloody remains, she later recalled, still wafting around her body, the drain of the public and private acts of mourning of the last seventy-two hours, the emotional toll on Caroline and John, the weight of the blow to Bobby and the rest of the Kennedys so heavy, that just four days later, Jackie could muster the clarity, grace, and strength to help Lady Bird into her new role.[20] Jackie's empathy for the Johnsons' atypical ascent, and her assistance in curtailing West Wing staff chatter belittling the Johnsons for their purported cultural and intellectual inferiority, was not only a product of Jackie's good breeding and commitment to Jack's presidency, but also a result of a long-accumulated genuine fondness for both Lady Bird and Lyndon.

During JFK's presidency, Jackie and Lyndon had kept a regular, affectionate, gracious, and often very humorous correspondence. Lady Bird and Jackie seemed constantly to be exchanging gifts and cards, with Jackie thanking Lady Bird for stepping in on many occasions in her stead, and there had been mutual plaudits exchanged between the two for various public events and entertainment. It could all seem the stuff of formalities required of public figures, but the *x*'s and *o*'s, the "much love"s, the effusive expressions of affection, the teasing about longhorns, and the sharing of implied understandings of the political prickliness of others—all these added up to a genuine and mutual appreciation. The lightness of heart between the two couples also yielded to compassion during painful moments. When Jackie's son Patrick died, Lady Bird and Lyndon wrote her, "You give so much happiness—you deserve more. We think of you—pray for you and grieve with you. Would say more but you would have to read it—and I fear want to answer it—don't."[21] In a note to

Lyndon following the assassination, Jackie would write, "I always thought way before the nomination that Lady Bird should be First Lady—but I don't need to tell you here what I think of her qualities—her extraordinary grace of character—her willingness to assume every burden—She assumed so many for me and I love her very much."[22] Each, then, perhaps out of fondness for the other, mustered the courage to carry out the dignified transition steps they might have undertaken had Bird become First Lady by an act of the people whose home—the "people's home," as Jackie had called it—she would now inhabit.

On Tuesday, November 26, the day of the personal White House tour, Bird found Jackie "orderly, composed and radiating that peculiar sort of aliveness and charm and warmth." And though it was Lady Bird who felt it her role—she was older and her husband still alive—to console Jackie, it was Jackie who tried to reassure the new First Lady. "Don't be frightened of this house," she told Bird, as "some of the happiest years of my marriage have been spent here." In "repeating that over and over," Bird felt, it was as if Jackie's excess of reassurance somehow glossed over the essential truths each knew directly and indirectly of the other's life: marriage to a powerful spouse with significant health issues and with barely concealed and apparently unapologetic infidelities could not but carry a special burden and a very unique charge. "You *will* be happy here," Jackie implored.[23]

Walking through the family sitting room, known as the West Hall, past the Cézannes and into the Yellow Oval Room, repeating the pattern of musical bedrooms established during the 1960 campaign, Jackie helped Bird plan which Johnson family member would come to occupy whose room. LBJ to JFK's, Bird to Jackie's, Lynda to Caroline's, and Luci to John-John's. And Jackie's dressing room, "one of the most exquisite rooms" Bird had ever seen, the room with a view out to Andrew Jackson's magnolia trees and the Washington Monument beyond them, would become Bird's private office, her chosen spot for recording her diary entries. And so we have the sound of Lady Bird's voice, just four days after Dallas, punctuating the cultural divide as she describes the WASPiest of Bouvier décor: photographs of the yacht in Hyannis Port and of the cover of JFK's *Profiles in Courage* and "the closets all covered with trompe l'oeil," pronounced in Mrs. Johnson's adamant, deep southern inflection "trump leyaya."[24]

They ended their afternoon at the White House in the East Room, where Jack's body had lain in state just two days earlier. The gears of the White House machine were already grinding though, with an event for the Alliance for Progress, where Lyndon sought to assure his audience of his continued support for a signature JFK program. Jackie's appearance changed the energy in the room at once. "It is doubtful," Bird reflected, "that anyone else is a star when she [Jackie] is present." And in that light, and aware of Lyndon's consciousness and insecurity with the cultural divide, Bird directed her recorded thoughts for the first time to her husband. Especially in light of Jackie and Jack's star power, "my heart went out to the bravery of Lyndon, who marches into this circumstance with so much determination and not all the preparation that one would have sought if one could have foreseen one's destiny" as, she implied, JFK had, at just sixteen years of age.[25]

* * *

The next day, November 27, 1963, Lyndon delivered his first speech to Congress as president of the United States. At least by the absence of reference to it in her diary and documents in the archival record, by day four of his presidency, Lady Bird did not yet participate directly in drafting or revising LBJ's speeches—Lyndon had asked Kennedy's speechwriter Ted Sorensen to knit the speech together from several drafts. But she was thoroughly steeped in Lyndon's preparation. Her insistence on the importance of "drama and pacing" made itself manifest in a speech widely lauded by a very skeptical and still-shell-shocked Washington commentariat, whose denizens praised the new president for conveying emotion, sincerity, and gravitas. "All I have I would have given gladly not to be standing here today," Johnson solemnly began. And in what was perhaps a rare, public admission of his own weakness, he implored, "I am here today to say I need your help; I cannot bear this burden alone. I need the help of all Americans, and all America."[26] Though Johnson had, at the very outset of this unwelcome plot twist, been certain that he would commit the remaining year of JFK's term to Kennedy's policy agenda, his promise to continue what President Kennedy had started, an ambitious agenda on civil rights and taxes, brought a sigh of relief among the coterie of Kennedy's devastated advisers, those whom LBJ had beseeched to remain in the White House and the loyalists beyond. These two issues, Johnson stressed, would not only "eloquently honor President Kennedy's memory" but also "fittingly continue [his] work."[27]

After the speech, Lyndon worked the phones, having Lady Bird jump on calls with their long-cultivated network of political, business, and media contacts. Lyndon's dexterity and reliance on his ubiquitous telephones is legendary, and Lady Bird became accustomed to him handing her the phone with no notice. The couple's use of the joint telephone call served their political objectives, but it was also the style of the time: like many Americans in the middle of the twentieth century, the Johnsons took keen advantage of the novelty of having more than one phone line and telephone installed in their homes and of using them simultaneously to make joint calls or to listen in on their teenage daughters' calls. By 1963, the Johnsons' seamless telephonic timing reflected their shared understanding of the moment, and of what they wanted to get from the person on the other end of the line. That afternoon, they were set to capitalize on the enthusiastic, relieved reviews of the new president's speech.

Lyndon's political career reached its crescendo during the age of broadcast television, when the three national networks, ABC, CBS, and NBC, commanded the public's attention, never more so than during coverage of the Kennedy assassination and its aftermath. Only two years earlier, in 1961, the first presidential press conference was broadcast on live television. But Lady Bird and Lyndon had been in the public eye for almost thirty years. Between the market dominance of their company in radio and television and Lyndon's political power in their home state, Lyndon personally, confidently, and at times aggressively managed his relationship with the Texas press. But going forward they had the national press to worry about. They understood how little time they had to keep, win, or lose the sympathies and favor of the national television networks and newspapers. LBJ's call list that afternoon covered top executives at NBC, ABC, and CBS and publishers and editors at the *LA Times, The Washington Post, The Washington Star,* and Condé Nast. Bird joined two of the calls, to Frank Stanton, president of CBS, the network affiliate of the Johnsons' KTBC in Austin, and to David Sarnoff, the founder of the Radio Corporation of America (RCA) and chairman of NBC, both of whom had been business partners with the Johnsons for decades. "I never needed you more than I need you now," Lyndon told Sarnoff, and introduced the First Lady as "a young lady who has been in love with you for a long time." Lilting and emphatic at once, Lyndon's best closer didn't miss a beat: "That's because I'm in love with optimism and a forward thrust," Bird offered.[28] Both Johnsons were keenly aware of the need to keep media coverage on their side, and believed they had a unique understanding of the television and radio industry.

Back in 1943, the Johnsons had purchased KTBC, a nearly bankrupt local Austin radio station, for $17,500, financing the purchase with Lady Bird's family money. For three months that year, Lady Bird drove the five-day, fifteen-hundred-mile stretch between Washington and Austin to clean up and renovate the decrepit physical plant, review the station's contracts, scrub the books for extra pennies, and keep an eye on personnel. From her equity and sweat during this grungy, unglamorous beginning, and during the ensuing decades until they entered the White House, the Johnsons built a multimillion-dollar Texas media, land, and cattle empire. Their status as political insiders boosted their fortune-building prospects—with FCC licenses and coerced discount advertising rates among the perks they leveraged. Bird might not have known the details of the financial and bureaucratic shell game Lyndon orchestrated to build their media holdings, or she well might have. But she was a full beneficiary, and often participant, taking the business from near death to solvent start-up. Within five years of acquiring the debt-ridden station, the Johnsons began to turn a modest profit, and by 1964 they were netting some $500,000 per year. The station's market value was estimated at $7 million.

Much has been written about the air of impropriety related to the financial benefits the Johnsons derived from leveraging LBJ's political influence in Washington.[29] Because the Johnsons' business records remain permanently closed, one can only surmise the considerable scope of Lady Bird's activism as a businesswoman running the company. Her own words over the years suggest she considered KTBC radio (and, later, KTBC TV) very much her project, one that Lyndon's political ties may well have helped advance—a fact about which she was not naïve but one on which she kept a close, detailed watch. During LBJ's vice presidency, well before vice presidents began the practice of placing their investments in blind trusts, Bird kept Lyndon closely informed about their media businesses. In fact, the business is a prime example of their partnership: Bird's money financed the acquisition; Lyndon's political clout in Congress and the Johnsons' close relationship with Clifford Durr, a civil rights lawyer in Alabama who was the FCC commissioner at the time, helped secure the proper license; and her acumen and instincts, and LBJ's close watch on all of it, helped grow the company. Their collective political weight in Austin and Washington brought in and kept advertising revenue and otherwise kept competitors at bay.[30]

In speaking to Sarnoff, Bird switched codes from saccharine to serious, appealing to Sarnoff's ego, media executive to media executive. Referring to the last few days, her voice deepened: "I couldn't help but take my hat off to our industry for the coverage of the whole dreadful thing."[31] As Stanton had, Sarnoff pledged his ongoing help, the objective of the afternoon's calls. But in Washington, the request for help and advice by the politically powerful often masked a demand for compliance and implied an expectation of deference. Helping a new president establish himself in the aftermath of an assassination was hardly an unreasonable expectation. But Sarnoff had already given the Johnsons reason to expect his help: in the 1950s, as the head of RCA, he had agreed to Senator Johnson's request that RCA, which also had military contracts pending before the federal government, sell its broadcast equipment in Texas only to the Johnsons' stations. Like Stanton, Sarnoff pledged his ongoing support.

* * *

Nine days after the assassination, after a short Sunday morning service at St. Mark's, the Johnsons returned to John F. Kennedy's grave site. A white picket fence, evocative of Cape Cod, formed a large rectangle, in the center of which burned the eternal flame. By the time the Johnsons arrived, the entire area inside the fence was already filled with flowers left by mourners—some 2,500 people per hour were visiting that weekend. Deepening her voice, Bird described the "long, long lines of solemn respectful people all along the hill of Robert E. Lee's home, as we wound up to the gravesite."[32] The color footage shot by the White House Naval Photographic Center, the principal presidential videography shop of the era, shows a big-sky day, cold and clear. Men, women, and children; black and white; young and old, file past and lay flowers on the grave. The Johnsons are dressed in black. Lyndon holds a bouquet of long-stemmed red roses. He walks alone, with only an officer beside him, while Lady Bird and the girls walk in step behind him. But when he reaches the opening to the grave site, he turns around, and Lady Bird joins him. With the cameras rolling, the new president bends down and places the flowers, and as he does so, Bird bows her head. Then Lyndon bows his and turns to depart, the Lincoln Memorial deep in the background of the shot. As Lyndon turns to walk down the hill, the camera pans in slightly closer to Lady Bird as she looks up and then farther up—with a look of one who possesses but also needs whatever strength she can find.[33] Taking in "the beautiful vista of Washington as it lay spread out below," Bird meditated on the tasks ahead as she walked back down the hill with her family to the cars waiting to take them back to the White House, and to the delicate diplomacy of transition.[34]

Chapter 3

Transition, Succession

The big-shots in Congress and even the right honorable gentlemen in the White House and the Cabinet moaned bitterly about all this, but it's perfectly obvious who had the worst deal of all. It was their women. For the women had to deal with the practical consequences of everybody else's stupidity, as usual. They not only had to mourn for the country, and help each other, but worry about the house in Washington and the house back home and the kids in both places. The country therefore owes them a special Christmas toast. They are unpaid and unappreciated, and they are married not only to their favorite baboons, but to Washington, which is more than any gal ought to tolerate.

—James "Scotty" Reston, "The Women of the Capital Pick Up the Pieces," *The New York Times*, December 24, 1963

Bird's diary entry for two days later, December 3, contains all the practical, professional, emotional, and psychological elements animating her understanding of her role in the Johnsons' transition to the presidency. Her love of language, her skill at turning a phrase, her feel for the urgency and hazards driving Lyndon, and her self-awareness regarding the need to seize the opportunity the new platform provided her while differentiating herself from Jackie—all these come across. Ever since she first ran Lyndon's office in the 1940s while he was stationed in the Pacific, Bird remained vigilant about personally responding to constituent mail—and never more so than now, as she and Lyndon singularly focused on solidifying the nation's belief that they represented continuity of government and a commitment to the Kennedy White House legacy. So that warm-for-December day began with a crowd of women friends helping her answer letters in her attic office at the Elms, followed by a scouting mission for the proper window dressings for the bedrooms that Luci and Lynda would soon occupy in the White House. The worthy causes of constituents and chintz, however, faded by comparison to the emotional and practical navigation required of her that afternoon, when JFK's personal lawyer, Clark Clifford, came to the Elms on a mission to work through some of the more foundational aspects of continuity and transition between Lady Bird and Jackie.

During her tenure, with Clifford's legal and political guidance, Jackie had launched several initiatives focused on restoration and preservation of the White House—among them the White House Fine Arts Committee and the White House Historical Association. Clifford, "so suave and persuasive and handsome with an almost Shakespearean delivery" in his signature baritone, pressed Bird to continue both, in particular the Historical Association, which he had helped launch to increase public understanding of and appreciation for the White House; he thus held a "deep, visceral feeling" that LBJ continue it. But it was Jackie herself who had suggested that Lady Bird discontinue the Fine Arts Committee. It had already raised funds and acquired art to hang throughout the White House. Fine arts would not be her métier, Bird thought, and with Jackie's blessing, the First Lady took Clifford's advice only on the Historical Association. At least for the time being, Bird "wanted Lyndon's"—she paused and corrected herself—"our administration's appearance in the public eye" to continue to convey the openness at the White House that Jackie had begun, and which she intended to expand.[1]

In an eight-page handwritten letter, Jackie thanked her successor and set forth her advice and wishes in exacting detail—including where and how to hang JFK's and LBJ's presidential portraits: next to each other.[2] Although the dispositions of Jackie's various committees did not represent an existential matter for the country, the discussion with Clifford and the letter from Jackie illuminate Bird's broader consideration during the delicate transition: Jackie's wishes, the best interests of the very new Johnson presidency, and Bird's own personal ambitions. Recording her diary with a weary sigh of self-doubt, Lady Bird "began to have the feeling that I was living in a jungle of which I was not very well prepared to fend for myself." Yet her emotional uncertainty was belied by the experience and self-knowledge she brought to that "jungle" of her new job. She already knew she wanted to carve out her own advocacy niche, "a love of my own," she called it, and "one that deserves the same sort of high class treatment with a custodian and a saver of its history as the White House had" in Jackie. Although the target of her formidable discipline and energy, beyond Lyndon's political success and health, had not yet come to the fore, Lady Bird's affinities for conservation of the natural environment and attention to redressing the dehumanizing effects of city life would soon take root well beyond the confines of 1600 Pennsylvania Avenue.[3]

Despite her uncertainty, Bird privately vowed to make the "new resolve" Lyndon had asked of Congress and the country her own mantra, too. As he had beseeched during his speech, her own mandate was "not to hesitate, not to pause, not to turn about and linger over this evil moment, but to continue on our course so that we may fulfill the destiny that history has set for us."[4] Bird seemed to be settling into the demands of the American presidency with the same care she had displayed in her past roles alongside Lyndon. Reflecting on the day, she felt a flicker of hope flash through her mind, replacing the gloom that had dominated her thoughts in the weeks following the assassination. "If he can just rest enough to think enough, it just might be wonderful," she considered.[5]

* * *

Orchestrating the delicate move to the White House was the first, and most visible, sign of Lady Bird's new resolve, even as she urged Lyndon to exercise a modicum of patience in doing so. In describing Jackie's demeanor after the assassination as one of great "steel and stamina," Lady Bird was not overstating her enormous reverence for the young widow when she marveled at her toughness and grace during those days.[6] Just fourteen days after the assassination, on December 6, Jackie, Caroline, and John-John moved out of the White House and into the Georgetown home of Kennedy confidant, former New York governor and now undersecretary of state for political affairs, Averell Harriman. But by the time they left, it was too late in the day for the Johnsons to move in. Lady Bird and Lyndon instead met for a swim in the White House pool and to survey the family quarters. Lyndon's impatience and his wife's own consciousness of how difficult it must have been "for Mrs. Kennedy to gather everything together in the agonizing aftermath of the assassination" left Lady Bird with no choice but to move into the Executive Mansion on Pearl Harbor Day, December 7, a date she and Jackie had hoped to avoid. The Japanese attack was barely twenty years past, and for both First Ladies, and Americans of both their generations, the date still resonated. The surprise nature of a direct attack by a foreign power had again been brought to the top of the public's mind with the possibility of a foreign power's involvement in JFK's assassination.[7]

But there they were. On that sunny and unseasonably warm morning, Saturday, December 7, 1963, Lady Bird arrived with Luci, the two dogs, and, under Bird's arm, a photograph of Sam Rayburn, the only political hero whose image traveled with the Johnsons from home to home as they moved from 30th Place to 50th Street and now to 1600 Pennsylvania Avenue. Chief White House usher J. B. West greeted Lady Bird and Luci. In his memoir, West recounts that the new First Lady's message to him was "Anything that . . . needs to be done, remember this: my husband comes first, the girls second, and I will be satisfied with what's left."[8] This hierarchy of needs and their tending to had reigned from the start in the Johnson household. Four decades later, while her own husband was running for the Senate, Michelle Obama again made explicit what for Lady Bird was a given: an awareness of this ranking. "What I notice about men, all men, is that their order is me, my family, God is in there somewhere, but me is first . . . and for women, me is fourth, and that's not healthy."[9] Lady Bird actively cultivated and sustained her husband's "me is first" primacy. She occupied that last place fully aware of the cost of doing so, but her embrace of the role was less a source of self-criticism or criticism of Lyndon than the result of an awareness of and, at times, fatigued pride in her own near-bottomless capacities. West also recalled that although she instructed him to run the White House, as she had run many households already and now had other things to do, "there was nothing tentative about Claudia Alta Taylor Johnson. During those difficult days of transition, she quickly organized her staff, her way of living, her family responsibilities. . . . And I did not run the White House, Lady Bird Johnson did—and in a way no other First Lady had done. She was rather like the chairman of the board of a large corporation."[10] She often credited Lyndon for "stretching" her, but it was she who also stretched Lyndon, by giving him the myriad resources he depended upon to battle his demons, those both within him and in the American body politic.

Over the next few weeks, while Lyndon focused on securing foreign aid funding from Congress, an important early demonstration of his legislative strength, Lady Bird managed the transition between two houses—she still had to sort, store, or give away the contents of the Elms and prepare to put that house on the market; decorate the family quarters at the White House; and get to know the White House staff. Now, with a degree of autonomy but a dearth of privacy, Lady Bird had a public persona that, even if clearly in the service of her husband, of the president, and of the country, also became a means to assert her own identity.

In handling the vast contingent of female journalists eager to cover her, Bird, savvy media operator, concluded early on that it was better to feed than to starve the beast of the fourth estate. She had trained as a journalist in college, rehabilitated and managed a media empire in Texas, and grown up politically in Washington surrounded by journalists, male and female. Women journalists at the time, with only some exceptions—Nancy Dickerson, Helen Thomas, Frances Lewine, Doris Fleeson—were assigned to "women's topics"; the pool of reporters on the Lady Bird beat were all female. Bird had known many of them for years and valued their friendship. She wanted a "workable formula," as her press secretary, Liz Carpenter, set out to craft her image. Knowing that her prime constituent had an appreciation for the profession and for working under deadline, Liz polled the journalists who would be covering the new First Lady and crystallized their advice: "Be available" and "Never lie—tell us you can't tell, but never lie."[11] Although she often found their coverage shallow, Bird obligingly, often self-critically, granted interviews to newswomen writing profiles and hagiographies about her. The new First Lady took Liz's advice and, in the early days of the Johnson administration, made herself available—to the point of near-total exhaustion.

Just one day after they moved into the White House, Lady Bird and Lyndon hosted the first of many women of substance as an overnight guest in the White House: Mary Lasker. Lasker, whose late husband, Albert, had once worked as a public relations whiz for tobacco, directed her philanthropy and prodigious networking chops toward advocacy for greater government funding for cancer and other medical research. Lasker had lobbied Lyndon since his days in the Senate, when he passed legislation to fund polio vaccines and medical research, and Bird was cognizant that Lasker regarded her as a conduit to Lyndon. Putting in time helping Lady Bird make decorating choices was part of the choreography of staying in Lyndon's good graces, and Bird understood her role in the dance. Lasker, for her part, knew how to make Bird her champion, and Bird praised Lasker's ability to bring out in Lyndon "the oddest combination of cynicism and undying belief in the mind of man."[12] Lasker's smarts and interests appealed to both Johnsons, and she would become a regular and reliable resource for Lady Bird's East Wing.

Though she would draw upon Lasker's connections in philanthropy, culture, and education as part of her network outside the White House, Bird had a long tenure on the Hill as the wife of a powerful senator. The experience gave her clarity about the distinctions between friendliness and friendship in Washington. She was keenly aware that there was a gulf of difference, and she had become increasingly adept at navigating it, having put in thousands of hours servicing constituents, listening to debates in the gallery, counting votes with her husband, and leading the Senate Wives Club. She knew how quickly allies could become adversaries, and how a change in one's job description could transform a relationship from "one of us" to "one of them." Nowhere was this truer than in the halls of the U.S. Congress.

Yet, now in the executive, she saw that "two great monolithic structures," the House and the Senate (albeit both under Democratic control), stood "between us and some degree of success" in achieving the toughest of JFK's still-unrealized policy goals, those LBJ had vowed days earlier to embrace as his own, civil rights and tax reform.[13] In previous decades, led by LBJ's mentor Richard Russell of Georgia, a coalition of Republicans and southern Democrats had managed to stymie social reforms in education, health, and housing and to stall progress on civil rights legislation hostage to tax cuts and other bills. Both Johnsons therefore readily grasped that LBJ would have to seize the momentum of the national tragedy to break through the congressional impasse that JFK's policy agenda had faced. They took nothing for granted. Watching Lyndon gear up to dislodge legislation in both arenas from the stasis of various committees, Lady Bird was now uncertain which Democrats, long-standing allies, would support them on civil rights or which Republicans would cross over to "our side" on passing JFK's once-stagnant tax reform. She sensed the adrenaline behind LBJ's momentum of recent weeks wearing thin. Her husband "was becoming more worried about little things" and visibly frustrated that a complacent Congress, whose legislative maneuverings he had once so deftly commanded, threatened to become a roadblock to his ambitious national agenda.[14] Always tuned in to Lyndon's moods, Bird prayed into the tape recorder for Lyndon to pace himself over the next thirteen months, asking "for him to be able to help himself and for me to be able to help him."[15] She couldn't quite allow herself to look beyond the year ahead.

And what of her own mood? In the early weeks of December, Lady Bird had to oversee a proper handoff from Jackie's staff to hers, host several meals and "breeding" events between the Kennedy and Johnson staffers, mingle over cocktails with members of Congress, and get Luci settled into their new home. The tedium of endless decisions, the consciousness of the need to project gravitas and continuity, the weight of it all, left Bird feeling exhausted, as "a blur of fatigue" set in.[16] "I gave less than brilliant answers," she lamented, referring to questions posed by one author on deadline to deliver a book about her. More letters, cards, and public activities filled her days. "My intake of life and my reaction to life is slow when my vitality is low," and though her staff worried about her, Lady Bird stuck to a relentless schedule.[17] In their transition dance,

Jackie had made only one request of Lady Bird: she hoped Caroline and her playmates could finish the year at the small school on the third floor of the private quarters that Jackie and her Georgetown friends had started. Bird readily agreed to Jackie's request: "[I]f it had been to chop off one's right hand one would have said 'sure' just that minute." When she visited Caroline, Bird was reminded of her own loss—at age five, just a year younger at the time than Caroline was now—of her mother. Caroline "stood and looked at me the longest of anybody, I think." Her gaze, with "the most beautiful eyes," touched Lady Bird deeply. But she steeled herself against feeling too intensely, reminding herself "not to be too sorry for Caroline, though, because there's an insulation, something that protects you when you're only six and the griefs of the world happen."[18]

In these tense and unrelenting December days, swimming would become one of Bird's principal forms of stress relief. Long a swimmer, she found consolation doing thirty laps in the White House pool. Surrounded by paintings donated by JFK's father, Joseph Kennedy, depicting serene spots in the Virgin Islands, she took solace in the solitary, quiet, body-and-mind relief of regular lap swimming. The White House pool would become one of Lyndon's zones of both recreation and business. But while Lyndon seldom swam laps—he tended to just float around, often naked—Bird came to rely on the pool for her solitude and wellness. After a swim one night late in December, she found herself alone with Lyndon at the White House kitchen table, eating a snack of oysters and leftover dessert. There they were, reenacting a scene together of many years, only now not in the modest kitchens of Kalorama or farther up Connecticut Avenue at the Kennedy-Warren apartment building or in the even ritzier Elms, but in the kitchen of 1600 Pennsylvania Avenue. Bird knew LBJ was wrestling with Congress, wanting an early show of force and unity before that body's return in January. He still hadn't been able to get much out of the institution he had once dominated, save approval to print a fifty-cent coin in JFK's honor. With irony, she wanted to rib Lyndon, "Who do you think you are—majority leader?"[19]

Just a few days later, December 23, marked the official end of the monthlong period of mourning. The White House could emerge from its stupor: the black crepe came down from the chandeliers, a decorated Christmas tree emerged, and with just a few hours' notice, the West Wing alerted the East Wing that Lyndon had invited the entire Congress plus spouses eager to leave town for Christmas recess for a holiday party that evening. Early on the morning of Christmas Eve, the House finally passed a foreign aid bill, and "released from our bondage," the Johnsons departed for two weeks at the Ranch.[20]

* * *

The Ranch had been transformed since November 22, 1963. Instead of fretting over stocking JFK's favorite beverages and Jackie's preferred hand towels, Lyndon, Lady Bird, and their household staff were now preoccupied with establishing new security protocols, communications systems, and administrative structures to parallel those in Washington. The new technologies took hundreds of technicians, multiple new outside structures, and over a month to install. Although Lady Bird wasn't a native of the Hill Country, she had come to love its open skies, clear air, big vistas, wildlife, vastness, and sense of freedom. For Lyndon, being at the Ranch was like "getting out of jail finally," from the frenetic pace and confining spaces of the capital.[21] The Ranch had been an escape for Lady Bird as well, but now, after making her usual rounds to deliver holiday poinsettias and check in on neighbors and friends on Christmas Day, she found Lyndon playing ringmaster to a vast traveling circus: journalists, at his invitation, paraded through their quite small home, each gifted by the president himself with an LBJ Ranch ashtray as a souvenir, while dinner for twenty-seven of his kin waited to be served.[22] Secret Service agents, guardhouses, all kinds of electronic security, and so many permanently lit outdoor spotlights took front and center at the Ranch these days that now "you never do quite settle into the anonymity of darkness" for which Lady Bird so yearned.[23]

The Ranch also became the location for the first state visit of the Johnson presidency. In an effort to avoid returning to meet Chancellor Ludwig Erhard in Washington, LBJ invited West Germany's head of state, one of Washington's most important Cold War allies, to the Texas Hill

Country to serve up a plate of Johnson "barbecue diplomacy."[24] The visit enabled LBJ to signal not just his commitment to continuity of government, but also his readiness to put his own stamp on the American presidency by showing the American public and a global audience that it was possible, and even a source of strength, to be presidential and assert one's identity. In hosting the chancellor and his ministers, five busloads of two hundred journalists, and much of Lyndon's cabinet at the Ranch, the Johnsons remained unflinching in "charging through that silken curtain of reserve" that Americans had come to expect from their First Families.[25] Perhaps, they thought, it was possible that the once-dilapidated Ranch and the accompanying 233 acres of land, bought for ten dollars from Lyndon's widowed aunt in 1951, could represent a popular alternative to Kennedy's Camelot.[26] Perhaps Lyndon Johnson's beloved Texas, the state held responsible for the horrific assassination of JFK just a month before, could rehabilitate its tarnished image in the hearts and minds of the American electorate.

After the Johnsons met Chancellor Erhard at Bergstrom Air Force Base, the entourage drove the sixty-two miles to the Ranch for an afternoon of meetings between heads of state and their cabinets. For the evening entertainment before a working dinner, Lady Bird invited Ezra Rachlin, pianist and conductor of the Austin Symphony Orchestra, to perform. Born in Los Angeles in 1915, Rachlin had studied in Berlin and, at the age of twelve, made his debut at Carnegie Hall. Soon after, at just thirteen, he became the youngest student ever to enter the Curtis Institute of Music in Philadelphia. In 1949, Ezra shifted his focus to conducting, and took the post of musical director and conductor of the Austin Symphony Orchestra, positions he would hold for twenty years.[27] Rachlin cultivated and expanded the appetite in Austin for high culture, and attracted a diverse following. Beginning in his first year as conductor, he staged concerts with full orchestras at drive-in movie theaters in Austin and around the state. With his ushers on horseback and musicians in blue jeans, he conducted Bach, Brahms, and Beethoven to local and national acclaim. Drawing on his Berlin conservatory training and his eye for crossover talent, Rachlin treated Chancellor Erhard and his diplomatic coterie to a recital and invited Linda Loftis, Miss Texas 1961, also an accomplished vocalist, to join him for the cocktail hour recital.[28]

The next day, a Sunday, the Johnsons continued the display of high/low culture by bringing Chancellor Erhard and his entourage on a visit to the local German community of Fredericksburg, a short drive west of the Ranch. In the 1840s, some 120 German families had settled there. They had not been LBJ's natural constituents during his earlier years in Congress, but the local *dorf,* where German was still actively spoken, had come around to him during the 1960 campaign, Lady Bird felt, and embraced him as one of theirs now that he was president. The first stop took the chancellor to visit a replica of an original 1847 church, a memorial to the town's original German "pioneers," where, with the Holocaust still a recent memory, a local historian made a point of stressing that the Germans of Fredericksburg "stand shoulder to shoulder with all faiths."[29] In the nearby community of Stonewall, Bess Abell and Liz Carpenter (Lady Bird's "generals," as the permanent White House staff described them) had taken over a not very large school gymnasium for a lunch of barbecue, beans, and beer. Outside, a giant sign over the doorway of the gymnasium splashed "Willkommen." Embracing the region's history and multiculturalism, a Mexican mariachi band serenaded the arriving guests. The White House's Naval Photographic Center's cameras lingered over the enormous hunks of fatty, fleshy ribs.[30] Red-and-white checkered tablecloths, red kerosene lanterns, and plastic cups sat on tables inside the gym. Bunting in the red, yellow, and black of the German flag and in the red, white, and blue of the American draped the ceilings and walls. Germany's enormous eagle insignia towered over the head table. With the protocols of the usual state dinner cast aside, the guests instead helped themselves from a buffet. The guest of honor, too: "I steered the chancellor into the chow line," a deadpan Lady Bird recalled.[31] Bales of hay decorated the stage, along with a mock-up of a wooden fence, slung with a leather saddle, lasso, and saddle blanket. "This is Hill Country," the décor screamed. And so did the entertainment: the Wanderers Three (plus a bass) played; girls folk-danced in traditional German dress; and a coed choir dressed in bolo ties and cowboy hats sang the 1940s hit "Deep in the Heart of Texas," in German.[32]

But not all the entertainment played to the world's caricature of Texas, or the European fascination with the American West. To follow Rachlin, Lady Bird had invited an almost neighbor from her own "Deep East Texas," a thirty-one-year-old concert pianist of already global renown. Van Cliburn, who had grown up forty miles from Lady Bird's Karnack, performed Beethoven and Schumann on a grand piano brought to the gymnasium for the occasion.[33] Surrounded by bales of hay and banjos, with a saddle and wagon wheel framing his tall, lean body, Van Cliburn performed pieces that contrasted with the eat-with-your-hands, bone-slurping cacophony of the lunch, offering an authentic, if paradoxical, glimpse into the complexity of American life in the 1960s. The German chancellor told a petite, tired-looking First Lady that he felt right at home. *The New York Times* called the state visit "an outstanding success—a new and relaxed kind of welcome from a chief executive for a visiting head of state," and wholly credited Lady Bird for its "gemütlich" atmosphere.[34] Very much the anti-Camelot, it was a tour de force for the Johnsons' first state visit and a sign of their natural ability to blend their roots with the role demanded of their new status.

As 1964 began, the Johnsons celebrated the New Year apart. Preferring to stay at home with her family in front of the fire, Lady Bird declined Lyndon's invitation to a party at the aptly named Forty Acres Club on the UT Austin campus. With no date for the event, Lyndon instead took off by helicopter with three of his secretaries, who were working at the Ranch over Christmas. It came as no shock to Lady Bird that Lyndon would recruit the three women, Marie Fehmer, Juanita Roberts, and Geraldine "Gerri" Whittington, to join him. But it was a shock to Austin society—Gerri Whittington was black. Radiant in yellow, Lyndon's favorite color, she danced that night on the president's arm. There to celebrate the birthday of LBJ's aide Horace Busby, Whittington and LBJ effectively desegregated one of the most important social institutions in his state.

Born and raised in Maryland just outside Washington, D.C., Whittington was the first African American woman a U.S. president had hired as his secretary. Qualified for the position by her background working as a secretary at the State Department, Whittington was also part of LBJ's public move to establish his bona fides on race and civil rights. Before leaving for the Ranch, the president let Roy Wilkins of the NAACP know he had hired her, and before the Forty Acres New Year's Eve splash, Lyndon had called to let the club know what to expect. Later, his office pressed the point, relishing Whittington's appearance the next month on *What's My Line?*, a game show popular in the 1950s and '60s. The panel of hosts—actress Arlene Francis, television and radio personality Steve Allen, journalist Dorothy Kilgallen, and Random House founder Bennett Cerf—quizzed her about her "line" after the television audience read the bland but pathbreaking description onscreen: "Secretary to President Johnson."[35]

Chapter 4

"Thank You, Mrs. Vice President"

Who knows of the possibilities of love when men and women share not only children, home, and garden, not only the fulfillment of their biological roles, but the responsibilities and passions of the work that creates the human future and the full human knowledge of who they are?

—Betty Friedan, *The Feminine Mystique*

Why not an LBJ and LBJ ticket? . . . Look no farther, Lyndon. Your big problem of a running mate for this fall is now solved. It's none other than that charming Texan, Lady Bird Johnson!

—Editorial, *Lexington Herald,* May 20, 1964

Lyndon Baines Johnson understood that Claudia Alta Taylor Johnson served to extend and magnify his power and reach. Once in the White House, by appointing Liz Carpenter as the First Lady's chief of staff and communications director, the Johnsons expanded the policy operation of the West Wing to the East Wing, more a nod to Franklin and Eleanor than to Jack and Jackie. Though all three presidential couples believed in the power of government to make lives better, emotionally and experientially, Lady Bird and Lyndon were more New Deal than New Frontier. FDR's success in leading the country out of the Great Depression and Eleanor's ethic of hard work in the service of the public good resonated with both Johnsons.

The dynamic of the Roosevelts' partnership, at once symbiotic and autonomous, was rooted in the intimacy of their shared aristocratic upbringing and noblesse oblige, and manifested itself in the rules they developed for their marriage. Eleanor adjusted to Franklin's infidelity and gained considerable independence, punctuated by heartbreak, in turn. Bird admired Eleanor for her work ethic, depth of knowledge, and humanitarian commitments, and paid public tribute to her early in her own tenure as First Lady. At the first anniversary lunch of the Eleanor Roosevelt Memorial Foundation in 1964, Lady Bird gave the keynote address. She recalled how, "as she did to many very young and very timid Congressional wives, she extended her hand and hospitality to me . . . and Washington was warmer." She lauded Eleanor for the "goodness that made her so great."[1] Although Lady Bird shared many of ER's values and was, to one observer, "the doingest woman that ever sat in the [White House] since Eleanor," Lady Bird and Liz understood that there was no mold: the First Lady to President Lyndon Johnson would necessarily have to reflect and reinforce the president's agenda; suit her own temperament, character, and interests; and manage the dualities and polarities of her husband's character.[2] Lyndon could be simultaneously brilliant, intuitive, largehearted, perceptive, charismatic, and energetic while also needy, entitled, heavy-handed, insensitive, insecure, inappropriate, withholding, and morose. Handling—indeed, loving—the very study in contrasts that made Lyndon Lyndon and President Johnson President Johnson would prove, perhaps, to be the toughest part of her job.

The political partnership between Lady Bird and Lyndon began within their marriage in the late 1930s, as did the constant process of accommodation Bird made to the knowledge of his sexual infidelities. Whereas Eleanor addressed FDR's dalliances head-on, and built an autonomous world for herself of intimate personal and political friendships outside the marriage, Lady Bird adjusted not by retreating, but rather, by making herself increasingly indispensable to Lyndon in business, politics, and family. By the time they reached the White House, LBJ's reliance on her for the emotional stability he required was total.[3]

Lady Bird seemed to accommodate Lyndon's history with other women by distinguishing between the mere sexual liaisons and the more serious interests, selectively deciding which to plainly ignore and which merited her recognition. Early in the presidency, when Lyndon invited his onetime mistress Helen Gahagan Douglas to spend the night at the

White House and "had supplied her, apparently, with my nightgown and robe," Lady Bird appeared not only unflinching but also readily accepting.[4] The two women spent breakfast the next morning together—"the most stimulating hour of the day," which Lady Bird had "simply *loved*," Bird recorded in her diary. She spoke rapturously of the onetime actress and member of Congress, of her intelligence, her breadth and depth of knowledge, even invoking, though not quite verbatim, Shakespeare's paean to Cleopatra ("time does not stale nor age . . . something . . . thou infinite variety") to describe her husband's former lover.[5] Perhaps Lady Bird was claiming a level of dominance over her husband's paramour, or perhaps she was dissimulating entirely, but consciously or not, she understood in her bones that the totality of Lyndon's dependence upon her since his 1955 heart attack and certainly by 1964 helped her claim a degree of influence and power over the thirty-sixth president of the United States that was vastly more potent and enduring than any paramour could achieve. Over the course of their marriage, Lyndon had taken ill with appendicitis, kidney stones, and the aftereffects of too much eating, drinking, and smoking. But it was the heart attack he suffered in 1955 that almost killed him, and that instilled in both Johnsons a new and permanent vigilance and anxiety over his health. At the time, he was only forty-six, and Lady Bird forty-two. Seeing Lyndon at the hospital "gray as a cement sidewalk," Lady Bird felt "embattled against death and absolutely enraged" at the thought of losing him and the life they were only in the middle of building. That health crisis, his struggle with depression that followed, and his extended recuperation at the Ranch under Lady Bird's watch, shifted something in Lyndon and between the two. He began to take greater pleasure in his family and to feed off the prospect of another kind of dominion: over the space and endless to-do lists of the Ranch. A near-death experience had forced him for a time to dial back the exercise of his newly acquired power as Senate majority leader, and it also leveled and clarified the distribution of power within the marriage.[6]

Lady Bird was a student of history, and she understood that it was the very qualities her husband and his predecessors possessed, grandiosity and entitlement, that had also helped compel these political animals to seek the power of the American presidency in the first place. However painful or embarrassing her husband's assignations could be, by 1963, when they moved into the White House, Lady Bird had no equal, and Lyndon made that clear to her. And he was not shy in talking about his wife's critical role in his career. At an event filled with ambassadors, Lyndon once recalled "how, at the end of an evening . . . when he had been out with Mrs. Johnson at a party where there were some very famous people, or [with] some special person, he would say to her, 'How is it that the most important man in the room is always talking to you all evening?'" With this anecdote, he concluded to the group gathered in the Rose Garden, "The strongest thing I can tell you is that the wife, your wife, is the most important asset you'll have."[7] Lady Bird Johnson's eye for spotting and understanding power was rivaled by only one, that of her husband.

* * *

By the spring of 1964, invitations for Lady Bird to speak were pouring in. Most of her time was earmarked for either ceremonial events or travel with LBJ. For solo appearances where she could exercise some control, Bird gravitated toward opportunities that allowed her to keep the focus on the status and prospects of American women. In late April, Radcliffe College president Dr. Mary Bunting, a geneticist by training, invited Lady Bird to deliver the baccalaureate commencement address that June. Lady Bird, a history major and journalism minor, was eager to accept the opportunity to speak to some of the most promising young women of that time, women who had arguably bucked traditional expectations of marriage above all else in order to graduate from a prestigious university. At the time, a middle-class girl was expected to go to college, but as a 1959 study showed, 37 percent dropped out before graduating.[8] In fact, the number of women enrolled in higher education had been dropping since the 1920s, when women earned approximately half of all bachelor's degrees and approximately 17 percent of doctorates. By the 1950s, those numbers had plummeted to 24 percent and 10 percent, respectively. By 1960, women made up a mere 6 percent of doctors, 3 percent of lawyers, and less than 1 percent of engineers. As a *Newsweek* article from 1946 pointedly stated, "For the American girl, books and babies don't mix."[9]

At Radcliffe, where, one reporter noted, women held "a long tradition of academic supremacy over the brother institution" of Harvard, the story was slightly different: unlike many academic institutions at the time, Radcliffe was serious about educating the next generation of female leaders.[10] Its students were trained in the sciences and mathematics, in law and literature. Radcliffe women were supposed to shatter glass ceilings and make history. The 1964 graduating class consisted of 252 students drawn from across the United States. More than 75 percent were graduating with honors (a higher rate than graduates at Harvard), and 40 percent were moving on directly to graduate studies.[11]

Lady Bird felt the pulse of history from the moment she arrived in Massachusetts, her first visit since the 1960 campaign planning session in Hyannis. Her trip to Kennedy territory, to Cambridge, to the Northeast, created its own special kind of dread and anxiety for her. More confident than her husband in the world of ideas, and an avid reader herself, she still felt intimidated by what she imagined to be the intellectual heft emanating from the Charles River set. Sitting on the pulpit in the small, high-ceilinged, "rather rococo" Memorial Church alongside an ancestor of Abigail Adams, her most literate diarist and letter-writing predecessor, Bird searched "the faces of the 250-odd girls, to see what it was that made them different from and smarter than most of the girls, because this certainly is Olympian ground, intellectually speaking, and I was never so awed in my life by both audience and pulpit."[12]

Speechwriting for Lady Bird took an enormous amount of time and energy. She'd worked harder on this speech than on almost any other. The process generally involved a sit-down with her team, sometimes recruited from the West Wing or from longtime friends around town, to write and rewrite her speech until it perfectly suited the audience in mind.

The challenge Mrs. Johnson faced with the Radcliffe speech was to acknowledge feminism, albeit indirectly, by also making very explicit to her Cambridge "Olympians," and to a national female audience, that she stood with young women and believed totally in their capacities—not just as Lyndon's voters, but as individuals with boundless abilities to realize their full and daunting potential as wives, mothers, professionals, and community activists.[13] Six years before Hillary Rodham gave the student commencement address at her graduation from Wellesley (a somewhat elliptical speech about sharing, and assuming, "power and responsibility" in which she did not explicitly mention women at all), the First Lady of the United States placed young women, not Lyndon Johnson, at the center of her remarks. Looking out at her captive audience, she vocalized the challenge they faced: "This is no easy task in a world of experts on women with every bookstore offering up the joys of emancipation and every newsstand proffering the delights of femininity. But actually, amid all the worries and uncertainties—and the provocative doctrines about the role of the educated woman today, a quite remarkable young woman has been emerging in the United States."[14] As if speaking directly to each graduate individually, she added,

> She is your sister, your roommate, and if you look closely enough, probably, yourself. She might be called the natural woman, the complete woman. She has taken from the past what is vital and discarded the irrelevant or misleading. She has taken over the right to participate fully—whether in jobs, professions, or the political life of the community. She has rejected a number of overtones of the emancipation movement as clearly unworkable. . . . She wants to be—while being equally involved—pre-eminently a woman, a wife, a mother, a thinking citizen.[15]

Acknowledging the difficulty inherent in such a complex juggling act, and well aware of her own limitations in that regard, Lady Bird noted,

> It is an awesome task, but you can organize life as you have learned to organize study. It is important to retain those qualities of warmth and tact and sensitivity which a real woman possesses. The man you marry will want you to be what you are—not only his wife and the mother of his children, but a person in your own right, with drives

> and desires, talents and skills of your own.... Ultimately, it comes back to the spirit in which you can direct your own life—how happily you can marry both man and job; or how happily you can marry one of them.[16]

Perhaps in her most pointed break from gendered orthodoxy of the day, Lady Bird applauded the young women who might choose not to follow a traditionally delineated path: "Not all of you, of course, will contribute to our society as young married women. There will be many whose contributions will grow from their job or their profession—very often after years of meeting intense demands of graduate training. I salute you because the world needs your talents."[17]

Like most commencement speeches, hers was in large measure autobiographical, if understated. "I urge you to enter outlets not as [a] superwoman, but as the total woman, a natural woman, a happy woman. If you can achieve the precious balance between woman's domestic and civil life, you can do more for zest and sanity in our society than by any other achievement." She could not of course reveal to her audience just how "total" her own experience had become, with her unique role in Lyndon's presidency and its future. Instead, Bird praised Bunting as having achieved all of it—a stable home and family life, an education with a terminal degree, a college presidency, and most recently a groundbreaking appointment by LBJ as the only woman on the Atomic Energy Commission, all while raising four children.[18]

Always allergic to the doctrinaire, Bird obliquely drew the line at stridency, bristling at the need to concede the "emancipation movement" as the sole terrain of the "long-striding feminist in low heels, engaged in a conscious war with men." Rather, her progressive message was that women from her generation and generations younger could well embody a feminist identity without needing to become militant about it. Beyond that, her claim that young women graduates could become "the complete woman," "the natural woman," while rejecting the impossibility of the superwoman, placed her at the center of debates not just in the 1960s but in every decade in American history since.[19]

On her way back to Washington, the First Lady stopped for a moment at the "noble, peaceful" place along the Charles River designated as the site for the JFK Presidential Library. Always one to look ahead well in advance of the next task, she had already begun to think about Lyndon's library and was taking mental notes. Bird began the day intimidated, ill at ease. Flying the Johnson flag right in the heart of Kennedy territory, she felt her confidence grow. "When I actually get down to talking to people," she concluded, "the gap between Karnack and Cambridge can be bridged, and I'm not quite so in awe of them."[20] Emerging from the shadow of Camelot by embracing the matter of women's role in the economy and society, Lady Bird further distinguished herself from Jackie—at the same time giving considerably more substance to Lyndon's attempt early in his term to bolster women's representation in senior federal jobs—by addressing the need for the administration to focus on the multiple roles of women, including as the providers of income in poor families. The First Lady understood the centrality of women to redressing poverty and, early on, sought to call attention to the economic, social, political, and even national security significance of women in the home and women in the public square.

* * *

Lady Bird Johnson came of age when laws, culture, and expectations for women in the United States yielded few options. She graduated as a history major from the University of Texas at Austin in 1933 and completed a second major in journalism in 1934. Dreading the thought of returning permanently to the isolation of Karnack, Texas, she laid the groundwork to follow the route of the well-educated women of the era and become a teacher. But she looked beyond Karnack or even remaining in Austin for her teaching career. Instead, Bird planned a flight that for the times would take her as far away as imaginable—to Hawaii or Alaska, neither of which was yet a state in July 1934—when a friend fixed her up with an ambitious congressional staffer named Lyndon Baines Johnson.

Her parents had married and migrated from Alabama to East Texas in 1900. Minnie Lee Pattillo came to the marriage with the wealth her father had acquired after the Civil War from thousands of acres of cotton and pine for timber and the labor and debt of its tenant farmers. Thomas Jefferson Taylor, Claudia's father, grew up working some of that Pattillo land under the tyrannical watch of his stepfather after his own father died when he was just a year old. T.J. and Minnie married against her father's wishes—not in a church, but in T.J.'s brother's home. Once settled in Karnack, Texas, fifteen miles from the Louisiana border, T. J. Taylor rapidly built his own wealth. The very well-read Minnie brought four crates of books from Alabama, and once there, bought herself a car, delved into the occult, and announced her belief in women's suffrage. She gave birth to two boys, Thomas Jr. in 1901 and Antonio in 1904. But their father soon became involved with other women, and the alienated and unhappy Minnie brought her two young sons back to her father's home in Alabama. After recuperative visits to the Kellogg sanitarium in Battle Creek, Michigan, Minnie returned to T.J. and Karnack, where the family moved into a seventeen-room mansion, the Brick House. Claudia, named for Minnie's brother Claud, came along on December 22, 1912. The only daughter and youngest of three, Claudia was raised by black women, the descendants of formerly enslaved people, their children her daily playmates. One of these women—or perhaps it was a playmate—seeing that Claudia was far too weighty a name for such a sprightly child, named her Lady Bird. When Claudia was almost six, with her brothers already away at boarding school in the Catskills, her learned, eccentric mother, while pregnant again, fell, was hospitalized, and died. T.J., or "Captain Taylor," Claudia's father, allowed for little mourning, even waiting a full year to tell Thomas and Antonio about their mother's death. He brought his daughter to his general store with him at first—she slept in the attic adjacent to the empty pine coffins in stock—while he worked. Soon, Minnie's sister, Effie Pattillo, a Juilliard-trained pianist, moved from Alabama to help with her young niece's upbringing.

Spending hours on end in the woods alone or in her room reading, Lady Bird—by this time, the nickname had stuck—developed an inner life that taught her how to take emotional sustenance from nature and books. Her outer life was blunted by social isolation—school in a one-room schoolhouse until, at age fifteen, she moved to Dallas to attend a junior college for girls. Like many smart southern girls in the 1930s, Bird consciously concealed her intelligence, to dodge public recognition and the pressure to speak or to avoid antagonizing her more socially adept, popular peers. Her years at the University of Texas at Austin pulled her further from her shy habits. Lyndon Baines Johnson would draw her further away from them still, and to a place where she might comment on the role of women in the nation's future, rather than only inhabit the more conventional role slated for the majority of women of her generation.[21]

* * *

Lady Bird's initial interest in women's issues stemmed not just from her own experience but also from the awareness that she needed to identify a set of priorities to call her own—those that would reinforce LBJ and, though she had her doubts that women could be treated as one homogenous voting bloc, his presidential bid. The First Lady and her staff initially turned the East Wing's focus to women, a safe zone few in the West Wing harbored any territorial instincts to protect. Other than Lyndon's stated commitment to hire more women as senior administration officials, and other than women's voting potential, the far broader and politically fraught matter of securing women's equality (rights, pay, status, and standing in society and the workplace) was not, in 1964, a significant policy priority for her husband's West Wing.

At the time, the discourse on women's rights was shifting dramatically, and the East Wing advanced Lady Bird (devoted wife, doting mother, businesswoman, and policy veteran) as a possible voice to nudge the public dialogue along. In August 1963, Betty Friedan, a not especially high-profile journalist of labor newsletters and women's magazines, published *The Feminine Mystique*. Perhaps the title's use of the word *mystique* should have appeared in quotes. For, rather than an ode to the aura of femininity the word implied, the book put forth the message that, popular mythology to the contrary, American women could not possibly realize their full human potential within the cultural confines and material trappings of postwar, middle-class America.

The Feminine Mystique offered women, long relegated to talk of their roles as wives and mothers, the vocabulary to more deeply analyze and articulate their grievances. At the time, responding to the small number of feminist activists in Washington and to garner the coveted "women's vote," the government began to devote energy to the study of "women's issues." In 1961, President Kennedy launched the Presidential Commission on the Status of Women to evaluate the legal, social, civic, and economic status of American women, with Eleanor Roosevelt serving as its honorary chairwoman. Just a few weeks before JFK's assassination, the commission issued its findings. The principal recommendations centered on steps the federal government should take to guarantee equal pay. It also advocated a number of major policy reforms, many of which remain elusive today, including paid maternity leave, universal childcare, an end to sex discrimination in hiring, and recognition of women's equality under the Fourteenth Amendment.[22] At the time the report was issued, women made up only 2 percent of U.S. senators, 2 percent of U.S. ambassadors, and 2.5 percent of U.S. representatives. Women did not have rights within their marriage other than to be "properly supported." Only four states allowed women the right to separate residences from their husbands, and many states required a woman to take her husband's surname. At least five states required that women receive court approval before opening a business in their own name.[23] Women in many states were legally barred from many of the freedoms that would have made it possible for them to live without a husband. Divorcées and single women often needed their father's name on house deeds and credit cards. In short, legally, economically, and culturally, women were a marginalized population that had only just begun to feel free to talk about and see themselves as such. *The Feminine Mystique* helped to open the floodgates.[24]

Lady Bird understood that she was among the tiny minority of American women who had been able to dodge the oppressive effects of the "strange stirring" that Friedan identified, precisely because of her partnership with Lyndon. In the first half of 1964, though never stated as such, she and her team envisioned making the East Wing a platform for promoting precisely the direction for American women that Friedan pointed toward in her bestseller. Less than two months into the presidency, Lyndon declared that he intended to boost the number of women in senior administration positions to at least fifty. "This is no sporadic election year gimmick," LBJ warned in a signal of his commitment to the issue.[25] But not everyone believed the president sincere. Columnist Charles Bartlett remarked, "It's ridiculous. A President ought to spend more time on policy than on public relations stunts."[26] Yet JFK's limitations with respect to women in government afforded LBJ an opportunity for improvement on his predecessor's frontier-pushing policies. And recruiting women to his administration might be less a political lift than actually changing the law to guarantee equal pay for equal work, or equal rights across the board.

Lady Bird's deft approach to highlighting women as professionals was both a direct, if unstated, reply to Betty Friedan's clarion call and a natural and logical way to harness her own very extensive network of women developed over decades. Segregation was not only racial but also a matter of gender in the nation's capital. In politics and in most professions related to the business of the federal government, men dominated. But women, perhaps at a disproportionately higher degree than in other comparably populated American cities at the time, did have a presence in the federal bureaucracy, the judiciary, journalism, and politics. In 1964, Washington women still observed, albeit grudgingly, certain enduring orthodoxies of subordination to men and exclusion from the institutions they dominated. Yet, in a way, these very orthodoxies also provided a protective pool of "influencers" upon whom Lady Bird drew during her early White House months, when the prospect of election to a full presidential term loomed large, but was, in Bird's mind, still uncertain.

Lady Bird's interest in the intellectual contributions of influential, even pioneering women began long before her tenure in the White House. During her travels around the world as Second Lady, and also on 50th Street, or stepping in for Jackie, Bird had grown impatient with the tea/flower/gift exchange protocol events expected of the spouses of senior government officials. Before that, as wife of the majority leader, she had clocked many hours rolling bandages and gathering (and likely spreading) political intelligence for Lyndon with her fellow spouses in the Senate Ladies Red Cross Unit, also known as the "Ladies of the Senate." Now, as First Lady, she had the chance to align her desire for substance with her innate political instincts. In the first six months of 1964, she hosted six gatherings of professional women for lunch and conversation in the Yellow Oval Room on the south side of the second floor of the White House. She and Lyndon made much of their affinity for "can-do" people on their staff, and so the series of women's confabs was thus dubbed "Doers Luncheons."

The somewhat patronizing, hokey sound of the gatherings, like so much that carried Lady Bird's touch, lightly laid a cloak of benign protection over an exercise that helped differentiate her from previous First Ladies by offering the platform of White House legitimacy to an issue that no First Lady since Eleanor Roosevelt had had the context, concern, or backing of her husband to spotlight. As the East Wing's press announcement described them, the luncheons would unfold "in a spirit of intimacy . . . where women with ideas can talk," and, initially, without press coverage or photos or much made public by way of who attended.[27] The meetings immediately evolved beyond the caricature of ladies taking tea together and instead reflected, in content and (occasionally) controversy, the political dynamics of the day. During the first six months of 1964, Lady Bird held six of the thirteen Doers Luncheons she would hold before leaving office. At each one, professional women of substance, all of whom worked in precisely the arenas of Lyndon's domestic policy agenda, spoke to an audience of their peers—as many as one hundred women drawn from local and national politics and government, science, education, media, the arts, and urban planning, including the likes of barrier-breaking African American contralto Marian Anderson and prima ballerina Maria Tallchief, daughter of an Osage Indian, who had debuted the *Firebird Suite* for George Balanchine and several other major roles for the New York City Ballet.

Some of the trailblazing women who spoke at the early Doers gatherings included Eleanor Pressly, the director of a rocket and spacecraft integration division at Goddard Space Flight Center in Greenbelt, Maryland; Kate Tuchman, principal of P.S. 184, a public school in Manhattan; and Professor Barbara Solomon, associate dean of Radcliffe College and since 1959 director of the archive of women's history at Radcliffe. First launched as Radcliffe's research library in 1943 with the holdings of the Women's Rights Collection of the National League of Women Voters, it is now the Arthur and Elizabeth Schlesinger Library on the History of Women in America. Beyond the archive's suffrage-related manuscripts, at the time of Solomon's White House speech, holdings featured collections related to women in medicine, law, education, politics, social service, and business. And the archive held the papers of the Presidential Commission on the Status of Women and of leading American women in twentieth-century government and politics. Solomon later became the first woman appointed as assistant dean of Harvard College, taught Harvard's first course on the history of women in America, and helped lay the groundwork for the creation of women's studies departments around the country. At the White House, Solomon implored her audience to "'save those letters, diaries, and other mementos' for they are the stuff of history." She continued: "[W]hat I would like to think the Radcliffe Women's Archives is telling [is] how American women did it.... What were the thoughts and actions of the women on the frontiers, the immigrant women who came over in steerage with their husbands, the women in seminaries? We want to tell what made the American woman independent and resourceful, interested not only in her own needs but in the needs of others."[28] Lady Bird, the active diarist and correspondent, committed already to documenting her husband's presidency and planning for his library, embraced Solomon's advice.

* * *

As the East Wing emerged as a permanent and valued addition to the Johnson White House, Lady Bird and Liz worked tirelessly to introduce the new First Lady to the American public. With a series of interviews, almost all by women journalists and writers whom Lady Bird had come to know during her many years in Washington, the East Wing sought to shape the narrative around Bird's public image. Among many others, the women who covered Lady Bird early in her White House tenure included columnist Katie Louchheim, a frenetic, striving almost-member of the "Georgetown set" who served simultaneously as vice chairwoman of the Democratic National Committee, director of Women's Activities of the DNC, and deputy assistant secretary for public affairs at the State Department under JFK; Doris Fleeson, a devoted feminist, avid New Dealer, and the first female journalist to become a nationally syndicated columnist, once called "a tiger in white gloves" for her tenacious and impartial reporting; and Nancy Dickerson, a Johnson insider who had recently moved from CBS (where she had become the first woman network television anchor) to NBC. Her coverage of the 1960 Democratic convention, including her exclusive interview with LBJ after he accepted the vice-presidential slot, and her marathon coverage from Washington of the Kennedy assassination and its aftermath, solidified her in the national media as a journalist who called it straight despite her status as a consummate insider.[29]

For a program to be aired the weekend after Lyndon's State of the Union address, NBC filmed Lady Bird meeting with labor leaders by day and with CEOs by night before Lyndon joined them for dinner to preview his message to the U.S. Congress. As Dickerson noted in the spot, "A Week in the Life of Lady Bird Johnson," the First Lady was the only woman in rooms filled with men. Indeed, we see a woman at ease, an active listener clinking her glass with the heads of U.S. Steel, Merck, the U.S. Stock Exchange, and Continental Oil, among others. Without the sound and only Dickerson's voiceover, Lady Bird, in a timeless black sleeveless sheath, pearls, and heels, comes off as very much a peer, another CEO, and, in a way, fulfilling the very role that a vice president otherwise might have performed for the president.

But she was "bone tired" that week. And her exhaustion showed as she faced the camera directly for an interview. Watching the program from Camp David, she described her own performance as "catastrophic," finding the interview "about as bad as I had thought it would be."[30] Bird,

Dickerson narrated, "may well be the hardest working First Lady in history. None before has ever been so closely identified with her husband's career."[31] None, perhaps, other than Eleanor. However, differentiating herself from Eleanor, Lady Bird, with one teenage daughter still living under her roof and the other away for her sophomore year of college, wanted also to project to American women, through her female boosters in the press corps, her desire to perform the traditional job: "to be balm, sustainer, and sometimes critic to my husband" and to "help my children" revere the presidency while retaining "the lightheartedness [to] which every teenager is entitled." For this early public display, she emphasized, ever so gently and with total sincerity, the role of wife and mother. And "as to my role, it will have to emerge in deeds, not words."[32] Gone was the breathy, haute-feminine voice and cosmopolitan diction of Jackie Kennedy. Instead, Americans heard and saw a tight, heavily accented, self-consciously emphatic, awkward-for-the-close-up effort to communicate confidence, readiness, and femininity, all marshaled in service of her husband, her children, her fellow citizens, and their president. But the new First Lady also looked frazzled, even a little shell-shocked, by the demands of the juggling act she was now forced to perform in the public spotlight.

Another portrait of Bird was drawn by Elizabeth "Babs" Janeway, the Brooklyn-born Barnard graduate and novelist who covered the Lady Bird beat early on and who wrote for *Ladies' Home Journal* what would become the most telling portrait of the First Lady to result from Liz Carpenter's early press strategy. Married to a man with a reputation for working hard to stay close to power, and having been close to it herself—she was at Lady Bird's side in the Los Angeles hotel suite while the Johnsons absorbed the impact of accepting the vice-presidential slot on the 1960 Democratic Party ticket—Janeway brought to her writing an appreciation for how women wielded and yielded marital power. In a fitting sign of the journalistic times, she hooked her reader not by leading with a description of Bird's prodigious energy, her capacity for professionalism, or how her emotional compartmentalization helped her manage and weather the fits and rages of the president whom Janeway later called, plainly, an "ogre." Rather, in 1964, Janeway led by indirection, praising Mr. Johnson for choosing Mrs. Johnson.

> "Washington is full of brilliant men—and the women they married when they were young." The cynical authority who voiced this was right in part. Washington does have its share, and more than its share, of faded, once pretty women who have not kept up with their husbands. Conversation after dinner can be sheer agony. Across the room the men are reporting the latest news from Capitol Hill, or discussing next week's appointment to an ambassadorship or a commission. The ladies, however, are comparing hairdos or recipes or nursery schools—fascinating topics in their place, but maddening when one is trying to follow political gossip of brilliant men.
>
> But there are a few brilliant men in Washington who apparently had as much taste and discernment in their twenties as they do in their fifties. They fell in love with pretty girls who grew up to be women of character and intelligence, of dignity, culture, humor and good sense. One of these lucky men is President Lyndon Baines Johnson.[33]

Janeway's portrait of Lady Bird covers the usual ground of early childhood and the accumulation of skills—personal, political, diplomatic, social, psychological. For an American readership still hooked on Jackie Kennedy's savoir faire, Janeway also took pains to address the cultural bias against the South. "Her voice is Deep South—so Southern that some Northerners say apologetically that it 'puts them off.' But Lady Bird Johnson is neither a Southern Belle nor a Southern Bigot. People who have begun to listen to her words instead of her accent find that her speech is tangy, terse and individual."[34] And Janeway addressed another elephant in the popular imagination at the time: how could Lady Bird—nay, anyone—have the constitution and patience to be married to Lyndon Johnson? The journalist had asked a number of sources how Lady Bird could excel so totally, and with such equanimity. Her conclusion:

> It's as if she had simply dropped somewhere, years ago, that irritable top bit of oneself that we all know so well, the part that says, "I want—I must have—I won't be happy without this or that." Her self discipline, I think, began with the decision to do what her husband needed, to accept the demands made on her, and to find in them not irritation nor disruption of her own inner life but instead its very purpose. This is neither easy nor impossible—it is simply hard. I believe that Bird Johnson's astonishing energy and strength of character stem from an old decision to forget about herself.[35]

What a younger feminist writer might have seen as submissiveness under the weight of an oppressive and domineering husband for Janeway amounted to a near-Buddhist inner calm, nonattachment, selflessness, service to others, to Lyndon. In her influential book *Between Myth and Morning,* Janeway cautions younger feminists coming of age in the 1960s and '70s not to mistake flying under the feminist radar as a rejection by their elders of the fundamentals of feminism—a view that endorsed Lady Bird's hard-won success.

* * *

Two weeks after crossing the Karnack-Cambridge divide at Radcliffe, Lady Bird traveled to Michigan for a speech at the annual convention for the Home Economics Association in Detroit. Given the awkward task of pushing female empowerment to a group of home economists, Bird was again heavily involved in the drafting of her speech and spent several hours practicing its delivery with her speech coach, Hester Beall Provensen. Barbara Ward, a visiting Harvard fellow, friend of JFK and LBJ, and early influence on LBJ and Lady Bird's thinking about the quality of life in America's urban centers (and who had also assisted with her Radcliffe speech earlier that month), had arrived for another White House visit the day before Detroit and helped the First Lady fine-tune her message.

Conscious of the need to project her voice to the back of the enormous auditorium, the First Lady went big, announcing that a "quiet revolution of emancipation has been taking place in the lives of women everywhere—from Detroit to Delhi. Millions of women have achieved the right to vote, to own property, to be educated." Technology in the home had freed "women from the total bondage of home chores."[36] Overstating her case, an idealistic Lady Bird declared that "with these newly won rights and with a rising standard of living, women can move beyond the struggle for equal status and for material goods to the challenge and opportunities of citizenship."[37] Perhaps praising home economists for their role in helping women obtain the yet-to-be-achieved "equal status" seems like a swipe at Friedan's point; indeed, Friedan's book had posited that the very life that home economists sought to enhance actually drove middle-class American women toward mental exhaustion and social alienation.[38] But such an audience provided an almost subversive platform for Mrs. Johnson to associate herself with those "doctrines of emancipation" she found too doctrinaire. "As American women, we hold a tremendous potential of strength for good. I do not refer to the sense of power that comes from flicking a switch or turning an ignition key. But to the force we exert when we mark a ballot, teach our children, or work for a better community."[39] Equal status had yet to be achieved, but Bird's message was that the women most associated with extolling the virtues of home life must leave their homes to actually obtain such equality.

How, she asked, can women "practice citizenship to the fullest extent, both at home and abroad"? Again, her answer was self-consciously autobiographical and equally telling. College, but also marriage—to a "tall Texan"—had broadened and deepened her "sense of power," her horizons, from the moss and alligators of East Texas to every corner of the country and around the world. Her close-up encounters with poverty in the developing world and in Appalachia had given her the opportunity to "draw the curtain open a little more"; and such experience "exposes us to ourselves" and "gives national attention" to her message: "This is the other side of America. Look! And act!" She addressed the need for women to involve themselves in redressing the "unfinished business of America." By that she meant "the fact that poverty roots are deepest in the family structure," whether in urban slums or in Mexican American border towns. She exhorted the home economists to turn their attention from the middle class to low-income women. She also praised the association for having mailed a bilingual instruction booklet, *Food for Fitness,* to El Paso families, a strategy focused on food and nutrition that her successor Michelle Obama would later deploy. But she questioned whether the curricula at American colleges "may be geared too much to the values of the middle-income family" at the expense of the poor. Wonky to the core beneath her pillbox hat and poise, she argued that fighting the War on Poverty, achieving the vision of the Great Society, would require not just more government funding, but a realignment of local, state, federal, and volunteer organizations, and the ability of individual women to reach outside their homes to mobilize or benefit from these institutions. Speaking to the multitasking capacity of women, she exhorted the audience "of women who manage several lives successfully" also to consider going into politics. And Lady Bird extolled the crowd above all, "Don't hold back. Don't be shy. Step forward in every way you can to plan boldly, to speak clearly, to offer the leadership which the world needs."[40]

Before she met Lyndon, and even after she fell for him, Lady Bird anticipated living a life of passivity. "For me, and probably for most women, the attempt to become an involved, practicing citizen has been a matter of evolution rather than choice." At the time, this was certainly true: women's agency in their own lives remained highly constrained. Twenty-five years earlier and given the choice, she said, she would have opted for a fantasy of "lying in a hammock under an apple tree with a book of poetry and watching the blossoms float." But the ensuing decades of marriage to Lyndon, whom she had initially implored not to go into politics, left her no choice but to embrace the life of a public citizen, often speaking to thousands and forgoing the quiet existence she had once hoped to live in Texas. Invoking the threat of nuclear warfare as yet another mobilizing call for women to act, she paraphrased Edmund Burke: "The only thing necessary for the triumph of evil is for good men *and good women* to do nothing."[41] Delivering such a progressive message to home economists, without insulting their profession as backward or crippling, exemplified the tightrope the First Lady walked as she gently subverted the established norms of her generation.

* * *

Related to the East Wing's early focus on women, Lady Bird's efforts stood squarely to amplify the Johnson administration's declaration of an "unconditional war on poverty in America," first articulated in his State of the Union address earlier that year.[42] In elaborating on this vision—one that for all good measure resembled a refashioned New Deal for the 1960s—LBJ argued that the social woes of the nation, ranging from civil rights to inadequate education and healthcare, were the result of extreme poverty. His objective would be to introduce a range of legislation, programs, and politically necessary tax cuts to alleviate these burdens. For Lady Bird, the speech represented "a good synthesis of his living and working over the last thirty years" and the beginnings of a blueprint for her time in the White House.[43]

That spring of '64, as Lyndon pushed to outmaneuver the forces of opposition to civil rights legislation drafted to eliminate employment discrimination and racial segregation in public spaces, and as movement leaders and activists mobilized to force Washington's hand, racial injustice and white resistance to change had become an inescapable feature of the South and of the American political canvas writ large. But Lady Bird Johnson was not yet ready to enter the fray. In planning a trip to Alabama to highlight her husband's patronage of the budding aerospace industry there, and the role of women in it, she met with their close friend, the Democratic Party's czar of southern supremacist politics, Richard Russell, for his advice.[44] Social change for Lady Bird came through the courts and the halls of Congress, not from the streets. Would it be possible, she wondered, for her to travel to the epicenter of the country's racial conflict without making herself a lightning rod for civil rights activists? If she stuck to government buildings where security could be assured and carefully curated whom she spoke to and about what, Russell told her, the answer was yes. But did her strategy during the first half of 1964, to wall herself from the issue on which her husband was attempting to define himself, betray a certain ambivalence about race? Or was she simply holding back until she had something more concrete around which to rally the southern constituents whom she knew so well? Did this Texan with Alabama roots simply feel more comfortable speaking to white women about white poverty rather than about black poverty and injustice?

More a matter of White House political strategy than a question of her discomfort, in early 1964, while LBJ pushed for civil rights legislation, the First Lady brought her lens to the social and economic conditions of poor whites to bolster the efforts of the War on Poverty. She visited job training institutes and a local college in Wilkes-Barre, the Eleventh District of Pennsylvania, coal country. She earned rave reviews from members of Congress on both sides of the aisle, one of whom wrote the president that Lady Bird was a "smash hit."[45] And one constituent, *The New York Times* reported, had "light-heartedly suggested that the president run on an 'LBJ and LBJ' ticket" that year, given Lady Bird's success in connecting with the American public.[46] The trip to Wilkes-Barre marked the beginning of dozens of such trips to promote Lyndon's signature legislation to tackle poverty and inequality.

Prior to the Democratic National Convention in late August 1964, Lady Bird would log 35,405 miles alone and 9,433 miles with Lyndon. Her domestic travels would take her to twenty states across the country, including to the Cumberland Plateau, in eastern Kentucky, that May. With her "incongruous army of newspaper people and cameramen trailing behind," she spent the day traveling by car, on foot, and by helicopter in the "beautiful but economically depressed" heart of Kentucky. And here, Lady Bird the endlessly open witness, the anthropologist, and the emerging nature writer comes through:

> I *love* the picturesque names—Troublesome Creek, Lick Branch School, the community of Quick Stand, Stray Branch. It was a country of hills and hollows, emerald green with spring, swift rocky streams crossed by foot bridges and occasionally a hillside blighted by strip mining—the process of simply scraping off the top of the

> earth by machinery, to get to coal, and leaving it looking wounded and ugly, with no reforestation. It's a beautiful country with a sad history of a declining economy that's gone on for the last three or four decades.[47]

Rather than risk a school bus breaking down, the First Lady pulled on the black boots she'd brought along and hiked the mile up Warsaw Branch Creek to visit one family, press army in tow. Standing on the porch of the family's three-room house to greet her were Mr. and Mrs. Robertson, their six sons, and Judy Ann, the lone daughter, "scrubbed and dressed up for the occasion." Judy Ann delighted Bird with a bouquet of red and yellow snake tongue and rooster comb, wildflowers whose names the First Lady had memorized as a young, comfortably prosperous girl during her childhood in Karnack, Texas. "Thin, wiry, gaunt-faced Arthur Robertson was easy to talk to and full of ginger although he looked like he hadn't had a square meal enough of the days of his 36 years," Bird recorded. Liz, Bess, and the various government agencies planning the trip had chosen the Robertson family for the First Lady to highlight as something of a poster child for successful rural poverty programs. Arthur showed Bird the house, which he had repaired and insulated, and the privy and well, which he had built, all with a seven-hundred-dollar federal grant, and the three-fifths of an acre of tobacco he had planted, also with Department of Agriculture assistance. He told her about the part-time job he also now held reforesting pine trees along Stray Branch Creek.[48]

After the Robertsons' home, Bird visited a one-room schoolhouse, one that reminded her of the Fern school she attended between the ages of five and eleven—only, this one was packed with twenty-five students, not the handful of classmates she had studied beside as a girl. She joined the kids and washed her hands where they washed theirs: with water from a tin can punched with holes. And she sat with them for a lunch of canned pork, green beans, hot cornbread, gingerbread, and milk. Food was a big part of educating poor children: most of the students also ate a hot breakfast provided by the school, their families too poor to feed them before the school day. With very tough living conditions (outdoor toilets; muddy, impassable roads; and not much of a social life), teacher retention was also a major impediment to rural education. In 1939, one of Lyndon's signature accomplishments as a junior congressman had been rural electrification for the residents of his native Hill Country. Almost three decades later, this Kentucky hollow still lacked electricity: one of the big moments of the day was when the First Lady flipped the On switch to light up the school, for the first time ever.

When she reflected on her trip a few days later, Bird's authority as a savvy American politician and policy wonk permeated her diary recording: "The bet we are making, the government—and it is a large bet, because the federal government is pouring about 200 million a year into Kentucky since 1961 to improve health, housing, for job retraining, for school lunch, public works, and similar pubic service programs—is that you can do this without destroying the character, the self-reliance of American citizens."[49] The First Lady was a creature of the New Deal's emphasis on the human, moral, and practical value of government programs for Americans at the margins of society. Yet she grasped that the programs her husband's administration would later implement also encroached upon the psychological and mythological resonance of individualism, especially in a rural America suspicious of but desperate for government help. Some twenty-six years earlier, Eleanor Roosevelt, who had inspired Lady Bird with her emphasis on how government could ease the burden of impoverished Americans, inaugurated the high school gymnasium where Lady Bird spoke that day, a facility built with federal New Deal public works and local funds.

Lady Bird had grown up around, but not in, rural poverty, both black and white, and the Republican Party had recently attacked her for the impoverished conditions of the tenants living on her Alabama property. A deft political operative, she had managed, with her trip to eastern Kentucky, to reinforce the value of her husband's poverty programs in the very home state of one of the Republican congressmen who had traveled to Alabama weeks earlier to charge Lady Bird Johnson with hypocrisy for renting run-down shacks with no electricity or running water to destitute tenants.[50] She capped the day dining with the Kentucky Federation of Women's Clubs, itself focused on charitable fundraising for rural medical clinics and literacy programs, to address the rather stunning fact of some 407,000 illiterate adults in the state (13 percent of the state's total population at the time). Lady Bird sensed that the women in her audience nevertheless "were not too much in sympathy" with her account of "the really very thrilling day" she had spent in their home state, with "the need and the progress I had seen," or with her pitch on behalf of the Johnson administration's War on Poverty. Kentucky, she observed, and her day there, was divided between "some of the most lush and beautiful and wealthy country and some of the most hilly and poor and backward country to be found in the Union." On that "dressed-up evening," she told the "nice ladies," whom she found charming enough, that charity was not enough—government must play a vital role in helping the poor.[51]

LBJ did not appoint a new vice president when he succeeded JFK. By the spring of 1964, as the president campaigned for his legislative agenda and looked with no small measure of dread to the November election, Lady Bird had become a stand-in for the absent vice president, and the press had started to notice. Yet on her return to Washington, she observed in her diary that the demands of the American presidency really did require two people, one of whom, she noted, would act like the "president for ceremonial purposes." This, she said, is "a substitute role that I try to fill," lacking "the aura of office" and Lyndon's "really overwhelming personality."[52] On her plane returning from Kentucky, a press gaggle with the First Lady ended when UPI's Helen Thomas quipped, "Thank you, Mrs. Vice President."[53] But Bird laughed off the suggestion: the role of vice president didn't appeal to either Johnson. This was, as she later described it, "our presidency," and Lady Bird much preferred the powerful role she was developing to the powerless slot designated by the Constitution.[54]

The next day, in a commencement speech at the University of Michigan that came to be known as his Great Society speech, Lyndon Johnson unleashed his most ambitious plan for eradicating poverty through government initiatives aimed at transportation, public health, aging, education, and urban and rural issues. Laying out a far more sweeping agenda than the New Deal or the New Frontier, Lyndon proclaimed the "three places where we begin to build our Great Society: In our cities, in our countryside, and in our classrooms."[55] But it was the Great Society's focus on the environment and conservation, a focus frequently lost in the telling, that grabbed Bird's attention. "I decided that's for me."[56]

Chapter 5
The Urban Environment

Many of you will live to see the day, perhaps 50 years from now, when there will be 400 million Americans four-fifths of them in urban areas. In the remainder of this century, urban population will double, city land will double, and we will have to build homes, highways, and facilities equal to all those built since this country was first settled. So in the next 40 years we must rebuild the entire urban United States. Aristotle said: "Men come together in cities in order to live, but they remain together in order to live the good life." It is harder and harder to live the good life in American cities today. The catalog of ills is long: [T]here is the decay of the centers and the despoiling of the suburbs. There is not enough housing for our people or transportation for our traffic. Open land is vanishing and old landmarks are violated. Worst of all, expansion is eroding the precious and time honored values of community with neighbors and communion with nature. The loss of these values breeds loneliness and boredom and indifference.

—Lyndon Baines Johnson, Ann Arbor,
"Remarks at the University of Michigan," May 22, 1964

Traffic had stopped us on the usual route and we had detoured through Harlem, that much-talked-about district of New York. It looked like there had not been a trash collector in the vicinity for two months. It was the bleakest, grayest mass of concrete and bricks, refuse and crumpled papers. No sprig of grass or trees. I hate to think what I might grow to become if I lived there. . . . I remembered the figure that this was the most concentrated area of population in the world. To look at it is to understand it better than you would from the newspapers.

—Lady Bird Johnson, White House diary,
September 10, 1964

In the spring of 1964, while on the lecture circuit in Washington, Barbara Ward took up residence at 1600 Pennsylvania Avenue, sipped tea with Lady Bird, and dined with the presidential couple. A native of Yorkshire, England, the third-floor guest at the White House had studied as a teenager at the Sorbonne, in Paris, and in Germany before graduating from Oxford in 1935 with a degree in philosophy, politics, and economics. She then served as foreign editor for *The Economist* and organized Catholic anti-Nazi resistance during World War II. She became known as Lady Jackson after marrying Sir Robert Gillman Allen Jackson, an Australian civil servant and peripatetic administrator of large-scale technical assistance projects all over the developing world for the United Nations. In 1958, Ward became a visiting professor at Harvard and Radcliffe, where she collaborated with John Kenneth Galbraith, author of the seminal critique of American inequality, *The Affluent Society,* in his seminar on developing countries. From there, her relationships with American politicians blossomed: she considered herself an adviser and friend to JFK and shared an extensive correspondence with Adlai Stevenson, one that reveals a substantive intellectual bond over policy and politics.[1] Ward became a regular on the D.C. speaking circuit, where her case for development assistance, her elaboration of nuclear strategy, and her advocacy on behalf of a trading model that would ultimately look much like the European Union were covered only in the "For and About Women" section of *The Washington Post.*

In 1962, Ward published her best-known work, *The Rich Nations and the Poor Nations,* in which, without coining the phrase, she identified the challenges of what came to be known as the North-South divide and also what today would be described as "megacities" in the global South. Ward argued that the concentration of populations in urban centers in the developing world had already begun to impose major stress on the use of resources—water, land, population, technology, and food.[2] Having witnessed the positive impact after World War II of major foreign aid programs in rebuilding Western European cities, Ward argued for a similarly strong government role in America, a message that resonated with the Johnson White House. Over dinner with Ward and the First Lady, "Lyndon listened," Bird recorded in April, "something he doesn't always do, especially to women. But he is fascinated by her and so am I."[3] Referring often to Ward's book as "the bible," the president embraced her rallying cry. "It's right here in one sentence," he told Liz Carpenter. And quoting Ward, he read, "[T]he mission of our times is to eradicate the three enemies of mankind—poverty, disease, and ignorance."[4]

Ward's access to the Oval Office was unusual for a woman of her interests and training at the time: learned male policy wonks and wordsmiths were welcome, but it was not yet commonplace for women with Ward's credentials to have the ear of an American president or of his advisers. But with Lady Bird's encouragement, and White House aide Jack Valenti as her interlocutor, Ward played an informal role, drafting speeches and memos for the president—some solicited, some not—on civil rights; global finance; demographics; urban planning and suburban sprawl; India, Pakistan, and South Asian geopolitics; African postcolonial development challenges; foreign aid; peacekeeping; and Russian nuclear strategy. Although Ward was not a staff member, a man, or even an American, the First Lady had been right about her: Lyndon had indeed absorbed her ideas on urban renewal as he and his staff congealed around the concept of the Great Society to embody his domestic agenda. Valenti explained to Ward that

> he has been using the term "the Great Society" to synthesize the themes you stated. He wants to seize the opportunity now to lay some hard foundations of the Johnson structure of imaginative and sensible government. . . . But to repeat, he wants to build on the ideas of Barbara Ward's—abolishing poverty, beautifying the land, giving medical assistance to the aged, giving jobs to the jobless, housing to the unsheltered, making available food to the unfed, assisting underdeveloped countries to find new pathways to prosperity, etc.—while

at the same time keeping our defenses strong and our economy healthy.[5]

LBJ would echo many of these ideas for the American public in his Great Society speech in Ann Arbor: Ward was not the only influence on the speech—Richard Goodwin and Bill Moyers, LBJ's aides; Tom Hayden, one of the founders of Students for a Democratic Society (SDS); and Michael Harrington, author of the 1962 book *The Other America: Poverty in the United States,* all could rightly claim to have shaped the president's thinking or given words to the thoughts he would set forth that May.

Lady Bird didn't attend Lyndon's Ann Arbor commencement speech, but its emphasis on the nature of cities and its soaring rhetoric resonated with a First Lady who yearned to find that "love of her own"—a policy agenda that, as Liz Carpenter recalled, "wasn't separate so much, but underlining the President's dreams and goals and purposes."[6] The Great Society speech gave Bird an opening for an agenda she could own: the environment. Speaking to many graduates who would go on to work for his Great Society programs or against his war in Vietnam, or both, LBJ warned, "We have always prided ourselves on being not only America the strong and America the free, but America the beautiful. Today that beauty is in danger. The water we drink, the food we eat, the very air that we breathe, are threatened with pollution. Our parks are overcrowded, our seashores overburdened. Green fields and dense forests are disappearing." Where once Americans worried about "the Ugly American," the president now called on them to "prevent an ugly America."[7] Clean water, air, and food; affordable leisure amid natural beauty protected from deforestation, overfishing, and clear-cutting—these concepts formed the foundation of LBJ's environmental agenda.

Ward also fundamentally shaped Lady Bird's thinking about the role of government in exacerbating or alleviating poverty and inequality, and protecting the environment, in the American urban landscape. When traveling across the country, Lady Bird noted, "I find myself now whenever I go to a city looking to see what they have done in urban renewal"—by which she meant the increasingly controversial postwar boom in public housing and urban freeways that destroyed poor (and often brown or black) neighborhoods—"and looking at it either with a criticizing or approving eye, but certainly a more alive eye" thanks to Lady Jackson.[8] Indeed, Ward's ideas filtered into Lady Bird's own speeches, at Radcliffe, at the YWCA in Cleveland, and in Detroit before the Home Economics Association. In Cleveland, Bird drew from Ward's emphasis on the strain placed on the human spirit from urbanization, and she pointed to LBJ's War on Poverty and the role of women in mitigating both. In Detroit, she somewhat subversively pressed the case for the whizzes of home economics seated before her to get out of their homes and become community activists. The goal she articulated of "[m]aking our cities clean, functional and beautiful" recognized the need for an alternative to the *Metropolis*-scaled, people-displacing, tower-in-plaza model envisioned by the modernist Le Corbusier and infamously implemented in Manhattan (by Robert Moses), in New Haven and, later, Boston (by Edward Logue), and in Washington.[9] In the nation's capital in the 1950s, albeit on a smaller scale, city planners (with Congress and the Supreme Court behind them) undertook to eliminate slums of considerably decrepit conditions, bulldozing streets, buildings, and landscapes and displacing residents and businesses in a five-hundred-acre sliver of Southwest Washington, D.C., south of the National Mall, along the Anacostia River.[10] But those slums were also communities.

What sounded on the surface like a paean to middle-class domesticity, the phrase "clean, functional and beautiful" that the First Lady had often used actually hinted at a broad debate among the leading lights of American architecture, landscape design, and public policy in the 1960s.[11] By then, some eight hundred American cities in nearly every state had used federal housing funds to finance new private and public housing. Few outcomes could be considered triumphs, or even modest successes, in engineering social, racial, and environmental harmony. But there was one private housing complex that replaced some of the demolished communities in Southwest Washington that did stand out as an exception for Washingtonians and for Lady Bird. River Park was a 1962 cooperative of townhouses and apartments sited on eleven acres of grass, greenery, and trees. Designed by the midcentury architect Charles Goodman, the space was marketed as "open-occupancy," meaning desegregated, to attract both black and white families. Liberal Washingtonians like Lady Bird saw River Park as a successful outcome in the nation's capital. Near the water, economically accessible, aesthetically pleasing, and somewhat funky, the modern three-story, barrel-roofed townhouses and window-filled apartment buildings had been constructed with public subsidies by private developers.[12] She would return to its example when thinking about D.C. as a potential model for the rest of the country.

By 1964, the concentration of Americans living in cities had grown from just under 40 percent of the population in 1900 to over 70 percent. By 1965, one of every seventeen dwellings in American cities had been bulldozed to make way for new housing or new freeways under the new federal laws. Some two-thirds of the people displaced as a result were Americans of color, and of these, the majority moved not to better housing, but into conditions equally as bereft as the dwellings they had left, or worse. When the Johnsons moved into the White House, the racially disproportionate displacement in New York, New Haven, Boston, and San Francisco was being roundly condemned by voices as diverse as the novelist and critic James Baldwin and the conservatives in *Commentary* magazine.[13] That so many of the communities most directly and negatively affected by massive urban renewal programs were black, poor, or often both added urgency to the intellectual and policy ferment of the time—and spoke directly to the necessity of LBJ's civil rights agenda.

In addition to Ward's tutorial on cities, Lady Bird was steeping herself in the thinking of urban policy critics and planners of the day. She mentions them often in her diary: of reading their work, studying staff memos about them, speaking of them in speeches, and working with many of them during her tenure in the White House. These included Lewis Mumford, critic and author of the 1961 bestseller *The City in History,* which topped the stack of books on the coffee table in the family's sitting room; Louise Bush-Brown, founder of Philadelphia's City Beautiful Movement; Victor Gruen, the Vienna-born architect and designer of the first American mall; Ian McHarg, Philadelphia-based landscape architect and author of the landmark *Design with Nature;* and Lawrence Halprin, a San Francisco landscape architect and author of the 1961 book *Cities* who designed and led the repurposing of Ghirardelli Square in Fisherman's Wharf from abandoned chocolate factory to a mixed-use public and commercial space. Halprin, in particular, would strike a chord.

With different matters of emphasis, these architects and planners shared the belief that to bring a measure of functionality, beauty, and aesthetic and social peace to American cities, government (municipal, state, and federal) had to play a major role in urban planning, with funding, regulation, and services. As important, they agreed on one core lesson of the failure of postwar urban renewal: community participation in decisions affecting that most intimate of environments, the home, was essential. Because the relationship between the built and natural environment in American cities was inextricably linked to poverty, race, and class, trying to solve the urban crisis in America through architecture, landscape, or even the most constructive of criticism meant climbing a mountain of complexity. When the Johnsons moved into the White House, none of these individuals could know that in the First Lady they would find an open mind, a champion for the social content of their profession and the values they advocated, and a direct line to the president of the United States.[14]

Out of the ferment of debate over urban life, and with her interest in giving a White House platform to professional American women, one woman in particular caught Lady Bird's eye. In 1961, Jane Jacobs, a self-taught architecture critic, had published her landmark *The Death and Life of Great American Cities,* which argues that American cities must reconcile the basic values of humanity and nature with the strain wrought by urban life. By 1964, Jacobs had become a superstar and a vocal opponent in New York of "master builder" Robert Moses. Her work stressed the organic choreography of the city and challenged the inflated perception of urban planner as God, capable of designing and building spaces that anticipated, resolved, and imposed upon city dwellers some omniscient understanding of their fundamental needs. Jacobs's influential book praised the semi-anarchy of city life, the messiness and unpredictability of diverse, accidental communities, and offered a sharp critique of the meticulously designed aesthetic that had dominated many American cities, including Washington, D.C.

By Jacobs's telling, Liz Carpenter called her one day and said, "Mrs. Johnson would really appreciate, honey, a nice, nine-minute talk on beautification" for one of the Doers Luncheons the First Lady had begun to convene.[15] Jacobs was initially dismissive of the First Lady's plans, associating them with Band-Aid flower planting to make poor people feel better about their dreadful living conditions. She expected an audience of garden lady beautifiers. She agreed to speak, but with a wider lens, telling feminist journalist Susan Brownmiller that her goal was to "talk sense to those women" and avoid the "inspirational stuff about tulips."[16] With the Doers gathered in the White House State Dining Room, the First Lady framed the discussion far more broadly than Jacobs had expected, with references to Thomas Jefferson, Carl Sandburg, and Walt Whitman. Lady Bird thought of herself as a country girl—she leaned more toward Jefferson's concern about the city's corrupting influence on the spirit than toward Whitman's and certainly Jacobs's embrace of cities' chaotic, organic vitality. "The question now," she raised in introducing Jacobs to her White House guests, "is how to keep size from smothering the individual into an impersonal and uncomfortable mold, and how to make a city beautiful. This is a question which writer, planner and citizen must answer. And one of the front-runners with the possible answer is Jane Jacobs, who is all three."[17]

With both women delivering their remarks seated at their tables rather than from a lectern, to ease their shared discomfort with public speaking, the atmosphere lent itself to a more conversational give-and-take. Jacobs spoke to what she regarded as the downside of government meddling and spending to bring nature into cities.[18] She argued for "the profound need we have for character, convenience, visual pleasure and vitality," what she called, in the vernacular of her field, "amenity."

> This is an age when we talk more and more about city amenity and produce it less and less. Many outrages are committed in its name. Poor people, Negroes, and businesses on which many livelihoods depend are tossed out of their neighborhoods in the name of somebody's idea of amenity. Here and there our cities are given a slick, artificial mask.... The amenity of cities cannot possibly be planned or bought wholesale. It is so much more complicated and quicksilver than a choice between wall-to-wall pavement and wall-to-wall grass.[19]

The First Lady found in Jacobs a "forceful, articulate, salty[,] somewhat controversial speaker."[20] Having clocked several hours that spring over meals and tea and walks around the White House grounds absorbing Barbara Ward's urgency about the ravages of urban renewal, Lady Bird found that her consciousness largely aligned with Jacobs's analysis.[21] What she found controversial in thinking about how to redress those recent wrongs was how strongly Jacobs objected to the allocation of massive municipal, state, or federal resources to those very ends.

The women the East Wing had assembled to listen to Jacobs—many of whom were journalists, writers, economists, or veterans of the New Deal—had lived, worked for, or documented the positive effects of public support for rural and urban poor, and they challenged Jacobs's allergy to similar programs. While Jacobs had wrongly assumed the room would be filled with the garden club set, she was correct that her audience held a strong bias in favor of dealing with the failures of government-sponsored, midcentury urban renewal with more, albeit better, government programs, planning, and spending. Jacobs did advocate for jobs and job training for city residents to take care of their parks and gardens. But she warned that a "great unbalance has developed in cities between money for building things and money for running things," meaning too much of the former and not enough of the latter.[22] She cautioned Lady Bird's guests about programs that would throw out "the good with the bad, the beautiful with the ugly, and the productive with the unproductive. We see," she said, "the paradox of cities actually impoverishing themselves by capital improvements," a phenomenon under way across the country and one caused in part by the requirement under the 1949 and 1954 federal housing laws that for every new unit constructed with federal dollars, one unit had to be destroyed.[23] Lady Bird and Lyndon had spent their entire adult lives believing in the moral case for government intervention to advance human progress—from rural literacy and electrification programs in the 1930s to the legislation now in Congress for civil rights and economic opportunity at home and foreign aid abroad. Jacobs's "salty" argument that when it came to cities, less could very well be more, may well have challenged their first principles about the fundamental role of government in the American social contract. But Jacobs's counterintuitive logic in fact aligned with the values LBJ had recently articulated. Bringing the good life to American cities, the president said, distilling the argument, meant serving "not only the needs of the body and the demands of commerce but the desire for beauty and the hunger for community."[24]

Race played a role in the women's discussion as well: Were pretty parks and flower boxes really enough to redress the profound inequities faced by black communities in the housing projects of New York, Chicago, and Philadelphia? What to do about the lack of fair-market mortgage financing for black families? On the eve of the first race riots of the Johnson presidency, and as LBJ pushed his civil rights legislation through Congress, the gap between Jacobs and Lady Bird's Washington policy pundit posse was not in fact so yawning. The very programs Jacobs did advocate (pilot efforts at community involvement in neighborhoods and the establishment of cultural and other institutions to address local needs) would emerge at the center of Lady Bird's work in the District of Columbia, where beyond monuments, tourism, and the federal government lay one of the most segregated cities in the United States. But in the middle of 1964, not six months into Lady Bird Johnson's White House tenure, the potential for the Great Society zeitgeist to resonate in residential Washington, D.C., remained inchoate.

* * *

Lady Bird soon found the institutional ally she needed in order to make headway on her budding interest in the quality of life in American cities and in environmental conservation more broadly. Of the ten members of JFK's cabinet, only four would remain with Johnson throughout his tenure in the White House. One of them was Secretary of the Interior Stewart Udall, Arizona native and member of an extensive Mormon family. In Lyndon Johnson's Southwest Texas sensibilities, Udall had seen early on an opportunity to advance the process he began under JFK of land, water, and natural resource conservation and the establishment of new national parks.[25] He would soon awaken to the prospect that another resource, the new president's wife, was primed to become his partner in advancing his ambitious environmental policy agenda. On the Sunday before Jacobs's White House talk, Secretary Udall and his wife, Lee, joined the Johnsons for church, lunch, and a swim. The Udalls piqued Lady Bird's curiosity: they spoke in a "detached and respectful way" about the role of the Mormon Church in American life; about their family—"their grandparents were polygamists!"—and about their embrace of the American West and its national park system as a source of beauty, family recreation, and treasure to be preserved. With passage of the Federal-Aid Highway Act of 1956, the federal government had become the primary arbiter of disputes over where to build national highways. While some resisted a blanket policy to avoid building them through parks, preserves, national monuments, or "historic shrines like the Frank Lloyd Wright House," Bird summarized, the "young and imaginative Stewart Udall" made himself a strong advocate for such a ban and "a loud voice for preserving the wilderness, the national parks, the shrines, many of the jewels of America."[26] Washington residents since 1954, when Udall was first elected to the House of Representatives, Stew and Lee packed their six children and their sleeping bags into the station wagon every summer for trips to national parks out west and to the Pacific Ocean—as Tom, the eldest of the kids, recalled, to "look at the sea anemones and the starfish."[27] In a matter of months, he morphed from the formal "Secretary Udall" to the familiar "Stew" in Lady Bird's diary entries.

Udall was an amateur naturalist, a devoted conservationist, an effective policy advocate, and a serious intellectual. As JFK's secretary of the interior, he assembled a working group at the Department of the Interior offices to help him write a book setting forth the historical and practical underpinnings of and rationale for placing environmental conservation at the center of twentieth-century American public policy. At first, it was a group of one: twenty-seven-year-old Sharon Francis, a Washington-born Mount Holyoke College graduate who worked for the Wilderness Society. An accomplished and record-setting mountaineer herself, Francis would become an essential liaison for Udall and Lady Bird's environmental partnership, for their work around the country, within the federal government, and in the District of Columbia. Later in the Johnson tenure, she would move into the East Wing and become the key point person for the First Lady's extensive environmental portfolio.

The book the working group produced—whose authors, besides Udall and his team, came to include Pulitzer Prize–winning historian and novelist Wallace Stegner—was published in 1963 as *The Quiet Crisis.* For an American public just awakening to the "New Conservation" (as opposed to the early-twentieth-century version that emphasized land preservation as the core of conservation), the book provided a history of American land use and abuse, rural and urban, and of the rise of a conservation consciousness. Native Americans, Thomas Jefferson, Daniel Boone, Henry David Thoreau, Teddy Roosevelt, John Muir, and Frederick Law Olmsted—all make an appearance, along with the politicians, philanthropists, and activists in whose hands the future of conservation and the environment would then lie. Echoing Jacobs, Udall's *Quiet Crisis* also sounded the alarm about the destruction of urban life in the name of progress; about the blow to mental health from the lack of affordable housing and natural beauty in American cities; and about the "explosive pressure of expansion" from highways, cars, and traffic in and out of suburbia. It also helped further legitimize the criticism of the perils of DDT first leveled by Rachel Carson in her pathbreaking book *Silent Spring,* published in 1962.[28] Written in language invoking the contrast between "natural beauty" and the specter of a future in which "ugliness" defined the American urban and rural landscape, Udall's overarching message was that the "New Conservation" would not come about as an accident or afterthought, but required planning, a critical eye on the temptations of technology, responsible management of natural resources, coordination between business and government, and public support. In producing the book, Udall sought to push back against the political backlash brewing in his own and neighboring western states against federal involvement in national stewardship over parks and other natural resources.

During the first half of 1964, Udall sent LBJ a progressively urgent stream of memos on legislation and resource management, attempting to draw the West Wing's eye to the intersection between politics and the environment. During this same period, the White House created fifteen task forces on various public policy issues, including on environmental pollution, urban problems, and the preservation of natural beauty. With LBJ focused on passing civil rights legislation, and thus unlikely to put his time into conservation before the November election, Udall began to press for Lady Bird, whose campaign chops were widely known, to travel with him across the country as Lyndon's surrogate. Throughout the Johnsons' tenure, Lady Bird and Stew would take several trips in support of the White House's environmental agenda—from Wyoming, Montana, and Utah to Big Bend and coastal California. Flying, driving, and rafting together created a bond of friendship and mutual interest that neither anticipated in early 1964, but that also began to pay dividends in raising the public's environmental consciousness as they paired the power of their offices to advance the Johnson environmental agenda.

Chapter 6
"We Might Have a Small War on Our Hands"

The whole question, as I see it is, is it more dangerous for us to let things go as they're going now, deteriorating every day . . . than it would be for us to move in?

—Lyndon Johnson to Richard Russell, telephone call, May 26, 1964

I'll tell you the more that I stayed awake last night thinking of this thing, the more . . . it just worries the hell out of me. I don't see what we can ever hope to get out there with, once we're committed. . . . I don't think it's worth fighting for and I don't think that we can get out. It's just the biggest damned mess that I ever saw.

—Lyndon Johnson to McGeorge Bundy, telephone call, May 26, 1964

I wish there was some honorable way out of it. With Vietnam and Laos, and Cyprus, with the summer's turmoil that faces us if Civil Rights passes, including the public accommodations portion, and worse, the boiling over if Civil Rights doesn't pass. Will it be months or years before this change is absorbed in our society, and whose hand is wise enough, and whose head and heart to guide it? How can anybody blame him for wanting to be anonymous, alone, and back at the Ranch? And yet, caught at this pinpoint in history, what exit is there?

—Lady Bird Johnson, White House diary, June 14, 1964

In early 1964, Vietnam appeared to Lady Bird still as just one part, albeit often the main course, of "my husband's diet."[1] Also crowding LBJ's plate, civil rights legislation at first moved quickly, passing in the House by early February, and by wide margins. But by spring, when what became a seventy-five-day debate in the Senate threatened to derail the components eliminating employment discrimination and abolishing Jim Crow laws, the world outside had begun to corrode Lady Bird and Lyndon's aspirations for that election year. The Viet Cong, the insurgency against the South Vietnamese government, was growing in strength, especially after successive coups in Saigon.[2] The conflict now peppered LBJ's press conferences, dominated his weekly Tuesday lunches with his national security team, and occupied conversations at the Sunday lunches and dinners the Johnsons hosted for their longtime friends, professional staff, and Washington opinion makers. At one such gathering, in March, back from one of his many trips to Vietnam, the secretary of defense, Robert McNamara, gave Lady Bird and Lyndon a "pretty terrifying" account, she recorded, "of how dedicated the opposition soldiers are" in the North, with "an intensive training in ideals that is lacking on our side." Even oral hygiene, she noted, was part of the Viet Cong's training, military intelligence reported. That Ho Chi Minh's warriors displayed their toothbrushes in their front pockets impressed Lady Bird as a detail reflecting the very kind of conscientiousness —"we belong to the up and coming"—that the boys her husband might send to fight might well lack.[3] By the middle of May, the Senate civil rights filibuster was into its sixth week, the North Vietnamese Army appeared to be mobilizing, and the insurgency it supported against the South had stepped up its attacks. The CIA predicted that by the end of 1964, "the anti-Communist position in South Vietnam is likely to become untenable."[4] The consensus of LBJ's war council shifted from launching aggressive anti-Communist propaganda and sabotage at North Vietnam to ramping up a vigorous program of U.S. military and economic support for the South Vietnamese.

Throughout the spring of 1964, Lyndon's political objective with Vietnam had been to keep the simmering conflict out of the public debate and the presidential campaign until after the November elections. He had rejected a State Department recommendation to ask Congress for a broad-based resolution authorizing presidential action on behalf of peace and security in Asia. Though his longtime mentor Senator Richard Russell now vehemently opposed Johnson on civil rights, he set aside his bitterness over domestic differences to counsel LBJ against taking on the Chinese presence, advising him to stay out of Vietnam.[5] Furthermore, public opinion leaned against greater American involvement. Yet, for the Johnsons, treating Vietnam as a "constant, low-level irritant" was becoming untenable.[6]

The very weekend the First Lady asked her husband's physicians to deliver Lyndon her pros-versus-cons Huntland strategy memo on the consequences of running or stepping away from the 1964 campaign, she returned to a Washington Sunday spent with fewer close friends from their usual circle and more talk of war. Lyndon had asked Robert and Margy McNamara; Secretary of State Dean Rusk and his wife, Virginia; and National Security Advisor McGeorge "Mac" Bundy and his wife, Mary, to join them for church at St. Mark's, followed by lunch and a swim. McNamara had just returned from Vietnam and sent the president a long memo laying out in exceptionally minute detail the political conditions, including religious conflict, contributing to the fragility of Saigon and the growing strength of the nationalist insurgency.[7] And so, the usual Sunday swim was overtaken by the "much more important and deadly serious business" of beginning to consider how increased American military assistance—air strikes, naval attacks, and possibly more "advisers" for the South Vietnam Air Force might be deployed.[8] A troop increase, though not yet formally on the table, was already on Lyndon's mind. No one that Sunday but Lady Bird understood "the depth of his pain, when and if he faces up to the possibility of sending many thousands American boys to Vietnam or some other place."[9] And that time would soon come. Yet Lady Bird found herself having to temper her own misgivings about Vietnam with the far more abiding instinct to support Lyndon. And Lyndon was dead set on achieving greatness in part by closing the breach of his predecessor's ambivalence—JFK had been eager to prevent a Communist victory in Vietnam but unwilling to "turn the conflict into America's war."[10] Three days after JFK's assassination, LBJ had vowed to Rusk, Bundy, McNamara, CIA director John McCone, and ambassador in Saigon Henry Cabot Lodge, Jr., "I am not going to lose Vietnam."[11] But the awareness that Vietnam could become his undoing lay just ahead of his initial burst of bluster. The presidency, Lady Bird decided, "is a killing job" for the individual in the Oval Office. When she recorded this entry, she was reading *When the Cheering Stopped,* the brand-new biography about the last years in the White House of a physically disabled Woodrow Wilson, when his second wife, First Lady Edith Wilson, essentially ran his presidency.[12] Lady Bird could see her husband increasingly boxed in, and she wondered if they would find "any technique for living peacefully" with "as many clouds of destruction hanging overhead as there are today." Trapped by the circumstances of a GOP primary campaign baiting LBJ from the right and the habits of a Washington political and national security culture that told the Johnsons that if they wanted a liberal domestic agenda they'd have to go hard on anticommunism abroad, Lady Bird worried that "we may not see soon the end of the acceleration of troubles."[13]

* * *

The violence and promise of Freedom Summer and the logjam in Congress over passing civil rights legislation jeopardized the legacy of LBJ's still-brief presidency and perhaps his proper election later that year. But it was the very awareness of that hazard and his battle to resist the prospect of loss that helped energize the president to press his Senate allies to break Senator Robert Byrd's filibuster: on June 10, 1964, just after the senator from West Virginia wrapped up his fourteen-hour, thirteen-minute filibustering address, with the backing of the Senate minority leader, Illinois Republican Everett Dirksen, 27 Republicans voted with the Democrats, the majority party, to override the sixty-seven-day filibuster. Never in history had the Senate been able to muster enough votes to cut short a civil rights–related filibuster. Nine days later, the Senate passed the boundary-breaking legislation by a vote of 73–27. On Thursday, July 2, 1964, the House of Representatives voted 289–126 to endorse the Senate version of the Civil Rights Act of 1964. The bill survived the longest filibuster in Senate history, a series of floor fights, and a number of eleventh-hour amendments, including one related to discrimination on the basis of sex, designed to torpedo the bill altogether but that ultimately became enshrined in law. In the spring and summer of 1964, the Johnson administration (LBJ and RFK, their deputies, and their congressional allies) had responded to the activism of the civil rights movement and the political analysis of its leaders to align around the same message: public support and passage of a serious civil rights law allowing the federal government to act against racial discrimination in schools, employment, voting, and public accommodation. The new law sent a message that the middle ground, of change through Congress and the courts, could prevent white and black extremists from further polarizing the country. At the very moment that LBJ was achieving a historic victory in Congress, pressure was building within his administration for a tougher stance on Vietnam, with the CIA ratcheting up warnings about the collapse of American credibility among American allies abroad should Washington allow Saigon to fall.[14] Emotionally, the accomplishment on civil rights could not be separated from the "depth of pain" that Lady Bird anticipated Lyndon would experience from Vietnam.

At six-thirty P.M., the East Room of the White House filled with more than one hundred government officials, civil rights leaders, foreign diplomats, and the entire White House press corps—print and television, men and women. Recording her meditations on the momentous occasion, Lady Bird focused on the weight of history burdening the South and on the trajectory of Lyndon's past and future. Although the room was filled with the visionary civil rights leaders who had made passage of the bill a political possibility, Lady Bird zeroed in on Bobby Kennedy, who had worked aggressively to pass it. She "particularly noticed the Attorney General sitting in the front row, and wondered what was going on in his mind, this bill that his brother had sponsored so ardently, had pinned so much hope on, that he himself had pushed and [that] had finally come to passage, I believe, with the earnest, dogged help of Lyndon."[15] She thought herself a good judge of character, and a good judge of Washington power brokers. But Lady Bird found Bobby inscrutable: "I haven't the vaguest idea what is going on in his mind." The eagle-eyed First Lady now surmised that Kennedy could not take pleasure in or give Lyndon credit for this moment. "I watched the Attorney General's impassive face and the very measured clapping of his hands, which would not have disturbed a gnat sleeping calmly in his palm."[16]

It had been seven months in the White House and seven months of distance from JFK's assassination, and with the passage and signing of the Civil Rights Act, the Kennedy eggshells beneath the Johnsons' feet were beginning to yield to solid ground. Yet the constant talk of putting Bobby on the ticket as Lyndon's vice president, and Bobby's refusal to affirmatively take himself out of the running, drained and infuriated the president. Although to many pundits and supporters Bobby was arguably a shoo-in for the vice-presidential slot, if he wanted it—carrying with him the Catholic, black, and northeastern vote—LBJ believed that Kennedy hadn't truly earned the second spot on the ticket.[17] As Johnson told one staffer, "That upstart's come too far and too fast. . . . He skipped the grades where you learn the rules of life."[18] Although Lady Bird felt a "peculiar unease around him which [she] did not feel around his brother," unlike Lyndon, she wanted to give Bobby the benefit of the doubt about his intentions toward what was now unmistakably her husband's, not his brother's, presidency.[19] Still, Bobby's apparently joyless reaction to Lyndon's success on civil rights did not obscure for Bird that, "in cold fact," he brought qualities to the national stage that her husband just would not and could not muster. Lyndon "needs many of the things that Bobby Kennedy has and is able to attract"—more charisma, more young people, for starters. But "it would take an agonizing wrench of the spirit on the part of either one" to "try honestly to feel close to the other," not to mention to join political forces at the convention the next month.[20]

Though Bobby may have resented LBJ's credit for the achievement in reaching the Civil Rights Act milestone—after all, JFK had introduced his own civil rights legislation in June of 1963—Lady Bird was keen to highlight her husband's historic accomplishment, which was rooted in what she saw as nearly a decade of hard work. Bird told a journalist from the black press about the marathon of passing far more limited civil rights legislation in 1957. The first such since Reconstruction, that earlier law had established the Civil Rights Division of the Department of Justice and given federal prosecutors the power to prosecute voter suppression. Bird recalled Lyndon spending "something like 37 nights" on a cot in the Capitol, where she had taken "hot meal after hot meal, and change of clothes after change of clothes down to him, and so this was just one step in a long chain of steps" of Johnson coalition building and vote counting, albeit now for a much more expansive law.[21] Appreciating the law's place in American civil rights (and her husband's) history, the First Lady also identified with the sentiment and logic expressed by one of the only seven House members from the South who had voted for the bill. Charles Weltner, a thirty-five-year-old newly elected Democrat from Georgia's Fifth District, had unseated a virulent segregationist in 1962. In explaining his own trajectory from opposing to supporting the bill, Weltner—who in 1966 withdrew from his House race to protest the Democratic Party's segregationist gubernatorial candidate, Lester Maddox, and later became chief justice of the Georgia Supreme Court—Bird recorded, had told the press that he "could have voted no today with tradition and safety," but

> I believe a greater cause can be served. Change swift and certain is upon us and we in the South face some difficult decisions. We could offer resistance and defiance with their harvest of strife and tumult. We can suffer continued demonstrations with their wake of violence and disorder, or we can acknowledge this measure as the law of the land. We can accept the verdict of the nation. I will add my voice to those who seek reasoned and conciliatory adjustment to a new reality.[22]

Weltner's assessment to Lady Bird represented a cautious yet clear recognition of her husband's legislative and political victory; it also tapped into her awareness of the potential backlash the new law might engender in challenging the white supremacist status quo her fellow southerners had gradually imposed since the end of the Civil War.

Like LBJ, Lady Bird was concerned that the very activism on the ground (voter registration, civil disobedience), though politically essential to helping LBJ mobilize votes in Washington, might also alienate the

Democratic Party's traditional white base in the South. "Remember the 90 percent," Bird reminded a visitor to the White House heading to Mississippi to register voters. This was the base she had grown up around and whose cultural leanings and party loyalty she had watched Lyndon navigate, fund government programs for, and pander to. Now he wanted to push them toward supporting desegregation and opportunity for all races. But however much she felt at home in the Deep South, and whatever ambivalence she felt about the out-of-the-courts-and-into-the-streets shift in strategy of the nonviolent protest movement there, the First Lady also understood and supported the momentous shift her husband's legislation portended for their party and her region. She also praised Weltner over "a pretty courageous decision for" a politician from such a backward district. The consequences of his decision she would undertake to explain later that year on her own campaign through the South.[23]

Yet even with LBJ's place in American history sealed by the monumental passage of the Civil Rights Act, Lady Bird watched over a Fourth of July weekend at the Ranch as Lyndon descended into "the Valley of the Black Pig," the William Butler Yeats phrase Bird often quoted to describe her husband's depression. Even among their closest advisers, her husband, Lady Bird saw, put on an act, appearing to be relishing his public battles and triumphs. But privately, the two had embarked again on the wrenching discussion about whether Lyndon could muster adequate energy and confidence to run for election that fall. "I suppose I was probably the only one who caught the full irony of the situation," Lady Bird recorded when the press reported that "Lyndon Johnson obviously enjoyed the job of President and was obviously going to run once because he wanted to be elected on his own." But "I could really believe that Lyndon didn't want any of that at all."[24]

There was only one other person whom Bird felt understood, even believed, that Lyndon might really walk away, and that was Walter Jenkins. Born in Jolly, Texas, Jenkins had been at Lyndon's side almost as long as Bird. He attended the University of Texas and, in 1939, at age twenty-one, joined Congressman Johnson's office as staff assistant. Over the years, Jenkins had become one of the most trusted members of LBJ's staff: It was Jenkins whom LBJ asked to get Attorney General Bobby Kennedy on the phone right after the JFK assassination. It was Jenkins whom the president first turned to when he needed someone to attend congressional breakfasts and cabinet and NSC meetings and to see to all manner of minutiae, from the trivial to the trenchant. And it was Jenkins who, very much like Lady Bird, "knew when to ignore what [Lyndon] said and not do it." During his tenure, Jenkins left Johnson's side only twice: first during World War II, to serve in the army, and again in 1951, when then-senator Johnson urged him to run for a House seat in Wichita Falls, where he finished second out of eight candidates. Following his failed election bid, Jenkins served as a top aide during LBJ's years as a senator and as vice president, becoming senior White House aide to President Johnson in November 1963 and LBJ's main contact with J. Edgar Hoover at the FBI. Like Lady Bird, Walter rode and tamed Lyndon's emotional roller coaster, but unlike Bird, he would soon pay a huge personal and professional price for the very humanity that allowed him to carry so much of LBJ's political, administrative, and emotional weight.[25]

* * *

By August 1964, the president's goal of keeping Vietnam off the radar until after the election was becoming hard to sustain. Accepting the GOP nomination, Barry Goldwater goaded Johnson to stop the "failures [that] infest the jungles of Vietnam" and blamed the Democratic Party for casting "a billion persons" into "Communist captivity."[26] Backed by Hanoi, Beijing, and Moscow, an ideologically tough and coherent nationalist insurgency rattled a weak and divided government in Saigon. To both signal American resolve and attempt to preserve a relatively light footprint, LBJ authorized covert military operations (raids along the Ho Chi Minh Trail), backed by American advisers, to counter the infiltration of North Vietnamese soldiers and matériel into South Vietnam, and he also authorized patrols by American destroyers off the coast of North Vietnam. Where the Americans regarded these operations as low-key, intended to let Hanoi know that Washington would not remain passive, the North

Vietnamese understood that asymmetry in power with respect to the most powerful nation in the world required a demonstration of force, lest the appearance of passivity be mistaken for intimidation.[27] In late July and early August, exchanges of fire between North Vietnamese torpedo boats and American destroyers operating in international waters in the Gulf of Tonkin produced a set of decisions in the White House later regarded as a turning point in LBJ's escalation of the Vietnam War.

The president's caution in not allowing himself to be prodded by Goldwater or provoked by the Viet Cong had kept a lid on more overt aggressive action in Southeast Asia—until exactly one month after the passage of the Civil Rights Act and three weeks before the Democratic National Convention in Atlantic City was set to begin. On August 2, naval intelligence reported a possible attack in the Gulf of Tonkin on the U.S.S. *Maddox* by three Soviet-built North Vietnamese torpedo boats. LBJ and his team didn't want to retaliate until, and unless, they were sure the *Maddox* had actually been attacked, and by whom. His advisers warned him against leaving himself vulnerable to the accusation of having fabricated an attack as a pretext for escalating the war. None of his military, intelligence, or national security staff could unambiguously confirm that the North Vietnamese had intentionally (or even actually) carried out an attack. The information leaned heavily toward an attack, one intended to show the Americans that the North Vietnamese had the wherewithal to take on a superpower. And all day that Tuesday, the momentum in the White House moved toward undertaking a greater and more public show of force than the low-level operations Johnson had authorized the previous month. Well before Congress or the public learned of the "U.S.S. *Maddox* incident," Lady Bird had already surmised from a conversation with "an extraordinarily grave"-looking McGeorge Bundy, and from his "portentous answer" to her question about Vietnam, that "we might have a small war on our hands." Yet she approached the moment with a measure of almost casual naïveté: "I can't think of anybody I would rather go into battle with than those three," she said, meaning Bundy, Rusk, and McNamara. While the men met with the president, Lady Bird went sunbathing, allowed herself a long nap, and plowed through her ubiquitous straw bag of papers for review and signing. The forced obliviousness was just that. "I can relax at the most amazing times occasionally, almost as though you'd have to wake me up in order to get me to the execution on time." The proximity to "great decisions," some shaped "completely beyond the control of any of us," but "some that have to be decided by the man closest to me," was offset by a welcome measure of the prosaic. "[Y]ou go right along doing necessary and frequently rather trivial things"—tea with visiting Texans or trying on ensembles designed for the convention by the Japanese American designer Kandi Ohno.[28] But sartorial choices would be among her easier tasks in advance of Atlantic City.

Lyndon's very long lunch with "those three" had indeed produced a consensus—that pending further, credible confirmation from the ground, it was time for the president to ask Congress to grant him the very authority to act that he had resisted requesting earlier that year. On the afternoon and evening of August 4, congressional leaders, cabinet members, and the Joint Chiefs came and went from the Oval Office, while the president deliberated over when he should go public with what had happened in the Gulf of Tonkin and begin to explain his military response. Immersed in the details, Lady Bird saw the timing of LBJ's statement, his decision to wait until very late that evening—11:36 P.M., she noted—to make his radio and television statement, as designed to achieve two ends. It would provide ample time to confirm the American response, air strikes against North Vietnamese targets and the location of American planes afterward, and it would allow LBJ to take control of the narrative with his own public statement before Hanoi could do so.[29] The president also needed the time to corral bipartisan congressional support, including from Senator Barry Goldwater, for a resolution that would give him broad authority to do whatever was necessary, including the use of armed forces, and, notably, without a formal declaration of war.[30]

Bird knew the tender emotional state Vietnam had stirred in her husband long before the war would polarize the nation or lose the Johnsons more friends than any other political decision they had made or would make. She seized upon LBJ's logic as a "limited and fitting" response.[31]

Her favorite lines from his statements echoed her husband's own favorites: "We Americans know, although others appear to forget, the risks of spreading conflict. We still seek no wider war."[32] But however sensitive she was to Lyndon's psychology around the war, whatever awareness she felt that even a limited war could amount to "a perilous path to tread," neither Lady Bird nor the nation had yet to fully awaken to those perils.[33] The military's actions of the night before, according to the reluctant commander in chief, had been in the service of preserving peace. In reality, the counterstrike would represent the first major escalation in an increasingly bloody and, eventually, unwinnable war in Southeast Asia.

* * *

On Thursday, August 6, 1964, four days after the Gulf of Tonkin incident, the Johnsons welcomed U Thant, the secretary-general of the United Nations, to the White House to discuss various peace initiatives in Vietnam. At the time of his visit, the Burmese diplomat was exploring several avenues for bringing Hanoi and Saigon to the negotiating table, he hoped with Chinese, Soviet, and American support. Joined by Adlai Stevenson, the U.S. ambassador to the United Nations, and a half dozen other American and UN officials, as well as the First Lady for part of the meeting, LBJ told Thant, "We are ready to get out tomorrow if they [the Communists] will behave."[34] With the escalation in Vietnam, and with Lyndon stewing in his ambivalence about the Democratic National Convention a few weeks away, Lady Bird thought of the state dinner that night as "probably the last during our tenure."[35] She seemed really to believe that Lyndon might actually decline to run again.

The guest list, however, indicated less a final act than a prelude to the main event: The governors from California, Missouri, and Indiana flew in with their spouses as overnight guests, triggering speculation, Lady Bird recorded, about their candidacies for the vice-presidential spot on the ticket. The top dogs of the Senate and the House arrived. Plus, there were longtime friends who were also friends of the United Nations and a gaggle of media heavyweights, including executives and journalists from all the major networks. Leaders in the fields of science and entertainment were there, including actors Gregory Peck, Fredric March, and Johnson stalwart Boston Symphony Orchestra conductor Erich Leinsdorf, whom LBJ had helped escape deportation (when the orchestra season was over) back to Nazi-occupied Austria. Also present were representatives from labor and industry, as well as a few blacks and Jews, Bird recorded, her eyes always peeled for a show of diversity in her husband's White House.[36]

With the vote on the Gulf of Tonkin Resolution coming the next day, Lyndon needed bipartisan support, so he stuffed his toasts not only with pabulums on peace and security for the secretary-general's benefit, but also with paeans to Republicans and Democrats in the room whose endorsements he needed to pass the consequential resolution. An escalation of American involvement in Southeast Asia, peace talks involving the great powers and the warring Vietnamese, a national party convention weeks away and a presidential election in a matter of months—despite the "perilous path" her husband had reluctantly embarked upon twenty-four hours earlier, Lady Bird was still able to savor the "enchantment of the strolling violins" and the "yellow, white and pink of stock roses, carnations, daisies, chrysanthemums in little bamboo Vermeil containers."[37]

It fell to the First Lady to introduce the evening's entertainment. The cultural tides had yet to shift against the White House, but the choice of one of the country's leading folk groups to serenade the war- and peacemakers could not have been more laden with significance. Civil rights activists already, and still unabashedly enthusiastic about Lyndon Johnson's legislative muscle on that front, "Peter Yarrow and Paul Stookey, with their slim bearded faces, looked like minor modern prophets, and Mary, in an Empire crepe gown fashioned with puffed sleeves, with her long, uneven, golden chopped bangs, looking like a slightly rakish Princess," better known as Peter, Paul and Mary, performed for the 142 guests.[38] The group, whose music later became synonymous with anti-Vietnam protest songs, had a history of ties to the Democratic Party. They'd performed at a fundraiser for JFK at the D.C. Armory in 1960 and become friendly with the Johnsons after accepting an invitation to the after-party hosted at their home.[39]

Despite the intense focus on Vietnam among their audience that summer evening, Peter, Paul and Mary did not intend for their playlist four years later to make a political point about the war. "We were not troubled by the surrounding events of the Gulf of Tonkin." Vietnam had yet to "penetrate our consciousness as the debacle it was to become," Peter Yarrow explained.[40] The group performed "Puff, the Magic Dragon" before the song became a popular reference for both marijuana and napalm. But of all the songs the trio performed that night, it was their cover of Bob Dylan's chart-topping "Blowin' in the Wind" that most resonated with Lady Bird. The song was first released a week before the March on Washington for Jobs and Freedom of the previous year, and the trio sang it on the steps of the Lincoln Memorial as a civil rights protest song. A year later, just a month after the Civil Rights Act passed, singing the song at the White House for them marked a celebration of progress by Lyndon Johnson, not protest against him. But for the audience, and for Lady Bird, the trio had conveyed an entirely different message that evening. The next day, the First Lady recorded into her diary a quote from a press report that "every one of the 142 guests sensed the winds of danger now blowing around the world from crisis-torn Vietnam." It was, Bird recorded with unease in her voice, "a very haunting song"—perhaps an omen, she felt, of what was yet to come.[41] The next day, Congress passed the Gulf of Tonkin Resolution, authorizing President Johnson to use military force in Southeast Asia.

Chapter 7

The Strategist: The 1964 Campaign

Mrs. Johnson represents a political asset for the campaign which is unique in Presidential history. She is highly appealing and effective on the platform. She comes across as intelligent and knowledgeable and unlike Eleanor Roosevelt thoroughly feminine. She maintains grace under the most hectic conditions. Politicians and reporters alike felt she would be more sought after than the Vice Presidential nominee for many occasions. The consensus was that she should make a number of treks apart from you—that she could give the extra push in critical states, visiting communities that lie outside the Presidential circuit.

—Douglass Cater to Lyndon Johnson, August 18, 1964

Somebody else can have Madison Avenue. I'll take Bird.

—Lyndon B. Johnson

Even after his Civil Rights Act achievement, a morose LBJ ruminated over his future in the White House. At a rare summer dinner alone together, Bird found her husband once again in the "throes . . . of what may be the last desperate turning away—the desire to escape being the Democratic candidate this fall." And she carried the weight of his equivocation. She knew it would be "mighty hard, almost impossible, for Lyndon to turn away and walk out at this stage of the game." Although she often shared his anxiety and ambivalence, on this round she felt he must settle, and settle soon, on the fact of his candidacy. The echoes of the consequences he suffered from his late declaration just before the 1960 Democratic convention were strong enough. But Lady Bird also feared that the backlash they felt then from their friends, patrons, and constituents in Texas, by first losing to JFK and then still accepting the vice-presidential slot, would now balloon onto a national stage if Lyndon stepped out of the race. Yet there was no "honorable escape." There was nowhere, Bird feared, they could go where the bitterness of betrayal would not stalk them.[1]

By August 1964, the time of the convention, Lyndon's acceptance of his party's presidential nomination seemed far from certain to Lady Bird. But to the party delegates and the American public, the Democratic National Convention offered little in the way of drama, at least as far as the identity of the presidential nominee was concerned. Not so the vice-presidential selection. As he mulled his own political fate, LBJ also held back on deciding who would serve as his running mate, exercising what Katie Louchheim described as "marvelous miraculous leger-de-main, sleight of hand, with all kinds of rumors, trial balloons, stories in confidence that are written in betrayal of confidence, all purposely divulged by the Master Impresario."[2] Only once all the delegates were assembled in Atlantic City did Lyndon signal his selection of Senate majority whip, policy ally, and perennial Minnesota candidate Hubert Humphrey as his vice-presidential running mate.

More unexpected was the challenge to LBJ and to the Democratic Party by the Mississippi Freedom Democratic Party (MFDP), an integrated alternative to the official Mississippi delegation. The latter, flouting federal law, had remained segregated—for whites only. Leery of further alienating the party's traditional southern support, LBJ offered an unpopular response to the prospect of a major floor fight: he offered the MFDP two at-large seats, with a promise that future conventions would be integrated, while also letting the original segregated delegation take their state's seats.[3] The proposed compromise drew upon input from his staff and also from Lady Bird. During the negotiations under way between Lyndon in Washington, D.C., and his deputies and the MFDP in Atlantic City, the First Lady, despite her sympathies for the MFDP's overarching objective of representation, argued for rules over emotion. The MFDP's members had argued that the Mississippi Democratic Party itself had violated its own rules by keeping black voters out of its caucuses and primaries. But in a draft LBJ statement bearing her edits, the First Lady suggested that only the state's "legal delegation" be seated under the Democratic Party's rules, and she positioned Lyndon against allowing "emotionalism" to alter that orthodoxy.[4] Unwilling to see LBJ yield to pressure from the floor of the convention, and seemingly out of step with the party's more liberal wing herself, the First Lady urged the president instead to emphasize the "steady progress that has been made in the area of human and equal rights," to remind the public of his leadership since 1957 on civil rights, and to commit to "lead[ing] the way within the guidelines of the law and within the framework of justice."[5] Yet, for Lady Bird, the defection from the national ticket by Mississippi and Alabama delegates to protest Lyndon's proposed compromise; the bitterness toward him among black activists; the disappointment in him by party progressives; and even the dread of anticipating what Bobby Kennedy might say at the convention—all this paled in comparison to the turmoil afflicting her husband on the eve of his appearance in the perennially "rundown and glamourless" Atlantic City.[6]

Despite his achievements—passing a civil rights bill and funding the War on Poverty—Vietnam, racial tensions, and anxiety over his physical health plagued Lyndon with doubts about his capacity to stand for election.[7] He was uncertain that a country still in need of unity "would unite indefinitely behind any Southerner." In his 1971 memoir, he would write of seething at the time about the "metropolitan press on the Eastern seaboard" all but ensuring a lack of public confidence in his leadership, with "tireless assaults" deriding "my style, my clothes, my manner, my accent, and my family." It was, as LBJ recalled, a "deep-seated and far-reaching attitude," "a disdain for the South that seems to be woven into the fabric of Northern experience," and a perception that might permanently undermine his ability, if not to be elected, then certainly to govern.[8]

As speaker after speaker stood before the convention podium the morning he was supposed to arrive, the president, still in Washington, undertook one final exercise to discharge his doubts. It was a practice Lyndon and Lady Bird had adopted over many years to think through the consequences of their decisions. On a yellow pad in the Oval Office, Lyndon wrote out a statement that portrayed his argument for leaving as a patriotic move intended to hand the country to a leader with greater capacity to unite, with greater public confidence, and with fewer enemies than those he'd accumulated over thirty-three years in public service:

> The times require leadership about which there is no doubt and a voice that men of all parties, sections and color can follow. I have learned after trying very hard that I am not that voice or that leader. Therefore, I shall carry forward with your help until the new President is sworn in next January and then go back home as I've wanted since the day I took this job.[9]

Lyndon's draft statement drew a swift reaction from his press secretary, George Reedy—"You'll just give the country to Goldwater"—and from Walter Jenkins, who told the president that though it might have been possible to withdraw in May, now it was just too late.[10] Over the phone, Lyndon read the draft to a close political and financial collaborator, A. W. Moursund, already with the Texas delegation at the convention. Moursund likewise cautioned Lyndon against issuing it, as did Dickie Russell, notwithstanding his anger over civil rights. Still, as LBJ told it in his memoir, it wasn't these men who persuaded him to board the plane for Atlantic City. It was Lady Bird. Where her Huntland strategy memo of three months earlier had taken a measured approach in laying out degrees of pain associated with the choice to stay or get out, and believing he could still abruptly abandon the race, Bird now allowed Lyndon no wiggle room, painting a picture of only the bleakest consequences of withdrawing. After reading Lyndon's statement and talking with Walter, she wrote:

> *Beloved,*
>
> *You are as brave a man as Harry Truman—or FDR—or Lincoln. You can go on to find some peace, some achievement amidst all the pain. You have been strong, patient, determined beyond any words of mine to express. I honor you for it. So does most of the country.*
>
> *To step down now would be wrong for your country, and I can see*

nothing but a lonely wasteland for your future. Your friends would be frozen in embarrassed silence and your enemies jeering.

I am not afraid of Time *or lies or losing money or defeat.*

In the final analysis I can't carry any of the burdens you talked of—so I know its only your choice. But I know you are as brave as any of the thirty-five.

I love you always.
Bird[11]

"In a few words," Lyndon wrote in his memoir, Bird had "hit me on two most sensitive and compelling points," evoking the good of the country and his personal courage (or, by implication, lack thereof) should he step out of the arena. "The message I read most clearly in her note to me was that my announcement to the 1964 convention that I would not run would be taking the easy way out."[12] Thrust back onto his feet by his wife's love and fearlessness, and by her suggestion of his "cowardice," Lyndon traveled to Atlantic City for the last day of the convention. In Boardwalk Hall, Lady Bird sat right next to Bobby, again with his impassive expression and his barely clapping hands, as Lyndon delivered a not-so-rousing speech to an only mildly aroused audience—the day before, the same audience had given RFK a twenty-two-minute standing ovation for his tribute to JFK, in which he recited from Juliet's monologue in act 3 of *Romeo and Juliet:* "When he shall die, take him and cut him out in little stars, and he will make the face of heaven so fine that all the world will be in love with night and pay no worship to the garish sun." The selection was purportedly chosen by Jackie.[13]

But during the final day of the convention, Lyndon's birthday, the Texas native son soon eclipsed Bobby's elegiac Shakespearean night. Where the Kennedys went high, the Johnsons' entertainment that day went, if not low, then emphatically mainstream. For the twenty thousand tired, sweaty, and cramped delegates, Mike Nichols, then an up-and-coming Broadway and film director, recruited Paul Newman as master of ceremonies and lined up something for everyone: a rabbi delivered the invocation; the pop crooner Vic Damone sang; Barbra Streisand dropped in between a matinee and evening performance of *Funny Girl;* the jazz vocalist, lyricist, and actor Oscar Brown, Jr., performed; and just weeks since their "haunting" White House rendition of "Blowin' in the Wind," Peter, Paul and Mary brought the entire hall to their feet singing along to the trio's cover of Bob Dylan's "The Times They Are A-Changin'."[14] Dylan had first performed this generational anthem (written and recorded in the fall of 1963) on the night after JFK's assassination. In less than a year, the song had become a fixture of protest and a harbinger of a fracturing decade. For her part, Lady Bird perceived the cataclysmic changes afoot, but she admitted to not understanding the nature or direction of the country's transformation. "I hoped I lived long enough to see what was boiling up in this period, because it might be the dawning of a new great era, one of the fastest thrusts forward that the world has seen since the Renaissance time."[15]

* * *

After a short break at the Ranch following the convention, the First Lady began planning the primary focus of her fall campaign, a solo whistle-stop tour of the South. By early 1964, the White House had already begun to make space for the vital role Lady Bird Johnson would play in the campaign later that year. Barely a month after the Johnsons moved into the White House, Pierre Salinger concluded that it was "becoming more obvious each day that not only will we have to contend with campaign trips of the President, but separate and equally important trips by Mrs. Johnson."[16] By the summer of 1964, Lyndon had given his West Wing staff the green light to put forward the best political operatives and resources to back Lady Bird and her team in their stab at the southern vote.[17] Indeed, it was during a four-day "land and people" campaign with Stewart Udall to shore up Senate Democrats in the West right before the convention that Bird's prowess as a national political figure stood out. Together, she and Stew covered 4,200 miles over four days in four states: Wyoming, Montana, Utah, and Idaho. The political goals of the trip were twofold: to dedicate the Flaming Gorge Dam and to hold the line against Barry Goldwater.[18]

Lady Bird emerged from her western campaign swing a widely desired surrogate, no longer for Jackie, another presidential candidate's wife, but for her own husband, the president of the United States. As Lyndon's "secret weapon," she prepared not only to carve out a major public role for herself during the campaign against Goldwater, but also to serve "as a conduit, a link between the President and the people he represents."[19] Drawing upon her training in journalism, she prepared to

> act as a reporter to my husband on the opinions and aspirations and moods and problems the people have. Actually in many ways I am a reporter on a closed circuit of course or for a very private editor because I try to report to him factually what I see and hear in places I visit, and I try to give him insight into the feeling of those I meet.[20]

"Mrs. Johnson was extremely effective," Udall wrote the president, "in her appearances on her 'land and people' tour in the West. . . . I am confident Mrs. Johnson could win the West all by herself if we gave her the opportunity."[21] "If we gave her the opportunity"—a turn of phrase that spoke volumes about the times, when a woman had to be given, rather than simply take for herself, the opportunity to shine on the national stage.

With Lyndon's imprimatur, his staff's support, and an experienced advance team and speechwriters, Lady Bird, Liz Carpenter, and Bess Abell set out to plan the First Lady's solo whistle-stop tour. Well before First Lady Hillary Clinton amassed her own team in the White House, "Hillaryland," Lady Bird and her team were navigating the spoken and unspoken sexism in Washington. They enlisted Lindy Boggs to run the operation. At the time, the Democratic National Committee ran a separate operation to reach women voters, and Boggs served as its chair. Married to New Orleans congressman and future House majority leader Hale Boggs, Lindy—who in 1973 ran for and won her by-then-deceased husband's seat in Congress—instructed her advance team that their first order of business was to "fight the lack of imagination in men" and their "idea that this is just a group of ladies sipping tea."[22] Tea, coffee, cigarettes, and drinks at the appropriate times may well have animated the effort, but Bird's team, and the network of congressional spouses Lindy led, took on bias and sexism without feeling, in the doing, that they needed to name them as such. Bird and Lindy and their teams considered themselves political operatives for LBJ and the party, and they understood the historic resonance of their undertaking: not even Eleanor Roosevelt, the most independent First Lady in American history, whose social reforms they hoped to deepen, had campaigned separately to elect Franklin. Though Lady Bird understood the value of the "women's vote" in national elections—and both political parties now competed for that vote—she did not believe that women voted "singly and alone" based on their gender, but rather, considered a whole range of issues at the ballot box. "I don't believe we are a herd of cows chomping along behind some petticoat general," she recorded.[23] But Bird was a team player and knew how the party machine operated, even if she doubted some of its assumptions that gender alone could predict how women would vote.

For Lady Bird, the objective of the solo tour, while broadly political (to fly the Johnson flag and make the case for his presidency and for civil rights), was also personal. She wasn't prepared to simply write off the South as a homogenous voting bloc, either, and surmised that LBJ's campaign might neutralize opposition by sending the message "that we love the South. We respect them." And even as LBJ had taken a major step toward leveling the racial playing field for black Americans, she wanted to show southern whites, whose mentality she well understood, that "we have not turned our backs on them."[24] Nor was Bird naïve about the election's likely outcome, however many speeches she would make in Klan-clogged towns along the route she chose. Indeed, it was Bird's fearlessness and "real moral courage" to boldly call into question the Deep South's racial attitudes and resistance to the civil rights movement that struck a chord with those who worked for her or ranked among her southern friends. Among them was Virginia Durr, a native of Alabama who, with her husband, attorney Clifford Durr, had been a longtime friend of the Johnsons and an activist, first against the poll tax and then for civil rights.[25] The signing of the Civil Rights Act had been extremely unpopular in the South, and in particular in Alabama. Ground zero for the civil rights movement, it was also the state of Lady Bird's ancestors, where she had spent summers as a girl, and where she had recently come under attack by Kentucky Republicans for the hypocrisy of neglecting her black tenants all while advocating for Lyndon's War on Poverty in predominantly white Appalachia. Realistic about Lyndon's prospects in the South, she mused, "I don't think there's much chance of carrying it for Lyndon, judging by the letters I get from my Alabama cousins." Pausing, she added, "But at least we won't lose by default."[26]

The Johnsons wanted to show that the problem of racial apartheid in America was not so intractable, and that under Lyndon's leadership, the South itself might accelerate the wheels of history in doing and undoing what had to be done and undone. With the passage of the Civil Rights Act, Lyndon, who understood the vulnerability of poor and working-class white voters to the appeals of race-based hate, pledged to "close the springs of racial poison" and "eliminate the vestiges of injustice in our beloved country."[27] By undertaking the reinvention of the country's racial norms and laws, he had risked his electability and the viability of the Democrats nationally and in the South. "I think we've just delivered the South to the Republican Party for the rest of my life, and yours," LBJ had confided to Bill Moyers when the Civil Rights Act passed.[28] Before the law's passage, Lady Bird had steered clear of race with a caution that stemmed from her own familiarity with racism in the South. But with a run at a legitimate shot at the presidency now the White House's singular focus, and the Civil Rights Act the law of the land, Bird, LBJ, and their staffs intended to quell the reactionary impulse and sense of betrayal among state officials and their constituents and to demonstrate to Richard Russell and his minions the seriousness of their intentions to keep the South with the Democrats, even while knowing they had likely already lost.

Working with the DNC, Lindy Boggs assembled an army of (mostly) women in every state and town Liz had identified for potential stops on the tour. Already, at the Atlantic City convention the previous month, the wives of Democratic governors in North Carolina and South Carolina, despite their husbands' opposition, had given their green light to a solo tour by Lady Bird, keenly aware that the best shot for the Democrats to keep the South was a southerner herself. Lyndon might have seemed to the northeastern liberals like a southerner, but the Texas Hill Country where he grew up was considered more West than South. Although also born in Texas, Lady Bird was more of a southerner than a westerner. The town of Karnack, where she was born, sat only eleven miles from the northeastern border with Louisiana. Between the ages of five and fifteen, Lady Bird spent her summers and many holidays in Autauga County, Alabama—adjacent to the county where her contemporary, author Harper Lee, was born—where her mother and father both had vast extended family, albeit of widely different social strata. Bird spoke like a southerner and possessed, even after almost thirty years in Washington, the feel for and air of the South. Where that very quality had caused her no amount of self-scrutiny and social awkwardness in the Washington milieu, and especially as First Lady in the shadow of Camelot's cosmopolitan culture, it now was considered invaluable. The Johnsons and their advisers in and outside the White House understood, as LBJ put it to Bird, "If you can't carry the South, no one can."[29]

* * *

It had been twenty years since American men and women last accommodated a politically active and outspoken First Lady. Eleanor Roosevelt had hosted weekly press briefings for women reporters—promoted as "teas" and attended by then–cub reporter Liz Carpenter—pioneered the solo poverty tour during the depths of the Depression, and lobbied FDR on matters of high policy, domestic and foreign. But while she stumped for decades alongside her husband during FDR's numerous political campaigns, and traveled alone for her own speaking tours, she never went out on the election campaign trail for FDR on her own.[30] Bess Truman and Mamie Eisenhower avidly avoided the spotlight and professed, and certainly appeared, to have little if any interest in the potential of their East Wing platform. Jackie Kennedy, pregnant and worried about more miscarriages, mostly stayed out of the 1960 campaign, relying on Lady Bird to traverse the country with her Kennedy in-laws.

There would be many ways in which Lady Bird Johnson redefined the role of the First Lady. Although the whistle-stop tour was first to break the mold for First Ladies, it was not out of character for Bird. Other than Lyndon's 1937 campaign, his first for the House of Representatives, when women campaigning "simply was not done in Texas," Bird threw herself into all of Lyndon's campaigns.[31] Recognizing her campaigning prowess, Bobby Kennedy credited the Lone Star State's 24 electoral votes in 1960 to Lady Bird's capacity to connect with voters. "Lady Bird carried Texas for us," he told *Time* magazine.[32] Once part of the Johnson presidency, albeit unelected, as she would frequently acknowledge, she professionalized the office of the First Lady with a chief of staff and press secretary, a social secretary, and their own staffs. She also drew from Lyndon's staff and from an informal group of outside advisers to help her write her speeches. A solo campaign to elect her own husband seemed the logical next challenge for the First Lady.

* * *

Lady Bird's skepticism about the "women's vote" notwithstanding, to make her active campaigning more palatable to the reactionary elements inside her party, and even to her husband's own West Wing, the East Wing team created "Women for Johnson" to stress the very general point that "women have a greater interest—and greater stake" in the 1964 election than any "since women received suffrage."[33] In the 1960 election, the majority of the women's vote went to the GOP. Now, as conservative women's organizations lined up behind Barry Goldwater, Lady Bird's team in the East Wing instructed the DNC, which had downplayed the women's vote in 1960, that its outreach materials to women should compliment "Mrs. Johnson on her courage and her sense of commitment to the major issues of our time." At the same time, they should emphasize, almost as if to underplay her very obvious political role as LBJ's most sought-after proxy, that "all American women realize intuitively that the

First Lady is a wife and mother before she is a political person—and they admire her all the more for the bravery and courage of her outstanding example."[34] That balance—between bolstering Bird's marital and maternal duties and framing her political pursuits as an outlier, or even as a step requiring a special kind of courage—permeated Carpenter's press strategy, one that, like Lady Bird herself, both asserted and deflected the First Lady's standing as a formidable public figure.

Despite Bird's active role in the 1960 campaign, the few Kennedy men still around for the 1964 campaign cringed at the thought of women running a major electoral effort in the South.[35] Kenny O'Donnell, in particular, could not fathom how LBJ could give so much authority (political, financial, scheduling, messaging, and organizational) to his wife and the women of the East Wing. O'Donnell, who had worked as JFK's special assistant, had spent the early transition months playing games with Carpenter and Abell's budget requests for social events, office space, supplies, transportation costs, and other matters large and small relating to East Wing operational needs.[36] As Carpenter described it, the Kennedy men gave Bird's staff the impression that "they didn't want Mrs. Johnson to do anything," and really didn't think she could. O'Donnell "had no respect for any women in politics whatsoever" and refused to meet about whistle-stop planning "until I laid the whole plan in front of the President. The president yanked him up there on the second floor of the White House, and we got out maps, and the President was obviously so enthusiastic about what Mrs. Johnson could do on a train trip that we sat there and planned." Carpenter, who went on to lead the national campaign for the Equal Rights Amendment, later recounted, "I enjoyed watching Kenny O'Donnell being brought around by the president of the United States on the value of women, and he had to suffer three of them—Mrs. Johnson, Bess, and me, for that period."[37]

In Lady Bird, LBJ had found someone who knew how to reach housewives in the rural Midwest; who could quote Whitman, Eliot, and Thoreau in the West; and who could stump before factory workers in the industrial Midwest and switch codes for the deep dive into her home turf.[38] Liz Carpenter, for her part, set out to prove O'Donnell wrong about women—and to prove the Washington elite wrong about the South. "The South may have its shortages—in nutrition and education," she acknowledged, "but I will match the political talents of Southern women against any others, any time and any place. They have the uncanny ability to look fragile and lovely as a magnolia blossom, and still possess the managerial ability of an AFL-CIO organizer."[39] And in Lady Bird, by appearances a quintessential southern woman, she had the perfect vehicle for rupturing the northeastern mythology about women, about the South, about southern women, and indirectly, about Lyndon Johnson's purported reactionary cultural biases.

* * *

In planning the whistle-stop tour, Liz and Lindy deployed a team of forty, among them Lyndon's most experienced advance men, old party hands, and new recruits, to lay the groundwork for Lady Bird's trip.[40] Known as "Operation Skyhook," their mission involved working with the Secret Service to ferret out security threats to the *Lady Bird Special*, as her train had been dubbed, and to make sure the crowds were populated by "salt and pepper." Translation: that the crowds included both white and black supporters.[41] Lady Bird was hands-on, too, instructing Liz not to send her to the easy spots like Atlanta, but to "let me take the tough ones," like Mobile, Savannah, and Charleston. Fresh from her western-state tour, Lady Bird put in six hours straight one Friday in September personally calling elected officials in the states she would visit, using the time-tested feint of a politician looking for political support by couching the ask as a request for "advice." She sweetened the pot by inviting them and their wives to join her for a leg of the train ride through their state.[42] Not everyone found it difficult to say no to the especially saccharine-sounding Lady Bird. Senator Willis Robertson of Virginia declined, citing a long-planned antelope hunt in Montana. "A lovely place, and I'm sure he'll have fun," Bird quipped. Another politician deflected the invitation, claiming to still be mourning his wife, although she had died two years earlier.[43] Bird's overtures to South Carolina senator Strom Thurmond, already preparing to defect from the Democratic Party, constituted, she recorded with irony, "the most hilarious call" of the day. And, recognizing the limits of her persuasive power, of Alabama governor George Wallace she concluded, "There was no use in calling . . . not even for courtesy's sake."[44] More personally, Georgia's senator Dick Russell, the Johnsons' increasingly embittered mentor, declined, to Bird's sadness, but her close friend and bridge partner Betty Talmadge (whose husband, Herman, a former Georgia governor, was a staunch segregationist and Senate opponent of LBJ's Civil Rights Act) readily agreed to join Bird on the train.

Less than a month before Election Day, between October 6 and 9 of 1964, Lady Bird Johnson set off on her whistle-stop tour. In the span of 1,682 miles, she made forty-nine stops, delivering forty-seven speeches in eight states: Virginia, North Carolina, South Carolina, Georgia, Florida, Alabama, Mississippi, and Louisiana. Some nineteen cars decked out in red, white, and blue were stuffed with 30,000 whistles printed with "Lady Bird Special," 12,800 pieces of saltwater taffy in wrappers marked "Choose Lyndon," plus buttons, matchbooks, postcards, straw hats, books, and records for the crowds. At each stop, "hostesses" dressed up in costumes of matching blue button-down shirt dresses and bright white sailor hats perched on their heads—ensembles that seemed purposely to echo the outfits of "the Goldwater Girls"—hopped off the trains to sprinkle the crowds with campaign propaganda and souvenirs as they waited eagerly, and sometimes angrily, to get a glimpse of the First Lady.[45]

Lady Bird had her own train car, and the whole *Special* included two cars dedicated to Carpenter's communications war room, into which she stuffed as many as 150 journalists at a stretch, including foreign press. While the official fact sheet emphasized the First Lady's clothes—"which she selected for their good style, for their usefulness, and for varying weather"—and the menus to be served on board, far more of Lady Bird's voracious energy went to digesting the extensive briefing materials she had her staff prepare for every single state and town where she would speak. She wanted to know whom she was talking to, the material and social conditions of the day, and how the local economy had grown under the Democratic Party, in order to make the case that Lyndon's election would represent continuity in the best, material sense. She knew full well that emphasizing a positive economic story would not gloss over the roiling polarization of the struggle for civil rights. The message: the president and his wife regarded the South as a "respected, valued and beloved part of the country" that stood to benefit economically from greater racial equality.[46]

Bird would typically tell her speechwriters what she wanted to say and then, once she received a draft, would undertake a light edit or substantial rewrite. For the whistle-stop, she was most concerned with conveying sympathy to her predominantly white audiences, regarding the difficulty of change, and empathy as a native daughter. Joining the advance team in the White House Mess before they deployed to organize the trip, Bird explained her perspective:

> I know the Civil Rights Act was right, and I don't mind saying so. But I'm tired of people making the South the whipping boy of the Democratic Party. There are plenty of people who make snide jokes about the cornpone and redneck. I'm no hard-sell person. But what I want to say to those people is that I love the South. I'm proud of the South. I know there have been great achievements there. And I want them to know that as far as this President and his wife are concerned, the South belongs to the United States. For me, it is going to be a journey of the heart.[47]

In Alabama, for example, her strategy to support civil rights and undercut both George Wallace and Barry Goldwater was to highlight the modern economic and scientific achievements of the "New South." Surely, she suggested, a state able to integrate NASA's Marshall Space Flight Center, America's largest space research facility (funding for which, as majority leader, Lyndon had advocated), could also assimilate the Democratic Party's embrace of civil rights. In Mobile, perhaps her most emotional stop, she added:

> Standing here today, I feel that having spent so many summers of my past here and having traveled quite some since, I can speak of what the New South means to the nation. I can talk about the warmth and courtesy of the South of my youth, which will never change, and about the New South that I saw at Huntsville where man turns his face to the moon, and the New South I see here in Mobile.[48]

Bird repeated her gently prodding message of respecting continuity and appealing for change, but as she traveled south and the days passed, the public's reactions intensified and became increasingly mixed. In Richmond, Virginia, a relatively benign banner read, "Fly Away Lady Bird: Here in Richmond, Barry Is the Cat's Meow."[49] In fact, Democratic senator Harry Byrd of Virginia was widely supported by the Dixiecrat set there as a possible running mate for Goldwater. When Bird's advance team stayed overnight in the home of North Carolina governor Terry Sanford, a Democrat, they awoke to a burned cross on the governor's front lawn. In Columbia, South Carolina, Liz Carpenter and the advance team "noticed as they landed at the airport in the early afternoon, a carload of six men in shirtsleeves there. They sat, silent, sullen and stared at us. I had an eerie feeling I was seeing the face of hate."[50] And when Bird's train stopped there, young white men "scarcely old enough to vote and dressed in the cashmere-sweaters-and-loafers uniform of the affluent teenager" showed up chanting for Goldwater and yelling, "[Lyndon] Johnson is a Communist. Johnson is a nigger-lover."[51] Protesters showed up with placards demanding "Black Bird, Go Home."[52]

But Lady Bird's concern was not with how nasty signs and baby-faced critics might affect her personally, but how they might affect the country politically.[53] Maintaining a sense of numerical proportion—she wrote to the Democratic National Committee of finding "thousands of friends and dozens of articulate opponents" on her route. "At times," she added, "the heckling went beyond a mere difference of opinion, and because young people, many of them too young to vote, were being used to express the enmity of others." Her antennae were out for groups associated with the Klan and other white supremacist organizations; she was "afraid some of them," some of the clean-cut-looking agitators in her audiences, were being used and were actually "the unsuspecting victims of hate organizations whose vehemence," as in Dallas during the 1960 campaign, "the President and I have met before."[54] No stranger to the virulence of an easily stirred-up right-wing mob and conscious of how easily political constituents could be manipulated, Bird held tight to the idea of "decency and fair play." Despite direct threats to her security, she implored the DNC chair to instruct his ground forces not to allow themselves to be provoked or intimidated by the "angrily unrestrained."[55] While the *Lady Bird Special* was crossing from southern Alabama into Florida, an anonymous tip alerted the Secret Service to a bomb threat. Bomb-sniffing dogs, dummy cars, a sweep of a seven-mile bridge on her route, and security escorts by boats and helicopters advanced and escorted the train.[56] But Bird was unflappable—perhaps naïvely so, worried more about the safety of the engineer in the dummy train than about her own. It would not be the last bomb threat against her.

Lyndon joined her for three of her forty-nine stops: at the outset in Alexandria, Virginia, then in Raleigh, North Carolina, and finally in New Orleans. He had entrusted his political partner of nearly thirty years with arguably the hardest, most thankless, and personally riskiest task of the 1964 electoral campaign. Joining Bird and their twenty-year-old daughter, Lynda, on the platform in New Orleans at the end of their trip, a beaming Lyndon summed up their collective and national message:

> We are going to have a government of all the people, and your President is going to protect the constitutional rights of every American.... Those that have other views are welcome to them, and this is a free country. They can express them as strongly as they want to with such vehemence as they may choose and we will listen, but we will not follow. Because this democratic land of ours is going to be a United land. In the words of Robert E. Lee, I am going to say tonight,

let's try to get our people to forget their old animosities and let us all be Americans.[57]

The received wisdom about this moment has left the impression that when Lady Bird took the stage in New Orleans, Lyndon somehow resented her for her success. But that day was one of enormous pride, Lyndon's and her own, in the universal praise she received for the courage, heart, and stamina she showed and in the unflappable discipline with which she undertook "those four most dramatic days in my political life."[58] And although there was no way to directly connect the dots between her whistle-stop campaign and the election results, LBJ did win in three of the eight states Lady Bird visited. In Virginia, by a margin of 54 percent to 46 percent; in North Carolina, where there was almost no local party apparatus until Bird's advance team arrived; and just barely in Florida, where by October, it was predicted in an internal White House memo that "only a miracle" would deliver the state for Lyndon. That miracle was arguably Lady Bird Johnson.[59]

* * *

While "hate organizations" confronted Lady Bird's campaign in South Carolina, in Washington, police arrested Walter Jenkins as he left the men's bathroom at a YMCA. With both Johnsons and the press that covered them campaigning outside the capital—Lady Bird in the South and LBJ in Iowa—the news of Jenkins's arrest for illicit homosexual activity did not begin to surface until October 14, when a reporter from *The Evening Star* spotted the Johnsons' closest aide and confidant on the D.C. police blotter and called Liz Carpenter to confirm the story. Fresh off the success of the whistle-stop tour, Carpenter called Jenkins for an explanation of the charges of "disorderly indecent gestures."[60] Just three weeks before the election, it fell to Liz to give Lady Bird the news.

For a period in American history when public attitudes were decidedly negative toward homosexual activity, such an exposure had the potential to balloon into a scandal nearly as great as the corruption and bribery charges surrounding another Johnson aide, Bobby Baker, which the JFK assassination had moved to the back burner of public discussion following a *Life* magazine exposé in early November 1963. Bird had acquitted herself with spectacular aplomb and to widespread acclaim in the public arena by campaigning for LBJ in Goldwater territory out west and down south. But it was the private counsel revealed in the secretly recorded LBJ tapes Mrs. Johnson decided to release three decades later that show not only her humanity toward Jenkins and his family, but her political savvy about how to neutralize the potential backlash of his arrest, and in so doing, manage LBJ's standing with the public, the Johnson White House staff, and the Jenkins family. Most starkly, the LBJ tapes reveal the skill with which Bird handled her number one and most important constituent, Lyndon Baines Johnson.

With Jenkins sedated and on suicide watch at George Washington University Hospital, and LBJ eager to have his resignation, Lady Bird telephoned Lyndon's suite at the Waldorf Astoria in Manhattan, where he was campaigning. LBJ had already asked adviser Clark Clifford and longtime Johnson lawyer and confidant Abe Fortas to shut down the story by appealing to the press on humanitarian grounds—to no avail. Lady Bird devised the better approach. She told Lyndon flat out and in precise and swift delivery exactly the steps they must take: "I would like to do two things about Walter," she began. "Offer him the number two job at KTBC," the radio station the Johnsons owned in Texas. She continued: "Second, when questioned, and I will be questioned, I am going to say that this is incredible for a man I have known all these years, a devout Catholic, father of six children, a happily married husband. It can only be a small period of nervous breakdown." But Lyndon pushed back, telling her that he already had "the best minds" on the case and that nothing good could come from a generous public response: "I don't think that's right," he argued. A White House statement calling more attention to Jenkins, LBJ thought, would make things worse for Walter and for the Johnsons. "I don't want you to hurt him more than he's hurt.... We'd blow it up more," said LBJ. But Bird was unrelenting: "I think if we don't express some support to him, I think that we will lose the entire love and devotion of all the people who have been with us," including, although unstated as such, other closeted staff or those whose own family members led closeted lives—a reality all too common in the 1960s.[61]

Bird told Lyndon that Marjorie, Walter's wife, already blamed them for the decades of overwork and exposure, and believed her husband had been set up by the Johnsons' enemies. Lady Bird recounted their conversation: "[S]he said, you ruined my life, and you ruined my husband's life and what am I going to tell my children?" To Marjorie, Bird reported that "overwork, and overstrain" in service to the Johnsons had "caused him to do whatever he did." Acknowledging as much, she added, "Their life is ruined and it has all been laid at the altar of working for us." But LBJ responded by asking Bird if Marjorie understood that Walter had "walked into the YMCA voluntarily." The two agreed that someone had to make that fact plain to Marjorie, but Lyndon didn't want Bird to deliver the message. He did ask the First Lady to vet her proposed job offer and public statement with Clifford, Fortas, and Ed Wiesel, one of their personal lawyers. Prescient and prepared, the First Lady had already done so, and reported their concurrence with her approach. Over the thirteen-minute phone call, she moved Lyndon from a decision to quickly distance the White House from Jenkins (no job offer, no public statement, no direct contact with Walter's wife by the president or First Lady) to agreeing to send Lady Bird herself to visit the Jenkinses, to find a suitable job for Jenkins in Texas, and to craft the public message that would ultimately become not just the First Lady's but that of the entire White House.[62] "My heart is aching today," read Bird's statement to the press on Jenkins, "for someone who has reached the end point of exhaustion in dedicated service to his country"[63]—and to her husband's unrelenting demands.

She released the statement before the West Wing could release its own. Within a matter of days, Billy Graham, the chief morals crusader of the era and an increasingly close friend of the Johnsons, echoed Bird's tone of sympathy rather than shock, calling the president to say, "You know, when Jesus dealt with people with moral problems, like dear Walter had, he always dealt tenderly. I just hope if you have any contact with him, you'll give him my love and understanding."[64] *The New York Times* reported that the American Mental Health Foundation, not known as a safe harbor for gay men and women at the time, sent President Johnson a letter reinforcing Lady Bird's and the White House's message of compassion: "The fact that an individual is homosexual, as has been strongly implied in the case of Mr. Jenkins, does not per se make him more unstable and more a security risk than any heterosexual person."[65]

Because of Lady Bird's management of the White House message, five years before the Stonewall riots, national editorial opinion telegraphed compassion rather than shame. Barry Goldwater knew Jenkins from his Senate years, and Jenkins had served under Goldwater's Air Force Reserve Command during World War II. Though Goldwater dealt in moral outrage over LBJ's use of political influence to benefit his media company during his years in Congress, the man who would later endorse gay rights in the 1990s refused to use the Jenkins affair as fodder for political gain. By 1973, the American Psychiatric Association concluded that homosexuality should no longer be considered a psychiatric disorder, defining it instead as a sexual orientation "disturbance." It wasn't until 1987 that homosexuality was completely removed from the *Diagnostic and Statistical Manual of Mental Disorders*.[66]

Bird and Lyndon's closest aides mourned the enormous hole left by Jenkins's absence. His preference for anonymity over credit, his allergy to gossip, and his ability to navigate "the shark-infested waters of the Potomac" while keeping his integrity intact were rare commodities in Washington.[67] Other than the First Lady herself, only Jenkins had been able to manage and overlook Lyndon's roiling emotions and badgering abusiveness in order to help him summon his enormous energy and talents. For Lady Bird, losing Jenkins weighed heavily. "I cannot measure the suffering he has gone through, but for me it's been one of the two or three most painful things in my life—more painful than the deaths of many close to me."[68] Reeling, too, from the loss of a trusted political adviser, Lyndon was equal parts draconian in distancing himself from Jenkins, eager to move on from the incident, and personally surprised that there had been any kind of secret between him and his close confidant.

The loss of Jenkins rendered the Johnson machine incomplete and weakened. Reflecting on the incident later, George Reedy, LBJ's press secretary, lamented, "A great deal of the president's difficulties can be traced to the fact that Walter had to leave. . . . All of history might have been different if it hadn't been for that episode."[69] Who would fill the gaping void? Lady Bird, for her part, was keen to try.

Chapter 8

"Our Presidency"

When I look at the newspapers and read, "President Comes Back from Texas," "NATO, Vietnam Among Problems Crowding Calendar," and I can think of all those that I could add to that calendar, I know why there was no sense of elation as we walked in the door, fresh from a victory of over 61 percent.

—Lady Bird Johnson, White House diary, November 15, 1964

He lives in constant concern that somebody somewhere in his periphery will be mixed up, fairly or unfairly, in some shady business. I'm probably the only living person who would attest, believe, swear that he never wanted to be president. But now that he's in it, he wants history to record a record of a hardworking President, a "people-loving" president, and a president who believes that man can solve his problems.

—Lady Bird Johnson, White House diary, January 13, 1965

On November 3, 1964, Lyndon Baines Johnson won 44 states, racking up 61.1 percent of the popular vote and 486 electoral votes to Barry Goldwater's 38.5 percent of the popular vote and 52 electoral votes. The win marked the highest percentage of the popular vote received until then by an American president since James Monroe's reelection in 1820. For the first time since winning suffrage in 1920, women turned out to vote in higher numbers than men, and for the first time in a presidential election, more women voted Democratic than Republican.[1] Until the 1964 election, there was no federal data on voting by race. The NAACP estimated that only about one-quarter of black Americans voted in the 1960 election. By contrast, and as a result of grassroots voter registration drives since 1963, black turnout reached almost 44 percent in the South and 72 percent nationwide.[2] In the Senate, Democrats took Republican seats in Arizona, Tennessee, Maryland, New Mexico, and New York. In the House of Representatives, specifically in the South, as widely expected, the party of Lincoln took seats from the Democrats in Alabama, Georgia, Mississippi, and South Carolina, where Strom Thurmond had led the unsurprising defection by the Democrats to the GOP over the Civil Rights Act earlier that year. Lady Bird's whistle-stop tour had managed to soften the blow: of the eight states she visited, LBJ narrowly hung on to Virginia, North Carolina, and Florida. But he lost the remaining southern states she traveled to by significant margins—as much as 73 percent in Mississippi. In Alabama, he did not even appear on the ballot.

As LBJ had anticipated, the backlash in the South against the Civil Rights Act launched a massive political realignment. The 1964 election marked the first time that Republican candidates won majorities in Georgia and for the first time since Reconstruction in Mississippi, Alabama, and South Carolina. The election also marked one of the first major pushes to attract Latino voters to register and vote for Democrats. Taking a cue from Jackie's more limited campaign role, Lady Bird recorded Spanish-language radio ads for broadcast in Puerto Rican and Mexican markets in New York City, Los Angeles, New Mexico, Colorado, California, Kansas, Illinois, and Arizona.[3] As a result, voter registration climbed higher among Puerto Ricans in New York City than in any previous year, with Bird's recordings "perhaps the most significant single factor," wrote Pedro Sanjuan, a DNC official working on the Hispanic vote. And the outreach also allowed the Johnson campaign to reach "the majority of the 6.5 million Mexican Americans in the United States."[4]

The Johnsons celebrated their victory in Austin, followed by eleven days at the Ranch combining rest, regeneration, and, as always, work. The Ranch provided its now-customary mix of geographic and emotional distance from Washington, even with a visit by the president of Mexico, the flurry of cabinet members and advisers flying in and out, and, on a separate track, the Johnsons' efforts to recruit new members to Lyndon's cabinet. Solitude was one thing the Ranch could no longer reliably offer. "Sometimes it is very comforting to be by oneself. My life does not have enough of that," Bird recorded in her diary.[5] Indeed, she craved time alone; LBJ loathed it. The constant entertaining, the work renovating Lyndon's childhood home, coordinating the planting of thirty pounds of bluebonnet seeds along the fence line, and always with a budget in mind—all this left Bird returning to Washington irritable, unrested, and full of dread.[6]

Their arrival at the White House on a Sunday afternoon was met with a raucous welcome by staff and aides—"very different from the way we entered it almost a year ago on December 7, but still no moment of high ecstasy."[7] Despite their win, Lady Bird felt "a curious pall of sadness and inertia" enshrouding her.[8] The adrenaline release after the full physical and emotional sprint of getting her husband elected on his own accord could explain her mood. Just a year earlier, the Johnsons had begun to put the pieces in place for Lyndon to become president of his alma mater, San Marcos College, beginning in January 1965. JFK would have been reelected, and they had planned for the possibility that he might replace LBJ with a different vice president on the party's ticket. Instead, winning the presidency also meant facing loss: of the respite of the Ranch "and its expansive way of life"; of Bird's business of twenty-two years and potentially of her family's financial future; of the departure of senior trusted staff; of her privacy; and of her close friend and confidant in all things Lyndon, Walter Jenkins.

Two days after arriving back in Washington—the Johnsons' thirtieth wedding anniversary—Bird visited Walter and Marjorie. "Whatever we have they have," Lyndon had promised, and Bird tried to telegraph that concept to the Jenkinses with offers of land, the accounting business for their "private account," and the use of the Ranch and a few other opportunities. Her diary recounts a conversation touching on the kids and "this and that." She found Walter "detached and disassociated." The chitchat left Bird with the feeling "of no estrangement between us three—none at all—but there is a complete understanding that everything has changed, or so it seems to me," she recorded.[9] Although the First Lady felt at ease around the Jenkinses, it was clear that with Walter's abrupt departure, everything was different now. Lyndon, too, felt the tremendous vacuum left by the loss of a loyal longtime staffer, and shared the malaise his wife felt and "the aura of uncertainty and stalemate" that greeted them in Washington.[10]

* * *

During the month of January 1965, Lady Bird recorded a diary entry on all but one day. Most of the entries pull the curtain back in sometimes eye-glazing detail on the preparation and execution of all the galas, parties, receptions, award ceremonies, parades, and balls surrounding Lyndon's inauguration, on January 20, as the thirty-sixth president of the United States. The time-consuming selection of clothing for the First Lady, Luci, and Lynda; the constant primping of hair by Jean Louis, Bird's longtime Georgetown hairdresser—the very activities that usually felt like obligatory drudgery requiring a "ridiculously inappropriate percentage of time and attention," took on, in Lady Bird's telling, an air of excitement: costumes, makeup, hair for a family that had thoroughly mastered the art of the public stage.[11] The First Lady's humor helped her undertake the many "fringe duties" of her office, but the ceremonial, time-consuming hostess activities she loved less were amply compensated for by her participation in the process of reviewing and refining Lyndon's State of the Union and inaugural addresses that year. She could pivot from the duties of hosting their extended families for the three-day inaugural to a deep appreciation of her moment, of theirs.[12] It was, after all, the American presidency they had finally and legitimately won. Anxiety and fatigue yielded to pride, and to an awareness of their place in history.

The marathon of activities leading up to the inauguration of Lyndon Baines Johnson unfolded over two days: the Distinguished Ladies' Reception at the National Art Gallery; pre-gala dinners; and the Inaugural Gala at the National Guard Armory. The latter featured a star-studded lineup, including director Alfred Hitchcock as master of ceremonies; comedy duo Elaine May and Mike Nichols; Carol Channing, of *Hello, Dolly!* fame; Barbra Streisand, the lead in the Broadway show *Funny Girl;* Julie Andrews, whose 1964 hit, *Mary Poppins,* was on the cusp of sweeping that year's awards; and native Texan and comic actress Carol Burnett.[13] But for Bird, the performance that left the greatest impression came from a "forlorn, undernourished little comedian" who "looks like you want to give him a blood transfusion": Woody Allen.[14] The premise of Allen's five-minute bit "The Moose," delivered to a National Guard Armory stuffed with the country's top political, financial, and media brass, implied that the only way a Jew could gain entrance to gentile culture was by dressing up as a moose, getting shot, and then being mounted as a trophy on the wall of a private club. For the First Lady, who knew something about outsiders breaking into exclusive clubs, the humor of a Jewish comic carried the evening, despite the too-tepid reaction to the star-studded entertainment she observed from the crowd.[15]

The next day meant more activity, including a reception to honor the winners of the Presidential Medal of Freedom, which included the contralto Marian Anderson; Dr. Lena Edwards, one of the first African American women to become a board-certified obstetrician and the founder of a clinic in Texas serving migrant workers; Ralph McGill, the Pulitzer Prize–winning journalist and antisegregationist editor of *The Atlanta Constitution;* A. Philip Randolph, the labor and civil rights leader behind Harry Truman's desegregation of the American armed forces; and the abstract expressionist Willem de Kooning.

On Monday, January 20, 1965, Inauguration Day, Washington sparkled under a bright sun. Just prior to the ceremony, the president and First Lady rode, this time alone, in the same limousine used by JFK at his inauguration—now bullet-resistant with its armor-plated sides and heavy armor plate in the floor. Their daughters followed separately as the president-elect made the journey from the White House to the Capitol Building to take the oath of office. The last time the Johnsons had made the two-mile trek down Pennsylvania Avenue with such large crowds surrounding them, the atmosphere had been dark and somber, Lady Bird feeling the crowd's grief and her own shame. Now she saw thousands of eager onlookers hoping to get a glimpse of the proud and rightfully elected president and the First Lady.

This time, LBJ's swearing in would not be held rushed or haphazard on a hot, crowded airplane, but instead in front of 1.2 million spectators. This time, after Leontyne Price serenaded the record-setting crowd with a gorgeous rendition of "America the Beautiful," LBJ stepped up to the lectern. As Chief Justice Earl Warren issued the oath of office to a triumphant Lyndon Johnson, Lady Bird Johnson became the first First Lady to hold the Bible used during the inaugural ceremony.[16] After he was sworn in, Bird glanced at Lyndon, her face "half-adoring, half-quizzical," with a mix of "pride and 'I-told-you-we-would-make-it,'" wrote one observer.[17]

* * *

Two days later, Lady Bird set off for Camp David, in Maryland's Catoctin Mountain Park, for a "postponed self-indulgent vacation" with Lynda and a friend.[18] Lyndon stayed behind and got back to work. Although the days away were meant as a respite from the chaos of Washington, the First Lady brought along briefcases filled with files to read, mail to respond to, and environmental projects to explore. But snug in front of a fire as a winter fog settled over the mountains, she allowed herself an unusual moment of emotional pause, brushing aside her work files and instead opening a small "metal box full of letters that will someday rest in our library."[19] They were love letters. Lady Bird leafed through the romantic exchanges with Lyndon from their short courtship of three decades past. I "have been intending to tell you everyday about a little orange comb I carry in my billfold," LBJ wrote from Washington in October 1934. "It is the only thing I have from my little girl at Karnack, and when I get lonesome and blue or happy and ambitious I always get pleasure when I look at the little comb and think . . . just think."[20] Less than a month later, Lady Bird and Lyndon would marry on the spur of the moment, in San Antonio with only two friends as witnesses by their side.

The box had traveled with Bird between sixteen different homes; it had been at least a decade since the First Lady had read the letters inside. After thirty years of marriage, she now possessed an unrivaled knowledge of the "importunate young man of 26." Now, whether "lonesome and blue or happy and ambitious," he depended upon her more than ever.[21] And she thrived on how fully he relied on her. She was clear-eyed about the full spectrum of his character. "Swift, generous deeds are typical of him, just as are swift, sometimes cutting words." She worked to protect herself, and many others, from the emotional whiplash of his personality and behavior. And she told him so. She loved Lyndon for his loquacity, but it could also annoy and worry her: It depleted his "amazing energy," which he needed to preserve for "the toughest times."[22] And she told him so. But Lady Bird fully recognized that "one can't be the person one is and change radically, and within the limits of a little moderate molding I'll have to let him remain the person he is."[23] Her realism about her husband's character, his enormous strengths and his always palpable weaknesses, gave her the judgment to know where she could influence him and where she could not. And at the thirty-year mark of their marriage, and the start of their official presidency, they had grown more in sync than ever before, stretching and molding each other to be better and to do more, separately and together.

* * *

At three A.M., Lady Bird awoke suddenly to a call she had always dreaded and, since Lyndon's heart attack in 1955, prepared for and expected. The president had been hospitalized in Bethesda after a cold and cough began to cause him chest pain. His doctor reassured Bird, but her thoughts turned to Lyndon—alone "in that vast museum, the White House," with "no wife, no daughter Lynda, no daughter Luci." Their younger daughter had been on a date, but rushed to Bethesda to meet her father. The thought of Luci's "presence to comfort and pet and reassure" Lyndon calmed Lady Bird's nerves. Now a practiced, media-wary celebrity, the First Lady decided it would be better to travel first thing in the morning, rather than set off a panic by arriving clandestinely in the middle of the night. The next morning, she entered through the front door so as not to cause alarm among the press. The president and First Lady spent several days in the hospital. Her worst fears allayed, she could feel instead "that the Lord is giving him an enforced rest."[24]

The day after Lyndon's hospitalization, a ninety-year-old Winston

Churchill died of a stroke at his home, Chartwell. Hearing of Churchill's death, Lyndon spiked a fever, a reaction his doctors attributed to the news. To prevent the president from flying off to Churchill's funeral, Lyndon's doctors "skimmed around the word *pneumonia*" as a serious health risk. Lady Bird encouraged the hyperbole, content with Lyndon to rest, and fearful of what might come should a more serious illness plague the president.[25]

Act II

February 1965–December 1967

Chapter 9

Beautification, Euphemism by Design

Getting on the subject of beautification is like picking up a tangled skein of wool. All the threads are inter-woven: recreation and urban renewal and mental health, and the crime rate, and rapid transit, and highway beautification and the War on Poverty, parks, national, state and local. It is awfully hard to hitch the conversation into one straight line because everything leads to something else.

—Lady Bird Johnson, White House diary, February 3, 1965

This means that beauty must not be just a holiday treat, but a part of our daily life. It means not just easy physical access, but equal social access for rich and poor, Negro and white, city dweller and farmer.

Beauty is not an easy thing to measure. It does not show up in the gross national product, in a weekly pay check, or in profit and loss statements. But these things are not ends in themselves. They are a road to satisfaction and pleasure and the good life. Beauty makes its own direct contribution to these final ends. Therefore it is one of the most important components of our true national income, not to be left out simply because statisticians cannot calculate its worth.

And some things we do know. Association with beauty can enlarge man's imagination and revive his spirit. Ugliness can demean the people who live among it. What a citizen sees every day is his America. If it is attractive . . . it adds to the quality of his life. If it is ugly it can degrade his existence.

Beauty has other immediate values. It adds to safety whether removing direct dangers to health or making highways less monotonous and dangerous. We also know that those who live in blighted and squalid conditions are more susceptible to anxieties and mental disease.

—Lyndon B. Johnson, "Special Message to the Congress on Conservation and Restoration of Natural Beauty," February 8, 1965

While the president was on bed rest at Bethesda Naval Hospital, "Mac" Bundy and Bob McNamara had set forth options for him to either escalate or get out of the conflict in Vietnam, where the United States had already stationed twenty-three thousand American "advisers." To add to the Johnsons' woes, racial tensions were again beginning to boil in the South. Following the passage of the Civil Rights Act, activists set their sights on challenging voter suppression policies, such as the literacy tests and poll taxes that targeted African American voters across the South. Peaceful demonstrations in early February in Selma, where just 2 percent of the African American population of the city was registered to vote, quickly descended into chaos, resulting in more than a thousand arrests, including that of Martin Luther King, Jr. Although depression frequently accompanied Lyndon's bouts of physical illness, in this moment, Lady Bird read her husband's mood as an expression not only of his own demons, but also of the nation's—"The obstacles indeed are no shadows; they are a real substance. Vietnam, the biggest. Walter. . . . The carping of the press. The latter I must honestly assess as very small indeed. And someday we may really know a storm."[1] Lyndon had not yet recovered from the loss of Walter Jenkins, and with his absence, Bird had no one to share in the task of Lyndon's mood management. This was particularly true as she endeavored to carve out her own policy niche, one that would tie the affinity she felt for the solitude and peace of the natural environment with the values of the Great Society.

Lady Bird credited her solitary girlhood experiences on Caddo Lake and in the moss-covered forests along the Texas-Louisiana border with her gravitation toward environmental policy. "My heart," she told students at Yale University in 1967, "found its home long ago in the beauty, mystery, order and disorder of the flowering earth."[2] But it was the crossroads of western, central, and southern Texas, the Hill Country, that gave her a taste for the scale and raw power of the physical environment around her. She was married to a force of nature, and that very fact gave her the capacity to appreciate scale and nuance both in human nature and in the natural environment. During a visit to the Ranch just after LBJ's electoral victory, Stewart Udall had grabbed Lady Bird's attention with ideas for planting native flowers and shrubs along the country's newly built highways—the state of Texas had been doing so for decades. They could use such plants to "screen from public view the dreadful graveyards of wornout automobiles, the acres of junked cars, that dot the landscape" and to make Washington, D.C., "the most beautiful city in the country." She also took a shine to his proposal to popularize the idea of family vacations in the country's national parks. Lady Bird found Udall to be "one of the most imaginative idea men in the administration," and soon considered him a good friend. After their campaign trip to the western states, and now with the time for planning her focus as First Lady, Udall's ideas tapped into her emerging environmental sensibilities. And he astutely saw that her formidable influence with Lyndon could serve as a vital channel to advance his own ambitious environmental policy agenda.[3]

No sooner had LBJ won the November election than Udall wrote him a memo laying out options for linking the Great Society agenda to the conservation focus of the Department of the Interior, which he led. It wasn't a hard sell. Among the dozens of policy task forces in 1964, designed to lay the philosophical and political groundwork for related legislation, Lyndon had already convened one on environmental pollution, another on the preservation of natural beauty, and a third on urban problems—the "tangled skein" of inextricably intertwined issues, in Lady Bird's words. And a few days before the election, the administration issued a policy paper extolling LBJ's legislative and executive achievements already and laying out the foundations of a "new conservation," one full of the ideas and language Udall had articulated in *The Quiet Crisis.* Population, technology, and urbanization had put enormous pressures on the country's and globe's natural resources, the paper argued, with "poisons and chemicals, the junked automobiles, and the waste products of progress . . . threatening the destruction of nature." Salvaging cities, maintaining access for their inhabitants to natural beauty, and developing policies on water, chemicals, weather, recreation, energy, and national parks reflected a strikingly holistic view that, in short, "we are the creation of our environment." In both cities and countryside, the task at hand was to preserve open spaces, carefully develop scenic parkways and river ways (such as the Potomac and, later, Anacostia rivers), and, among other items on a long to-do list, ensure that highways and urban and industrial construction advanced "with reverence and regard for the values of nature."[4] Udall had managed to memorialize nearly his entire wish list with LBJ's policy paper and moved quickly after the election to solidify his relationship with both Johnsons, for whom stewardship of the natural environment was at once intuitively appealing and, they thought, politically doable. But the Johnson in the White House who most embodied these values was the CEO in the East Wing.

* * *

As Lady Bird focused on schooling herself in the debates about urban planning and environmental projects, she wavered between the thrill of mastering a new subject and a near-relentless self-doubt about her abilities—imposter syndrome, perhaps: "I am no authority, just an interested, enthusiastic citizen," she claimed. She acknowledged the potential of her political clout: "I recognize I do have a sort of tool in my hands, by this title I carry, and I want to use it, but I quake at the thought of putting myself forward as a sort of city planner, landscape architect, pedagogue." In her early White House years, by speaking about her environmental agenda with words like *beauty* and *beautification,* she was able to take the measure of the public's appetite for environmental action and at the same time adjust to her newfound power. "I still find it very difficult—very distasteful, in fact—to say 'First Lady,'" she lamented. Lady Bird viewed the orthodoxy of some of her duties as tedious, if politically useful—congressional prayer breakfasts, where men and women sat separately and listened to separate speakers, for example, could be "saccharine, sophomoric."[5] The idea that beautification might be regarded as such unsettled her, too.

* * *

When she felt her own strength falter, she reminded herself of Lyndon's burdens. As the Vietnam crisis encroached on his presidency, it wasn't always easy for her to anesthetize herself to the tension and shadows of Lyndon's mood. She felt the "weight and burden" of those around her as "an almost tangible experience."[6] She wavered between the ability to remove herself and her preternatural tendency to internalize Lyndon's every shift in mood.

Nor, in early 1965, could Lady Bird shield her own work from the larger forces welling up against her husband. In December 1964, kneeling in the snow outside the White House, antiwar protesters sang "We Shall Overcome" as an emotionally transfixed First Lady gathered her staff in the unapologetically pink Queen's Bedroom to begin planning her beautification programs. The Udalls and Liz Carpenter, and also Libby Rowe, chair of the National Capital Planning Commission, and Nash Castro, the National Park Service liaison to the White House for the Washington region, joined her. Udall brought Sharon Francis, the young conservation policy expert who had helped draft *The Quiet Crisis*. They discussed the possible long-term impact on the country of a public opinion campaign designed to awaken an environmentalist ethos from the Atlantic to the Pacific. As a practical matter, however, there was no one specifically designated in the East Wing to staff the First Lady's environmental programs. Over the course of the year, Sharon gradually shifted from working directly with Udall at the Department of the Interior to working directly for the First Lady, and as her liaison to Udall and the rest of the government. The East Wing had a social secretary and press secretary—each with staff and plenty of women to attend to the mundane task of constituent mail. Lady Bird worried about boredom and drudgery setting in for these "bright young folks" and bemoaned the departure of staff for "the sparkle and excitement of the West Wing"—and, pointedly, access to the men working there. With Sharon coming on board, at first dressed up as yet another letter writer, Lady Bird was creating the first East Wing policy shop in American history.[7]

Even with Lyndon's trust in Stewart Udall's conservation vision, Lady Bird maneuvered with caution in assembling a diverse coalition for her initial environmental kitchen cabinet. Her work would fall under the umbrella term *beautification*, and her advisers and collaborators would join what was an anodyne-sounding Beautification Committee. To Lady Bird, the choice of the term *beautification* was all a part of a politically expedient song and dance. "I'll never forgive Lyndon's boys for turning my environmental agenda into a beautification project," she later recalled. "But I went ahead and talked about wildflowers so as not to scare anybody, because I knew if the people came to love wildflowers they'd have to eventually care about the land that grew 'em."[8] In focusing first on the nation's capital, at least, Lady Bird chose a city she knew well. She had lived there, when not in her home state of Texas, since Lyndon was first elected to the House in 1937, and during his political climb by 1955 to Senate majority leader, she developed a commanding knowledge of Capitol Hill, the geography of the federal bureaucracy, the landscape of national monuments, and several neighborhoods of Northwest Washington, where the Johnsons lived over the years. She was also aware of the entrenched nature of racial segregation, economic marginalization, and the lack of representation and political control for the city's black majority and was intent on putting a direct spotlight on the very issues that had both local and national resonance. In focusing first on Washington, D.C., she stood in good male company. Pierre Charles L'Enfant, who designed the original plan for the new "Federal City" of Washington, wrote to Thomas Jefferson in 1792 of the imperative to "beautify" the city "to that degree of perfection, necessary to receive the Seat of Government of so extensive an Empire."[9] In the early twentieth century, when the modern City Beautiful Movement took off, the male-dominated American Institute of Architects backed Senator James McMillan, and the National Parks Commission he created, to beautify Washington with monuments and public green space, albeit with extensive plans that reinforced and extended Washington's already segregated geography. That movement stretched beyond to Chicago, Detroit, Cleveland, Madison, Memphis, Philadelphia, and several other smaller American cities. Underlying it was the suggestion that the European emphasis on monuments, parks, walkways, and other public spaces would not only provide aesthetic pleasure but also reflect a modern social order and civic virtue, and would redress the squalor of tenement life for the urban poor. The early proponents were virtually all men, and *beauty* was less a surrogate for the female and the feminine domain than for the requisites of urban life in an emerging industrial empire, an antidote to *ugly,* a term also then in heavy rotation. By the 1960s, the term *beautification* had taken on a feminized ring. And by 1965, as Rachel Carson's environmentalism and Betty Friedan's feminism began to shape American cultural debates, *beautification* increasingly evoked a feminine space—one in which suburban ladies in garden clubs occupied a geographical, social, and cultural zone light-years away from the human beings, disproportionately poor, brown, and black, who experienced the gritty, dehumanizing conditions of urban life.

In setting out to preserve a "green legacy for tomorrow," the Johnsons tried to place people at the center of their effort to bridge the gap between the beautiful and the useful, between the natural and the built environment. Beautifying green spaces and monuments for the tourists in Washington was the easy part. More difficult would be the effort to redress what was described as Washington's "disgraces": its "many lawns, dilapidated sidewalks, ugly and confusing clutter of traffic signs, decrepit benches, forbidding trash baskets, hideous parking lots, poorly lit, deserted, and crime-ridden city parks, and a desperate dearth of amenities."[10] It would take more than flowers to make the lives of Washington residents more beautiful—meaning more economically solvent, more racially harmonious, more politically representative, more broadly accessible to leisure and recreation, as LBJ described it in the numerous decrees, messages, speeches, and executive orders issued and legislation introduced that year.

In early 1965, Lyndon's formal presidential messages to Congress, the first on "conservation and restoration of natural beauty" and the second on the "needs of the Nation's capital," helped deepen the political support for Lady Bird and Stew's beautification work. For LBJ, environmental policy was not only about "man's welfare" but also about "the dignity of man's spirit." In a special message to Congress about Washington,

D.C., that year, he was the first American president to connect the idea of home rule in the District with the need for the natural and built environment of the nation's capital to be a "living expression of the highest ideals of democratic government."[11]

Home rule was an important issue for the Johnsons in Washington, if not necessarily known to the country as a whole. In 1964, LBJ won the District's 3 electoral votes with 85 percent of the vote; his inaugural parade featured a "Home Rule Now" float. Between 1948 and 1966, the U.S. Senate passed legislation granting some form of self-government to residents of the District of Columbia. Yet the House of Representatives' District of Columbia Committee, which controlled the federal city's budget and was traditionally ruled by conservative southern Democrats, repeatedly killed the bill. In 1961, both chambers passed the Twenty-third Amendment to the Constitution, giving D.C. residents the right to vote for president and vice president of the United States for the first time since 1800.

While it might have seemed only a provincial concern, there was a strong connection between home rule and national civil rights. By 1965, Washington, D.C., was the only big American city with a majority African American population. That year, in a statement on home rule to Congress, President Johnson noted the injustice that District residents "are asked to assume the responsibilities of citizenship while denied one of its basic rights. No major capital in the free world is in a comparable condition of disenfranchisement." The District of Columbia Charter Act that LBJ introduced called for representative local government and an elected delegate to the House of Representatives for Washington, D.C. The bill passed the Senate, but the House stripped it of the substance LBJ and local home rule activists had fought for, even as the entire Congress soon passed the 1965 Voting Rights Act. By 1966, Martin Luther King, Jr., began to focus on the lack of franchise in the District as part of his focus on American cities outside the South. In 1967, under the guise of "reorganization," and once Congress had repeatedly thwarted home rule legislation, the White House appointed a mayor and a nine-member city council, a move eventually approved by Congress.[12]

LBJ addressed the dearth of services that kept the District from realizing its potential: decent and dignified low-income housing, education, jobs to redress poverty, fair wages, safe streets, and health and recreation facilities for Washington residents. In essence, he would bring the Great Society to the nation's capital, with programs intended to endure for decades. "The new awareness of our urban environment" nationally, LBJ emphasized, could well "make the District the symbol of our best aspirations."[13] For the East Wing, planting massive beds of flowers and blooming shrubs with private funds on public grounds in Washington, D.C., gave surface expression to the concept of natural beauty advanced by the Johnson administration. But the effort embodied a broader philosophical approach to social change that would touch on and, for some, touch off the crisis in American cities.

* * *

Repairing the fault lines between beautification and segregation would take local activists and political actors possessing depth of experience in the District and a clear vision for its future. Two such advocates stood out. The first was Walter E. Washington, at the time chair of the National Capital Housing Authority. Washington had moved in 1933 from an upstate New York of relative racial peace to the heavily segregated District of Columbia to attend Howard University. Active in the New Negro Alliance, he worked with Thurgood Marshall, then a young attorney, to advocate for fair hiring practices. He met and married D.C. native Bennetta Bullock, the daughter of a prominent Washington minister and herself an expert on jobs and poverty with a master's and a doctorate in hand. In 1941, while balancing a new wife, his own graduate studies, and later a baby daughter, Washington went to work full-time as a junior assistant in the Alley Dwelling Authority (ADA), a federally funded government agency established in 1934 to find homes or improve conditions for the thousands of D.C. residents living in the cramped alleys of Southwest, Capitol Hill, and Foggy Bottom. A precursor to the National Capital Housing Authority, the ADA sat at the center of the debates, steeped in race and class politics, over whether residents living in often-wretched conditions would most benefit from the improvement of existing conditions or their removal to new, modern housing. These were the very alleys that First Lady Eleanor Roosevelt had written about and advocated for, the very alleys that she had taken Lady Bird to visit in the 1930s. And those in Southwest in particular were the very alleys and alley dwellings that had been demolished, their residents displaced and businesses disrupted, with urban renewal in the 1950s—and whose disappearance would radically alter the demographics of Washington, D.C., by accelerating white flight and uprooting black residents.

As Walter Washington climbed up the ranks of the white-led agency over the next twenty years, he worked to move residents into affordable housing and create jobs and other social programs for the poor and working poor. He also schooled himself in the art of navigating the white supremacist impulses of the congressional overlords who controlled the budget for his and every other District agency. By 1965, when Washington made his way through the District's snowy streets to the White House to launch the First Lady's Beautification Committee, he and Lady Bird had accumulated a sometimes-overlapping history outside politics, one peppered by their experiences as parents whose daughters went to school together and of D.C. as both a federal district and their home.

Another player uniquely positioned to support Lady Bird's Washington, D.C., agenda was Elizabeth "Libby" Rowe. A third-generation Washingtonian, Rowe was educated in journalism and labor rights during the interwar Depression era, but turned toward Democratic Party politics after World War II. This was especially so after she married James "Jimmy" Henry Rowe, a Montana transplant whom FDR hired as his special assistant in 1939. Growing up steeped in Washington politics, Libby became a Democratic Party insider. In 1961, President Kennedy appointed her to the National Capital Planning Commission, the federal agency that oversaw and funded the District of Columbia's public spaces. Soon after her appointment, she became its chair. Libby's tenure on the commission marked a decided pivot away from the experimentation with at least one aspect of urban renewal of the 1940s and '50s, new federal highways. Instead, Rowe put her political skills and knowledge of the

District into trying to block plans to run federal highways through the four quadrants of Washington, D.C., and emphasized preservation and restoration of neighborhoods, along with mass transit, the development of riverfront property in Anacostia and Georgetown, and investment in public spaces. Despite off-and-on personal conflict between their husbands, their own letters show that Libby and Lady Bird maintained a close friendship, having raised kids together and thrived on and also endured the larger-than-life antics of their power spouses. With Walter Washington's credibility and reach into District neighborhoods beyond the wealthy Northwest enclaves and Libby's leadership at the planning commission, their membership in the Beautification Committee had the potential to make a tangible impact on a city once derided by author Mark Twain as "the grand old benevolent National Asylum for the Helpless."[14]

* * *

In the first quarter of 1965, Lady Bird convened several White House gatherings of the Society for a More Beautiful National Capital, intended to build political and philanthropic support for the idea that the East Wing of the Johnson White House would begin to engage in certain quite visible public policy matters. As a standard big-tent operation, these early gatherings were designed to signal a consensus-driven approach by including everyone, ranging from the president of the National Capital Area Garden Club League, to the president of the American Petroleum Institute, to some of the District's leading advocates for fair housing, school desegregation, family planning—universal access to birth control was soon to become a goal of the president and First Lady—healthcare, jobs, culture, and home rule. Joining the core cohort was Laurance Rockefeller, the third son of the Standard Oil titan, John D. Rockefeller. Laurance believed that philanthropy could play a vital role in stewardship over public lands. Possessing a vast accumulation of prime American land around the country, he continued his family's tradition of promoting a proto version of the public-private partnership, whether by donating lands directly for national park designation and federal stewardship or by investing Rockefeller family capital into the conversion of wilderness, mountain, and oceanfront properties into high-end resorts—or a hybrid of the two. He had developed a close relationship with Stewart Udall during the Kennedy years and served on LBJ's White House Task Force on Natural Beauty. His participation in the Beautification Committee and his role as adviser to Lady Bird would evolve into a lifelong camaraderie around the "tangled skein" of beauty, the environment, and quality of life.[15] Rounding out the group were two leading architects, Nathaniel Owings and Victor Gruen. Owings and his partner, Louis Skidmore, had earned national acclaim with their buildings at the 1939 World's Fair; had designed the town of Oak Ridge, Tennessee, and the production site for the Manhattan Project; and were now involved in the revitalization of Pennsylvania Avenue. Owings had become a prominent environmental activist on California's Central Coast, home to Big Sur. Udall had tasked Gruen with giving the opening remarks to the group. Raised and educated in prewar Vienna, the Jewish Gruen (once "Grunbaum") fled to the United States in 1938. His treatise on America's urban crisis, *The Heart of Our Cities,* argued that the city "should serve man and should be molded to do so." Though he would later recant some of his own less-humanizing designs around the country (among them, the first commercial malls), Gruen insisted on a holistic approach to environmental urban design—flowers, yes, but people, too, a conviction that would gradually dominate the First Lady's thinking.[16] Imposter syndrome notwithstanding, Lady Bird's hours of preparation before the first gathering left the impression of a First Lady in total command, her mood as bright as the winter white wool outfit adorning her tiny frame. And yet, she found fault. She reprimanded herself for reading, rather than simply delivering, her opening statement at the first meeting, a statement brimming with references to observations by visiting Europeans taken by both the beauty and missed potential of the nation's capital city.

When the group gathered again, this time for a more public exercise, they left the White House to embark on the first of many field trips. On the Mall, a kneeling, gloved First Lady, foreshadowing a pose taken by Michelle Obama in her White House Vegetable Garden, planted purple and yellow pansies near the Smithsonian Museum of American History and Technology (now the National Museum of American History). The group also stopped near the building housing the Department of Health, Education, and Welfare, where Nash Castro, born Ignacio Castro, a native of Arizona, planted several azalea bushes. The First Lady's decorative beautification photographed and documented, the group then drove just one mile—though it might as well have been one hundred, or even to another planet—to Greenleaf Gardens, a six-year-old public housing project of mid-rise apartments and two-story townhouses in Southwest D.C.[17] This was another example of urban renewal. Though the process had taken twenty years, cost approximately $500 million, and displaced 23,000 residents, for Lady Bird, Walter Washington, and many white Washingtonians, Southwest Washington's transformation from slums lacking running water and electricity to a fifty-six-acre "model redevelopment" boasting subsidized low- and middle-income housing served as a paragon of interracial, multiclass harmony—and even hope for what D.C. might become.[18] Although most of Southwest's previous residents had been relocated as a result of the District's first experiment with residential urban renewal, the near- and long-term consequences of that displacement had yet to be fully digested by the reform-minded enthusiasts on hand, including Lady Bird. They had not fully, or collectively, connected the dots between race, poverty, local control, and the potential for "beautification" to act as mere window dressing, incapable of getting at the deeper challenges of segregated housing and racial discrimination in Washington, D.C., or, for that matter, in cities throughout the country.

At the third gathering of the Beautification Committee that spring, while Lyndon met with his cabinet about Vietnam, Laurance Rockefeller announced that his family foundation had donated $100,000 for the National Park Service to clean up and develop a public park out of thirty-six acres along the Watts Branch tributary of the Anacostia River, a polluted expanse flowing through an underserved black working-class neighborhood virtually devoid of public services.[19] Rockefeller's office, consulting with Udall, guided the selection: Like much of the District of Columbia public property outside the Northwest quadrant of Washington, the

Park Service owned but had long neglected much of the ravine and riverfront areas in the Northeast quadrant. The plan represented an early indication of the East Wing's awareness of the environmental and social conditions outside tourist and monumental Washington and hinted at the committee's future direction.

At the same time, a conflict within the committee began to surface, one that offered a window into the broader conflict emerging in the country between environmentalists and the auto industry. While a representative from a gas station lobbying association laid out plans by Texaco and the other major companies to begin planting flowers outside gas stations along new interstate highways, the industry's push to put more and more Americans into cars came under attack. With a "dour face and a very articulate tongue," Bird noted, Victor Gruen railed against the proliferation of cars in American cities and against the cynicism of brightening the "sidewalk" appeal of gas stations to attract more drivers or to make for more enjoyable travel on America's burgeoning interstate highways.[20] Lady Bird had spent years driving on roads and highways between Washington and Texas, often accompanied by her African American staff. Through their experience, she saw how the cultural, social, and practical prohibitions of Jim Crow made highway travel both risky and humiliating for black Americans. She also well knew the limited options for aesthetic or hygienic roadside alleviation on American roads and highways, and the dreary experience of spending hours looking at nothing or enduring the visual assault of unscreened junkyards and obnoxious billboards that had become ancillary components of the burgeoning automobile industry. Although far from resolving the tension emerging between Gruen's aesthetic sensibilities and the car industry's economic interests, she was determined to start somewhere. The practical and public awareness benefits of community cleanup and planting flowers and shrubs, she thought, seemed an approachable launching point for what would become a deeper exploration of the environmental, economic, and psychological impact of "beautification," very much along the lines of Gruen's critique.

* * *

The initial objectives of the committee—to support "beauty" on the Mall, advance Jackie Kennedy's projects to renovate Pennsylvania Avenue and Lafayette Square, plant flowers and shrubs on the triangles and squares dotting Washington's main thoroughfares, involve local communities in beautification, and engage volunteer landscape architects to draw up plans for Washington's neighborhoods—all sounded benign enough. Yet, for Lady Bird and Lyndon, and for the country, the ensuing months were neither. A week after her first White House beautification convening, police in Marion, Alabama, shot Jimmie Lee Jackson, a twenty-six-year-old church deacon, during a nonviolent protest. He died eight days later, adding more tragedy and urgency to an already catalytic voting rights campaign in Alabama. On Sunday, February 21, as the Johnsons listened to a message about reconciliation from the minister at Christ Church in Alexandria, Virginia, Malcolm X was assassinated in New York City at the Audubon Ballroom in Washington Heights. The day after the assassination, LBJ approved General William Westmoreland's request for two marine battalions to fortify the American air base outside the city of Da Nang, on Vietnam's central coast. And on March 2, the first bombing campaign of the war, Operation Rolling Thunder, began with one hundred American fighter-bombers attacking targets in the North, especially along the Ho Chi Minh Trail. The air campaign marked a major turning point in the escalation. Martin Luther King, Jr., death threats following him, spoke at Howard University. "I know that President Johnson has a serious problem here, and naturally I am sympathetic to that," King told the Howard convocation, but he said he saw no solution in violence. "[T]he war in Vietnam is accomplishing nothing," King warned.[21] And three days later, King returned to Washington to meet with his then-ally President Johnson. On Pennsylvania Avenue, uniformed Nazis greeted King with picket signs, "Down with Martin Luther Koon" and "Who Needs Niggers."[22] The President's Daily Diary records that in their eighty-eight-minute conversation, they discussed Dr. King's perspective on the escalation of conflict in Alabama, President Johnson's timing for sending a voting rights message to Congress, and the larger policy context the president regarded as relevant to the lives of black Americans: his programs and legislation on poverty, health, education, low-income housing; his appointment of black professionals to senior posts; and even his administration's emphasis on the environment and the quality of life in American cities.[23] Leaving the White House, King announced that LBJ had communicated, without reference to timing, Republican senator Everett Dirksen's commitment to a voting rights bill. He then caught a late flight back to Atlanta.

To dramatize the demand for voting rights and protest the fatal police shooting of Jimmie Lee Jackson, the Southern Christian Leadership Conference (SCLC) and the Student Nonviolent Coordinating Committee (SNCC) called upon clergy and students from around the country to join a march from Selma to Montgomery that Sunday, two days after King met with LBJ. On March 7, some six hundred protesters, including civil rights leaders John Lewis and Hosea Williams, marched through Selma to the Edmund Pettus Bridge, named for a Confederate general and seared in the First Lady's consciousness since her childhood summers in Alabama. More death threats against King kept him off the streets that day. Journalists from the major television and radio networks from around the country converged at the bridge, where they broadcast to the American public live images of state troopers and mounted police as they brutally bloodied the protesters with whips, tear gas, and batons.[24]

That very Sunday in Washington, Lady Bird and Lyndon attended church with Lynda and her new boyfriend. Afterward, Lyndon met with McNamara; Lady Bird bowled with Lynda and swam laps with Margy McNamara; dinner with the Cliffords and Valentis followed. Lady Bird's day sounds routine, and appropriately uneventful for a Sunday. Though she makes no mention of the violence she and her husband likely watched on television that afternoon and evening, her diary entry for what came to be known as "Bloody Sunday" gives a direct line of sight into her particular angst about the moment, about Selma, about her husband, about the presidency, and about her countdown to the moment three years off when she planned for the Johnsons to get out of Washington.

> For quite some time I have been swimming upstream against the feeling of depression and relative inertia. I flinch from activity and involvement, and yet I rust without it. Lyndon too lives in a cloud of troubles, with few rays of light. Now it is the Selma situation. Negroes are demonstrating for the right to vote, and the cauldron is boiling. Out in front of the White House pickets are marching—a not unusual sight, but in this context with more poignancy than before, I think, because Lyndon is a southern president, because he won with such a great vote from the Negroes last fall, because the right to vote has been the key to the whole civil rights issue that he has hammered and hammered since '57. I am counting the months until March of '68 when, like Truman, it will be possible to say, "I don't want this office, this responsibility, any longer, even if you wanted me. Find the strongest and most able and God bless you. Goodbye."[25]

The very next day, Monday, March 8, as King's forces planned a second attempt to cross the bridge in Selma, marines invaded a beach near Da Nang, crossing the psychological barrier provided by the euphemism of "advisers," or the distance of an air war, and marking the first American combat boots on the ground in Vietnam. And on March 9, while Martin Luther King, Jr., held marchers back from crossing to the other side of the Edmund Pettus Bridge, the president authorized the use by American fighter-bombers in Vietnam of a gel-like substance made from extracts of petroleum and coconut oil. It was called napalm.

* * *

Violence at home had also increased pressure on LBJ. On the one hand, he faced a bloodied and determined civil rights movement agitating for evidence that the White House would support more legislation, this time on voting rights. Likewise, LBJ knew that authorizing any kind of federal intervention to protect the protesters from local police risked further white supremacist charges of excessive federal overreach. On the morning of Saturday, March 13, LBJ's "gloom" over how to handle his dilemma had become "thick enough to cut with a knife," Lady Bird recorded. Voicing her own sensibilities about how to advance civil rights without inflaming the southern whites she had grown up around, she wondered what LBJ could say "that will pull together these broiling masses of humanity, the Negroes in Selma and the white folks in Selma and the preachers and students and folks from all over the United States." Lyndon needed rest and sun, his doctors were telling him, but he "felt chained" to the White House and weighted by the "fog of depression." He was planning a television appearance before the American people, although he and Lady Bird both knew that television had never been his strong suit. But a three-hour meeting with Alabama governor George Wallace, a staunch segregationist and Johnson adversary, brought LBJ the kind of challenge he relished and one that dissipated his gloom. Wallace was threatening to again block civil rights marchers from actually crossing the bridge. But LBJ forced the governor to relent and stand aside as the president federalized the Alabama National Guard to protect the protesters in order to stifle further violence and humiliate Wallace. When Lady Bird next saw LBJ, in the Oval Office just after the meeting, she found that the fog had lifted. "Lyndon must have touched some inner spring, some untapped resource, because he sounded ready to go out and face the world, to take it on."[26] With the governor out of the White House and on his way back to Alabama, Lady Bird watched an energized Lyndon, "composed, in charge, in command of the situation," as he updated several hundred journalists on the situation in Selma. Attorney General Nick Katzenbach then briefed the press on voting rights legislation. A thousand antiwar protesters continued their chants on Pennsylvania Avenue, but Lady Bird had already learned not to let the noise bother her.[27]

That evening, the presidential couple entertained the country's aristocrats: Bird watched in disbelief as Lyndon rallied again to convey such a fine countenance to this crowd; she even felt uncharacteristically confident in her own skin. But she paired her usual diet of self-criticism with an even more severe regime to control her weight, periodically putting her petite self on a restrictive nutritional budget of black coffee, dry toast, grapefruit, and just a hard-boiled egg for lunch to offset the gastronomical indulgences of her White House hostess role. She needed to balance the pleasure of eating chicken-fried steak, Tex-Mex, or peach cobbler with abandon while at the Ranch with the constant scrutiny of her clothing and appearance by the public, her daughters, and her husband. Caffeinated but barely fed, she stayed under the covers until ten the next morning, sharing in the adrenaline of her husband's high and enjoying a sense of achievement and control from the approval of her aristocratic guests. "With the feeling of being really alive and really working in spite of mounting troubles," Bird headed to Sunday services at St. Mark's. Her pastor, Bill Baxter, had just returned from marching with Dr. King in Selma.[28]

As protests unfolded across the country over violence in Selma, LBJ convened a meeting with the vice president, the attorney general, and the House and Senate leadership. Bird recognized that Lyndon's work on civil rights was still inadequate to the task of empowering all Americans to exercise their right to vote. Rather like "deciding to climb Mount Everest while you are sitting around at a cozy family picnic," it was decided that evening that Lyndon would appear the next day before a joint session of Congress to personally introduce the new voting rights legislation long under discussion. Bird felt enormous relief at seeing Lyndon thrive, "glad that he is launched, that he is being intensely active," she recorded. "It is the milieu for him." Whether his improved mood was a result of prevailing in his confrontation with George Wallace, placing himself on the moral side of American history, or simply taking charge (or all of it at once), Bird wasn't quite sure what had "sprung him," but her husband was now "loosed from the bonds of depression," when not two months ago, when he fell ill after his inauguration, he had been lying in a hospital bed questioning his own resolve.[29]

Now, clad in his pajamas, Lyndon read page after page of the draft speech as quickly as his staff could write it, scratching out sentences, adding new ones. With her husband surrounded by assistants, speechwriters, telephone operators, and valets, Lady Bird, who over the years had fulfilled all these roles, felt she could begin to "divorce myself far more from" the mounting tensions leading up to LBJ's appearance that evening in Congress. Just before nine P.M. on Monday, March 15, a relaxed and elated First Lady entered the chamber of the House of Representatives, where the entire body rose to applaud her.[30] As Lyndon delivered his message, Lady Bird counted applause lines and ovations, watched for the reactions of the Republicans and southerners, and regretted certain absences, including that of their friend and now adversary "dear Senator Russell" and of Robert Kennedy, anything but a friend, but still a staunch advocate of civil rights. LBJ's awkward delivery notwithstanding, the substance of his speech was crystal clear.

> There is no Negro problem. There is no Southern problem. There is no Northern problem. There is only an American problem. And we are met here tonight as Americans—not as Democrats or Republicans—we are met here as Americans to solve that problem.
>
> This was the first nation in the history of the world to be founded with a purpose. The great phrases of that purpose still sound in every American heart, North and South: "All men are created equal"—"government by consent of the governed"—"give me liberty or give me death." Well, those are not just clever words, or those are not just empty theories.[31]

More than seventy million Americans watched. The press and pundits heaped praise on the president's speech. Historians ever since have counted it among the greatest ever delivered by an American president. It was also the speech that LBJ had the most sustained and direct hand in drafting, although he deleted a line in one draft making explicit the link between the two greatest challenges of his presidency: "Americans are risking their lives today in Vietnam and Selma."[32] Bird offered a more qualified, unvarnished reaction: the speech was too long by a good fifteen minutes, and Lyndon's delivery too slow. But "all in all," she conceded, "it was a magnificent speech. . . . And now what can be done has been done, and we shall see."[33]

* * *

With LBJ's mood restored by his taking a stand against Wallace and putting his political capital behind voting rights legislation, the First Lady turned back to her own portfolio. Still, it was impossible for her to separate herself entirely from the other major source of tension in the Oval Office, the escalation of the war in Vietnam. As the Johnson White House came under increased scrutiny, Lady Bird explained the problem not as a matter of a sound or a reckless foreign policy, but rather, as "a failure" to adequately explain American involvement in Indochina to the press and the public. What had once stirred inside her as a creeping feeling of doubt about the war now morphed into a stance of unequivocal support for the president's choices. Lyndon, she thought, must seize the political advantage with the public, and whether with editorial writers, the press pool, or members of Congress, he must try "to put Vietnam in true perspective, to win the war of words in which we have faltered even more than on the battlefield itself."[34] And this he did.

In the aftermath of a Viet Cong bombing of the U.S. embassy in Saigon at the end of March, Lyndon had secretly authorized sending two additional marine battalions and another forty thousand logistical personnel to Vietnam. A week later, without acknowledging his approval of more troops, the president made two extensive statements to the public—one, in a speech at Johns Hopkins University, billed as a commitment of massive economic assistance to the Mekong Delta, and the next in a press conference in the Cabinet Room, where he laid out plans for economic development generally and in Southeast Asia and Vietnam in particular.[35] Like many Americans, both Johnsons carried in their bones the creed and the blind spot of American exceptionalism. They held firm to the Wilsonian conceit that the purpose of American power, power they now had the chance to exercise, was to project the American experience of progress—in their case, their success in bringing electricity and literacy to the poor in Depression-era Texas—to somehow settle a conflict unfolding worlds away. Hearing the president in Baltimore invoke his own biography to explain his administration's offer of peace talks and proposals for massive development assistance in Vietnam, Bird felt

> the high thrilling feeling that we have taken the initiative. We are beginning to really explain to the world about Vietnam, about what we can do, about the promise of this epoch in history that we were on the move against the negation of war and communism. It was exciting. I felt like stalemate had had a firecracker put under it.[36]

An olive branch to some, a fig leaf to others, LBJ's proposal for economic aid received almost uniformly positive reaction nationally and internationally. Still, Ho Chi Minh, now in his third decade of battling foreign powers for Vietnam's independence, rejected the idea that the United States could act as a partner in development—a poison pill, in his view. A week later, American fighter-bombers dropped a thousand tons of explosives on villages controlled by the Viet Cong.

Over Easter weekend at the Ranch, Lyndon slept little—"I want to be called every time someone dies"—taking calls in the middle of the night. But as much as she feared the toll on his health and resented how former Senate friends like William Fulbright, refusing her husband the benefit of the doubt, had become critics, Lady Bird saw that Lyndon could not separate himself from the ticktock of the war. "Actually," she recorded, "I don't want him to, no matter how painful."[37] She understood the gravity of Lyndon's decisions, and she supported them even as she harbored doubts about whether American soldiers possessed the will to fight against an anticolonial insurgency, but it was the risk to his mortality that was most vivid for Bird in those early years of the Vietnam escalation.

At the Ranch, Lady Bird exulted in Lyndon's ability to take in the pleasures of the Hill Country of Texas, but she also worried that the very conditions that gave him such comfort in his life were the same that might cut it short.

> I look at him in profile. He is so much too heavy. I do not know whether to lash out in anger or sarcasm or gently remind him for the

> ninety-ninth time. But now I see him yearning toward the days of peace and retirement toward a life much along the pattern of these three days. I strain even more that what I know is an obstacle to such a life—these twenty-five pounds or so overweight.[38]

Excess weight in pounds could stress his already tested heart; his mood, weight, sleep, and drink fluctuated with the fits and starts of Vietnam bombing.

But both Johnsons had learned to compartmentalize, and allocate their energies to matters beyond the complexities of foreign war. This was especially true, and palpably easier, for Lady Bird, whose portfolio of preservation and institutionalization, of beauty and the environment, provided, by definition and design, an antidote to the emerging cloud that would soon hover over the Johnsons throughout their presidency. The First Lady found herself at ease with people around whom, and in circumstances in which, just a year earlier, she had flinched with self-consciousness and self-doubt. Travel to New York City for wardrobe, theater, museums, and schmoozing with aristocratic philanthropists, for example, had become second nature. "I'm moving in different circles from any I have known!"[39] She, in turn, drew New Yorkers to Washington to participate in a series of high-profile conferences meant to shore up public support for the president's domestic policy initiatives.

A major priority for Lady Bird and her growing cohort of policy allies in and out of government was the White House Conference on Natural Beauty. Chaired by Laurance Rockefeller, the conference included fifteen separate sessions featuring some 120 panelists and was attended by 800 participants. Beauty and beautification may have given off a feminine aura, but nearly all the attendees were men. And behind the label was an ambitious understanding of the concept of beauty, one encompassing the intersection between the natural and built environment and defined by the leading conservationists of the time. The federal government had barely begun to scratch the surface of how environmental conditions shaped the daily life of every American, urban or rural, black or white. Now, with Lady Bird's political backing and Lyndon's policy pronouncements, the White House made itself the country's central platform for debate on environmental policy (barely a term of art at the time) and more so than any American presidency in history.

The conference brought together a hugely disparate group of individuals and interests, ranging from the president of the National Association of Gravel Producers to the governor of California; from the executive director of the Sierra Club and the presidents of the Nature Conservancy and the National Geographic Society to the Automobile Manufacturers Association and its industrial progeny, the Junkyard Dealers of America, strip miners, and a number of advertising executives. Many of Lady Bird's closest collaborators, including Barbara Ward, Jane Jacobs, Libby Rowe, Louise Bush-Brown, Nancy Dickerson, Walter Washington, Nathaniel Owings, and Victor Gruen, spoke or attended.[40] Notably absent was Rachel Carson, who had sounded the alarm about industrial contamination with her 1962 book, *Silent Spring,* but who had died of cancer a year earlier; and Lewis Mumford, whose essays and books about cities, architecture, and the public environment left analytic and intellectual fingerprints throughout the two-day affair. Just days earlier, Mumford had gone public with his anger at the Johnson presidency over Vietnam, his broadside the canary in the coal mine of American arts and letters. Soon he would find himself in equally esteemed company.[41] Despite Mumford's telling and highly political absence, the ambition and substance of the White House conference unfolded remarkably free from the antiwar cultural zeitgeist then taking shape beyond Pennsylvania Avenue.

* * *

President Johnson had since 1964 begun to put his presidency behind a vast and ambitious environmental agenda for the cities, towns, parks, parkways, highways, waterways, farmlands, and skies of the United States. But it was Lady Bird who managed to elevate the need for federal, state, and municipal planning, hailing the value of her own approach: a focus on individual citizen and community action. Her ubiquitous presence those two days, taking copious notes in shorthand and popping in and out of various panels, reinforced the credibility and seriousness of the White House effort. In her comments opening the conference, she set forth the challenges addressed by the beautification agenda and the urgent need to prioritize action: "Our peace of mind, our emotions, our spirit—even our souls—are conditioned by what our eyes see. Ugliness is bitterness. We are all here to try and change that."[42] LBJ had positioned the office of his presidency behind the environment and natural beauty as a matter of priority. But preoccupied as he was by foreign policy crises and getting a second major civil rights bill passed, he could not relish the pioneering promise of his own White House's environmental ambitions. That portfolio he happily turned over to his wife.

The nation's leading landscape architects and environmentalists were peppered throughout the mammoth conference and its proceedings, their ideas about the social and political value of citizen participation and community action echoing and elevating the First Lady's own concerns. Despite her fears to the contrary, the conference was not simply about lofty goals and flowery rhetoric. At the time of its convening, there were at least a half dozen bills before Congress (or close to being introduced) that might put laws on the books that integrated "beauty" into national policies—in cities and along the nation's highways.[43] Keyed to the imminent expiration of a 1958 law intended to pay states a small bonus for regulating billboards, the White House used the natural beauty conference to introduce four new bills to regulate the placement and size of billboards on American highways and to require the screening of junkyards.

Of all the issues the White House might have chosen as a signature matter to associate with natural beauty and with the First Lady, billboards and junkyards required taking on two powerful industries, advertising and, indirectly, the automobile industry. Neither was in the habit of self-policing, and both had powerful lobbying operations and allies on the Hill.[44] Politically innocuous as they seemed, billboards and junkyards were not nonissues. And for the First Lady, the seemingly modest effort offered a vehicle to help cultivate public investment in, and consciousness about, broader and more entrenched environmental matters. But it wasn't until the fall of 1965 that Lady Bird became directly involved in calling members of Congress and otherwise promoting what on the Hill, her "home," came to be known as "Lady Bird's bill." More important, while the beautification bills were only beginning their trek through Congress, the White House learned that the Senate had overridden a filibuster threat to the Voting Rights Act: the day after the Conference on Natural Beauty concluded, in a vote of 77–19 (including four southern Democrats voting in favor), LBJ's second signature civil rights bill passed the Senate.

Chapter 10

"We Could Fall Flat on Our Faces"

In a society which has always been marked by that special disorder which comes of vast spaces, a highly diversified people, great natural and technical resources, and a rapid tempo of historical change, the Arts are here of utmost importance—not only as a moral force, but as a celebration of the American experience which encourages, clarifies and points to the next direction in our struggle to achieve the promise of our democracy.

—"First Annual Report to the President's National Council on the Arts," September 1965

In a moment of self-preservation for the First Lady who often contented herself with "what's left," Lady Bird seized upon an invitation to escape Washington and travel to the Rockefellers' Caneel Bay Resort in early June 1965. While Bird was snorkeling and hiking in the Virgin Islands, the pressures of Vietnam saw a resurgence of Lyndon's depression and volatility. General Westmoreland's cables painted a dire portrait of the campaign in Vietnam. "Desertion rates are inordinately high. Battle losses have been higher than expected. . . . Troops are beginning to show signs of reluctance to assume the offensive and in some cases their steadfastness under fire is coming into doubt." He requested 41,000 more U.S. troops, with an additional 52,000 later—more than doubling the total on the ground. One cable ended with an ominous warning: Washington should be ready, if needed, "to deploy even greater forces, if and when required."[1] LBJ had turned over every stone in deciding how to proceed with the consequential, perhaps legacy-defining, decision of meeting Westmoreland's request. He sent Bob McNamara to Saigon and Averell

Harriman to Moscow, and enlisted the views of other "wise men" in foreign policy who had served prior presidents. He asked for paper after paper from the Pentagon and State Department, arguing the cases for withdrawal, status quo, or escalation. Of all the views he solicited, only two made the case for drawing down, or at least not escalating, the American presence in Vietnam. As cognizant as he and his advisers were of the weakness of the South Vietnamese government, collectively they did not—maybe even could not—internalize the lesson of French colonialism there: the nationalist drive for independence, now dressed up in Communist attire and with the support of the Chinese and Soviets, was strong enough to outlast even the mighty resources of postwar American power.

Allowing the corrupt and disorganized South Vietnamese regime to fall to the North was not, LBJ's advisers and their mentors argued, a matter of sealing the fate of a single country somewhere in Asia of no direct challenge to American interests, but rather, of preserving American preeminence and the geopolitical balance of power of the Cold War. To withdraw, the argument went, would bring catastrophic consequences to the United States. The American public still supported U.S. involvement in Vietnam, but public skepticism about President Johnson's intentions had begun to grow. LBJ repeatedly eluded press questions about his aims in Vietnam, less to obscure his plans than because he hadn't yet decided what to do and because he didn't want to jeopardize his Great Society initiatives or the political support he'd need to get Congress to finance them.

Brewing doubt about foreign policy notwithstanding, LBJ's domestic legislative agenda still advanced rapidly and robustly in 1965: by the time the Eighty-ninth Congress broke for its August recess, the president had signed into legislation several major bills, including on education, public health, Social Security, and civil rights. Among them was the National Foundation on the Arts and the Humanities Act of 1965, which laid the groundwork and financing for what became the National Endowment for the Arts (NEA) and the National Endowment for the Humanities (NEH). The act resonated more as a legacy of Camelot than with the Johnson ethos. The Kennedys had elevated high art to the recital rooms of the White House and masterfully used the occasions and the press's love affair with Jack and Jackie to equate their administration with high culture. In 1962, Kennedy's advisers urged the president to evaluate areas where the objectives of government might overlap with the arts and to set up what they called a "national cultural policy."[2] Jackie, whose studies in France had familiarized her with the concept of a state cultural policy, embraced the idea. But it wasn't until after JFK's assassination that momentum picked up in Congress to vastly expand the role of the federal government in promoting the arts. One year later, with this act, Congress put taxpayer dollars behind the arts, which led to the creation of national and regional theaters; supported dance companies, operas, and symphonies; funded new works by composers; and helped found the American Film Institute. All this happened not only in major American cities, but also in small towns across the country.[3] Not since Franklin Roosevelt's Works Progress Administration (WPA) had federal funding for the arts found such support from the White House.

Although the Johnson White House had begun to accelerate the pace, the intersection of arts and business, at least as old as the Sistine Chapel, remained a relatively recent phenomenon for Washington, D.C. Plans to raise money for a National Cultural Center, first enacted while Eisenhower was in the Oval Office and LBJ in the majority leader's suites, had stalled until JFK appointed Roger Stevens to chair the effort and really got off the ground only after the assassination. Stevens was a self-made real estate developer who became an advocate for new playwrights and a successful producer of plays and musicals. Throughout his career, he produced more than one hundred plays, including *Cat on a Hot Tin Roof* (1955) and *West Side Story* (1957). He also added politics to his portfolio, chairing Adlai Stevenson's finance committee in 1952 after Truman declined to run again and, four years later, that of the Democratic Party. At the nexus of art, politics, and philanthropy, Stevens became the first chairman of the board of the newly named John F. Kennedy Center for the Performing Arts, an Edward Stone–designed building for which LBJ broke ground with a gold spade at the end of 1964. With LBJ's dedication to the project, and a clever funding scheme to allow the government to match private donations, Stevens raised millions in corporate, government, and private philanthropic funds to support the construction of the world-class performance center.[4]

In early 1965, the Johnson White House had also toyed with another way to bring art to the masses. Before approving the use of napalm in Vietnam and before sending 24,000 troops to the Dominican Republic, purportedly to prevent a Communist takeover, the president had asked the First Lady her opinion about a memo sitting on his desk proposing a White House Arts Festival to be held that spring. Eric Goldman, a Princeton professor of history hired by LBJ as an in-house intellectual, had authored the proposal with his chief assistant, a young art history PhD, Barbaralee Diamonstein. The two envisioned opening the White House to a marathon of events over the course of one full day to showcase contemporary American art: music, dance, theater, and letters as well as paintings, sculpture, film, and photography; the event would be hosted by the president and First Lady. Such an event, especially with an effort at geographic and artistic diversity, would spotlight the nascent National Arts Council; Stevens, its chair, agreed. With his decision-making energies and angst elsewhere, Lyndon asked Lady Bird to weigh in. The First Lady had spent the last year and a half schooling herself on contemporary art, architecture, theater, and music—initially, simply by inheriting Jackie's White House art acquisitions program, but also through numerous trips to New York City to see theater, opera, and art; or while basking in the beauty and social message of Marian Anderson and Leontyne Price performances at state dinners; or during semisecret tours of the newest architecture in the country to select the architect for her husband's presidential library. Lady Bird seized upon the festival as a chance to elevate the Johnson White House's commitment to the arts on the national stage, and advised the president to approve the undertaking. Only with her blessing in hand did LBJ give his green light to the proposal.[5] Bearing the burden of her husband's decision to go forward in a space that pointedly elevated the Johnson White House to the cultural heights the Kennedy White House had once occupied, Bird viewed the festival with nervous apprehension, knowing "we could fall flat on our faces, or it could be great."[6] But she had already undertaken a separate initiative in the arts that would turn out to be of far more lasting significance.

Roger Stevens and Dillon Ripley, the secretary of the Smithsonian, were at the time positioning the United States to compete for a large and diverse private collection of sculptures, paintings, and drawings housed on an estate in Greenwich, Connecticut. The collection was owned by Joseph Hirshhorn, an immigrant from Latvia. The youngest of twelve children, he had arrived in the United States when he was six years old. Skirting the ravages of the Depression, the five-foot-two-inch-tall Hirshhorn made his fortune investing in uranium, gold, and oil, mostly in Canada. Self-taught, he turned his investment eye toward art early in his business career, while still in his twenties. A recent heart attack had prompted him to accelerate his plans for finding a permanent home to display his vast holdings: more than 1,500 pieces produced by sculptors such as Rodin, Degas, Sir Henry Moore, Brancusi, Calder, Renoir, Giacometti, Marini, and Matisse; and more than 4,800 paintings, including works by Picasso, Eakins, Munch, Wyeth, Dalí, Bacon, de Kooning, Pollock, and Hopper. The Smithsonian had no contemporary art holdings on the National Mall—the National Gallery's modern wing did not yet exist—and the case for an American institution to become home to Hirshhorn's vast collection of contemporary paintings and sculpture piqued his interest. After several meetings with Stevens and Ripley, Hirshhorn offered his collection with the caveat that the museum housing it bear his name—another American financier, Andrew Mellon, who had donated his collection of 126 paintings and 26 sculptures to create the National Gallery of Art in 1937, had pointedly declined such a tribute in order to encourage other collectors to donate their art.[7]

To satisfy Hirshhorn that the Smithsonian had the political clout to deliver on such an arrangement, Stevens and Ripley organized a lunch with the president for Joe and his new wife, Olga. Producing a successful outcome from a meeting between a man of Lyndon Johnson's scale and southwestern sensibilities and one with the ambitious eye for art possessed by the diminutive Hirshhorn required the touch of LBJ's best ambassador, Lady Bird. Before their first meeting, Bird did her homework on Hirshhorn, comparing the vastness of his art collection to Lyndon's own ambitions for the country, and drew a connection between their shared story of "poor beginnings, intelligence, and drive." Her job that day was to show the Hirshhorns that the Johnson White House stood behind the Smithsonian acquisition. Whether by design or natural affinity, during a tour of the White House, Hirshhorn gravitated to the same works Lady Bird treasured most—James Whistler's *Nocturne,* Rembrandt Peale's portrait of Thomas Jefferson, David Martin's portrait of Benjamin Franklin, John Singer Sargent's portrait of Teddy Roosevelt and his ethereal painting *The Mosquito Net.*[8]

Over lunch, LBJ asked Hirshhorn to donate a Thomas Eakins portrait to the White House collection, and the collector agreed. But Lady Bird made the more ambitious ask. Would Mr. Hirshhorn, she inquired, allow the announcement of the Smithsonian's acquisition of his collection to take place at the White House Arts Festival? A one-day White House extravaganza celebrating the country's artistic talent would be an unmistakable signal of the Johnson administration's support for legislation to endow the arts and humanities with real money. Using the event to showcase LBJ's role in acquiring the Hirshhorn collection, Bird recognized, would make it "a coup, a crowning event."[9] But the deal still wasn't ready, and Hirshhorn said no.

Nevertheless, with the Johnsons' green light, their staff had only twenty-two days to pull off the massive logistical requirements for the festival. White House staff working directly and indirectly for the president and the First Lady provided the ideas, energy, and hours necessary for an endeavor of such scale. The festival boasted an astonishingly diverse lineup: Ansel Adams, Josef Albers, Richard Anuszkiewicz, Richard Avedon, Milton Avery, Leonard Baskin, Thomas Hart Benton, Harry Bertoia, Alexander Calder, Robert Capa, Imogen Cunningham, Stuart Davis, Willem de Kooning, José de Rivera, Richard Diebenkorn, Alfred Eisenstaedt, Walker Evans, Sam Francis, Robert Frank, Morris Graves, Grace Hartigan, Hans Hofmann, Edward Hopper, Robert Indiana, Jasper Johns, Ellsworth Kelly, André Kertész, Franz Kline, Dorothea Lange, Jacob Lawrence, Jack Levine, Jacques Lipchitz, Barbara Morgan, Robert Motherwell, Louise Nevelson, Isamu Noguchi, Georgia O'Keeffe, Jackson Pollock, Robert Rauschenberg, Man Ray, Larry Rivers, Mark Rothko, Ben Shahn, David Smith, Edward Steichen, Alfred Stieglitz, Paul Strand, Edward Weston, Garry Winogrand, and Andrew Wyeth—a testament to the convening power of the White House as an institution, and certainly to Lady Bird's vision and her Texan appetite for scale. One art critic called it "an artistic barbecue, Pedernales River–style."[10] A huge, splashy marathon, Lady Bird thought, but also one of impeccable taste, might position President Johnson as the country's artistic patron in chief. The painters, sculptors, and photographers whose galleries and museums from around the country had readily agreed to send their most iconic work to the White House indeed represented the highest quality of American artistic creativity of the era.[11] The works were paired with readings from plays by Arthur Miller, Millard Lampell, and Mildred Dunnock; dance pieces by the Joffrey Ballet and American Ballet Theater; film screenings by Alfred Hitchcock and Elia Kazan; and vocal performances by Marian Anderson, Leontyne Price, and Sarah Vaughan. The thirty-three-year-old Barbaralee Diamonstein, who had worked to engage museums and galleries from almost every state of the Union and all the major New York and Washington art museums and who pioneered the inclusion of cinema as an American art for display that day, was spot-on when she described the White House Arts Festival as "one of the most signal days in the history of federal relationship to the arts, to the creative America of the 20th century."[12]

Although, of Eric Goldman's staff, it was Diamonstein who worked to identify the painters, sculptors, photographers, playwrights, and filmmakers to showcase and invite, it was Goldman himself who filled in the literary side of the festival program. He invited Pulitzer Prize–winning poet Mark Van Doren; novelist Saul Bellow; novelist and nonfiction essayist John Hersey; poet Phyllis McGinley; National Book Award winner Catherine Drinker Bowen; the seminal strategist behind the Cold War's containment strategy, George Kennan; and Pulitzer Prize–winning poet Robert Lowell.[13] Campus teach-ins against the Vietnam War had begun that spring, but public opinion nationally still backed President Johnson's foreign and domestic policies by two to one. The anxiety Bird felt about the festival derived not so much from a concern that it would induce a backlash against the Johnson White House over foreign policy as from doubts that such a monumental undertaking could be pulled off in so little time. But her worries missed the mark. Following Lewis Mumford's stirrings of dissent earlier in the year, a few weeks before the festival, Robert Lowell sent a letter to the president voicing his despair over the prospect that the United States might become an "explosive and suddenly chauvinistic nation, and may even be drifting on our way to the last nuclear ruin." Lowell had already accepted the invitation, but he now withdrew: Without mentioning Vietnam by name, he wrote the president, "At this anguished, delicate and perhaps determining moment, I feel I am serving you and our country best" not only by not attending the arts festival, but also by sharing his letter with *The New York Times*, a story that landed on the front page. Lady Bird, the woman who served as Lyndon's extra pair of eyes, found herself totally blindsided.[14]

Lowell's public dissent set off a cascade of further reprimands, not of Lowell for snubbing the White House, but of the White House over LBJ's war in Vietnam and recent military intervention in the Dominican Republic. On the heels of the Lowell letter, John Hersey and Saul Bellow gave statements to the *Times* supporting Lowell, although they stopped short of withdrawing altogether. Hersey cited the "drift toward reliance on military solutions" as "deeply troubl[ing]," but felt that withdrawing might make less of a point than reading passages from "Hiroshima," his 1946 multipart *New Yorker* essay, in front of the president at the White House. Bellow, for his part, derided the interventions in Vietnam and the Dominican Republic as "wicked and harmful," but added that he intended to "honor [the president's] high office" by participating in the White House festival.[15] Robert Silvers of *The New York Review of Books* organized a statement reiterating Lowell's broadside, stressing that artistic participation in the festival should not be mistaken as an endorsement of America's "increasingly belligerent and militaristic" foreign policy.[16] Twenty cultural and intellectual luminaries signed the Silvers telegram, among them six Pulitzer Prize–winning poets; philosopher Hannah Arendt; satirist and cartoonist Jules Feiffer; playwright Lillian Hellman; essayist Alfred Kazin; novelists Bernard Malamud, Mary McCarthy, Philip Roth, William Styron, and Robert Penn Warren; critic Dwight Macdonald; and artists Larry Rivers and Mark Rothko. What's more, Hersey had, as a courtesy, sent Goldman the text he planned to read at the festival, an excerpt from "Hiroshima" and a separate essay, "Here to Stay."[17] Hersey's reporting from Japan had left an indelible imprint on his American readership, and seemed to resonate once again. Indeed, Truman's use of the bomb was fresh enough in the American mind to haunt LBJ as well. Until the day he left office, he feared that an escalation of fighting in Vietnam might inevitably lead to his finger not only on the button, but also to pressing it.

Six days before the festival—with her husband threatening to boycott or even cancel the event, deploying his staff to vet the FBI's background checks on the invitation list, and angling for a press blackout—Bird invited Goldman to lunch to discuss what had now become, as she described it, her "bête noire."[18] Meeting in the Queen's Bedroom, where Lady Bird frequently held private meetings, the First Lady, by Goldman's account, rather quickly and directly got to the point. Making clear that she spoke for herself and for the president, she told Goldman that the passage Hersey planned to read amounted to an attack not only on President Truman but also on the Johnson presidency. "The president is being criticized as a warmonger. He can't have writers coming here and denouncing him, in his own house, as a man who wants to use nuclear weapons," the First Lady said over a meal that no one was eating. Surrounded by her political staff, Mrs. Johnson, Goldman wrote, was unambiguous: Hersey must not come to the festival and read his "Hiroshima" passages. Goldman attempted to explain that censoring Hersey would promote the view that protecting a thin-skinned president from criticism was more important than respecting artistic freedom at the very event meant to signal the White House's embrace of it. Despite Goldman's concerns, the decision was made: "angry and taking charge," the First Lady insisted that Goldman stop Hersey from reading the "Hiroshima" passages. But he refused.[19] The First Lady's diary leaves out this color, lamenting only that she felt "a little, though not much, reassured" about the festival after the meeting. "The Lowell affair has gotten us off to a bad start."[20] But Bird had allies in the West Wing who were intent on preventing a complete free fall. Richard Goodwin, then LBJ's principal speechwriter, and Jack Valenti, the president's special assistant, recognized the high quality of the art and artists amassed for the festival and pleaded with the president not to boycott the event. "I prayerfully suggest you may want to reconsider and be present for your brief remarks at the Festival of Arts," Valenti wrote LBJ. Lady Bird would attend all twelve hours of the event—the president need only appear briefly, at an afternoon reception. "First," Valenti told him, "your absence will look deliberate, no matter what we say. It will be asserted that this is the President's way of reacting to Robert Lowell and the others who sent a wire backing Lowell. Second, it will be interpreted as a withdrawal of presidential attention to the arts because of sniping by certain artists at the President's Vietnam and Dominican program. Third, the President's absence will become the lead in the story and diminish an otherwise first-rate program." To let "one erratic, unstable poet"—a reference to Lowell's manic depression—"plus a dozen headline-seekers damage a truly high-quality enterprise" would overlook the fact that of the hundreds invited to exhibit and attend, only a few had taken an active posture of dissent. "The rest of those invited are delighted to attend and participate—and the majority of the art world," traveling from cities around the country, among them presidents of symphonies and operas, critics of every genre from the top magazines and newspapers, "are overjoyed at" what Valenti insisted was "this administration's fruitful favoring of the arts."[21]

The letter, the petition, the threatened "Hiroshima" passages, a few more withdrawals by invited guests, the growing din of criticism that LBJ was planning a propaganda festival meant to dupe artists and their patrons into looking like supporters of his war effort—all these denied the Johnson White House the splashy triumph for which Bird had originally hoped.

Lady Bird and Lyndon spent the weekend before the festival at the

Ranch.[22] Arriving back in Washington, they found the entire South Lawn and Rose Garden displaying the modern sculpture of Alexander Calder, Isamu Noguchi, and David Smith, among others. Unable to land amid the art, she and the president alighted in their helicopter onto the National Mall, where the Joffrey Ballet was in the middle of a dress rehearsal. "Here I am to face it," Bird thought, "for better or worse."[23]

The First Lady sat stone-faced during the opening session of the festival as the audience applauded Hersey's "Hiroshima" passages. And no wonder: the passages Hersey read cut to the quick of the White House and Lady Bird's focus on natural beauty. Hersey described a woman returning to Hiroshima to find that the bomb had caused a profusion of wildflowers growing even in the most inhospitable nooks and crannies of the city's wreckage, "grotesquely stimulated by the destructive blast," *The New York Times* reported.[24]

Beyond "Hiroshima," there was the spectacle of the critic Dwight Macdonald, on assignment for *The New York Review of Books* and circulating an anti-Johnson petition, his wide-striped shirt unbuttoned toward the bottom, exposing his portly belly, and of Charlton Heston and art and architecture critic Aline Saarinen challenging Macdonald's manners; of Saul Bellow, who read a passage from *Herzog* and worried about the pressure he felt from his New York literary pals over his decision to participate; of Lyndon showing up not once but twice, first in the morning to take in the sculpture on the South Lawn with his old Senate ally, now Vietnam nemesis, Bill Fulbright, and then for a twelve-minute appearance that evening; and of several guests leaving midstream.[25] All these atmospherics, and the wider cultural breach they portended, took place in a White House resplendent with the greatest American art and artists of the time. More than three hundred art enthusiasts, funders, and critics attended, alongside a number of the artists whose works were on display.

In his memoirs, Goldman describes the White House Arts Festival as an abject failure. Goodwin's and Valenti's memoirs do not mention the event at all. Nevertheless, despite having also signed the Silvers petition, the White House exhibited canvases by both Rothko and Rivers, along with dozens more contemporary works set up on false walls and partitions in the West and East wings. Twenty-nine sculptures were on display throughout the Jacqueline Kennedy Garden and the South Lawn, including William Zorach's *Affection* and David Smith's *Lectern Sentinel*. Throughout the day, guests zigzagged from the East Room for poetry readings, to the National Gallery of Art for lunch, and back to the White House for an afternoon session of music. There, in a tall black turban, Marian Anderson introduced the Louisville Symphony and the Metropolitan Opera's soprano Roberta Peters. Following a buffet dinner on the South Lawn, with Alexander Calder's massive sculpture *Whale II* on display nearby, LBJ sounded a note about how breathing life into America's artistic achievements requires "great responsibilities that can no longer be cast off on others."[26] Duke Ellington, whose father had once worked as a butler in the White House, closed out the thirteen-hour affair well into the night to a celebratory crowd, playing excerpts from his *Black, Brown and Beige* in a temporary bandshell constructed on the South Lawn.

Lady Bird dubbed the day after the festival "Black Tuesday." Yes, "Lyndon's dark countenance was dour and grim" because of it, but it was a "mere pebble in the shoe," she recorded, compared to the "real rocks [that] are the constant black background of Vietnam and Santo Domingo." Her efforts to comfort Lyndon went off "without too much effect." She would have preferred "the complete oblivion" of sleeping in, but instead, called on Liz and Bess for a postmortem on the festival.[27] How had they fared in the papers? Coverage in the Washington, New York, and national press focused largely on Lowell's, Hersey's, and Macdonald's acts of resistance far more than the artwork of Georgia O'Keeffe, Edward Steichen, Ellsworth Kelly, Robert Motherwell, Louise Nevelson, or Jacob Lawrence, the African American artist who, at age twenty-three, took the art world by storm when he painted a series of works in 1941 known as *Migration*.[28] The creative and artistic resonance of the day, or the Johnson administration's push that year for federal funding in the arts and humanities, would not, could not, be felt the morning after.

Reading the coverage, Bird observed a study in contrasts. Generally written by men, the front-page stories, she summarized, focused "only on Robert Lowell's not coming, John Hersey's coming and lecturing,

Dwight MacDonald's passing around a petition. . . . [T]here is some uncertainty whether he got four or seven signatures out of the three hundred or so guests. I'll take two-ninety-three-to-seven majority anytime!" Yet, even on such a dark day, her abiding sense of proportion led Bird's gaze to an alternative interpretation. "Oddly enough, the women reporters saw it in perspective. As their stories came in, one by one—Isabelle Shelton, Marie Smith, Gerry Van der Heuvel, Miriam Dobbin . . . All the women . . . gave the great good parts their due and the small dissensions their due."[29] From the beginning of Bird's tenure, the First Lady and Liz had cultivated a reputation for transparency and access to the female press corps, and Bird waited anxiously for Washington's *Evening Star* to come out. The opinion of reporter Mary McGrory, "the best writer of all," mattered to her. The Boston native wasn't writing for the ladies or arts section, but for the news section. But, Bird found, "hers was as cruel and cutting a story as ever I remember."[30] McGrory's piece pulled no punches: Her report depicted a weak and censorious White House that she found lacking in the taste or touch of the Kennedys'. For McGrory, the festival displayed middlebrow artistic work aimed, she thought inappropriately, at a mass audience. Unable to neutralize dissent or control those even on its own payroll, the White House had produced, she thought, what amounted to, notwithstanding the defense from Johnson literary stalwarts Ralph Ellison and John Steinbeck, a "canned" exercise.[31] McGrory was an astute observer of presidents and politics, and the Johnsons may not have showcased American art with the panache of the Kennedys (or the sparkle of the Obamas decades later). But McGrory's affinity for the Kennedys and her grief over JFK prevented her from seeing past the dissent over Vietnam to the significance of the Johnsons' willingness to promote and finance some of the most cutting-edge American art of the era. The First Lady tried to ignore McGrory's attack, aligning herself instead with the verse of Phyllis McGinley, who had captured Bird's frustration with "those who wear tolerance as a label but find some other views intolerable"—a cliché, but one that, Bird found, "fitted the whole occasion."[32] The emotional toll of Lyndon's mood and of her own disappointment with what she saw as the fiasco of the festival, including the failure to announce the Hirshhorn acquisition on that day, accumulated for Lady Bird into an irresistible need to sleep, to escape from the way in which Vietnam was, as the Johnsons foresaw, drowning out their domestic achievements. "Drenched in weariness," over the next two days, she allowed herself to collapse into several long-elusive afternoon naps.[33]

* * *

Although the disastrous turn of the arts festival may have served as a momentary, if unwelcome, distraction, Lyndon still faced the decision of sending yet more troops to Vietnam. In summarizing his anguish, while away from Washington at the Ranch, Bird recorded his thoughts:

> Things are not going well here.... Vietnam is getting worse by the day. I have the choice to go in with great casualty lists or to get out with great disgrace. It's like being in an airplane and I have to choose between crashing the plane or jumping out. I do not have a parachute.

Bird felt helpless: "[W]hen he is pierced, I bleed." Punctuating her awareness of Lyndon's loneliness was a dinner they hosted for Walter and Marjorie Jenkins. After the Jenkinses fled Washington, Lady Bird had continued to feel responsible for their happiness. With Walter's accounting business thriving at least financially, the Jenkinses, with some help from the Johnsons, had landed well. But for "some hold-backs, some little slurs," their "acceptance" in Austin after Walter's arrest and departure from the White House eight months earlier had been "mostly good."[34] Nevertheless, Bird was filled with anxiety. She was "getting frantic for sleep. I shamelessly take a sleeping pill each night." But they didn't seem to work, and for several weeks now, she found herself "awake and awake and awake," sleeping only "scantily and not that deep, refreshing sleep." She woke one night at two in the morning, "with a fluttery, pounding, nervous feeling," but read herself back to sleep with an Agatha Christie novel.[35]

Although it may have felt like it to Lyndon at times, not everything in Washington revolved around Vietnam—at least not yet. On July 9, in a vote of 333–85, the House of Representatives, with significant southern and Republican support, passed the Voting Rights Act. The same day, the Medicare bill also passed in the Senate. On July 13, with an eye toward an eventual Supreme Court appointment, the president appointed Thurgood Marshall, then a JFK-appointed judge on the U.S. Court of Appeals for the Second Circuit, to the position of solicitor general of the United States.[36] On the same day, and helped by public momentum built by the Conference on Natural Beauty, the Johnson White House announced the creation of the Environmental Science Services Administration, the first U.S. government organization with the word *environment* in its title and a precursor to the Environmental Protection Agency and the National Oceanic and Atmospheric Administration. A day later, the U.S. spacecraft *Mariner 4*, part of the space program LBJ had ushered in while in the Senate and as vice president, took the first-ever photographs of Mars.

* * *

> I woke up about 5:30 to hear Lyndon say—almost as though he were in the middle of a sentence, but he had been interrupted—"I don't want to get in a war and I don't see any way out of it. I've got to call up 6,000 boys, make them leave their homes and their families." It was as though he was talking out loud, not especially to me. I hope the refrain hadn't been in his mind all night long. Feeling like the boy that leaves the burning deck, I went to my own room to try to get another hour or two of sleep. Fitful and unsatisfactory, and so I got up and started a busy day devoted entirely to beautification.[37]

Lady Bird's growing recognition that her own self-preservation was required to ensure Lyndon's longevity gave her an escape from the ugliness of his Vietnam torments. The floral focus of beautification's early stages offered the perfect antidote. Back in Washington after the Fourth of July break at the Ranch, she spent a morning with Mary Lasker and Nash Castro planning fundraising campaigns for cherry blossom trees and other plantings at Washington's monuments and along Hains Point (the confluence of the Potomac and Anacostia rivers), at the long-neglected, southern tip of East Potomac Park, in Southwest. They called Walter Washington to see if he could break free for a drive to take a look at schools, playgrounds, and parks her committee might choose for fall plantings.

Driving around the Cardozo school district, just up the hill from Shaw, Bird saw "dreary and ugly" schools with "a little woe-begone grass in front, no planting," and sparely furnished concrete playgrounds.[38] Decades before the much-debated "broken windows theory" emerged as an influential social science explanation for crime and disorder, she observed a spate of broken windows on these schools. She spoke with Washington about the reason young people in the District found themselves bored and frustrated enough to turn their energy to damaging their own schools. Washington pointed out that it was at many D.C. schools where students themselves had participated directly in the landscaping and care of donated plantings where he had seen an almost complete absence of damage—he thought, as a result. As the First Lady had insisted at the White House Conference on Natural Beauty, citizen participation, Bird knew in her bones, was key to the shift to a sense of stewardship, of ownership. However significant donations from New York philanthropists and liberal-minded D.C. family businesses could be, anything beyond bulbs and trees—namely, land acquisition or designing and building new parks for underserved District residents—would require a degree of decision-making autonomy, revenue collection, and budget authority that would be, by and large, out of reach without home rule for D.C. citizens. Although LBJ was actively pushing to get a home rule bill through the House and Senate, even with the West Wing and East Wing behind him, there was only so much that Walter Washington could make happen from his post then as director of the National Capital Housing Authority. Along with White House backing, coordination with federal agencies would be vital. And Washington would find the champions he needed in two new members of Lady Bird's Beautification Committee: Robert Weaver, who in 1966 would become the first African

American to hold a cabinet-level position, and Stephen Currier, a philanthropist with a passion for civil rights and a humane urban environment. There would be a third champion, a true outsider, Larry Halprin, the San Francisco landscape architect. Halprin's emphasis on bringing nature into cities and on citizen participation in urban design would help him to become an ally and partner in Lady Bird's emerging focus on the built and natural environment for Washington's most underserved residents.

* * *

But no amount of attention to beautification could shield Bird from a feeling of helplessness when it came to Lyndon. As they approached the end of July 1965, and a decision about sending more troops to Vietnam, neither slept well. "For an extraordinarily healthy, tough, reasonably happy person, sleeping is becoming the hardest thing for me to do, particularly when I feel that I have not played my role well, that I have been a hindrance, not a help," Bird lamented.[39] She could not console Lyndon, and she hoped a weekend away at Camp David would help them both. Gatherings there often combined business and pleasure, and on the last weekend of the month, a hodgepodge of guests ventured with the president and First Lady to Maryland's Catoctin Mountains for "a parade of people, work, talk and exercise."[40] Later that day, a helicopter brought the McNamaras and their teenage son, Craig; the Cliffords; and Luci and her new beau, Pat Nugent. After an evening of burgers and bowling, their minister from St. Mark's performed a service the next morning for the entire entourage, "including two Jews and a few Catholics."[41] More naps helped Bird feel herself again, and time away freed her to spend several hours with Luci and Pat. The two in some ways were polar opposites, she observed. Luci was "a lark, a sprite—sometimes very intuitive, deeply feminine and quite mature. Sometimes flying off the handle"; whereas Pat was "clean and blonde," and a Catholic. He had just graduated from Marquette University and signed up for service with the Air National Guard Reserves. His service would begin at the end of the year.[42]

Decision time was at hand. It had been almost two months since General Westmoreland requested an increase of troops from 81,000 to

175,000, with 41,000 immediately and 52,000 by the end of the year. LBJ had already shifted the marines' mission on the ground from defensive to offensive operations, but given the French experience of a decade earlier, the president sensed that the escalation had all the trappings of an adventure "waist deep" into what Pete Seeger by 1967 would coin as "the big muddy"—a military, political, and diplomatic quagmire. But in the middle of 1965, Johnson's domestic agenda still held promise: he had dozens of pieces of major legislation before Congress, covering health, immigration, poverty, the arts, and voting rights. He wanted to preserve the political space for winning votes on his domestic legislation and associated budgets. Taking some time to weigh the decision about a major troop escalation represented both prudence and political shrewdness.

Still, his war council pushed for escalation. In early July, his national security advisor, "Mac" Bundy, delivered four papers to the president: Three of them (from Bundy, Rusk, and McNamara) represented the case for granting Westmoreland's request, and the fourth, written by Undersecretary of State George Ball, warned that the war was unwinnable and that exceeding the 100,000-troop mark would pave the way for as many as 300,000 or 400,000 troops and as many as 50,000 American deaths.[43] Washington could no longer protect South Vietnam from itself, Ball argued. Another voice from outside his direct staff also weighed in. Clark Clifford, Bird's partner in securing plans for the LBJ presidential library and public policy school, pressed the president, even more strongly than Ball, to find a route to a settlement between the North and South and then to draw down the American presence—by year's end, if possible. Over the next few weeks, LBJ made public reference to increasing demands for resources, human and otherwise, in Vietnam and spoke about the stakes there in terms of protecting national honor. He probed his national security staff for all the arguments for and against and sent McNamara to Saigon for more consultation with Westmoreland, Taylor, and their teams. But even though McNamara shared his pessimism with the president upon his return to Washington, he, like Rusk and Bundy, nevertheless pressed for an increase in American troops, lest South Vietnam fall. By the twenty-first of July, though fully cognizant of the risks abroad and of the political, policy, and public opinion backlash at home, the president decided to authorize more troops.[44]

When the Johnson parade arrived at Camp David for the weekend, Lady Bird knew Lyndon was still wrestling with the magnitude and implications of this decision and that he wanted to hear again the arguments for and against escalation. She'd seen time and again how the release of tension that comes with a difficult decision could ease Lyndon's torment, self-doubt, and depression. But this one was too momentous to produce such a ready release. At five in the afternoon that Sunday, when LBJ summoned McNamara and Clifford from their cabins to meet him in the Aspen Lodge, the table was set for each to make his final case before an unusually subdued president.

Sipping his Fresca, LBJ listened first to Clifford, who retraced the arguments he and George Ball had set forth over the summer: this was not "the last inning" in the fight against communism, the war was unwinnable, and the North Vietnamese, with China and Russia backing them, would match any American increase and then some. McNamara followed, pinning his argument to grant Westmoreland's request on the risk to American global standing should Washington allow the increasingly vulnerable South Vietnamese government to fall to the North. Clifford had prepared to debate the secretary of defense, but the president had heard enough and ended the meeting. He left the lodge and took a drive around the Camp David campus alone. And then he walked for another hour, also, and unusually, alone.[45]

On the helicopter ride back to Washington a few hours later, Clifford, the "absolutely cool symbol of discretion," gave Bird the impression that some portentous decisions had finally been reached. "It's been a good weekend for us all. It's been a good weekend for the country," she recorded his saying. A characteristically cautious comment, but with "his tone so weighted," she recalled, "you can feel the inescapable weight of decisions upon you, and you know they must be reached soon."[46] In a final step to dispense with his feeling of ambivalence, the president asked

Clifford the next day to once more restate his case for scaling back in Vietnam, against the troop increase, this time in front of a larger group of advisers.

But the decision had been made. Mac Bundy had already sent out telegrams to American embassies around the world with talking points on how to explain the new policy. LBJ then briefed congressional leaders, but asked them to keep the details of the discussion confidential. Finally, on Tuesday, July 28, in a press conference that included other announcements, President Johnson revealed his decision to send forty-four new combat battalions, increasing American troop strength to 125,000. "Additional forces will be needed later, and they will be sent as requested," he coolly added. And, buried deep in the press briefing, was also an announcement of an expansion of the draft—"This will make it necessary to increase our active fighting forces by raising the monthly draft call from 17,000 over a period of time to 35,000 per month, and for us to step up our campaign for voluntary enlistments."[47] Perhaps more than any other issue related to Vietnam, the draft would emerge as a target and source of major public outrage.

Over the summer, LBJ had navigated the thicket of preserving his options, protecting his domestic programs, neutralizing his conservative critics who were pressing for action, and keeping the American public in his corner. His still-new press secretary, Bill Moyers, attempted to reassure the president with a strained but nuanced take on reaction to his Vietnam announcement: "I don't think the press thinks we are going to change basic policy"—framed at the time as shoring up the government of South Vietnam—"but the requirements to meet that policy."[48] But the lines between that "basic policy" and its "requirements" had clearly begun to blur.

Chapter 11

"Impeach Lady Bird"

There's nothing to give you a feeling of self-control, self-assurance, of being able to face life and love it like exercise. And swimming in a lake, where you can go on and on, and watch the sky and the birds, and lose yourself in peace, is something I love dearly.

—Lady Bird Johnson, White House diary, August 1, 1965

Beauty cannot be set aside for vacations or special occasions. It cannot be for the occasional privilege of those who come long distances to visit nature. It cannot be reserved, "For nice neighborhoods ONLY." I am quite sure that ugliness—the grey, dreary unchanging world of crowded, deprived neighborhoods—has contributed to riots, to mental ill health, to crime.

—"Remarks by Mrs. Lyndon B. Johnson to the National Council of State Garden Clubs and American Forestry Association," Jackson Hole, Wyoming, September 7, 1965

President Johnson ricocheted between the escalation of war abroad and the expansion of social peace at home. On August 6, he signed the Voting Rights Act into law. The achievement temporarily helped shift the national conversation away from Vietnam. By providing the legal foundations to enforce the voting rights guaranteed by the Fourteenth and Fifteenth amendments, the act allowed the federal government, through the Justice Department, to identify discriminatory voting laws, monitor elections for voter suppression, and review any proposed changes to voter laws before they went into effect. The new law was one of the most consequential pieces of legislation passed since the Civil Rights Act. To historians it would represent a turning point. According to Carol Anderson, author of *One Person, No Vote,* it was a "seismic shift in thought, action, and execution for the US government."[1] But Lady Bird did not join Lyndon, Martin Luther King, Jr., Rosa Parks, Roy Wilkins, and John Lewis, among many others, in attending the signing ceremony. Instead, Luci accompanied her father to the Capitol rotunda. Lady Bird had left for New York City two days earlier and, in a lapse, forgot to watch the televised event.[2]

Missing the signing of the historic Voting Rights Act did have its purpose: to secure the Smithsonian and White House's objective of acquiring for the American people the nation's first major modern art collection. Since being thrust into the spotlight following JFK's assassination, Bird found her definition of the First Lady's role evolving from that of quasi–vice president during the thirteen months of transition to one that balanced her ceremonial duties with a sizable, substantive, and often autonomous portfolio. This increasingly meant sticking to her own schedule, a move supported and encouraged by the president. From Manhattan, Bird set out with Lynda to the estate of Joseph Hirshhorn, in Greenwich, Connecticut.[3] The visit with Joe and his wife, Olga, was too short for Bird's taste—her always rushed schedule gave her too little time wherever she was and felt to her, in this case, like "something of an insult—it should be savored slowly, luxuriously, like a delicious candlelit banquet, instead of gulped like a hamburger." Up a winding driveway lined with rhododendron and elm trees, Bird found Hirshhorn's "dignified, impressive residence," a twenty-four-acre estate that embodied everything about the world of philanthropy and art that Bird now navigated with aplomb. There, she recorded, "all similarity to anything I have ever seen before ended. Right in the middle of the circular driveway, in a plot of green, were five or six huge figures in chains, marvelous expressions—agony, dignity, endurance, self-sacrifice, by Rodin!" For $250,000, Hirshhorn had purchased the seven-foot-tall, nine-foot-long *Burghers of Calais* to decorate his lawn, one of six original works cast by Rodin himself. During her short visit, the First Lady found herself "pelted by impression after impression" as her "five foot two, bouncy, delightful" host, along with his curator, wife, and attorney, walked her through part of his vast outdoor sculpture collection. There, works by Daumier, Giacometti, and Marini dotted the "beautifully kept lawns, sloping off into misty vistas, visible between tall trees, a rose garden."[4] Inside Hirshhorn's Tudor-style mansion, a massive estate with more art than many museums, Hirshhorn showed Bird works by Thomas Eakins—he owned more than thirty of them—Robert Henri, and Childe Hassam. Sloans, Wyeths, and Hoppers decorated bedrooms and hallways. In the mansion's eleven bathrooms hung paintings by Max Ernst and Jack Butler Yeats. English antiques and pre-Columbian clay figurines lined the mantels. Negotiations with the Smithsonian were still under way—one reason that Hirshhorn, on his White House visit, had rebuffed Lady Bird's request to announce the acquisition at the arts festival that spring. Rather than make a direct pitch now, the First Lady spent her too short visit taking in the art, and showing Hirshhorn her appreciation for it, to again signal the Johnson administration's commitment to the collection and to neutralize any lingering competition from the Tate and New York museums. And though she berated herself for poor salesmanship, she was right to hold back at the moment.[5] In May 1966, the Smithsonian and Joseph Hirshhorn finalized the donation of his entire art collection, along with a contribution of a million dollars to buy more art for the collection. And by November 1966, Congress would pass the law formally establishing the Hirshhorn Museum and Sculpture Garden and authorizing fifteen million dollars for planning and construction. With a call to Secretary McNamara, Lady Bird helped secure the land on the National Mall, at the time occupied by a Defense Department museum, in order to designate it for construction of Gordon Bunshaft's circular museum and adjacent sculpture garden.[6]

* * *

Over the summer of 1965, before the escalation of major ground operations in Vietnam, and as riots erupted in the Los Angeles neighborhood of Watts just one week after LBJ signed the Voting Rights Act, Bird wrote her own copy for a ten-page *Life* magazine article: "Watching Lyndon in the Presidency, there is something a wife feels which is quite apart from devotion. It is deep compassion for the man who must cope with problems from Vietnam to Appalachia."[7] As pressure on Lyndon built, the First Lady's near-constant diet of black coffee and hard-boiled eggs and her trouble getting a good night's sleep, along with her disciplined fitness routine, intensified. Activities like swimming were "a shot of adrenalin." Keeping herself productive, busy, and fit was her antidote to succumbing to the weight of the world Lyndon carried, a way of expressing her compassion by staying as healthy as possible, and thereby helping to lighten his burden. Over the summer, she traveled to Milwaukee, Peoria, Syracuse, Buffalo, Denver, and Jackson Hole to raise public consciousness and press her case for public participation in community planting programs.[8] She hosted the U.S. Postal Service at the White House as part of her campaign for the 34,000 post offices in the United States to beautify their public spaces and to serve as a model for other federal agencies. She reviewed and gave notes for every word and image of a pamphlet, *Toward a More Beautiful America,* a key publicity document the Beautification Committee developed to promote its efforts. The emphasis of her travel, message, and publications at the time hewed strictly to the idea of citizen participation in local beautification. But her outreach began to broaden beyond garden clubs: she targeted labor unions, for example, and met with Walter Reuther, head of the United Automobile Workers (UAW), to secure his commitment to make environmental cleanup part of his public message to the union's rank and file.[9]

But even as her public messaging hewed to the more intrinsically pleasing value of beautification, the First Lady was also putting in many, many hours taping voiceovers, reviewing drafts, and filming a Thanksgiving documentary for ABC. By the mid-1960s, postwar urban renewal had invited considerable scrutiny and criticism for its displacement of communities and for the inhuman public housing towers mushrooming in American cities. Lady Bird wanted to begin to show the public that beneath the surface of the beautification efforts she promoted were deeper, structural dimensions to the urban crisis that connected to housing, industrial pollution, race, and economic inequality. In the documentary, she highlights the environmental threats to the rivers and public spaces specifically in Washington, D.C., and the squalid conditions in the built environment experienced by the most underserved of the city's majority-black residents. The images and voiceovers depict "blight" and describe "ugliness," phrases once in vogue in the world of urban policy reform, but increasingly under attack for their implication that black and brown people living in such communities were themselves blighted and ugly. But the documentary also shows, as a model of an ideal urban oasis, the newly opened mixed-use, integrated, architecturally pleasing, green-space-filled River Park cooperative complex built in Southwest on land where slums had been razed a decade earlier. When the documentary aired at the end of the year, Bird could barely bring herself to watch it. She didn't like how stiff she appeared on camera, to be sure. But she also found it nearly impossible to find the right voice and emphasis—wanting to reach a broad, suburban audience and, without alienating them, tell them that too many of their fellow American citizens had yet to benefit from the promise of American prosperity and democracy. However flawed, Lady Bird's focus on how people in Washington, D.C., lived marked a real and, Bird knew, risky departure from Jackie Kennedy's wildly successful 1962 network documentary showing Americans the art, antiques, and china surrounding the residents of the cloistered White House.[10]

Yet, for all the talk, words, images, and activity feeding her public campaign, and for all her efforts to serve as an antidote to Lyndon's travails, it wasn't only for his benefit that she sought to physically embody the cool and calm on which he relied. Keeping herself in the public spotlight, working to popularize her husband's far-reaching social programs, gave the White House and the Johnson presidency a near-continuous stream of positive print, radio, and television coverage. This was particularly true for programs like Head Start, a local effort run by volunteers, but with the guidance and backing of the federal government, which aimed for national expansion. As LBJ proclaimed from the Rose Garden earlier that year, the program would "make certain that poverty's children would not be forever more poverty's captives."[11]

Head Start expanded on the recommendations of the Cooke Report, produced in 1964 by a panel of experts in early child development at the behest of LBJ and Sargent Shriver, then recently minted as the director of the Office of Economic Opportunity. First envisioned as an eight-week summer program run by volunteers, Head Start grew into a year-round, permanent pillar of the Great Society. Initially, the program provided preschool children from low-income households with access to education, nutrition, and health and emotional care in an effort to support them as they entered kindergarten. Although the program was Kennedy territory, under Shriver's leadership, it found its most ardent and active champion in Lady Bird. She understood her added value and willingly supported any effort to highlight this aspect of LBJ's domestic agenda.[12] As the public face of the early childhood, antipoverty literacy effort, Lady Bird received more than six hundred letters from volunteers and recipients related to Head Start, some in Spanish, some in English, many of which compared her work favorably to Eleanor Roosevelt's advocacy during the Depression. Some highlighted the needs of individual Head Start centers: for teachers, space, or money for breakfast. Others simply gushed with praise and congratulated the First Lady on her "brain storm."[13] Head Start's budget and mandate came directly from the Office of Economic Opportunity—the First Lady hadn't come up with the idea; her role was simply to amplify its message.[14]

Although she frequently incorporated visits to rural and urban Head Start centers into her travel schedule, the rapidly expanding early childhood education initiative was Shriver's program, and it did not occupy her passionate gray matter in the way that the tangible and aesthetic benefits of natural beauty and environmental consciousness-raising did. But despite her intense public campaign on that front, by late summer, precious little energy had gone into direct lobbying for highway beautification legislation, first announced at the White House Conference on Natural Beauty earlier that year. When the White House submitted the draft laws to Congress, there were four separate bills that addressed outdoor advertising, junkyard control, scenic roads, and highway landscaping. Later, the White House sought to combine all four into one stand-alone bill. At the time, the highway beautification bill stood out as one of the few potential new laws on the national environmental policy landscape that held out the prospect for federally funded, legally binding, and thus potentially lasting consequences.

The First Lady and her staff directly lobbied several senators over the course of August.[15] But with no champion in Congress, they were no match for the billboard lobby, a powerful force with auto industry backing. The lobby negotiated hard with the White House, and by the fall, it had prevailed with a watered-down bill, one that somewhat restricted the size, spacing, and lighting of roadside billboards. Even worse, the consolidated highway beautification bill had been stripped of meaningful funding and would require reauthorization after only one year.[16]

To add to the challenge of building public support, the First Lady had to fight with not only the Hill, but also the West Wing, over resources to advance the president's agenda. Earlier in August, Liz had sent a memo to LBJ adviser Marvin Watson about travel for East Wing staff—for advance trips on behalf of Lady Bird and the First Daughters. "Is the East Wing always to be considered 'second class citizens'?" she asked.[17] Her request was met with resistance—"Previous First Ladies had not had their travel expenses paid for out of the $25,000 travel allotment for the White House" staff, she was told. Up until this point, Lady Bird had been paying for her own and her staff's travel out of her pocket from her KTBC severance, which was about to end. In Lyndon's bedroom, Bird laid into the president: "They work for the White House, the whole overall operation. Should their travel be paid for, just as the male members' would?" Defiant and angry, Lady Bird left Lyndon's room, only to be called back later to his office. The East Wing, she needed Lyndon to remind his West Wing staff, was part of the White House policy and political agenda, and should be treated with due professionalism. "I'll get you whatever you need," Lyndon reassured her.[18]

* * *

Lady Bird's "personal problems," as she described her budget battles, may have appeared minor to a thinly stretched president.[19] Between the Fourth of July and Labor Day weekends of 1965, the Johnson presidency had seen both tremendous highs and devastating lows—and the First Lady shared completely in both. By the time LBJ arrived at the Ranch in early September 1965, the military had authorized Operation Starlite, the first offensive action conducted by U.S. Marines during the Vietnam War. But in the wake of the national success of the Voting Rights Act, the president also planned to push Congress to legalize home rule in the District, a now imaginable step toward local democratic control. LBJ had also successfully settled a nationwide steel strike waged by six thousand steelworkers against Worthington Corporation, for an increase in their hourly pay. Public support for Johnson still hovered at around 60 percent, but it fell steadily throughout the year as criticism mounted over the administration's foreign policy.

The Johnsons spent their last weekend of the summer boating and swimming on LBJ Lake (renamed that year to commemorate his role in bringing electricity to the Hill Country and in damming the Llano River), touring LBJ's boyhood home with visitors, and lounging by the pool.[20] Amid all the weekend's carousing, Bird revised and edited six drafts of a speech she was scheduled to deliver right after Labor Day in the heart of Wyoming's Grand Tetons.

On the morning Lady Bird was set to travel to Jackson Hole and LBJ to Washington, the president awoke before dawn complaining of stomach pain. Coming in waves, the symptoms were indistinguishable from those he had experienced just prior to his heart attack a decade earlier. But Lyndon encouraged a worried Bird to keep her travel plans. To cancel at the last minute would signal to the press waiting to fly to Wyoming with her that something was awry.

Lady Bird left Lyndon and joined a plane full of journalists en route to the Tetons that same morning. It had been a little over a year since her last trip to Wyoming, where, against "this magnificent setting—God's handiwork," she stumped successfully for Lyndon.[21] This time, she had returned to the stunning landscape with a different agenda. Speaking to the National Council of State Garden Clubs and the American Forestry Association, two nonprofits given an unexpected national platform by her conservation campaign, Lady Bird stressed the role of local organizations, "where inspiration becomes action and results take shape." She extolled the push for environmental action by capital and labor—by General Electric, to bury transmission lines underground; by the United Automobile Workers, to push beautification on a national scale; by the National Association of Home Builders, to preserve trees while rebuilding cities; and by volunteers, activists, scientists, and young people, who at every level were working to "preserve and enhance" America's beauty. It was this type of local activism that would drive change at the national level. In advocating for the Highway Beautification Act, she conceded that, though imperfect, "it will be a step forward" and only one part of a much broader effort. "For the purpose of this great land is not simply to pile up wealth and power," the First Lady concluded, long concerned about the concentration of capital and the unregulated construction of environmentally destructive freeways.[22]

Pleased with her speech, Lady Bird breathed a deeper sigh of relief that evening when she received word of Lyndon's diagnosis: gallstones. Liberated from the anxiety of public speaking and with a clear course of action for Lyndon's health, she spent the next day with Laurance and Mary Rockefeller, exulting in the beauty of the Tetons. She returned to Washington, D.C., expecting to find a sick and needy husband, but with his condition diagnosed, pain largely managed, and plans secretly under way for surgery, Lyndon had rallied and flown to New Orleans for a laying on of presidential hands: Hurricane Betsy had killed eighty-one people and caused $1.43 billion in damages.[23]

LBJ and Lady Bird decided not to announce the president's planned surgery until the fifth of October, nearly a month after the gallstone attack. In the days leading up to the operation, they filled their schedules with a frenzy of activity. On October 1, Lady Bird traveled to Syracuse and Buffalo, stopping at Niagara Falls to highlight her natural beauty campaign. On October 2, Lyndon signed the Water Quality Act of 1965, which required states to issue water quality standards, and released a statement on the early findings of a joint report on "Natural Beauty in America," citing progress in bringing "the full resources of this Government to bear on the problem of dwindling beauty."[24] That day, the First

Lady placed calls to the House and Senate to press for passage of the highway beautification bill. The Johnsons flew the next day to New York City. From John F. Kennedy Airport, they took a helicopter directly to Liberty Island, where President Johnson signed the Immigration and Nationality Act of 1965, the most progressive legislation on immigration perhaps ever. With the Hudson River and the Statue of Liberty framing him, LBJ proclaimed, "Our beautiful America was built by a nation of strangers. From a hundred different places or more they have poured forth into an empty land, joining and blending in one mighty and irresistible tide." The Immigration and Nationality Act, also known as the Hart-Celler Act, dismantled the more than thirty-year-old national origins quota system, designed to restrict immigration from countries in Asia, Africa, the Middle East, and Western and Southern Europe. The goal of the new law was to eliminate prejudice from the American immigration system and to put in place a set of criteria that favored family reunification and employment-based migration. But the law was not without its skeptics. In his dissent on the Senate floor, Sam Ervin, a Democrat from North Carolina, scoffed, "With all due respect to Ethiopia, I don't know of any contributions that Ethiopia has made to the making of America."[25]

In a bit of understatement, LBJ reassured Congress that the act would not "reshape the structure of our daily lives or add importantly to either our wealth or our power."[26] In fact, his law did change the country—its labor force, its language base, its demographics. It also increased America's wealth and, arguably, its power as a diverse democracy. As important, it opened the doors to immigrants from around the world by ending the emphasis on Northern European migration, creating the family-based system of "chain migration"—the very system that, like many of LBJ's transformative domestic programs, would come under assault decades later.

* * *

On the day the White House planned to break the news that the president would undergo gallbladder surgery, an anxious Lady Bird sat down at her desk to conquer stacks of paperwork, feeling as if she was moving "automatically through the prologue toward the real beginning," the imminent public announcement of LBJ's surgery. Again, the hairdresser; a diplomatic reception; photos with Alabama notables and with a mayor, a senator, and the (former Nazi) space engineer Wernher von Braun, now helping the First Lady build public support for burying power and telephone lines underground in American cities; then five minutes at the Metropolitan Washington Board of Trade, with holly trees and chrysanthemums—another beautification ceremony. Feeling "heavy with failure" after working on her ABC documentary on the urban environment, she returned to the White House depressed by her performance.

The control she exercised that day had taken its toll. At five-thirty in the afternoon, Bird told Bess and Liz that they would announce Lyndon's surgery thirty minutes later, and that she planned to move into the hospital for the duration of the president's two-week stay there. "When I finished, I felt like I had just coughed up a time bomb that I had been carrying." With the air cleared, her stunned staff could now deal with the mounting stacks of unanswered invitations, arrange for the First Lady's absence from Pennsylvania Avenue, and go ahead with plans for two massive, back-to-back receptions for members of Congress and their spouses. As soon as Lyndon announced the surgery, Bird drove out to Bethesda Naval Hospital to make sure his quarters there were properly outfitted: with a carpet for the bathroom floor, a reclining chair to be brought over from Camp David, pillows (hard, not soft), the three-screen television set, and his family pictures. They would move in a few days later.[27]

* * *

With the Johnsons preparing to retreat to the hospital while the highway beautification bill moved toward a vote in the House, Bird's recent activism on behalf of the bill became a target of GOP ridicule and the media. Never before had a First Lady been so intimately tied to a single piece of legislation, and seldom had a First Lady become such clear fodder for political scorn. Before the congressional reception, Lady Bird learned that she was the latest subject of a cartoon by Bill Mauldin, an editorial cartoonist with the *Chicago Sun-Times* known for his acerbic political commentary. The cartoonist came to the White House to present an original autographed image to the First Lady, which depicted her driving on a winding highway peppered with billboards, one of which read "Impeach Lady Bird"—a satirical comment on her unusual political influence in the Johnson administration. Though she was surprised to be the subject of a political tussle and uncomfortable with the added visibility, she brushed off Mauldin's drawing with a laugh. While Republicans in Congress were mocking Lady Bird as a too-powerful surrogate for LBJ, Supreme Court justice Earl Warren also came under fire for the liberal bent of his Court. Responding to Mauldin's cartoon not with outrage but, rather, with pride, the First Lady crowed, "Imagine me keeping company with Chief Justice Warren!"[28]

* * *

Before LBJ went under the knife, he signed a $340 million spending bill to fund medical centers working on heart disease, cancer, and stroke.[29] But Congress was less eager to deliver on "Lady Bird's bill," as Kansas representative Bob Dole called it. An easier focus of partisan opposition than medical research, for example, highway beautification and Lady Bird had become Republican marks, surrogates for LBJ's broader agenda. But LBJ doubled down on the attack by essentially daring House Republicans to vote against his wife, and on the eve of his imminent surgery, no less. "You know I love that woman and she wants that Highway Beautification Act, and by God, we're going to get it for her." At 12:07 A.M., the watered-down highway beautification bill passed by a vote of 245–138, with 49 abstentions.[30] By the time the vote came in, the president had left the national stage for the surgical theater in Bethesda.

Although the president and First Lady stayed in the hospital for nearly two weeks during his recovery from gallbladder surgery, Lady Bird returned to the White House for a few hours each day to "see what the outside world was doing." With such a long convalescence for what has since become outpatient surgery, Lyndon transformed his hospital suite into a West Wing of sorts. From his hospital bed, he signed thirteen domestic policy bills. Sometimes, as he recuperated, Bird sat beside him simply to hold his hand; other times, she retreated to her room to catch up on episodes of *Gunsmoke* recorded for her by White House techies of the era.

In the early days of his recovery, Lyndon made progress, even famously showing off to the press his enormous scar. His spirits seemed high, and his appetite improved. But the constant threat to his emotional equilibrium of overexertion—too much and too soon—dogged the First Lady. After a few days in, with Lyndon in good hands, Lady Bird took off for a full day of errands. Exhilarated by the fall colors of sunset, a "magnificent parade of crimson and russet and gold," Bird found upon her return to the hospital that LBJ's mood had dramatically shifted. In a meeting described in the President's Daily Diary as "OFF RECORD," and in a section of her own diary she marked "close for ten years, and review then," the First Lady describes the "somber atmosphere" she found in LBJ's room at dusk that day. Abe Fortas, Lyndon's recently confirmed Supreme Court associate justice, sat by his bedside. They had been speaking for twenty minutes before Lady Bird came in. Understanding that the burden of managing Lyndon's mood would ultimately fall to the First Lady, they encouraged Bird to join their conversation.[31]

There was no specific incident that had triggered the shift in Lyndon's mood. It was the whole of it. And LBJ was asking his wife and his closest consigliere "advice on how he could escape from the burdens of the presidency for the next indefinite period." With some eighteen domestic policy task forces operating simultaneously, a State of the Union address to be written, a weakening dollar, new demands for foreign aid, and a budget due to Congress, Lyndon confided to Abe and Lady Bird that he felt he could handle "not one more piece of paper, not one more problem." Any decision he had to make now, he assured them, would be the wrong one. "I want to go to the Ranch. I don't want even Hubert to be able to call me. They may demand that I resign. They may even want to impeach me," Bird recorded her husband as saying. "He was like a man on whom an avalanche had suddenly fallen," Lady Bird observed. For

Abe, she recorded, it was an "awesome feeling," because he had never seen this side of LBJ. But the self-doubt, the crippling depression, were "not entirely new to me." She had seen them in 1955, after the heart attack that nearly killed him. Back then, though, Lyndon could step away from his duties as majority leader—when "it was much more a personal decision and not a national one or even global." Not so now. The three confidants "sat in an atmosphere of numbed silence, with Abe offering quiet legal observations," until their conversation was interrupted. After dinner, the associate justice, the president, and the First Lady returned to LBJ's private room. There, Lyndon had Abe write out in longhand some of his thoughts. "Lyndon speaking at random gave us a glimpse of the most painful things on his mind," most prominently, in Lady Bird's telling, about the boys whose lives he was risking in Vietnam. Although his secretary typed up two copies of Abe's longhand note, we do not know its exact contents. The Fortas papers at Yale University remain closed, and the LBJ Library either does not have the document in its possession or has not made it available to the public. "So here is the black beast of depression back in our lives," Bird recorded. Though she had grown accustomed to anticipating Lyndon's mood swings, the First Lady conceded that this time she had missed the signals. Resigned, she readjusted her focus, knowing that after a period of rest, albeit perhaps impossible to carve out "when you are president of the United States" rather than the majority leader, he would soon bounce back and require "activity to feed on." If she couldn't help him "buy a little time of quiet," she could at least provide him that other reliable resource: her own knowledge of him.[32]

Chapter 12

"Little Flames of Fear"

> *We had to walk past the eleven cars. That was good, because the stinging cold air and the snow sifting into our faces made us all feel brisk and alive again. Then I looked on my right. There was a freight car with a door open and lights inside. I could see three oblong boxes. Seven or so feet long. On top of one there were sprays of flowers. Rather wilted gladiolas. I suppose their destination was Arlington. Hard to think of anything else.*
>
> —Lady Bird Johnson, White House diary, January 29, 1966

Public life in the White House had become as routine, and sometimes as tedious, as the constant trips to Jean Louis to have her hair permed (a four-hour affair) or teased (brief by comparison), to New York to keep her wardrobe updated (usually an overnight jaunt), to the White House pool for the solitude of thirty or forty sanity-keeping laps, or to the bowling alley, alone or with whomever she could grab, to improve her game. She had mastered traditional First Lady duties: a dinner with a head of state, tables sprinkled with cabinet members, Supreme Court justices, members of Congress, and their wives; preparing herself for informed conversation, usually with a Supreme Court justice or head of state seated next to her; minding the flow and interactions among the curated guest lists, the seating she had meticulously arranged, the entertainment, the speeches; the post-event rehash over drinks with friends spending the night. Even as Bird took comfort in the intimacy of those postmortems with close friends, she knew she would not miss the White House once she and Lyndon were gone.[1] And she had already begun counting the days until their exit. With the modernist Gordon Bunshaft the definitive choice as architect to design the LBJ library and the adjacent school of public affairs, working with Clark Clifford; Harry Ransom, the chancellor of the University of Texas; and the Austin architect Max Brooks, the Johnsons made public a relatively fast time line for completion: by May 1969, after LBJ would have served just one term. Perhaps it was an overt clue to their plans for an early exit, she thought, but no one seemed to notice.

Mustering the energy, interest, and enthusiasm to keep herself and her husband mentally focused and physically and emotionally well became an increasingly difficult task. Neither of them slept enough. A Christmas bombing pause in Vietnam and a parallel surge in diplomatic talks with allies at the United Nations or in back-channel messages to the North Vietnamese offered "flashes of hope"—despite what she registered in the press's growing skepticism over her husband's intentions in Southeast Asia.[2] But stalled progress on the domestic front deflated her. Interagency briefings her staff had arranged for the First Lady revealed that her husband's Great Society Job Corps programs had yet to make much progress in incorporating humane design and green public spaces—urban, rural, highway, or otherwise. "It all sounds rather dead," she recorded in her diary. "Discouragement settles like a fog over the whole poverty program unless you have got the energy and faith of an evangelist."[3] The Highway Beautification Act was weak at birth. Even so, the law had antagonized the country's scrap metal and iron dealers, who dominated the American junkyard business and who would have to spend money to comply with the law's limited regulations requiring them to screen their otherwise exposed junkyards. Bird was an evangelist for the environment, and with the smarts of a politician—"I would rather enlist them than insult them"—she hosted a reception for five hundred wives of junkyard dealers, "a heavy percentage of them well-dressed Jews," she observed, to try to win them over to her cause.[4] At the time, Jewish businessmen, who had brought the trade with them from Europe, dominated the American scrap metal business. In the 1950s and '60s, urban environment advocates had targeted junkyards as a real symbolic testament to the environmental hazards of the American auto industry. In shaking hands and greeting each personally, Lady Bird sought to put them and their husbands on notice that the White House regarded their junkyards, still ubiquitous eyesores in the nation's cities and along its highways, as a prime target for reform. It was her own version of the "Johnson treatment."

Although the visual and environmental scars on the national landscape (whether unscreened junkyards, garishly massive billboards, exposed transmission lines, or polluted water supplies) might not be remedied overnight, by the beginning of 1966, Lady Bird had set in motion plans not just to plant flowers, trees, and shrubs in Washington, D.C., but also to press the social dimensions of that word she hated, *beautification*. She spent the gray day in January of what would mark the first color broadcast of an American president's State of the Union address enticing socialite Brooke Astor to invest in public projects in the District of Columbia. The New York philanthropist had come to Washington, bringing with her Simon Breines, one of the two architects whom New York City had tapped to work with the Astor Foundation to design what they described as an "outdoor living room" at Jacob Riis Plaza, a neglected public housing complex space on the Lower East Side. Breines's sensitivity to urban quality of life resonated with Lady Bird—he was a pioneer in pushing New York City to create pedestrian zones free of cars and an advocate for keeping disproportionately tall skyscrapers from dominating streets scaled to the size of human beings.

Sharing a meal of Lobster Newburg, Bird, Brooke, and Breines, along with Walter Washington and Nash Castro, discussed locations in the District of Columbia where they might focus their resources and design energies. After lunch, they piled into an unmarked station wagon to scout out possible spots for a Breines-designed public recreation area. One stood out: the Buchanan School, located on Capitol Hill, at 13th and E streets, in Southeast. Washington, Lady Bird, and Kay Graham, the publisher of *The Washington Post*, had made frequent visits there. Now, even within the limits of his congressionally controlled budget, Washington had been able to channel funds to the late-nineteenth-century large brick school to replace the "almost jail-like" window screens with something less oppressive and to repair and paint the Romanesque Revival woodwork.[5] The group stopped at several more schools and public housing developments, discussing which location best lent itself to an outdoor living area combined with plantings and modernized play equipment.

That evening, President Johnson began his third State of the Union address by rattling off ten major asks of Congress, among them several frequently in the First Lady's purview: the quality of life in American cities and especially for the urban poor, industrial pollution in American rivers and the country's water supply, and family planning. The speech was also, Bird recorded with pride and approval, "the first time" that "a president has declared himself on birth control," and she applauded the move, having made sure, with her own notes on the speech draft, that the president made the statement.[6] The FDA had approved "the Pill" in 1956 for hormonal disorders and in 1960 for contraception. In 1965, in a 7–2 decision, the Supreme Court ruled in *Griswold v. Connecticut* in favor of a married couple's right to privacy. The Court's decision struck down the state of Connecticut's "bedroom patrol laws," known formally as the Comstock Laws of 1873, which, among other things, had criminalized the use of contraceptives. The Court ruling deemed this a violation of the Fourteenth Amendment's right to privacy, thus finding all such laws unconstitutional and effectively clearing the way for legal use of contraception. *Griswold* set the precedent for a future landmark ruling, the 1973 *Roe v. Wade* decision granting women the right to an abortion.

After the 1965 Supreme Court ruling, the "Never-Never Committee," a group of federal government policy analysts, convened secretly to plan the administration's contraception policy, followed by the public White House Conference on Health that drew on input from doctors, economists, social workers, and activists to broaden the legitimacy of family planning. The White House placed itself firmly behind access to contraception, not only on the market, but also via subsidized programs so that poor, unwed women might also benefit from their use. The Johnsons' perspective on family planning had been shaped in part by their conversations with development economists and informal advisers such as

Barbara Ward and John Kenneth Galbraith. Both Ward and Galbraith regarded universal access to contraception as a tool to redress the global "population explosion"—code at the time for too many babies born to poor women in the developing world or in the United States.[7] In 1966, the Johnsons would publicize their birthday wishes to Margaret Sanger and, with bipartisan support in Congress, promote appropriating federal funds for Planned Parenthood. At the innocuous-sounding conference titled "Women and the Changing Community: A Conference on the Responsibilities and Opportunities of Alabama Women in the 1960s," held in Tuscaloosa the very next month, the First Lady, without making explicit reference to the Johnson administration's push for universal access to birth control, obliquely pressed the issue of women's rights to an audience that, she understood, required gentle prodding to see themselves as changemakers. Drawing again from her personal story as the foundation for her broader message, Lady Bird emphasized the right of women to control their destinies and the broader benefit to society when they did so:

> I have made a discovery in my life that I am sure many of you have made for yourselves. It is a life-renewing discovery. There is some magical energy—a secret chemical more powerful than adrenalin—which pushes me on when I am doing something I love. Someday I believe that medical researchers are going to isolate "habitual fatigue" only to find that it is the presence of nothing. What else can explain the fact that the men and women who love their work are able to work twice as hard and twice as long and yet remain refreshed? We have all had periods of nothingness in our lives when we felt too tired to begin to do something. But if there is one message that I would like to give you today, it is this: be aware of your hidden strengths. You have the capacity to change the face of your community, to elevate the level of life around you. Through the centuries, women have been the prodders. Good works go forward in proportion to the number of vital and creative and determined women supporting them. When women get behind a project, things happen.[8]

Her take on women's empowerment—don't be afraid of your own strength, of women's strength—articulated for the White House a perspective that no one else in the Johnson cabinet had ventured to set forth, but with her trademark gingerly approach. To her Alabama audience, she stopped short of making explicit the link between her message of women's empowerment and her own husband's support for women's access to such a key tool, birth control, even though she had made certain LBJ promoted his support for family planning in his State of the Union. But in Tuscaloosa, Lady Bird assessed she didn't need to say more. By April, two women journalists, Nan Robertson and Jane Brody, would report in *The New York Times* that as a result of the work of the White House to convene the "Never-Never Committee," new federal guidelines and funding would make it possible for women, married or unmarried, to have access, free of "judgmental restrictions," to federal funds for "birth control advice, pills or contraceptive devices."[9]

Delivering a message of autonomy and ambition for women was especially significant in the state run by George Wallace, but for reasons that in the moment were almost impossible to see. In the American South, in Alabama, and in George Wallace himself, white supremacy was the twin pillar of tyranny with another form of repression, misogyny. Both phenomena related to control: over black Americans and over American women, black and white. In 1961, when Wallace's wife, Lurleen, gave birth to their fourth child, her doctors found she had uterine cancer. At the time, the practice of male physicians' keeping information from their female patients and, in turn, of revealing that information only to their husbands was common across the United States.[10] Lurleen's doctors informed only Governor Wallace, who decided to withhold from his wife the knowledge of her life-threatening illness. Four years later, in November 1965, a bout of unexplained bleeding forced the issue: in January 1966, now informed of her diagnosis, Alabama's First Lady had a hysterectomy. On the day before Lady Bird Johnson arrived in Alabama in February, a still-recovering Lurleen Wallace announced that she would run for her husband's office, a strategy intended by and for George Wallace to keep control of the Montgomery State House, where the law prevented the governor from running for two consecutive terms. Lurleen was inaugurated in January 1967, but her cancer returned five months later.[11] She died in office, three months after George Wallace entered the 1968 presidential primaries. While enabling her husband's political ambitions by running for governor, she exercised a degree of agency and autonomy by seizing the limelight; but in dying in office from a disease that could have been treated six years earlier, she was also the most proximate victim of his ambition and paternalism.[12]

At the same time, and with the backing of another man from the South married to a woman with Alabama roots, American women were agitating for more direct control over their own bodies, including over their reproductive choices. In her message to her audience in Tuscaloosa, delivered with all the trappings and tone of a proper southern lady, Bird stood in sharp contrast to Alabama's First Lady. And the White House built on her efforts. By April, the president had made sixteen statements favoring access to birth control, four times the number in 1965. And the number of states following suit had more than doubled from thirteen to thirty. Alabama was among them.[13] Over the next few years, especially as access to safe abortions became a major demand of the American women's movement—the underground Jane Collective in Chicago, for example, founded the same year, helped put safe abortion on the public policy map—the president's stance represented a major step forward in public health and women's health.

But on the night of the State of the Union address, with 182,000 troops on the ground in Southeast Asia, it was not Lyndon's transformative stance on family planning that dominated headlines. It was Vietnam. The geopolitical context that came to frame the president's rationale for intensifying the American air and ground strategy in Vietnam received only the lightest of touches: LBJ emphasized the U.S. interest in preventing the South from losing to the Communist North, with only an indirect reference to the Chinese or Soviets. Yet, for someone with so much inner turmoil about the risks to his domestic programs of escalation in Vietnam, the president staked out a very open-ended, eye-of-the-beholder commitment: "[W]e will stay as long as aggression commands us to battle," he affirmed. Still, LBJ's awareness of his impossible position came through in the substance, tone, and delivery of his message. He acknowledged that the members of Congress might well "share the burden" with him of *knowing* that war and madness still plagued the world and deprived American soldiers of their future. War, he said, "is young men dying in the fullness of their promise." Speaking of his own torment, Lady Bird knew, President Johnson described war as "trying to kill a man that you do not even know well enough to hate."[14]

LBJ's World War II service in California, Australia, and New Zealand had not involved having to muster such blindness to the other's humanity; he never saw combat. Now, as president, Bird's husband felt virtually alone with the burden of sitting at the top of the country's national security and foreign policy hierarchy. Indeed, he stood a world apart from his former colleagues in Congress, "[for] finally," he intoned, sharing some of the pain he expressed to Abe and Lady Bird in the hospital after his gallstone operation, "I," not his former colleagues, "must be the one to order our guns to fire, against all the most inward pulls of my desire. For we have children to teach, and we have sick to be cured, and we have men to be freed. There are poor to be lifted up, and there are cities to be built, and there is a world to be helped."[15] As the president explained the difficulty of his dilemma, the First Lady scrutinized the House chamber for reaction. Gone was the spirit of unity that had animated the address in January 1964. Gone was the enthusiasm that had followed that year's biggest landslide election, when LBJ took the podium in January 1965. She found the audience "cold and lethargic" and, as the New Year unfolded, felt that way herself.[16]

* * *

Still, there were high points to the start of 1966. The president swore in the first African American cabinet secretary in American history, Robert Weaver—born and raised in Washington, D.C., and with three Harvard degrees, including a doctorate in economics—as secretary of the newly created Department of Housing and Urban Development. "It was one of those moments when a sense of history hung in the air," Bird recalled.

"He comes to his job with a heavier obligation than most. He has just got to be good because he is the first Negro. He looks solid. The acceptance by Congress and the country has been good; our hopes are high."[17] Walter Washington, executive director of the National Capital Housing Authority; Roy Wilkins, president of the NAACP; and Whitney Young, Jr., president of the National Urban League, joined the Johnsons for the occasion. During FDR's presidency, Weaver had served under one of LBJ's New Deal–era allies, Harold Ickes, who hired him as an aide at the Department of the Interior. A pragmatic activist who preferred to work within the system to catalyze change, in 1944 Weaver was appointed director of the Mayor's Committee on Race Relations in Chicago, and then hired as the director of the American Council on Race Relations. In 1955, he became the first African American to hold a state cabinet-level position when New York governor Averell Harriman named him state rent commissioner.

Coming on the heels of the murder in Tuskegee, Alabama, of Sammy Younge, Jr., an enlisted service member and the first college student to be murdered for civil disobedience (for using a "Whites Only" bathroom), and the denunciation of the Vietnam War by SNCC, of which Younge had been a member, Weaver's appointment, confirmation, and swearing in cast light on the divisions within organized black politics of the era. Some argued that the new agency he would lead might perpetuate the kinds of alienating and discriminatory housing policies urban renewal had brought about in recent decades. Would Weaver be able to direct legal and financial resources to end the practice of redlining neighborhoods (i.e., withholding home loans and insurance from areas considered a poor economic risk, code for black neighborhoods) and channel funds for more humane urban policies? As a light-skinned black man who was highly educated and who possessed a history of working institutionally for reform, Weaver faced opposition from black militants and elected members of Congress, such as Adam Clayton Powell, Jr., of New York, who opposed the appointment altogether.[18]

Beyond the historic advance Lady Bird saw in Weaver's appointment, she also had high hopes for him for another reason. His agency's budget now had a line item allocating $483,000 for beautification in the District of Columbia, where civil rights activists new to the District, like Marion Barry and others long in the trenches (e.g., Walter Fauntroy, a Baptist minister and activist in urban renewal in D.C.'s Shaw neighborhood and Reverend King's Washington liaison), were gearing up to press D.C.'s white power structure for financial resources and political representation for the city's black majority.[19] The Johnson White House backed their efforts. LBJ heralded his 1965 legislation for home rule in the District of Columbia again in his 1966 State of the Union. His embrace of home rule in a majority-black federal city paralleled his support for civil rights and voting rights across the South. Separately from Weaver's budget, the Johnson administration's Office of Economic Opportunity, created with War on Poverty funds, had begun to channel funds to D.C. to redress the profound deprivation of black residents, whether in the matter of social services, education, housing, healthcare, jobs, infrastructure, justice, or policing, issues SNCC and the SCLC were focusing on. For Lady Bird's agenda, Weaver's overlap with Walter Washington's remit, and their shared history toiling in the white-led local and federal agencies of D.C., might boost the East Wing's effectiveness in the District's schools and housing. It would also become relevant later, as the First Lady reached for ways to more publicly and effectively emphasize the social content of "beautification" by expanding the space for desegregated public recreation projects.

Still, aside from the lack of institutional capacity, bureaucratic challenges to working in Washington abounded. There would be no Department of Transportation until later that year, meaning every road or highway beautification project required a local angle and ally. There was no mayor's office or city council, meaning the National Capital Planning Commission both depended for political and financial resources on the federal government but could operate somewhat autonomously from it. Although there was plenty of momentum behind planting pansies, tulips, daffodils, azaleas, and cherry blossom trees in public spaces and parkways, the First Lady worried that far less progress had been made in implementing her deceptively simple concept that planting plants is "not only for people but by people too."[20] Bereft of a willingness to empower, educate, and employ (especially D.C.'s young black male population), beautification, she had begun to see, might easily be dismissed as a liberal fancy, the ultimate surface answer to some very profound, and largely unanswered, social questions. During this period, white people were moving to the suburbs, and black communities were being displaced by the Southwest Waterfront project. This transformation of the population brought new pressures to the city government, which at the time was run through an appointed board of commissioners and Congress.

Working with the Johnsons to make the First Lady's vision a reality, Polly Shackleton, a longtime Democratic Party and D.C. home rule activist, proposed in a 1966 memo to Lady Bird a way to connect the values and programs of the Great Society with the challenges of achieving better living conditions for residents of Washington's poor neighborhoods and advancing the goal of local political power through District home rule. She reassured Lady Bird that adequate funds had been raised to implement job training programs in the District. Hardly one to flatter, the future D.C. council member credited the First Lady's public stance for giving these programs, and their employment impact, a huge boost. As Shackleton noted, Lady Bird created the demand not only for more plants but also for many vocational and job opportunities, ranging from the basic to the specialized.[21]

Many of the programs Shackleton described to the First Lady echoed those of the New Deal era and involved linking labor with skills and skills with consciousness and confidence. But Shackleton was also a pragmatist, the ultimate LBJ-style "doer." To redress the gaps in these and other services, she wrote Lady Bird about tapping into the then-nascent "Operation Pride," a broader, more targeted, and better-paying D.C. jobs program still in the concept phase, for the Northwest neighborhood of Shaw.[22]

The Washington Post started to notice this shift toward the more substantive aspects of beautification and reported that the District was planning to double spending on additional landscaping, not in the tourist areas of town but in poor neighborhoods, a move "designed to prove that beautification has far reaching social and economic—rather than merely cosmetic—effects." Crediting Lady Bird with the change in focus, her friend Kay Graham's paper reported that direct participation by students, parents, and teachers in school cleanup (part self-help, part community action) might mitigate the usual pattern of municipal authorities swooping in with cosmetic changes, quickly to be undermined by the lack of local involvement.[23] All this came on the heels of the launch by Marion Barry of "Free D.C.," a public campaign run out of SNCC's local office to spotlight the countless ways in which the lack of home rule in the District made "it impossible for us to do anything about lousy schools, brutal cops, slumlords, welfare investigators who go on midnight raids, employers who discriminate in hiring, and a host of other ills that run rampant through our city."[24] The flow of War on Poverty funds, federal money beyond the control of the usual congressional committees overseeing District spending, now created an opportunity for local activists, black and white—those inside the bureaucracies, on the streets of Shaw and Capitol Hill, and in the cossetted neighborhoods of Georgetown and Upper Northwest—to raise money privately and mobilize public funds for a host of social issues that reinforced the legal and political significance of home rule.

* * *

Although the substantive aspects of the beautification agenda, finally, had begun to pick up steam, both in D.C. and potentially beyond, Lyndon's ongoing troubles in Vietnam muted Lady Bird's ability to appreciate her own potential successes. Vietnam had become pervasive in Lady Bird's consciousness, and by her count, it now filled up at least two-thirds of her conversations with Lyndon.[25] Their morning routine of papers and breakfast together in Lyndon's bedroom now regularly resembled a full-blown West Wing staff meeting, often lasting hours and increasingly focused on the war. In late January, Lyndon authorized Operation Masher, a name that quickly changed to the more benign-sounding White Wing, large-scale search-and-destroy missions against the Viet Cong and the

North Vietnamese Army (NVA).[26] Lady Bird had long since assimilated Vietnam as a fact of Lyndon's presidency, but she, too, grappled with many of his tactical decisions: troop escalations, the start and stop and start again of bombing, the international diplomacy. With two feet of snow outside, in the pool with Lyndon and Bundy one afternoon in February, the First Lady absorbed the strategic justification for a much more portentous announcement planned for the next day: the resumption of bombing after a thirty-seven-day pause over Christmas and the New Year. And as with previous momentous decisions on Vietnam, judging from her diary entries during the first quarter of 1966, Bird seemed to focus as much on the relief at the release of tension for Lyndon that came with such decisions as on their domestic political implications. Bobby Kennedy, now representing New York State in the Senate and eyeing a presidential run, predicted that the resumption of bombing would lead "to catastrophe for all of mankind."[27] Hearings in William Fulbright's Senate Foreign Relations Committee—featuring testimony from George Kennan, the architect of American Cold War containment strategy and a Vietnam skeptic from the outset—and the growing cacophony of what Lady Bird saw as an increasingly hostile press brought considerable strain and sleeplessness to both the Johnsons.

The public pushback against escalation also brought out an unusual defensiveness and protectiveness in the First Lady. She wanted her husband to be correct as far as strategy—she records her conversations with Bundy and McNamara about the tactics and timing of bombing as if to reassure herself of the soundness of their advice—and held out hope that her team would prevail. But she also worried about the emotional toll on Lyndon, for whom the responsibility of returning two hundred thousand American boys to safety made him feel, she thought, their collective loss even more strongly than the boys' own mothers. The job had become an "endurance contest" for both of them. "I count the months and the weeks until the time I have set [to exit the presidency], but I have not the force of character, and not really even the desire, to try to make Lyndon work less hard." She believed in her husband's vision for the United States. And though she resented what the job had become, she also believed that the strain, tension, and toll were "worth every last atom of whatever he has to give."[28] Both Lyndon and Bird felt alone at this moment, Lyndon feeling the weight of his national responsibility and Bird the isolation of her role and soon-to-be-empty nest. Her own life had become a study in contrasts: bombing strategy in Vietnam; poverty and polluted rivers in the District; clothing selection from Neiman Marcus; dinner on President Grant's china with her daughter's Hollywood beau, George Hamilton; and of course a Dubonnet to accompany her favorite television series, *Gunsmoke*. She often felt "divided, sundered," unable to be everything to everyone at once.[29]

Vietnam, a topic on which Lady Bird remained publicly silent, was causing her husband to rapidly lose the goodwill he had earned in the aftermath of the JFK assassination and in plowing forward with a revolutionary social contract and long-suppressed civil rights agenda. Bombing raids had just destroyed twenty thousand acres of food in North Vietnam, drawing harsh condemnation from the U.S. academic community. The Buddhists in South Vietnam had begun their campaign in Saigon, Da Nang, and Hue to topple Washington's ally, the politically weak premier Ky, setting off a wave of unrest and interfering with American military operations. And thousands of Americans were now demonstrating against the war on the streets of New York, Washington, Chicago, and Philadelphia.

On March 13, 1966, as Lyndon prepared to meet with nearly fifty governors to brief them on Vietnam and enlist their support for his policies there, Lady Bird entered Lyndon's bedroom to find Richard Nixon, "looking relaxed and affable and well dressed," by her husband's bedside.[30] Still wearing her nightgown, Lady Bird crawled into bed next to Lyndon and joined their conversation. Nixon and Johnson had known one another since overlapping in Congress beginning in the late 1940s; both had served in the thankless role of vice president. By Lyndon's own account, Nixon—LBJ couldn't bring himself to call him Dick—was only sort of practicing law in New York after his loss to JFK.[31] Mainly, he was traveling around the country speaking and raising money for the 1966 midterms and, ultimately, for his own run at the 1968 presidency. They complained together about the treachery of *The New York Times.* Nixon, evincing an attitude of sportsmanlike competition, alerted LBJ that while tough on the Democrats, his campaign speeches would stop short of attacking the president personally. Lyndon, for his part, remained unfazed: "We politicians are just like lawyers who get together for a drink after fighting each other like hell in the courtroom," Nixon recalled the president saying. The former vice president put in a plug to another former vice president to treat his own, Hubert Humphrey, a little better. On Vietnam, a topic on which he himself would later commit a major act of treason during the 1968 campaign, Nixon pressed the president to hit even harder.[32]

LBJ hardly needed the encouragement. Although he professed to want basics like food and medicine and running water and electricity to change the hearts and minds of the Vietnamese people, he still viewed himself as a prizefighter, "in the ring, the right fist is the military, the left fist is aid, washing, agricultural, education." But however strong his humanitarian impulse, the president was, at the end of the day, right-handed. "And so," the First Lady conceded, "the Ides of March passed, a good, full, happy day, except that little flames of fear begin to lick at me, about what's going on within Vietnam. . . . If this government falls in Viet Nam, we've had it, at least where I sit. I cannot see what happens next."[33] The next month, her husband authorized B-52 bombing raids, each with a capacity of a one-hundred-pound bomb, to target North Vietnamese power grids, transportation lines, ground and air military installations, and fuel storage. By the end of April, American troops in Vietnam would reach the quarter-million mark.

Chapter 13

At Home

One of the greatest needs of our society is to teach people to be intelligently alone with themselves.

—Marie Larkin, recipient of the National Gallery of Art Teaching Award, White House, March 17, 1966

[A]ll this time the most magnificent drama was happening in the sky above us. Sundown and twilight—the unceasing play of lights and shadows and the nuances of colors in the sky and on the sides of the mountains. Sometimes I think the Lord made up in this western big sky for what he didn't give us in rainfall, in verdant vegetation, with the glory of the sky. It was the most superb theater. Fit subject for a symphony or a poem but for me just an hour of delight that was almost tangible—of the heightened feeling of being alive.

—Lady Bird Johnson, Big Bend National Park, White House diary, April 2, 1966

By 1966, Lady Bird had spent almost three decades in Washington and almost three years in the White House. Since the minute they married three months after they met in 1934, supporting Lyndon's career became her full-time job. After 1944 and 1946, when her daughters were born, it was Lyndon's ambitions that demanded her constant nurturing. To build and sustain a vast network of political contacts and financial patrons, and to cultivate journalists and confidants among the semipermanent establishment of Washington, required nights and weekends of socializing, often out of the house, for both Johnsons. Lady Bird's days were also filled with giving tours around the Capitol to their visiting Texas constituents, attending countless luncheons and charity events with the spouses of the men who populated Lyndon's orbit, monitoring KTBC's growth, and supervising her staff at home. This last dimension included the girls' caregiver, Helen Williams; gardener and handyman Gene Williams; and her cook, Zephyr Wright. After 1951, when they bought the Ranch in Stonewall from Lyndon's ailing aunt Frank, overseeing the renovation of the main house and ongoing upgrades and maintenance to the land, fence lines, roads, and other buildings on the Hill Country property added to Bird's portfolio. "Washington," Bird frequently quoted Lynda as saying, "was no town for children." Until they moved to the White House, parenting her daughters left Bird feeling constantly pulled, inadequate to the task, conscious of her inability to satisfy their needs. She was aware, too, especially as her daughters reached adolescence, of how much her political partnership with Lyndon meant missing out on the spontaneous, unexpected bursts of conversation and shared intimacies between a parent and a child that come simply from a spell in the same physical space.

The second-floor quarters and third-floor solarium of the White House, proximate as they were to the West and East wings, gave the four Johnsons the chance to have more impromptu time together under one roof than ever before. Between the end of 1963 and June of 1964, Lynda returned to Washington from college in Austin and spent spring semester of her sophomore year at George Washington University. Luci lived at the White House for half her sophomore year and the rest of high school at the National Cathedral School. Even after Lynda returned to UT for her junior and senior years of college, she saw her sister and parents frequently, on weekends at the Ranch or the White House or on trips to New York with her mother. Lady Bird savored the time with her daughters, time to make up for so many lost moments during their childhood, when Lyndon, always her first priority, occupied the majority of her psychic space and most of her waking hours. Lyndon's absorbing requirements hardly lessened with the move to the White House, but now he had ready access to his daughters, and they to him. In turn, Lynda and Luci had adopted their mother's modus operandi: part of their role, especially as they grew older, would be to help manage their father's emotional highs and lows and care for him during frequent bouts of minor maladies or major surgeries. But if Lyndon was the sun and the three Johnson women the planets in his direct orbit, they also found many ways to nurture one another. Girl talk about boys, clothes, and school came easily for Bird and both her daughters. In turn, with only three years separating the girls in age, their mother felt doubly needed, at times the referee of the natural competition between the two: Lynda, the intellectual with top grades, an aspiring journalist (like her mother once was), with an appetite for travel, who could engage any of her parents' guests in serious policy conversation; Luci, the freer spirit, who, diagnosed with dyslexia, compensated for her struggles with schoolwork by deploying her innate charisma to collect streams of friends from many walks and generations and to command her parents' attention with large, identity-defining gestures, including, at age eighteen, her conversion to Catholicism. And whether for the cumulative emotional solace of sharing last-minute lunches; late-night dinners; Sunday morning church services; an anonymous trip to the Arena Stage for theater or the National Gallery for art; bowling; swimming; or trips to Camp David, the early years in the White House felt to Lady Bird like a rich reward for the decades of frenetic, frequently alienating time apart.

But that snug feeling of family togetherness wasn't to last. In June, Lynda graduated cum laude from the University of Texas and spent the summer in Spain. She had started dating the perma-tanned actor George Hamilton that spring, after they met at a White House event a year earlier. In his memoir, he recalled Lynda as "brainy and bookish," but he "sensed that somewhere inside that bookworm was a babe trying to get out."[1] Hamilton doted on the elder Johnson daughter and, with his taste for glamour, Bird felt, helped the sometimes awkward-in-her-own-skin Lynda carry herself and dress with a newfound air of confidence. "George is easy, smooth," Bird recalled; he is "worldly and has had quite a few too many women crazy about him."[2] Between chaperoned trips to Acapulco, to the Oscars in Hollywood, or to New York for theater and to interview for jobs in journalism and philanthropy, Lynda was spending less and less time either in Washington or at the Ranch. But it was Luci's wedding to Pat Nugent, at the National Shrine of the Immaculate Conception, the largest Catholic church in the United States—the ceremony could not be held at the Cathedral of St. Matthew, site of Luci's baptism; too many Kennedy ghosts—that screamed the end of an era for her mother. The wedding was now set for August 6, one month after Luci's nineteenth birthday. For a woman even of Bird's discipline, who prized her devotion to physical fitness but whose body was nevertheless sending signals of aging (fitful sleep, the need for hours and hours of dental work, the unavoidable prescription eyeglasses), planning it struck a deeper chord.

The loss of her own mother at five years old, even with the dominant presence of a father drawn straight out of a Tennessee Williams play (she once remarked), and with her elder brothers both off at boarding school, Lady Bird's upbringing and daily care were overseen by paid staff, very likely the descendants of enslaved people; by her aunt Effie; by extended family in Alabama; by dorm parents at St. Mary's College, an Episcopal boarding school in Dallas; and by resident upperclassmen at the University of Texas at Austin. Although her mother's death deprived her of many things, she had instilled in her daughter the habit of reading and of listening to music and the comfort she then found in nature—all of which set the stage for Lady Bird to master the art of being "intelligently alone" as an adult. It was a skill that contrasted wildly with her husband's inability to be alone, and one that provided Bird with the inner resources to seek and find solitude both within and outside the circus her life had become.

Attending Lynda's graduation from college brought Bird back to her own graduation thirty-three years earlier. "The campus was full of ghosts" from her past, but there were marks everywhere of a modern era. Babies and children of married graduate students cried during the ceremony—an occurrence "as rare as an elephant when I was on campus" and a sign to Lady Bird that young women no longer had to sacrifice an education in order to have a family. She took pride in seeing degrees offered in aerospace engineering, a recent effort by the university regents to attract the best scientific talent in the country, and she recorded her pride in seeing "a negro woman getting a Ph.D. . . . ," a sign to a fifty-year-old "born and raised in deep East Texas" of "the most miraculous change in the life of our country."[3] Bird felt herself strongly moved by the institutional and social changes she observed at Lynda's graduation ceremony—milestones for Texas, for the country. Yet it was the same country where, the next day, 6,400 teachers and professors from around the country took out a three-page advertisement in *The New York Times* protesting her husband's war in Vietnam. Lynda's graduation was a front-page story in the same issue. And the same country where, two days after the graduation, civil rights activist James Meredith, the first African American man to enroll at the University of Mississippi, was shot from behind by a sniper and suffered wounds to the back, head, neck, and legs on the second day of his solo "March Against Fear" from Memphis to Jacksonville.

It was less Lynda's commencement per se that marked a family milestone for the Johnsons—they slipped in quietly because Lynda told them to come as parents or not to come at all. Instead, it was how she would balance her desire for personal autonomy and a professional life with her duty to the family, the First Family of the United States, that seemed to most preoccupy her mother. With the younger Luci's wedding approaching, Lady Bird seemed focused, perhaps inevitably, on Lynda's love life. Her elder daughter had already broken off a previous engagement while she was still in college. Was her current beau, George Hamilton, the right fit? "He and Lynda seem remarkably companionable. I think it's a play between them of things the other didn't have," Lady Bird surmised. "For Lynda, the excitement, freedom, somewhat spicy life of show business. For him, could it be perhaps a solid education, the real interest in learning, and I would hope the fairly deeply rooted family life that she has had?"[4] Although Hamilton's attempts to avoid the draft caused a minor public relations kerfuffle for the White House, the Memphis native had impressed Lady Bird as a gentleman genuinely in thrall with Lynda, doting and present, as he was for the graduation and its surrounding festivities. Or was his Hollywood life too fast, too superficial, for her daughter? These were concerns she once had for herself, journalism and history degrees in hand, about a different city, a different suitor, and in a different time. With a whiff that perhaps gaps in geography and compatibility might make for some insurmountable hurdles, Lady Bird reasoned, it was, on balance, best for Lynda to defy her father's call for Americans to vacation in their own country that summer. Lynda, she decided, should spend hers abroad, whatever the press blowback, before resuming a search for the right job and, if not George, then the right man.

Watching Lynda graduate from college and head off on her own stirred memories of Lady Bird's first adventure after her own graduation. In the summer of 1934, two young college graduates, Claudia Alta "Lady Bird" Taylor and Cecille Harrison, traveled from Texas to Washington to see the sights, celebrate their graduation, and imagine their future. The final touches were being put on the Supreme Court Building, its neoclassical style and imposing marble façade conveying all the gravitas of a republic whose constitutional strength depended on an independent judiciary and the adjudication of disputes by reputable jurists sitting on the highest court of the land. Recently in Austin, one of the two women had just met a young congressional aide, Lyndon Johnson. Although he, too, was in Washington at the time, she ignored his invitation to pay him a visit while in D.C. Instead, she and her friend toured the New Deal–era capital and found themselves meandering through the Supreme Court. Carpenters and workmen were still installing pieces of the interior, filled with marble largely quarried from Alabama. No one asked what they were doing there, no security guards shooed them away, and the young grad from Karnack explored every nook and cranny. The two young women sat in the justices' chairs. A fellow Alabamian, and the man with whom together Bird had helped "make Lyndon," Hugo Black, would sit in one of those chairs in just three years' time.[5]

"Farthest from my dreams," Bird recorded thirty-two years later, "was that I should ever return here for a party given by one of the justices in honor of my daughter and the young man she was going to marry!" That justice, a Texas native and close political ally and personal friend of the Johnsons, Tom C. Clark, while serving as the U.S. attorney general, had led the commission in 1947 that published "To Secure These Rights," a report that identified race discrimination in virtually every area of American life. The report recommended that President Truman establish a Civil Rights Division in the Department of Justice, secure federal protection from lynching, and abolish poll taxes, among other measures. Truman promoted Clark to the Supreme Court in 1949, a year into Lyndon's tenure in the Senate. When Justice Clark and his wife, Mary, threw Luci Baines Johnson and Patrick John "Pat" Nugent an engagement party at the Court, Clark was poised to retire in just one year, a step that would clear the way for Lyndon to nominate Solicitor General Thurgood Marshall to the Court.

Lady Bird's own short engagement didn't allow for her father's circle of friends to host a party. Less than twenty-four hours elapsed between Lyndon's proposal to her, her acceptance, and their wedding in San Antonio. She had no mother to help her vet her fiancé, choose a dress, draw up invitations, curate a guest list, or plan a honeymoon. Deprived of these rituals of the modern bridal era, Lady Bird indulged her daughter Luci in all of them, perhaps to excess, organizing and supervising the execution of the first White House wedding in over sixty years. The night of the Supreme Court party, Lady Bird arrived with Pat's parents. Luci, seldom punctual, arrived with Pat ahead of schedule, in a fairy princess dress of embroidered white lace with sleeves to the elbows designed by Molly Parnis, one of the East Wing's go-to designers. Lynda allowed her sister her grand entrance; dressed in a black cocktail dress, her hair in an elegant chignon, she arrived on her own time. Lyndon, who at the start of the party was watching the AP ticker boards for updates from Vietnam, joined the festivities an hour late.[6]

An engagement party at the Supreme Court was the first of its kind. The marble hall was filled with Luci's friends and teachers and with the Johnsons' Texas stalwarts, too. But the elegant, candlelit affair also brimmed with Washington's political establishment and high-society members, and all the justices but one. Lady Bird embraced it all. She had become the queen of her own court, and even as Lyndon reportedly cringed at the public glare of the nuptials planning, of the press's insatiable need for details, Lady Bird seemed to take it all in with pride and pleasure, but also without her usual caution about excess public scrutiny. As the doting mother of the bride, the occasion allowed her to fulfill the maternal duties her mother's death had deprived her of, and also give her own daughter the lavish affair Lyndon's hurry-up insistence had prevented her from experiencing three decades earlier.

* * *

Although Luci's engagement festivities provided a moment's respite, Vietnam and civil rights again tore at Lyndon's mood. His once ally in the GOP who had cosponsored the Voting Rights Act, Senate minority leader Everett Dirksen, now joined with a young congressman from Michigan, House minority leader Gerald Ford, to attack the president for his lack of candor and bipartisanship on Vietnam. Election-year politics would normally shake any White House's ability to count on support from the opposing party on its major initiatives. Gallup had specifically linked LBJ's decline in the polls to the American public's uncertainty over Vietnam, but the White House pinned its problems on pressure from hawks for a more aggressive approach to the war.[7] There were real reasons beyond partisanship to resist LBJ's assumption of a foreign policy blank check when it came to Vietnam: American casualties, protests, humanitarian concerns, the potential for a Korea-like stalemate, and the internationalization of the war—the Chinese, Soviets, and even the PLO (founded just two years earlier) were lining up to support the Viet Cong, for geopolitical, ideological, or domestic political purposes.

As criticism of the war grew, Lyndon became increasingly entrenched and defensive about the escalation of the conflict. In a speech at Princeton, he challenged critics of the war: "Surely, it is not a paranoid vision of America's place in the world to recognize that freedom is still indivisible—still has adversaries whose challenge must be answered."[8] More friends abandoned LBJ. John Kenneth Galbraith, whom both Johnsons once considered a reliable source of ideas, went on the attack at a graduation speech in Rhode Island. With a weak, corrupt, and divided South Vietnamese government barely worthy of that characterization, he argued, and little doubt in the public's mind that Washington had nevertheless pulled out all the stops on its behalf, the Harvard professor called for an end to bombing and the reduction of "all military action" by American troops.[9]

As criticism over Vietnam weighed on Lyndon, the emotional energy to support him took its toll on the First Lady. Her own all-too-frequent exhaustion still caught her off guard, even though she had been wrestling with fitful sleep for at least a year. Like Lyndon, regular afternoon naps proved essential to sustaining packed days that regularly ended well after midnight. And now, also like Lyndon, Lady Bird found herself taking staff meetings in her own bedroom: she'd lie flat on her back and toss around ideas with speechwriters, policy gurus, and press aides poised on chairs circling her bed. When possible, she escaped from the turmoil of Washington through books, whether the pure entertainment of *The Night Visitor and Other Stories* (all set in Mexico), by B. Traven, the pseudonym for the German author of *The Treasure of the Sierra Madre,* or Albert Camus's more serious novel *The Plague.* And when she could afford to get out of town, she ventured into nature. In the vast expanses of the Chisos Mountains, along the border with Mexico in Big Bend National Park, she rafted down the Rio Grande with Stewart Udall; and in the Hill Country of Texas, she even managed to steal away from Lyndon for a week of hiking, walking five and ten miles a day accompanied by local naturalists, her own camera, and her Secret Service detail, and enjoying the prosaic luxury of cracking open a cold beer along the trail.[10]

For all her efforts at self-preservation, by the summer of 1966, Bird recorded, "Dog days have set in. There is an air of weariness, irritability, tenseness around the White House."[11] On July 15, U.S. Marines launched the largest joint military operation yet against the North Vietnamese Army in Quang Tri Province. With the decline in LBJ's polls, the press battered the president with questions about whether he would run in the 1968 presidential campaign. Hanoi Radio reported that captured American pilots had been paraded past jeering crowds; the images were widely circulated in the U.S. press. Washington stepped up bombing raids along the Ho Chi Minh Trail. George Hamilton's draft deferment, Lynda's tussle with the press during her summer in Spain (defying her father's "See America First" wishes), and Luci's "insistence on a big wedding while the boys are dying in Vietnam" gave journalist Drew Pearson plenty of political soft spots to hit. All of it unsettled the Johnsons. In the face of Lyndon's volatile temperament, the confidence and sense of well-being Lady Bird had cultivated through solitude at the Ranch yielded to her other persona—dutiful spouse and soldier.

"How," she recorded, "can I combat" the ugly White House mood? "Two ways for myself and my side. I can thank all those people who do such a good job day after day all year unnoticed. I don't do enough of that. This is one of Lyndon's wonderful qualities. He roars when he is angry—he thanks sweetly the moment that he feels like it in colorful language. In his life he has endeared a host of people to him that way." The woman known for preemptively thanking her own staff, and making a point of seeking out the staff in the pantries and kitchens of the embassy residences and private homes that hosted her, could not bring herself to record a negative word about her husband's bad temper. Instead, she explained his ferocity and sensitivity as two inseparable facets of his total being and pushed herself to compensate for the former by demonstrating more than her share of the latter.[12]

* * *

As anxiety once again enveloped Lyndon, plans for Luci's wedding day consumed Lady Bird. Getting to know Pat's parents, Gerard and Tillie Nugent (Pat's elder brother, Gerard Jr., was already in Vietnam); combing through numerous invitation lists; house hunting in Austin for the newlyweds; scrutinizing seating charts at the "staggeringly immense" Shrine of the Immaculate Conception; working with the wedding cake and bridal gown designers, calligraphers, florists, and chefs; vetting Liz's screening of the press as they clamored for details; establishing the protocol for often outlandish gifts sent by heads of state to the newlyweds; instructing Luci and her staff on how best to cope with the thousands of letters coming in; choreographing the angles and staging of the wedding and reception photography; and conspiring with the Secret Service to ensure the newlyweds' surreptitious departure for their honeymoon at a ten-room villa in the Bahamas—the shock and awe of nuptial planning "carrie[d] its own anesthesia," the exhausted mother of the bride recorded. This was a wedding of quasi-royal (or, at the very least, Texan) proportions. And it was also a political affair, with opponents in Congress scrutinizing each and every gift (a ten-thousand-dollar Ethiopian costume with accompanying bangles and earrings from Emperor Haile Selassie, a caftan from King Hassan II of Morocco) for any opportunity to cry foul play.[13]

Getting to Saturday, August 6, required an absolutely herculean effort by Lady Bird to make infinite decisions about those mostly prosaic details that so often distract from and absorb the nerves and emotions surrounding such a monumental moment. It also required a certain amount of sophistry: Lady Bird repeatedly told herself, and a skeptical press, that the younger Johnson daughter's big day was simply a personal, family wedding. History pointed toward a more mixed reality. While some White House brides, such as Elizabeth Tyler and Alice Roosevelt, had failed to shield their nuptials from the public gaze, others, like Maria Hester Monroe, were more successful. For the first White House wedding, the Monroe family in 1820 managed to limit the guest list to just forty-two people and the press coverage to a mere thirty-four words. Whether a grand affair or an intimate gathering, Bird told one journalist unapologetically, "the wedding day will be something to remember, and I want Luci to have it."[14]

Beyond creating a memorable experience for both of them, the First Lady's own family history shaped Bird's impulse toward pageantry. It wasn't only Lady Bird who had married below her station, on short notice, and with none of the pomp and circumstance now planned for Luci. Lady Bird's mother, Minnie Pattillo, had married Thomas Jefferson Taylor against the wishes of her own parents and their wedding was an austere, private, low-key affair.[15] Yet Lady Bird felt that Luci deserved to have the kind of wedding she desired, and at some level she understood that, as the matriarch of the family, she now had the chance to set a different course for her daughters. Nor could Bird have missed another parallel to the women in her family: Like her mother and grandmother, Luci had grown up with material conditions far superior to those of her father and grandfather. And like Lyndon Johnson before him, Pat Nugent, who grew up in a small bungalow in Waukegan, an industrial suburb of Chicago, would have to accept the complicated truths of marrying above his station.

Producing a presidential wedding and White House reception for 750 guests in the sticky heat of a Washington summer swamped the Johnson women and their staff with its numerous logistical demands. Outside the nation's capital, that summer's leitmotif of simmering violence was unrelenting. Five days before the wedding, a marine-trained sniper with a history of threatening violence climbed to the top of the clock tower at the University of Texas campus with two rifles, two pistols, a carbine, and a shotgun. From the second-tallest building in Austin, Charles Whitman opened fire at 11:48 A.M. Central Time, killing sixteen people and injuring thirty-one others. "It was incredible—too hideous to believe," Lady Bird noted; she knew the exact spot Whitman was shooting from, had been there many times, and thought back to the gorgeous view of the blue Austin hills from the twenty-eighth-floor observation deck.[16] The first victim the sniper hit was Claire Wilson, an eighteen-year-old Dallas freshman from a Democratic family of civil rights activists. Eight months pregnant, she survived, but her baby did not. Another victim was the grandson of Paul Bolton, a Johnson family friend and a news executive and employee of KTBC. The tower shooting was the first mass shooting of its era, and the first to target a school. American campuses had already seen their share of student agitation, but gun violence on campus, on *her* campus, was still beyond Bird's and the country's imagination.[17]

* * *

"Nobody is invited except the immediate country," quipped comedienne Edie Adams. And no piece of coverage better captured the flavor of the Johnson wedding spectacle than *Time* magazine. Cast as a "semi-monarchical event" and inviting irresistible scrutiny, Luci's wedding in Northeast Washington, D.C., drew swarms of press to the largest Roman Catholic church in the United States. American network television broadcast the ceremony live. In the pews, guests included friends and family from Texas, Alabama, and Illinois; White House staff; the Catholic clergy; plus a sizable representation of the LBJ cabinet, the Supreme Court, and Congress—the separation of powers melting together as the temperature indoors climbed to a humid eighty-five degrees during the ceremony.[18] The "personal, family wedding," as Lady Bird described it in her thirty-four-minute diary entry recounting the day, was a local, national, and global story for its intrinsic interest and the inevitable chatter that flowed from it. The wedding date, August 6, 1966, also marked the twenty-first anniversary of the day President Truman dropped the atomic bomb over Hiroshima.[19] Protesters in dozens of cities across the country, some fifteen thousand in New York City's Central Park alone, expressed outrage over the apparent indifference on display in the Johnson family's choice of wedding dates. Stokely Carmichael threatened to lead a protest in front of the White House over Hiroshima, Vietnam, and what he regarded as a stalled civil rights agenda. But Martin Luther King, Jr., Roy Wilkins, and other movement leaders insisted that Luci and her family have their day in church. They denounced the protests as a "futile and unflattering exhibition of the egos of the demonstrators, with no practicable effect upon the objective, the ending of the war."[20] Ultimately, Carmichael, the man who that summer had coined the term *black power,* stayed away from Washington that day. But protests spanned both coasts, accompanied by flags in support of the Viet Cong and signs taking direct swipes at Luci: "How Many Hiroshimas Will Luci Johnson Celebrate?" read one. "Happy Wedding Day, Dirty Bird," read another.[21]

Still, the criticism failed to quash the "warm tide of love" Bird felt walking up the aisle, seeing lifelong friends, hers and Luci's, and thinking about the loss of a daughter, the "giving away," in conventional marriage vernacular of the era. Wearing a daffodil-yellow chiffon dress, overcoat, and, in the couture style of the times, a yellow turban—Anne Bancroft would mimic the look the next year as Mrs. Robinson in *The Graduate*—in the limousine with Lyndon and the Nugents on her way back to the White House reception, Bird took stock. Protesters? Relative to New York, San Francisco, Los Angeles, Denver, Pittsburgh, Atlanta, and Cleveland, she saw very few. But as the car drove south along Rhode Island Avenue back to the White House, she counted each of the sixty-one dying or dead cherry trees her Beautification Committee had planted—another loss and an "aesthetic psychological blow," she recorded, a hint of frustration in her voice.[22]

* * *

Three days after the wedding, American jets attacked two villages in South Vietnam, killing sixty-three civilians and wounding one hundred. The Pentagon and the White House described the attack as a mistake. A *New York Times* headline suggested that President Johnson stood ready to respond to "any signal" that the North Vietnamese might be interested in negotiating, "from whatever source and no matter how faint or indistinct."[23] The "unrelieved pressure of Vietnam" kept Lyndon up at night, whether he was at the White House or the Ranch. He was overeating, though drinking very little. The demands on him were such that Bird forswore her planned post-wedding vacation. But for a short visit to Huntland and a dive into Irving Stone's *The Agony and the Ecstasy,* she mainly stuck with Lyndon for the rest of the month, at the Ranch, in Washington, or traveling around the country. Helping her daughter set up her own home, prepare for married life, for children, gave Lady Bird a glimpse of her own middle age and mortality. She had absorbed Lyndon's always-in-a-rush, striving energy, but could feel, with Luci entering a period of domesticity and Lynda professionally launched as a journalist for the women's magazine *McCall's,* a sense of "a second chapter, a turning point," and of fleeting time. Yet her own vitality remained a huge source of relief. Hiking along the Pedernales River again that August, at times up to her waist in or swinging from the limb of a cypress tree across, she relished "the euphoria of being physically tired." While seeding the next year's wildflower harvest with Indian blanket, pink Texas star, and always more of the ubiquitous blue bonnet, she documented the abundant wildlife around her (from rattlesnakes to armadillos to spotted deer, all under the big West Texas sky) with the same eagle eye she lent to Lyndon's presidency.[24]

Chapter 14

Protest and the Urban Crisis

We need once again to evaluate our urban open spaces and to design them to perform ecologically for the good of the community. We must realize, too, that open spaces in a city are not decorative frills which can be added or subtracted at whim. Adequate open space is a hard biological necessity, essential to life. We know, for example, the exact number of square feet per individual needed for other animals to live a normal existence. . . . We do not yet know the exact ratios of open spaces which people need biologically for their lives and personalities to be fulfilled. But we do know of their importance, and of our need for constant contact with the elements of the natural environment.

—Lawrence Halprin, *Cities,* 1963

Bird's organic connection to the natural environment gave her an internal sense of personal authenticity, one that freed the now-confident First Lady to shine in her public role alongside Lyndon. The strength she drew from the alignment between her inner life and her public persona allowed her to better connect with the matters she cared about in Washington, and helped her offer the president some necessary perspective. His presidency, indeed the country over which he presided, had become a study in contrasts at every turn. Lyndon allowed himself to feel the torment of terrible choices. Bird felt them, too, and felt deeply for him. Of course she also had the easier job, and as urban uprisings and campus protests broke out across the country, and Vietnam could now be called a morass, the First Lady responded by raising her public profile and expanding her activism on behalf of the social and environmental dimensions of the Great Society's "natural beauty" portfolio, in the District of Columbia and in cities from coast to coast.

The contrasting elements of the portfolio began to hint at the issues of racial, class, geographic, and demographic diversity that shaped the Johnson White House perspective on the American experience in the 1960s. For example, in the scorching, sweaty heat of that 1966 summer, the First Lady hosted some five hundred young Americans representing long-established youth organizations, such as the 4-H network of clubs, the Boy Scouts of America, the Girl Scouts, Future Farmers, and Future Homemakers, to rally them to organize local community action on air and water pollution and litter cleanup in their cities and on their roadways.[1] Her guests were the starched, A-lined, bobbed, and crew-cut youth who had stayed on the straight and narrow, living embodiments of the Norman Rockwell fantasy of midcentury American comity. Her largely white audience had not, or had not yet, joined the culture of protest. The scene looked and sounded very square, but the concept of citizen advocacy for new laws and regulations for reform represented for Bird the bedrock of democratic change. In supporting such change, she was promoting local activism as a means to expand environmental consciousness and, ultimately, action and policies across the country. The First Lady's approach also made clear her awareness that young Americans were living in a decade of powerful transformation, and of youthful agency in that transformation. Drawing from Ralph Waldo Emerson, she encouraged a combination of independence and patriotism, of self-reliance, conviction, and community action. Though she sensed the tectonic cultural shifts afoot, she was not fully prepared for the anti-establishment counterculture rebellion soon to envelop the country.[2]

The very next day, in the Jacqueline Kennedy Garden, Lady Bird greeted several hundred more guests, only now they were residents of the District of Columbia, and predominantly black. Her message likewise sought to encourage local participation as a means toward empowerment. The First Lady passed out bronze plaques and dozens of certificates to schoolchildren and their teachers and parents, recognizing beautification programs at some of D.C.'s public schools. Awarding mainly African American residents of the District of Columbia for their efforts to transform their long-neglected physical environment placed the spotlight on the essential truth about the absence of home rule by and for the people in the nation's capital. Recognition for participating in the aesthetic shift from "ugliness" to "beauty" at schools in the era of Head Start conveyed something larger than a politically neutral approach to "flower power." Lady Bird well understood that even without direct political participation and oversight on budget priorities in D.C., the citizens of a majority-black city—especially those living on the margins, those displaced by urban renewal, and those who could not afford to send their kids to the handful of Washington private or parochial schools that had begun to integrate even before *Brown v. Board of Education*—had begun to view the beautification programs as a step, if a modest one, toward achieving the respect they'd long been denied.[3]

It was a big summer for home rule activism in the District in 1966. The local Baptist minister and close MLK ally, Walter Fauntroy, made the case within the walls of the White House at the civil rights conference "To Fulfill These Rights," and local activists organized home rule rallies in the streets and along the National Mall. Lady Bird's Beautification Committee members were beginning to acknowledge that there was only so much impact the riotous colors of the azaleas, daffodils, and tulips they planted could accomplish to materially improve the well-being of a fundamentally disempowered citizenry in the District of Columbia. Aware of the need for a new approach to beautification, Laurance Rockefeller brought to the First Lady's attention the work on civil rights and American cities of another New York philanthropist, Stephen Currier. It was an introduction potent with promise for the enhanced quality of life the First Lady wanted her platform and clout to deliver for the unrepresented citizens of Washington, D.C.

Stephen Currier, a descendant of the New York printmaker Nathaniel Currier, was nine years old when his mother, then an editor for *Vogue* magazine, divorced and married Edward M. M. Warburg, of the Viennese banking family. As a Harvard undergraduate, Stephen met and married Radcliffe student Audrey Mellon Bruce, the daughter of the diplomat

David Bruce and Ailsa Mellon Bruce and the first grandchild of Andrew W. Mellon. Progressive in their politics, the couple made a significant decision: to spend their considerable inherited wealth, most of it Audrey's, in their lifetime. They created the Taconic Foundation in 1958, directing their philanthropy to social programs and policy issues related to equality, child welfare, and mental health, though initially only in the New York City area. By the early 1960s, their foundation had begun to fund direct organizing by the civil rights movement. In 1962, after talks with then–attorney general Bobby Kennedy and with leaders of the country's most prominent black civil rights organizations, including the NAACP, SNCC, and CORE, Taconic underwrote the Voter Education Project, to register voters in the Jim Crow South. In 1963, following the assassination of Medgar Evers in Jackson, Mississippi, and a meeting with Martin Luther King, Jr.—and with more than $500,000 in pledges from ninety-six corporations and foundations, including the Ford and Rockefeller Foundations—the Curriers funded the Council for United Civil Rights Leadership (CUCRL), the civil rights umbrella organization that produced the March on Washington for Jobs and Freedom.[4] By the time Laurance Rockefeller introduced the thirty-six-year-old Currier to the First Lady, Currier also presided over Urban America and the Potomac Institute, both of which focused on the relationship between racial justice, equal opportunity, and the quality of life in American cities.[5]

Since the 1965 Watts riots in Los Angeles, the urban crisis in America had become a source of intense concern and urgency for the Johnson White House. Progress on civil rights early in Johnson's tenure had opened a tap of demands for deeper reforms—in better housing, credit, jobs, education, healthcare, nutrition, recreation, transportation, representative juries, fair trials, and impartial policing. By the summer of 1966, frustrations over the failure of new philosophically, if not financially, ambitious government programs to deliver whole-cloth structural change in these arenas sparked confrontations with local police forces and morphed into all-out race riots in Chicago, Omaha, Brooklyn, Jacksonville, Cleveland, Lansing, Waukegan, Philadelphia, Atlanta, and twenty-nine other cities around the country. The violence resulted in hundreds of wounded and arrested and significant destruction of property—but not in the District of Columbia. With D.C.'s relative absence of militant black activism compared to other cities—and a solid black professional class practiced in the pursuit of a national legal strategy for broadening civil rights—the potential for full-blown riots to occur in Washington was deceptively easy to underestimate.[6]

There was no getting around the fundamental disconnect between professing equal rights around the country while they were so obviously neglected in her adopted hometown, and Lady Bird empowered Rockefeller, Shackleton, Washington, and now Currier to help highlight, and perhaps even improve, the conditions Washingtonians had long come to endure. Catalyzed by Shackleton's prodigious energy and vast network of contacts across the District's racial, class, and geographic cleavages, the Beautification Committee began to direct some of its resources into the Northwest neighborhood of Shaw. The neighborhood was bound by 14th Street, Florida Avenue, New York Avenue, and M and N streets, and encompassed 150 city blocks that were home to twelve thousand families. Throughout most of the twentieth century, especially in the 1930s and '40s, the area on U Street between 9th and 16th streets, NW, was a mecca for black culture and commerce—"Black Broadway" it was called. The jazz greats of the era, Duke Ellington, Count Basie, Billie Holiday, and Pearl Bailey, were regulars at the Howard and Lincoln theatres, and if Washington could be said to have had a fashionable neighborhood in the first half of the century, it was Shaw that took the prize. But by the 1960s, now dubbed "Shameful Shaw," it had begun to lose its appeal. The black middle class that had long lived in its nineteenth-century row houses had begun to flee to the suburbs. Liquor stores, heroin use, and violence proliferated. After mixed results in Southwest and the possibility that the federal government would engineer another experiment in urban renewal in Shaw, Walter Fauntroy organized a coalition of churches, businesses, and civic groups to press Secretary Weaver's new Department of Housing and Urban Development to get it right this time. "We have taken urban renewal, a tool often used to destroy black neighborhoods, and fashioned it into an instrument by which the people can preserve and upgrade their own community. We shall not be another Southwest," declared an editorial in the local paper, *Shaw Power*.[7]

With the goal of local participation now key, Fauntroy's coalition, the Model Inner City Community Organization (MICCO), found allies in the federal government who had money to spend and were eager to improve on the ravages of the first wave of urban renewal. That summer, MICCO received a staggeringly large federal grant of $1.8 million to engage local residents, businesses, and community groups in grassroots planning for urban renewal to save Shaw.[8] Fauntroy envisioned Shaw as a neighborhood with potential, for its residents and for the entire District. Renovated schools, appealing public spaces, jobs, housing, and transportation could help revitalize the community. Construction for a subway in D.C., known as the Metro, had yet to begin. And although he did not foresee how gentrification would eventually displace its residents, he argued with some prescience that a Metro stop in the heart of Shaw would help residents find employment outside their neighborhood and also attract new middle-class residents and professionals, businesses, and other commercial activity. But until that vision could be realized, Shaw citizens still faced the daily insult of living without even basic local services of regular garbage collection and cleanup of public spaces or control of Washington's perennial plague: rats.

The District's own government, then called the Board of Commissioners, was notoriously inefficient, bureaucratic, and underfunded. What funds it did have for upkeep and hygiene of the physical environment in Washington's neighborhoods tended to go to the Georgetowns, the Cleveland Parks, the Spring Valleys, and the Forest Hills of Upper Northwest. Even those neighborhoods often pooled their own money—and still do—to hire private contractors to provide services the District could not or would not. With a budget of seven thousand dollars from Stephen Currier and a rented work space at 9th and P streets, NW, Shackleton launched "Project Pride" to coordinate and deliver a host of services to Shaw residents. Over the summer of 1966, Project Pride worked together with MICCO on the practical aspects of beautification and set out to put meaning behind the concept advanced by Jane Jacobs: in essence, that cities are their people. Volunteers donning Project Pride T-shirts placed rat bait throughout 86 city blocks; ran rat and vermin education programs; removed 163 truckloads of trash, including old refrigerators and dead plants; and replaced vacant lots serving as public dumping grounds with community gardens. All this provided jobs and training for students at Howard University and Cardozo High School. Project Pride also partnered with the D.C. government's tree division to redress damage from drought, sponsored a National Youth Corps program to train boys in basic home repair skills, and ran clinics on lawn and plant care for church and school custodians.[9] Shackleton and her team recruited soil conservationists, science teachers, police captains, and landscape architects to volunteer their time. Also, *Washington Post* art and architecture critic and *Cityscape* columnist Wolf Von Eckardt, in covering Pride's progress, shamed the D.C. government for its passivity, helping to cajole some degree of assistance from half a dozen district government agencies.[10] With Shackleton as the First Lady's D.C. community liaison, her advocate from the inside was Walter Washington, still leading the District's National Capital Housing Authority. By 1966, Washington had come to acknowledge the shortcomings of the Southwest experience and backed Project Pride as part of a transition to "a new, decent neighborhood life we expect from urban renewal" and mildly noted in Shaw "a most significant expansion of the beautification effort."[11]

* * *

The expanding intensity and violence of convulsions in American cities, and Lady Bird's consciousness of the social and racial divides in Washington, D.C., made her commitment to public service both more challenging and more relevant. The Johnson administration's early focus on the environmental components of "natural beauty" had spurred American foundations to invest in new academic and policy-oriented initiatives in urban planning and social policy. At Currier's suggestion, President Johnson gave his green light to convening yet another White House conference on American cities, "Our People and Their Cities." In the run-up to the conference, Urban America held a series of roundtable discussions around the country with architects, landscape architects, urban planners, and community groups about the impact of the built environment on how urban residents live and feel. The agenda for the September 1966 conference emerged out of those discussions: housing, work, transportation, leisure, and how public policy, private initiative, and citizen action might coalesce so that cities might better meet the aspirations of their residents and their need for human dignity.[12]

Whereas the 1965 White House Conference on Natural Beauty made little if any explicit reference to race, by 1966 it was now impossible to ignore the racial and class-based dimensions of the crisis in American cities. Indeed, many of the speakers addressed the disproportionate impact on Americans of color of segregation and shoddy services in American cities. Yet, in kicking off the conference and serving as the president's surrogate, Lady Bird trod carefully.

> Our challenge is not how to build, for no nation in history has had greater technical resources at its command; nor is it entirely money, for the richest nation on earth has money to spend, and is spending it; but the challenge to America's cities is how to govern their growth boom with beauty and compassion for every life and its fulfillment. Can we do it? Dare we do less? The clamor of city victims is a spur to progress. You have seen the beacon of achievement in small and large measure. In a downtown plaza, along a waterfront, in a city block program. You know how much that means.[13]

Like the president, the First Lady worried about how white Americans would react to the specter of black Americans rioting in the streets, that such uprisings might cause funding for Great Society programs intended to benefit the urban poor to lose political support. But she revealed none of this in her public remarks. Instead she projected hope that significant public, private, and philanthropic investment in the design of American cities might itself redress the doleful conditions that had wrought such a direct rebuke, or "clamor," from their inhabitants, that summer's "city victims."

The conference made clear that the Johnson White House recognized the interwoven dimensions of the urban crisis. But as important for Lady Bird was Currier's private suggestion that she meet with a brilliant landscape architect from San Francisco, Lawrence Halprin. Raised in Brooklyn and on a kibbutz near Haifa in the British Mandatory Palestine, Halprin had developed a collaborative approach to landscape design for public spaces, an approach heavily influenced by the postmodern choreography of his wife, dancer Anna Halprin, and by his very close proximity to nature in California. By the 1960s, he had opened a studio in downtown San Francisco and taken on private and public projects around California, including some to remedy the destructive impact on San Francisco's African American neighborhoods of the early postwar iterations of urban renewal. Halprin was an erudite and learned student of the public space, with a keen understanding of how people define and are defined by it. He published accessible books on cities and freeways that earned him popular and critical acclaim at the time, and he had begun to consult on major national and state-funded projects across the country and around the world. He was also in the midst of projects to design both the UN Plaza adjacent to San Francisco's city hall and the Sea Ranch, a utopian vision of human interaction with the natural environment located along a privately owned eleven-mile stretch of raucous, craggy coastline north of Marin, in Sonoma County.[14]

At the time, California's architects, landscape architects, and urban planners were experimenting with how to manage, restore, conserve, and commercialize the state's sites of natural beauty and historic value. Halprin's practice of community consultation as part of his design process reflected the aspirations for a greater democratic culture then permeating his Northern California setting. The public, private, and hybrid projects he ultimately developed, ranging from Ghirardelli Square to the Sea Ranch to St. Francis Square, an integrated housing complex in San Francisco's Western Addition, showed his entrepreneurial energy and conceptual flexibility.[15] More important, his fine-tuned aesthetic and urban philosophy were catching on across the country, with his most powerful potential patron residing in the nation's capital.

Lady Bird was keen to find a creative and experienced partner for her work in the District. The day after she spoke with Currier about him, Halprin received a confidential phone call. "Mrs. J is aware," one of Currier's minions explained, that the emphasis on flowers and "fancy" women "is now being laughed at and joked about." The First Lady "now wants serious, imaginative program[s] set up." Noting the "great financial latitude" backing Mrs. Johnson, would Halprin consider proposing ideas for the District of Columbia?[16] After a promise of a private meeting and tour of the city with the First Lady, East Wing aide Sharon Francis followed up with some crucial advice. "Mrs. Johnson does not need convincing of this need for amplification" of the committee's portfolio and focus. But it would be "fatal" and unnecessary, Sharon warned, for Halprin the outsider to arrive in Washington and deride as "lousy" the work to date of the Beautification Committee. Currier would fund the new initiative well beyond the token amounts he had already contributed to Project Pride in Shaw. Halprin and Sharon spoke initially of Halprin's developing just a few pilot programs for public spaces in low-income neighborhoods. But by the end of the call, the scope had expanded. In his signature, almost calligraphic handwritten notes, Halprin wrote the phrase "carte blanche," and noted that with Currier and the Taconic Foundation's financial backing, the First Lady had invited him to propose as "broad and creative and imaginative" a vision for public spaces in the District of Columbia as possible. He booked a flight from San Francisco to Washington.[17]

Claudia Alta "Lady Bird" Taylor, teenager.

August 1958, on Capitol Hill, Lady Bird's political home until the vice presidency.

Lady Bird with a pregnant Jackie, October 29, 1960, ten days before Election Day.

May 24, 1961, President Kennedy greets the Johnsons upon their return from a visit to Southeast Asia. Among the group, Deputy Assistant Secretary of State Carl Rowan (far left, back), Speaker of the House Sam Rayburn (blocked by Lady Bird), Congressman Carl Albert of Oklahoma, and Senator Everett Dirksen of Illinois.

The Johnsons face a phalanx of press when they arrive at Andrews Air Force Base outside of Washington, D.C., after the assassination of JFK in Dallas on November 22, 1963.

The four Johnsons joined thousands of mourners at the gravesite of President Kennedy on Sunday, December 1, 1963. Back at the White House, still dressed in their mourning attire, they posed for Yoichi Okamoto, who began covering LBJ during the vice presidency and developed virtually unfiltered access to the president as the White House official photographer. Cropped, this image of Lady Bird was used as the backdrop to the 2012 commemorative edition of the 1969 beautification stamp series.

Working the phones at the Ranch on Christmas Day 1963. Their joint call list that day included Dwight and Mamie Eisenhower, Robert McNamara, *New York Times* reporter James "Scotty" Reston, syndicated columnist Walter Lippmann, and Al Friendly of *The Washington Post*.

Greeting the press for a barbecue and tour of the Ranch in advance of the visit of German chancellor Ludwig Erhard, December 27, 1963.

Lady Bird was known for shaking every hand while on the campaign trail. In Georgia during her October 1964 whistle-stop tour through the South.

March 24, 1964, at the Marshall Space Flight Center in Huntsville, Alabama. "I'm really proud of the vital role that women are playing in space . . . ranging all the way from clerks and typists to aerospace engineers. . . . In any of my trips to the South, I want to accent its future and not its past. What better springboard than space?" Standing off to Lady Bird's right is Wernher von Braun, "the German scientist we virtually kidnapped."

Women dominated the leadership and local organizing for the whistle-stop tour and turned out to greet Lady Bird in Greensboro, North Carolina, on October 7, 1964.

October 15, 1964, after the news about Walter Jenkins broke, Lady Bird met LBJ and RFK the next day in New York City. There the two held a rally in Madison Square Garden campaigning for LBJ's presidential election and for Bobby's election to the Senate representing New York. In the limousine on their way back to Washington, along with White House aide Jack Valenti.

In Lyndon's bedroom, the Johnson family prepares for the inauguration of the thirty-sixth president of the United States, January 20, 1965.

February 11, 1965, at the White House shining a light on Washington's hidden, underserved neighborhoods with Walter Washington and Stewart Udall (middle and far right, foreground). Beautification was not just about flowers.

April 16, 1965, Lady Bird Johnson poses for Okamoto at the Ranch. In her diary she recorded, "The day was remarkably free of the worries of the office—a jewel of a day but it would not be such a jewel if it were not in the setting of hours and days of toil and worry. Is it the cessation of pain, of trouble like Schopenhauer says that makes it so valued?" The next day, more than twenty thousand in Washington, D.C., protested the war in Vietnam.

At the White House Arts Festival on June 14, 1965, Lady Bird brought hundreds of the country's most celebrated contemporary artists to the White House. A dancer from the Joffrey Ballet leaps across the South Lawn in front of a sculpture by Alexander Calder.

August 9, 1965, at the signing of a bill for the National Institutes of Health (NIH) biomedical research laboratories, one of thirty-two Great Society bills passed in 1965. In signing the bill, LBJ said he had asked his speechwriters to incorporate a passage from Barbara Ward's book *The Rich Nations and the Poor Nations,* but they would not, so LBJ went off script and read a passage of her book to the audience.

March 1, 1966, with Muriel Humphrey, Lee Udall, and several other cabinet wives in the White House bowling alley to celebrate Humphrey's birthday.

Hiking in the Chisos Mountains of Big Bend National Park with Stewart Udall, April 2, 1966.

June 6, 1966, at the Ranch.

August 5, 1966, Liz Carpenter commanded Lady Bird's political operation and went on to lead the national campaign for the Equal Rights Amendment. Here (seated right, middle) she directs her team of deputies assembled on the steps of the National Shrine of the Immaculate Conception in Washington, D.C., one day before Luci Baines Johnson's wedding.

Part of a three-day tour through North Carolina, promoting Teacher Corps and Job Corps programs, March 14, 1967.

June 1967, with John Hechinger, Jr., a Washington, D.C., business owner and philanthropist, on a visit to the River Terrace School in Northeast, along the Anacostia River. The surrounding neighborhood was first built in 1939 and prohibited black residents. The Supreme Court ruled against the enforcement of exclusionary covenants in 1948, and the first black families bought homes in 1949; KKK violence followed.

April 27, 1967, with Stewart Udall (left) and Laurance Rockefeller (right) at a Beautification Committee meeting in the White House. Larry Halprin (bearded and gesturing with his hands) talks in the background, facing camera.

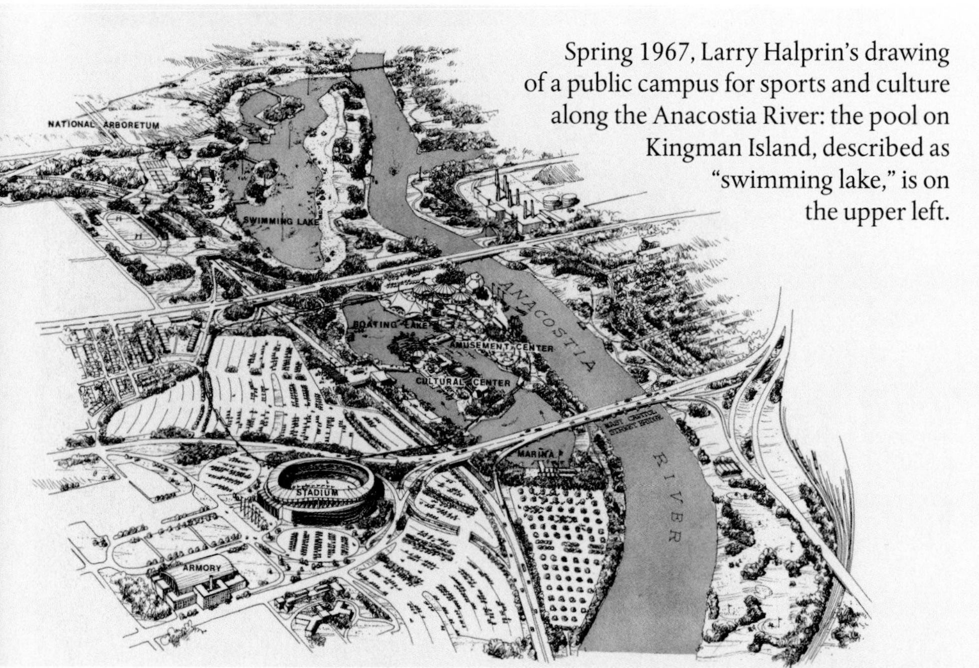

Spring 1967, Larry Halprin's drawing of a public campus for sports and culture along the Anacostia River: the pool on Kingman Island, described as "swimming lake," is on the upper left.

Returning from a summit with the Soviets in Glassboro, New Jersey, aboard Air Force One with Secretary of Defense Robert McNamara, Ambassador Llewellyn Thompson, and President Johnson. "The first word I remember Lyndon saying was, 'well, I'd say we didn't budge an inch today,'" June 25, 1967.

Working in the Oval Office with President Johnson and aides Juanita Roberts, Charles Maguire, and Larry Temple, November 3, 1967, the day of the swearing in of the nine members appointed by LBJ to the newly created District of Columbia city council. In the evening, Lady Bird attended a party in Georgetown with novelist Harper Lee and vocalist Marian Anderson.

With Eartha Kitt and Katherine Peden at the White House, January 18, 1968.

With Nash Castro overlooking the Potomac River, March 30, 1968.

In the Oval Office, March 31, 1968, before President Johnson went on live television to announce a bombing halt in Vietnam and his decision not to run in the 1968 election.

"And there we were in the familiar Oval Office of the President, the floor a jungle of cables, the brilliant glare of the TV. What a stage setting! . . . I went to him and said quietly, 'Remember—pacing and drama,'" March 31, 1968.

Fielding calls from around the country together in LBJ's White House bedroom after his bombshell announcement, March 31, 1968.

Walking along a portion of the eighty miles of newly inaugurated Padre Island National Seashore, April 8, 1968. Back in Washington, D.C., police clashed with rioting residents in the aftermath of the assassination of Martin Luther King, Jr., four days earlier.

June 7, 1968, the day after RFK's assassination and before his funeral, with President Johnson while he sits for Madame Elizabeth Shoumatoff, the artist who painted, but could not finish, FDR's portrait in Warm Springs, Georgia, days before he died in April 1944. During his own sitting, LBJ reads aloud from a letter he received from his is son-in-law Captain Chuck Robb. Shoumatoff also painted Lady Bird's official portrait.

At the Ranch, watching the Democratic National Convention in Chicago on LBJ's birthday, August 27, 1968; working the phones the next morning, August 28, 1968.

Walking on the White House grounds, October 31, 1968, on their way to greet Lynda and her new baby girl, Lucinda, the president tells the First Lady about his plan to announce another halt to bombing in Vietnam.

In her October 31, 1968, diary entry, she recorded, "He kept on trying to get his grandfather's attention, and Lyndon said, 'Lyn, go kiss grandpa,' and pointed to the screen. And Lyn went over and gave him a big kiss, first on one screen, then another, and then another."

During a visit to the coastal redwood groves north of Eureka, California, in Humboldt and Del Norte counties. After a two-mile hike and a lunch of local fare, smoked salmon and hot clam juice, to celebrate the creation of Redwood National Park, November 25, 1968.

In the second-floor White House family quarters, December 25, 1968. Luci's and Lynda's husbands, Pat Nugent and Chuck Robb, shared Christmas together in Vietnam and spoke to the family that night. Left to right: Luci, Lyn, Lady Bird, Lyndon, Yuki (on the floor), Lynda, and Lucinda. The star on the top of the family Christmas tree topped FDR's tree during World War II.

Goofing off at the LBJ Library and Museum in Austin, Texas, January 9, 1971, four months before its formal opening.

May 11, 1977, telling an audience at the Kennedy Center in Washington, D.C., that regarding the Vietnam War, she felt, like Lyndon, "just as sorry, just as strained, just as ripped and not knowing the answer but feeling this country had to live up to its commitment." Continuing, she said, "It was extremely painful, of course, because he could not find an honorable way to end that war and he wanted this country to be united. So of course, it was a very eroding, wearing, painful period."

With Coretta Scott King, Rosalynn Carter, and Betty Ford at the National Women's Conference in Houston, Texas, November 18, 1977.

Chapter 15

"This Is a Stepchild City"

[W]e had a long talk about . . . college campuses in general and California campuses in particular. It was a shattering hour, LSD and marijuana are real, and our nice young folks know them or know people who know them, and it is a quagmire to walk in. . . . Very dimly seen by me, it sounds like bright young people, imaginative young people, sensitive and searching, are quite likely to meet up with such a milieu. . . . What is lacking? An anchor? Constant old-fashioned discipline?

—Lady Bird Johnson, White House diary, September 18, 1966

The center was not holding. . . . Adolescents drifted from city to torn city, sloughing off both the past and the future as snakes shed their skins, children who were never taught and would never now learn the games that had held the society together. It was not a country in open revolution. It was not a country under enemy siege. It was the United States of America . . . and the market was steady and the G.N.P. high and a great many articulate people seemed to have a sense of high social purpose and it might have been a spring of brave hopes and national promise, but it was not, and more and more people had the uneasy apprehension that it was not.

—Joan Didion, "Slouching Towards Bethlehem," 1967

While Halprin began to digest the magnitude of the opportunity in Washington the First Lady had just offered him, Lady Bird embarked on a long-planned visit to California, a state abundant with natural beauty and the lodestar of the national conservation movement. An invitation by a state senator, Fred Farr, to dedicate the Big Sur Coast Highway, California's first scenic highway, fit squarely within Lady Bird's remit and gave her a chance to see the city where Halprin had already made such a mark.[1] It was an election year in California, and throughout most of the summer, a second-tier Hollywood film actor, Ronald Reagan, campaigning against free speech and the redwoods, had led the incumbent governor, Pat Brown, by double digits; by early September, that lead had been cut to just 3 percent—well within the margin of error. Campaigning for Farr and Brown's reelection gave the First Lady a platform to promote California's conservation-oriented public policies as a model for the country. Inhaling the crisp champagne air of the "cool grey city of love" when she arrived in San Francisco, Lady Bird praised the state for its financial backing of design excellence in the built, public environment; for its scenic trails and roads; for its measures to prevent pollution of its rivers and lakes, to preserve the redwoods, to protect the shoreline of San Francisco Bay, and to plan the first new rapid-transit system in the country in the last fifty years.[2]

After her arrival, she flew west over the Marin Headlands to one of the newest publicly protected coastlines in the country, the Point Reyes National Seashore. With some 53,000 acres and 80 miles of undeveloped Pacific coastline, the area was home to over 45 percent of North America's bird species and nearly 18 percent of the state's plant life and an ideal climate for cattle grazing and dairy farming. Stewart Udall had worked since the Kennedy administration with a constellation of California politicians and activists set on protecting the seashore with national park status. In 1962, thirteen months after signing into law the Cape Cod National Seashore in Massachusetts, President Kennedy did the same for the exquisite stretch of coastal land in Northern California. But it fell to Lady Bird Johnson to inaugurate the new national treasure.

Already a big backer of expanding the national park system, she praised Point Reyes and its dramatic cliffs, its rustic beaches, its estuaries and bays, as the embodiment of her belief in the value of public access to the natural environment and leisure as a necessary component of a healthy society. And with its proximity (thirty-five miles and a one-hour drive) to a major American metropolis, Point Reyes offered a balance between urban productivity and environmental conservation. But for a few "Stop the Genocide" signs (a show of dissent Bird expected but on this occasion did not seem to notice), a large and largely benign crowd (kids and grown-ups from the Audubon Society, the Sierra Club, and several local unions of carpenters, plumbers, and butchers) gathered in front of the tan cliffs of Drake's Beach, named for the explorer Sir Francis Drake, to hear the First Lady: "One of the dominant facts of modern times," she noted, "is that Americans . . . are now more and more divorced from natural surroundings." The density of American cities was top of mind, and she regarded national parks as a recognition that "[e]very person needs a place where he can be at repose and peace. For many, many Americans that 'place' of recreation will be public land—parks, seashores, refuges of one kind or another." She worried that "the growing needs of an urban America are quickening the tick of the conservation clock" and insisted that only places like Point Reyes and other national parks and seashores make "bearable" the "crushing forces of our age." She took particular aim at one of Ronald Reagan's favorite attacks on environmentalists, placing herself squarely behind the creation of a national park to protect the redwood trees—"immortality living amongst us"—inhabiting the forests along the Northern California coast.[3]

At the San Francisco Opera that night, a bomb threat against an unperturbed First Lady's own mortality soon emerged as a publicity stunt, but protesters carrying signs reading "Lady Bird, Bring Our Troops Home Now" and "Beautify America, but Defoliate Vietnam?" managed to get under her skin with their "aura of madness, sort of a mob spirit."[4] Lady Bird Johnson found California, with its scale of natural beauty, its ambitions for the good life, and its lack of inhibitions for expressing all of it, both off-putting and enticing.

Before heading the next morning to Monterey, Carmel, and the Central Coast, Bird sneaked out to see Ghirardelli Square. More than a year before Lady Bird saw it, *The Washington Post*'s Wolf Von Eckardt had lauded Halprin's transformation of the chocolate factory into a mixed-use public and commercial space for preventing "another aseptic, slick affair, another one of those better mousetraps, a well-designed moneymaking machine"—and suggested that Washington, D.C., might benefit from a similarly inventive approach to repurposing its dormant, decaying public spaces.[5] With a view down to Fisherman's Wharf below her, Lady Bird concurred.[6]

California was also setting the national standard for scenic highways, parks, and resource conservation. Especially as Congress threatened to defund the Highway Beautification Act, the First Lady wanted not only to campaign for Fred Farr and Pat Brown, but also to bring the national spotlight to the fifteen-mile stretch from Carmel along the Big Sur Coast Highway. Her fifteen-car entourage stopped at Hurricane Point, on the south side of a WPA project, Bixby Creek Bridge. "As we rounded every corner of the hairpin curves, another magnificent view of towering cliffs and rolling surf below came into sight. You exhaust all the superlatives! You can *feel* but you can't *talk*." There were no demonstrators this time when she spoke. On the cliff looking out at Bixby Creek Bridge, Ansel Adams, California's greatest living photographer and environmentalist, stood apart from the horde of photographers there to capture the red-bedecked First Lady standing on the very edge of the continental United States. As she absorbed the overwhelming majesty of the Pacific coastline, Bird, with her capacity for seeing contradictory qualities in people and in nature, came to appreciate California's complexity even as she recoiled at its culture of protest:

> It was a country of artists and poets and writers. John Steinbeck, Robinson Jeffers, and Joan Baez of today. Someone told me only rich people live here and people with *no* money. The bearded ones come on motorcycles and live under the bridges or in tents or in the parks, and we did see a few of the bearded ones along the way, looking very much at home, and I don't blame them—it is a land you can love.[7]

Northern California and the Central Coast were not only havens for environmentalists. And they were not immune to the social upheaval and racial violence erupting first in Los Angeles and then throughout the rest of the country. Toward the end of the First Lady's trip, while she was heading from San Francisco down the Bayshore Freeway to San Francisco International Airport, the governor's wife, Bernice Brown, pointed out, along the highway embankments, the hardy, bright yellow and pink blooming succulent native to South Africa known as the ice plant, a result of California's own beautification efforts.[8] But the extremely observant First Lady could not have missed a part of the built landscape just past the ice plants, on the hills looking over the highway. Hunters Point was inhabited mainly by African Americans who had migrated west to San Francisco for jobs in the ports and shipping yards during World War II. It was also the neighborhood where African Americans who lost their homes to urban renewal in the city's Western Addition had recently moved.

There in Hunters Point, just days after Lady Bird's visit, San Francisco police shot and killed a sixteen-year-old boy as he ran away from the car he and two friends had stolen. The next day, the temperature an uncharacteristically hot eighty-four degrees, civil rights activists gathered at a jobs hall funded by Lyndon Johnson's Great Society programs. They demanded that the commanding officer of the local precinct arrest the policeman who had shot the young man; they were told the case was under investigation and were rebuffed. Within hours, Hunters Point erupted in a riot lasting for three days. It was the worst racial violence in San Francisco since the anti-Chinese riots of ninety years earlier.[9] Two weeks later, Huey Newton and Bobby Seale founded the Black Panther Party in Oakland.

Lady Bird's visit to California roughly converged with that of another documentarian of the time, Joan Didion. The two appeared to have little in common, but in her devastatingly critical essay "Slouching Towards Bethlehem," published in 1967, Didion, like the First Lady, was also trying to sort through the confounding and contradictory qualities that made her native state such an absorbing national experiment for testing the boundaries of ideas and change.

* * *

Back in Washington, Lady Bird wrote Larry Halprin to praise him for his "ingenious" design and for salvaging a potentially "blighted" part of San Francisco. Anticipating their meeting and tour of the District, Halprin had sent Lady Bird his 1963 book, *Cities,* full of his photographs, drawings, and analysis of cities around the world, especially those built to a human scale with amenities designed for community interaction. Importantly, Stephen Currier publicized his commitment to underwrite Halprin's initial study and proposal for the District of Columbia. At first, Lady Bird Johnson's partnership with Halprin aimed to identify ways for the Beautification Committee to broaden its remit, to be sure. But in ultimately commissioning the designs for what came to be known as a "master plan" for Washington, D.C.'s neighborhoods, parks, commercial areas, playgrounds, rec centers, highways, and waterfronts, Lady Bird Johnson and, by extension, the Johnson administration had undertaken a far more financially and politically ambitious plan. In California and in Halprin, Bird had found her muse.

On the surface, Lady Bird and Larry seemed an unlikely pair—she the southern Episcopalian, he the New Yorker/Californian and Jewish socialist Zionist. The experience of traveling through the great capitals of Europe and living in Jerusalem of the 1920s and '30s—before cars had disrupted city life and where community and commerce were both accessible to people's homes—had left indelible marks on the younger Halprin's design imagination. But as a comfortable country girl, Lady Bird saw the car as part of her coming-of-age in Texas: she began driving her first at age thirteen, without a driver's license, to travel the fifteen miles back and forth to school each day. Driving vast distances (from Karnack to Marshall, from Karnack to Austin, and back and forth between Washington and Austin) gave her a sense of freedom and also of the country, the scale of its distances and the scale of the segregation that defined it. By contrast, Halprin, like many New Yorkers, didn't own a car until graduate school. Instead, he hitchhiked when he needed to travel farther than he could cover on foot or by bus or subway.

An aspiring horticulturalist who once dreamed of returning to the kibbutz to help develop its burgeoning orange groves, Halprin instead gravitated toward the newly emerging field of landscape architecture. On the eve of World War II, he transferred to Harvard, where the founders and leading figures of the German Bauhaus movement, Walter Gropius, Marcel Breuer, and László Moholy-Nagy, had sought refuge from the Nazi regime. After a stint in the Pacific during the war, and a near-death experience when the Japanese bombed his destroyer, Halprin found himself living with his wife in a Quonset hut while stationed at a base looking out over the shipyards of the San Francisco Bay: It was pre–urban renewal Hunters Point, the very place where the riots of twenty years later would take place.

Before his Ghirardelli Square and other public-private commissions, and now living across the Golden Gate Bridge from San Francisco, in Marin County, by 1965 Halprin had designed more than three hundred residential gardens in the Bay Area. His frequent pairing of inorganic concrete (a new, inexpensive, and modern material) or asphalt with natural stone and water, elements he had studied and sketched in notebook after notebook while hiking in the Jerusalem Hills, Yosemite, and the Sierra, testified to his hybrid sensibilities.[10] He and Anna Halprin had participated in sit-ins and happenings; their collaboration in choreographing "scores" for both dance and landscape design had transformed them into California cultural heavyweights known for blurring lines between disciplines and across other once-indelible norms. Though Halprin was steeped in a California gestalt of experimentation and participation, the very nature of his profession, in which to thrive involved competing for federal, state, and municipal contracts, required him to develop the practical and political skills of a successful businessman and an entrepreneurial public arts advocate.

By the early 1960s, the displacement caused by San Francisco's own experiment with urban renewal in the neighborhood known as the Western Addition and in another, the Fillmore District, had come under fire. When the Japanese community living in the Western Addition after the 1906 earthquake was forced into internment camps during World War II, African Americans who had come west as part of the Great Migration or who had moved to San Francisco for jobs in the shipyards during World War II moved into the Western Addition and into the Fillmore, making the latter a thriving, if underserved, community of black-owned businesses and culture. It is the Fillmore where James Baldwin, in his

1963 documentary, *Take This Hammer,* coined the term *Negro removal* to characterize black residents' displacement from the neighborhood's iconic Victorians, then regarded by policy reformers as substandard housing, to the boxy, alienating public housing model cropping up in so many American cities at the time. Halprin was not an architect, but by the mid-sixties, his designs came to represent a pivot in urban planning. Financed by the International Longshoremen's Association to provide integrated housing for retired members, Halprin devised a far more humanly scaled housing development in the Western Addition, one intended to mark a departure from the blanket destruction that came with the first phase of urban renewal after World War II. With its emphasis on access to both community and private outdoor space and its multiracial composition, St. Francis Square, at the time of its inauguration in 1966, would have communicated to the First Lady, had she visited it, echoes of D.C.'s River Park in Southwest.[11]

Both avid recorders of their observations, Larry and Lady Bird had separately come to very similar conclusions about the role of cities in American society. An additional dimension of the national landscape also preoccupied them: freeways and how the boom then under way across the country, and the irresistible glut of federal dollars to finance new construction, might harm the established social and physical environment of American cities. Highways, Halprin argued, ought to preserve the distinct character of neighborhoods, both physically and ethnically. They should not alter existing land use. And they should avoid the destruction of topography, such as hills, valleys, riverfronts, and their views.

During her tenure in the White House, Lady Bird, too, set out to exert her influence over how freeways, and not just the great interstates, were shaping lives in American cities. The conventional narrative about the First Lady is that planting flowers and minimizing visually obnoxious billboards along highways in rural America predominated in her environmental policy priorities and represented the lion's share of her contribution to the Johnson administration. But this telling leaves out her role as a back channel to relevant cabinet and subcabinet members about the placement and design of highways often in and around American towns and cities. She received and responded to hundreds of letters from the public asking her to intervene when the planned placement of a highway or a seemingly inconsequential choice by a disconnected engineer or bureaucrat threatened to destroy or uproot people's natural environment and lives.[12]

Halprin had already begun to tackle these questions in San Francisco, where he had worked with local citizen groups, in what was known as the Freeway Revolt, to stop the placement of a freeway along an extended stretch of the peninsular city's waterfront. In the early 1960s, he and architect Mario Ciampi worked with engineers to bring "conscious aesthetic design" to Interstate 280, a new artery exiting south from San Francisco down the peninsula, landscaping it with durable native plants and lining it with an irrigation system. In *Freeways,* his 1966 treatise on how to tame their inevitable proliferation, the always optimistic Halprin argued that "freeways could become a new art form, if they were thoughtfully designed." He had made it his mission "to show that it was feasible to handle freeways in such an elegant manner that they could improve, rather than destroy, the cities they served."[13] The rapid expansion of freeways across the country posed a challenge that both he and Lady Bird were keen to redress in Washington, D.C. "Most cities," Halprin wrote, "have a fine grain, particularly [the] older more urban parts," such as public squares, parks, plazas, and waterfronts, and are also most vulnerable to destruction from new freeways, because, as Jane Jacobs also suggested, once urban public spaces are established, they often are left unimproved. These established cities also had existing street systems that "function beautifully for older methods" of transportation, but become altered, negatively so, through the introduction of the automobile and, now, the rush to build freeways not just on the edges but within cities themselves. Drawing from the negative experience of urban renewal in San Francisco, Halprin stressed that preserving the "quiet residential" quality of old city neighborhoods and the communities living in them would be key. Just as important were buildings and landmarks, which "must not only be preserved intact themselves, but views of them and their relationships to their surroundings *must* be preserved." Evoking Franklin Roosevelt, an icon of his youth, Halprin imagined "a series of freedoms" for American cities. In notes for a talk he delivered at a 1965 conference on freeways, under a column he titled "Freedom From," Halprin listed all the elements of a city that made it inhospitable to personal enjoyment: asphalt, grids, mercury vapor, and so on. The freedom "to want," as he described it, included waterfront promenades, pedestrian precincts, and sidewalk cafés, aspects of the very urban planning agenda Washington, D.C., would eventually follow, albeit not in his lifetime and not in Lady Bird's.[14]

* * *

When Halprin arrived in Washington to meet the First Lady, the District's residents were waging a protracted battle to prevent the construction of at least three separate highways and superhighways ringing or running through the District, in addition to another half dozen projects to expand lanes, extend parkways, and build on- and off-ramps and extensive tunnels through their city. As with almost every development proposal in Washington, a searing racial component permeated the clash. In the absence of home rule, the channels for citizen input into, let alone control over, such consequential decisions were decidedly weak, despite advocates for managed growth and public transportation (like Libby Rowe) occupying some positions of power.

In one plan, a mini-Beltway would have encircled the District just a half mile north and south of the White House. Another plan would have built a tunnel under the Mall starting from the Lincoln Memorial, running under the Tidal Basin, and rising out of the ground at the Jefferson Memorial. Another proposed an eight-lane superhighway under K Street. In yet another, a highway would extend north from a proposed new bridge (then called Three Sisters), across the Potomac to the Georgetown waterfront, and straight up the Northwest quadrant of white Washington through Bethesda and north onto the Maryland freeways. In still others, a ten-lane freeway would link Silver Spring, Maryland, and Capitol Hill, with the potential to destroy four thousand homes of low- and middle-income African American and white Washingtonians living in some of the few semi-integrated communities of D.C., Takoma and Brookland. A proposal for a massive waterfront highway in Anacostia would likewise have gobbled up potential open space and parks otherwise there to be enjoyed, if properly cleaned up, developed, and desegregated, by the predominantly African American residents of the Northeast and Southeast quadrants of Washington. Although urban renewal in Southwest initially had few opponents among the Georgetown and Cleveland Park set, preventing highways from carving up the city and their own neighborhoods became one of the few issues that unified black and white Washington.

For Halprin's first visit to Washington under his new commission, to give him a sense of the city's social and geographic landscape, Sharon Francis arranged a driving tour with the First Lady's key allies. Nash Castro took the wheel, Larry sat in the passenger seat, and Polly Shackleton, Walter Washington, and Francis rode in the back. They drove from the White House through monumental Washington and then out along the Potomac to National Airport. At the time, some members of the Beautification Committee, like Castro and Mary Lasker, were not ready to focus on residential Washington as much as on the areas designed for tourists. Halprin quickly concluded that his services really weren't needed for those sorts of public spaces; they already had ample political support and sizable budgets. Listening to Shackleton and Washington describe the vast needs of D.C. residents, the proliferation of bureaucratic politics to navigate on their behalf, and the paucity of collective vision and resources, Halprin settled his focus on the schools, parks, and neighborhoods.[15]

Although Project Pride was a Shaw project, most of the Beautification Committee's work to date, and Lady Bird's focus now, was on Capitol East.[16] Capitol East contained several neighborhoods within it, not all African American and not all poor, but predominantly both. Lady Bird had come to know it because her favorite church, St. Mark's, was located in its more materially secure, racially integrated part. The farther east Nash drove them, the more Halprin saw how little there was by way of entertainment, recreation, parks, green space, food, or accessible public transportation. The neighborhood was vast, comprising parts of Northeast and all of Southeast Washington. It extended east from the U.S. Capitol to the stadium then known as the District of Columbia Stadium; south through the Navy Yard, along the Anacostia River; and north beyond Union Station to Florida Avenue and Benning Road. Construction of the Southeast Freeway, running from South Capitol Street across the 11th Street Bridge, completed in 1958, had already destroyed several schools and parks.

Buoyed by the White House backing for D.C. home rule, a group of some fifty volunteer residents from Capitol East—frustrated with the failure of the District recreation department and the National Park Service to deliver pools, parks, and playgrounds, especially for young, restless residents fearful of more freeways—had come together in 1965 to produce a thirty-two-page survey of their neighborhood.[17] The report they created gave Halprin a detailed description of the entire area, including the population, median income, number of children, and list of schools, parks, playgrounds, and potential playgrounds and other recreational facilities in each census tract. Playgrounds of public schools in many American cities frequently offered little more than asphalt, a chain-link fence, and possibly a basketball court and some basic play equipment. Both New York City and Washington, D.C., had begun to incorporate a far more multidimensional and multigenerational view of the benefits of play for child development and community connection. The Kennedy Recreation Center in Shaw, for which LBJ and Lady Bird had taken pains to raise funds and invite public attention, seemed downright avant-garde in comparison to the barely human status quo in Capitol East.

Kids living in underserved neighborhoods of Washington, D.C., and their parents and grandparents, still required more public spaces, besides streets and alleys, where they could play and gather after school and work. To endure Washington's oppressive summer heat and humidity, and unable to afford travel to beaches three hours away, they needed public swimming pools, a largely segregated and, in any case, virtually nonexistent amenity. At the time, the District had only nine public pools, five in Northwest, three in Northeast, and one in Southeast. The last, a pool in Anacostia, had shut down in 1949 when white patrons, outraged over its recent desegregation, attacked black patrons and caused a race riot. Bird wrote often in her diary about the well-being she derived from swimming, about its giving her "such a sense of self-mastery, of strength, and of being able to cope with my environment."[18] She understood the reasons that such an enormous segment of Washington's population had little if any such opportunity, and it pained her. She hoped the White House could help change things.

The Emergency Recreation Council for Capitol East, the group behind the push for public services, wanted to make better use of vacant lots and corner triangles (the latter a design element dating back to L'Enfant) and called for staff to supervise recreation not in accord with the "white collar" schedule of the D.C. rec department but by providing for supervision on evenings and weekends, when kids most needed to be outdoors. The community's demands were relatively modest: one pool, four new rec centers, and six renovated playgrounds, plus more "tot lots" and staff. "With imagination, energy, money and without destroying people's homes, the present picture could be greatly improved," the Capitol East volunteers concluded.[19] Sharon arranged for Halprin to meet with the community in order to better understand its needs. With its up-to-date, meticulous detail, their report laid the groundwork for a portion of what would become Halprin's master plan for the District.

In 1966, when ideas about community action and democratic participation were the stuff of SDS, SNCC, and the SCLC, the White House, not generally regarded at the time as a champion of such goals, commissioned a cutting-edge, globally recognized landscape architect and arranged for him to meet with a racially and economically mixed neighborhood group in the nation's capital. That individual listened to and incorporated the community's needs directly into the design he would present to the White House. Mrs. Johnson didn't quite think of herself as the democratic activist she was becoming, and perhaps, in the absence of home rule, she knew it may well be impossible for such an approach to have any chance of empowering local citizen activism. But the residents in the neighborhood thoroughly grasped the potential value of the East Wing's clout. As *The Capitol East Gazette* remarked, "[T]he power of White House backing and the personal interest of Mrs. Johnson cannot help but improve the chances of these plans becoming reality."[20]

The First Lady and her California muse took many scouting expeditions around Washington, D.C., during Halprin's several research trips. The most important was one to Southeast, a quadrant of the city that had experienced considerable white flight since World War II. Standing on the crest of a hill along the banks of the Anacostia, Larry and Lady Bird, together with Stewart Udall and Libby Rowe, began to imagine the possibilities Halprin might incorporate into his master plan. A giant swimming pool sunk into the spit of land known as Kingman Island, along the banks of the river? Or how about a public amusement park inspired by Copenhagen's Tivoli Gardens, the sprawling complex of rides, restaurants, and gardens bankrolled by the Danish king Christian VII in 1843? Lady Bird and Stew embraced the scope and vision of Halprin's suggestions, and they well understood the political implications of such a boundary-breaking endeavor. But Libby offered a dissenting view.[21] The District of Columbia was no Copenhagen, LBJ was no king, and a year out from the Voting Rights Act and two years out from the Civil Rights Act, Washington was still very much a southern city. Libby could remember the segregated Washington of her youth and young adulthood, when Garfinckel's Department Store kept separate entrances and water fountains for black and white patrons, and when the maids working in white Washington crossed the color line every day to work. For Libby, it may well have been hard to imagine a certain breed of white Washingtonian and her children at an amusement park or swimming in the same pool with the kids who actually lived in Southeast. Her concern about racial violence over integrating a swimming pool nearby, manifest in 1949, would play out soon enough: in 1968, riots at a segregated amusement park, Glen Echo, near the Maryland border with Upper Northwest, resulted in its permanent closure as a private park. It would reopen to the public, both black and white, three years later.

But Lady Bird's ambition prevailed. She was fully aware of the racial fault lines that prevented most D.C. residents from having access to recreation and other services that white Washingtonians and visiting tourists took for granted. The political hurdles to integrating public recreation in the racially tender 1960s were multiple. Buy-in from Congress, Bird understood, and cabinet-level stewardship would, therefore, be essential for countering the entrenched interests opposed to integrating public recreation in the politically neutered District, in particular, for one of the most neglected and segregated parts of the city. In contrast to the Georgetown waterfront along the Potomac River, the Anacostia River, which spans the edges of Northeast and Southeast D.C., remained—but for a golf course, park, stadium, and municipal landfill—largely undeveloped. It begged to be transformed.[22]

By the time Lady Bird and Larry met, each had cultivated a lifelong affinity for nature and design. Each, from opposite coasts and quite different urban environments, believed in the importance of community participation in creating public and commercial space for the benefit of the human spirit and for the common good. Larry Halprin recalled his encounters with Lady Bird Johnson as a meeting of the minds. They spoke, according to the blue notebooks Sharon Francis used to keep a record of their meetings, "of creating spaces that would foster interaction and be anchored with natural commons, about creative treatment of commercial corners, about improving playgrounds and pools, among a range of ideas."[23] He observed in the First Lady her signature style of strategic reticence. Although she was clearly knowledgeable about urban design and opinionated about her tastes, when Larry sought her views directly, she professed not to be an expert. "This is a stepchild city," she told him, so any plan Halprin devised should be easily maintained, broadly accessible, and also fun. "My only qualification," the First Lady said with characteristic understatement, "is knowing how to live." She reminded him, "I rely on experts to make the choices."[24] That was certainly true.

Lady Bird's expression of confidence in Halprin's expertise reinforced not only his ambitions for Washington, D.C., but also her objective of leveraging his credibility to redirect the priorities and resources of her

Beautification Committee toward socially meaningful initiatives. Halprin saw beyond the surface of the self-effacing First Lady and appreciated her form of projecting gravitas and deploying power. The two, he wrote in his memoir, had "struck up a close, friendly, and collegial relationship that led to my involvement in a project of great personal importance to her. . . . I was astounded by the First Lady's interests and energy and particularly by her wide-ranging concern for civil rights."[25]

Halprin planned to present the White House with a draft of a master plan in early January 1967. Working with Sharon Francis, he developed a three-phase process of assessment, analysis, and preliminary drafting to encompass the aesthetic, financial, transportation, and environmental consequences (e.g., pollution, flood-control) of building new recreation facilities and parks. He would also offer ideas on how to mitigate the impact of new freeways and a mass transit system in Washington. To build support for all of it in advance of presenting the report to the Beautification Committee, the East Wing would arrange further input from local communities, the National Park Service, pundits, and other stakeholders in the D.C. government and federal agencies whose political support and financing the plan would require.[26]

Halprin filled his Washington notebooks with sketches for new designs: a reimagined interior block in Shaw similar to his design for St. Francis Square in San Francisco; an area northeast of Union Station that might contain a complex of playgrounds and community centers anchored by three high schools; and ideas for the park along the Anacostia River. Incongruously perhaps, tucked in toward the back of his Washington sketchbook, Halprin included a drawing of the National Gallery of Art's fifteenth-century terra-cotta bust of Lorenzo de' Medici. In addition to Lady Bird's political support, Halprin needed financial assurance from Stephen Currier, the Medici of this project. Currier, Halprin believed, had committed up to $100,000 to the initial phase. But he, too, wanted assurance that Halprin would stick with the project, and that the East Wing was adequate to the task of shepherding such an ambitious plan. Like many philanthropists with vision, Currier was uncomfortable with the idea of serving as the only source of funding, and the prospect of having "the whole thing dumped in his lap" worried him.[27] But with the First Lady's endorsement and Currier's initial backing, Halprin flew back to San Francisco and quickly set to work; Sharon booked his return flight to Washington for right after the New Year.

* * *

The Johnsons spent the last few days of 1966 at the Ranch, facing what they felt to be an inexorable path deeper into Vietnam. They saw no face-saving exit. By the end of the year, American troop levels had climbed to nearly 400,000, with 5,008 combat deaths and 30,093 wounded. Still, LBJ showed no sign of relenting and, two days after Christmas, authorized a large-scale napalm bombing along the Mekong Delta. It was a major contrast with the bombing pause he had authorized over the previous Christmas. In her last diary entry of the year, Lady Bird recorded her disappointment that "the press seemed apathetic—dully interested if at all" in interviewing the thirteen young people she had invited to the Ranch to celebrate their environmental activism.[28]

President Johnson declared 1967 as the "Year of Youth for Natural Beauty and Conservation." The proclamation sounded dreadfully tin-eared and hypocritical coming from a commander in chief sending American youth to risk their lives in Indochina. But despite the president's declining credibility with the American public, Mrs. Johnson still possessed the political standing to lead "the fight for conservation and beauty," and she anticipated, *The New York Times* reported, a "collision with powerful and entrenched forces" in Washington, D.C., and beyond.[29]

Chapter 16

"Not a Luxury . . . but a Necessity"

The pretty community plazas, the city park on Kingman Island and the other amenities landscape architect Lawrence Halprin proposed . . . are not luxuries. They are vital necessities if this city is to avert the malaise and the ugly rioting which plagued so many other large cities last summer. It doesn't take experts to realize that at the beginning of "upward mobility" must be motivation—motivation for education, jobs, decent living conditions and good citizenship. And the key to motivation and the key to a well-functioning and attractive city, is giving each citizen a sense of belonging to his community and outlets for his individuality and creativity. This takes community facilities for spontaneous gathering, recreation, culture and education, both indoors and out. Halprin's great achievement is that he has shattered the myth that there is no space for this sort of thing in the city. What is lacking is only imagination. . . . Halprin would put these spaces to use in a new kind of "functional beautification" that goes deeper than sprinkling daffodils around and yet saves the agonies of conventional "urban renewal." For rather than "clear" the homes of people and displace them, he would give them some of the things that a joyful and constructive community life is built on. The things that cities are all about.

—Wolf Von Eckardt, *The Washington Post,* January 13, 1967

Halprin's outings with Lady Bird Johnson and Walter Washington had changed his view of the District of Columbia. Whereas he once "thought everyone lived in Georgetown," he came to see Washington not simply as the seat of national government, but as a complex urban center with "the same problem tormenting every other American city."[1] Yet he also quickly came to see how the District's unique lack of local franchise further institutionalized the economic and environmental dimensions of its segregation and racial polarization.

Meanwhile, civil rights leaders like Martin Luther King, Jr., had long understood D.C. as much more than the seat of national government. Within the sixty-eight-square-mile stretch of land along the Potomac and Anacostia rivers, the local and the national could play out simultaneously. In 1965, during the push for the Voting Rights Act, King led a march from Shaw to Lafayette Square, across from the White House, to support the home rule legislation LBJ had introduced earlier that year. King compared D.C.'s semicolonial status to the poll tax, to stress the continued disenfranchised status of black majorities outside the Deep South. As urban riots threatened the civil rights agenda and radicalized black politics, King's focus on conditions of northern city dwellers in Chicago, Cleveland, and Philadelphia primed him as well to see the District of Columbia as a litmus test for the rest of the country.

The vision of a Washington, D.C., with democratic access to public spaces, humanizing amenities, and services for all its residents, then, offered a potential road map for other cities. But because of the control exercised by the politically retrograde southern members of Congress who dominated the House committee overseeing District affairs, Washington, D.C., also served as a cautionary tale about the political obstacles to real progress. Although the Senate had twice passed home rule legislation, in both 1965 and 1966, the House passed only a watered-down version, one essentially shorn of the attempt to legalize meaningful local or congressional representation, and thereby effectively stalling progress just as it had on civil rights legislation before 1964. But even when local D.C. agitation had petered out, LBJ kept up his vocal stance on home rule as both a local and national civil rights issue.[2]

Without local control, without an institutional center of gravity such as a mayor's office or a city council, the task of building political and financial support for Halprin's master plan throughout the diffuse bureaucracy running the District fell to the East Wing of the White House. Currier had made it clear that he did not want to be the sole backer beyond the initial phase of Halprin's work. With standing but no real legal status in the administration, the East Wing would have to raise funds for the project from a blend of urban renewal grants from HUD and the National Capital Planning Commission and private funds from homeowners and local businesses. The legwork for this effort fell to the twentysomething champion mountain climber, young mother, and environmental policy dynamo whom the First Lady empowered as her emissary. Anticipating an uphill battle, and working with Udall's team at the Department of the Interior, Sharon Francis again organized back-to-back meetings for Halprin to expand political buy-in before his formal presentation at the White House. The First Lady, who despite her influence, occupied an informal position in the administration, would need broad and diverse support if she hoped for any kind of short- or long-term traction to finance and implement even segments of Halprin's master plan. Halprin also previewed the report privately for Mrs. Johnson, Secretary Udall, Stephen Currier, and Carol Fortas, a prominent Washington attorney and spouse of Abe Fortas.

For the formal presentation of the plan, the East Wing invited the directors and staff of twenty-two federal and D.C. agencies. Mrs. Johnson sat in the front row, but her calculus about when to make the case herself and when to let others do so drove her choice to ask Stewart Udall, the cabinet secretary, to kick off the briefing. He made clear that Halprin's mandate was not to raze Washington neighborhoods, but to offer prototypes to help "refurbish, restore and renew" them.[3] By 1967, Halprin had become, if not quite a household name, then someone whose work was indeed nationally known and whose books had made it onto *The Washington Post*'s Christmas book list in 1966, for example. But he was from San Francisco, a city at the heart of the American counterculture movement and one that few Washingtonians, including Lady Bird, fully understood. Grasping the gravity and potential of the moment, the bearded Halprin shed his sandals, striped pants, and turquoise jewelry and opted instead for an understated suit and tie. With the visual aid of easels placed in a semicircle from one side of the State Dining Room to another, he summarized for his audience the context and concept behind his vision. The future of Washington where its citizens might feel both "joyful" and "significant" would be determined by separate geographies. Halprin delineated those already with some degree of public policy attention: monumental Washington, which he described as "under control"; commercial Washington; the Potomac, where Libby Rowe and Stew Udall were overseeing a study of the river's water quality; Shaw, which had money (from HUD) but still little community participation; and Southwest, where Washington's first and most contentious experiment with urban renewal had spawned displacement followed by controversial redevelopment.[4]

But in Southeast Washington, Capitol East, and the undeveloped green space along the Anacostia River, Halprin described what he saw as achievable needs: community support, which it had, and financial resources, which as yet it did not. Backed by detailed maps and indexes, his sixty-six-page report focused on spaces that were already in the public domain, either controlled by the National Park Service or owned by the District of Columbia; if privately owned, they could be readily purchased. Precisely because there was no need to start from scratch, a vast area of Washington, D.C., invisible to most of the people in the room, invisible to most of the country, offered a prime arena for improving the existing environment and, more important, possessed an active and well-organized multiracial and multiclass community. Shaw had money without community participation, and Capitol East had participation without money. The initial report laid out plans for a new parkway along the Anacostia River as pleasing and green as Rock Creek Parkway, in Northwest; for a riverfront pool and recreation area on the forty-acre Kingman Island; and for appropriately scaled small businesses and residential upgrades. Halprin's plan also included drawings for a community garden to replace the city's highly toxic riverfront Kenilworth Dump.[5]

Halprin's White House presentation marked a major turning point for Lady Bird Johnson and the focus of her Beautification Committee. Securing the express interest of the federal and District agencies attending that day would be no small achievement and the sine qua non to advance such an ambitious agenda. But it was members of her own committee whose skepticism Mrs. Johnson anticipated and sought to neutralize. They pressed Halprin not about design or the social content of his proposals, but about the reliable deal breaker in any visionary project: money. The answer came not from Larry, but from his professional colleague and occasional competitor and committee member, the Vienna-born landscape architect Victor Gruen, who had long worried about the superficiality of flower planting alone. Now Gruen stepped in. He urged the doubters in the room to forget about whether the committee, with its reliance on private, philanthropic, and small-business donations, could afford a $20,000 spray pool or a $200,000 swimming pool. In his thick Viennese accent, Gruen made the case for focusing not on how this or that aesthetic upgrade might be bestowed upon the poor, striving residents of Capitol East or Shaw as an act of charity, but rather, on how a scaled effort at truly beautifying the District represented no less than "improving the physical and mental health of the nation. . . . Not a luxury . . . but a necessity." It was time, Gruen preached, to stop denying the scale of the urban challenge and diminishing the suffering of America's urban youth by thinking small. The members of the committee, now in its third year, must see themselves and Halprin, Gruen said, as the "instigators and catalysts of new ideas, taking advantage of all the existing federal, state and government agencies in the city of Washington . . . to work with us . . . and with the various urban neighborhoods, as closely as we can." If the committee takes on that challenge, Gruen concluded, "then I believe we can prove that beautification . . . is the very heart of the health of this country."[6]

Seated on their delicate bamboo party chairs, the First Lady's guests erupted in applause. Always measuring how to translate the emotion of an audience into her desired response, she allowed the moment to continue, uninterrupted. When the room finally quieted, all eyes focused on Mrs. Johnson. By socialization, political instinct, and years of experience, Lady Bird had the wisdom to let others do the talking and take the credit in order to advance her agenda, less out of shyness at this point in her career than as a matter of strategy. And with her own cultivated sense of theater and drama, she also knew that less, in this case, was undoubtedly more. "That was great," she said.[7]

With a knowing nod to the secretary of the interior, the First Lady designated a core group of her beautification companions to integrate Halprin's plans—not just one vest-pocket or triangle park, but as many as possible of his ten proposals, including for Anacostia—into the District government's preparations to apply for Model Cities monies and other HUD funds. The consummate Great Society strategist, Mrs. Johnson had articulated two ambitious and sensitive criteria for the next phase. Assuming Lyndon would not run for a second term, and thus with a short period of time remaining to solidify her own legacy, she wanted to see the proposals completed by November 1968, and her criteria for such initiatives must involve community participation and "minimal displacement of people and reflect wants as expressed by the people in the neighborhoods rather than as assumed by others."[8]

Glaringly absent from the White House meeting and from the planning for this next phase, however, were two individuals, two prominent African Americans whose participation in knitting together support from local and federal players would be crucial. The first was Walter Washington, who had joined Halprin and the First Lady on many of their drive-arounds. Lyndon Johnson had recently passed over Washington to become one of three D.C. commissioners, leaving an opening for New York City mayor John Lindsay to hire him away to lead the New York City Housing Authority: Walter had departed Washington, D.C., Lady Bird, and his many fans in the East Wing just weeks earlier, leaving the First Lady's committee without an experienced local official with standing among the District's black residents. Also absent was Walter Fauntroy, the minister, Yale theologian, MLK ally, and MICCO founder whose home base at the New Bethel Baptist Church was located just a few blocks from the two projects Halprin had proposed for Shaw. Either by error of commission or omission, the man who harbored high hopes and who had procured major resources from HUD for his community appears neither on the list of those invited to the White House that day nor among those whom Sharon had Halprin brief in advance of his meetings with the First Lady. Mrs. Johnson would soon make her move to remedy Walter Washington's absence, but the political cost of excluding the other Walter would reveal itself in short order.

Halprin flew back to San Francisco "astounded" by the reaction of his Washington audience. Gruen's soliloquy had the intended effect of elevating the committee's sense of possibility beyond its horticultural, fiscal focus. It was now determined "not to let problems of money and land ownership get in the way of determined action."[9] Lady Bird's willingness to go well beyond a few neighborhood pilot programs and back his entire master plan elated Larry. His outsider status and national stature provided not only the "fresh eyes" Lady Bird had been looking for, but also the ballast in what she anticipated would be a "collision with 'powerful and entrenched forces'" and, quite possibly, community resistance.[10] Still, even with Halprin's credibility established, the much more ambitious objective he had laid out would have no chance of getting off the ground without a reliable claim to his increasingly demanding schedule. And for that, a commitment of financial support was essential, indeed existential.

Fortunately, Stephen Currier, who also attended Halprin's White House presentation, came away satisfied with the results of his initial $23,000 investment and confident that the First Lady possessed the convening power to move forward and the political cachet to organize major public financing. Their encounter at the White House was not the appropriate time for Halprin and Currier to nail down the dollars and cents or to discuss in any detail the scope of Halprin's future with Lady Bird's committee. But on that January afternoon, Currier left Sharon, Larry, and the First Lady with the distinct impression that going forward he intended to cover Halprin's growing fees. And time was short, given the necessarily limited period of the First Lady's mandate.[11] Halprin seized upon the urgency. Only four days after his presentation in Washington, his San Francisco studio delivered an itemized bid for design and other consulting services for the first phase of work: helping the understaffed recreation and education agencies of the District of Columbia shape the District's Redevelopment Land Agency's application for HUD Model Cities funds for Capitol East, a real bureaucratic tangle. Addressed to the Taconic Foundation on behalf of Lady Bird's committee, the proposal topped out at $46,000 to convert Halprin's initial sketches into detailed site-specific drawings for Capitol East, Anacostia, and Shaw. The proposal was dated January 17, 1967.[12]

After attending Halprin's White House presentation, Stephen and Audrey Currier traveled to Florida and then to Puerto Rico, where they chartered a six-seater Piper PA-23 Apache twin-engine airplane for the seventy-mile, forty-five-minute flight from San Juan to the Virgin Islands. Their nine- and ten-year-old daughters stayed in Manhattan—second semester at the Brearley School had already started—but their six-year-old son waited with friends in St. Thomas to join his parents for a ten-day cruise around the Caribbean. Thirty minutes into their flight on the very day, January 17, 1967, that Halprin submitted his bid to their foundation for the next phase of work in Washington, the Curriers' plane disappeared.

With no radio contact and no airplane in sight, the Coast Guard launched a search, sending planes and helicopters to cover a 2,500-square-mile stretch of the Caribbean. The next day, a guided missile cruiser and four submarines joined the Coast Guard and expanded the search to 5,000 square miles. Search teams turned over every stone on each of the tiny, mostly uninhabited islands along the route from San Juan to St. Thomas, but not a scrap of metal nor any sign of survivors materialized. By the end of the week, the search widened still, now to 48,000 square miles, roughly the size of the state of New York. This was no ordinary search-and-rescue operation. Perhaps because of the First Lady's particular concern for the plane's passengers, it was carried out with resources generally not heard of for this scale of loss. But this was no ordinary loss, and Lady Bird let the president know how strongly she felt about the tragedy, and of course its potential consequences for the District and for her impact and legacy therein. By the weekend, though, it became clear that no amount of submarine and air power would bring the Curriers back.[13]

Chapter 17

Chaos or Community

Sixteen per cent of Washington's children (and the poorer ones) should have 16% of the city's public recreation facilities and programs instead of having to rest content with less than 5% of its supervised play space and 10% of its full-time recreation supervisors. While the recreation situation in Capitol East is bleak, it is not hopeless. With imagination, energy, money and without destroying people's homes, the present picture could be greatly improved.

These recommendations will, however, remain but words and hopes unless the Recreation Board and Department tackle the problem with unaccustomed energy and determination. Finally, of course, until Washington manages its own affairs, the ultimate arbiter will remain Congress, which bears the responsibility for providing appropriations needed to assure that inner city neighborhoods, including the Capitol's back yard, have adequate public facilities.

—Emergency Recreation Council for Capitol East,
"The Capitol's Backyard: A Citizen's Survey of Recreation Problems and Possibilities," October 31, 1965

Six weeks before their deaths, Audrey and Stephen Currier's Christmas card to Lady Bird accompanied a gift of two miniature topiaries. In Renaissance art, Audrey explained, each herb carried a specific meaning. For Lady Bird's topiaries, the Curriers chose rosemary, for remembrance.[1] Writing in her own longhand alongside the cursive, typewritten thank-you note she had dictated earlier, Lady Bird praised the couple for their support of Halprin's exciting, "catalytic" work. Invoking that new urban planning buzzword, Lady Bird indicated that she fully understood the value of urban design with a "strong sense of place and authenticity," in lieu of traditional, large-scale urban renewal and redevelopment.[2] Just nine days before their deaths, the First Lady wrote the Curriers, "I hope we can be forceful enough to make some part of it at least a reality."[3] Without the man whom she had described as a "modern Medici," her own catalytic impact on Washington, D.C.'s future now stood in jeopardy.[4]

At first, Lady Bird's staff and her "little David of a committee" clawed through the maze of local and federal bureaucracy, assuming that even without Stephen and Audrey, their Taconic Foundation would not abandon the First Lady, and that its seed grant would indeed help the East Wing leverage federal funds for the District. With outreach to local communities a key criterion, Sharon Francis's first order of business was to report back to the organizers of the Emergency Recreation Council for Capitol East, whose ideas now had the potential to materialize, with a push from the other LBJ.

Seizing on support from the White House, the Capitol East organizers plastered their neighborhoods with fifteen thousand flyers inviting residents to attend a town hall meeting at the integrated Hine Junior High School, where the First Lady's aide would seek the community's input.[5] *The Capitol East Gazette* grasped the significance: "[T]he power of White House backing and the personal interest of Mrs. Johnson can not help but improve the chances of these plans becoming reality."[6] On a snowy night in February, just eight blocks from the Capitol dome, hundreds of people packed the school gym. Prim in her sweater set, her headband holding her long, blond hair away from her face, the twenty-nine-year-old Sharon Francis, now the mother of a young toddler, stood before the assembled community members. After a short presentation on Halprin's Capitol East ideas, ideas that had been drawn directly from the community, she opened up the evening for comment.[7] Feedback was largely positive, some downright exuberant, but there was also some resistance in the crowd, though not from the most disenfranchised African American families. The "white, Capitol Hill Restoration types" of the Capitol Hill Restoration Society and the Capitol Hill Southeast Citizens Association balked at the idea of desegregated, publicly funded recreational facilities in their midst, Sharon later told the First Lady.[8] Yet, in a letter to the editor published by *The Evening Star,* Capitol Hill resident Jesse Locke wrote to correct the impression that black residents also opposed the Halprin plan. He minced no words:

> If these purse-proud segregationist haters of the Great Society who are against the swimming pool for our neighborhood, who have opposed a decent-sized and integrated Hine Junior High School, who don't care about the poor people whose houses are being torn down to make way for the freeway, don't want beautification, that's ok. But the rest of us—the majority—who live between the Capitol Building and the Anacostia River do want more recreational facilities for all ages and a better neighborhood in which to live. The public and Mrs. Johnson ought to know that.[9]

The Capitol Hill Restoration Society's stated concerns, that Halprin's plan stood to *decrease* the value of residential property, was a dog whistle that hardly concealed a deep resistance to altering the established racial order of the neighborhood. It was a perverse objection. But one that went to the heart of the powerful potential of beautification, unobjectionable as the term appeared on the surface. In reporting to the First Lady and to the Taconic Foundation about the clash of opinions at the town hall, Sharon acknowledged, "It was the first time their opinions had been publicly sought . . . and they expressed years of pent-up advice on crime, police, lighting, litter, franchise, and everything else, including what we asked for: open space." "The restoration society people," she surmised, "were insulted that we had not praised their achievements more: the hard core, middle-aged segregationists were in opposition; the deprived were impatient. . . . But even before the marathon meeting of February 9th was over (but after the reporters filed their stories), the frustration began to spend itself and constructive comments" began to flow.[10] Following the community meeting, two hundred proposals from twenty-five more community groups reached the White House. The open invitation to participate had struck a chord.[11]

The same could not be said for Shaw. There is no evidence that Walter Fauntroy or any of the other Shaw community activists working under the MICCO banner had the opportunity to weigh in on Halprin's ideas for interior blocks or school renovations, for example. Perhaps Shaw's blackness; Fauntroy's alliance with Martin Luther King, Jr., and well-established access to the West Wing; and King's condemnation of the Vietnam War and focus on living conditions in American cities made Shaw just too political for the East Wing. Or perhaps the Beautification Committee simply didn't think to reach out to Walter Fauntroy. Or perhaps, knowing MICCO's adamancy about Shaw community participation in shaping any future "renewal" projects, and absent a living, breathing document yet to have been produced by Shaw activists along the lines of the Capitol East road map, and without Walter Washington's bridge building to rely on, the White House simply stayed away.

There is another reason that the East Wing may have limited its involvement with Shaw. Though decrepit with slums and devoid of decent schools and other services, when it came to a newer, better version of urban renewal, Shaw, by comparison to Capitol East, was about to benefit from an embarrassment of riches. Walter Fauntroy's relative prominence helped place the neighborhood first in line for Model Cities appropriation of close to $2 million for MICCO to organize direct community participation in the renewal process.[12] Still, given the West Wing's delay in moving ahead on fair housing and other measures proposed in the 1966 White House civil rights conference Fauntroy had attended, when Halprin presented his report in January 1967, MLK's ally in Shaw had reason to doubt the potential for Congress or the White House to deliver.

Living conditions in the District were a matter of both local and national interest, to the White House and to the national civil rights movement. Just weeks after the Capitol East town hall, on a gray, chilly Sunday, Martin Luther King, Jr., returned to Shaw. He had just spent two months in Jamaica to rest and write his fourth book, *Where Do We Go from Here: Chaos or Community?* Riding in a convertible, flanked by Fauntroy and the nine-year-old Martin Jr., King led a parade of 350 cars, 1,000 marchers,

7 bands, and 12 floats through 16 blocks of the 145-block neighborhood, winding up at Cardozo High School. He spoke to a crowd of nearly 4,000 gathered in Cardozo's outdoor stadium, the U.S. Capitol dome visible just three miles in the distance. Striking the chords Lady Bird was now also striving to sound, King vowed that there was "no more serious domestic problem than that of the crisis in our cities." With Fauntroy standing behind him and his son to his right, MLK made an impassioned plea for the federal government to make Shaw a "laboratory for urban renewal and a prototype for Model Cities" nationwide, one that would, importantly, be a "massive Negro-initiated" version of urban renewal. Sounding much like Victor Gruen, King said that such a project would represent a "comprehensive assault on the central city problems of human despair and physical decay." He praised the "courageous response" of Shaw's community organizers in showing "the ability of Negro people to unite together in shaping their own destiny." But Fauntroy had already grown frustrated—Shaw's residents had yet to really take a direct, participatory role in shaping that destiny. So, King's stem-winder was also an attempt to shore up tangible community action and place the District of Columbia's problems of representation, participation, and now living conditions onto the national stage. "We did it in Montgomery and we did it in Selma." In what sounded more like a plea than reassurance, he urged his audience, "You are going to do it here in Shaw."[13]

The day before King's appearance at Cardozo, LBJ had made his own surprise trip to Shaw's LeDroit Park neighborhood. In a ceremony to mark the one-hundredth anniversary of Howard University, LBJ defended his administration's record and affirmed his commitment, despite the "retrenched and tough" opposition of his adversaries, to giving "20 million Negroes the same chance as every other American to learn, to live, to grow, to develop his abilities to the fullest . . . to pursue his individual happiness" and to addressing the still-squalid living conditions of America's urban and rural poor.[14] Although LBJ's words were well received, King's exhortation the next day, "Prepare to Participate!," his pithy slogan plastered by MICCO on posters around the neighborhood, came from a far more credible orator than the president. Bird knew her limits and knew that neither she nor Lyndon had the power to resonate with Shaw residents the way that King did. In the political spotlight for most of her adult life, the First Lady believed in the value of the rope line, of shaking every hand, in the duty to ensure universal suffrage and voter registration and to eliminate Jim Crow. Though her office and Beautification Committee were now engaged in extensive consultation with black citizen groups in Capitol East, by excluding Shaw from consultation after Halprin's initial ideas for the neighborhood, she had inadvertently widened the distance between the White House and an important hub of local activism in the District's urban planning. Yet Lady Bird believed deeply in the power of individual and community participation: in that sense, there was little distance separating the outdoor stadium where King spoke on that dreary Sunday in March from the two-lane bowling alley at Camp David where the First Lady had spent that afternoon.

* * *

Over the course of the spring, at Lady Bird's insistence, Francis worked to keep the D.C. Department of Recreation and HUD engaged. And she pressed Currier's staff for an answer about funding Halprin's proposal, warning them, by invoking Vietnam, that a "credibility gap" between talk and action was beginning to undermine the East Wing's standing with the Capitol East community.[15] The question of Taconic Foundation funding aside, the weakness of local government offices in Washington, the racism of the congressional committee that controlled the city's budgets, or the sheer lack of institutional capacity and human capital might alone torpedo the time line Halprin and Lady Bird aspired to. Under the best of circumstances, the idea of completing projects in three socially underserved, politically underrepresented D.C. neighborhoods in just eighteen months was highly ambitious. Capitol East represented the best shot at success, particularly given that the community had already organized itself. And though the initial response to Halprin's plans had produced some backlash from white and some African American residents there, the broader prospect of a boost from the White House to their community development dreams resonated with the vast majority.

To keep the embers burning that winter and spring, Kay Graham at *The Washington Post* published profiles on both Sharon and Halprin.[16] In May, Halprin returned to Washington to review the designated sites. In June, with his help, the District's Redevelopment Land Agency filed a formal application for HUD funding of over half a million dollars, to finance the development of several interior blocks in Capitol East. And in August, while multiple uprisings in American cities in the North were gripping the nation, LBJ found a way to get around House opposition to home rule by presenting a reorganization plan by executive order to create the post of mayor and by naming a nine-member, majority-black city council for the District of Columbia. With Lady Bird's strong endorsement, LBJ put aside his annoyance with Walter Washington for leaving to work for Mayor Lindsay in New York City and tapped the First Lady's longtime ally as mayor; he also appointed Walter Fauntroy and Polly Shackleton among the new council members. Even if the process itself clearly circumvented Congress, LBJ's move was the strongest sign yet of White House commitment to creating some sort of democratic local control for the District, an objective of his presidency since 1964.

But in the fall of 1967, as the White House pressed Congress for more funds for Vietnam, and in the aftermath of the summer riots in Detroit (one of the first cities to receive Model Cities funds), a House-Senate conference committee stripped 90 percent of HUD's appropriation for demonstration projects and 25 percent of its total budget, forcing a substantial reduction for the Capitol East project. Just as it was all beginning to gain traction, the death of a patron and now the budget politics of guns and butter threatened to thwart the clear material, barrier-breaking momentum behind building a more humane, community-based environment in the District of Columbia.

As enticing as the prospect of designing and overseeing upward of a dozen demonstration projects in Washington was, Halprin had other plans on deck in the Bay Area and in New York. After the Curriers' plane crashed, he stayed in close touch with Sharon, and the two coordinated their attempts to get an answer from the Taconic Foundation about what they believed to be Stephen's intentions before he died. Although Audrey had allocated half her inheritance, $300 million, for the couple's philanthropic activities, the board of the Taconic Foundation now had only limited funds to disperse after the Curriers' deaths and allocated not Halprin's full eighteen-month fee of $46,000, nor even his initial phase-one drawings, priced at $18,000. Instead, Taconic split the difference to pay Halprin for his work up until Stephen's death and an additional $10,000 for his design services through 1968, for a total of $24,000. It was a dream-killing decision. To cover the deficit, Lady Bird went to Laurance Rockefeller with a request for funding, to no avail. His regard for the First Lady was high and his largesse ample, but he preferred to choose his own projects, not inherit those orphaned by other donors. But even before Rockefeller's decision not to fund the project and the Taconic Foundation's lowball grant, Halprin had grown resigned. The fates, not the lack of money, had intervened. "Sic transit gloria mundi," he wrote, Latin for "Thus passes the glory of the world."[17]

For a deflated Lady Bird, Stephen Currier joined the list of those people, beginning with her mother when she was five years old and through to JFK when she was fifty, whose untimely deaths shaped her life and, ultimately, her legacy. By 1967, Lady Bird had felt the confidence to use her platform to make manifest her hopes that the most neglected citizens of the District of Columbia might, by virtue of living in a more humane physical environment, begin to possess a sense of hope and opportunity about their future. In Larry Halprin, Mrs. Johnson had found not only her urban design muse, but someone whose social sensibilities spoke to her own. By valuing community participation and integrated, democratic access to public spaces, Larry's aspirations paired squarely with her own, for Washington and for cities around the country. Another tragic death a year later would rekindle the potential of their partnership.

Chapter 18

"Without the Momentum of Success"

I simply did not want to face another campaign, to ask anybody for anything. Mainly the fear that haunts me is that if Lyndon were back in office for a four-year stretch—beginning when he was sixty years old—that bad health might overtake him, an attack, something not quite incapacitating, and he might find himself straining to be the sort of president he wanted to be—to put in the eighteen hours a day—and not be able to draw enough vitality from the once-bottomless well of his energy. A physical or mental incapacitation would be unbearably painful for him to recognize, and for me to watch. . . . He has had the most roaring energy and will of anybody I have ever observed. But these are not inexhaustible.

—Lady Bird Johnson, White House diary, September 8, 1967

Throughout 1967, Vietnam and uprisings in American cities had stripped momentum to renew and expand funding for the White House's domestic agenda and eaten away at LBJ's standing in the polls. The Johnsons spent much of 1967 feeling "tense, tired, and harassed," trying to beat back the "swarm of troubles" closing in on their White House.[1] With the Beautification Committee's now more ambitious objectives facing a protracted, perhaps indefinite, slowdown, Lady Bird turned her time and energy increasingly away from Washington and toward the Ranch; toward the Johnsons' new grandchild, Luci's son, Patrick Lyndon, nicknamed "Lyn"; and toward her husband's legacy. She had been working since 1965 on plans for LBJ's presidential library, researching and selecting an architect, negotiating the arrangement with the president and regents of the University of Texas at Austin, and now beginning to acquire collections for the library's holdings. In doing so, the First Lady recognized the impossibility of keeping their work under wraps. With Lyndon still in office, the "pitfalls of going public now" were "prickly with problems." Did it sound, she asked, "like self-glorification for a man in office"? Maybe so, but how, really, could they plan for the future without public scrutiny over their every move? The far thornier matter, as Lady Bird framed it, was "does this herald a decision not to run in 1968?"[2] To Bird, the clues were now obvious. But no one seemed to notice, because no one could fathom LBJ volunteering to give up on a second term.

During a press conference in March, one journalist did ask the president about his plans for a second term. "It was like a play," Lady Bird recalled. "This was one of the big lines, and the audience was very quiet. Lyndon rose to it like a good actor," replying, "I am not ready to make a decision about my future after January 1969, at this time. I think that down the road—several months from now—would be the appropriate time for an announcement of my future plans."[3] Case closed. Though out of the White House for nearly a year by then, Jack Valenti joined the Johnsons for the postmortem after the press conference. "Never has one President done so much and ignited so few," Bird recorded Valenti's take. He had put his finger on the matter that dominated Bird's thoughts as she mulled over plans for the library and, of more immediate concern, their exit from Washington. It was one thing for her husband's deeds to go unrecognized in the heat of the moment. "But will the *doing* be recorded in history? That is one of today's puzzles that I hope to live to see tomorrow give an answer to. Or does it matter if you get the *job* done, whether you get the *recognition*?" She answered her own question, and it was an answer that would animate her escalating focus, her near fixation, on how to get out of Washington without running for a second term, where she could not see a clear prospect of greater achievement for her husband. "I think it does, because you don't have the fuel to continue getting the job done without the momentum of success."[4]

The political ground had begun to shift ever since the midterms in November 1966, when the Democrats lost 47 seats in the House, 3 seats in the Senate, and 8 governorships, including California. And though the party that LBJ led still held a solid majority in Congress, many of its members now felt emboldened to challenge him. The cultural winds had also begun to shift away from the Johnson White House's claim as the standard-bearer of American liberalism. Peter, Paul and Mary had once celebrated LBJ for his civil rights victories of 1964 and 1965, and even attended Luci's wedding in 1966. Now their hit single "Blowin' in the Wind," a cover of Bob Dylan's classic, had risen to the top of antiwar protest songs. By 1967, a veteran of the Berkeley Free Speech Movement, Barbara Garson, published a feminist satire, *MacBird!*, depicting Lyndon and Lady Bird as rivals of the "amoral, calculating efficiency" of the Kennedys and the masterminds behind JFK's assassination. Garson transformed Lyndon into a "fat, yet hungry looking" caricature and, perhaps obliquely recognizing the First Lady's centrality to the White House, drew Lady Bird as "a full-blown Lady Macbeth, the prime mover toward evil of a weak, indecisive husband"—longtime White House critic Dwight Macdonald relished in "Birds of America," an essay in *The New York Review of Books*.[5]

It wasn't just the cultural elites who had their talons out. Network television coverage of the war, of the brutality of American losses and the violence inflicted by American soldiers on Vietnamese civilians, had given the lie to the White House spin that the United States was fighting a winnable, limited war, with bombing and ground operations somehow poised to cajole the Communists into peace talks. At one dinner with journalists, Lyndon, Lady Bird reported, had "very succinctly expressed" his view that coverage from Vietnam was so "prejudiced, one-sided" that "you doubted whose side the reporters were on." The president pressed his case, reading aloud from a letter that their friend John Steinbeck, then reporting from Vietnam, had written him about the war. The Johnsons and the Steinbecks had been friends since Lady Bird and the novelist's third wife, Elaine, were in college together. John Ford's 1940 film version of Steinbeck's *Grapes of Wrath*, she wrote, had "anchored" Lyndon "emotionally" to FDR's New Deal.[6] In 1964, Lady Bird arranged to distribute a folksy Steinbeck hagiography about LBJ, "A President, Not a Candidate," at the Democratic National Convention.[7] She trusted Steinbeck's loyalty to the president now and hoped again to harness his reporting and literary prowess on LBJ's behalf. Though Steinbeck's letter from on the ground in Vietnam was captivating even to the ear of the president's amazed and alarmed dinner partners, Lady Bird observed, she suspected that the novelist on this round was not getting much of a hearing by the American public. But in fact, Steinbeck's field reports and dispatches from Saigon, the last of his writing before he died the next year, did not lack for readership, reaching an audience of more than four hundred thousand. The American public, Bird agreed, simply didn't see the rationale for war now as it had during World War II, when Steinbeck had also reported, and no amount of sympathetic dispatches from either of the Steinbecks—Elaine was also writing from the field—could change public opinion. Lady Bird didn't allow herself to acknowledge that Steinbeck's literary flourishes fell flat not because of censorship or a media conspiracy against LBJ. Still, watching her husband perform that night, she did begin to recognize that his bearing on Vietnam had plainly become too forced. He had grown too unyielding in pressing his case against the American media. "I wondered," Lady Bird added, whether the guests that evening "might say to their wife when they got home that night that some folks were looking for Communists under every bed."[8]

Over the next few months, the growing din of protest against the war, against the draft, reinforced Lady Bird's focus on getting out of Washington. In Nashville, a naked man and woman, clothed only in antiwar signs, jumped at the president and First Lady's car. The Johnsons had planned to participate in ceremonies honoring Andrew Jackson, but instead, LBJ's speech before the Tennessee General Assembly transformed into an announcement of further escalation in Vietnam. Weeks after his Cardozo rally in D.C., speaking at Manhattan's Riverside Church, Rev. Martin Luther King, Jr., denounced the Vietnam War and called for the community to support draft resisters. More than one hundred thousand protesters in New York and San Francisco marched against the war the next week. Addressing a joint session of Congress, General Westmoreland urged domestic support for the war: "Backed at home by resolve, confidence, patience, determination and continued support," he asserted, "we will prevail in Viet Nam over the Communist aggressor."[9] For all his spin, Westmoreland made little headway in persuading a skeptical public to consider the war effort's alleged degrading of enemy forces as a positive development. The next day in Houston, heavyweight boxing champion Muhammad Ali appeared at a local draft board only to claim exemption on religious grounds—"as a minister of the religions of Islam," he wrote on his draft form.[10]

* * *

Though resolute in her advocacy to make Washington humane and livable for its most deprived residents, as early as 1964, Lady Bird had begun to feel that her appetite for inhabiting Washington's world of ideas and politics would at some point begin to subside. Her girls would mature and build their own families, and she wanted to reserve the time and psychic energy for them that she had lacked when they were younger, when building Lyndon's career took precedence. She had grown up largely without a mother herself, and raised her own daughters without a maternal grandmother, as Bird's own mother had done until *her* early death at age forty-four. By becoming a grandmother herself, Bird had disrupted the pattern and now counted the months and conspired with her closest confidants, and with Lyndon, over when and how to tell the American public that their presidency would soon come to an end.

In the three years since her Huntland strategy memo to Lyndon first placed a date for withdrawal on their calendar, the country had changed dramatically. And Lyndon's mood and erratic behavior increasingly reflected his immense frustration over and exhaustion from trying to lead a country he felt he misunderstood and that misunderstood him. With war abroad and riots at home, and cleavages of race and class roiling both conflicts, especially at home, the Johnsons felt that the very people whose lives they'd hoped to improve with new civil rights laws and billions in Great Society programs were now sabotaging political support for those programs by ravaging American cities and inflaming white reaction against government largesse. In Selma two years earlier, the president had federalized the Alabama National Guard in order to protect civil rights activists against local police violence. But the federal intervention he authorized in Detroit that July to join forces with the Michigan National Guard to suppress the predominantly African American uprising exposed the limits of LBJ's tolerance for protest. The Detroit riots left 43 dead, 1,189 injured, 7,200 arrested, and 2,000 burned buildings in their wake, the bloodiest uprising since the New York City draft riots in 1863 and certainly since the Watts riots began the surge two years earlier.

In the immediate aftermath of Detroit, Lyndon and Lady Bird gathered before dinner one late July evening on the Truman Balcony with Oveta Culp Hobby, chair of the board of *The Houston Post,* and Abe and Carol Fortas, most all of them southerners who understood the intensity of the American apartheid system Lyndon was trying to undo. A Supreme Court associate justice at the time, Abe sought to bring some context to the mystified Johnsons. They had shared his liberalism and relied on his loyalty and counsel since Lyndon's 1948 Senate race. Blurring the separation of powers, he now served not only on the highest court in the land but also as an undeclared senior adviser on matters large and small in the executive branch. Abe's counsel on race relations in the United States struck a chord with the Johnsons, and it made its way to Lady Bird's diary that night.

> I remember at one point something that Abe said about the country's whole handling of racial inequality and injustices, and the monumental attempt we have made in the last few years to even things up. I gathered from what he said that the very fact that we had tried so hard and done so much in the last few years might be the forerunner, even the cause, of this rioting now.[11]

She had it half right—Bird agreed with moderate and even radical black critics that the reforms were not enough, but from where she sat, she did not see how the machine of government, given the palpable racism and bias in Congress and the country, could bring about deeper changes, advance the hands of time, any more quickly. Lady Bird pressed for more reassurance, cold comfort though it was. "Yes, it's like steam accumulating in a boiling pot. If you lift the lid it comes out in a great 'whoosh' that may be destructive. The other way to handle it is like they do in South Africa, where they don't even lift the lid at all," Abe offered. At dinner afterward, and dieting yet again, Lady Bird "succeeded valorously," limiting herself to eating only meat and salad, no starch. And for her drink, no gin, just tonic. Despite the deprivation, she "felt very self-satisfied." It wasn't just the nutritional self-control she exhibited—she had demonstrated as much time and again—but the awareness of the immense privilege of finding herself sitting on that Truman Balcony, gazing out over the South Lawn at the Washington Monument, knowing that in Washington, she could partake in the most consequential conversations of the day. In preparing to "come down from the mountain" and walk away from it all, Bird "began to feel a sort of comfort in saying goodbye . . . curiously light and free."[12]

Indeed, it was during a recent Saturday afternoon conversation with Abe that Bird sorted through the various elements she felt would condition the timing of Lyndon's announcement. The First Lady typically reserved her Saturdays as "a blank day on the calendar—a sort of creative day—to think, to plan," to regenerate, to walk the Mall with Libby Rowe, to talk through her Washington projects with Polly Shackleton, to escape to the National Gallery with Lynda when she was in town. Bird had invited Abe in confidence to discuss the "subject that has engaged so much of my thinking ever since Lyndon got into this job—how to get out and when." She summed up the thoughts she shared with him: "Many, many months ago I set March '68 in my own mind as the time when Lyndon can make a statement that he would not be a candidate for reelection." She explained that she had "counted first the years and then the months until that time. Now it is ten months away," and she had begun to imagine Lyndon as a "happy retired man," busy with the Ranch, with the school of public affairs, an occasional lecture. But there was more than the prospect of a happy retirement that concerned her. Their health preoccupied both Johnsons, ever more so as Lyndon approached age sixty, the age his father died of the heart disease that brought early death to all the men in his family. "I do not know whether we can *endure* another four-year term in the presidency. And I used that word in Webster's own meaning—'to last, to remain, continue in the same state' without perishing." Aside from her ongoing dental issues and adjusting to what appeared to be signs of menopause, Lady Bird's own health was superb. But she confided in Abe, who was raised in an Orthodox Jewish home, "The prospect of another campaign I face like an open-ended stay in a concentration camp." Throughout 1967, she had thought that "Lyndon was of the same mind as me—that he would at some time announce that he would not be a candidate for reelection." Despite her repeated insistence, Lady Bird could not at that moment be entirely sure of the path Lyndon would take—not until he made his decision public. As she saw it, there were two factors that perversely enough might push him to run for reelection. One was bad polling numbers or, more specifically, "if Bobby Kennedy's lead was so strong that it looked like he, Lyndon, could not be elected. That might force him to try" to prove he could nevertheless beat RFK. The second factor was Vietnam. In Lady Bird's assessment at the time, the prospect of a victorious end to the war was still imaginable, and could set up a winning platform on which to run again, providing "a wonderful beckoning hope that the enormous economic muscle of this country which in the past six or seven years has grown so vastly could be harnessed to achieving the goals of the Great Society, rebuilding the cities, and work on health and education and conservation. That could be really a siren song" to compel Lyndon toward running for a second term.[13]

Abe, Bird recorded, believed that "Lyndon had done enough—and worked enough with his life—so that he could, about next March, make that announcement if things in the war were going good." The prospect that the war in Vietnam could be brought to an honorable conclusion as soon as March 1968, just ten months away, gives a sense of how even Lyndon's closest confidants so thoroughly misjudged the potential for American military power to tame Vietnamese craving for sovereign independence. But Abe did raise the alternative. Should things in Vietnam stay "as bad as now or worse," there was no way Lyndon could stand not to run again. He would have to "try for the nomination," which he may or may not obtain. And also for the election, which he may or may not win, Fortas reasoned. The "solemn, rather sad talk" with Abe reinforced and boosted Lady Bird's confidence that Lyndon's "place in history was assured, whether he served out this term or was elected again or died tonight." But it also alerted her to the daunting possibility that should the war go from bad to worse, at least from Abe's perspective, Lyndon would have no choice but to stay in the game. At all costs, though, Abe insisted that Lyndon make neither a decision nor an announcement before the following March, as doing so could "hamstring, almost immobilize, the war effort and Lyndon's domestic leadership in the country."[14]

The ninety minutes with Abe had helped her rethink and revise the conditions and timing for Lyndon's decision about a second term: Bobby Kennedy's entry into the race might compel Lyndon to run again, of this she was already thoroughly aware. But what now became a new part of her thinking was the prospect that an ugly, protracted war in Vietnam might likewise oblige Lyndon to stay the course. Gone now was the bouncy lilt and lift. Her tone both low and serious, and audibly allowing a beat between each of her words, Bird reflected that her, *their*, presidency's conundrum "was never far from my thoughts. I cannot control the outcome, though I will have some effect on it. And it will not, I hope, be decided until next March." Yet she found it impossible to suppress her desire for assurance that, come March 1968, Lyndon would follow through with their understanding and enable her to begin her final countdown. And she channeled her uncertainty into conversations that focused on not if, but on how and when Lyndon would exit center stage.[15]

Though unpredictable, the anticipation of getting out of the White House buoyed Lady Bird's spirits with the passing of each day. Over Labor Day weekend with Luci—whose baby boy, Lyn, born in June, increasingly became the center of the First Couple's family life—mother and daughter found themselves "in a deep, deep discussion of her daddy's problem." As her daughters grew into adults and Lady Bird into middle age, the confidences they shared morphed from the patient, often amused listening and guidance of adolescence to much more of a give-and-take. Lyndon and Luci had become increasingly close during the White House years of family life under one roof: she had become, Bird observed, Lyndon's "most understanding champion." As a new mother herself, Luci was adamant and unequivocal that he not run again. Late one night in the guest room of Pat and Luci's Austin townhouse, Luci told her mother, "I want my daddy alive." Lady Bird slept well that night, her belly full of a bucket of her favorite Youngblood's Fried Chicken. She felt "an increasing glow," a "sort of relief that expands into confidence" that elections two days earlier in Vietnam might signal a politically stable future and pave the way for an American exit, and thus factor into Lyndon's own withdrawal from public life. But the elections were followed by a show of force from both Hanoi and Washington, moves intended to ensure the strongest possible position during negotiations should satisfactory terms for peace talks finally emerge.[16]

* * *

Vietnam remained a major, though not the only, consideration dictating the timing of the public reveal of the Johnsons' plans to leave politics. Texas governor John Connally had long tied his political fate to LBJ's, dating back to 1939, when a freshman congressman Johnson hired the twenty-two-year-old Connally as his aide. Shot but not mortally wounded in Dallas on November 22, 1963, Connally in 1967 was completing his fourth year in the governor's mansion and contemplating his own future, one inextricably entwined with Lyndon's. Over the course of several conversations in the fall of 1967, Connally pressed Lyndon to announce his decision not to run as early as October at a major Democratic Party fundraising event, which would thus free Connally to preserve the option to run in 1968 as a conservative Democrat—and an alternative to Bobby. One September afternoon at the Ranch, the president, the governor, and Congressman J. J. "Jake" Pickle, also a former aide, spent eight hours driving around in Lyndon's white convertible Cadillac, churning over every element of his decision and its timing. The president called the First Lady on the business telephone. Where was she? "It was the wrong thing to do," but she had been working on yet more house renovations and, at the moment of Lyndon's call, was having her hair done. Her perspective was essential, so wearing her yellow silk robe, her hair still rolled into sausage curls, Lady Bird joined the three men for what she regarded as the most consequential conversation that year about her and Lyndon's future.[17]

LBJ grasped for the explanation he would proffer to the public. Connally tried his hand, suggesting that the president "wanted to devote all his time, his brains, his energy, in the coming fifteen or sixteen months to bringing the war in Vietnam to a successful conclusion, to attacking the problems of the cities—in short, to working on the major difficulties that face this country. A campaign would necessarily siphon off hours and days of time and energy and brainpower. He wanted to be free to do his best in the time he had"—and, as LBJ later told historian Doris Kearns Goodwin, without the partisanship that a campaign would necessarily entail. This formula, for domestic political, if not international, peace, had been months and months in the making, and the product not only of the Johnsons' waking hours of deliberation, but also of sleepless nights and taunting nightmares for both of them.[18] "I think we all knew," Lady Bird surmised, "that we would only really know what was going to happen when we heard it happen."[19] The marathon session concluded over dinner—shrimp curry eaten off TV trays.

During a sleepless night together later that month, "one of those bleak nights when the shadows take over," Lyndon and Bird again ran through their options. They had missed two chances to announce his decision—his birthday at the end of August and the Vietnamese elections earlier that month. Now the party fundraiser in October, Connally's preference for LBJ's announcement, was around the corner. Lady Bird felt that disappointing the party's most loyal donor base at an event of that scale would be a political misfire and also, following Abe's logic, simply premature. "In these discussions I felt that Lyndon reaches out to me more than ever, and yet I do not have the wisdom, the foresight for the answer. The only gift I have is the assurance that I will be content and happy saying goodbye to all this, much as I have loved it, deeply immersed as I have been in every day, even the painful ones."[20]

And not all of them were painful. Judging from her diary, on many days, maybe even most, Lady Bird's idealism about the possibility of LBJ's and her advocacy for the urban environment amply compensated for the constant undertow of Lyndon's depression and uncertainty, or for the public backlash against the war and against the depletion of resources at home. In New York City earlier that year, the First Lady was honored by the Citizens' Committee for Children for her work with Head Start. Inside the ballroom of the Pierre hotel, Lady Bird saw not the hypocrisy claimed by her husband's critics but a who's who of New York's "power structure . . . oriented toward the legal and educational and social rights of children." She yearned to immerse herself in "the brains, the hopes, the works, and experiences in the past of so many of these people," and she tried to come to terms with the contradiction she was living: that the rancor her husband's presidency had uncorked could coexist "in the midst of the utmost affluence, opportunity, hope that the world perhaps has ever known." Antiwar activists from Women Strike for Peace, among them Head Start teachers, had issued a press statement describing the bestowal of the award on Mrs. Johnson as "tasteless" and "morally outrageous" given how the war was denying Vietnamese children a decent life and sapping funds from Head Start. With protesters chanting the now-familiar "Hey, hey, LBJ, how many kids did you kill today?" as she accepted her award, the First Lady delivered a speech about early childhood education holding the key to breaking the cycle of poverty. She ticked off a by-the-numbers account of the impact of Job Corps, Community Action, and Head Start programs. But Lady Bird knew that the real star of the show that evening wasn't the president's wife. It was Thurgood Marshall, the solicitor general of the United States. The First Lady had never heard him speak, and he dazzled her with his control of the audience, beginning "in a quiet manner" and allowing his voice to "crescendo powerfully." "[P]retty soon I realized I was in the presence of an orator." High praise from a severe critic of public speech—her own, her husband's, and that of whoever else crossed her path. "There is a real emergency involved," Marshall admonished the audience. "Children cannot be held up in their growth. With or without justice or equality of opportunity they will grow up. They will grow up into either the reformatory or college." Watching him up on the stage, Bird wrote of the pioneering jurist, "I was proud that he was in the Administration."[21]

The next month, LBJ nominated Marshall to fill the seat on the Supreme Court of the retiring associate justice, Texan, and close Johnson friend Tom Clark. By nominating Marshall to the post, LBJ wanted to leave no doubt in the public's mind about his commitment to racial equality, and no other contender possessed the stature or the name recognition of Thurgood Marshall. But Lady Bird, despite her reverence for the West Baltimore native, had a dissenting view, at once both overestimating the near-term impact of LBJ's civil rights policies and also progressive in her desire for him to expand upon that agenda. The president's staff assistant Joe Califano recorded the First Lady's approach: "Oh Lyndon, you've done so much for the negroes, isn't it time to nominate a woman to the Supreme Court?"[22]

But in 1967, the country's focus on civil rights in America remained squarely on race, not yet gender. The National Organization for Women (NOW) was only one year old, and the Supreme Court was still six years away from handing down an 8–1 decision on *Frontiero v. Richardson,* one of its first rulings on gender discrimination, specifically in the military. That case was brought in 1973 by the forty-year-old ACLU lawyer and future Supreme Court justice Ruth Bader Ginsburg. It would be fourteen years until a president appointed a woman to the Supreme Court, when Ronald Reagan nominated Sandra Day O'Connor to replace the retiring Potter Stewart.

Although LBJ did not yet see the women's movement as the major social and political force it was becoming, he did not miss Bird's broader point. Later that year, Lyndon and Lady Bird hosted more than one hundred women in the military for a ceremony to mark the signing into law of a bill two years in the making, one that provided equal opportunity in promotions for women in the armed forces. One of its major advocates,

Oveta Culp Hobby, director of the Women's Army Auxiliary Corps, joined the Johnsons in the East Room for the signing ceremony. Although at the time the bill served the primary purpose of expanding the pool of possible soldiers available for Vietnam, it paved the way for women to be eligible for promotions beyond the rank and pay of major or, in rare cases, colonel, the limit since 1948, when President Truman first opened the officer corps to women. The law had cleared Congress earlier that spring, but LBJ waited until November 1967 for a public signing ceremony. Surrounded by a number of women in the military, including fifty who had flown in from Vietnam, and Republican senator Margaret Chase Smith, the first woman to serve in both chambers of Congress, LBJ made a small, albeit significant gesture to support women with aspirations toward military service.[23] With the opportunity for officer promotions generally tied to combat experience, and combat open to women only in 2013, the new law, LBJ acknowledged, did not result in an immediate breaking of the glass ceiling in the leadership of the American armed forces, but it served as a step in the right direction.

Lyndon gave one signing pen to Oveta, surprised Lady Bird by handing her another, and gave the last to his secretary, Juanita Roberts, one of the first officers of the Women's Army Auxiliary Corps to be promoted to colonel. But to Lady Bird, "really the most touching part of the day" was when the president presented the Bronze Star to Major Marie Rodgers, a fifteen-year veteran of the U.S. Army Nurse Corps, to honor her distinguished service. In 1966, Rodgers volunteered for service in Vietnam, where, as the lone African American on the medical staff in her unit, she supervised the operating room at an evacuation hospital located about twelve miles outside Saigon and known unofficially as Long Binh Junction, or LBJ. It was an honor, Bird recognized, that "struck just the right note," one punctuated, she thought, by the fact that just the day before, voters in Gary, Indiana, and Cleveland, Ohio, had elected their first African American mayors.[24]

Although LBJ's nomination of Thurgood Marshall to the Supreme Court reflected his desire to secure his own legacy and to further institutionalize the country's civil rights progress, an objective Lady Bird thoroughly shared, he was aware of the power women represented, or could represent, in American political life. The president shared with his audience that day his vision for a far less discriminatory future for American women, however distant. "The bill does not create any female generals or female admirals—but it does make that possible. There is no reason why we should not someday have a female Chief of Staff or even a female Commander in Chief." Though reported by the major wire services, LBJ's really quite radical statement—followed by a male chorus singing, in grudging recognition of female power, "There Is Nothing Like a Dame," from Rodgers and Hammerstein's Broadway musical *South Pacific*—was drowned out by the dissonance of Vietnam and obscured by profound distrust of the White House, including by the country's leading women's rights groups.[25]

Chapter 19

The Generation Gap

If I had to capsule these two days in academia, how would I? For one thing, both campuses seemed quite set apart from the world—insulated, encased in gelatin with the window on only one issue—Vietnam. There was also that feeling of a fascist society where everybody that thinks the same and does the same thing and everybody who dares not has to be pretty brave—a sort of McCarthyism in reverse.

—Lady Bird Johnson, White House diary, October 9, 1967

With Luci easing into motherhood, Lady Bird's focus shifted toward Lynda's future. After graduating from UT, Lynda traveled, dated, and took a stab at journalism. Although she had a taste for glamour and for surrounding herself with the beautiful people in Acapulco, Hollywood, and Madrid, she soon settled down with a steady boyfriend, marine captain Chuck Robb, at the time detailed as a social aide to the White House, and she set her sights on looking for a job in New York City. Lynda entertained offers from the Ford Foundation and *National Geographic*. Ultimately, the best fit came in the form of a job as a part-time editor for *McCall's* in its Washington office. The magazine created a new section for and by young American women and hired the president's elder daughter as its first editor. "Women are interested in thinking—civil rights, peace. They are interested in people, but on a more sophisticated basis. They want substance they can relate to in their own lives," editor Robert Stein told *The Christian Science Monitor* in 1966. In 1956, as editor of *Redbook* magazine, Stein had commissioned "Our Weapon Is Love," a profile of Martin Luther King, Jr., and he ran King's columns in *Redbook* for years thereafter. Stein had a knack for hiring, and later firing, a number of young writers who would rank among the most influential in their fields: he fired film critic Pauline Kael over her scathing criticism of popular American softball hits such as *Born Free* and *The Sound of Music*, and Betty Friedan over an offensive analogy she drew between the oppression of women in suburbia and concentration camps.[1]

Friedan went on to describe *Redbook* and *McCall's* as "propaganda organs" for domesticating American women. And *McCall's* did steer clear of openly declaring its allegiance in the cold and hot wars between races, genders, and nations then causing such turbulence in the American identity. But with *Ms.* magazine's debut still years away, *McCall's* stepped in, offering writing by a slate of serious, predominantly female authors—Barbara Tuchman, Rachel Carson, and an author whose Alabama roots paralleled Bird's own, Harper Lee—that reflected an awareness of how much the country was changing. In articles by guest writers, the magazine sought to explain those changes to its predominantly female, educated audience: Gloria Steinem published a string of profiles—on Truman Capote, Margot Fonteyn, and Hugh Hefner. James Baldwin published fiction dealing with interracial relationships, bisexuality, and Christian fundamentalism; and the conservative Catholic writer Clare Boothe Luce gave her two cents on the righteousness of the Pill over the rhythm method. A regular *McCall's* feature, called simply "Medicine," in 1967 ran pieces on the Pill, IUDs, breast cancer research, LSD and pregnancy, sleep, midlife crises, the sexual revolution, psychiatry, and the pope's views on family planning.[2]

McCall's readership counted themselves less as changemakers than as those who wanted and needed to understand the changes being pushed by their daughters and even by some of the magazine's authors. It was an audience that, having read excerpts in *McCall's* and in its rival publication, *Ladies' Home Journal*, of Friedan's *Feminine Mystique* earlier in the decade, was attuned to the somnolence of living the "problem that has no name." Although Lynda's readers likely agreed with the feminist call for equal opportunity, they were not exactly the ones out in the streets demanding that change.

Like the First Lady herself, *McCall's* might have appeared as an emblem of a traditional take on the American woman, but its progressive impulses suggested otherwise. The job at *McCall's* gave Lynda a vehicle to explain her generation's choices to her readers, to herself, and, notably, to her parents, especially her mother. The country was undergoing a massive cultural transformation, and the institution of the widely circulated women's magazine served as one barometer of that change. The draft, the war—these were the polarizing policies for which the public now hated LBJ. But for young women in 1967, one of the most culturally transformative policies Lynda's parents had also advocated for, albeit with little public credit, was universal access to the Pill.

The 1965 *Griswold v. Connecticut* Supreme Court ruling had established a constitutional right to privacy, but the ruling for which *Griswold* would lay a foundation, *Roe v. Wade,* was still six years away. Thus, the Pill marked the innovation that made possible both the racy liberation of free love and the autonomy to choose when to have children. American women, the advertising and lifestyle articles in *McCall's* conveyed, might still hold forth as hostesses and homemakers, but the magazine's content showed that American women were also Vietnam War correspondents and sharp-witted political analysts, and now with the potential for reproductive autonomy.[3]

For her very first cover story, Lynda and her boss, *McCall's* Washington Bureau chief, Christine Sadler, traveled together to Palo Alto, California, to conduct a series of interviews. The discussions offered a glimpse into a very narrow swath of young American women and their mothers, ten from each generation. Still, they provided material for Lynda to make some observations about the issues dividing and uniting the generations in the state, now led by Governor Reagan, that Lady Bird and much of the country closely identified with the confluence of environmental conservation, conservative politics, protest, and radical culture.

Although none of the young Stanford women would admit to the president's daughter that they had actually done drugs, and maybe they had not, they did express strong criticism of their parents' snap dismissal of hypothetical drug use. As for the Pill, they found their mothers to be more accepting of their choice to have sex but avoid pregnancy. Their mothers confided separately, though, that they nevertheless believed that easy access to birth control and thus multiple short-term relationships risked leaving their daughters unprepared for the hard work, self-abnegation, and emotional dimensions of marriage. For the daughters, sex and drugs were hardly novel phenomena in American society, and the young women resented the hypocrisy of their parents for suggesting otherwise. Even as the mothers criticized their daughters as the self-centered "*me* generation and the *now* generation," they were sympathetic to the desire to find an escape from problems "like the war and having to go to war and the tragedy of all kinds in the world today." Lynda concluded, perhaps autobiographically, "The girls saw themselves flexible, receptive to new ideas and intellectually imaginative, while they thought of their parents' generation as essentially inflexible, set in its ways and seriously behind the times." The young women she had spoken with believed it was their role to guide their parents through the new realities of the country. "Many of the girls felt the necessity of 'bringing up' their parents, of acquainting them with the new ideas and events that concern young people." On Vietnam, the Johnsons' elder daughter would come to do the same with her own parents.[4]

Lynda's fair-minded, though somewhat anodyne, generation gap reporting and, more important, their private catch-ups may well have served to "bring up" and gently alert her mother to those uncomfortable truths in the realm of "lifestyle choices," a term much in vogue at the time. But it was Lady Bird's own visits to college campuses in New England that fall that delivered a far more unvarnished picture of just how yawning the American generation gap had become.

* * *

For Lady Bird, the fall of 1967 solidified her growing belief that the presidency was no longer a place from which she and her husband could do their best for their country or their family. Their lives in Washington, she vividly described, had grown rank from the stench of an "avalanche" of "pernicious fruit," poisoned by a "tidal wave of stories, murmurs, whispers that create distrust, frustration, and uncertainty."[5] Lyndon himself began to float with a wider circle the idea of forgoing a second term. He sent his press secretary George Christian to Texas to work with John Connally on a draft resignation statement. He pointedly raised the prospect of not running again in the middle of a meeting on national security and foreign policy with Secretaries Rusk and McNamara, Special Assistant for National Security Affairs Walt Rostow, and Director of Central Intelligence Richard Helms, but they didn't yet take the president seriously.[6] The antiwar movement was planning its biggest protest yet, a march to the Pentagon set for late October, and Lyndon's doctors were growing increasingly concerned about the president's health. After examining him, his longtime cardiologist J. Willis Hurst asked to see the First Lady so that he could confide in her:

> [The president's] feeling of mere anxiety had not abated. He did not see the bounce, the laughter, the teasing quality in Lyndon that he has watched over these twelve years. He thought he was running on marginal energy—quite simply that he was bone tired. . . . He kept on saying that he expected a part of it must be a psychological result of seeing four papers every morning and three screens of television that kept shouting all of the troubles of the world and all the things he was doing wrong—the declining polls, the rising frustrations.[7]

Although she was careful not to let on exactly why, Lady Bird jumped at the opening to press Dr. Hurst about their future. "I asked him point blank if he thought as Lyndon's doctor that he ought not to run again because of his health." This was the first time Hurst had raised such concern about Lyndon's condition with Bird. Yet she didn't get the answer she might have expected or hoped. "And here," the First Lady recorded, "he came to a dead stop." Hurst told Bird that "it was beyond medical knowledge to determine what result" not running again might yield for Lyndon, adding, "I don't think he can quit. . . . Because he hasn't done everything he wants to. That will never happen."[8] Hurst, who admired the First Lady for her "poise and stature and presence," did offer one uncomfortable piece of advice: "I think you ought not to travel so much. I think it matters to him for you to be with him. Stay home."[9] She was supposed to leave town the next morning.

Though Lady Bird reminded herself of Hurst's cautionary note about the perils of working on "marginal energy," the doctor's visit the day before had in fact left Lyndon feeling better, his spirits high. He was looking "jovial, full of controlled energy, cool and tough." And so, Mrs. Johnson decided to follow through with a trip to New England to speak at Yale University and Williams College. With possibly only fifteen months remaining of the Johnson presidency, the First Lady didn't want to "stay home"; she wanted to raise the profile of her portfolio focused on making American cities livable, not only in the flyover states where she was more comfortable, but also before the coastal elites, or at least their draft-age children. That summer, she had reached that very audience through a three-part *New York Times* series by Nan Robertson, reporting, before Congress drastically cut funds, on the scope of HUD's grants for green spaces and other urban beautification projects, an accomplishment the First Lady regarded as a feather in her cap and evidence that policy and political space for such projects might still be expanded. But this campus trip provided a novel opportunity to amplify her message—especially to the younger generation whom she often found hard to understand, despite her daughters' tutorials.[10]

At Williams, presidential historian James MacGregor Burns had become involved in launching one of the country's first environmental studies centers at an American liberal arts college: the country's leading environmentalists, landscape architects, architects, and philanthropists would convene for the weekend, and the First Lady would speak. Yale was also a pioneer in environmental studies, and New Haven an early recipient of now-much-criticized urban renewal funds. The Yale Political Union offered Lady Bird a platform to make her case for municipal, state, and federal involvement in making cities livable for all citizens. Against a backdrop of the yellows, reds, and oranges of the New England fall foliage, campus-wide resistance over Vietnam greeted the First Lady at both stops.

By the eve of her arrival, the Williams faculty had circulated a petition signed by more than half the 1,225 undergraduates and 56 of the 113 professors, protesting Vietnam and the "diversion of funds that are needed for urgent urban and environmental problems at home" and objecting to Mrs. Johnson's appearance there.[11] Although picket signs and protesters accompanied her throughout the duration of her stay in Williamstown (even from the National League for Freedom from Vaccinations), so, too, did townies hoping to catch a glimpse of the First Lady, providing Bird with a benign, even comforting alternative to the "furies" escorting her around campus. Though she credited the protesters with emboldening her during her speech, she couldn't escape the "ugly murmur" or the chants of "shame, shame" by the Williams Committee for Action and Resistance crowding her airspace. Playing to stereotypes, the *Williams Newsletter* published a photograph of the First Lady speaking to the college president, the crowd in the backdrop. Its caption describes her as "seemingly oblivious."[12] Hardly—Lady Bird was taking it all in, and found something "weird and animal about mob psychology." Though she thought momentarily about fleeing the scene, she mustered a smile instead and kept to her "dignified gate." As she walked among the protesters, she felt "cool and firm and determined to maintain dignity." As tough an exterior as she managed to muster, she found herself unsettled: "[T]hrough every pore you sense a sort of an animal passion right below the surface."[13] It wasn't the intensity and anger that threw her for a loop—in fact, their display seemed to harden her resolve—but rather, it was the way the venom spread among the student body, unrelenting once it started to take hold, that gave her real pause.

Protest was hardly new to the First Lady: for years now, she had heard it nearly every day in Washington, wafting from Lafayette Square, on Pennsylvania Avenue, just beyond the White House grounds. But the Williams visit marked the first time since the whistle-stop tour in 1964 that Lady Bird herself had been the direct target of the public's sustained wrath. Back then, touring through the South, she had held the high ground while preaching the message of progress embodied by her husband's civil rights agenda to a skeptical, reactionary public. Now, to this generation, no matter the forward-looking vision of her environmental message, she and her husband stood on the wrong side of the moral issue of the day—an unfamiliar, even unsettling place for a public servant who had grown accustomed to quietly breaking down barriers. "All in all," she concluded, "I guess I lost this round."[14]

Lady Bird loved New England's charm, "but did not feel the least kinship to it."[15] But she did feel a connection to Yale, or so she thought. She had been to New Haven and to the Yale campus several times over the years, to meet with Mayor Richard Lee, one of the early champions and beneficiaries of urban renewal and later her push for beautification in American cities, and to scout out potential architects for the LBJ library. But on this occasion, it was only a matter of minutes after she arrived that she began to sense that this visit would be different.

As with her stop at Williams, when Lady Bird arrived at Yale, a crowd of protesters greeted her. Gathered outside the home of Yale president Kingman Brewster, they waved signs—"Stop Beautifying Vietnam," "Tell LBJ to Withdraw Now"—some bearing photographs of napalm victims. But Vietnam wasn't the only issue. The *Yale Daily News* also reported protests accusing the university of practicing discrimination in hiring and promoting "apartheid" practices by denying access to Yale housing for New Haven residents attempting to flee riots earlier that summer. It also charged Mayor Lee with relegating the city's black residents to ghettos. For Lady Bird, the message was clear: at least in New Haven, and perhaps in the rest of the country, the Great Society had failed.[16]

Once inside President Brewster's home, Bird right away became aware that "my presence here was really an imposition on him." Brewster looked and acted the part of an old-school Ivy League college president: urbane, articulate, elegant, utterly establishment. (He displayed none of these qualities in excess, one undergraduate at the time later recalled.)[17] But Lady Bird saw through his practiced affect. "His manner was absolutely correct, but if I have any antenna at all, I sense that he wished he had no part of it" and would rather have been in Paris, on a trip he had reluctantly postponed in order to host the First Lady.[18]

Under Brewster's leadership, the school known for its secret societies had just begun to open its doors beyond New England's elite prep schools—to young men, some Jewish, some African American, some from Chicago, Muskegon, and as far west as Los Angeles. Coming from small towns, with parents who were recent immigrants who ran their own businesses, or with relatives that were union members or were serving in Vietnam, the new undergrads injected the elite community with what at the time stood out as a significant dose of diversity—one if not yet based on gender or much on race, then certainly derived from their families' ethnic, geographic, demographic, and life experiences.

The Yale Political Union, a politically diverse debating society, had extended the invitation to the First Lady, and Bird found herself in impressive company by accepting it. In 1966, the group had brought Strom Thurmond, Thurgood Marshall, James Reston, Roy Wilkins, and William F. Buckley to speak. Lady Bird would be the first sitting First Lady to speak before the group; Eleanor Roosevelt had done so after FDR's death. Yale began admitting women into its graduate programs in 1892, but it wasn't until 1969 that Yale would admit its first female undergrads, a fact the Yale Political Union president noted in his invitation to Mrs. Johnson. "Even though Yale does not yet seem prepared to welcome its first co-ed, it is always prepared to welcome its First Lady."[19] But Yale's gender homogeneity at the time was the least of the controversies. Neither Eleanor nor any of the speakers the previous year had provoked the outpouring of protest that Lady Bird incited.

Prior to her visit, the Ad Hoc Committee for Peace in Vietnam organized a demonstration to greet the First Lady and collected more than six hundred signatures for an open letter about Vietnam published in the *Yale Daily News* on the day of her visit. Though commending the sincerity of the First Lady's work on beautification, the committee took her visit as an opportunity to denounce her husband's policies in Vietnam. "Those who participate in the vigil," the letter noted, "will be demonstrating on behalf of the same humanitarian values which Mrs. Johnson herself has championed. They are asking that these values apply to America's conduct in a far-off country as well as to preservation and reconstruction of our own country."[20]

Ten days away from the biggest antiwar mobilization of the Johnson presidency, the media-savvy First Lady wanted to avoid offering herself up as "camera bait for the students' demonstration." Instead of walking the short distance through Beinecke Plaza to the Freshman Commons, the venue for her talk, the woman once eager to shake every hand, now chose to drive rather than cross paths with students protesting in silent vigil. From the backseat of the car, she saw "students running pell-mell like on the football field with their signs up high and their hair flying." The woman who labored to keep every hair in place found the display of untethered anger just a little too wild.[21]

At the time, Bird recorded no doubts about the rationale behind her husband's escalation that fall, about the dead and wounded, about the blow to his cherished Great Society programs. Rather, she wielded against the students the very critique their generation now aimed at hers: conformity. She found their display "very interesting," as it "seemed a curiously fascist sort of atmosphere—very conformist. And I wondered how anyone would dare speak out on the other side for fear of ostracism by his fellows." But a car carrying pro-LBJ placards did offer a note of comfort. "I guess even in this atmosphere, there are dissenters," Bird recorded.[22]

Inside the imposing, high-ceilinged Freshman Commons, "aptly named War Memorial Hall," she recorded, Bird found herself surrounded by portraits of "long dead presidents of Yale" and some eight hundred students and faculty seated at tables throughout the wood-paneled hall. Outside, another two thousand students stood in silent vigil. Inside, President Brewster flattered the First Lady with a "generous, even eloquent," although she felt undeserved, comparison to Eleanor Roosevelt. But she resented his show of sympathy toward the student demonstrators—they had begun to chant "Hell No, We Won't Go!" and "Peace Now!"—even as she empathized with the leadership challenge he faced. Bird simply doubted this president's sincerity. His attempt to bridge the generation gap, to her ears, fell flat.[23]

The chanting outside and the tension inside the hall again pushed Bird to outdo herself. She had worked on many drafts of her speech and, against her own instincts, took the advice of her team by opening with humor. Like Lyndon, she could be stilted and stiff at the lectern or in front of the camera, and she knew it. Striving for authenticity, she told a joke about the generation gap her daughter Lynda had tried to educate her about. "I belong to the generation which thinks that when you take a trip, you go on a barge down the Mississippi River." She didn't get much of a laugh. But the substance of her speech, a pitch for integrating environmental concerns into the study of business, economics, art, or any other major, earned her a prolonged standing ovation that was "long and loud and clear," she recorded, "and I hope they heard it outside. And I was never so glad to be finished with a speech in my life." In 1972, Yale launched one of the most comprehensive environmental studies programs in the country, an approach that aligned with the interdisciplinary approach the First Lady had called for. But in 1967, what she saw as the "gelatin encasement" of American campuses, with the focus on Vietnam to the exclusion of all else, and the negative press she received, left Bird feeling alienated from a portion of the American public with which she once identified. She found herself unable to grasp the rationale behind the intensity of draft-age students, even those protected by their status or enrollment, objecting to her husband's war. Although the resounding rejection of the war still had not recast her own thinking about it, she did draw a lesson from her experience on New England campuses: "I must not live in the White House, insulated against life. I want to know what's going on—even if to know is to suffer."[24]

And suffer she did. The blinders were beginning to come off. She continued to attribute Lyndon's decline in the polls and the public's rejection of Vietnam to a "veritable propaganda war" more than to the possibility that her husband was just plain wrong and the war unwinnable. But her heightened awareness that the status quo, whatever she thought of the war's merits, had simply become unsustainable animated her pursuit of an exit from the White House. On the day before the antiwar movement would gather in Washington for its biggest national mobilization yet, Lady Bird and Lynda ate lunch in Dupont Circle at the Jockey Club. Lynda periodically brought her mother there for a quiet escape from the White House, "a kind of therapy." This time, the ripple of reaction to the First

Lady from the other patrons, Bird recorded, had tipped toward the decidedly hostile. The First Lady hated to see her daughter's plan spoiled, but "we both understood . . . [that] we are in the eye of the hurricane, and in a way helpless. But I do not want to be ignorant, I want to know." Returning to the refuge of the White House, she met in the West Hall of the family's private quarters with the second of Lyndon's long-trusted doctors, Jim Cain. She told him about "my own feelings that I did not want to go through the grueling six months of another campaign" or, if they won, have to endure "another four years as devouring as these last four years have been." But even worse to Bird was the prospect that a second term might inflict a debilitating illness on her husband, leaving him, like Woodrow Wilson, mentally or physically incapacitated but still in office. For all her activism, Lady Bird Johnson didn't see herself as Edith Wilson, as the president's gatekeeper, triaging cabinet inquiries and vetting policy proposals. An illness that might leave Lyndon deprived of strength or faculties while trapped in office "would be the most unbearable tragedy that could happen to him," she told Cain, and asked for his perspective. Cain agreed that the last four years had aged the president and "taken a lot from him."[25] Although Cain believed FDR's doctors should have cautioned against a fourth term because of Roosevelt's advanced heart disease, he was not prepared to caution Lyndon against running for a second.

Birth and death were much on Lady Bird's mind: Lyndon's health and the prospect of his survival, and by extension her own, but also the flowering of the next generation of their family. Luci and Pat began to periodically bring baby Lyn to the White House for overnights with his grandparents, and as he grew into a plump and amiable infant, he brought the president and First Lady profound joy. They sat for photographs throughout the summer. The candid shots show a family completely enthralled by their newest member, and especially a grandfather with an ease in playing with and comfort in holding and soothing his grandson. Often with Lyn's sleepovers, Lady Bird awoke to find the baby lying in bed next to his grandfather, gurgling happily, chewing on papers marked "Top Secret" while Lyndon plowed through his morning reading.

The campus tours had ruptured Bird's isolation, to be sure. "But one thing, within our own family circle, thank God, it's been good and strong and happy. All seven of us healthy, all seven of us loving."[26] After the arrival of Pat and Lyn added two to their original four, Lynda's announcement of her engagement to Captain Charles Spittal Robb, U.S. Marine Corps, made him the seventh.

Following lunch the Sunday before Lynda and Chuck's wedding, Lady Bird and Lyndon gathered their flock around the table in the third-floor White House solarium, where they embarked on "a family conference, unplanned, drifted into, deeply enjoyed, nothing settled." Lyndon and Lady Bird tried out arguments on one another, and on their kids, sometimes even trading sides. Lyndon quoted Lady Bird, "and it's true, that I had said that 'we were drifting into the posture of running again, that we were being forced into it.'" She had begun 1967 believing that political pressure would force Lyndon to run in 1968. But Lyndon, she recorded, now "didn't see that as the necessary outcome at all. He felt that we were heading toward announcing that we would not run." Lady Bird remained skeptical. Luci repeated her insistence that she liked her father and "wanted him with us and alive and having fun and helping raise Lyn and any other children she might have." She feared a second term would take him away from the family, but worse, that he wouldn't survive it. Lynda was of two minds. For herself, she hoped he wouldn't run. But for the country, she "could not see anyone else right now that she would feel good about taking over." However much the family indulged these discussions, Lynda believed her father would end up running again—her fatalism perhaps necessary to prepare for her now fiancé's deployment to Vietnam, set for March 1968. "As for me," Lady Bird recorded, "knowing it was no help, no comfort, no guidance to Lyndon, I could only repeat that I wish we could get out and I don't know how to get out, nor when, nor in what words to frame the decision."[27]

As the date for Lynda's wedding approached that December, Lady Bird shifted from fatigue, anxiety, and a bad stomach to again feeding off Lyndon's energy. "He's in a fighting mood," she recorded.

> I admire him fiercely. I want to see him spend himself almost whatever it takes against this miasma of despond, this virus, that is infecting our country. And yet it would be so easy, so happy to, as I have heard him say, "Let the bastards save the bastards," announce he would not be a candidate. Draw a circle for our energies, our brains, our hours, around our family, our business, our very personal friends, and have fun for what is left to us of life.[28]

Lynda's marriage to Chuck marked the second White House wedding in less than two years. In many ways, by comparison to Luci's, hers was equally elaborate if somewhat more intimate: its venue, the White House, lacking the cavernous, imposing feeling of the largest Catholic cathedral in America. In the lead-up to the wedding, more than five hundred journalists descended for daily Q and As, the questions ranging from the serious to the ridiculous: Would Captain Robb continue his scheduled deployment to Vietnam? Yes. How many raisins in the five-tiered wedding cake? 1,511. Would George Hamilton, Lynda's ex-beau, be among the guests? Yes. On December 9, 1967, at four P.M., Lynda Bird and Chuck Robb married in the East Room. They shared the day with five hundred invited guests, among them members of Congress, family from Texas, former significant others, college friends, and a few Hollywood stars. Although the winter-themed wedding—the décor featured holly sprigs and evergreen trees adorned with twinkling lights, and the bridesmaids dressed in red velvet—filled the Executive Mansion with a temporary spark, the shadow of Vietnam lurked close by. Chuck was scheduled to ship out for combat duty in four months. Pat Nugent, Luci's husband of a little over a year, would deploy a few weeks later.[29]

* * *

In the final months of 1967, conditions in Vietnam were growing increasingly untenable. In September, at a speech in San Antonio, LBJ offered to halt bombing in North Vietnam if Ho Chi Minh engaged in "productive" peace talks and also agreed not to use such talks as a chance to infiltrate more NVA troops into the South. Coined the "San Antonio

Formula," this proposal remained LBJ's principal paradigm for altering the prosecution of the war well into 1968. Yet the president correctly believed, especially with the American public turning against the White House, that Ho Chi Minh would never relent short of total victory—meaning Communist-controlled unification with the South. In the absence of a reply from Ho, LBJ continued to escalate bombing and send more troops. To add to the pressure on him, on October 21, the American people raised the volume on their opposition to the war when more than one hundred thousand protesters descended on the capital with calls to "levitate" the Pentagon. Though not a literal levitation, as Beat poet Allen Ginsberg explained, "The Pentagon was symbolically levitated in people's minds in the sense that it lost its authority which had been unquestioned and unchallenged until then."[30]

The massive antiwar mobilization paralleled a decision by the president to escalate the ground war in Vietnam. Battles, casualties, deaths, and bizarre assertions of optimism about the enemy's weakness by General Westmoreland and President Johnson instead registered with Hanoi as weakness. Lyndon's public convictions aside, like Bird, he was continuing to turn over every stone in deciding whether to gear up either to run in 1968 or to announce his retreat from politics. He asked Westmoreland if the troops would feel let down should he decide not to run. The general flatly told him no.[31] Over Thanksgiving at the Ranch, Lyndon drove to the top of the Edwards Plateau with the DNC's finance chair, Arthur Krim. With a 360-degree view of the Pedernales River Valley laid out before them, the two agreed that although Krim should move at once to put the machinery of fundraising and reelection in place for a 1968 campaign, he should be prepared to shut it down just as quickly.[32] By the end of November, two developments reinforced Lyndon's agony. Bob McNamara set a date to leave the administration for a position as president of the World Bank, a job LBJ had arranged for him. Having changed his assessment of Vietnam and now warning Johnson that he regarded the war as unwinnable, and with his wife in and out of the hospital with cancer all year, McNamara was being eased out by the president even as the defense secretary felt a growing pull to resign. Still, the Johnsons adored him. Lady Bird had "seldom felt as sorry for" Lyndon, and McNamara's departure caused great "loneliness and separation" for them both. And Eugene McCarthy, senator from Minnesota, declared his candidacy for president on an antiwar ticket.[33]

As 1967 yielded to 1968, John and Nellie Connally made their annual New Year's visit to the Ranch. John had announced in November that he would not run again for Texas governor, and Lady Bird found herself feeling envious of the couple's happiness; they were now liberated from John's own turmoil: the thirty-ninth governor of Texas had made his decision. To Connally, it seemed increasingly unlikely, whatever Lyndon decided, that the American public would be ready to embrace another Texan, and a foreign policy hawk at that, on the Democratic Party ticket in 1968. So, when the two couples spent the day together, Lyndon and Lady Bird felt at ease relying on their old friends' advice: now the Connallys' counsel would be shaped not by how the Johnsons' decision might affect their own political fate, but rather, by what they thought best for Lyndon and for the country. The four talked without interruption for three hours in Lyndon's newly decorated bedroom.

Lady Bird recorded the scene in her diary.

> John said, "You ought to run only if you look forward to being president again—only if you *want* to do it." I think he meant if there was an element of joy in the work, but you ought not to if the frustrations, the pain, the backbreaking work makes you dread it. You also ought not to run just to keep somebody else from being president. One of the most lucid and interesting words were spoken by Nellie, who said, "You will probably find after you've made the decision, if you decide not to run, that there is sort of an ephemeral period when you feel like everything has stopped. You are sad. You almost feel like you are dead and then when that is passed there is a great wave of relief." And looking at John, I myself see no hint, no likelihood that he will reconsider and run as some of the columnists in Texas are saying.
>
> Lyndon spoke of the simple fact that he feels older and more tired

> than he did ten years ago, five years ago, and what of the next five years? Suppose he runs and wins. Would he be able to carry the load in a way that he would be proud of and that the country deserves? For all of those years, most of all—always in the background—is the lowering shadow of nuclear power. Sometimes, somewhere will he have to make a decision on using that? Yet, if he chooses to get out, what will history say of him? What will his friends and those close to him who believe in him say of him? What will the soldiers in Vietnam say of him?[34]

It was impossible to answer all Lyndon's questions. "The only way," Connally summarized, "was to die in office"—precisely the outcome the president and First Lady wished to avoid. They made no decision, but they did come closer.[35] Maybe LBJ would announce his decision at the 1968 State of the Union address, now less than two weeks away.

Act III

January 1968–August 1968

Chapter 20

"Maggots of Doubt"

We drove to Luci's house and there was Lyn, all smiles, apparently over his ear infection, absolutely enthralled at seeing his grandfather. It is one of the pleasures of my life to see them together. Lyndon spends more time with him than he ever did with either of our children. He said there is one job I want and that is to be a full-time grandfather. It was both humorous and pathetic.

—Lady Bird Johnson, White House diary, January 13, 1968

After weeks of daily lap swimming and stationary bike riding over the holiday, Lyndon had managed to drop sixteen pounds, and seven inches around the belly. Competition and mutual scrutiny over inches, pounds, hairstyles, and clothing were a constant source of razzing between the president and the First Lady. And Lady Bird couldn't help feeling a little aggravated that he could so easily slim down without starving himself on black coffee and hard-boiled eggs, her go-to diet. With Lyndon's longevity constantly on her mind, Bird worried that at any moment, and under the unavoidable and avoidable stresses of his presidency in 1968, he might just as easily abandon his discipline and let his health decline. At the "beginning of the hardest year with our big problem still unresolved," Lady Bird was determined to find her baseline of compassion and patience for her husband's testiness and fatigue, for she "knew that his mind was leashed as though to a Siamese twin, with that inescapable problem of how and when do I face up to this running again or getting out."[1]

With the State of the Union address less than a week away, *The Wash-*

ington Post predicted that Lyndon would use his time before Congress to kick off the 1968 presidential race with a blueprint for reelection.[2] But much had changed since his last State of the Union. There were now more than 500,000 Americans and more than 850,000 South Vietnamese, South Korean, and other U.S. allied troops fighting in Vietnam, and with her own sons-in-law poised for duty, it was evident even to a First Lady still adamant in her defense of her husband and his national security team that there was no end to the war in sight. And although LBJ's bitter rival, Bobby Kennedy, had yet to enter the race by January 1968, Lady Bird and Lyndon felt the near-constant shadow of a potential RFK candidacy, and possible presidency. Such an outcome stood to diminish LBJ's legacy as a leader in both civil rights and in the far-reaching social gains of his domestic programs. Still, neither a challenge from his political rival nor the morass in Vietnam had slowed their momentum toward a decision not to run again.

Something else had also shifted in 1967: the electorate itself. Riots around the country and calls for law and order had triggered a political backlash aimed squarely at the Great Society government spending programs, to say nothing of antiwar and other social movements transforming the country from the left. The administration had responded by pressing Congress on gun control and crime bills, but in an election year, these actions were unlikely to stem the tide of a nasty, racist, antiliberal authoritarian impulse consuming the country. It was an impulse that men like George Wallace were eager to exploit, not just in the South, but nationwide. Against this backdrop, Lady Bird wondered if Lyndon could finally bring himself to decide once and for all. And if so, would he actually make his announcement during the State of the Union address, set for January 17, 1968, at the same time that he laid out his agenda, the Democratic Party's agenda, for a legacy-defining election year?

For Lyndon's entire presidency, Lady Bird had spent the day of the State of the Union address internalizing the adrenaline that pulsed through the West Wing. Each day was "always one of such tenseness for me, quite out of proportion to any responsibility I have for it"—a characteristic deflection.[3] In the past, she experienced the speech itself by counting ovations, and scrutinizing the faces of all of Lyndon's adversaries, especially those from the South and from their party. She assembled her guests to join her in the gallery to watch the speech, always a mix of cabinet and staff spouses and citizens from around the country who embodied issues important to the administration. Some years, she glanced at speech drafts, offering comments in the margins—on birth control, beautification, and urban quality of life. But this year, as Lyndon reread, rehearsed, and rewrote, and his staff and advisers ran through at least eleven drafts of the main speech, Lady Bird trained her focus exclusively on the final section of the address, a section that could provide an answer to their "big problem."

In preparing for the address, LBJ had asked both Mrs. Johnson and his press secretary, George Christian, who alone among his staff had been tuned in to his thinking since the fall of 1967, to each write a statement announcing that he would not run for reelection—one that the president could add to the end of his speech without letting on to anyone else on his staff. Around noon on January 17, with Christian's statement in hand, "his face calm, unrevealing, as it always is," the First Lady recorded, Lyndon tracked Lady Bird down at her desk and asked to see the text she had composed. Three and a half years earlier, in August 1964, Lyndon had drafted his own statement against running, and shared it with Walter Jenkins and Lady Bird.[4] She had briefly indulged his low then, but was adamant that he get himself on the airplane to Atlantic City for the Democratic National Convention and announce his run for the presidency. But exercising a masterful bit of marital and political psychology, she also drafted a statement to the contrary. She recorded in her diary that she had kept it all those years in the right-hand drawer of the desk in her bedroom. Now she fished it out. Together, Lyndon and Lady Bird read the three drafts: Christian's, her 1964 text, and her 1968 statement, written by hand on the same kind of stenographer's notepad of her earlier memos and drafts to and for Lyndon. In eight sentences that distilled the endless hours over the last year the two had spent analyzing, together and separately, every possible angle of his decision, Bird captured her husband's voice, mood, and intent:

> And now to my personal plans. I shall devote all the energy, the brains, and the heart I have, in the year ahead, toward achieving what all of us want most—a just and honorable peace and toward building/furthering the programs for our country to which I have devoted the four years of my Presidency.
>
> I know from 30 years experience the (crushing) demands of a campaign—from primaries, through convention, through the campaign itself—a nine-month involvement devouring hours of each day. I cannot use these same 24 hours of the day to do both. The time has come to look at priorities, quite clearly, for myself and for the country. I choose to fulfill, with all the strength I have, my first obligation—to the job of the Presidency.
>
> Therefore I will not be a candidate for re-election (and shall not permit my name to go on the ballot in any primaries).
>
> I also know the weight of today's problems, national and international in the chair in which I sit, that test the mind strength and use of time.[5]

But the woman who as a high school senior declined the nomination for class valedictorian found her statement "feeble." Aware of the historic gravity of the announcement ("If there was anything we ever ought to say—with words that have wings and fire—this is it"), she pushed for a better alternative. She and Lyndon decided that he should go with Christian's more concise version. Lyndon put it in the inside pocket of his suit, Lady Bird recalled. "If he made [the announcement], it would come at the end," they planned, but it would not show up in advance in his distributed remarks or on his teleprompter.[6] Nine hours before LBJ was scheduled to deliver the State of the Union, neither Christian nor Lady Bird could predict what he would do. Lyndon really was alone with his decision. "He looks," recorded Bird, "from one to another of those close to him for an answer—for some wisdom—beyond anything he can have. There isn't any. There is nobody but him."[7] Alone, yet surrounded by people, Lyndon left Bird and returned to the Cabinet Room. Alone, she ate lunch on a tray in her room.

Like the First Lady, President Johnson had an eye and an appetite for detail, and he hired staff who shared and could keep up with and record his meticulous penchant for exhaustive record keeping. But even LBJ's White House tapes, the historian's treasure of treasures (the release of which we owe to Lady Bird Johnson's 1998 decision), do not tell the whole story of life in the Johnson White House. For example, it was LBJ's secretarial staff who took the time to record in his President's Daily Diary that on the day of the 1968 State of the Union address, the president sat down at 3:47 in the afternoon to eat a late lunch. Marie Fehmer's notes record the still-dieting president eating veal chops; turnip greens; a tomato, lettuce, and onion salad; and Jell-O for dessert. He hated eating alone, so Lady Bird's secretary, Ashton Gonella, joined him, with Juanita Roberts, LBJ's longtime aide. Their meal was light, but the talk heavy.

Lynda Bird, now facing Chuck's deployment, barged into the family dining room carrying a bundle of letters written to her by wives of servicemen. She read one of them aloud to her father. It came from a fellow Texan whose husband had left for Vietnam two months after their wedding. He was killed just thirteen days before his tour of duty was scheduled to end. Lynda, Marie documented, told her father that she doubted she could display comparable courage in the face of such a tragedy. LBJ's staff did not record the president's expression at this moment, nor how he replied to his daughter's anguish. The discussion was certainly not the first time the president was forced to think about exactly what it might mean for his daughters to lose their husbands to a war of his making. Nor would it be the last to coincide with a day of monumental presidential decisions. Unable to provide any reassurance to his daughter, or control the outcome of the war, he shifted the conversation to more prosaic dimensions of the evening's speech. Looking across the table, he told his daughter and his wife, who had recently joined the conversation, to wear bright colors and get their makeup done professionally. He wanted "his ladies" to "look good" that night. His instructions about beautifying his own family seem, by today's lights, to reduce his wife and daughter to stage props. But Lyndon was a political micromanager, the White House a stage, and the members of the First Family actors in the live drama.

They would not have speaking parts, but the protagonist wanted to project authority and control not only through his own delivery at the podium in the Capitol that night, but in the images the cameras would capture of his family.[8]

In her accounts of state dinners and their other official duties, Lady Bird repeatedly marvels at how quickly Lyndon could switch gears and change clothes—he routinely sweated through several shirts a day—and still show up on time, whether to welcome an arriving head of state at the South Portico or to depart, always separately, for the short drive from 1600 Pennsylvania Avenue to the Capitol, for his State of the Union. The speech was scheduled for nine o'clock that evening. At 6:25 P.M. the president visited the White House barber. At 7:20 P.M., his makeup man, Lee Baygan, got to work—it wasn't exactly high-def TV, but the networks were to broadcast the address live, in color, and Baygan applied LBJ's makeup accordingly. Lyndon returned to the White House theater to rehearse his speech yet again, and Lady Bird hosted a reception for the guests she had invited to join her that night to watch the address. While getting ready for the evening, she found that George Christian's final draft announcing Lyndon's decision not to run again, the one Lyndon had earlier placed in the breast pocket of his jacket, was no longer with Lyndon, but stashed away in his desk. Before the West Wing's usual prespeech frenzy could commence, Lady Bird tracked down a rushed LBJ, catching him on his way from the Oval Office to the nearby Fish Room, where he was meeting with the congressional leadership of both parties.[9] She seldom interrupted such meetings, but "I had this memo in my keeping," she recorded, "and I held it like a coal of fire—and I wanted to get it back in his pocket, so I took it over."[10]

The two spoke for only five minutes—"It was hardly a conversation. It was just a few phrases"—but in their short exchange, they covered five years, or maybe even a lifetime, of accumulated knowledge about each other. Still, even after thirty-three years of marriage, there was only so much one individual in a lifelong partnership could provide for the other, and they both knew it. With his Secret Service and a clutch of assistants just out of earshot, Lyndon stood in the doorway between the Oval Office and his adjacent private office and asked his worn-out wife, "What do you think? What shall I do?" Feeling hopeless, Bird looked at him and ran through his options, yet again. "Luci hopes you won't run. She wants you for herself and for Lyn and all of us being together. She does not want to give you up. Lynda hopes you will run." Lynda had confided this to Lady Bird "with a sort of terrible earnestness" that afternoon, "because her husband is going to war and she thinks there will be more chance of getting him back alive and everything settled if you are president." As for her own view, she reverted to her baseline with Lyndon. "Me—I don't know. I have said it all before. I can't tell you what to do." And then she laid it out once more, separating her own desires from his options: "One, either you make a conscious decision to run in the same state of mind of a man who is becoming a monk or some such—just giving up your life, saying, 'Here it is. I will take whatever happens—I will try to do some pacing and have some humor for the next five years.' Or, two, simply make the announcement at a time and in words only *you* can choose, but as strong and as beautiful as we are capable of." Lyndon listened, and handed her a note, this one from John Connally, recommending that the president make the statement that night. The size of the national audience and a slight improvement in LBJ's poll numbers made it "a noble time" to announce his intentions, Bird surmised from Connally's message. When she left Lyndon, Lady Bird could not be certain whether her husband would or would not announce later that evening, but at least he now had the right words, properly expressed and in his jacket pocket.[11]

More than most years, for the First Lady's designated gallery seating that night, Liz and Lady Bird made sure that the ambitions and accomplishments of the Great Society were on full display, embodied by a VISTA and Head Start volunteer from Oklahoma; a reading teacher in the D.C. Public Schools with Job Corps; a seventeen-year-old Job Corps African American student now on track for college placement; and a Vietnam War medic, Lawrence Joel, to whom Lyndon had awarded the Medal of Honor in 1967 for his battlefield heroism, the first living black American to be so awarded. (After being shot twice, Joel had dragged himself over the battlefield and continued to bandage and treat his fellow wounded soldiers.) Walter and Bennetta Washington were also among the First Lady's guests.

The crowd greeted Lyndon, Bird recorded, with three minutes of thundering applause. His speech covered Vietnam, with a restatement of the San Antonio Formula promising a stop to bombing in exchange for peace talks. But it also touched on other issues close to the Johnson presidency: a call for measures to control pollution in American rivers and cities, to preserve the California redwoods, to fund the Highway Beautification Act, and for Congress to pass a spate of other environmental legislation. And he launched into a long meditation on American cities—not on the quality of life, but on the propensity for violence in them. "Last summer," LBJ began, referring to the "long, hot summer of 1967," "we saw how wide is the gulf for some Americans between the promise and the reality of our society. We know that we cannot change all of this in a day. It represents the bitter consequences of more than three centuries." But rather than call for more funds for Great Society programs, for equal and race-blind access to housing and mortgage financing, or for equal justice in the American judicial system, the president focused on juvenile delinquency, crime, and lawlessness; and on funding for police training, better pay, and equipment for suppressing rioters embodied by the Crime Control and Safe Streets Act, legislation first introduced during the 1967 riots. America would in time convert the despair and frustration of those uprisings into confidence and achievement, the president assured the country. But to thunderous applause, he also warned that "those who preach disorder and those who preach violence must know that local authorities are able to resist them swiftly, to resist them sternly, and to resist them decisively." The language might as well have come from a speech on Vietnam, but now it was the home front where the president sounded ready for battle, with policies to placate the conservative demand for law and order.[12]

At one point in his speech, Lady Bird noticed that the teleprompter had gone out. She saw Lyndon leaf through three or four pages of text. He spoke extemporaneously. Ever the honest critic, she credited him for ad-libbing "magnificently." But always the trained editor, she noted his use of extra adjectives "that I would have left off. I like the spare bones better." Thankfully, he wouldn't have to rely on the teleprompter for the final statement of the evening—he had it in his breast pocket. "As he approached the end, I tightened up in my seat," Bird recalled. "Will he reach in his pocket? Did I want him to? Would I be relieved if he did or if he didn't?" Did the woman who, since 1964, had been so strategic in her sustained campaign for her husband to get out in 1968 now allow herself to doubt her own desires?[13]

What happened next was what didn't happen. Lyndon "ended his speech on a strong high note, and there was a great roar of applause," but "he did not reach in his pocket for the draft that I knew was there." He simply turned and walked down the steps of the dais. A stunned First Lady showed no sign of her feelings. She simply bid goodbye to her gallery guests and walked to meet the president for the ritual visit to the Speaker's office. In the chamber, especially at the end of his address, she did allow herself to feel "a great surge of support" for her husband. But a few minutes later, with the Speaker, the congressional leadership, and Lyndon's cabinet, she wondered if she had "been off the beam," misreading the reaction to his speech. "The first little maggots of doubt began to erode the good feeling I had." Maybe her doubt had less to do with the tepid response she picked up on from the party's leadership than with her own disappointment with Lyndon, and with not knowing their future.[14]

The Johnsons spent the nine-minute drive back to the White House crammed into the presidential limousine with Chuck and Lynda and three close aides. They may have had a private minute in the elevator on their way up to the mansion's family quarters, where they would host their traditional postmortem drinks-and-buffet, enough time perhaps for a quick word or a glance acknowledging where they now stood. Lady Bird's diary entry offers no clues about whether they discussed why Lyndon had not reached into his pocket and read the statement they'd agreed to that morning. The specifics of what they said to each other are part of the secret history of their marriage. We do know that in LBJ's 1971 memoir he claimed he left the statement in the White House with Lady Bird, but the First Lady clearly recalled otherwise. Whatever the logistics, however distorted their memories, LBJ had somewhere decided that he could not, with one breath, ask the country or Congress to pass more bills, spend more money, fight more fights, and then, in the next breath, declare that he would be stepping out of the political arena in a matter of months.[15]

Had Lyndon read his statement, he and Lady Bird would have been greeted when they stepped out of the elevator by a gathering of their closest allies and employees, nearly all of them shocked by the political earthquake the president would have just unleashed. Instead, the shifting tectonics remained the Johnsons' to feel and conceal, and they carried on as they had in years past. Friends and staff floated in and out, watching the spin about the president's address on the three networks in LBJ's bedroom and on the LBJ-created National Television—NT was a precursor to PBS—in Lady Bird's. Bird approved of remarks on the public television panel by Bill Moyers; found those by Cleveland mayor Carl Stokes, who insisted on more funds for American cities, "reasonable and articulate and mostly fair"; and by William F. Buckley "amusing." She reserved a more biting review for Kennedy aide and historian Arthur Schlesinger, Jr.: "[S]o bitter I thought he was funny. Somebody said he looks like he is being milked, though the product must have been gall." By the time they went to sleep at nearly one in the morning, though her husband had yet to take the big step, Bird allowed herself to feel, after an evening with their closest supporters, "an air of elation, goodwill, relief, a brief short draft of the wine of success which we had tasted" in 1964 and 1965.[16]

Chapter 21

"Somewhere . . . Between the Words Gut and Pot"

White people have not experienced the hurts and humiliations at the hands of whites that are the lingering heritage of millions of people of color around the world. Because whites have not experienced the anguish, they do not understand the anger. Even those black, brown or yellow, who have managed to achieve every outward success in the white man's world bear the psychic scars of centuries of injustice. When these old wounds are reopened, sometimes by the most innocent act or word of a well-meaning white, all the accumulated venom of ages pours out. It may be and often is rude and irrational. It may be self-destructive. But it is there, and it must be faced—not with scorn or anger or bitterness, but with compassionate understanding.

—Editorial, *The New York Times*, January 20, 1968

The morning's headlines—"somewhat negative and unenthusiastic"—quickly dampened Bird's optimism. The president had barely touched on the topic of civil rights, once the epicenter of his legislative and national agenda, *The New York Times* pointed out, and then only with a line that "failed to arouse a ripple of applause."[1] Still, LBJ had not entirely exhausted his good standing with the black press. The *Afro-American* summarized the thrust of his speech, picked up on the Great Society substance behind Lady Bird's choice of guests that night, and praised the Johnsons for including a black "war hero" among those Americans whom the First Lady had invited to hear the president. But clips from the Baltimore paper very likely did not routinely make it to the expectant Johnsons' morning review of the news.

Especially since the protests at Williams and Yale had drowned out her message on the urban environment, other, more obvious disconnects had begun to shape Lady Bird's world. As she sat down in her private office to write Lyndon her version of an exit announcement, some five thousand women from across the country marched in snowy silence from Union Station to the Capitol to protest the war. Organized by Coretta Scott King and Jeannette Rankin, an eighty-seven-year-old lifelong pacifist and former member of Congress from Montana, the march offered a platform to "encourage women to express themselves." Outside, the women who gathered on that cold, sunny day in January, as feminist lore has it, together coined the phrase "sisterhood is powerful."[2]

But inside the ever-more-permeable White House bubble, a First Lady who had become increasingly powerful had also become increasingly distanced from the sisterhood outside. Following a dedicated focus on women in American society in the first two years of her tenure, she had let all of 1967 pass without holding one of her Doers Luncheons, the gatherings of professional women invited to the White House to tell their stories and amplify the administration's policy agenda. But for this election year, she and Liz planned to reconvene the speaker series. Tracking closely with the West Wing's political awareness of the Republican Party seizing on law and order in an election year, and to promote the crime bill the president had announced in the State of the Union address, Liz and Lady Bird titled the first lunch talk of 1968 "Crime in the Streets." They invited some fifty high-profile women: journalists, local and national activists, trade unionists, teachers and leading educators, authors, television producers, volunteers, and spouses of key administration officials and allies.

The East Wing slated three women to lead off the discussion: Margaret Moore, founder of an anti-crime women's group from Indianapolis; Martha Cole, a recent college graduate and VISTA worker in Atlanta; and Katherine "Katie" Peden, a longtime business and political acquaintance of the Johnsons from Kentucky. In 1963, Katie became the first woman in America to serve as state commerce commissioner and the first woman in Kentucky to hold a state cabinet position. Just a week before the Doers Luncheon, she had announced her candidacy for Senate as an "'All the way with LBJ' Democrat." Although she would go on to lose the election by 2 percent, Katie's primary victory against all rivals made her the first woman to compete for one of the Bluegrass State's seats in the U.S. Senate. LBJ had named her as the only woman to serve on the Kerner Commission, a task force he appointed to look at racial uprisings in American cities, then finalizing its report on race and racial violence in America.[3] As the butlers passed sherry and orange juice in the Blue Room, White House ushers led guests to the Green Room to sit for a photograph with Lady Bird and the panelists. Straight from a meeting at the Pentagon about performing for the troops in Vietnam, the Hollywood star and performer Eartha Kitt was among the last to arrive.

Kitt began her career dancing for the Katherine Dunham Company, the first African American modern dance company in the United States. As one of a few black students at the mostly white Metropolitan Vocational High School, precursor to New York City's High School of Performing Arts, Kitt had an early introduction to the powers of code switching. In a class called Speech (or Elocution), wearing dresses handed out by FDR's Emergency Relief Administration program, Eartha learned not only how to speak properly, but also about table manners: how to read the menu at a restaurant, order food from a waitress, and hold a knife and fork.

After running away from her aunt's home and dropping out of high school at age seventeen, she auditioned and won a ten-dollar-a-week stipend to study with Dunham's company. Six months into her training, Kitt performed for the first time as a professional dancer in the new Broadway show *Blue Holiday,* an all-black variety show with music by jazz artist Duke Ellington and folk musician Josh White. As the show toured America, Kitt's talent for singing in several languages and dancing across cultures distinguished her, earning her national stardom and invitations to perform abroad. Returning to the United States in the mid-1950s from half a decade of company and solo performances in the far less racially polarized London, Paris, and Berlin, she parlayed her success in Europe into gigs on television and in live performances. As her fortune grew, her activism expanded.

In 1954, she made her first major donation to the Northside Center for Child Development in Harlem. The nonprofit was headed by Kenneth B. Clark, the black educational psychiatrist whose research had been pivotal to the Supreme Court's *Brown v. Board of Education* ruling. The Northside Center's mission was to treat the psychological effects of racism and poverty experienced by Harlem's youth. After the Watts riots of 1965, Kitt turned her attention to job training and counseling programs in Los Angeles, and also in Washington, D.C. In a nod to her friend James Dean, she worked with a group in Anacostia dubbed Rebels with a Cause, which sought to prevent juvenile delinquency among D.C.'s inner-city youth. In 1967, her testimony before the House General Subcommittee on Education and Labor about the Rebels' work, and on youth issues more broadly, revealed her to be an astute observer of the social and political woes plaguing young, urban, mostly black residents and a shrewd tactician in agitating for change on their behalf. But Kitt was careful not to let her activism jeopardize her hard-won professional standing or career prospects. When she arrived in Washington for the Doers Luncheon, she was on a break during her tour of the play *The Owl and the Pussycat,* and her first episode as Catwoman, the sole African American in an otherwise all-white cast in the TV series *Batman,* had just aired to rave reviews.[4]

Eartha Kitt and Lady Bird Johnson had never met. On the surface, they had little in common. But they were both from the South and both raised by their aunts. They were both performers who had studied speech; and both were accustomed to the public spotlight and, generally, attuned to and able to readily adapt to their various audiences. And though neither seemed aware of it at the time, both had attempted to reach youth in Washington, D.C.—Kitt through the Eartha Kitt Foundation and work with Rebels with a Cause; and Lady Bird through the Trailblazer summer jobs project in Anacostia, Project Pride in Shaw, and planting programs at D.C. schools.

There the similarities mostly ended. As a child, Kitt picked cotton and lived through poverty, physical vulnerability, and the alienation of the Jim Crow South. As an adult, she developed into a charismatic talent onstage and onscreen—in the 1950s, she was known for iconic, suggestive renditions of the songs "Monotonous" (1952), "Santa Baby" (1953), and "C'est si bon" (1953). Her professional and personal life found her crossing over between races and cultures with what appeared to be extraordinary ease, but that surely required a wellspring of grit. Eartha made no secret of her alignment with the civil rights causes of midcentury America, but the closest she had come to the radicalism of groups like the Black Panthers was the dominatrix leatherette costume she wore as Catwoman. Still, the CIA had started a file on her during her years performing in European nightclubs, and the FBI surely kept an eye on her, given her artistic collaboration dating back to the 1930s with artists later blacklisted, such as Josh White and Orson Welles.[5]

The Johnsons' efforts to push for legislation on behalf of black Americans came at the expense of the Democratic Party's hold on the South and left little doubt about their commitment to end the legal dimensions of American apartheid. Lady Bird's Alabama kin, whom she visited every summer growing up, arguably embodied the suppression of African American opportunity and the very backlash against the Johnson policies designed to secure it. The First Lady's ties to and complicated political relationship with Alabama had given her unusual space to publicly address southern racism, but it also instilled in her a certain reluctance about directly confronting a culture she knew so well.

She had demonstrated this delicate balance during the whistle-stop tour in 1964, and again in 1966, during a visit to the University of Alabama in Tuscaloosa, where she gave a speech entitled "The South's Place in the Nation." According to reporter Nan Robertson, Lady Bird, "without once mentioning the words 'negro,' or 'integration,'" challenged her audience to leave behind "human backwardness."[6] Another reporter described her visit as a "skillfully contrived gentle prod" for Alabama to "get with" the twentieth century on race relations and in other areas.[7] Even though her advocacy in Alabama offered a master class in pointed indirection, the efficacy of Lady Bird's efforts in the formerly slave-owning state, one with deep roots in timber and cotton farming, also had its limits. Now, two years later and well aware that her husband's civil rights agenda had stirred the pot of the very white supremacism she had grown up around and feared uncorking, Lady Bird found herself lunching with Eartha Kitt (on seafood bisque, chicken, and peppermint ice cream), the two an unlikely pair, for a gathering billed as a conversation about kids, crime, and cities.[8]

The seating that day was especially cramped, with two head tables, set up on either side of the lectern, packed closely together. Lady Bird sat at one head table, along with the invited speakers. Eartha sat at the other head table, with NBC reporter Nancy Dickerson, *The Washington Post*'s Katharine Graham, and journalist Isabelle Shelton, who was covering the lunch for *The Evening Star*. A few minutes into the event, the president strolled in unannounced. Perhaps it was a conciliatory gesture, after he disappointed his wife just the night before with his silence about their quasi-promised departure from politics. Or perhaps it was just a sign of his understanding that women represented a key constituency in his party. Or perhaps he simply had eight free minutes and decided to drop by on a whim.

Standing at the front of the room, between his wife's table and the lectern, LBJ ad-libbed about police, both their power and brutality, and about juvenile delinquency. He flattered his audience for their "courage, stick-to-it-iveness, tenacity"—all necessary to address crime. He compared the doggedness of his two primary enforcers, Lady Bird and Liz, to that of a bulldog—even, he suggested, when pushed "out four different doors . . . [they] will find another one to come in." Notwithstanding the canine metaphor, LBJ's compliment telegraphed his admiration for his wife's toughness, resilience, and intelligence and for the capacity of women more generally.

The audience had no chance for a Q and A with the president. But as LBJ began heading out of the dining room, Eartha Kitt, as if to demonstrate his point about female tenacity, stood up from her chair and walked right up to him. In an institution where even an impromptu presidential appearance takes on a measure of staged choreography, the physical act of approaching the president without being called on marked Kitt's first departure from protocol. Stepping out of her lane may have been unorthodox, but the question she then posed was well founded: "Mr. President, of course there is delinquency across the United States which we are all interested in and that is why we are here today. But . . . what do we do with the children while the parents are off working?" If LBJ was surprised, he didn't show it. He looked Kitt in the eye, and answered her with a reference to the "millions of dollars for day care centers where mothers can take their children" recently approved by Congress. "I think that is a very good question for you to ask yourselves, you women here, and you all tell me what you think." With that, he left for his next meeting.[9]

Representing three generations of American women, the scheduled speakers resumed their remarks. Margaret Moore, a generation older than Lady Bird, invoked the crusades of early-twentieth-century women's organizations and the responsibility of American women to instill "the moral fiber in the next generation." Martha Cole, a recent graduate of the University of Michigan, where three and a half years earlier Lyndon had given his historic Great Society speech, described her experience in Atlanta with VISTA and Head Start. Lady Bird marveled at how her generation "walk[s] out of their comfortable lives and headfirst—unafraid apparently—into the problems of the ghettos trying to learn and work with them."[10] And Katherine Peden described spending the previous six months with the Kerner Commission, traveling around the country and taking testimony from activists, police, and parents in ghettos, about the causes of crime and uprisings in American cities.

Even as the headlines that week screamed war, protest, and politics, the ladies gamely played the role of amplifying the White House message: Mrs. Johnson cares not only about parks and flowers but about people, victims of crime and their perpetrators. As Lady Bird moderated, she kept one eye peeled for Eartha Kitt. "She smoldered and smoked," and raised her hand and "I knew I must, in turn, get to her. I did not know what to expect—only that it would not be good."[11] Kitt stood, walked toward the First Lady, "and look[ed] with intense directness at me (she is a good actress)," Lady Bird recorded. The floor now hers, Kitt made a very long statement, one that in its aftermath the White House painted in terse, gendered terms as "shrill." *The Evening Star* called it an "angry tirade," and *The Chicago Daily Defender* an "emotional display."

It is one that defies easy summary. As the full transcript clearly shows, Kitt that day was not appearing as an actress who had memorized and delivered a carefully blocked and scripted monologue. She was speaking her mind and, in doing so, touched on all the major social issues of 1968.

> I don't belong to the NAACP. I don't belong to anything; I just belong to America. As a matter of fact, the work that I have [been] doing is just in that vein.

Kitt located herself in the mainstream of the culture of volunteering and community action promoted by the Johnson administration.

> I have listened to the speeches here today. I feel that somewhere along the line, we have missed out on something. I think that we have forgotten or somewhere along the line, we have not realized that the reason, the main reason, why there is juvenile delinquency in America today is because the teenagers in the country—and I see youth of America today and I am saying this because I work with them.

Her activism on both coasts, she explained, derived not just from her well-earned means, but from her identifying with marginalized youth. "It's been talked about walking through the gutters," she noted. "I have lived in the gutters. That's why I know what I am talking about. The youth of America today are angry. They are angry because the parents are angry. The parents are angry for many reasons."

Though she could identify with alienated urban youth, she also represented herself as a parent—at the time, she had a six-year-old daughter—and one of means, frustrated by the government spending tax dollars on war.

> The parents are angry because we are so highly taxed and because there is a war going on that the Americans do not understand. I know that there have been many speeches and many discussions about the Vietnamese war, but basically we must all stop and realize and analyze our own selves and realize where the truth really is. The children of today, the youth of America today, are not rebelling for no reason at all. They are not hippies for no reason at all. We do not have Sunset Boulevard behaving the way they are behaving for no reason at all. They are rebelling against something and we all seem to camouflage this something. This something happens to be very basic to us, we who pay our taxes and who are very resentful of these high taxes. I am sorry, Mrs. Johnson, if I am going to offend the President or you, but I am here to say what is in my heart.

Returning to her contact with young people in the country, Kitt went on:

> I am speaking as a mini-mommy of America because that is what I am considered. I am in very close contact with the youth of this country and also with the young mothers of this country as well as the older mothers of this country. I go from school to school across the nation and I have listened to their problems, the problems of the children, the problems of the parents.
>
> Why are they so angry today? Why are the mothers so reluctant about taking care of their children today? Because when they get a $4 check per week and this is what the Welfare Department—when it adds up—when you break it all down, they get $4 a week. The other thing is, there are many, many things that are burning the people of this country and mostly the mothers because the mothers feel

> that if they are going to raise a son and you know, you have children of your own, maybe no boys, but there was a case like Israel where they said the girls of the war really feel this, too.

Attempting to connect protest, rebellion, education, welfare, jobs, taxes, poverty, race, class, crime, the draft, war, and the generation gap, Kitt told the women at the White House that day that, in essence, they and the Johnsons were out of touch.

> When we raise our children, our sons, we send them to school as best we can, whatever kind of schools they are. We send those children to school today. They do not want to go to school because they feel that no matter what kind of education they get, they spend a great majority of their lives getting an education and when they come out, they will be snatched away from the mother and sent off to Vietnam. They do not want it. The mothers don't want it and since the mothers don't want it, that emotional feeling goes right down into the children. Therefore, the boys of this country are doing everything they possibly can to avoid being drafted, and the mothers are helping them do it.
>
> They feel that if I have any kind of life at all, I am going to enjoy it as best I can because I may not be here tomorrow. This is what the youth of America is crying today. They also feel that if my education is going to only bring me a diploma, that I will not even have a job waiting for me afterwards, why should I even try to get a diploma? There are boys now that I know across this nation who feel it does not pay to be a good guy today, "Why should I be a good guy? If I am a bad guy, I get thrown in jail and I have a record or the Government is going to take care of me. I don't stand a chance of going off and being shot in Vietnam. Therefore, I am going to be a bad guy. It pays to be a bad guy." So this is where the juvenile delinquency lies, not only in the fact that parents are juvenile delinquents themselves.
>
> I am talking as a mother who has a child . . . so I know the feeling of having a baby coming out of my guts, particularly when it is a boy.

> This nation depends on strength; it depends on men who are strong. You take the best of the country and send them off to a war and they get shot. They don't want that. And particularly since the last world war, when they saw their fathers coming back from a war maimed not even being able to get themselves a job. The children see that; they don't want it now, and they are going to tell you about it. And the way they tell you, they can't come to you and tell you, Mrs. Johnson. They cannot get to President Johnson and tell President Johnson about it. They rebel in the streets; they will take pot. If you don't know the expression, it is marijuana. They will smoke a joint and get themselves high as they possibly can get in order to avoid whatever it is to get shot at.[12]

Although she went on for too long and appears to have lost her train of thought here and there, Kitt's main message, though buried in the coverage and spin that followed, seemed to be that whatever their economic class, America's youth, young boys especially, were expressing their opposition to the Vietnam War by rejecting American institutions writ large. The straight path offered little protection from the war, so why not "take pot" to enjoy life before being sent off to war—or commit a crime, land in jail, and avoid war altogether. Kitt believed she was well situated to serve as the messenger for the privileged hippies or rioting ghetto youth, but "somewhere along the way," Lady Bird recorded, "I think between the words gut and pot—I had a sense that maybe the feeling in the room was swinging to me. Miss Kitt stopped for a breath to a stunned silence in the room, and that second I was waiting to see whether it was a comma or a period."[13]

The First Lady needed time to formulate her response. So, she yielded the floor to Miriam Hughes, mother of eight and First Lady of New Jersey, who rose to Lady Bird's defense by attacking Kitt's attempt to connect the war in Vietnam to protest and racial conflict at home. She told the group that her first husband was killed in World War II, and that although her sons hoped for a deferment from fighting in Indochina, if they didn't get one, "they won't like it and I won't like it, but I'll kiss them goodbye. . . . I consider that anybody who's taking pot just because there is a war in Vietnam is some kind of a kook." Kitt insisted that she was at the White House to explain delinquency and rebellion, not to defend it. Not once during her monologue did she mention the word *black, Negro,* or *ghetto* nor make any reference to race; she didn't need to. By departing from the expected script, an African American woman from the South, trained since her teenage years in code switching, had managed to bring inside the most protected space of the White House, the women's space, all the pressing issues the country beyond Pennsylvania Avenue would wrestle with in 1968.[14]

Lady Bird's reply—misreported in clip after clip as delivered with tears in her eyes—revealed precisely who was the better actress that day. It felt like a nightmare, she later recorded, and the papers were indeed correct "that I was pale and that my voice trembled slightly as I replied to Miss Kitt."[15] But there were no tears. Mrs. Johnson was a skilled politician and a careful speaker and listener who had written drafts of speeches and practiced and studied their delivery, hers and LBJ's, for decades. She tried to draw upon the cardinal rule of a good politician: empathy.

> Miss Kitt, I believe that I should like to answer you. . . . Because there is a war on, and I pray that there will come a just and honest peace, that still does not give us a free ticket not to try to work on bettering the things in this country that we can better. Crime in the streets is one that I think we should try to solve and better. Better education is another. Health is another. I think we have made advances in those. Believe me, we are going to try hard to make more. I am sorry I cannot understand as much as I should because I have not lived in the background as you have. Nor can I speak as passionately or as well as you can. But I think we must keep our eyes and our hearts and our energies fixed on constructive aims and try to do something that will make this a happier, better educated, healthier land. That violence will not help it. It will call attention to the problem. I think all of us should put our shoulders to the wheel and try to solve the

problems. Violence alone will not solve it. Does anyone else have any remarks?[16]

And that was the prompt to rally the room. "Thunderous applause," she recorded, reinforced the First Lady's attempt at a course correction. She could see the journalists in the room scribbling madly. Conscious of the purpose of the lunch, to focus press coverage on American women's support for the president's crime bill, she opened the floor to a few more observations and promptly closed the three-hour lunch. Making her way through flattery, encouragement, and some discomfort, she made a point of saying goodbye to Eartha Kitt. But the White House had already begun to turn against the actress. There was no limousine waiting to take her back to the Shoreham Hotel, where over a scotch, Kitt contemplated sending a bouquet with an apology to Mrs. Johnson. But according to *The Chicago Daily Defender,* her manager objected to such a gesture. And there was certainly no White House car to drive her to Shaw for a meeting that afternoon with Stokely Carmichael.[17]

Why did this incident present itself as a "nightmare" to Lady Bird Johnson? Was it the substance of Kitt's muddled message? The fact that she had challenged the president's Vietnam policy on the First Lady's turf? Or blamed Vietnam for the riots engulfing the country? Or talked about how little the Johnson administration's social programs were actually helping the urban poor? Bird had listened to protests against the war outside her window and faced them head-on during her travels around the country for years now. She didn't like or agree with them, but she knew all the critiques backward and forward. Like Kitt, Bird had her own experience in crossing racial boundaries in her engagement with leading black (and female) professionals, and likewise speaking with and comprehending the fears, anxieties, and racism of southern white voters, among them her own family, as they moved increasingly away from the Democratic Party.

So why did this experience rattle such a skilled, thick-skinned veteran public figure as Lady Bird Johnson? Perhaps her reaction boiled down to losing control, or the feeling of losing control, when accustomed to exercising it so completely. In the postmortem retelling, the incident plays directly to stereotype: A black woman challenged a white woman, and not just any white woman but a southern First Lady of the United States, and not from a picket line but as an equal participant in a policy discussion at the White House. The only trouble with this rendition is that neither woman's actual words suggest a story of such obviously black-and-white contours. Yet that is how it played, almost immediately, and since.

By the next day, the White House press machine began depicting Eartha Kitt as "shrill" and "ill-bred." In an effort to control the narrative, Lady Bird issued a formal statement: "I am sorry that the good constructive things which the speakers on the panel said were not heard—only the shrill voice of anger and discord."[18] Wearing dark sunglasses as she arrived in Los Angeles, Kitt now played along with a narrative that had begun to spiral. Holding court on friendlier ground, she described Lady Bird as "a little flustered" and "emotional."

> I was not rude. I raised my hand and asked to be heard. I was recognized by the First Lady in order to give my opinion. . . . I said what is in my heart. . . . I think what I had to say is primarily on the minds of the people across the country. It was time that we began to examine our problems with the First Family. After all, the Johnsons are our family and as the head of the nation, who better to discuss the subject with?[19]

Kitt repeated her critique of the war in Southeast Asia, her exposure over the previous decade to a fading European colonial empire evident. "Why not just pull out of Vietnam and take a chance of 'losing face' as other countries have done, for instance England and France?"[20] The gendered and racial tropes about what each woman actually said and did went on for several days thereafter.

Some 1,900 letters and telegrams poured in; a blindsided Liz Carpenter supplied the First Couple with a steady, hour-by-hour count of reactions—90 percent favorable to Lady Bird—she reported from both white and black Americans.[21] No one in the White House appears to have reread the transcript to perceive, in all of Kitt's contradictions, that she had been speaking entirely for herself and as herself. But her speech did undermine the objective of these Doers Luncheons: to promote support for the White House policy agenda. And by connecting Vietnam to riots and poverty, by bringing the nation's pain right into the First Family's home, Kitt had touched a nerve. It was a nerve whose current ran between the East and West wings and that electrified and polarized the American body politic in 1968.

As the White House and most of the establishment press misrepresented the exchange, elevating Lady Bird and demonizing Eartha—perhaps the singer was adhering to Helen Gurley Brown's *Cosmo* "wine diet," Nancy Dickerson quipped to Liz, and woozy from hunger, she just couldn't think straight—leading figures in the black community as well as the black press rallied around Kitt. Martin Luther King, Jr., called the act "a very proper gesture" that "described the feelings of many persons."[22] Others weighed in, including Congressman Bob Kastenmeier, a liberal opponent of the war from Wisconsin; Rat Pack performer Sammy Davis, Jr.; and Bill Cosby, then costarring in *I Spy*, the first weekly network television program to feature a black actor in a lead role.

Their reactions reinforced Kitt's perspective that black parents have little incentive to work or to educate their children properly when white America gives them no opportunity, and that black anger is made worse when black soldiers return from Vietnam only to be shunned. Her words also revealed the contradictions at the core of Lady Bird Johnson's "beautification" policies and messages. The word *beautification*, despite two years of effort to undo its visceral connotations, still telegraphed white derision of black spaces and a painfully superficial, gilded do-gooder faith in the artifice of liberal reform. To Kitt, such women had "forgotten where the trouble is. They wish to plant flowers down the middle of the boulevards of America and build bigger lights, but that won't squelch juvenile delinquency."[23]

Dick Gregory, a comedian who explicitly built his career using satire to address race and racism in America, flew from Boston to Washington to join a small protest outside the White House. Gregory had spent much of the decade parlaying his stature with both black and white audiences into social justice and civil rights activism. Well before Lady Bird and Polly Shackleton brought Laurance Rockefeller to Anacostia to fund the Trailblazer Project, the First Lady had even chaired a fundraiser organized by Shackleton for Anacostia youth groups, where Gregory performed stand-up as the main draw. But Gregory appeared not to recognize the First Lady's efforts on behalf of social programs he championed. The First Lady's very acknowledgment that she could not possibly relate to Kitt's experiences growing up became, to Gregory, not an honest recognition of difference, but an expression of indifference. "People are shocked to hear a mother reacting as Mrs. Johnson did to this war. This is a war where just about everybody has lost a loved one, or knows somebody who has."[24] He was unaware, perhaps, that her two sons-in-law were preparing to deploy.

Another Gregory, Gregory Peck, then in his second year as president of the Academy of Motion Picture Arts and Sciences, chimed in to support the First Lady. His frequent presence at the White House or at the Ranch allowed the Johnsons to bask in the reflected glow of Peck's Atticus Finch, Harper Lee's champion of justice in *To Kill a Mockingbird*. Peck often talked about how closely he identified with his character's defense of a falsely accused black man. But as a private citizen, Peck's derision tracked more closely with the older, more conservative Atticus Finch of Lee's nearly posthumous *Go Set a Watchman*. "I regret the intemperate behavior of certain members of my profession in recent days," he cabled the First Lady. "I think I speak for the vast majority of Americans when I tell you that none of my children are smoking anything because the United States has problems at home and abroad. Nor are we weeping about high taxes."[25] The day Peck's telegram arrived, January 30, 1968, the Viet Cong staged a siege on the U.S. embassy in Saigon, launching a series of defining, devastating attacks against American targets that would continue for nearly a month: the Tet Offensive. And in a matter of weeks, Katie Peden and her colleagues would speak their own version of truth to power, writing in the Kerner Commission's final report to the president, "Our nation is moving toward two societies, one black, one white—separate and unequal."[26]

* * *

Eartha Kitt had taken a significant risk by speaking out at the White House event, even one at which her participation had been actively sought. She quickly found bookings dry up. Regular performance venues refused to invite her back; commercial sponsors pressured for her public appearances to be canceled. Radio stations stopped playing her songs. Although her European audiences continued to flock to her shows, she spent years in domestic professional exile. In 1975, the columnist Jack Anderson supplied Seymour Hersh, then writing for *The New York Times,* with Kitt's CIA file, purportedly created as part of a threat assessment after the White House lunch. When Hersh called Kitt about the document, she told him the *Times* could publish however much of it the paper saw fit, but she scoffed at its inaccuracies and the legacy of McCarthyist lies that African American leaders had been subjected to in the twentieth century. "As long as they're going to investigate any of us," she said caustically, "they should at least come out with the truth."[27]

However eloquent, controlled, and honest her reply to Kitt in the moment of their exchange, by participating, both actively and passively, in the White House's subsequent smear campaign, the First Lady had broken with her own sense of decorum. She came into office with the explicit goal of showing the public that "deeds, not words" would define her White House tenure. This was the same woman who had taken pride in LBJ's involvement, just after the JFK assassination, in rehabilitating Robert Oppenheimer's reputation after his blacklisting over opposition to nuclear weapons. It was the same woman who had successfully pressed her husband to assume a sympathetic private and public stance toward Walter Jenkins when his arrest for homosexual activity became public during the 1964 campaign.

Yet, for all her focus on action, and pride in her own demonstrable compassion toward others, she was unable to handle her own public embarrassment over Eartha Kitt's criticism with similar grace and thoughtfulness. Maybe it was her exhaustion from the job and her anxiety over not knowing when she would get out, or maybe it really was just the affront of having the unvarnished truth spoken in her own home. Kitt's fearlessness that day, not the women's march for peace the day before, exposed to Lady Bird how wide the breach, how big the disconnect, between her husband's administration, between their presidency, and the rest of the country. Lady Bird's lapse in both deeds and words represented a rare display of uncharacteristic cruelty and self-regard.[28]

In interviews over the next few decades, Kitt correctly insisted that her statements resulted from a White House invitation to participate in a discussion on the basis of her experience teaching dance in Watts and working with youth groups in Los Angeles and Anacostia. Her error on January 18, 1968, was no more than having accepted the White House offer. And there were other casualties. By 1968, the word *urban,* especially in white America, increasingly became a slur for "black" or "ghetto," and the term *beautification,* associated with colorful flowers, sounded not just prissy and ineffectual, but decidedly tin-eared and, as Dick Gregory disparaged, indifferent to the depth of black pain. Most of the public had little or no idea of the substance the First Lady had tried to bring to her own vocation since 1966, fully aware as she was of the need to bolster the floral façade of urban beautification with local and national policies designed to deliver major improvements in the physical environment surrounding the most marginalized residents in American cities. In talking about how her own career had suffered, Kitt delighted in mocking Lady Bird's as mere window dressing. However accurate Kitt's characterization of the Johnson administration or however earnest her condemnation, the White House spin caused irreparable damage to her burgeoning career.

Chapter 22

"Standing Still When I Should Be Running"

I have a growing feeling of Prometheus bound, just as though we were lying there on the rock, exposed to the vultures, and really not fighting back. . . . I had the feeling of wasted opportunities, of standing still when I should be running.

—Lady Bird Johnson, White House diary, March 17, 1968

The Eartha Kitt controversy had blindsided the Johnsons and tainted the East Wing's otherwise spotless reputation for public engagement. "We need a better system for an election year," Liz wrote Marvin Watson, a close LBJ adviser attuned to the president's thinking about a second term. "[A]s you know, the First Lady is a terrific asset for the president. He knows it better than anyone and certainly better than any staff members who seem to think that she should have a low priority rating."[1] Throughout the early spring of 1968, as part of her constant struggle for resources, money, staff photographers, office space, and, most precious, the president's time, Liz had been pushing the West Wing to spotlight the Johnsons' political partnership as an asset of his presidency. With the White House senior staff gearing up for Lyndon's reelection and planning a spate of promotional press coverage in advance of the Chicago convention that August, Liz finally made some headway. The president did spend fifteen minutes in an off-the-record interview with *Look* magazine discussing exactly what Liz had pushed for. The 1964 election had been a landslide for Lyndon, and his internal polling showed a narrow path to victory in 1968. Johnson could afford to leave no votes on the table, including the women's vote: showcasing the centrality of his partnership with the First Lady, Liz argued, would be critical come November.[2]

Vietnam had by then both defined and undermined LBJ's presidency. At the end of February, America's most trusted news anchor, Walter Cronkite, broadcast live from Vietnam and concluded that "it seems now more certain than ever, that the bloody experience of Vietnam is to end in stalemate."[3] Watching the CBS report from the White House, Johnson famously told one adviser, "If I've lost Cronkite, I've lost Middle America."[4] On Sunday, March 10, with rumors swirling of imminent escalation, NBC correspondent Frank McGee concluded that "the war, as the administration has defined [it], is being lost. . . . [T]he time is at hand when we must decide whether it is futile to destroy Vietnam in the effort to save it."[5] That same night, the highly influential weekly magazine *Newsweek* went to press with a special edition on Vietnam, with an editorial statement warning that unless the administration "is prepared to indulge in the ultimate, horrifying escalation—the use of nuclear weapons—it now appears that the US must accept the fact that it will never be able to achieve decisive military superiority in Vietnam."[6] Monday morning, Secretary of State Dean Rusk endured six and a half hours of televised Senate grilling over the administration's plans for Vietnam, while the very same body passed the Fair Housing Act, the administration's next step on civil rights that aimed to prevent racial or religious discrimination and harassment in the housing market.

Although LBJ had distanced himself from the Kerner Commission's stark condemnation of "two increasingly separate Americas" as the root of racial conflict in U.S. cities, two days after the Senate passed the fair housing bill, the president moved forcefully to press the House to do the same. He stated that in contrast with violent demands for change, "our national purpose is being served and the requirements of our national conscience met, through lawful democratic processes."[7] A fair housing law, he argued, in a stretch of hopeful imagination, would show the world that the United States was intent on deepening its values of equality at home. "America is determined to achieve racial harmony and social justice for all her people," LBJ's message to the Speaker of the House read. In particular, passing a new law intent on leveling the playing field in the highly segregated and discriminatory housing market would assure "one man, the Negro veteran of Vietnam . . . of the elemental rights in his own country for which he risked his life overseas."[8]

Despite accolades from many civil rights leaders for pushing the legislation, the politics of the country were moving beyond the thirty-sixth president. Eugene McCarthy lost the New Hampshire primary on the twelfth of that month. But the eight-point margin was narrow enough to demonstrate that the president was losing his grip on his own party. Bobby Kennedy's announcement four days later of his own presidential candidacy reinforced LBJ's vulnerability. Speaking from the same spot in the Senate Caucus Room where JFK had announced his own run eight years earlier, RFK cited the "perilous course" of the country as motivation for jumping into the race.[9] Lyndon was utterly unsurprised. But Bobby's concerns were not unfounded. Across the world in My Lai, a village in the South Vietnamese province of Quang Ngai, American forces, led by First Lieutenant William L. Calley, had that very day killed 347 of the impoverished hamlet's 504 unarmed men, women, and children.[10]

Although competition from McCarthy and RFK would pose a challenge to LBJ in the primaries, White House staff were already anticipating a much closer race against the GOP than in 1964. The field was led by two Californians—with Richard Nixon as the party favorite and Ronald Reagan as the dark horse. Lady Bird's personal favorite, New York governor Nelson Rockefeller, had announced that he would not pursue the Republican presidential candidacy. In "a very terse, forthright, manly, dramatic statement," Bird recorded, Rockefeller concluded that he did not have the party machinery behind him. As much as Lady Bird Johnson thought of herself as a New Deal Democrat, the time she spent with Nelson's brother Laurance and his wife, Mary, had shaped her into a bit of a "Rockefeller Republican" on domestic matters, with strong views on protecting the environment and liberal on social policy, the very stripe of the GOP that Goldwater, and soon Nixon and then Reagan, would begin to erase. That night, with Bird's encouragement, Lyndon placed a call. "I'm sorry," the president told the governor. "I sort of hoped the Republicans would field their best man"—or maybe one he believed he could beat were he to run.[11]

Since 1964, when it became clear to the Johnsons that the Vietnam War could derail their domestic agenda, Bird had believed that her husband would not stand for a second term and that LBJ's concern was over not whether but only how and when to tell the country.[12] Lyndon's obsessive attention to the tools of power, his paranoia, and his ego gave staff, friends, allies, and adversaries, perhaps everyone but Lady Bird, the impression that once in office, he would never voluntarily give it up. Rockefeller's announcement left Bird wondering whether she could really be so certain about Lyndon's intentions—more surprisingly, she even questioned her own desire to leave.[13]

The reasons against a graceful exit from the Oval Office seemed to mount: the January 23 capture of the U.S.S. *Pueblo* by North Korean patrol boats, Tet, skyrocketing casualties among the 510,000 troops already stationed in Vietnam, and General Westmoreland's ask for 206,000 more. Add to all that Cronkite's call for a noble exit from an unwinnable war, the defection of senior cabinet members, bitter internal debates, flags and draft cards in cinders, and Bobby Kennedy's entry into the race. At least a part of the country, and not just the free-loving, drug-doing country, but rather, the country of civil rights and social progress, was emphatically rejecting the Johnsons. The woman who possessed a modern vision of urban design and of the social and economic dimensions of environmental health, who once mused expectantly about what the 1960s might bring, now felt alienated by talk of revolution, mysticism, yoga, and nihilism. Most dismaying was that black Americans, including Martin Luther King, Jr., were angrily making demands of a president she believed had done the most on their behalf since Abraham Lincoln.

Vietnam may have exacted a very high price, but it had not changed her mind about the legitimacy of the war effort. Pat's and Chuck's imminent deployment, Lynda's growing identification with servicemen and their families, and the private gatherings Lynda and her mother hosted at the White House for wounded vets had brought the conflict much closer to home. These encounters were among the rare occasions when Bird seemed not to know what to say or how to act. "With each new face, an uncertainty as to whether I should stick out my hand or not," she recalled. "If you're new on crutches, can you take one hand away with ease, to shake hands?"[14] Precisely because her husband's administration had grown so embattled by his determination not to become the first American president to lose a foreign war, and precisely because of RFK's and McCarthy's critiques of it, the First Lady's field of vision about Vietnam further narrowed. In that regard, she was every bit as stubborn and proud as her husband. And yet, nightmares still plagued her sleep—in them, she found herself lost, wandering from room to room, unable to find her way.

* * *

One journalist in the female press pool reported that although "you can smoke out at any party" the concern from Johnson Washingtonians over LBJ's political future, "it does not show in the faces of either Mr. or Mrs. Johnson."[15] Writing for the *Washington Examiner,* Betty Beale reported this exchange at the White House: "Someone observed to [LBJ] . . . 'Some people think Mrs. Johnson is looking so relaxed these days they are convinced, sir, that you are not going to run again.' Both Johnsons laughed. 'The faster I run, the more she relaxes,' replied the president."[16] But the Johnsons' reality could hardly have been further from the reporting. Just the night before, they had lain awake agonizing over this "endless, murky war"; over Pat's and Chuck's imminent deployment; and over whether Bobby's candidacy had "finally slam shut any exit," since yet another Kennedy at the top of the party's ticket would necessarily frame LBJ's presidency as a mere placeholder and jeopardize his legacy.[17] By then, Secretary of Defense Robert McNamara had left to go run the World Bank. LBJ awarded him the Medal of Freedom for his seven years of government service. After the emotional ceremony, and alone in the family quarters, Lady Bird allowed herself a rare lapse: she cried. The next day, Lynda told her mother that she was pregnant.[18]

Within weeks of McNamara's departure, LBJ—prompted by Tet, battles at Khe Sanh and Hue, and Westmoreland's incendiary request for hundreds of thousands more troops—finally began the process of extricating the United States from Southeast Asia.[19] Lady Bird had imagined that Lyndon would bring the war to a just conclusion, allowing them to leave the presidency in 1968 on a high note. It was a bitter irony that instead, the war had become a source of agony and indecision, but had also granted him the certainty and resolve to leave. Perhaps they had finally reached the moment, Bird thought, when Lyndon might tell the country he would not run for president in 1968.

But how to frame this decision for the public? March 10, when news leaked of Westmoreland's outsize troop request, was a day of "deep gloom" for Lady Bird. She "felt it in my very bones." Yet she found Lyndon's demeanor animated and hardy. "I never took off my hat to him more," she recorded, "or felt more tender."[20] Moving ever closer to a decision about his future, Lady Bird and Lyndon circled back to the familiar theme of national unity. LBJ was proud of having defied expectations by unifying the country after JFK's assassination, knitting together a historic political coalition in Congress that delivered unprecedented gains for civil rights and social reform. Now, under relentless attack on all sides, he felt the kernel of self-doubt that had always plagued him again become the "nettle in his throat," impossible to swallow or to spit out.

Given how polarizing a figure he had become in a now-splintered nation, could LBJ possibly be the only one to unify the country? "Suppose," Lady Bird hypothesized, "someone else were elected President. What could Mr. X do that you could not do?" Lyndon replied, she recorded, "that Mr. X 'could unite the country and start getting things done.' That would last about a year, maybe two years." With Bird's prodding, LBJ was allowing himself to acknowledge what he had always understood on some level: that he was not indispensable and was possibly an impediment to seeing his own progressive vision manifest. Heaviest on his mind, Bird concluded, was Lyndon's doubt over his own leadership. "Can *he* unite the country, or is there simply too much built up—antagonism, division, a general malaise, which may have him, irrevocably, as its focal point?" Even with sties in both eyes, "like Job," LBJ was nevertheless "calm, even-tempered, rather serenely philosophic."[21]

On the day RFK announced that he would run, Lyndon left Washington, picked up his grandson, Lyn, in Austin, and flew on to meet Lady Bird and to celebrate Lynda's birthday at the Ranch. It was their last time together as a family before Chuck's deployment. With another civil rights victory in the air (the Senate had just passed the fair housing bill), they gathered for LBJ's second viewing of the 1967 Stanley Kramer film about intermarriage and race, *Guess Who's Coming to Dinner.* "It's odd," Bird recorded, "that Lyndon should admire it, and find it so interesting that he would see it twice, when he usually goes to sleep after the first 10 minutes of any movie."[22] The portrayal by Spencer Tracy, Katharine Hepburn, and Sidney Poitier of three serious adults trying to come to terms with a country reluctant, but very much needing, to change must have provided some consolation to a man who felt that he, too, had tried to reconcile the social cleavages embodied by each character in the story.

But the elegantly managed conflict and feel-good denouement of Kramer's Technicolor San Francisco utopia bore little resemblance to the gravity of white supremacist force endured by black Americans in cities around the country. As the Johnson family prepared for two of its members to deploy to Vietnam and watched a fantasy family find comity across the racial divide, Martin Luther King, Jr., was putting the final touches on an address to twenty-five thousand Memphis residents gathered in support of striking sanitation workers.[23] Earlier that year, to escape the deluge of torrential rains and flooding streets, two sanitation workers, required by the city's public works department to take shelter in the back of their own truck and wait out the rain, were crushed to death when an electrical switch malfunctioned and turned on the truck's compactor.[24] Memphis mayor Henry Loeb had rebuffed workers' efforts to unionize, greatly exacerbating racial conflict in the city. In the aftermath of the mayor's veto, King returned to Memphis to participate in the march supporting the workers' demands for representation, fair wages, and proper safety standards. The protesters carried signs asserting the devastatingly simple, poignant notion of their humanity, "I Am a Man," but the Memphis Police behaved otherwise. As violence and looting began, a police officer shot and killed a sixteen-year-old boy. Police fired tear gas into a church sanctuary and clubbed people as they lay on the ground gasping for air.[25]

As Memphis erupted in violence, Lady Bird focused on her beautification work in the capital with Mayor Walter Washington. She came away disappointed with the uneven progress and found herself tired out by the need to "project an animated, interested appearance all at the same time."[26] But she was reassured when she saw that everywhere they stopped, the mayor's deep ties with District residents were apparent. He was appointed, not yet elected, but short of a one-year stint in New York, he had spent his entire professional career trying to improve the daily lives and living conditions of residents outside the privileged enclaves of Upper Northwest.

Bird also believed she shared with Washington and other standard-bearers of more traditional national black establishments (the NAACP, say, or the Urban League) a concept of progress rooted in the patient reliance on judicial rulings and congressional legislation. She reluctantly accepted the role of activist movements such as those in Memphis pushing for change from the outside. But she couldn't fathom how nonviolent mobilizations, or how legislation her husband had passed, laws and policies that she had campaigned for and promoted, had somehow opened the door to the violence and racial animus engulfing the country since 1965.

Even with historic civil rights laws and unprecedented federal funding for Great Society programs, there just hadn't been enough time or money to heal the spiritual and economic wounds of slavery and Jim Crow. The bestselling report of the president's own politically moderate Kerner Commission said as much, and in unvarnished terms: "Segregation and poverty have created in the racial ghetto a destructive environment totally unknown to most white Americans. What white Americans have never fully understood but what the Negro can never forget—is that white society is deeply implicated in the ghetto. White institutions created it, white institutions maintain it, and white society condones it," the report concluded.[27] When the report was published in February 1968, replete with unanimous recommendations for substantial federal investments to redress discrimination in employment, housing, policing, and even the media, President Johnson first ignored and then attacked it, resentful over the report's lack of appreciation for his accomplishments. He professed instead that the riots were born of media hype and political conspiracy, not real conditions. But he knew better, and so did Lady Bird.

While momentum built for MLK's next phase of direct action, a Poor People's Campaign that would occupy the grounds of Washington's National Mall to demand economic justice, the First Lady did take some satisfaction from the fact that the District of Columbia appeared to be exempt from the tinderbox conditions of so many other American cities. By 1968, the hegemony that King and the Southern Christian Leadership Conference once exerted over the civil rights movement had frayed. Like LBJ, King had lost control over his base, a coalition of organizations whose mobilization and sacrifice had paved the way for the president to pass his landmark civil rights laws. And he'd certainly lost control over the forces, both organized and disorganized, that now agitated for more rapid, even violent change. Since King's Riverside Church denunciation of the war in Vietnam one year earlier, LBJ had soured on the thirty-nine-year-old leader. Dejected by the president's depletion of the nation's riches, both human and financial, and bereft over the backward momentum of violent urban uprisings, Reverend King had likewise soured on President Johnson.

* * *

Lynda celebrated her twenty-fourth birthday at the Ranch over steak, spinach, homemade peach ice cream, and a big cake. Already worn down by the fatigue of early pregnancy, she was consumed with anxiety about her new husband's vulnerability as they left for Camp Pendleton, in California. She had met with enough wounded vets, read enough in letters about the worries, heartbreak, and courage of the wives of servicemen, to know that even with the inevitable, though unspoken, protections her husband would enjoy, he was putting his life at risk not just for his country, but for a commander in chief who happened to be her father. It was a heavy burden for the newlyweds. When asked whether she thought LBJ should run for a second term, Lynda was emphatically positive, telling her father that she believed him to be the only man up to the task of keeping American soldiers safe in Vietnam. Now more than ever, she needed to cling to that faith.

After three days at Camp Pendleton, on March 30, Lynda traveled with Chuck to another base for his departure to Da Nang. A photograph in *The New York Times* shows her surrounded by a scrum of reporters. Her hair pulled back with a wide headband, she clings to a coffee tin filled with brownies for Chuck's send-off to active duty. After their emotional, all-too-public goodbye, she went to see *The Graduate,* crying through the entire movie. Spent, she caught the red-eye back to Washington to be present for what she believed was to be a major speech on Vietnam.[28]

As Lynda said goodbye to Chuck, the White House buzzed with speechwriters and advisers laying the groundwork for a Rose Garden press conference where LBJ would set the stage for a major speech scheduled for Sunday, March 31. But there was more to it than Vietnam. After three months of nightmares and sleeplessness, worrying about her daughters and Lyndon, Lady Bird could not quite allow herself to believe that the president would at last announce the decision they had been planning since 1964. He was finally ready. Lady Bird and Lyndon had breakfast together, posed for a photograph on the South Lawn, and went their separate ways. As the crocuses and daffodils of early spring in Washington began to peep through the barren soil, the First Lady felt the need to experience her own unambiguously tangible legacy as Lyndon prepared to announce plans for his. She didn't need to stick around to hear his press conference; she knew what was coming. Instead, the First Lady phoned her friend and ally at the National Park Service, Nash Castro: "Nash, let's go for a ride."[29]

With only the Secret Service accompanying them, the two set out for a three-hour ramble through Rock Creek Park, down Pennsylvania Avenue, to Pershing Park, and out to Columbia Island. The cherry blossoms in Washington were already in bloom. They strolled. They chatted with a teenager from Chevy Chase who sketched blooms at the park for an art class. The cherry trees around the Tidal Basin had also begun to bloom, and Bird posed stiffly for several photos with locals and tourists, with Nash and alone.

Lady Bird craved a burger, she confided, and Nash handed some money to the Secret Service. Surrounded by buds from among the nearly eight hundred thousand daffodils Nash's team had planted, Castro spread his jacket out for her to sit on. When an agent returned with a carryout burger, Castro watched her remove the top bun from the burger before she allowed herself to eat. "Mrs. Johnson, just imagine how much more you'll be able to accomplish over the next four years," he said as they viewed the scene. But Lady Bird had been working for two days on the statement Lyndon was preparing to deliver the next day. Hiding their secret and her anxiety, she turned her gaze away from Nash—and then turned back. "We'll have to see, Nash, we'll have to see."[30]

Meanwhile, just after noon, sitting at a table in the Rose Garden, the president announced that the next night, at nine P.M., he would deliver a speech to the American people. After a word on his budget for the coming fiscal year, the press moved quickly to politics and Vietnam. Who would win in the Wisconsin primary next week? LBJ said he didn't know. And what about rumors of a bombing pause? The White House had been involved in an extended review of Vietnam options ever since Tet, the president replied. Sounding blander than usual, he added, "It will be more or less a report on the reviews which have taken place, together with an announcement of some actions that we are taking." In light of the mêlée in Memphis of two days earlier, asked how he felt about the Poor People's Campaign heading soon to the capital, the president kept to his talking points, displaying respect for the lawful right to protest while pressing for marchers and law enforcement to avoid all violence. Attorney General Katzenbach and Mayor Washington had been given ample time to prepare, he noted. What's more, "we know of no way to prohibit people who comply with the law from exercising their rights."[31]

Under more favorable political conditions, the president might have used the mobilization in Washington, as he had marches in Selma, as an opportunity to press his case in the House for passage of the Fair Housing Act. Instead, he seemed to regard demands for deeper social change just a few hundred yards from the South Lawn as an outlier, rather than a sentiment that resonated nationally. He also had other matters on his mind. Asked if there was any validity to a rumor that he would not announce his 1968 plans until the August convention in Chicago, the president declined to comment, saying only that "we haven't made any decision on the matter yet." Perhaps that was still true.[32]

Chapter 23

March 31, 1968

It is interesting and perhaps significant that among the few well informed people in Washington who maintained that Mr. Johnson would not run again were some of the wives of men close to the President. While their husbands were saying that the President would never willingly give up the Presidency so long as the war was on, the women insisted that Mrs. Johnson would prevail on him in the end to avoid what promised to be a very bitter and maybe even dangerous campaign.

—James "Scotty" Reston, "They Didn't Believe Him,"
The New York Times, April 1, 1968

At seven the next morning, the White House operator called the Johnsons. Lynda's red-eye had landed, and her car would arrive at any minute. The president and First Lady went downstairs to the South Lawn to greet their daughter. Lynda "looked like a ghost—pale, tall, and drooping."[1] She'd taken a sedative to sleep on the overnight flight, but it hadn't eased her mood. After seeing Captain Robb off to war, she arrived in Washington on edge, aware only that her father was to make a major speech on Vietnam that night. Her parents hugged her. She turned to her father. "Daddy, I want to ask you a question. Why do we have to fight over there when so many people are opposed to the war?"[2]

There is no record of LBJ's reply, but in his memoir, he recognized that "war and separation were cruel intrusions into her young life. The divisions in the country had left their mark on her. . . . Lynda had been reading about those demonstrators and critics who looked on such sacrifices as hers and Chuck's as meaningless, or worse. The hurt that had been building up inside her was now released in a flood of tears." Describing his response, LBJ recalled, "I wanted to comfort her, and I could not."[3] He was unaware at the time, and wouldn't learn until April, that Lynda was pregnant. The president went back to his bedroom, and Lady Bird took Lynda to hers, the room she had inherited from Caroline Kennedy five years earlier.

Bird helped Lynda settle into bed. Lynda recounted the scene at Norton Air Force Base, with the press pushing and shoving, almost running over a child, just to get a shot of her goodbye to Chuck. This was the day Lady Bird would be most needed by Lyndon, to provide that "balm" and the strength he required to announce his decision. Yet, here she was, Lady Bird thought, pulled between husband and child, attempting to provide some measure of comfort to her distraught daughter just when Lynda had finally allowed herself to question her adored father's judgment.[4]

"When I went back into Lyndon's room, he was crying," Lady Bird recalled. It was the first time since mourning the loss a decade earlier of his beloved mother, Rebekah Johnson, that she had seen him in tears. "But he didn't have time to cry," and neither did she.[5] Lyndon's speech was still not done—not the part on Vietnam, not the statement about his future. His bedroom would soon begin to fill with aides laying out newly tailored suits; doctors incongruously scraping samples of skin cancers from his hands; staff bringing breakfast—and, for levity and pure play, his grandson, Lyn. Before the deluge of the day, and crying still, the president changed out of his pajamas, grabbed Luci and her husband, Pat, and went to church. On his way out, Horace "Buzz" Busby handed him a draft of his speech. An exhausted Lady Bird went back to bed and tried, unsuccessfully, to snatch some sleep in preparation for the emotional hours ahead.[6]

Mass at St. Dominic, the twin-spired, brick Gothic church built just after the Civil War, again provided the president with a moment of peace. In his memoir, he recalled that he also went there with Luci in June 1966, just after he had issued orders to bomb Haiphong harbor.[7] In less than twelve hours, he'd go on television and indirectly acknowledge the folly of the strategy behind that decision.

Before returning to the White House after Mass, the president traveled to the vice president's apartment to share the news. On the four-block drive through Southwest to see Hubert Humphrey, LBJ read Luci and Pat the draft of the statement he planned to deliver that night. As her eyes welled up with tears, his usually loquacious child sat silent. Lyndon broke the silence. "I thought this was what [you] wanted me to do." Indeed, Luci had been adamant that her father exit the White House after one term. But now her husband, the father of Lyndon's cherished first grandchild, would shortly ship off to war. "Trying to smile, she replied that her reaction was complicated," LBJ recounted. "I understood. No matter how strong and simple the conviction, when you got right to the finish line, it *was* complicated. Looking at both of them, I experienced emotions too overwhelming to express."[8] At the Humphreys', a large apartment with sweeping views of the Potomac, LBJ handed him the draft speech. The final paragraph blindsided the vice president. His face flushed, a "thunderstruck" Humphrey's eyes filled with tears. Hubert had taken a drubbing as LBJ's deputy, waiting in the wings for years for his moment to shine as the party's next and rightful standard-bearer. But in the moment, he implored the president not to step down. "You can't just resign from office. . . . There's no way I can beat the Kennedys," he said softly.[9]

Less than six miles away from the vice president's home, at the National Cathedral on Wisconsin Avenue, more than three thousand people packed its pews, stood along its aisles, and crowded into the back, while another thousand gathered on the grounds outside to listen to a guest minister deliver the Sunday sermon. The riots in Memphis earlier that week had thrown Dr. Martin Luther King, Jr.'s schedule into disarray, but he kept to his long-planned appearance at the invitation of the cathedral's dean, in order to speak about the Poor People's Campaign. "It is an unhappy truth," King lamented, "that racism is a way of life for the vast majority of white Americans, spoken and unspoken, acknowledged and denied, subtle and sometimes not so subtle—the disease of racism permeates and poisons a whole body politic. And I can see nothing more urgent than for America to work passionately and unrelentingly—to get rid of the disease of racism." King preached against the "myth of time," and against the "notion that only time can solve the problem of racial injustice." He preached against "those who often sincerely say to the Negro and his allies in the white community, 'Why don't you slow up? Stop pushing things so fast. Only time can solve the problem. And if you will just be nice and patient and continue to pray, in a hundred or two hundred years the problem will work itself out.'" But King had lost patience with both time and prayer.[10]

On this, he and the president had something in common. Lyndon was always in a rush, never believed time was his friend, and certainly, as president, seldom viewed his power or the policies that derived from it with an air of inevitability. But the two men bore a very different sense of what they must do with the time that remained. King's mission was to lay bare how the Vietnam War's erosion of the American dream "has put us against the self-determination of a vast majority of the Vietnamese people, and put us in the position of protecting a corrupt regime that is stacked against the poor." At home it has "strengthened the forces of reaction in our nation . . . and has played havoc with our domestic destinies." The time had come not only for King to oppose LBJ for reelection, but also to channel his energy into justice in Memphis, the Poor People's Campaign in Washington, and, he warned, toward a "real awakening in Chicago," should the recommendations of the 1968 Kerner Commission and the 1966 White House Conference on Civil Rights remain unmet.[11] Mobilization, protest, occupation—there were no more excuses for "remaining asleep through a revolution." For the once-conciliatory King, the time for collaborative change had long passed. "This time," he said, his voice rising in the massive Gothic space, "we will really confront a Goliath."[12]

* * *

Lady Bird awoke from a fitful nap with an hour to herself before Lyndon, Luci, and Pat would arrive back at the White House. She culled the day's news clips—and indulged in the women's sections of both *The Washington Post* and *The Star*. The papers published a spread about the wardrobe choices she had selected for a trip through Texas the next week; *The Star* featured a story, placed above her own, about another political spouse, Pat Nixon.[13] Her husband had also planned to give a speech that night about Vietnam and "deliver a sharp critique of the Johnson policy of gradualism," but he canceled it when he heard about the president's address.[14] In a matter of months, Nixon would find another way to thwart LBJ's efforts on Vietnam.

The president spent the afternoon between the Treaty Room, where Busby was working on his statement, and the family quarters. Buzz and LBJ refined draft after draft. Finally, the president asked his secretary to type it up, do a final word count, and provide him, and no one else, with several copies. Lyndon called Lady Bird and asked her to assemble Pat, Luci, Arthur Krim, and Krim's multilingual scientist wife, Mathilde, in the West Hall of the family quarters. Then the president began to read them his proposed speech. "There was no comment," his daily diary recorded. "Luci fought back tears." Lynda stayed away entirely. And Lady Bird, who "seemed engrossed," scribbled furiously, editing as she wrote on a five-by-seven White House–embossed pad of paper, taking yet another pass, as she had nearly four years earlier, at articulating their rationale for Lyndon's withdrawing from the 1968 presidential race.[15]

As the group dissected each word, Lyndon called for Buzz to join them for lunch. Luci allowed herself to cry without restraint. Mathilde's eyes brimmed with tears. Arthur, who in 1967 had pushed back when he first heard of Lyndon's desire not to run for reelection, now argued that LBJ's soon-to-be-publicized bombing halt would in fact strengthen his candidacy. But the president had settled the matter: he could work to resolve the Vietnam morass only if he could operate free of politicization and partisanship. The speech that evening announcing a bombing halt, he thought, would otherwise "be written off as a political gesture."[16]

Ever mindful of the weight of historical moments, and of her own perspective in and on them, Lady Bird recorded tersely, "And I, what did I feel—so uncertain of the future, that I would dare not to try to persuade him one way or the other."[17] From her scribblings, her edits, and the late nights awake together, LBJ knew exactly where she stood. "Lady Bird said nothing, but I already knew which side she was on," Lyndon recalled.[18]

She also felt "there was much that cried out to go on, to get every friend of ours, to give and work, and spend and fight, right up to the last, and if we lost, well and good—we were free. But we could be free without all this draining of our friends." For Bird, after Lyndon's health, after the emotional toll of Vietnam on her daughters and their marriages, it was the loss of friendships that hurt her most. "I think what was going over and over in Lyndon's mind was something that I've heard him say increasingly the last months." Bird summarized her husband's most compelling argument, the one that would allow him to unbind himself from the Promethean rock: "'I do not believe I can unite this country.'"[19]

* * *

For years, Lyndon had struggled to extricate himself from the White House. And for years, he had failed to settle on a satisfactory course of action. Tormented by nightmares, he realized his predicament only after one particularly bad dream, where "he was swimming from the center toward one shore. He swam and swam, but he never seemed to get any closer. He turned around to swim to the other shore, but again he got nowhere. He was simply going round and round in circles." How, then, could Johnson leave the White House, but do so honorably and without shame? "Looking ahead to posterity," Lyndon found his answer: "'If the American people don't love me, their descendants will.'"[20] It was a perspective fit for the Johnsons, meticulous curators of their legacy that they were, from the courtship letters of their youth to the hundreds of notebooks filled with Lady Bird's shorthand during Lyndon's congressional years, to the First Lady's diary recordings throughout the presidency, to the hundreds of hours of tapes LBJ recorded of his Oval Office conversations, and even down to the richly specific stenographic record preserved in the President's Daily Diary. Each source, loaded with detail, explanations, and, even, acknowledgments of their shortcomings, was meant to outlast them, to explain their actions more clearly than they ever could in their own lifetimes.

Finding the motivation to retire from Washington politics was one thing. Articulating the rationale of patriotism over partisanship in a way that would not only sound reasonable to a stunned nation, but also withstand the test of history, was another matter. Now, with yet another draft delivered by Marie Fehmer to the dining room table, LBJ again read it aloud, with Horace Busby providing "a very persuasive, almost poetic little explanation of how and why he had written the statement," the First Lady recorded. Although Lady Bird had made her case, argued against it, and then made it again, and written her share of drafts, for this version of the statement, she credited "Lyndon," who "indeed, was the architect, the planner," while Buzz "cloaked it in its final word."[21]

* * *

On a typical Washington Sunday, after the newspapers, church, and lunch with their ever-depleted circle of confidants, Bird would usually retreat to her sitting room to record her diary or to read briefing papers, sign letters, and autograph photos. Perhaps she'd swim or bowl, or seek out her daughters for quiet conversation. But after lunch on this particular Sunday, she was at a loss. "I must do something, but what, and how did I dare do anything, with the decision so momentous, and one I could by no means implement, or take responsibility of making it turn out right."[22]

She spent the rest of the afternoon immersed in the anxiety and tension of waiting, watching the clock, counting the minutes until nine P.M. "It was a strange afternoon and evening," she recorded. "We would meet in the West Hall by twos or threes, or all of us—Mathilde, Arthur, Buzz, Lynda, Luci, Pat and I, and look at each other, helplessly, silent, or exploding with talk." Her daughters were especially emotional—Luci crying, Lynda distraught, even bitter. Referring to her father's war, Lynda spoke her mind: "We've been scared into believing that what we are doing is wrong, by the Kennedy money, and the blitz of public opinion this last month." But for her this was above all a deeply personal jolt. "Chuck will hear this on his way to Vietnam," she told her mother. More unanswerable questions poured forth. "'What does this do to the boys? They will think—what have I been out here for? Was it all wrong? Can I believe in what I've been fighting for?'" Her daughters felt that "Lyndon had been something of a champion of the soldiers, that his getting out would be a blow to them."[23]

When LBJ woke from a nap after lunch, Bird shared Lynda's questions, but reminded him that their daughters "were looking at it from [the] closer range of the wives of two young soldiers." For all the bluster about imminent success in Vietnam, Lyndon told Bird that several months ago, when he asked General Westmoreland how a change in the Oval Office might affect the morale of the boys on the battlefield, the army commander had said, "It will not matter appreciably." Bird wrote, "He looked at me rather distantly and said, 'I think Westmoreland knows more about it than they do.'" Lyndon's tears of that morning had long dried. His daughters and their husbands were no longer a factor keeping him in office. Quite the opposite: He wanted to be around to see them flourish and his grandchildren multiply, and although he bristled at the idea of his sons-in-law seeing him as a "yellow-bellied S.O.B.," in his moments of most honest self-examination and reflection, he understood that leaving the presidency was the best way to secure not only the family peace, but that of the country.[24]

Finally, the energy in the White House began to shift. By six o'clock, the backstage preparations for the president's statement gave everyone a point of reference on which to project their feelings of shock, sadness, and relief. A full three hours before he would tell American citizens and the rest of the world, the president took the extraordinary step of sharing his decision not with his longtime confidant Secretary of Defense Clark Clifford, nor with the lawyer whose legal strategy twenty years before had cleared Lyndon to take his seat in the Senate, associate justice of the Supreme Court Abe Fortas, but with a foreign diplomat, Anatoly Dobrynin, Moscow's ambassador to the United States.

At 5:55 P.M., Lady Bird sat in the Yellow Oval Room with the Soviet diplomat waiting for the president. With her was a "gray and weary"–looking Walt Rostow, the national security advisor, and Averell Harriman, LBJ's choice as special envoy to future Vietnam peace talks. Bird found Dobrynin "affable and talkative," and she steered the conversation toward whether the Bolshoi Ballet might perform in San Antonio. Arriving a little late, "Lyndon came in with a jaunty step," the kind she'd seen him use to "rev up under the most intense tension."[25] Had the First Lady remained for the discussion, she would have heard the president explain that he was about to announce a partial, temporary bombing halt above the 20th parallel in Vietnam. Referring to Moscow's role in settling the Indo-Pakistani War of 1965 and its efforts to negotiate the Nuclear Non-Proliferation Treaty, Lyndon asked if the two superpowers might come together again for international peace.

With a copy of that night's speech in hand, a noncommittal Dobrynin began to leave. Johnson followed him into the hallway and delivered another piece of news, one that even his key cabinet secretaries and Harriman, one of the few foreign policy "wise men" whom he still trusted, were still hours away from learning. In Dobrynin's memoir, he described a president who "could hardly hide his emotion" and who "did not look well" when he told the Soviet ambassador "in strict confidence" of his decision not to run again.[26] Leery of leaks by his own people, LBJ sufficiently trusted the envoy of Washington's most devout global adversary to keep a lid on his secret, if only for the next three hours. If ever there was a sign of certainty that this time Lyndon would go forward and publicize his decision, this was it. But Bird had since left the scene.[27]

Busby and LBJ worked through two more drafts until finally, just after seven-thirty P.M., the president authorized his secretary to deliver the first part of his statement to the teleprompter, and forty minutes later, the crucial remaining two pages. In an Oval Office now crawling with cables and lit by the glare of television lights, Bird found "Lyndon, very quiet, at his desk. The lines in his face very deep, but a marvelous sort of repose overall. And the seconds ticked away."[28]

LBJ relished the surprise he was about to deliver. He took pleasure in watching the shock on the face of his deputy press secretary reading the text of the teleprompter minutes before they went live. He enjoyed imagining the reaction by the small press pool invited to watch from the doorway of the Oval Office as he delivered a speech they thought was only about Vietnam.[29] Now, with both daughters and one son-in-law gathered together, Lady Bird took her seat off camera, within the president's peripheral vision. She then got up and walked over to his desk. "Remember—pacing and drama," she whispered. He and Buzz had written "a great speech and I wanted to get the greatest out of it." Yet, for all the weekend's emotion, for all the tension and buildup, even while Moscow's ambassador already knew what LBJ had in store, Lady Bird recorded, "I still did not know what the end would be."[30]

When his live broadcast began, President Johnson declared a temporary halt to all bombing north of the 20th parallel. He also announced an initiative to launch talks in Paris, hoping that North Vietnam's president, Ho Chi Minh, would "respond positively, and favorably, to this new step toward peace." The president spoke for almost forty minutes. But the most shocking part of the statement, the part Bird claimed she still could not be sure her husband would actually read, lasted for less than two.

> With America's sons in the fields far away, with America's future under challenge right here at home, with our hopes and the world's hopes for peace in the balance every day, I do not believe that I should devote an hour or a day of my time to any personal partisan causes or to any duties other than the awesome duties of this office—the Presidency of your country.
>
> Accordingly, I shall not seek, and I will not accept, the nomination of my party for another term as your President. But let men everywhere know, however, that a strong, a confident, and a vigilant America stands ready tonight to seek an honorable peace—and stands ready tonight to defend an honored cause—whatever the price, whatever the burden, whatever the sacrifice that duty may require. Thank you for listening. Good night and God bless all of you.[31]

To his wife, watching from stage right, it was a "magnificently delivered" speech, emanating from a "calm, strong" man now "at his best." To those watching it on television, Lady Bird hoped "those that love him, must have loved him more, and those that hate him, must at least have thought—'Here is a man.'"[32] As soon as the cameras stopped, Lady Bird hugged and kissed LBJ, still standing behind his desk. The footage captures a glance between the two, a knowing exchange. Luci, holding back tears, kissed her father on the cheek. Lynda, too. For the moment, "the weight of the day and the weeks and the months had lifted. I had done what I knew ought to be done." He couldn't unsay it. "Now it was history and I could do no more," LBJ later wrote.[33]

Within minutes of going off the air, LBJ stopped with his family to watch the initial shocked reactions on the networks. The White House switchboard rang off the hook. The first call came from Chicago's mayor, Richard Daley. "You dropped the biggest bombshell," Daley told LBJ, and warned that at the Democratic convention in August, "we're going to draft you." At that moment, thoughts of the convention in Chicago five months out were still remote. The next calls came from Hubert Humphrey and, a minute later, John Connally.[34]

The president and First Lady then led their entourage up to the second-floor family quarters. LBJ changed out of his suit into a pale blue turtleneck. The first call Lady Bird placed was to a shocked Liz Carpenter. Bird had felt awful about allowing her staff to plan for the 1968 campaign—watching Liz especially rev herself up with reelection adrenaline, and knowing that the work was quite likely for naught. The first incoming call Lady Bird fielded came from Milwaukee, where Abigail McCarthy was campaigning for her husband. "Bird, Bird—you know what I've always thought about you. . . . When he made the announcement, I could only think of you standing in front of the Wilson portrait."[35] The two had known each other since Lyndon and Gene served together in the Senate. For a moment, McCarthy had thought that Lyndon might just choose him as a vice-presidential running mate in 1964.

Abigail didn't have to say more. Hanging in the Grand Staircase of the White House, F. Graham Cootes's portrait of Woodrow Wilson, painted after the twentieth president suffered a debilitating stroke, was a constant reminder to both Johnsons of the risks of becoming incapacitated while still in office. As Bird put it dryly, "I know what I always say in front of the Wilson portrait. Its message to me: 'The President should have his portrait painted reasonably early in office'"—a feat the Johnsons had yet to accomplish to their satisfaction.[36]

The barrage of calls continued: Dean Rusk, Bess Abell, Abe Fortas, Bill Moyers, Mary Lasker, special counsel Harry McPherson, Secretary of Labor Willard Wirtz, press secretaries George Reedy and George Christian, actress Tallulah Bankhead, CBS president Frank Stanton, UN ambassador Arthur Goldberg, OEC director Sargent Shriver, Nelson and Happy Rockefeller, plus a half dozen of the Johnsons' closest Texas friends from politics and business. As drinks and dinner circulated, and more friends came and went, LBJ stepped away from the phone to meet the journalists waiting for him in the Oval Office. Finishing a bowl of chocolate pudding, the president fielded their questions. Was his decision irrevocable? Completely. Can you see a scenario under which that might change? "No, I cannot."[37]

When Lyndon returned to the Yellow Oval Room, he appeared to Lady Bird "like there was a great load off his shoulders." The next day, *The New York Times* reported that the president said he "felt as good as a fellow could feel that's gone through what a fellow's gone through."[38] He had, Bird thought, "made it quite clear to 'them' that this was final, and that any talk of a draft [in Chicago] was foolishness."[39] In the family quarters, with official U.S. presidential photographer Yoichi "Okie" Okamoto taking photographs and most people speaking in hushed tones, the room looked and felt more like a funeral parlor. Lady Bird sat in a corner at a table, watching the scene unfold, trying to eat some dinner, while Walt Rostow kneeled next to her, speaking to her quietly. But LBJ seemed relaxed, leaning back in his chair and resting his chin on his hands, on the phone, off the phone, schmoozing with his shocked coterie. His humor and razzing elevated the group. Although she was still preoccupied with the morale of the troops, even Lynda's sense of humor seemed to return. That night, after their last guest left, and after Lyndon had gone to sleep, Lady Bird found herself feeling "immeasurably lighter."

At last the decision had been reached, and stated, and as well as any human can, we knew our future. It had been, I believe, his best speech, nobly done, and almost, in its way, as dramatic as our entrance into this job, although the actual exit is still nine months away, if the Lord lets us live. And to these nine months, I'm going to bring the best I possibly can. I went to sleep planning.[40]

Chapter 24

Assassination

It was a strange, mostly quiet meal. I thought—and maybe they did too—that we had been pummeled by such an avalanche of emotions the last four days, that we couldn't feel anymore, and here we were, suddenly poised on the edge of another abyss, the bottom of which we could in no way see. If we were silent, the TV was not, it blared constantly—statements from everybody, speculations on what would happen in various cities—fearful, heating up, and tensions. I do not remember when the first word came of crowds gathering in Washington on certain streets.

—Lady Bird Johnson, White House diary, April 4, 1968

In the aftermath of the JFK assassination, LBJ had focused on the two domestic policy issues that had remained stagnant during Kennedy's last year: taxes and civil rights. Foreign policy was not his forte, and after assuming the presidency, Lyndon wove together an agenda for the country that drew from his most searing experiences and beliefs. In the middle of the night at the Elms, after returning from Dallas, LBJ gathered his aides and began to visualize his presidency:

> I am going to get Kennedy's tax cut out of the Senate Finance Committee, and we're going to get this economy humming again. Then I'm going to pass Kennedy's civil rights bill, which has been hung up too long in the Congress. And I'm going to pass it without changing a single comma or a word. After that we'll pass legislation that allows everyone anywhere in the country to vote, with all the barriers down. And that's not all. We're going to get a law that says every boy

> and girl in this country, no matter how poor, or the color of their skin, or the region they come from, is going to be able to get all the education they can take by loan, scholarship, or grant, right from the federal government. And I aim to pass Harry Truman's medical insurance bill that got nowhere before.[1]

His successes had been breathtaking. Yet, as clear-minded and confident as LBJ was about his domestic ambitions for the country when he assumed power in 1963, in matters of foreign policy and national security he acted with the overreach and bluster of an insecure man. The Cold War's polemics made it that much harder to reject the relentlessly, if at times cynically, encouraging advice of Kennedy's foreign policy team when it came to involvement in Vietnam. They were creatures of World War II and, but for a few dissenting voices, could not fathom an American loss abroad. They also did not believe the United States could be susceptible to the kind of imperial ambitions that the British and French once faced. The French played for indecent colonial stakes, the thinking went, but America played to preserve and expand the benefits of its exceptionalism. LBJ recognized early on that Vietnam might well distract from his plans for a country with equal racial and educational opportunity, and this realization elevated the stakes of failure in Vietnam. In the end, only by setting a firm date to exit his presidency was he able to contemplate how to unhinge his legacy from the disaster in Indochina.

Lady Bird compared the 1968 transition with that of the transition foisted upon them by the tragedy in November 1963. In 1963, the couple found themselves thrust into the presidency under circumstances no one could have planned for. With Lyndon's announcement, they at last felt in their bones that they could exercise some control over their own future. Bird cherished the possibility that the feeling would endure for the rest of the year.[2] Everything she hoped to accomplish (desegregating public access to the natural environment and to better recreational conditions in the District of Columbia, curating exhibits for their presidential library in Austin, designing parks in and around Stonewall, and shaping the images and narrative the White House would produce about the president's last year) now had the perfect organizing principle: a deadline. After Lyndon's announcement, she consoled her shocked staff, kept an eye on her daughters' adjustment to their father's decision, and looked ahead, relieved that a decision long in the making had finally become irrevocable.

Her relief was short-lived. The bullet that killed Dr. Martin Luther King, Jr., at the Lorraine Motel in downtown Memphis at 6:01 P.M. CST on Thursday, April 4, also shattered all illusions of well-being. Home after two days of rest as the guest of Marjorie Merriweather Post at her ornate Palm Beach palazzo, Mar-a-Lago, Lady Bird was sitting in her flame-colored chiffon Stavropoulos dress, having her hair done and preparing to accompany Lyndon to a Democratic Party fundraiser, when Lynda Bird burst in: "Mama, Mama, Dr. King's been shot." King had been shot on a balcony in Memphis, Lynda reported, and was on the way to the hospital. "From that moment on, the evening assumed a nightmare quality." An hour later: "Mama, he's dead." And with that, Bird recorded, "Everybody's mind began racing off in its own direction as to what this would mean to racial violence in our country, to the work of so many to try to bring us together—how far would it throw us back?" And there she was, feeling ridiculous, with an elaborate hairdo, in an elegant dress. She changed, and with her daughters by her side and her grandson crawling on the floor, they waited in "a strange sort of suspended state."[3] Lyndon was in his office, talking on the phone with political allies in Atlanta.

Once more, LBJ found himself totally alone, as an overwhelming feeling of powerlessness set in. He called Coretta Scott King. No, there was nothing he could do, she told him, and thanked him for his call.[4] As grieving crowds began to pour into the streets of Washington, D.C., LBJ spoke to the nation on television with sadness and a very palpable sense of dismay. Although he urged against "lawlessness and divisiveness" following "this most tragic incident," what he did not articulate was the rawness of his fear of violent conflict in American cities.[5] On the phone with black leaders, he implored them to get out into the streets, denounce violence, and convey a message of restraint and empathy. To white law enforcement and mayors he begged for control over their police forces and also over white communities around the country, the Klan included, which had already begun celebrating the news of MLK's death.[6]

Lyndon canceled his upcoming trip to Hawaii to meet with South Vietnamese president Thieu. Lady Bird was scheduled to depart the next day for a long-planned trip to Texas, where with thirty-eight European journalists in tow, she would show them the Hill Country and the Ranch and would inaugurate the San Antonio "HemisFair," a world's fair extravaganza designed to put Texas on a more cosmopolitan map. Urged by Lyndon's doctors, she recently had scaled back her travel in order to be more present for Lyndon and her daughters. With LBJ's trip to Hawaii now canceled, and with an avalanche of troubles on the horizon, she was reluctant to leave Washington. Finally, after a very late dinner in the family dining room, no one really eating, only the sounds of Lyn padding around the floor and climbing onto his grandfather's lap punctuating the weighty air, Lyndon and Lady Bird were able to steal a few moments alone.

They may have talked about much more, but the only two items Bird felt strongly enough to record in her diary about this moment related to Bobby Kennedy and her trip to Texas. On the day before the assassination, when Bird had returned from Palm Beach, she had sat down to read through the newspapers. Staring out from the front page of *The Evening Star,* "Few Hear Kennedy, but Thousands Cheer" reported that despite a failure of the public address system to broadcast his speech, Bobby Kennedy encountered a "frenzied" response in Columbia Heights, the neighborhood bordering Shaw about two miles from the White House, and one of Bird's frequent stops with Mayor Washington. In a campaign appearance there with his wife, Ethel, RFK had promised a "jubilant" crowd of mostly black D.C. residents "to make the Nation's capital a place of pride" by bridging barriers of "race and wealth."[7] It must have irked the First Lady to hear Bobby extemporize on the very issues she had striven mightily, but perhaps too cautiously, to advance from her White House platform. As much as she had relished the new sensation of never having to campaign again, reading about RFK's eloquence and the popular response from the Washington residents whose lives she, too, had hoped to touch must not have sat well. Bird held no ill will toward the martyred JFK and reserved for Jackie every ounce of empathy she could muster. But ever since she observed how Bobby barely marshaled a clap for Lyndon when the 1964 Civil Rights Act passed, her views of Jack's younger brother tracked with Lyndon's: skeptical of his intentions, yet envious of his charisma.

Also on the day before MLK's assassination, RFK had visited the White House for what appeared to be a cordial meeting. But his goal was to gauge LBJ's support, or lack thereof, for his presidential run. The next day, Bobby flew to Indianapolis. Perhaps it was the residue of her pique over his hit performance up the street, or hearing now about his quoting Aeschylus in an extemporaneous, grief-filled speech before the stunned crowd gathered in the heart of the Indianapolis ghetto, but in the fog of the MLK tragedy, Bird had the New York senator on her mind. She asked Lyndon about his meeting with Bobby, and Lyndon replied that "he had never seen such arrogance," she recorded.[8] In one way or another, RFK had been stalking Lyndon for the better part of a decade. His ambition for the presidency had loomed well before he announced it weeks earlier, and well before the 1964 convention, when he recited Shakespeare and wept for his brother. More than McCarthy's reach for the top of the ticket, and even more than the prospect of losing the White House to a Republican, Bobby's opportunism—his assault on the Vietnam War and his deepening alliance with the very civil rights leaders LBJ now needed more than ever—was galling. Despite the pathbreaking social policy of the Johnson administration, Bobby had, first as attorney general and then as senator, staked out a position as the real changemaker for a black community disillusioned with the slow, if steady, progress made under LBJ. Now signs of support for RFK read, "Kennedy White but Alright."[9]

On the more prosaic matter of whether she should go ahead with her trip to Texas, a show of steadiness and stability was in order, and no one was more prepared to demonstrate White House resolve than the First Lady. The Texas trip was on. Thirty years later, talking with historian Robert Dallek, she described her time away from Washington over those next five days as "torture."[10] But Lady Bird was nothing if not a disciplined political wife, soldier, and member of the Johnson administration. As looting and protests erupted throughout Washington, and as the National Guard moved in, the next morning Bird gamely set out to perform her obligations on a jet lettered red with "Crossing the Trails of Texas."

* * *

Organized and funded by the same corporate sponsors behind a campaign to promote domestic tourism by Americans, "Discover America" (GM, Chrysler, Ford, Hertz, American Petroleum Institute, Hilton Hotels), the Texas extravaganza was designed to promote the United States as an international tourist destination. Bird had been eager to show the foreign press the country between the coasts, and with the HemisFair launch in San Antonio, the Johnsons' home state won out. That "the world had changed overnight," she recorded, required her to adjust her demeanor and the content of speeches. Stewart Udall and National Park Service director George Hartzog joined her for the trip. On board the TWA flight from Dulles, sensing "a feeling of uncertainty, tension in the air," Bird read "in a quiet serious voice" from a handwritten statement she had drafted earlier that morning and coordinated with Lyndon.

> We travel with a heavy heart today, because of the tragedy of Dr. King's death. Every man must look into his own heart, and ask himself, if his every word, every act, leans toward peace and healing in our country. This lays a demand on all Americans, for understanding, self-control, and steady, determined work to attack the problems that made possible such violence. The greatest tribute we could pay to Dr. King is to bring forth from this cruel tragedy some good action on our problems.

And then, conscious of her dueling roles, "I put it behind me," she recorded, and with what she described as "a change of tone," welcomed her travel companions to see the part of the country she knew best. There she was again, on an airplane right after a political assassination. The Bloody Marys failed to introduce the "jolly air of camaraderie" usually present on such trips.[11]

In a tense Cabinet Room back in Washington, Lyndon—flanked by Hubert Humphrey, Justice Thurgood Marshall, HUD secretary Robert Weaver, and Justice Earl Warren—met with prominent civil rights leaders, including Whitney Young, Jr., Dorothy Height, Clarence Mitchell, Bayard Rustin, Roy Wilkins, Walter Fauntroy, and Judge Leon Higginbotham. Also present were Walter Washington, Senate majority leader Mike Mansfield, and Senate minority leader Everett Dirksen. They spoke to the president not only about condemning violence, but also of the urgent need to improve the living conditions of the urban poor, most tangibly through legislative steps to redress housing discrimination. The issues animating the anger and fear of black families in America that an audacious Eartha Kitt had just three months earlier laid bare during what Bill Cosby had derided as a "mud pie" luncheon for the garden ladies, had now, with the MLK assassination and the country's reaction to it, forced themselves onto the high table of the Cabinet Room itself.[12] LBJ's domestic policy adviser Joe Califano summarized the president's exchange with the civil rights leaders: "Johnson warned that King's murder could reinforce those of both races who believe that violence is the way to settle racial problems in America. That, he said, would be a 'catastrophe for the country.'"[13] The president, who not six weeks earlier had ignored the "two Americas" analysis and recommendations of the Kerner Commission report, now demonstrated his keen understanding of the moment, telling those gathered, "If I were a kid in Harlem, I know what I'd be thinking. I'd be thinking that the whites have declared open season on my people, and they're going to pick us off one by one unless I get a gun and pick them off first."[14]

President Johnson then went to the National Cathedral for a memorial service. As he walked up the aisle, the congregation rose and sang "We Shall Overcome." After the choir's rendition of Dr. King's prescient choice for his own funeral, "Precious Lord, Take My Hand,"[15] D.C. councilman Rev. Walter Fauntroy prayed for collective forgiveness and called for passage of the fair housing legislation stuck in the House.[16] That afternoon, fearing an unstoppable wave of violent clashes, Mayor Walter Washington requested more troops from the president. And on April 10, the House finally passed the Fair Housing Act. LBJ signed it into law the next day.

With their civil rights laws and Great Society programs, the Johnsons attempted to remedy the social problems plaguing urban America. But unlike Bobby, they had resisted using the word *race* or *wealth* when speaking about racism and inequality. And that elision was exacting its cost. Just as Bobby's campaign stop in D.C. and his improvised eloquence before a grieving crowd in Indianapolis had bested both Johnsons in emotional cadence and literary precision, as she traveled in Texas, Bird was forced to acknowledge that while she could certainly feel the tragedy of MLK's death, she could neither understand nor relate to the black rage that followed. What she grasped quite viscerally was the pain of white Americans who wanted to feel hopeful but who also increasingly rejected the idea that government laws and programs could somehow advance racial equality unless also providing for law and order, a slogan that had increasingly become a message for police control of racial minorities.

The White House, Lynda told her mother, was "like a fortress. Nobody gets out and nobody gets in."[17] Trucks and jeeps from nearby army bases had begun to occupy the federal city, with the props of war (sandbags, machine guns, men in fatigues) stationed in strategic zones, including at the Capitol Building and the White House. The smell of burning rubble wafted through open windows and doors. Federal employees had begun to flee by foot and car to the Virginia and Maryland suburbs, and the president, surrounded by his staff, advisers Abe Fortas and Clark Clifford, and his daughters, had only to look out the window to see the chilling spectacle. By sundown, a curfew had done little to keep people off the streets. By midnight, the Secret Service reported "incident calls" coming in every eight seconds and a total of 1,008 arrests, 10 percent of them of juveniles. Also, as Lynda told her mother, 300 people were in D.C. hospitals and 7 had died in related fires. "[A]fter a day that ran the gamut of emotions against the background of mounting turbulence with our whole nation straining at the seams," it was nearly two in the morning in Washington, one in the morning in West Texas, when Lady Bird finally talked to Lyndon and then went to bed. She felt "a queer sense of ambivalence, because though I was right in the middle of it because of my husband's job and the presence in Washington of all my family, I, myself, was nevertheless removed and encapsulated in a different world where we were just hearing about them and reading about them [events in Washington], as though they lived on the moon."[18]

The next day, looting, property destruction, fires, and confrontations with police rippled through Chicago, Baltimore, Detroit, New York, Philadelphia, Pittsburgh, Daytona Beach, Tallahassee, and Nashville. There were no riots in Texas, but in a conference call, Governor Connally and Liz Carpenter told the First Lady to expect some "disturbances" on the fairgrounds in San Antonio, one "peace-loving" and two "militant," a Mexican American group and some fifteen hundred SDS protesters.[19] To avoid them, Lady Bird would shuttle, rather than walk, around the ninety-two-acre expanse. She rewrote her speech to christen the event, read it to Lyndon over the phone, and set off from the Ranch for the Texas happening.[20] During one of three speeches that day, in a subtle act of retaking a piece of cultural turf RFK had begun to stake out as his own, Lady Bird turned her gaze from the promise of the coming Olympics in Mexico City to the tragedy at home. Now a national political figure in her own right, and channeling her inner Woody Guthrie, she reassured her audience: "In these troubled hours, we need to remember that we are moving forward. This land is our land. It belongs to all of us. It is ours to rend apart—or to work for—and to keep strong."[21] With American flags flying at half-staff, the men seated on the podium behind the First Lady and the mostly white Texans in the arena before her, upon hearing the reference to Guthrie's 1940 anthem to American unity, erupted in emphatic applause.

* * *

In Oakland that day, Eldridge Cleaver led an ambush of local police. After a ninety-minute siege, the police shot and killed seventeen-year-old Panther treasurer Bobby Hutton as he surrendered. In Washington, a curfew had gone into effect at four that afternoon, with riots still raging and more than twelve thousand troops now occupying the streets. In New England, funk musician James Brown helped avoid a repeat of the 1967 Roxbury riots by imploring his audience at the Boston Garden arena "to pledge that no matter what any other community might do, we in Boston will honor Dr. King in peace."[22] As more than one hundred cities experienced more violence and unrest, Lyndon and Lynda ate dinner in the family dining room with General Westmoreland. Luci and Pat came by later. The four-star general was in town that week to brief the president and his advisers on Vietnam. LBJ wanted to assure his daughters that their husbands would be safe, even if he would no longer be their commander in chief. With Chuck already in Da Nang, and Pat soon on his way, their conversation focused on the general's assurances to spare no expense on regular mail, food, and medical care for wounded men. But would homemade cookies arrive unbroken? Westmoreland offered an unqualified no.[23]

That evening in San Antonio, costumed in a jacquard-patterned gown with chiffon and a fur wrap, Lady Bird attended the first-ever production in the United States of Verdi's five-hour opera *Don Carlos*. Under the circumstances, Verdi's themes of love, infidelity, and death during the Spanish Inquisition made for a dissonant choice. Although the final curtain did not fall until one in the morning, an exhausted First Lady, eager to speak to her family in Washington, took her leave after the second act and flew the short, bumpy ride back to the Ranch. The Secret Service had reported that "Negroes are pulling people out of cars [and] . . . out of buses" in Columbia Heights and Shaw. According to the FBI, "looters reported a plan to hit Georgetown area this evening" and target the predominantly white neighborhood of Cleveland Park. By the end of the night, 2,134 people had been arrested.[24] The annual National Cherry Blossom Festival was canceled for the first time since 1942. Palm Sunday became a day of national mourning for Martin Luther King, Jr.

At his New Bethel Baptist Church in Shaw, Walter Fauntroy gave Bobby Kennedy the pulpit. "We cannot tolerate violence and disorder," Kennedy said. "The disorder between races must stop. The preachers of violence must cease, I think that must be the lesson of events last week."[25] Bobby and Ethel received Communion, sang hymns, prayed, and shook hands with the entire congregation. After the service, Fauntroy and the Kennedys walked over to 7th Street, one of the main corridors of violence over the previous three days. They passed scores of burned buildings, shook hands, coughed from the smoke. Armed with bayonets, National Guard troops at first thought the crowds surrounding RFK threatened more violence, until the D.C. Police sped over to explain otherwise. Bobby told the crowd he would attend MLK's funeral that week. A local resident grabbed RFK's hand: "I have ten children too. I want a better life for my children."[26] At the time, Ethel, having shed her black mantilla of mourning, was pregnant with the couple's eleventh child.

President Johnson viewed the damage from a different vantage point. Smack in the middle of the meltdown in Washington, D.C., his meetings with General Westmoreland on Vietnam had consumed an enormous amount of LBJ's energy that week. At four in the afternoon, as a curfew was taking effect, the two held a joint press conference to describe the purpose of the general's visit. Westmoreland did most of the spinning: Tet was ultimately a defeat for the North, the South was a competent and reliable ally, and the end of a seventy-seven-day siege at Khe Sanh was a testament to the valor of U.S. troops. It sounded like fantasy.[27] But there was no way to put such a gloss on conditions just blocks away. LBJ had read reams of reports since April 4. But to get his own look, he accompanied Westmoreland to Andrews Air Force Base and then flew by helicopter up 7th Street and, at a lower altitude, down 14th Street, the very same corridors Bobby and Ethel had walked earlier that day. With a majority of the businesses damaged and many destroyed, it looked like a war zone. Within the same hour of the president's aerial tour, the Secret Service Command Post reported 13 incidents of looting in Northwest, Northeast, and downtown; 4 fires in Northwest and Southeast; and 4,291 arrests, 947 injuries, 54 "miscellaneous" incidents of snipers, and large crowds of young men gathering throughout the city. No names were put to their faces, but the FBI did report that "Stokely Carmichael has been hanging around" the Georgia Avenue Aunties Supper Club, near Howard University, his alma mater, driving a green-bottomed, tan-topped Dodge.[28] After his dinner, Lyndon signed an executive order sending the Maryland National Guard to Baltimore.[29]

* * *

On the flight back to Washington from Texas, Lady Bird sat with her old friend and companion Stewart Udall. Stew seemed distant in his conversation, as if he were dancing around something:

> He is a very articulate man. But I sensed that he could not quite get out all that he wanted to say. I feel there is a withdrawal from him in his enthusiasm for the Johnsons. I would not be surprised if he got out of the Cabinet, or if he stayed in, because there is a very real dedication in him for all the works of conservation and I think he gives credit for how useful and effective Lyndon has been in the field.[30]

In fact, although Udall probably intended to signal to Bird that his political allegiance bent toward RFK, he was clear with her that he hoped the Johnsons would take "the next months to further nail down the conservation program." When he first visited the Ranch at the outset of LBJ's presidency in 1964, and first laid out a strategy for "beautification" in Washington, D.C., Udall had recognized Lady Bird's standing in Lyndon's orbit and her potential as an environmental standard-bearer in the White House. He now hoped that she would remain central to his goal of concluding his eight years as secretary of the interior by persuading LBJ to add considerably more land to the national park system. Udall stood with Bobby, but he seemed to be hinting that he would remain loyal to the Johnsons until the end. Still, exhausted, and with her own mind very much on Atlanta, the site of MLK's funeral, Bird wasn't really sure what Stew meant to say.[31]

Other than Lady Bird and Lyndon, it seemed as if every major politician in the country attended the funeral. Mrs. Jacqueline Kennedy and Mrs. Ethel Kennedy had visited with Mrs. King and her children in their home. A half dozen presidential contenders (Hubert Humphrey, Bobby Kennedy, Eugene McCarthy, Nelson Rockefeller, who had jumped back into the race, George Romney, and Richard Nixon) were there to pay their respects. Justice Thurgood Marshall, Secretary Robert Weaver, and Mayor Walter Washington flew to Atlanta with the vice president. The most renowned figures of the country's black leadership in culture, entertainment, and sports attended, too, among them Eartha Kitt. Lyndon, who was at Camp David for talks on Vietnam, kept away because the Secret Service and FBI thought he could be the next target.[32]

But Lady Bird and Stew had instead spent the day walking the back roads to tiny villages of Southwest Texas with three busloads of European journalists. The political distance between Atlanta, Georgia, and Gonzales, Texas, was far greater than the actual 926 miles that separated Lady Bird from the center of the country's great trauma that day. Finally, as she drove back to the White House from Dulles, along the ambling George Washington Parkway and across Memorial Bridge, she looked, "with that sense of expectancy that you might have on a battlefield looking for trenches and gutted buildings and, of course, saw nothing except very silent and deserted streets." With 13 dead, more than 900 businesses and 700 homes damaged, and more than 7,600 arrests, Lady Bird noted, "The curfew was still on."[33]

* * *

While the First Lady had been urging her husband to withdraw from the presidency, her staff had begun planning for the final activities of her Beautification Committee of 1968 in order to showcase local achievements and help raise money and consciousness to support more substantial projects in East Capitol and to begin developing Kingman Island in Anacostia. In proposing the plans for one such activity (to include a combination of bus rides, boat rides, and walking tours), Lady Bird's staff suggested to her that the emphasis should be on the ghetto—for this is the year of the ghetto. By 1968, the word *ghetto* had become a common part of the American lexicon, but it was not a word Lady Bird used, and it barely shows up in any of her or her staff's documents. Though LBJ first protested and initially ignored the Kerner Commission's report, the specificity of its language and the directness of its message—that white institutions in America were responsible for black ghettos—may well have encouraged the generally cautious East Wing staff's linguistic shift to using the word. For one tour by her committee, the First Lady's team gave her two routes to choose involving public gardens and housing projects. In one of them, Lady Bird had envisioned a multigenerational play space with gardens and a community recreation spot serving the fifteen hundred residents of a housing complex in East Capitol's Southeast, near what is today Nationals Park and the recently developed mixed-use residential, commercial, and recreational space known as the Navy Yard. The second route added a bus trip to the relatively new Anacostia Community Museum (now under the umbrella of the Smithsonian), where the Beautification Committee had already financed plantings outside. This would be followed by a drive first to the Kenilworth Dump, the District's toxic open waste disposal site adjacent to District of Columbia Stadium, and then to the proposed construction site of the East Leg Freeway. A third alternative, her team wrote, "could be to not emphasize the ghetto" but instead blooms and travel.[34]

When Bird returned from Texas, the Washington, D.C., she had once considered immune to the destruction of rage and riots the rest of American cities had experienced was no longer. And what might once have been an easy programming decision, which route her committee's bus would take, now became freighted with meaning. She took a drive with staff around the proposed tour sites in order to map out a tour that would strike a balance between "ghetto" and "beauty." She was surprised to see less damage than she expected in "part of the disturbed area." Someone had painted "Soul Brothers" on two store windows; on another was "Please don't take our jobs away."[35] Though she saw some signs of looting and broken car windows, she did not see a full picture. She did not make the trek up 7th or down 14th Street as RFK and LBJ had, or she would have seen fires smoldering, buildings gutted, and bullet casings littering the streets.

The Giant supermarket on 14th Street, north of Florida Avenue, had not been a target of looting or fires—the chairman of the chain had hired a black manager who, over the previous two years, had involved his staff and the neighborhood in a steady stream of beautification-themed plantings and garbage cleanups.[36] This outcome suggested to the First Lady that community participation could indeed provide an antidote to rage-driven destruction. In fact, when King died, it was not the entire black population of Washington that took to the streets. But the pain expressed by those who did set fire to buildings, attack police, and loot businesses was widely shared.

Against this backdrop, Lady Bird's caution—to emphasize blooms over blight—guided her. She planned to narrate the tour herself, but the real work would come after the tour and after lunch, when she intended to allow the eloquence and direct experience of an exhausted Mayor Washington to help her make a pitch to the government and private sources of funding on hand to invest in the recreation project along the Anacostia River, stalled for over a year. With only eight months remaining in office, she wanted to secure her own legacy, and in the immediate aftermath of such tragedy, the Anacostia project Lady Bird and Larry Halprin had first envisioned in 1966 felt increasingly relevant, and urgent.

Although the Kingman Island project had real potential to provide underserved populations with access to swimming and recreation, its complicated ecology and geography, and the political and financial expense, had brought the project to a standstill. There were two substantial roadblocks. One was a decision by the House subcommittee that handled appropriations for the District of Columbia to withhold funds for a Metro system unless the city first began construction of several contested freeways as well as on the Three Sisters Bridge crossing the Potomac from Virginia into Georgetown. The other related hurdle was more specific and more existential: in order to build the freeway planned for Anacostia, the East Leg Freeway, local engineers had concluded they would have to obliterate Kingman Island altogether and fill in its adjacent waters to accommodate its original design and secure congressional funds. The ambitious alternative Larry had proposed, a tunnel stretching under District of Columbia Stadium and along the north edge of the Anacostia River, seemed beyond reach.

But MLK's death and the riots that followed changed the calculus in Washington. While Lady Bird and Stewart Udall were in Texas, the secretary of the interior's chief of staff wrote Halprin that the "events of the last few days in Washington must commit us all to further resolve in braking the financial deadlock in order that this project proceed with utmost speed."[37] Sharon and Larry seized the moment. Their proposals and budget together now well exceeded the initial idea, and very modest budget, for a few pilot programs of vest-pocket parks and play spaces for Capitol East. And with the National Park Service suddenly poised to underwrite the plan, Larry proposed a feasibility study for moving the proposed East Leg of the Inner Loop Freeway, a prerequisite for building the freshwater swimming lake on Kingman Island.

The woman who began her tenure in the White House by beautifying highways now staked her legacy, or at least part of it, on actually moving one. And just moving the still-unbuilt freeway, the National Park Service estimated, might cost between $15 million and $20 million. Developing a riverfront park along the banks of the Anacostia, to include Kingman Island; an amusement park; a renovated, desegregated golf course; and community gardens to replace the Kenilworth Dump, would cost, the National Park Service estimated, as much as $335 million, from feasibility study to shovel-in-dirt to completion.[38] Knowing such a massive cost might risk a collective retreat among the D.C. and federal bureaucracy, Sharon called the budget director of the Park Service to ask if he could find just $300,000 in the budget so that the First Lady could finally announce the launch of the Kingman Island project to her Beautification Committee. Once Secretary Udall pressed him, his budget director finally secured the funds. On April 18, the First Lady announced the launch of engineering studies, the first step in this long-coveted dream, what she described as a "huge fresh-water swimming lake—Kingman Lake—the equivalent of 100 swimming pools in size." Long a devotee of swimming's mental and physical health benefits, the First Lady of the United States was going to deliver to District residents—especially "for those who have nothing now," to those long deprived of this most basic human need—summer recreation in an urban park free of charge, free of highways, and free from the community-corroding legacy of Jim Crow.[39]

Mayor Walter Washington's staff wrote three versions of the speech he would deliver for Bird's donor lunch in the East Room. Not three weeks had passed since the MLK assassination, but troops no longer patrolled the main corridors into the District. The signs of occupation (sandbags, bayonets, and tanks) were gone; smoke and embers no longer wafted through the city. While the White House and the Congress celebrated the passage of the Fair Housing Act, much of the city remained tense with shock, wrecked by anger and anguish. "My eyes are bleary and I am moved . . . so I hope that you will bear with me," said Washington, "and that I will just talk a little with you and that you will understand this is a moving day." The New Yorkers in the room—Laurance and Mary Rockefeller, Mary Lasker, and Brooke Astor—sat riveted listening to the man who had abruptly left the leadership of the New York City Housing Authority to return to his home. He had accepted the president's offer to serve as an appointed mayor presiding over a similarly unelected city council and a bureaucracy that paled in comparison to those of New York City in terms of resources and experience. Mrs. Johnson prefaced her introduction of the mayor by saying that her "criteria for a project," such as the one in Anacostia, "is that it receives the fullest human use, that it be well cared for—and a third ingredient—that the desire for it emanate from the neighborhood and its users." Lady Bird had developed this paradigm from her exposure to Jane Jacobs, her collaboration with Larry Halprin, and her years of work with Walter Washington. He had become mayor in part because of the First Lady's influence on President Johnson during the appointments process. Now, she felt both relieved and responsible for Washington's presence in the District.

As he began to speak, Washington "looked so tired," Bird recorded, "that my heart ached for him." Speaking "almost in a poetic strain," he poignantly explained to the assembled audience of journalists, donors, diplomats, and landscape architects, Halprin among them, how he and the First Lady had come to develop a vision that combined the environmental with the social, beauty with well-being, and the importance of their investment in the District of Columbia.

> We have travelled through this city; we have been in the alleys, we have been in the byways and side streets, because it was very early that I think both of us determined that a certain part of what she wanted to do would be regarded as cosmetic and that really, behind the monuments there was a big job to do and that this job had to be done in the sense of identifying the individual with his environment. Her heritage as First Lady is not in beautification per se; it is in communication. It is in the hope and the desire to identify a human being with his environment.[40]

Washington challenged the notion that the amenities they brought were merely cosmetic. He acknowledged how he and the First Lady had endeavored to "make open spaces and recreational facilities a part of the daily living and a part of the daily environment of people." And he beseeched his audience to reflect on what had just transpired in the District. Because "the heart of turbulence and the turmoil we are going through now, the extent to which the people have been alienated from participation, alienated from what they call a piece of the action, alienated from the American dream, and I would like to think that here and now . . . we would reflect and know despair, simply reflect."

With the charge that the committee's investment was merely cosmetic put to rest, and with his audience asked to reflect on how much remained to be done, Mayor Washington closed his prayerful speech. "I think the greatest thing that we can do for the greatest First Lady I have ever known"—and he knew Eleanor, Bess, Mamie, and likely Jackie before Lady Bird—"is to dedicate ourselves to continue with her this great work, continue it in a way that will be meaningful, continue it in a way that will involve the people, permit them to participate . . . because no one destroys something they participate in building. That is the basic lesson."[41] The First Lady was taken aback by the "kind, warm, generous" chords Washington struck in speaking about her. "I began to shrivel and look at my plate." As she said goodbye to her guests, she could not shake the "undertone of sadness, because this was, in a way, an end."[42]

Chapter 25

Resurrection

There was nothing pretty about Resurrection City except the spirit of the people. There is nothing pretty about poverty. Poverty is an ugly blot on the face of this which we call the Great Society. But more ugly than poverty is the frustration of trying to explain Resurrection City to those who were glad to see it torn down. That ugliness may be buried in the mud which will be seeded over with new green grass between the Lincoln and Washington Memorials in Washington, D.C., but it will still be there like a brand on the heart of a nation.

—Gertrude Wilson [Justine Priestley], "Explaining Resurrection City," *New York Amsterdam News,* July 13, 1968

Before his death, MLK had begun to plan a Poor People's Campaign for spring and summer 1968. He wanted to put a human face to the poverty and other maladies, material and spiritual, plaguing American cities by bringing a prolonged act of "disciplined urban disruption" to the nation's capital. King had begun to use words like *sick* to describe American society. In his campaign, Bobby Kennedy echoed and reinforced MLK's "sick society" rhetoric to describe the very country whose president had expanded healthcare coverage to the young and the old in history-making numbers. Both laid blame at the feet of the Johnson presidency. With Vietnam draining the coffers and a shift toward law and order as the political response to three years of urban riots, it was Lyndon Johnson, they argued, who, despite the Civil Rights Act, the Voting Rights Act, Medicare, Medicaid, the Economic Opportunity Act, the Fair Housing Act, and a multitude of other laws on the books, had sickened American society.

The suggestion that the Johnson administration had produced the violence and polarization now roiling the country incensed the president and First Lady. When the Johnsons announced their withdrawal from the political arena, they expected their tenure to be subject to considerable scrutiny. But LBJ had risked the Democratic Party's long-standing hold on the South by going all in in 1964 and 1965 for civil rights, and he and Lady Bird could not accept now seeing that legacy largely dismissed. They could not abide being told that the antipoverty and other Great Society programs of their presidency not only were insufficient, but actually amounted to salt in the open wound of race and poverty in America. The attack was especially hard to digest coming from the Kennedy coterie of "self-styled intellectuals," as Lady Bird described them.[1]

After King's death, the Southern Christian Leadership Conference moved forward with plans for national mobilization. Fittingly, it was on Mother's Day in Washington, D.C., where Coretta Scott King led thousands, mostly women, to launch the Poor People's Campaign. She had agreed to participate before her husband's assassination, and decided to follow through as part of her healing process. "I just had to run on and let the healing catch up with me," she later wrote.[2] On a rainy Sunday morning, the march began in the heart of Shaw, near burned-out storefronts untouched since April. Comprised of white, black, Latino, and Native American women, men, and children, the march traced the path that RFK and Ethel had taken on Palm Sunday after the riots, making its way down U Street and up 13th to Cardozo High School, where MLK had urged the crowd to "prepare to participate" in designing their own version of urban renewal. Now they carried signs demanding "Income, Dignity, Justice, Democracy," "More Money Now," and "Bread and Justice Now." Betty Friedan, the National Organization for Women president, carried one that read, "Free Women from Poverty Now." Mrs. King, regal in her horn-rimmed sunglasses, a corsage of orchids and organza pinned to her black suit, took the stage before a crowd of six thousand spectators. Right behind her, in a simple navy mock turtleneck dress and a brooch, the same outfit she wore when she and Bobby visited Coretta in Atlanta after Martin's death, sat Ethel Kennedy. Bobby was campaigning in Nebraska.[3]

With the gravitas of her delivery, Coretta's oratory was unmistakably King. In her thirty-minute speech, Mrs. King called for a "campaign of conscience" by "black women, white women, brown women, and red women—all the women of this nation"—to roll back the age and funding limits established for welfare assistance from the federal government. "I firmly believe, our last and best hope for a future of brotherhood and peace lies in the effective use of woman power." King did not limit her critique of the U.S. Congress to a point of public policy. "Our Congress passes laws which subsidize corporation farms, oil companies, airlines and houses for suburbia, but when it turns its attention to the poor it suddenly becomes concerned about balancing the budget."[4] In her speech, Coretta made a much broader philosophical case, one that would remain at the core of the American debate on the purpose of government spending and in whose interests for the rest of the twentieth century and beyond. And to do so with Ethel Kennedy and two other Senate spouses at her side was to put the Democratic Party on notice that the policies and practices that made sense in the early 1960s were now inadequate to the task of closing the gap between rich and poor, black and white, women and men.

The day before the march for "Woman Power," as one of the banners read, the National Park Service issued a renewable thirty-seven-day permit to the Poor People's Campaign to build a three-thousand-person encampment along the length of the sixteen-acre West Potomac Park, stretching from the Lincoln Memorial to the Reflecting Pool. The proximity to the Lincoln Memorial was no accident. It had been five years since Martin Luther King, Jr., delivered his "I Have a Dream" speech there, and his successor at the SCLC, Ralph Abernathy, planned several events and mass meetings in the same spot to commemorate their fallen leader. The permit allowed for such events, and also for the construction of replicas of rural shacks on the Mall in front of the Smithsonian Institution. The day after Coretta Scott King's speech at Cardozo, union carpenters and volunteers began building Resurrection City.

Although LBJ was annoyed by what he saw as the Poor People's Campaign's "unattainable" asks on too many domestic fronts at once, politically speaking, he knew that he couldn't oppose the encampment.[5] Lady Bird Johnson stayed silent on the matter, but she was hardly in the dark. Stewart Udall objected entirely to allowing the encampment on the Mall—he wanted it far away, in Anacostia. Walter Washington had the unenviable task of not only welcoming the Poor People's Campaign, but also announcing that the District of Columbia's eighteen-hundred-strong National Guard unit stood ready, along with eight thousand regular army and Marine Corps troops at bases nearby.[6] Bennetta Washington hosted a one-day workshop to address tensions between the District's professional, middle-class black women skeptical about the campaign and the campaign participants and organizers from cities around the country, often very poor themselves. The well-to-do women faced considerable pushback from the meeting's less-well-off participants: "Some of the Negro people here are in places where they can change things for the poor. They sit on the same boards as the white establishment. It's time they stopped sitting on their furs and realized we're all black sisters. We've got to find out what the poor want and stop telling them what they ought to want."[7]

Walter Fauntroy was one leader in D.C. who had bridged these fault lines within the black community. From his seat on the city council, and his standing in his community, Fauntroy lobbied for the Mall over Anacostia as a site for the encampment and shaped the SCLC permit requests with the Justice Department. Nash Castro, the National Park Service liaison to the White House, meanwhile, felt livid and helpless as he watched the encampment's grass yield to mud from twenty-nine straight days of rain.[8]

On the day after Mother's Day, Rev. Ralph Abernathy dedicated the space "Resurrection City, USA." It even had its own zip code: 20013. He vowed to "plague the Pharaohs of this nation with plague after plague until they agree to give us meaningful jobs and a guaranteed annual income."[9] From the outset, the organizers split over whether their "city" should be a living example of how better to redress poverty or an example of how the poor actually lived. Even with all the services and service providers (doctors, teachers, barbers, cooks, etc.) built into the structure of the encampment, problems soon overshadowed solutions. The rain rapidly converted the ground into knee-deep mud. Mosquitoes multiplied. City "manager" Rev. Jesse Jackson had to send back home the gang members from Chicago and Detroit initially brought in to provide security. Fully one-quarter of the three thousand people who arrived and set up camp on the Mall were sick, unwittingly embodying the "sick society" concept MLK and RFK had promoted that spring.[10]

Under the pseudonym Gertrude Wilson, Justine Priestley, an Upper East Side mother of four and the only white reporter for the *New York Amsterdam News,* the oldest black newspaper in the United States, marveled at the SCLC's determination to carry on with the event without "indulging themselves in that period of grief and mourning which anyone who has loved someone and lost him knows is almost a physical and spiritual demand." In a column she occasionally titled "White-on-White," the Brown University graduate also criticized those who would call Resurrection City a failure. "It is easy to say that there were troubles in Resurrection city," she wrote. "For there were troubles. They were the same kind of troubles, 'family troubles and city troubles,' which all of the critics face behind the closed doors of their own more secure homes every day of their lives," troubles of coordination, communication, fatigue. In the face of shared adversity, in the makeshift community a sense of participation and place, of identity and agency, also took root. Priestley's essential point was that the racism and the lack of empathy that lay at the heart of much of white America had permeated the country's knee-jerk readiness to describe Resurrection City as a failure rather than draw from the entirety of the experience the blazingly clear lessons about the relationship among race, poverty, and the physical environment in which poor Americans lived in 1968.[11]

But most of federal Washington wished it would all go away. There were exceptions. Although the Department of Agriculture concocted a tortured rationale to prevent Resurrection City dwellers from eating in its federally subsidized cafeteria—for department employees only, a spokesman hedged—over at the Smithsonian, museum director Dillon Ripley took another view. Although the museum's board of directors wanted to close down during the Poor People's Campaign, Ripley ignored their wishes. He wanted the encampment's residents to "'come in, if only to use the restrooms,'" one of his aides recalled. "'How often are these people going to be in Washington?'" Instead of closing, Ripley kept the museums open later than usual. And Thomas Lovejoy, then Ripley's assistant secretary, to ease the worry about having to potentially arrest demonstrators and to "sensitize the Smithsonian guard force," lay down on the floor and made them practice on him.[12] The Smithsonian, which under Ripley had begun to bring its museum exhibits into D.C. neighborhoods, became a welcoming, air-conditioned resting place for protesters.

Some members of the Poor People's Campaign came temporarily to the nation's capital in caravans from geographies as varied as America's Indian reservations, West Coast cities, the Deep South, and Appalachia. Others wound up staying for good. Dallis Carr, a twenty-two-year-old from Marks, Mississippi, found a job at a gas station. In Washington, D.C., he told Nan Robertson, he would earn twenty-five dollars a day. In Mississippi, twenty-five dollars *a week*. But there was more about the District that struck Carr. "Look at this big, green park with green trees, birds flying and singing all over," he told her. "There is freedom in the air. I feel I am in the free world I heard so much about."[13] Relative to where he had come from, natural beauty and a decent wage offered by the District of Columbia provided one young black man from the South with the necessities Lady Bird believed so vital to the human spirit, yet so often neglected. The First Lady had worked for three years to convert this logic into the new conventional wisdom in zip codes outside Northwest Washington. But the mud, squalor, and skepticism engulfing zip code 20013 now eclipsed that effort.

* * *

Bringing the experience of black poverty to monumental, touristy Washington was arguably the ultimate rebuke of the East Wing's attempt to demonstrate the social context and potential of beautification. As Coretta

Scott King and Ethel Kennedy campaigned for far more tangible social progress than the Johnsons' Great Society had been able to deliver; as Bobby met in Oakland with Black Panthers and other militants; and as *Time* magazine portrayed Kennedy as a rebel on its front cover in a Pop Art portrait by Roy Lichtenstein, Lady Bird, terribly aware of her estrangement from the realities on display at Resurrection City, staged a retreat. During the "Woman Power" march, she was in Texas berating herself for not having written to Pat and Chuck in Vietnam—knowing that Lyndon was writing to each of them twice a week. She often felt tired but tried to keep herself busy. She presided over a series of "sad-happy" lasts: She ran the last meetings in the Treaty Room on the LBJ library, attended the last Senate Ladies Luncheon, convened the last Doers Luncheon, hosted the last White House reception, oversaw the always important seating arrangements for the last state dinner, and kept a frame-by-frame eye on the narratives and imagery of the last set of official monthly films from the White House Naval Photographic Center about the Johnson presidency. Even as it appeared that the entire black entertainment community was turning against LBJ (and toward RFK)—and as Sidney Poitier, Eartha Kitt, Bill Cosby, Nancy Wilson, Sammy Davis, Jr., Dizzy Gillespie, Josh White, Harry Belafonte, Ossie Davis, and Billy Stewart visited or performed in Resurrection City—the East Wing made a point of showing respect for, and asserting its claim to respect from, African American talent, inviting Arthur Ashe, James Brown, Alvin Ailey, Carmen De Lavallade, and Geoffrey Holder to attend or perform at state dinners.[14] In 1967, when Lady Bird first acknowledged that the anger on American campuses over Vietnam would drown out her message on the environment in American cities, she vowed not to stay in the White House bubble. She wanted to know where the country stood, even if assimilating that knowledge required a painful reckoning. By June of 1968, the painful reckoning had arrived. Once Lyndon announced his plan not to run again, Lady Bird began to clarify her analysis about the convulsions shaking American society. The American people as a whole were not collectively responsible for the social and racial upheaval rocking the nation, but in her view, the political consequences of such cleavages of race, class, and gender were likely to encourage a conservative backlash.

Always focused on Lyndon's legacy, Bird also allowed herself to grapple with her own. American historians, she felt, might not adequately capture the full range of her role in the White House. That mischaracterization had already begun. James MacGregor Burns, the Williams College presidential historian and the author of tomes on FDR, on a young JFK, on Congress, and on leadership, brought the First Lady galley proofs of a collection of essays about the Johnson administration. With the near-complete book in hand, Mrs. Johnson answered questions about her own role in the administration. But the revered historian framed his questions not about substance, but about staffing. What does Bess do? What does Liz do? To Lady Bird's mind, they "were not the sort of questions that got at the meat of the matter," she recorded. "And I, though I regard him with respect, and would really like him to understand what this is, and what it can be, this particular niche I occupy, I simply do not have enough energy left, to paint the word picture it deserves, so I answered in very simply, and briefly, on the bones of the set-up."[15] The skeletal nature of this renowned historian's questions gave Bird all the more reason to make sure that her diary would see the light of day. As she embarked upon her last six months of recording, and worried that perhaps "a thousand words might be better than the million I have recorded," Lady Bird Johnson also began negotiations with the first of several publishing houses about the editing and publication of her White House diary.[16]

Chapter 26

"Claudia All of My Life"

[The United States] is a land of violent people with a violent history, and the instinct for violence has seeped into the bloodstream of our national life. What sort of people are we? The answer is that we are today the most frightening people on this planet . . . because the atrocities we commit trouble so little our official self-righteousness, our invincible conviction of our moral infallibility. . . . It is almost as if a primal curse has been fixed on our nation, perhaps when we first began the practice of killing and enslaving those whom we deemed our inferiors because their skin was another color. . . . Now as our nation grows more centralized, our energy more concentrated, our inner tensions more desperate, we can no longer regard hatred and violence as accidents, as nightmares, which will pass away when we wake up. We must see them as organic in our national past; we must uncover the roots of hatred and violence and, through our self-knowledge, move toward self-control.

—Arthur Schlesinger, Jr., June 5, 1968

All day long I had heard this cacophony over and over—the reactions of people questioned. What is our country coming to? What is happening to us? In fact, at one point when I had listened to Arthur Schlesinger giving a graduation speech somewhere, I had felt like spitting on him. And so I welcomed it when Lyndon said after a condemnation of this assassination attempt on Senator Kennedy and of the spirit of violence that made such things possible that "200 million people did not shoot Senator Kennedy." We have to cling to the belief that the fabric of the American people is still good, that it's not the fault of every last one of the 200 million of us, that there is enough virtue and courage and discipline and hard work in Americans to solve our problems.

—Lady Bird Johnson, White House diary, June 5, 1968

On May 28, 1968, Bobby Kennedy lost the Oregon primary to Eugene McCarthy by 22,359 votes, nearly eight percentage points. For RFK, the stakes of the next Democratic primary, in California, were clear: he would have to win the state to stay competitive at the Chicago convention in August. Outside California, by going after the industrial states, Bobby's campaign strategy was no different from Jack's in 1960. But LBJ's decision to sacrifice the Democratic Party's historic hold on the South by pushing the 1964 and 1965 civil rights laws required a broader voter base than the party had relied on in prior presidential elections. California provided the opportunity.

In 1964, LBJ was the first Democrat since Harry Truman's 1948 election to win the state (and the last until Bill Clinton in 1992). California was almost a microcosm of America; home to Governor Ronald Reagan and presidential aspirant Richard Nixon as well as the heart of the counterculture, the New Left, and the American environmental movement. Some of Bobby's advisers there pressed him to focus less on drumming up crowd frenzy in the cities and more on pursuing white working-class voters fleeing to the Golden State's exurbs.[1] But RFK ignored their counsel and attempted to stitch together the threads of a new California political coalition. With unprecedented turnout in black and Mexican American districts, on June 4, 1968, Bobby Kennedy beat Eugene McCarthy by 4.5 percent. The California of 1960, where at the Biltmore Hotel in Los Angeles, LBJ had, over Bobby's objections, reluctantly joined the JFK ticket, by 1968 had morphed into a different state.

At the Ambassador Hotel the night of the primary, the crowd in the ballroom sang "This Land Is Your Land," now the Kennedy campaign's unofficial anthem. In the moment, Bobby's victory speech sounded like a total repudiation of Lyndon Johnson. He decried "what has been going on in the United States over the period of the last three years, the division, the violence, the disenchantment with our society," and called for unity across his hodgepodge California coalition.[2] Bobby's victory in California was about the transformation of the state and maybe, as California often presaged, the country. And even as they winced over their Great Society now being condemned as a "sick society," both Johnsons had begun to move on; LBJ focused on bringing North and South Vietnam to the table for peace talks in Paris and on a final raft of social programs before Congress, and Lady Bird worked through her list of lasts, with hope for one final success: the mammoth riverfront public swimming spot in Anacostia.

As the polls in California closed, Bird was making her peace with the campaign and its candidates. As for Lyndon and the thought of being drafted in Chicago, "I am more and more relieved every day that he has made his decision" not to run. Seeing Lyndon back in the race, she recorded, offered "absolutely no allure for me."[3] After plowing through an hour's worth of correspondence, she went to sleep at one in the morning, ten at night in Los Angeles.

But the bullets that hit the back of Bobby's head as he and Ethel made their way through the Ambassador Hotel's kitchen pantry immediately thrust both Johnsons back into a zone of emotional conflict far more complex than any they had experienced—more so than Jack's assassination and more so than Martin's. And Los Angeles came to represent another kind of symmetry: JFK had launched his presidential campaign there, and for a brief moment had consolidated his own path to the presidency. For the Johnsons, two Kennedy deaths, nearly five years apart, threatened to bookend their entire presidency.

The phone jarred Lady Bird awake. It was Lyndon. He sounded terse. "Will you come in here?" Resentful, Lady Bird looked at the clock: 4:23 A.M. She had been asleep for three hours. In his room, Bird found LBJ propped up on pillows, with all three TV sets on, looking as if he hadn't gone to sleep at all. "I am not sure whether I heard it first from the TV set or from Lyndon. Senator Kennedy had been shot." Each network was broadcasting the same footage. "The whole thing had taken place under the eye of the television camera, and we saw over and over film of the shooting itself and heard the light crack of the gun. We saw him lying on the floor, and a pool of blood under his head, and heard that he had gone to one hospital and briefly treated and dispatched to another."[4]

The horror on the televisions continued through the early morning. "There was an air of unreality about the whole thing—a nightmare quality. It couldn't be. You dreamed it. It had happened before," Bird recorded. "And then," unable to look away from the relentless broadcasts from Los Angeles, "every few minutes, there would come on the screen a smiling face of Senator Kennedy tasting the wine of victory, making little jokes with Ethel by his side. And then we would go through the whole thing over again."[5] The onetime media executive now recoiled at the power of television. As she watched, the president worked the phones, calling Attorney General Ramsey Clark, FBI director J. Edgar Hoover, and the head of the Secret Service. At the time, although the White House had sought congressional approval for candidate security after the King assassination, presidential candidates still did not travel with Secret Service security. The president ordered immediate protection—Secret Service, FBI, the marines: any would do until Congress passed a law guaranteeing it—for McCarthy, Humphrey, Nixon; for Nelson Rockefeller; for Harold Stassen, then in his sixth run for the GOP nomination; and even for the comedian Dick Gregory, who had declared his candidacy following a forty-day fast against the Vietnam War.

By seven that morning, Senate majority leader Mike Mansfield was in the family quarters with the president to discuss the best way to codify into law permanent Secret Service protection for all presidential candidates.[6] LBJ had just called Ted Sorensen in Los Angeles, Bobby's younger brother, Teddy, and his brother-in-law Stephen Smith. He reassured them that the Secret Service would protect Ethel and her children and deployed a government plane to send three of Bobby and Ethel's ten children to Los Angeles. Washington, D.C., was quiet, Walter Washington reported. Yet, given RFK's deep ties to the black community in Shaw and Columbia Heights, the mayor and the White House agreed on contingency plans that would allow for troop deployment at thirty minutes' notice should the news of the assassination provoke further violence in the District, particularly in Resurrection City.[7] LBJ spent the rest of the day and evening like the rest of the country, glued to the television set, waiting. All the while, the news reports "kept repeating the hideous story that the Senator was going in for brain surgery," Bird recorded.[8] Unlike JFK or MLK, who both died within an hour of being shot, RFK lingered through surgery and after. Unlike his command of the public eye after Jack's and Martin's assassinations, Lyndon waffled about a televised address to the nation about Bobby. Echoing his other advisers, Clark Clifford told the president that "he had to set aside his own feelings and speak against the forces of hatred and prejudice that had cost us another great national figure."[9] When LBJ went on live television at 10:07 P.M. on June 5, seventeen hours after the shooting and six hours before RFK actually died, he did so, according to Clifford, in a manner that reflected his ambivalence toward the younger Kennedy.

Lady Bird cleared her schedule. She and Liz drafted and sent telegrams from the president and the First Lady to Ethel, Rose, and Ted and Joan Kennedy. Bird drifted in and out of Lyndon's bedroom or the Oval Office. Luci called from Austin, crying, and made plans to fly to Washington with eleven-month-old Lyn. Lynda, who had just let the public know of her own pregnancy, focused on Ethel's ten children and the eleventh on the way. At one point, as five hundred Poor People's Campaign marchers wept and prayed at the Lincoln Memorial, Lady Bird talked with Lynda out on the Truman Balcony. In direct line of sight to the outdoor terrace at the Washington Hotel, Bird became conscious as never before of her own vulnerability. "Not that I myself ever feel any fear at all. It is absolutely foreign yet for me, or even really for Lyndon. But maybe neither of the Kennedys felt it either."[10]

* * *

Neither JFK's assassination in 1963, nor the University of Texas clock tower mass shooting in 1966, nor even the Black Panthers' 1967 armed protest in Sacramento had yielded meaningful legislation to regulate the sale of guns in America. In the wake of MLK's assassination, Bobby, too, had begun to speak on the campaign trail about gun violence in America. When the president appeared before the country to speak about the RFK shooting, the lion's share of his statement—he'd written nearly every word of it himself—focused on themes that Americans today would readily recognize: "Tonight this Nation faces once again the consequences of lawlessness, hatred, and unreason in its midst. It would be wrong, it would be self-deceptive, to ignore the connection between the lawlessness and hatred and this act of violence."[11]

The rivalry between LBJ and RFK has received perhaps more than its due in the telling of their shared history. And it is true that LBJ used his statement to push back on the Kennedy argument about the "sickness" of American society. "It would be just as wrong, and just as self-deceptive, to conclude from this act that our country itself is sick, that it has lost its balance, that it has lost its sense of direction, even its common decency."[12] After his speech and after Kennedy's death was confirmed, LBJ indulged his most petty self by waffling over whether RFK could be buried in Arlington Cemetery, and then slow-walking a plan to pay for it. But by today's lights, the rest of his statement displayed a willingness to use his platform and his rhetoric to speak clearly about the crisis in the country in language not so different from that used by Kennedy adviser Arthur Schlesinger, Jr., in a graduation speech that morning. President Johnson said:

> Two hundred million Americans did not strike down Robert Kennedy last night any more than they struck down President John F. Kennedy in 1963 or Dr. Martin Luther King in April of this year. But those awful events give us ample warning that in a climate of extremism, of disrespect for law, of contempt for the rights of others, violence may bring down the very best among us. A nation that tolerates violence in any form cannot expect to be able to confine it to just minor outbursts.

But like Lady Bird, and unlike Schlesinger, the president stopped just short of framing such violence as part of the American DNA.

> We cannot sanction the appeal to violence, no matter what its cause, no matter what the grievance from which it springs. There is never—and I say never—any justification for the violence that tears at the fabric of our national life; that inspires such fear in peaceful citizens that they arm themselves with deadly weapons; that sets citizen against citizen or group against group.[13]

It wasn't just three assassinations on LBJ's mind. It was a broader penchant toward white vigilante activism to which the president directed his message. George Wallace had recently declared his third-party candidacy for president—his traditional firebrand rhetoric and comical swipes at liberals as "pointy headed intellectuals" and the Warren Court as "limousine hypocrites" appealed to disaffected, rural, white law-and-order voters alienated from both parties.[14] LBJ also directed his words, if obliquely, to black activists who, long before MLK's death, had begun to push back against the reverend's strategy of nonviolence. "Let us put an end to violence and to the preaching of violence." And at a time when the prospect for an open market in semiautomatic weapons, AR-15s, AK-47s, bump stocks, and high-capacity magazines was totally unthinkable, President Johnson turned his sights toward gun control. "Let the Congress pass laws to bring the insane traffic in guns to a halt, as I have appealed to them time and time again to do. That will not, in itself, end the violence, but reason and experience tell us that it will slow it down; that it will spare many innocent lives. Let us purge the hostility from our hearts and let us practice moderation with our tongues." In a pointed push for Congress to pass more restrictive gun control laws, mindful of the conspiracy theories that continued to plague the Warren Commission's findings about the JFK assassination, and eager to counteract such speculation over RFK, the president appointed another commission to examine "the causes, the occurrence, and the control of physical violence across this Nation, from assassination that is motivated by prejudice and by ideology, and by politics and by insanity, to violence in our cities and even in our homes."[15]

In substance, the premise of the commission's work would be to explain "what in the nature of our people and the environment of our society makes possible such murder and such violence." A lethal alchemy of guns and violence in the media, combined with a long history of racial violence, had generated a public debate about the sources of violence in American society. To concede political assassination as an inherent byproduct of American society would be to implicate his own tenure in office. LBJ characterized political violence as more of an aberration, not a structural feature of the American creed. The president had largely dismissed the findings of the Kerner Commission, established in 1967 at another violent inflection point. His skeptics could be forgiven for seeing yet another commission as a superficially appropriate but empty gesture.

The next morning, LBJ sent a message to Congress calling for passage of a new gun control law "governing the full range of lethal weapons" and closure of the "brutal loopholes in our gun laws" that made it possible for two million guns to be sold in the United States in 1967.[16] Hundreds of protesters gathered outside the offices of the National Rifle Association at Scott Circle in Washington, D.C., including children carrying signs that read, "Don't use a bullet to kill again!" The Senate had already passed a watered-down version of the gun control law LBJ introduced in 1963: it covered only handguns but not rifles or shotguns. Hunters and sportsmen shouldn't fear such a law, aimed as it was at cracking down on the interstate "mail-order" gun industry, the president suggested. In October, when Congress finally did pass the Gun Control Act of 1968, the fingerprints of what would become the dominant political faction of the NRA could already be perceived. The law did establish new regulations on gun manufacturers and owners, but not a national registry of guns or requirements for the licensing of those who carried them. Weakened as it was, LBJ's legislation stood as the only comprehensive gun control law until the Federal Assault Weapons Ban of 1994, which has since lapsed.[17]

* * *

RFK's funeral at St. Patrick's Cathedral in New York City was scheduled for Saturday, June 8. Until then, a combination of grief, anxiety, and unsettling energy filled the White House. An awkwardly timed sitting for the portrait artist, Madame Elizabeth Shoumatoff, took part of the day before the Johnsons would travel to Manhattan. The first couple had rejected an earlier portrait of LBJ, and now, with their time in the White House brief and Shoumatoff already slotted into the president's schedule, the president sat for the artist, reading a letter from Chuck in Vietnam. The First Lady sat nearby, just out of the frame, but by his side. The result is the official portrait of LBJ that now hangs in the White House. Snapshots of the moment, caught by White House photographer Okamoto, wink lightly at Diego Velázquez's famed painting *Las Meninas,* a portrait of a portraitist painting her subject. Off in a corner, the executive producer of the Johnson legacy sits next to a window, morning light flooding in, helping to animate the object of her affection. Staged though the scene was, their fifty-five minutes together in the Lincoln Sitting Room would be the last moment of relative insularity, if not solitude, before the Johnsons had to muster the courage to participate the next day, as they had five years earlier, in yet another round of Kennedy death pageantry and ritual.[18]

The morning of the funeral, they turned to the usual review of newspapers, finding them "drenched with every aspect of the story." The relentless exposure on the television and in the papers to the violent details and painful displays of family and national mourning had exhausted the country and the Johnsons. It would be a long day: attending the funeral in New York, receiving the train carrying RFK's coffin and entourage later that afternoon back in Washington, joining the procession through the capital to the burial site at Arlington Cemetery. During his last trip to St. Patrick's Cathedral two months earlier for the ordination of the new archbishop of New York, the crowds greeted LBJ with a measure of respect and relief—reassured and impressed by the statesmanship of his withdrawal from the presidential race four days earlier. But the tectonic political and emotional shift of a country wrestling with the assassinations of two of its most promising national leaders, a country where LBJ had come to personify its maladies at home and abroad, was now palpable in the crowd inside and outside St. Patrick's.

"New York was a strange sight. The streets were lined with people who stood silent, motionless," numbed with grief after a three-day barrage of visual and audio footage from that night in the Ambassador Ballroom—"the voiceless chorus" of a Greek tragedy, Lady Bird thought. St. Patrick's Cathedral was filled to overflow with four thousand people. The First Lady no longer had to borrow a black dress and coat as she had for JFK's funeral. Inside, an "absolutely stricken" Pierre Salinger, RFK's campaign manager, escorted the Johnsons up the nave. They paused briefly as they passed Bobby's flag-covered coffin, before taking their seats in the front row, on the left side of the aisle. Just as they moved into their pew, the congregation "silently and without signal" rose to its feet. Lady Bird's predecessor, Jackie Kennedy, "in black and veiled," had entered, along with John Jr. and Caroline. JFK's widow and children walked past the Johnsons to take their seats in the front row on the right side of the aisle, the Kennedy family side. Bobby's widow, Ethel, until two days earlier perhaps Bird's successor, along with her ten children ranging in age from one to sixteen, sat to the right, also in front. A third widow, Coretta Scott King, sat a few rows back, also, Lady Bird noticed, on the Kennedy family side of the aisle.[19]

Under the cathedral's vaulted ceilings mourned members of Congress, current and former Kennedy and Johnson cabinet members—the Goldbergs, the McNamaras, the Rusks, the Dillons, the Harrimans—military brass, New York's scions of philanthropy, the country's leading journalists, artists and intellectuals. The pews were filled with campaign and policy advisers who just two days earlier had imagined themselves staffing an RFK White House, and with the leaders of the new American political coalition RFK had begun to stitch together during the primaries, including activists Cesar Chavez, John Lewis, and Dolores Huerta. Other than George Wallace and Dick Gregory, every 1968 presidential candidate sat among the mourners. And so, too, did each of Lady Bird's potential successors: Muriel Humphrey, Abigail McCarthy, Happy Rockefeller, and Pat Nixon. Bird could see him only from behind, but as Leonard Bernstein conducted a painfully beautiful rendition of Mahler's "Adagietto" from Symphony No. 5, at first she wasn't sure it was the revered conductor, but saw in him "an expression of the utmost of passion, of torment and talent," words Bird may well have reserved for Bobby himself.[20] In some ways, the gathering felt like a requiem not just for Bobby Kennedy, but for the Democratic Party—or for the Johnson chapter in American political history.

Senator Ted Kennedy's "most beautiful eulogy" equally moved the First Lady. Well practiced in scrutinizing how public figures delivered their messages and connected with their audiences, Lady Bird captured the moment: "partway through, his voice began to quiver, but then came under control and ended calmly." Teddy's eulogy included a composite of a number of speeches his brother had given—in South Africa, in Mississippi. She recited verbatim the eulogy's most memorable lines. His eyes "red-rimmed," Teddy "asked that his brother be remembered simply as a good and decent man, who saw wrong and tried to right it, saw suffering and tried to heal it, saw war and tried to stop it," she recorded. Another line of "sheer poetry" from George Bernard Shaw that Bobby had often recited, although the First Lady didn't know its provenance, was also memorable: "Some men see things as they are and say why. I dream things that never were and say why not."[21] At that moment, the purity of grief had transcended resentment.

The president and the First Lady were the first to exit the cathedral after the funeral. On their way, they walked over to the Kennedy family. The patriarch, Joseph Patrick Kennedy, Sr., who in 1955 had pressed LBJ to make Jack his presidential running mate, had been unable to travel to his son's funeral, his health severely diminished by a stroke. But LBJ shook hands and spoke briefly with Teddy, and Lady Bird grasped his hand. They stopped to speak with Ethel, Bobby's greatest advocate and protector, her face "beautiful, sad, composed." They spoke to several of her children, and also to Rose Kennedy, the matriarch, whom Lady Bird had admired when they first met at the Hyannis compound in August 1960. That was the time just after the Los Angeles convention, when, feeling they had no choice, the Johnsons painfully gave up the Senate leadership, accepted the vice presidency, and threw their lot in with the Massachusetts clan. During that first Hyannis visit, Jack and Jackie had hidden their toothbrushes, emptied their drawers, and squeezed into a twin bed in a guest room so the Johnsons could spend the night in their room. It was also where Jackie first saw, and misjudged, how Lady Bird deployed her 360-degree powers of observation and encyclopedic recall in the service of Lyndon's and her own sizable ambitions.[22]

It had been almost eight years since the Johnsons' late-night arrival in Cape Cod, when, her mouth watering, Lady Bird declined Jackie's offer of a lobster dinner. It had been almost eight years since a pregnant Jackie asked Lady Bird's advice on how best to help her husband's candidacy while sitting on the sidelines, minding her womb. And it had been almost five years since Jackie and Lady Bird navigated, together and separately, the brutal reality of Jack's assassination and the fourteen excruciating days of transition that followed.

In the early weeks and months after her exit from the White House and then her departure from Washington, the Johnsons had stayed in touch with Jackie with letters and with invitations, all declined. They named the garden designed and planted by horticulture guru Bunny Mellon, and filled with plants native to the United States, the Jacqueline Kennedy Garden. Even as she finally felt she had gotten out from under Jackie's shadow living at the White House, Lady Bird built on Jackie's art acquisition initiative and continued with her historical preservation projects. But there was only so much Lady Bird could do to heal the wounds of November 1963. By June 1968, Jackie had been living on Fifth Avenue in Manhattan for four years and had begun to date Aristotle Onassis, a Greek shipping magnate, far older and shorter than the multilingual equestrian debutante.

After the warm exchange with Ted, Ethel, and Rose, Bird perhaps expected to find a similar display of manners from the wounded yet ultracareful Jackie, the one Kennedy with whom she shared the most history. Not so. "And then," Lady Bird recorded, sounding a bit perplexed,

I found myself in front of Mrs. Jacqueline Kennedy. I called her name and put out my hand. I hardly know how to describe the next few moments of time. She looked at me as though from a great distance, as though I were an aberration. I felt extreme hostility. Was it because I was alive? At last, without a flicker of expression, she extended her hand very slightly. I took it with some murmured words of sorrow and walked on quickly. It was somehow shocking. Never in any contact with her before had I experienced this.[23]

Jackie's losses had again mounted. Two infants. One husband. Now a beloved brother-in-law. Defying the mythology of Kennedy stoicism in the face of tragedy, she had practically collapsed at one point during the ceremony. Making Lady Bird feel at ease, a skill Jackie had mastered between 1960 and 1963, was perhaps not her highest priority in 1968. Was it a measure of survivor's guilt that Lady Bird had projected onto this potent encounter? She had every reason to feel it. Her husband was still alive, even if his presidency was politically moribund.

As Jackie, Coretta, and Ethel mourned their fallen husbands, Lady Bird felt especially helpless and purposeless. "Once again, the country is being revived by the sight of a Kennedy wife, behaving with perfect nobility," the journalist Mary McGrory wrote of Ethel's grace at the funeral.[24] Perhaps the hardest truth was that there was nothing Lady Bird, in her capacity as First Lady, could do to provide comfort to the three widows or to a mourning nation. Back in Washington, she spent the rest of the day unable to concentrate on work; she played bridge with her daughters, "hung in this interval of time between the funeral and the burial with everyone in a sort of emotional trance."[25] Most inhabitants of Resurrection City had abandoned the encampment for churches, schools, and homes around the District, in order to watch live television coverage of the national trauma.

The train procession carrying Bobby in his coffin, Ethel and the Kennedy clan, and hundreds of friends, journalists, and political allies was scheduled to arrive at Union Station at four-thirty in the afternoon. But in Elizabeth, New Jersey, two bystanders waiting along the tracks to pay their respects were instantly killed by an oncoming train. In Trenton, another mourner, who had climbed to a high vantage point to get a better look at the train, grabbed a live wire and severely burned himself.[26] The television replayed Teddy's eulogy; commentators tried to fill the airtime until there was more live action to cover. As the images of Bobby's assassination played on a loop, the commentariat spun on about the implications of the tragedy for the Democratic Party. The California primary loss had torpedoed McCarthy's campaign, leaving Hubert Humphrey as the next viable contender, but they all knew that, as Hubert put it, "whoever gets the Democratic nomination, it will be a tarnished shield." And maybe no shield at all, Lady Bird thought. "It seems to me," she recorded, that "this whole tragedy turns the nation toward the Republican party." If her own instincts were any measure, during her travels after the 1967 riots and in Texas after MLK's assassination, the First Lady had already begun to pick up on the "silent majority" sentiment of rural and small-town law-and-order white Americans, who were angered by urban violence and resentful that tax dollars for the Great Society had raised expectations and then failed to deliver.[27]

After a family dinner with Rev. Billy Graham, now a regular at the White House, the Johnsons finally were summoned to Union Station, where Bobby's train would shortly arrive. From there, the president and First Lady would accompany the funeral cortege to the burial at Arlington Cemetery. The three flags outside flew at half-staff. Inside the huge concourse, the vaulted doorways were draped in black, as the White House had been in 1963. The last time Lady Bird had been at Union Station as part of a funeral was for General Douglas MacArthur in April 1964. She stood with Bobby Kennedy, still the attorney general, waiting for MacArthur's train to arrive from New York. Bobby turned to her and said, "You're doing a wonderful job." He paused and added, "and so is your husband."[28] It was a single kind moment in an otherwise fraught relationship.

Overcome by Rose Kennedy's suffering and also by her strength in the face of so much tragedy, Lyndon welled up with tears during the rainy ride to the station. Lady Bird tenderly touched his arm.[29] When they arrived, they found Hubert and Muriel waiting, and invited them into the presidential limousine. "The ever ebullient" Hubert "looked for once drained and empty."[30] The twenty-one-car train that finally arrived carried what only a few days before was the nascent RFK administration. Their job now was not to best Lyndon, but to bury Bobby. The president's limousine followed fourteen cars behind RFK's hearse. The motorcade's route traveled from Union Station along First Street, past his Senate office building; turned west along Constitution Avenue, where it paused at the Justice Department, where Bobby had served as attorney general; and then west to the Lincoln Memorial, past the Resurrection City encampment.[31] There, under a bright moon, the cortege stopped.

Onlookers, at times six people deep, lined the lawns and sidewalks nearby. From Washington, Maryland, and Virginia, some from the South, others from across the country, they'd been waiting all day. The raised fists of the crowd at Resurrection City cut a dramatic contrast with the Cadillacs and National Guardsmen posted nearby. The Marine Corps brass ensemble accompanied two local choirs to perform "Battle Hymn of the Republic." But the Secret Service cautioned Lady Bird against lowering her window to listen to the abolitionist Julia Ward Howe's classic of the American songbook. People, more people, candles in hand, lined Memorial Bridge across the Potomac to Arlington Cemetery. There, too, Americans had been waiting for hours to see the cortege pass. Inside the gates of the cemetery, more candles still. Kennedy friend Bunny Mellon had selected the grave site, on a slope shaded by two magnolia trees, "right close to President Kennedy's tomb," Bird recorded.[32]

Joe Califano had negotiated every detail of the Johnsons' role for that day. Going over the choreography, Califano had told the president that when the flag came off the casket, "they want you to present it to Mrs. Kennedy," to Ethel. "I'll be glad to do it, but I want you to make sure that this is what the family wants." Califano reassured him. "Yes, sir," he replied, "we have asked them three times."[33] LBJ said later that he was glad his last meeting with Bobby, the day before MLK's assassination, had been at least outwardly friendly. The *New York Times* journalist Max Frankel captured the two men's "braided" fates.

> Lyndon Johnson and Robert Kennedy thought of each other as unruly detractor and unqualified usurper and their thoughts of each other could provoke them to private profanity. Yet they fought by the proper processes and peculiarly respected even what they resented. For a decade their lives were tautly intertwined, and as they pulled apart politically, they managed only to strangle one another.[34]

Lyndon was confounded by his inability to read the Kennedy clan and deeply frustrated by their rejection of his talents. In the end, after a brief ceremony, the Johnsons hung back. They stood when the family stood, kneeled when the family kneeled, and watched as one of the pallbearers, astronaut John Glenn, folded the flag with military precision and handed it to Teddy Kennedy—and Teddy, not LBJ, carried it to Ethel. "This was," Lady Bird recorded, "as it should be." Knowing the family's wish to "linger alone," the president and First Lady said their goodbyes to Ethel and walked down the slope, Washington's monuments and the Capitol dome illuminated ahead of them. "There was a great white moon riding high in the sky—a beautiful night. This is the only night funeral I ever remember, but then this is the only time in the life of our country—an incredible, unbelievable, cruel, wrenching time."[35]

On the drive back to the sanctuary of the White House, the First Lady noticed they were not crossing Memorial Bridge. The Secret Service thought it better to avoid Resurrection City. But there was no security threat emanating from the Poor People's Campaign, this much Lady Bird understood. In the aftermath of the assassination, the force and power behind the zip code 20013 had steadily deflated.

* * *

On June 24, once the Department of the Interior announced that it would not renew Resurrection City's permit, the D.C. Police needed all of ninety minutes to clear the remaining occupants. Most had already left. Walter Washington enforced a curfew in the District, and National Guard troops deployed throughout Shaw. Police arrested and charged Ralph Abernathy for overstaying the permit. On June 25, two federal agencies and the D.C. Department of Highways sent four hundred men with bulldozers and crowbars to dismantle the encampment.[36] The next day, June 26 (the same day LBJ nominated Abe Fortas as chief justice and Homer Thornberry as associate justice to the Supreme Court), the First Lady set off with Sharon Francis for Portland, Oregon. Heading for the airport, they drove down Constitution Avenue, right past the former grounds of Resurrection City. Seeing the scattered remains of 20013, Lady Bird told Sharon that "she wished she could be inside those people to know what they were thinking and how they felt and what their images of themselves were and what their images of us were." Despite her work in the District for the past four years, her natural sympathies lay more squarely with Nash Castro, for the headache the encampment had caused to the National Park Service, and with Walter Washington, for the demands of public security required of his still-fresh leadership role. "She just wanted to have an empathy with them, and didn't know them well enough, realized she didn't," Francis explained in her 1969 oral history.[37]

It seemed fitting then, that she would choose to bring to bear this self-awareness and self-criticism before the annual convention of the American Institute of Architects (AIA) in Portland. There, Lady Bird Johnson finally shed the trappings of "beautification." There, she fully departed from euphemism in setting forth her environmental values and vision—delivering the longest speech she had ever given, and the one she worked on the hardest to convert from staff draft into her own voice. If ever there was a time to move beyond flowers and flowering shrubs, the summer of 1968 was it.

The lineup for the event spoke volumes. First, the president of the National Urban League, Whitney Young, Jr., followed by the no-longer-regular White House guest, the British development economist Barbara Ward, and finally, Lady Bird Johnson. Though regarded by some militants as too moderate and too intimate with the white corporate and government establishment, Young, an MIT-trained army engineer, minced no words. He forced his audience to reckon with the full-frontal activism of the civil rights movement, of the Poor People's Campaign, and of Resurrection City. He berated the AIA for the absence of black faces among their members, but offered praise for the early signs of readiness to communicate and even to explicitly name racism, as the Kerner Commission had, as the foundation of material disparities its members witnessed while touring American ghettos:

> We are a racist nation, and no way in the world could it be otherwise given the history of our country. Being a racist doesn't mean one wants to go out and join a lynch mob or send somebody off to Africa or engage in crude, vulgar expressions of prejudice. Racism is a basic assumption of superiority on the part of one group over another, and in America it had to happen because as a society we enslaved people for 250 years, and up until 1964 it was written into our laws.

But if that weren't enough for the shell-shocked crowd, Young then took aim more specifically at their profession.

> . . . You are not a profession that has distinguished itself by your social and civic contributions to the cause of civil rights, and I am sure this has not come to you as any shock. You are most distinguished by your thunderous silence and your complete irrelevance. . . . You are employers, you are key people in the planning of our cities today. You share the responsibility for the mess we are in [in] terms of the white noose around the central city.[38]

Young's electrifying speech changed the profession of American architecture. At the time he delivered it, black architects made up one-half of 1 percent of the AIA's twenty thousand members. Within two years, Robert J. Nash became the first African American to hold a national office in the AIA when he was elected vice president; he soon created a national scholarship fund to promote the study of architecture by minority groups. In 1970, the Ford Foundation made a grant to the AIA to fund young, talented minority designers in order to help them break into the segregated field.

After Young cast a spotlight on the dysfunction of the architecture profession, and Barbara Ward called for the United States to dedicate a Vietnam peace dividend to eliminate "the enemies of all human tranquility at home—ugliness, filth, rats, slums, wretched schools, unemployment, despair," it must have come as a relief to anticipate the carefully modulated, southern cadence of the First Lady.[39]

Secretary of Agriculture Orville Freeman introduced her as "one of [the] single most powerful influences on ornamental horticulture that this country has ever known." However much genuine pleasure she took in floral beauty, Lady Bird Johnson had no intention at this point in her tenure of staying in the lane of "ornamental horticulture," the field of flower arranging and garden design. This was a woman who had used her White House platform to help elevate and advocate the pioneering field of participatory design in urban planning. It was time for her to display her knowledge and perspective, and no longer defer to the guild's experts. In her remarks, she didn't once mention race. And her focus on the material and natural resource impact of capitalism itself is both subtle and, in the heightened polemic of the moment, perhaps easy to miss.[40] "I am one of millions of Americans who are troubled—and hopeful—about the physical setting of life in our country. As you may know, my concern has been expressed in an effort called 'beautification.' I think you also know what lies beneath that rather inadequate word." Finally, she had the forum to say what she meant about a term that had bothered and belittled her from the start. "For 'beautification,' to my mind, is far more than a matter of cosmetics. To me, it describes the whole effort to bring the natural world and the man-made world into harmony; to bring order, usefulness, and delight to our whole environment. And that of course, only begins with trees and flowers and landscaping." The First Lady had been trying for three years to raise the public's awareness about how "a preponderance of concrete and asphalt—of fumes, haze and screeches—go against our grain in a cultural way, as well as a biological way."[41]

Neuroscience has since shown that our physical environment conditions how we feel about ourselves as individuals and in relation to others.[42] Lady Bird was an early advocate of the public and environmental health significance of the connection. "Both dimensions of our makeup have been offended and poisoned. . . . Citizens everywhere in America are demanding that we turn our building to a sensible human purpose. They are asking—literally—for a breath of fresh air; for pleasant precincts in the heart of the city; for relaxation as well as excitement; for more reminders of nature in the city center. . . . The answers cannot be found in piecemeal reform," the very kind of reform the Johnson administration's critics now took it to task over. Rather, she argued, "The job requires really thoughtful inter-relation of the whole environment; not only in buildings, but parks; not only parks, but highways; not only highways but open spaces and green belts. When the New Conservation speaks of the vast rebuilding that America must undertake, it does not mean on the old terms of freeways ripping through neighborhoods and parks, or drab housing so all-alike that it reminds one of Gertrude Stein's phrase, 'There's no there there.'" But worse than the absence of a there there was the legacy of midcentury American urban renewal. "I earnestly hope that our civilization is remembered for more than its mammoth freeways and vast urban superblocks; for more than the isolated, impersonal, gigantic public housing projects of our cities. Too many of these great projects seem to me to be reproaches, not signs of progress."[43]

Directly and indirectly, Lady Bird's environmental policy statement broadly reinforced Young's attempt to focus the field of architecture not just on clients and contracts, but on the human cost and human consequences of their omissions and commissions. "So deep is the environmental crisis; so urgent is the demand for change, that architecture must become not only a profession, but a form of public service. When so many are affected by your work, you are serving not only the client who commissions your work and pays your fee: the public is also your client," she insisted. "If we are to obtain the vital balance of nature and architecture and man, architects must become thoughtful political activists," a call similar to Young's, only now by the First Lady of the United States, and a challenge to examine the profession's relevance to the material and spiritual needs of Americans and of American society.[44]

The audience delivered a standing ovation. Orville Freeman then took the podium to announce that the National Arboretum would name a white-budding azalea in Mrs. Johnson's honor, calling it "Mrs. LBJ." It was something of an anticlimax. The First Lady, who had never seen herself as a beauty, who measured her achievements less in how she looked or dressed than in how she thought and acted, wanted to be recognized for the seriousness and gravitas she brought to her environmental agenda. She had at long last said what she wanted to say, how she wanted to say it, but she could still not escape the essential liability of having her public identity so closely associated with the prettifying effect of a flowering plant. It was "another one of those times," she said, thinking back, "when I wished I hadn't acquired a nickname but had just been Claudia all of my life."[45]

Chapter 27

"Over by Choice"

And so we go on through this strange year. And personally it is a happy year, but in the close circle of our family, because I think we are proud of what each one of us is doing—all of us together. How strange that might sound from somebody on the outside who is looking at us. Yet it is true—the world is undergoing convulsions all around us—our Party, our Country—the whole world. And it seems to me Lyndon is plowing right along, working as hard as he can every day on those things he can control and assaulting those things most vigorously that he has even a little hope of controlling. I know that it is a racking year for Lyndon physically, and it must be mentally and spiritually. And sometimes I think the greatest courage in the world is to get up in the morning and go about a day's work. That is one of the things I like about him. He keeps on and on and on.

—Lady Bird Johnson, White House diary, August 27, 1968

Two assassinations and the national convulsions that followed had persuaded Lady Bird, if she needed any persuasion at all, that Lyndon's decision not to run again had been not just "irrevocable" but "providential."[1] Yet, after RFK's death, polls showed LBJ running substantially ahead of the GOP front-runner, Richard Nixon. Even Bobby Kennedy's and Eugene McCarthy's own advisers thought the best man to defeat Nixon was Lyndon Johnson, not Hubert Humphrey, and they communicated as much to the White House. As the summer months unfolded and Lady Bird continued to plow through her list of "lasts," Lyndon toyed with a continuum of options—from getting back into the race as the party's unity candidate to appearing in Chicago for a valedictory speech on his sixtieth birthday, August 27, 1968, where just maybe the delegates would draft him on the convention floor. He kept a hand in virtually every aspect of the convention: the choice of its venue, the chairs of its various committees, who got to speak when, and of course, the party's platform plank on Vietnam. Secretly, he sent aides to Hollywood to commission a twenty-eight-minute legacy film narrated by Gregory Peck. Before the GOP convention in Miami, he met with George Wallace, Nelson Rockefeller, and Richard Nixon. Like LBJ, Nixon had been a member of the House and the Senate, and a vice president. Although LBJ knew that Nixon would likely try to roll back some of his signature domestic programs, he regarded Nixon's Cold War credentials as unimpeachable. As were his skills at ingratiating himself with sitting presidents. Of all the candidates, Republican or Democratic, it was the Orange County, California, native whom LBJ regarded as the most likely to continue his hybrid strategy of bombing in North Vietnam and peace talks in Paris, the very strategy that ultimately weakened the Democratic Party going into the convention.[2] By preventing the party's Platform Committee from approving a Vietnam plank favoring an end to the war, LBJ effectively strengthened Nixon's shot at the presidency.

On the first of August, as Lady Bird prepared to spend most of the month in Texas, she found Lyndon in the family dining room eating lunch with Richard Daley. That morning, the Chicago mayor had attended the signing of the gutted Housing and Urban Development Act at the recently completed modernist HUD building in Southwest D.C. In a few weeks, he would host the Democratic National Convention at the decrepit International Amphitheatre near the Union Stock Yards, on Chicago's South Side. "The mayor," Lady Bird recorded, "was giving Lyndon a sales talk about coming to Chicago. The Democrats wanted to give him a rousing welcome, they wanted to show their appreciation." Daley had pressed for LBJ to revoke his decision not to run for reelection since that night in March when he announced it. In classic Johnson treatment, Lady Bird observed, "Lyndon gave him little encouragement that he would come. He stopped just short of a definitive 'no.'"[3] But unlike the months leading up to his March 31 announcement, despite LBJ's end-stage equivocations, Lady Bird felt certain that this time they really were done. She'd already started packing up and shipping their things from the White House to the Ranch, where the Johnsons planned to spend the month of August watching the conventions on television.

As the GOP gathering concluded in Miami with Richard Nixon and Spiro Agnew headlining the 1968 ticket, the Johnsons hosted a spate of visitors. Although Lady Bird was not one prone to illness, after a week in Texas she found herself often writhing with stomach pain so intense she thought she might faint. Perhaps it was adrenaline simply leaving her system, or maybe it was her body rebelling—or, potentially, it was some kind of stomach bug she had picked up during a trip to Central America. Doctors had also found a growth on Lyndon's colon, and put him on a liquid diet ahead of more testing. It was far from the ideal conditions to play host, with their usual mix of work, play, cocktails, and meals.

One of their first visitors was Senator James Eastland of Mississippi, a plantation owner bitterly opposed to desegregation. In unflattering terms, LBJ had once said, "Jim Eastland could be standing right in the middle of the worst Mississippi flood ever known, and he'd say the niggers caused it, helped out by the Communists—but, he'd say, we gotta have help from Washington."[4] Yet the president had invited Eastland down to try to neutralize his opposition to the nomination of Abe Fortas as chief justice. Lady Bird met Eastland when his plane arrived and took him on a drive to Lyndon's birthplace. "Senator Eastland was determined to talk politics" and to pitch Lady Bird. "You know your husband is going to be nominated, don't you?" Eastland asked her. "No, Sir, not at all. There is not going to be any movement of that sort—that is not with any force behind it. And if he were, he wouldn't accept." Perhaps unaware of Lady Bird's clout with the president, Eastland, she recorded, "seemed somehow taken aback—a little disbelieving." And that was her intention. The First Lady wanted to make perfectly clear to a key southern delegate of her own party that Lyndon would not accept any such draft. "You know Hubert can't make it. He's not catching on," Eastland insisted. Nor, despite his own segregationist inclinations, did Eastland hold any enthusiasm for George Wallace, who had recently taken to the airwaves to convince Americans that he was not, as popular sentiment held, a racist.[5] As little as Eastland had in common with LBJ, and as strongly as he would soon and successfully oppose the Fortas nomination, he told the First Lady that he wanted Lyndon at the top of the ticket. But Lady Bird pushed back.[6] Lyndon would spin his wheels, change leads, dodge and parry on the phone and with visitors, and maybe they'd go to Chicago for a birthday fête. But on the matter of another run, as far as Lady Bird was concerned, that question had been asked and answered. She was now focused on successors, Lyndon's and hers. Hubert and Muriel came and went. Nixon stopped at the Ranch on his way back from the Republican National Convention in Miami. He did not bring his wife, who would be Lady Bird's successor. But he did bring Spiro Agnew.

Aside from the requisite politicians, Lady Bird had hoped to host Larry Halprin at the Ranch that August. She had wanted him to help her make a last-ditch pitch to LBJ to veto the highway bill then making its way through Congress. The bill would require the District of Columbia to construct freeways in Washington as originally proposed in 1959, and threatened to strip the D.C. government and the Department of the Interior of the power to amend or end plans for the Three Sisters Bridge in Northwest, for the inner loop in Northeast, for a tunnel under the Lincoln Memorial, and for the East Leg of the freeway in Southwest. But with Lady Bird sick when Larry was supposed to have visited Stonewall, and Lyndon running the presidency, orchestrating the convention, and planning his transition, the window had closed for Halprin to make a final case against tearing up the city so dramatically.

Among the First Lady's posse of collaborators, there was a complete consensus against the highway bill. Udall described it to LBJ as an "arrogant, calculated effort to undermine critical conservation victories achieved during your Administration" and advised the president to veto it. Robert Weaver agreed with Udall and sought to enlist Mayor Washington "on behalf of the negro citizenry who would be affected," to press him to ask LBJ for a veto. The mayor had, according to Weaver, surprisingly, "copped out."[7] Lady Bird sympathized with the arguments against the bill, and with the people making them, but she wondered if the president could afford a veto given such a strong showing in the Senate for the federal aid the bill promised. "While not trying to make the decision for him," the First Lady did lay out the case to LBJ for a veto. But without Halprin there at the Ranch to push with her, Lady Bird's advocacy on behalf of the citizens across the District of Columbia ultimately failed.[8]

As convention delegates and protesters flooded Chicago for the start of the Democratic National Convention, the Federal-Aid Highway Act of 1968 reached the president. The law secured three years of funding to complete the interstate highway system under more stringent environmental and design standards and with funds for families displaced by new construction. There was little more positive to say about it, as LBJ's lengthy, nose-holding, near-repudiation of a signing statement set forth.[9] He signed the bill over the objections of his wife, many among his staff, local politicians, and key cabinet members. The weakened version of its beautification components (reduced funding and little federal enforcement of billboard height) was the least of its problems. The major offense was the requirement that the District of Columbia move forward with the construction of bridges and highways through and within Washington's neighborhoods, rich and poor, white and black.

The Johnsons, however, still had options for helping their city. It wasn't lost on them, both advocates of home rule, that precisely because the District of Columbia did not have the powers of a state, the administration could, in Lyndon's remaining months in office, rely instead on a combination of executive orders, public hearings, community protest, and, ultimately, challenges in the courts to stop the environmental and social disaster promised by new highway construction in the nation's capital.[10] Nevertheless, when Lyndon Johnson signed the bill into law, he signed away the likelihood, remote and ambitious though it was, that his wife's signature legacy project, the Anacostia River/Kingman Island swimming and recreation space, would ever see the light of day.

* * *

The Democratic National Convention opened on August 26 in the sweltering heat and humidity of the Chicago summer. During the Johnson tenure, Chicago had both benefited and suffered from the largesse of urban renewal funds, but Mayor Daley's boss leadership had come under growing scrutiny for the city's heavily segregated neighborhoods and the racism and economic inequality that permeated its ethnic politics. The White House had no problem persuading Daley, a staunch advocate of law and order, of the wisdom of deploying the city's entire police force of 12,000 officers, along with 5,600 members of the Illinois National Guard and 5,000 Army Reserve troops, during the convention. With an eleven P.M. curfew set for the city's public spaces, police officers were given permission to "shoot to kill" if protesters defied their orders.[11]

Aretha Franklin opened the 1968 Democratic convention with a powerful rendition of "The Star-Spangled Banner"—so powerful, in fact, that she was quickly derided for bungling some of the lyrics (practically a national pastime) and for putting too much soul into her rendition of the anthem. The reaction to Aretha was only the start of a stream of invective and violence that flooded the convention halls and the streets of Chicago that week.[12] That first night, the Johnsons settled into their living room, trays on their knees with a dinner of steamed beef; macaroni and cheese; spinach, carrot, pineapple, and raisin salad; peach preserves; and cookies. They watched the convention on a three-screened console, each screen carrying one of the major networks. They kept NBC and ABC on mute and listened only to Walter Cronkite on CBS.[13] Cronkite's denunciation of the Vietnam War notwithstanding, he was an old friend (a classmate of Lady Bird's at UT) and remained, even to the Johnsons, the most authoritative voice on television. On the second day of the convention, Lyndon's sixtieth birthday, the president deployed John Connally to probe for interest by southern states and the Texas delegation in drafting LBJ to the ticket.[14] The answer was decidedly negative. Had it been positive, LBJ would then have been able to magnanimously reject such an entreaty. With that scenario off the table, the Johnsons began the week of the Chicago convention with only one element of suspense. At the 1964 convention in Atlantic City, Lyndon had combined the celebration of his nomination with a raucous fifty-sixth-birthday bash. Would he accept Richard Daley's invitation to fly to Chicago to celebrate his birthday and deliver a valedictory speech?

Luci described the week of the convention as "the longest wake I ever attended."[15] But the black-and-white candid photos of the Johnson family shot by Okie at the Ranch and in Austin have a settled, unperturbed quality: Lyndon and Lyn playing in the pool; Lady Bird, rubber bathing cap secured under her chin, hanging off the side of the pool, pushing Lyn back and forth in a floaty to his grandfather or his mother; Luci, in a bikini, holding Lyn; her father, in his bathing suit, goofing with the one-year-old; all of them arrayed around a sleeveless, tanned Lady Bird reading something aloud to them; Lynda, in her maternity clothes and glasses, diligently riding a bicycle to help ward off the weight of pregnancy; Lyndon, in Luci's Austin neighborhood, helping Lyn onto his new banana-seat Schwinn bike. The "wake" Luci described also suggested a series of last suppers. The president's secretarial staff made note of each meal, each dish devoured by the First Couple and their guests. Perhaps the photographs were taken to reinforce for the American public what Lyndon was himself keen to transmit: "I'm not a candidate for anything, except maybe a rocking chair."[16] But if the beautiful candids were part of some public relations jujitsu, they also, and quite accurately, reflected Lady Bird's mindset.

> Lyndon's 60th birthday—Tuesday, August 27th—was probably as strange and dramatic and in a way sad birthday as any he will ever have. For me it was a sort of suspended in space time—this whole week. The decision had been made irrevocably on March 31st. But somehow there was a special saying goodbye this week to our whole political life. The Convention would be choosing from among others, and for us it was over—no matter that it was happily, cozily over by choice. There was still a special aura. There had been talk about going to the Convention to make a sort of valedictory speech, to receive good wishes on our birthday—Lyndon's birthday I mean. No

> decision. And gradually as the days passed, my betting was more and more that we would not go. And when the convention virtually erupted on Monday, the chances of making our trip seemed to me to dwindle to almost nothing.[17]

While Lyndon spent much of his birthday behaving as if he might actually fly to Chicago that night—tweaking his valedictory speech; having his aides call Chicago while listening in on the other line; or calling directly to Humphrey, Daley, and his other soldiers on the ground—Lady Bird, "with all vestige of any possible trip to Chicago ruled out," called their Texas friends to join them for a convention-watching birthday dinner. And to keep the press away from the Ranch, Luci threw a birthday party for LBJ at her home in Austin, and invited several dozen journalists. It was yet another family affair, this one purposely staged, with coconut chocolate rum cake, candles, soda, and gifts. The press sang "Happy Birthday." Lyndon held court from a rocking chair. "It was all very low-key, which somehow in a way added to the sad atmosphere." Asked if he would attend the convention, he replied, "I have not decided yet."[18] But Bird certainly had made up her mind.

In Chicago, in what was billed as a "freak-out of the biggest freak of all," the National Mobilization Committee to End the War in Vietnam staged a "top velocity, high-decibel, multi-media" anti–birthday party "tribute to Mr. Johnson's historic career all the way from the first election he stole in Texas to the new anti-personnel weapons his Administration developed for use in Vietnam and the ghettos."[19] An exhibition hall at the Chicago Coliseum displayed gory photos of American and Vietnamese war dead, of refugees streaming from Vietnamese villages, and of kids in American cities running from helmeted police. Singer-songwriter Phil Ochs sang "I Ain't Marching Anymore," and Beat poets William S. Burroughs and Allen Ginsberg and French dramatist Jean Genet ridiculed the Johnson war machine. Dick Gregory, now a write-in candidate for the presidency, closed out the event. On the convention floor, a security officer punched Dan Rather in the stomach as he tried to interview a Georgia delegate whom police were dragging out of the hall.[20]

From her remote outpost in the Hill Country, Lady Bird could afford a measure of curiosity. "From afar [Chicago] seemed like a seething caldron of emotions and striving peaks—of every stripe of Democrat—and hippies and yippies and police standing by. If I could have been there without being me I would have liked very much to see what is looming—one of the spectacles of our time."[21] Live footage of police, many with their badges removed, attacking protesters with billy clubs in Grant Park and marching with .30-caliber machine guns along Michigan Avenue, made the prime-time news. The whole world was watching, and so was Lady Bird Johnson.

In the weeks before the convention, Mayor Daley had denied permits to demonstrate. Now, as protesters hurled bags of urine and rocks, police officers indiscriminately beat anyone within baton's reach. Bird didn't understand the impulse or passion driving protesters to put their bodies on the line, and she likely would have agreed with Mayor Daley's police crackdown. The gravitational pull she felt toward law and order as a response to such mayhem spoke to her sympathy toward voters drawn to the hard-line notes George Wallace was sounding. She could understand the message but never relate to the messenger. Her prescient sympathy was also part of something bigger, representative of a turn voters (many like Bird, perhaps) would soon take in electing Nixon. She found herself amused by the now-legendary ABC debate from Chicago between William F. Buckley and Gore Vidal. Over the course of one broadcast, Vidal called Buckley a "crypto-Nazi" over his defense of Mayor Daley's police tactics and of LBJ's war in Vietnam; Buckley hit back, calling Vidal a "queer" and threatened to "sock you in your goddamned face."[22] Bird was happy not to be present for the "three-ring circus," happy to be done. Still, the natural sadness she felt arose not only from the ending of an era, an end that in any case she had been crucial in orchestrating, but from seeing Lyndon struggle to come to terms with the consequences of his choice. Surrounded by his wife and daughters, his beloved grandson, his most loyal staff, and his closest Texas friends, LBJ observed his birthday that night still unable to fully give up the fantasy that the chaos in Chicago, inside and outside the convention hall, and the weakness of the party's support for Humphrey might somehow still convert him into the nominee of last resort.[23]

Lyndon did eventually come to grips with the inevitable and arranged for the convention chairman to read a statement to the delegates expressing the irrevocability of the president's March 1968 decision. The balloting, nomination, and formal acceptance by Hubert Humphrey and Edmund Muskie as the party's candidates for president and vice president unfolded over two days and two nights. Outside, protesters had planned a march on the International Amphitheatre, but police sprayed tear gas to keep them away. Lady Bird, her family, their friends and staff, floated between coffee and newspapers in Lyndon's bedroom, walks around the property, dashes into Austin to measure the space for Bird's new office above the KTBC station, and dips in the swimming pool. They took their meals on trays in front of the television, their relief reinforced and their anxiety alleviated by ample servings of fried chicken, creamed potatoes, pineapple salad with cottage cheese, turnip greens, brown-and-serve rolls, lemon sponge cake, shrimp curry, homemade bread, tossed salad with pineapple and pears, and chocolate soufflé with vanilla sauce. On the last night of the convention, they gathered again in the living room to watch Humphrey and Muskie deliver their acceptance speeches. Thanksgiving was a few months off, but Lady Bird's choice of a menu of turkey and dressing, beans, and sweet potatoes expressed her gratitude at the successful outcome of a strategy years in the making: to get Lyndon out of Washington still alive, if ever broken.[24] At midnight, letting down her guard, Bird raided the refrigerator.

LBJ's family (and staff) often convened in his bedroom, in the morning over coffee, breakfast, and papers, or late at night for television, talk, and planning. At one such gathering—in the morning, during the balloting, or perhaps in the evening, after Humphrey's acceptance speech—the photographer Okamoto captured the moment.[25] In one of the stills, one that perfectly represents how the Johnsons combined familial intimacy with business, Lyndon and Lady Bird sit under the covers in bed in their pajamas. Lyndon aims the remote at his television, at the foot of the bed. Lady Bird talks on the telephone, spiral phone cord stretching from the bedside table across Lyndon's lanky frame to reach her, watching the set, too. A new watercolor painting of Lyn, a birthday present for LBJ, hangs on the wall above a bedside table full of the usual quotidian clutter of pencils, pens, papers, and a glass of water. Lynda stands next to the bed, socks unevenly scrunched at her ankles, dressed in an Empire-style maternity top and shorts, hair pulled back, glasses affixed—also watching the set. Luci, in a bralette and shorts, sits on a chair against the wall, gazing not at the television but across the room toward Lyndon's massage table on the other side of the bed. Two male staffers in short-sleeved plaid shirts are perched nearby—one writes on a notepad, the other leans on the doorframe, watching television. The other photos in the series show Lyndon on the phone, Lady Bird's gaze fixed on him. By aligning the dates of the photos with the time stamps on LBJ's call records, it appears that in this moment, the Johnsons were on the phone congratulating Hubert Humphrey, or maybe Edmund Muskie, or someone else. But does it really matter?

Over the course of four days, Chicago had concentrated all the forces pulling American society apart, violent and nonviolent, institutional and anti-institutional, convulsive and corrupt, racial and ethnic. The generation gap Lynda had written about during her year as a single woman barely touched the scope and intensity of the paroxysm displayed on Michigan Avenue, in Grant Park, or even inside the convention hall. In the muggy heat of the Chicago summer, the Democrats had chosen the party's next presidential candidate. In the arid Hill Country of Texas, two Americans who had made their fortune from the media, and for whom the media had become a reliable foil, much like so many in the nation now, sat at home in their pajamas with their kids close by, glued to their television set, watching as their country left them behind.

Epilogue

To Survive All Assaults

January 1969–July 2007

I came very late and timorously to the uses of power. I really turned aside from it, half knowing what could be done with the leverage of the White House.

—Lady Bird Johnson, White House diary, December 12, 1968

I think when this is over I want to declare a long moratorium on several words—"last," "historic," "feel," would be among them.

—Lady Bird Johnson, White House diary, January 4, 1969

On the short drive from the White House to the Capitol, Lady Bird Johnson and Pat Nixon barely managed to conduct a real conversation. Eight years earlier, the two had made the same trek along Pennsylvania Avenue when Richard Nixon turned over his vice-presidential duties to LBJ after a bruising defeat in the 1960 campaign against John F. Kennedy. The two Second Ladies had known each other for years during their husbands' parallel ascents from House to Senate to the vice presidency and now to the highest office in the land. Since Nixon's election, Lady Bird and Luci had given Pat and her daughter Tricia the requisite orientations to the family quarters and otherwise executed their roles in the presidential changeover with order and planning—a far cry from the fraught, abrupt transition required of Jackie and Lady Bird in 1963. All the Johnsons' belongings had been packed and shipped to Texas. On January 20, 1969, Mrs. Johnson and Mrs. Nixon, their husbands, their two families, their dogs, and their senior staffs had already survived the ritual pre-inauguration gathering for coffee and sweet rolls over a warm fire in the Red Room.

On a frigid, overcast day, Lady Bird and Pat sat together again in the backseat of a limousine, joined by the Speaker of the House and Johnson ally John McCormack. A station wagon stuffed with Secret Service agents separated them from their husbands' limousine, just ahead. Since March 31, 1968, Lady Bird had allowed herself to feel the emotions of so many lasts and goodbyes. But not now. "For me," she recorded, "in any day of crisis, all the real emotions, all the leave-takings or whatever-it-is, have already been lived through at a quieter time."[1]

During the last months of "this most awful year," and for the first time in as long as she could remember, Lady Bird had stopped exercising. She boomeranged from feeling confident, even youthful, in her middle-aged body to feeling stiff and "disdainful of the encroachment of the years." Since August, she had been hospitalized twice with repeated bouts of severe stomach pain and muscle spasms, as if her body were finally rebelling against her exacting control. "When there have been enough troubles—mental and physical—one's body finally presents the bill in some way," she recorded. But over the holiday season, even beginning to practice a new kind of exercise called aerobics, the Johnsons began to ready themselves for the final burst of energy required to reach January 20, 1969.[2]

And then, the day that marked the marathon's finish line finally arrived. Bird joined Lyndon in his bedroom for one last breakfast over coffee and the papers, looking out over the South Lawn, past the Ellipse, toward the Jefferson Memorial. During her "last little pilgrimage" to take in the mansion's public and private quarters, the detoxifying odor of ammonia, the ultimate olfactory mark of finality, wafted through the White House. The smell was inescapable, but of the sensations ahead for her that day, Lady Bird vowed, "From now on, one is sort of anesthetized—in armor—and still there's the feeling of 'going to the fair,' and wanting to absorb, take everything in, but not to feel it."[3]

Pat Nixon's stomach was "knotted with excitement." During their drive to the Capitol, she picked up on Lady Bird's control. Pat didn't keep a diary, but she later told her daughter Julie that she sensed that "behind Lady Bird Johnson's detached smile and soft answers in her carefully modulated southern voice, she too was concentrating on keeping her emotions in check."[4] Bird's diary in the last months of Lyndon's presidency is filled with her consciousness of the presidency as performance, and flows with the language of theater: drama, stage, scene, costume, action, audience reaction. Riding down Pennsylvania Avenue along the parade route, Bird noticed the ceremonial banner and bunting, but sparse crowds. "Our conversation was desultory and trivial," she recorded, "we were glad it wasn't sleeting; we might even avoid rain although it was a gray brooding day. I said I felt sure that the stands were going to be full by the time they rode back. Somehow I felt vaguely sorry that they weren't."[5]

The stiff formality of the presidential transition continued; the separation of genders resumed. Both donning fur hats, Mrs. Johnson and Mrs. Nixon were escorted to the office of Senator Margaret Chase Smith, the only female senator at the time, a Republican from Maine and the first woman to have her name placed in contention for the GOP presidential nomination at the party's 1964 convention. Muriel Humphrey and Judy Agnew arrived as well. Mamie Eisenhower had left her ailing husband at Walter Reed—he would die nine weeks later—in order to greet the incoming and outgoing First Ladies.

As the group engaged in well-practiced conversation, Lady Bird Johnson and Muriel Humphrey received the signal. They walked together, side by side, out the door and down the steps of the Capitol. From her seat in the front row, the First Lady was surprised to recognize so few faces in the crowds below her. Accompanied by "Hail to the Chief," the president, she thought, looked "very tall and handsome and impressive, and very relaxed," as he walked by himself down the steps, "truly for the last time." The platform built for the live television broadcast of the inauguration seemed much bigger compared to four years earlier. "The great eyes of television trained down on us." From behind bulletproof glass, the First Lady took in the moment with, *The New York Times* observed, a "smile [that] has never been freer."[6]

The ceremony seemed short, its brevity matching its tone, "low key, restrained," Lady Bird recorded, and with "none of the youthful ebullience, the poetic brilliance of the Kennedy inauguration, or the warm roaring Jacksonian quality of ours." Nixon's inaugural address contained "no high trumpet calls to action, and probably that is just as well. God knows there's been plenty of striving in the last five, yes, eight years, and probably the country is tired of striving—maybe they just want to hold still—absorb the deluges of change for a while." For Lyndon's speeches, Bird counted applause lines; for Nixon's, she noted "no great surge of emotion that swept the sea of people in front of us."[7] Though Lady Bird well understood the appeal of candidate Nixon's call for law and order, and while his outreach to middle, rural, silent-majority America resonated strongly with her, his electoral victory over Hubert Humphrey, by a mere 0.7 percent of the popular vote, still stung. Like a Democratic president almost fifty years later, reasonably informed but lacking "absolute proof" of a Republican campaign's potential treachery with respect to a foreign power, and not wanting to be accused of trying to throw the election to his party's candidate, on the day before the 1968 presidential election, LBJ opted not to tell the public about Nixon's treasonous attempt to undermine South Vietnam's participation in peace talks on the eve of the November election.[8]

After the thirty-seventh president of the United States swore to uphold the Constitution, the thirty-sixth president and First Lady walked up the Capitol steps to take their leave by car. In his memoir, Lyndon recalled his relief that "the nightmare of having to be the man who pressed the button to start World War III was passing." He told Lady Bird he felt he had ended his tenure in office without having to "haul down the flag, compromise my principles, or run out on our obligations, our commitments, and our men who were upholding those obligations and commitments in Vietnam."[9] Among those men were his two sons-in-law. "I realize that it may be difficult for people to understand how I felt. As discerning and perceptive as the American people are, I believe that very few of them have ever been able to grasp what transpired in the minds and hearts of the thirty-seven men who have served them in the Presidency."[10] But Lady Bird Johnson, the most discerning and perceptive of all of LBJ's constituents, grasped it all.

Following the inauguration, Clark and Marny Clifford hosted a fifty-person goodbye luncheon for the former president and First Lady at their Greek Revival home in Bethesda, Maryland. Upstairs in the Cliffords' bedroom, Lyndon and Lady Bird gathered LBJ's most loyal civilian soldiers (Dean Rusk, Clark Clifford, Averell Harriman, Walt Rostow, and William S. White) so that he could personally award each of them the Medal of Freedom in a ceremony at once intimate and idiosyncratic. (He had signed the presidential decrees before Nixon's inauguration that morning.) As recognition of the East Wing, he also gave Medals of Freedom to two of Lady Bird's most important allies, Mary Lasker and Laurance Rockefeller. After a quick bite, Lyndon, Lady Bird, Lynda, her infant, Lucinda, Luci, and Lyn made their way by car the short distance to Bethesda Naval Hospital, where they boarded a helicopter to Andrews Air Force Base.[11]

Thousands of supporters greeted them in the hangar there, including a Republican congressman representing Midland, Texas, who had begun his own political career campaigning against the Civil Rights Act and, then, four years later, voting in favor of the Fair Housing Act. In the coming years, George Herbert Walker Bush would continue his political trajectory with a stint as head of the CIA, as vice president, and as president of the United States. Lady Bird and Lyndon were touched by Bush's presence and by his show of support. The band played, a twenty-one-gun salute followed, and Air Force One, on loan from President Nixon, took off to Texas with the Johnson family on board.[12]

Four hours later, two more crowds of Johnson loyalists greeted them in Texas when their plane arrived. First, nearly three thousand people met them at Bergstrom airfield, outside Austin, and a second group of some five hundred friends from the Hill Country, waited to greet them at the Johnsons' own hangar, at the LBJ Ranch. By nine o'clock that evening, everyone had finally gone. After a drink and dinner, with a huge pile of suitcases waiting to be unpacked on the floor and a new moon above,

Lady Bird went to sleep "with a line of poetry reeling in my mind," she recorded. "I think it's from 'India's Love Lyrics,' 'I celebrate my glad release, the tents of silence and the camp of peace.' And yet for me it's not quite the exit line because I have loved almost every day of these five years. A better go-to-sleep line was one of the signs I had seen today, my favorite, 'LBJ, You Were Good For The USA.' "[13]

* * *

On August 27, 1969, exactly one year since the Democratic National Convention in Chicago had marked the beginning of the end of the Johnson presidency, the Johnsons flew to San Clemente, California, to visit the Nixons at the Western White House. It was Lyndon's birthday. They sang "Happy Birthday," blew out candles, and together flew eight hundred miles north up the Pacific Coast to dedicate the Lady Bird Johnson Grove, part of Redwood National Park. By the early 1960s, the redwoods faced extinction, with only 15 percent of the original two million acres of trees remaining. The California lumber industry had found its champion in Governor Ronald Reagan, but with the Johnsons' support and the public's demands, in October 1968 Congress passed legislation creating the 58,000-acre Redwood National Park. Lady Bird had inaugurated it before she left the White House.[14]

Nine months later, standing among the ancient trees, President Nixon delivered a speech placing Lady Bird in the long line of presidential conservationists that began with Teddy Roosevelt.[15] "A tree is a tree—how many trees do you need?," the future President Reagan had once said.[16] But surrounded by the giant living creatures, many more than ten times older than the American republic, Lady Bird reminded everyone that conservation is a "bipartisan business."[17] And indeed, during her White House years, she had laid the groundwork in public awareness to ensure that President Nixon could and would build on her environmental success. In his first year in office, Nixon established the Council on Environmental Quality. Shortly after, Congress passed the Environmental Policy Act of 1969, and in 1970 the Clean Water Act. In his 1970 State of the Union address, Nixon placed himself squarely behind Lady Bird Johnson.

"The great question of the seventies is, shall we surrender to our surroundings, or shall we make our peace with nature and begin to make reparations for the damage we have done to our air, to our land, and to our water? Restoring nature to its natural state is a cause beyond party and beyond factions.... Clean air, clean water, open spaces—these should once again be the birthright of every American. If we act now, they can be."[18] Four months later, some twenty million Americans celebrated their first Earth Day, and in the face of massive public pressure, by executive order Nixon created the Environmental Protection Agency, which began operating at the end of the year.[19]

Also in 1970, President and Mrs. Johnson inaugurated the Lyndon B. Johnson School of Public Affairs: Elspeth Rostow, a Barnard and Radcliffe graduate whose intellect and equanimity Lady Bird had come to deeply admire during her husband Walt's tenure as national security advisor, became the school's first dean. That year, Lady Bird Johnson published her 806-page *A White House Diary*. It stayed on the *New York Times* bestseller list for thirteen weeks. Seven months later, in May 1971, the Johnsons presided over the opening of the Lyndon Baines Johnson Library and Museum. As Vietnam veterans and antiwar protesters clashed with police nearby, President Nixon and First Lady Pat Nixon attended, along with men from several chapters of Lyndon's life: Robert McNamara, Averell Harriman, Dean Rusk, Hubert Humphrey, John Connally, Gregory Peck, Hugo Black, and Thurgood Marshall. Theodor Geisel (better known as Dr. Seuss) was there and donated the original manuscript of *The Lorax,* his children's book about the hazards of environmental neglect. Later that year, Lyndon Johnson published his memoir, *The Vantage Point: Perspectives of the Presidency, 1963–1969*.

In many ways, Lady Bird replicated her life of national public service on a state and local level in Texas, albeit at a far more human pace. She began a six-year term on the board of regents of her alma mater, the University of Texas, in 1971, and the next year, she turned her focus on urban green space to her beloved town of Austin, joining the public campaign to finance and transform a river-like reservoir on the Colorado River known as Town Lake into a more beautiful and accessible space for public recreation. Fed by the wildly popular three-acre outdoor natural-spring swimming hole Barton Springs Pool, the lake is nearly six miles long, with ten miles of adjacent bike trails; it was renamed Lady Bird Lake following the former First Lady's death. In 1972, while still living on the Ranch in Stonewall, the Johnsons donated the "Texas White House" and its surrounding land to the nation, making the National Park Service its permanent steward.

Those three years back in Texas, living the post-presidency period Lady Bird had begun planning just weeks into their White House tenure, were marked by contrast: between the peace and happiness of new grandchildren and LBJ's depression and declining health. It all came to an abrupt and shattering end on January 22, 1973. Lady Bird was attending a regents meeting in Austin when she received the urgent but not surprising call from the Secret Service. Lyndon had suffered a massive heart attack. After leaving the White House, he had picked up smoking again, and his overall health, physical and emotional, had noticeably weakened. He died at age sixty-four. Lady Bird Johnson was barely sixty years old.

Lady Bird lived for thirty-four years after Lyndon's death, spending many of those years deeply involved in the LBJ Presidential Library and LBJ School of Public Affairs and traveling around the world with her daughters, grandchildren, and great-grandchildren. (They called their grandmother by yet another nickname, "Nini.") Other honors and activities punctuated that time as well. A woman as compulsively engaged as Lady Bird needed channels for her still-formidable intelligence and energy. In 1974, she began her fourteen years of service as a trustee for National Geographic Society, only the second woman to serve on its board. That year, she also joined Gordon Bunshaft and Joseph and Olga Hirshhorn at the unveiling in Washington, D.C., of the Hirshhorn Museum and Sculpture Garden. Five years before, during their last week in office, she and Lyndon had joined the couple for the museum's groundbreaking ceremony.[20]

More initiatives that Bird and LBJ had championed from the White House began to see real results. In 1970, as the ethos of home rule took root and Congress passed the District of Columbia Delegate Act, Walter

Fauntroy became the first-ever nonvoting D.C. delegate to Congress and a founding member of the Congressional Black Caucus. With a focus on increasing black voter turnout in the South, Fauntroy devised a successful strategy to defeat South Carolina's John McMillan, the long-presiding segregationist chair of the House District Committee and opponent of home rule for Washingtonians. McMillan's ouster in the 1972 Democratic primary cleared the way for passage of the District of Columbia Home Rule Act in 1973.[21] In a city whose black population stood at 71 percent, the new chapter in local control provided for the democratic election of Mayor Walter Washington and of a black-majority city council.[22] Despite numerous local referendums favoring greater autonomy, and still well short of full statehood for the District of Columbia, Congress retains its veto power over the D.C. budget and over all legislation passed by the city council.

Just a few months after the Johnsons left office, Mayor Washington brought Richard Nixon and George Romney to visit a still rubble-strewn Shaw; the Department of Housing and Urban Development had authorized new funds for urban renewal there. A slow resurgence of the neighborhood, including of black-owned design and architecture firms focused on humane and affordable housing, began to emerge before LBJ's death. It would take another three decades, and in some cases more, for Shaw, Southwest, and Anacostia to begin to experience the kind of aesthetically appealing growth in residential, commercial, and recreational development that Lady Bird Johnson and Larry Halprin had envisioned in 1968. Despite greater political representation, the disproportionate impact of gentrification on poor African American residents relegated to the margins the criteria of community participation and democratic access the Johnsons had hoped to engender. By the end of the Johnson administration, the lack of local sovereignty in Washington, D.C., had become inseparable from the threat that Congress would force the construction of new highways throughout every quadrant of the District. But a combination of protests in the streets and lawsuits in the federal courts stopped construction of the Three Sisters Bridge and all the proposed new highways, including the East Leg Freeway threatening Kingman Island, in Anacostia. In August 1970, the chief judge of the U.S. District Court, John J. Sirica, ordered a halt to all construction; and in 1972, the Supreme Court upheld his ruling.[23]

When Barack and Michelle Obama moved into the White House forty years later, they inspired in Washington, D.C., something of a renaissance in artistic and entrepreneurial activity among D.C. residents. But with private capital and profit margins driving a construction boom, rates of gentrification and displacement in the District reached among the highest in the country. Unlike most other major American cities, Washington, D.C., remains relatively free of urban freeways. In a twist of history, the very gentrification that has displaced so many Washingtonians in the twenty-first century has occurred in and around many of the historic neighborhoods the freeways would otherwise have demolished in the twentieth century. In 1995, the National Park Service turned over Kingman Island to the District of Columbia. There is no gigantic urban swimming lake as there is in Austin, but a nature trail, an environmental education center, vibrant flora and fauna, and an annual blues festival have transformed the spot into a broadly accessible public park for residents of Northeast and throughout Washington. For the area where the East Leg Freeway had been slated for construction, in 2019 the D.C. government announced a $500 million plan to build a 190-acre campus for professional and amateur sports, community recreation, restaurants, and public parks, including a moat connecting the Anacostia River to the new campus. The preliminary designs are strikingly similar to the drawings Lawrence Halprin produced for the same area more than half a century earlier.[24]

* * *

Lady Bird Johnson broadened her policy interests beyond women's issues soon after LBJ's 1964 election. But in 1977, on the eve of her sixty-fifth birthday, she joined First Lady Rosalynn Carter and former First Lady Betty Ford in Houston to attend the National Women's Conference. The energy that the women's movement had created during the Vietnam War continued long after the United States evacuated all American military and civilian personnel from Saigon in 1975. Gloria Steinem, Congresswoman Bella Abzug, and Coretta Scott King led the planning for the conference. It was a gathering of two thousand voting delegates and twenty thousand women observers set to discuss twenty-six major topics, including the Equal Rights Amendment, and to develop a National Plan of Action for policies on reproductive freedom, sexual preference, rights for women with disabilities and for minorities, childcare for working women, sexual assault, healthcare, and a cabinet-level women's department. *Roe v. Wade* had been decided by the Supreme Court the day Lyndon died, but four years later, women's reproductive freedom was still under attack.

Pro tennis player Billie Jean King carried a torch set aflame in Seneca Falls to the opening ceremonies, and Maya Angelou presented her poem "To Form a More Perfect Union" to the three First Ladies. Lady Bird Johnson's close friend Barbara Jordan, who in 1973 became the first African American woman from the South elected to Congress, delivered the opening address. With her daughter Lynda looking on, Lady Bird delivered her own remarks before the convention, speaking directly to her own evolution. "I once thought the women's movement belonged more to my daughters than to me," she said. "But I have come to know that it belongs to women of all ages. I am proud to say, and I want you to know, that Texas was the ninth state to ratify the right of women to vote, and the seventh state to ratify the Equal Rights Amendment."[25] The woman with the habit of counting applause lines would have been thrilled by the sustained, roaring ovation that followed. Lady Bird had enjoyed a rather direct point of access to the women's movement. In the 1970s, Liz Carpenter had become the founder of the National Women's Political Caucus and joint chairwoman of ERAmerica, an organization campaigning to pass the ERA. By 1978, ratification had stalled at thirty-five states, only three short of the three-fourths majority required to amend the Constitution.[26] On January 15, 2020, the Virginia General Assembly became the thirty-sixth state legislature to ratify the ERA.

The roles of former First Lady, patron of the arts, keeper of the Johnson historical flame, academic trustee and feminist, notwithstanding,

Lady Bird was ever and always known for her leadership in preserving and enhancing the natural beauty of the United States, especially in American cities, a theme explored periodically in seminars she presided over at the LBJ Library and the LBJ School of Public Affairs. In 1977, President Gerald Ford awarded Lady Bird the Presidential Medal of Freedom, and in 1988, at seventy-five years old, she became the first First Lady (and second woman) to receive the Congressional Gold Medal.[27] In 1982, with her friend actress Helen Hayes, and working with her longtime aide and friend Nash Castro, Lady Bird established what is now the Lady Bird Johnson Wildflower Center, an educational and research center, public garden, and nursery of nearly three hundred acres dedicated to ecological diversity in Texas and in North America, to rare native plant conservation, to the preservation of water and other natural resources, and to the environmental impact of climate change. According to the National Park Service, by 2012, Lady Bird was responsible for the planting of some two million daffodils and thousands of other bulbs, trees, and shrubs in Washington, D.C.[28] That same year, the U.S. Postal Service unveiled a collection of stamps to commemorate her centennial: one stamp reproduced her official portrait painted by Madame Shoumatoff; several more replicated the beautification watercolor postage stamps of Washington, D.C., first issued in 1969. The 2012 commemorative stamps are presented on a sheet printed with an enlarged black-and-white photo of the very new First Lady, cropped from a family portrait taken after returning to the White House from a visit to JFK's grave in Arlington Cemetery nine days after his assassination. In the photograph, and still dressed for the period of mourning, Lady Bird wears a black sheath dress, a triple string of pearls, and a broad, even radiant, smile, but with the adrenaline of shock and exhaustion all too evident in her eyes.[29] In 2013, Mrs. Johnson was posthumously awarded the Rachel Carson Award by the National Audubon Society for "women who have made outstanding contributions to the conservation and environmental movement."

The decades of Lady Bird's life after Lyndon's death passed with the same dignity and engagement with public service that had characterized her life with him. During the 1980s, she spent many summers on Martha's Vineyard, where she and Jackie Kennedy Onassis periodically got together for a day and found a way to revive their friendship.[30] When Jackie died in 1994, Lady Bird attended her funeral. Aging for Lady Bird required her to gradually give up the mastery over her body she had long cultivated and treasured. In 2000, while the country waited for the Supreme Court to rule in *Bush v. Gore,* two elderly women, both in wheelchairs, attended a book reading by a visiting author at a lakeside spa outside Austin. They were the only two people to attend the talk by Terry Tempest Williams, and one in particular caught the nature writer and environmental activist completely off guard with her question. An eighty-eight-year-old Lady Bird, by then nearly blind from macular degeneration and having suffered the first of two strokes, leaned forward and said, "Thank you, Mrs. Williams, that was a lovely piece of writing. But now, can you tell me again, in your own words, why I should care about your desert?" Thinking this was precisely what she had just accomplished in reading aloud "about why America's red rock wilderness mattered," the award-winning author found herself at a loss for words. Lady Bird knew the challenges of writing and communicating about nature and the environment, having struggled to master both skills for much of her life. "Make me see it, make me feel it," she advised. "Tell me, how are you going to translate those words for real people in real places in real time."[31]

Whatever formality had existed before then disappeared, as the three women talked well into the night. Lady Bird dazzled her audience with her intelligence, her humor, and her take on politics, women's rights, the environment, and especially language and public policy. Sitting beside her friend and lifelong adviser and confidante Liz Carpenter, she explained, "I'll never forgive Lyndon's boys for turning my environmental agenda into a beautification project. But I went ahead and talked about wildflowers so as not to scare anybody, because I knew if the people came to love wildflowers they'd eventually care about the land that grew 'em." Mrs. Johnson urged Williams not to be seduced by the grandeur of her own prose. "Beautiful language isn't enough. You have to be very smart about what you are doing when talking about the environment," she urged. "You have to reach people where *they* are—not where you are. You must find out what they care about and build relationships with them, involve them in your cause." And summarizing the lessons she had drawn from her years in the White House, always laboring to find language to communicate with the public and to tell her own story, to craft and cement her husband's legacy and her own, Lady Bird Johnson added, "Then you can speak like a writer, but until then, you must speak like one of them."[32]

* * *

In early July 2007, as the Democratic presidential primary race was gaining momentum and the competition appeared to be breaking between an African American senator, a long shot with astonishing appeal, and a woman and former First Lady who was clearly the front-runner, and as America was embroiled in another forever war, this one in Afghanistan, a ninety-four-year-old Lady Bird Johnson, grandmother of seven and great-grandmother of ten, lay dying at her home in Austin. Incapacitated by a weakened heart and a series of strokes, she continued her sheer engagement with life until the afternoon of Wednesday, July 11. In Austin, during a twenty-one-hour period of mourning, thousands lined up to pay their respects at the LBJ Library and the Wildflower Center. There was also the inevitable outpouring of tributes and remarks: "Mrs. Johnson was an implementer and translator of her husband and his purpose," Liz Carpenter told *The New York Times.* But in a separate tribute, Liz drilled down on Lady Bird's own accomplishments: "[W]ith her own strong words," Bird had rallied "not only powerful allies but millions of unknown followers" to lift "the stature of those environmentalists who had been struggling at city halls and state legislatures. As a result of her courageous voice and national following, she put the environment on the agenda of every person in public life—where it remains."[33] At the funeral, Lady Bird's granddaughter Lucinda explained the nature of her grandmother's power and influence. "My grandfather was famous for his persuasive abilities, for the Johnson treatment," she began. But Lady Bird Johnson "was his equal in influence, I suspect, but we'll never entirely know, because her touch, while mightily effective, was so light. She believed in, and appealed to, the best in people, to allow them to rise to the occasion. Perhaps the key to her success was that she really didn't care who got the credit."[34] Mastery, leadership, influence, power, the very attributes long associated with the presidency, captured by two women, about a third who worked so hard, yet also so naturally, to exercise those qualities.

Yet there was a very significant part of Claudia Alta Taylor, Lady Bird Johnson—the journalist, the historian, the strategist, the businesswoman, the political partner, the environmentalist, the wife, the parent and grandparent—who did want us to know those qualities and actions that made her very much Lyndon's "equal in influence," and who did take pains to leave a substantial record of that influence in her diary and in the voluminous body of documentary evidence at the LBJ Presidential Library. The duality of the Johnson partnership, he with that heavy hand, she with that light touch, makes all the more complex the work of disentangling Lady Bird Johnson's life and legacy from that of her husband. In that fact she would no doubt take great pride. But just as she appreciated the complexity of other public figures, starting with her husband, Lady Bird Johnson well understood—indeed, hoped—that at a certain point in history the breadcrumbs she left us would allow us to see, assess, and appreciate her place in American history.

Acknowledgments

I am privileged to count so many people in my corner, individuals who offered their support and encouragement as I researched and wrote Lady Bird Johnson's story. My gratitude and appreciation truly know no bounds.

Marianne Szegedy-Maszak has been an unstintingly generous friend and partner on this project. This is not the first book of mine that has benefited from her skill and experience as an editor, journalist, and author. On this one, however, Marianne became the person I relied on often for a daily morning call, when she helped me sort out matters of emphasis, pacing, and plot—the elements of storytelling that only a brilliant writer and reader of her acumen could possibly have the talent and stamina to offer. Credit to Marianne for the best of this book, from conception to completion and everything in between.

My hardworking research team helped me survey and digest vast quantities of material from several archives around the country, especially from the holdings in the Lyndon Baines Johnson Library in Austin, Texas. Max Scheinin took the first dive with me, imposing order to the material and helping organize the story line. Valerie Wirtschafter picked up the reins from Max, and even while earning her doctorate and becoming a published author in her own right, she lent her scrupulous editorial eye and, where necessary, unsparing scalpel to nearly every draft of this book. Isabel Dorval brought her considerable research chops to this effort, along with technical and organizational prowess without which this book would not have been possible. Their contributions merit the highest of praise. For additional research and support, thanks to Hannah

Altman, Caroline Bowman, Pilar Fitzgerald, Teresa Garcia, Claire Mufson, Abby Roberts, and Leah Roberts.

The archivists at the LBJ Library assisted me and my team with their expertise and unfailing dedication at every turn. Barbara Cline, Claudia Anderson, Sarah Cunningham, and Alexis Percle embody the vision Lady Bird and Lyndon Johnson had for the professionalism and rigor of their presidential library. Our presidential libraries are a national treasure—one of the foundations of the democratic tradition of transparency and of learning from our history. The LBJ Library Foundation's support for that mission, including the hard work of transcribing all 123 hours of Mrs. Johnson's White House diary and releasing for public consumption those transcripts as well as the original audio, made this book possible. That dedication reflects just how vital, how central, Claudia Alta "Lady Bird" Johnson was to the presidency of Lyndon Baines Johnson and to the documenting and telling of the Johnson history. Mighty thanks to Larry Temple and Mark Updegrove and the staff and board of the LBJ Foundation for that decision. Thanks to the good graces of Shirley James, I had the privilege of meeting and interviewing Harry Middleton, the library's founding director and Mrs. Johnson's partner in so many dimensions of her post-presidency, including her decision to open the LBJ tapes to the public.

My greatest thanks go to Darren Walker and his able colleagues at the Ford Foundation. When I decided to pivot from a professional career in foreign policy, Darren, another visionary Texan and Head Start and UT alum who knew Lady Bird Johnson, immediately grasped the importance of telling her story and provided the philanthropic wherewithal to make it happen. Also at the Ford Foundation, my friend and collaborator of many years, Mario Bronfman, likewise encouraged me in so many ways. My friends and colleagues Bruce Byrd, Pat Grant, and Kenneth Siegel also helped sustain a project of this scale.

Many thanks to the deans of the LBJ School of Public Affairs, first Robert Hutchings, and now Angela Evans, for providing me with an institutional home during this project. Tom and Jill Udall, Larry and LouAnn Temple, Sam Farr, Sharon Francis, and the late Nash Castro were either participants in this story or related to them. Separately from their generosity in granting me interviews, each helped with multiple gestures of confidence in this endeavor. In Austin, Marlee Mendelson, Suzanne Mitchell, Barbara and Ted Owens, Judith Coffin, and William Forbath provided friendship and shelter. Beyond Austin, a giant thank-you to Zoe Mendelson.

I benefited from input along the way from a number of individuals. Most especially, I send thanks to the presidential historian Robert Dallek for all of the expertise and advice he imparted since our very first lunch. Thanks to Kai Bird, Blanche Wiesen Cook, Charlie Edel, Jeffrey Goldberg, Robert Kanigel, Debra Katz, Jennifer Klein, Felicia Kornbluh, Daniel Kurtz-Phelan, Jane Mayer, David Rothkopf, Jeff Shesol, and Scott Stossel for encouragement, for opening new doors, and for helping me think parts of this through along the way.

For reading and commenting on portions of the manuscript, thanks to Michael Abramowitz, Wynne Bailey, Heidi Bourne, Kate Collins, Anita Elliott, Andrea Freedman, John Gray, Sophia Heller, James Lawry, Judy Minor, Adam Pincus, Jaimie Sanford, Janet Shenk, Carol Sweig, Michael Sweig, Agnes Tabah, Robert Taren, Larry Temple, LouAnn Temple, Alexander Thompson, Isabel Thompson, Reed Thompson, Meryl Unger, and Darren Walker.

A bad car accident interrupted research and writing for more than a year. Recovery would have been impossible without a team of health professionals to whom I am so very grateful: Carlisle Bland, Marie Connor, Craig Faulks, Carole Horn, Lindsey Lampel, Judy LaPrade, Brooke Merriweather, David Moss, Jeff Robinson, Roberta Stiehm, and Deborah Tabb. Mila Kagan's support meant and means the world. My friend Rachel Kronowitz led me to Richard Silber, who, with great humor and forbearance, helped bring the whole ordeal to a welcome denouement.

At Random House, I found a home. I had the good fortune of working with Jon Meacham, who opened the door for this project when he first acquired it. I did not know Susan Kamil personally, but I treasure the encouragement and warmth she conveyed at the outset. Kate Medina readily embraced the objective of bringing dimension, humanity, and substance to Lady Bird Johnson and offered wisdom and vision at so many crucial moments. She also provided me with a brilliant editor, Molly Turpin, whose energy and talent in the process of sculpting a book out of a manuscript dazzled me every day. Great thanks go to Dennis Ambrose, Jennifer Backe, Jenna Dolan, Ayelet Gruenspecht, Jane Hardick, Belina Huey, Barbara Jaktola, Greg Kubie, Virginia Norey, Anna Pitoniak, and Robert Siek.

At the literary agency Sterling Lord Literistic, its president, Philippa "Flip" Brophy, told me when we first met that it was time for me to write what she called "the big book." Having Flip in my corner has been the greatest of gifts. She is the best advocate an author could hope to find. Also at SLL, big thanks to Nell Pierce. My thanks as well to Adam Pincus and Best Case Studios for collaborating in new media platforms, and to Ellen Goldsmith-Vein and Victoria Cook.

For encouragement and friendship, major thanks to Mark Angelson, Mary Davis, Elizabeth Economy, Ellen Futter, Jeffrey Garten, Lisa Gugenheim, Fred Hochberg, Richard Plepler, Carol Stacks, James Stavridis, and Meryl Unger.

To Les Gelb and Saul Landau, two mentors who both died before they should have. Their sharp, skeptical minds, twinkly eyes, and work ethic inspire me every day.

Thank you for so many forms of kindness to me and to our family: Heidi Bourne, Liz Britton, Robert Brown, Susan Collins, Christopher Dorval, Peter Fox, Steven Goldstein, Aurie Hall, Sophia Heller, Jennifer Klein, Rachel Levy, Jim Margolis, Judy Minor, Steve Mufson, Christine Neptune, Beth Parkinson, Jamie Raskin, Sarah Bloom Raskin, Vicki Seyfert, Todd Stern, Michael Sweig, Agnes Tabah, Marcy Wilder, and Josh Wyner.

San Francisco, my California outpost, is my West Coast home. Jaimie Sanford, a native of that "cool grey city of love," spent a week with me in Abilene in 1993 and a week with me in Austin in 2013 in the presidential archives: She has been part of my book-writing odyssey since the very beginning. Before and since, Jaimie's intelligence, critical eye and ear, faith and generosity, have been my daily ballast. One of her editorial suggestions in particular now anchors the arc of this book. Without her dedication and inspiration, I could not have started, nor surely finished, this undertaking. Ted, Abe, Ella, and Nathan Storey, and now Lucy, have opened their home to me and to my research team, and with generosity and humor given us the support and infrastructure we've needed over the years. My deepest gratitude for so much love, kindness, and fun. Also in San Francisco, Mathea Falco and Peter Tarnoff have given me the gift of friendship, love, and support, and often their home, where I wrote and edited large portions of this book. Their loyalty in friendship and example in living mean the world to me.

Across the Golden Gate Bridge and west a bit, adjacent to the Point Reyes National Seashore Lady Bird Johnson inaugurated in 1966, my parents, Carol Sweig and James Lawry, are the anchors and the animators: Their embrace of a life of creativity, literature, storytelling, music, theater, poetry, writing, painting, and natural beauty have inspired three generations of us, with more to come. Thank you, beautiful parents.

Ricky (RIP), and now Charlie, have been my constant feline companions.

Our children, now adults—Isabel Thompson and Alexander Thompson—bring love and inspiration every day. With his giant heart and freeing spirit, Reed Thompson, my husband and partner, makes *everything* possible.

Notes

Abbreviations Used

AP: Associated Press
AWHD: *A White House Diary*
CTJ: Claudia Taylor "Lady Bird" Johnson
CTJ DD: First Lady's Daily Diary
EX: Executive File
JFK: John F. Kennedy
JFKL: John F. Kennedy Library
LBJ: Lyndon Baines Johnson
LBJL: LBJ Presidential Library
MLK: Martin Luther King, Jr.
NYT: *The New York Times*
OH: Oral History
PDD: President's Daily Diary
RFK: Robert F. Kennedy
SF: Subject File
UPI: United Press International
WHCF: White House Central File
WHD: White House Diaries
WHSF: White House Social File

Lady Bird Johnson's White House Diary

1. "Statement of Mrs. Lyndon B. Johnson," in *Investigation of the Assassination of President John F. Kennedy: Hearings Before the President's Commission on the Assassination of President Kennedy,* vol. 5 (Washington D.C.: U.S. Government Printing Office, 1964), pp. 564–67.
2. Introduction to *AWHD,* p. viii.
3. Christopher Lehmann-Haupt, "Book of the Times: My Husband Right or Wrong," *NYT,* November 2, 1970.

Preface: The Huntland Strategy Memo

1. "Transcript of Goldwater Address at Rally Here," *NYT,* May 13, 1964.
2. "Notes Prepared by the Secretary of Defense (McNamara)," Document 154 in Edward C. Keefer and Charles S. Sampson, eds., *Foreign Relations of the United States, 1964–1968,* vol. 1, *Vietnam, 1964* (hereafter cited as *FRUS: Vietnam*) (Washington, D.C.: U.S. Government Printing Office, 2010), https://history.state.gov/historicaldocuments/frus1964-68v01/d154; Jack Ray-

monds, "McNamara Urges Further US Aid for Vietnam War; Back from Saigon, He Gives President a Plan to Send More Money and Men," *NYT*, May 15, 1964; AP, "McNamara Begins Visit to Vietnam" *NYT*, May 12, 1964.

3. J. Willis Hurst interview 2 (II), June 16, 1970, by T. H. Baker, Oral Histories, LBJL.
4. Annotated transcript of audio diary, Lady Bird Johnson, May 14, 1964, Lady Bird Johnson's WHD, LBJL.
5. Ibid.
6. Ibid.
7. Letter, Lady Bird Johnson to LBJ, Reference File, "CTJ to LBJ on decision to run," May 14, 1964, "Mrs. Johnson 1964 Campaign (letters to LBJ)," LBJL; Lady Bird Johnson to LBJ, Memo, May 14, 1964, as reprinted in LBJ, *The Vantage Point: Perspectives of the Presidency, 1963–1969* (New York: Holt, Rinehart and Winston, 1971), pp. 93–94.
8. Ibid.
9. Ibid.
10. Ibid.
11. WHD, May 14, 1964.
12. Ibid.
13. LBJ, "The President's Address to the Nation Announcing Steps to Limit the War in Vietnam and Reporting His Decision Not to Seek Reelection," Washington, D.C., March 31, 1968, American Presidency Project, https://www.presidency.ucsb.edu/documents/the-presidents-address-the-nation-announcing-steps-limit-the-war-vietnam-and-reporting-his.
14. There are three partial exceptions—Robert Dallek, *Flawed Giant: Lyndon Johnson and His Times, 1961–1973* (New York: Oxford University Press, 1998), p. 523; Betty Caroli, *Lady Bird and Lyndon: The Hidden Story of a Marriage That Made a President* (New York: Simon & Schuster, 2015), pp. 244–45; and Irving Bernstein, *Guns or Butter: The Presidency of Lyndon Johnson* (New York: Oxford University Press, 1996), p. 312.
15. LBJ, *Vantage Point*, pp. 93–95; In 2013, Michael Beschloss published in *Texas Monthly* excerpts from an audio transcript of LBJ speaking candidly about his time as president. The recording was originally made in 1969, only seven months after LBJ left the presidency, and was expected to be a starting point for Lyndon to write his memoirs. In the summer of 2002, Harry Middleton, the retiring director of the LBJL, found the transcript while cleaning out his office. Among the published excerpts, LBJ once again acknowledges the importance of May 1964 in his decision not to run in 1968: "The best way I know to put it is this: My best judgement told me in 1964 in the spring—May or June—that if the good Lord was willing and the creeks didn't rise, if

we had the best of everything, I could get the job done. I could get my ideals and wishes and dreams realized to the extent I would ever get them realized by March of 1968. The odds were that I could survive that physically—but there was no assurance, and there were grave doubts." Michael Beschloss, "Lyndon Johnson on the Record," *Texas Monthly*, January 20, 2013.

16. Letter, Lady Bird Johnson to Jan Jarboe Russell, December 5, 1997, in Jan Jarboe Russell, *Lady Bird: A Biography of Mrs. Johnson* (New York: Scribner, 2016), p. 13.
17. WHD, January 9, 1964.

ACT I: August 1960–January 1965

Chapter 1: The Surrogate

1. Transcript, Claudia Alta "Lady Bird" Johnson, recorded interview by Sheldon Stern, March 9, 1979, JFKL.
2. Ibid.
3. Robert A. Caro, *Means of Ascent*, vol. 2 of *The Years of Lyndon Johnson* (New York: Alfred A. Knopf, 1990), pp. 3–34, 303–18; Robert Dallek, *Lyndon B. Johnson: Portrait of a President* (New York: Oxford University Press, 2005), pp. 15–70.
4. Lady Bird Johnson, in Michael L. Gillette, *Lady Bird Johnson: An Oral History* (New York: Oxford University Press, 2012), p. 316.
5. Ibid., p. 323.
6. Ibid., p. 316.
7. Transcript, Lady Bird Johnson OH Interview, March 9, 1979, JFKL, p. 12.
8. Gillette, *Lady Bird*, p. 322.
9. Jacqueline Kennedy Onassis, quoted in *Jacqueline Kennedy: Historic Conversations on Life with John F. Kennedy: Interviews with Arthur Schlesinger, Jr., 1964* (New York: Hyperion, 2011), p. 85.
10. Gillette, *Lady Bird*, p. 322.
11. Ibid., p. 317; Claudia Alta "Lady Bird" Johnson OH, March 9, 1979, JFKL.
12. Nancy Dickerson, *Among Those Present: A Reporter's View of Twenty-five Years in Washington* (New York: Random House, 1976), p. 49.
13. OH transcript, Jacqueline Kennedy Onassis, interview 1 (I), January 11, 1974, by Joe B. Frantz, LBJL.
14. Kennedy, *Jacqueline Kennedy: Historic Conversations*, p. 85.
15. Dickerson, *Among Those Present*, p. 49.
16. Claudia Alta "Lady Bird" Johnson OH, March 9, 1979, JFKL, p. 12.

17. Gillette, *Lady Bird*, p. 325.
18. Ibid., p. 326.
19. Ibid., p. 324.
20. These spiral notebooks have not been open to researchers at the LBJL.
21. Kennedy, *Jacqueline Kennedy: Historic Conversations*, p. 85.
22. Liz Carpenter, *Ruffles and Flourishes: The Warm and Tender Story of a Simple Girl Who Found Adventure in the White House* (College Station: Texas A&M University Press, c. 1970, 1993), p. 19; "Alumni Profile—Liz Carpenter," Moody College of Communications, UT Austin, https://moody.utexas.edu/alumni/outstanding-alumni-award/liz-carpenter.
23. Carpenter, *Ruffles and Flourishes*, p. 18.
24. OH transcript, Elizabeth (Liz) Carpenter, interview 1 (I), December 3, 1968, by Joe B. Frantz, LBJL.
25. Joe Holley, "Liz Carpenter Dies; Former Aide to LBJ, Lady Bird Johnson," *Washington Post*, March 21, 2010.
26. Enid Nemy, "Liz Carpenter, Journalist, Feminist and Johnson Aide, Dies at 89," *NYT*, March 20, 2010.
27. Isabelle Shelton, "Newswoman Appointed: Mrs. Carpenter to Help 'Lady Bird' on Campaign," (Washington, D.C.) *Evening Star*, August 16, 1960, Box 192: "Records of the DNC," LBJL.
28. "President Lyndon B. Johnson Walked with Destiny," *Galveston Daily News*, December 1, 1963, EX PP, WHCF, Box 64, "11/22/63–2/10/64 [Green/General]," LBJL.
29. Press clippings from Records of the DNC, Box 192, LBJL: Gene Britton, "Lady Bird Beams Charm, Optimism," *Atlanta Constitution*, October 7, 1960; Inez Robb, "Of Politics and Marriage," *Chicago Daily News*, August 24, 1960; Bess Furman, "Bigotry Scored by Mrs. Johnson," *NYT*, August 24, 1960; Carol LeVarn, "Ladybird Is Democrats' Answer to GOP's Pat," (Washington, D.C.) *Evening Star*, August 24, 1960; Marjorie Farnsworth, "It's an Adventure, Lady Bird Reveals: Accepts Rigors of Campaign," *New York Journal-American*, October 5, 1960, Records of the DNC, Box 192, LBJL; Patricia Jansen Doyle, "Lady Bird Shows Color and Wit," *Kansas City Times*, September 23, 1960; Emma Harrison, "Mrs. Johnson Campaigns Here, Giving Praise to Mrs. Kennedy," *NYT*, October 5, 1960; Nancy Osgood, "Lady Bird's Trouper on the 'LBJ Trail,'" *St. Petersburg Times*, October 13, 1960; Trudy Cargile, "Alabama Land of Kissin' Kin to Lady Bird," *Birmingham News*, October 14, 1960; Alyce B. Walker, "Johnson's Biggest Booster—Lady Bird Brightens Rough Campaign Road," *Birmingham News*, October 14, 1960; Julie Hollabaugh, "Mrs. Johnson Finds Race Grueling but 'Wonderful,'" *Nashville Tennessean*, October 19, 1960; Gwen

Gibson, "D.C. Wash," *New York Daily News,* October 29, 1960; Marie Smith, "In Second Lady Role—Lady Bird's Ready for Lyndon's Lead," *Washington Post, Times Herald,* November 13, 1960; Marie Smith, "Faces Taunting Texans with Courage—Lady Bird Combs Mob Right out of Hair," *Washington Post, Times Herald,* November 5, 1960.

30. Memo, George Reedy to Doug Cater, Joe Frantz, and Ernest Goldstein, "Oral History Outline for Vice Presidential Years," July 1, 1968, EX FE 12, WHCF, Box 20, "L.B./2–4, Manila Envelope no. 2 [Memos on Oral Histories Project]," LBJL.
31. Bess Furman, "Bigotry Scored by Mrs. Johnson," *NYT,* August 24, 1960.
32. OH transcript, Elizabeth (Liz) Carpenter, interview 3 (III), May 15, 1969, by Joe B. Frantz, LBJL.
33. Doyle, "Lady Bird Shows Color and Wit."
34. Ibid.
35. OH transcript, Elizabeth (Liz) Carpenter, interview 3 (III), May 15, 1969, by Joe B. Frantz, LBJL.
36. Farnsworth, "It's an Adventure"; Harrison, "Mrs. Johnson Campaigns Here."
37. Harriet Stix, "Claudia Taylor Johnson Makes Appearance at Sheraton on Park Avenue and 57th," *New York Herald Tribune,* October 5, 1960.
38. Letter, LBJ to Lady Bird Taylor, October 27, 1934, Personal Papers of Lyndon and Lady Bird Johnson, 1934–1968, LBJL.
39. Letter, LBJ to Lady Bird Taylor, n.d., Personal Papers of Lyndon and Lady Bird Johnson, 1934–1968, LBJL.
40. Letter, LBJ to Lady Bird Taylor, September 18, 1934, Personal Papers of Lyndon and Lady Bird Johnson, 1934–1968, LBJL.
41. Letter, Lady Bird Taylor to LBJ, September 17, 1934, Personal Papers of Lyndon and Lady Bird Johnson, 1934–1968, LBJL.
42. Letter, Lady Bird Taylor to LBJ, October 22, 1934, #2, Personal Papers of Lyndon and Lady Bird Johnson, 1934–1968, LBJL.
43. CTJ in Gillette, *Lady Bird,* p. 81.
44. CTJ quoted in Gillette, *Lady Bird,* p. 335.
45. Lady Bird Johnson to Bill Moyers, in Dickerson, *Among Those Present,* p. 48.
46. Marie Smith, *The President's Lady: An Intimate Biography of Mrs. Lyndon B. Johnson* (New York: Random House, 1964), pp. 161–81.
47. Elizabeth Singer More, "Report of the President's Commission on the Status of Women: Background, Content, Significance," Radcliffe Institute for Advanced Study, Harvard University, Cambridge, MA, https://www.radcliffe.harvard.edu/sites/default/files/documents/report_of_the_presidents

_commission_on_the_status_of_women_background_content_significance.pdf.

48. Claudia Alta "Lady Bird" Johnson OH, March 9, 1979, JFKL.
49. Ibid.
50. "Planning the Texas Trip," in *Report of the President's Commission on the Assassination of President John F. Kennedy* (Washington, D.C.: U.S. Government Printing Office, 1964), p. 28.
51. John Norris, "A Boston Girl from out of the Blue," in *Mary McGrory: The Trailblazing Columnist Who Stood Washington on Its Head* (New York: Penguin Books, 2016), p. 17.
52. Stephen Labaton, "Ralph Yarborough Dies at 92; Cast Historic Civil Rights Vote," *NYT*, January 28, 1996.
53. Sally Bedell Smith, *Grace and Power: The Private World of the Kennedy White House* (New York: Random House, 2004), pp. 393–95.
54. Dallek, *Flawed Giant*, pp. 46–47; Caro, *The Passage of Power*, p. 299.

Chapter 2: "Shame for Texas"

1. WHD, November 22, 1963.
2. WHD, November 24, 1963.
3. Ibid.
4. Lawrence Wright, *In the New World: Growing Up with America from the Sixties to the Eighties*, 2nd ed. (New York: Vintage/Random House, 2013); Warren Leslie, *Dallas, Public and Private* (New York: Grossman Publishers, 1964).
5. OH transcript, Elizabeth (Liz) Carpenter, interview 1 (I), by Joe B. Frantz, LBJL; Donald Janson, "Jeering Texans Swarm Around Johnson and His Wife on Way to Rally," *NYT*, October 1964.
6. Luci Baines Johnson, interview with Mark K. Updegrove, "Luci Baines Johnson Interview: Nov. 22, 1963 and the Transition," November 12, 2013, LBJL, https://www.youtube.com/watch?v=Tu7ZC94MCho; Lynda Johnson Robb, interview with Mark K. Updegrove, "Lynda Johnson Robb Interview: Nov. 22, 1963 and the Transition," November 12, 2013, LBJL, https://www.youtube.com/watch?v=v-Wfl2GEBV0.
7. Liz Carpenter's husband, Les, pressed her after the assassination to record her experience. In 1966, she returned to the tape and transcribed it into a twenty-eight-page first-person account from which this quote is drawn. "Liz Carpenter's Recollections of President Kennedy's Assassination, December 1966," Special File on the Assassination of JFK, Box 4, LBJL. In Robert A. Caro, *The Passage of Power*, vol. 4, *The Years of Lyndon Johnson* (New York: Alfred A. Knopf, 2012), p. 366.

8. WHD, November 23, 1963.
9. WHD, November 24, 1963.
10. Ibid.
11. Ibid.
12. Ibid.
13. Ibid.
14. Mary McGrory, "A Young Widow Brings Meaning to Tragic Chaos," November 25, 1963, in *The Best of Mary McGrory: A Half Century of Washington Commentary*, ed. Phil Gailey (Kansas City, MO: Andrews McMeel, 2006).
15. Donald Wilson, "John Kennedy's Lovely Lady," *Life*, August 24, 1959.
16. Hugh Sidey, "First Lady Brings History and Beauty to the White House," *Life* 51, no. 9, September 1, 1961.
17. "A Tour of the White House with Mrs. John F. Kennedy (Best Quality)," Dailymotion, https://www.dailymotion.com/video/x74jyr0 "Jacqueline Kennedy: White House Tour"). First broadcast February 14, 1962, on CBS as *A Tour of the White House with Mrs. John F. Kennedy.*
18. Betty Beale, "Jacqueline Kennedy Set Unusual Record," (Washington, D.C.) *Evening Star*, November 24, 1963.
19. WHD, November 26, 1963.
20. Transcript, Jacqueline Kennedy Onassis OH Interview, LBJL, p. 9.
21. Letter, Lady Bird and LBJ to Jacqueline Kennedy, August 22, 1963, White House Famous Names, Box 7, "Kennedy, Mrs. John F., 1963," LBJL.
22. Letter, Jacqueline Kennedy to LBJ, November 26, 1963, White House Famous Names, Box 7, "Kennedy, Mrs. John F., 1963," LBJL.
23. WHD, November 26, 1963.
24. Ibid.
25. Ibid.
26. LBJ, "Address Before a Joint Session of the Congress," Washington, D.C., November 27, 1963, American Presidency Project, https://www.presidency.ucsb.edu/documents/address-before-joint-session-the-congress-0.
27. Ibid. For an account of LBJ's middle-of-the-night epiphany the night after JFK's assassination on how best to enact JFK's unfulfilled policy agenda, see Doris Kearns Goodwin, *Leadership in Turbulent Times* (New York: Simon & Schuster, 2018), pp. 308–9.
28. Telephone conversation #83, sound recording, LBJ and David Sarnoff, November 27, 1963, 2:13PM, Recordings and Transcripts of Telephone Conversations and Meetings, LBJL.

29. Louis M. Kohlmeier, "The Johnson Wealth," *Wall Street Journal,* March 23, 1964. See also Caro, *Means of Ascent,* pp. 80–119; Dallek, p. 177; John Barron, "The Johnson Money," (Washington, D.C.) *Evening Star,* June 9, 1964; Keith Wheeler and William Lambert, "The Man Who Is the President," *Life,* August 14, 1964.
30. Kohlmeier, "The Johnson Wealth."
31. Telephone conversation #83.
32. WHD, December 1, 1963.
33. Video, "Vice President Johnson Visits JFK Grave Site," December 1, 1963, Outs Reel #1211-60-63, White House Naval Photographic Center Films, YouTube, https://www.youtube.com/watch?v=08cw8uidFOA.
34. WHD, December 1, 1963.

Chapter 3: Transition, Succession

1. WHD, December 3, 1963.
2. Letter, Jacqueline Kennedy to Lady Bird Johnson, December 1, 1963, White House Famous Names, Box 7, "Kennedy, Mrs. John F., 1963," LBJL.
3. WHD, December 3, 1963.
4. LBJ, "Address Before a Joint Session of the Congress," speech, Washington, D.C., November 27, 1963, American Presidency Project.
5. WHD, December 3, 1963.
6. WHD, November 26, 1963.
7. *AWHD,* December 7, 1963, p. 14; CTJ's entry for this day is not in the notebooks released by the LBJL.
8. J. B. West and Mary Lynn Kotz, *Upstairs at the White House* (New York: Coward, 1973), p. 290.
9. Jodi Cantor, "Which Michelle Obama Will We Get When She Leaves the White House?," *NYT,* January 6, 2017.
10. West and Kotz, *Upstairs at the White House,* p. 285.
11. Liz Carpenter, quoted in *AWHD,* December 7, 1963, p. 15.
12. WHD, December 9, 1963.
13. WHD, December 10, 1963.
14. WHD, December 11, 1963. For more on LBJ and the Congress he inherited in 1963, see Caro, *Passage of Power,* pp. 419–35; Dallek, *Flawed Giant,* pp. 63–74.
15. WHD, December 11, 1963; WHD, December 14, 1963.
16. WHD, December 19, 1963.

17. Ibid.
18. WHD, December 18, 1963.
19. WHD, December 20, 1963.
20. WHD, December 24, 1963.
21. Hal K. Rothman, *LBJ's Texas White House: "Our Heart's Home"* (College Station: Texas A&M University Press, 2001), pp. 131–35; WHD, December 25, 1963.
22. WHD, December 25, 1963.
23. WHD, December 24, 1963; Edwin C. Bearss, "Historic Resource Study: Lyndon B. Johnson National Historical Park—Lyndon B. Johnson and the Hill Country, 1937–1963," National Park Service, 1984.
24. Jim Shahin, "Smoke Signals: Presidential Grilling," *Washington Post,* February 21, 2012.
25. In her diary entry of December 3, 1963, Lady Bird recounts LBJ's directness with Katharine Graham about her husband Phil's recent suicide. "One thing so typical of Lyndon, he just charged right in through that silken curtain of reserve that one draws around such matters, and said to Kay, in his peculiarly innocent and typical fashion: 'I thought about Phil the whole time. He'd be right here by me; he was always here whenever anything was in trouble. You just don't know how much I've thought about him these last seven days.' Kay, she may have been taken aback, but I think she was appreciative. And I liked it, because it had been there in all of our minds, too."
26. Bearss, "Historic Resource Study"; Rothman, *LBJ's Texas White House.*
27. See "Family Background," "Child Prodigy," "Pianist," "Conductor," and "The Texas Years," Ezra Rachlin, ezrarachlin.com.
28. WHD, December 28, 1963; "The Texas Years," Ezra Rachlin.
29. WHD, December 29, 1963.
30. Daniel Vaughn, "King of Barbecue: Walter Jetton's Rise to National Fame," *Texas Monthly,* July 23, 2015; Caro, *Passage of Power,* pp. 508, 513.
31. WHD, December 29, 1963.
32. Ibid.; Caro, *Passage of Power,* p. 513.
33. WHD, December 29, 1963.
34. Nan Robertson, "The First Lady Takes Huge Guest List in Her Stride," *NYT,* January 3, 1964.
35. Caro, *Passage of Power,* pp. 536–537; "'What's My Line?'—Van Heflin; Steve Allen [panel] (Jan 19, 1964)," Season 15, Episode 21, aired January 19, 1964, CBS, https://www.youtube.com/watch?v=iyTsMTPExWA.

Chapter 4: "Thank You, Mrs. Vice President"

1. Press release, "Tribute to Eleanor Roosevelt by Mrs. Lyndon B. Johnson, Eleanor Roosevelt Memorial Foundation First Anniversary Luncheon, Hilton Hotel," New York, April 9, 1964, "Mrs. Johnson—Speeches," Reference File, LBJL.
2. Letter, Katie Louchheim, March 20, 1965, Papers of Katie Louchheim, Box 79, Library of Congress, Washington, D.C.
3. Blanche Wiesen Cook, *Eleanor Roosevelt,* vol. 2, *The Defining Years, 1933–1938* (New York: Penguin Books, 2000).
4. WHD, March 5, 1964.
5. Ibid.; Robert A. Caro, *Master of the Senate,* vol. 3 of *The Years of Lyndon Johnson* (New York: Alfred A. Knopf, 2002), pp. 139–46.
6. Gillette, *Lady Bird,* pp. 291–95. See Caro, *Master of the Senate,* pp. 650–53, for more on the impact of LBJ's heart attack on the Johnson marriage.
7. OH transcript, Katie Louchheim interview 1 (I), April 1, 1969, by Paige E. Mulhollan, LBJL, p. 19 (hereafter Louchheim OH interview).
8. Brett Harvey, *The Fifties: A Women's Oral History* (New York: ASJA Press, 1993), p. 47.
9. Ibid., p. 70.
10. Anne Wyman, "Radcliffe Girls Excel in Brains," *Boston Globe,* June 10, 1964.
11. Ibid.
12. WHD, June 9, 1964.
13. Ibid.
14. Lady Bird Johnson, "The Total Woman—Baccalaureate Address, Radcliffe College," Cambridge, MA, June 9, 1964, printed in *Addresses by the First Lady Mrs. Lyndon Baines Johnson, 1964* (pamphlet), WHSF LC, Box 11, Whistle Stop [10/6–9/64], LBJL; Mary Hughes Nash, "Mrs. Lyndon Baines Johnson at Baccalaureate: 'You Don't Have to Build Rome, You Can Build Lick Branch,'" *Radcliffe Quarterly,* August 1964, Radcliffe Archives, Harvard University; press release, "Mrs. Lyndon B. Johnson, Baccalaureate Address, Radcliffe College," Cambridge, MA, June 9, 1964, "Mrs. Johnson—Speeches," Reference File, LBJL.
15. Lady Bird Johnson, "The Total Woman."
16. Ibid.
17. Ibid.
18. Ibid.
19. Ibid.
20. WHD, June 9, 1964.

21. Caroli, *Lady Bird and Lyndon*, pp. 8–26; Robert A. Caro, *The Path to Power*, vol. 1 of *The Years of Lyndon Johnson* (New York: Vintage, 1990), pp. 294–300.
22. More, "Report of the President's Commission on the Status of Women."
23. Stephanie Coontz, *A Strange Stirring: "The Feminine Mystique" and American Women at the Dawn of the 1960s* (New York: Basic Books, 2011), p. 4.
24. Ibid., pp. 4–5. See also Gail Collins, *When Everything Changed: The Amazing Journey of American Women from 1960 to the Present* (New York: Little, Brown and Company, 2009); Gail Collins, *America's Women: 400 Years of Dolls, Drudges, Helpmates, and Heroines* (New York: HarperCollins, 2003).
25. LBJ, quoted in Patricia G. Zelman, *Women, Work, and National Policy: The Kennedy-Johnson Years* (Ann Arbor, MI: UMI Research Press, 1982), p. 50.
26. Charles Bartlett, quoted in ibid., p. 40.
27. Winzola McClendon, "U.N. Aide: Baby-Sits 10 Gallon Hats to Nurse Friendships," *Washington Post, Times Herald*, January 17, 1964.
28. Susan Ware, "Barbara Miller Solomon, 1919–1992," *Jewish Women's Archive*, https://jwa.org/encyclopedia/article/solomon-barbara-miller; Obituary, Bruce Lambert, "Barbara Solomon, 73, Educator and Pioneer in Women's Studies," *NYT*, August 23, 1992; Isabelle Shelton, "Women Doers Are Told History Needs Records," (Washington, D.C.) *Evening Star*, February 20, 1964.
29. Nancy Dickerson, *Among Those Present*, pp. 35–37; John Dickerson, *On Her Trail: My Mother, Nancy Dickerson, TV News' First Woman Star* (New York: Simon & Schuster, 2006), p. 107.
30. WHD, January 9, 1964; WHD, January 12, 1964.
31. "Nancy Dickerson Profiles Lady Bird Johnson," January 12, 1964, NBC News, http://www.nbcnews.com/video/icue/33108396.
32. Ibid.; Marie Smith, "First Lady Mrs. Lyndon B. Johnson: Political Know-How and Southern Charm in the White House," *Washington Post, Times Herald*, December 8, 1963.
33. Elizabeth Janeway, "The First Lady: A Professional at Getting Things Done," *Ladies' Home Journal*, April 1964. The comment by the "cynical authority" has been sometimes attributed to Gregory Peck, another frequent White House guest.
34. Janeway, "The First Lady: A Professional at Getting Things Done."
35. Ibid.
36. Press release, "Remarks by Mrs. Lyndon B. Johnson, National Convention of American Home Economics Association," Detroit, June 24, 1964, "Mrs. Johnson—Speeches," Reference File, LBJL.
37. Ibid.

38. Katherine R. Conafay, "Homemaking and Wage Earning Through Home Economics," Association for Supervision and Curriculum Development, 1965. http://www.ascd.org/ASCD/pdf/journals/ed_lead/el_196501_conafay.pdf.
39. "Remarks by Mrs. Lyndon B. Johnson, National Convention of American Home Economics Association."
40. Ibid.
41. Ibid.
42. LBJ, "Annual Message to the Congress on the State of the Union," Washington, D.C., January 8, 1964, American Presidency Project, http://www.presidency.ucsb.edu/ws/?pid=26787.
43. WHD, January 8, 1964.
44. WHD, February 12, 1964.
45. Letter, Congressman Daniel Flood to LBJ, January 14, 1964, EX PP 5 WHCF, Box 64: "11/22/63–2/10/64 [Green/General]," LBJL.
46. Nan Robertson, "First Lady Wins Friends on Trips," *NYT*, May 22, 1964.
47. WHD, May 21, 1964.
48. Ibid.
49. Ibid.
50. Marjorie Hunter, "Two Will Make Report Today on First Lady's Tenants," *NYT*, May 14, 1964; Marjorie Hunter, "2 Decry 'Poverty' on Johnson Land," *NYT*, May 15, 1964.
51. Ibid.
52. WHD, May 22, 1964; Pierre Salinger to E. C. Chamberlin, January 11, 1964, WHCF PP, Box 64, "11/22/63–2/10/64," LBJL.
53. UPI, "Lady Bird Vice President?" *Fort Lauderdale News*, May 22, 1964.
54. OH transcript, Lady Bird Johnson interview 23 (XXIII), September 5, 1981, by Michael L. Gillette, LBJL.
55. LBJ, "Remarks at the University of Michigan," Ann Arbor, May 22, 1964, American Presidency Project, http://www.presidency.ucsb.edu/ws/?pid=26262.
56. CTJ, quoted in Gillette, *Lady Bird*, p. 357.

Chapter 5: The Urban Environment

1. Jean Gartlan, "Barbara Ward—Lay Woman Extraordinaire," *U.S. Catholic Historian* 29, no. 3 (2011): 9–16.
2. Barbara Ward, *The Rich Nations and the Poor Nations* (New York: W. W. Norton and Company, 1961).

3. WHD, April 16, 1964.
4. "Lyndon's Other Bible," *Time,* September 3, 1965; LBJ, quoted in Carl M. Brauer, "Kennedy, Johnson, and the War on Poverty," *Journal of American History* 69, no. 1 (1982): p. 115.
5. Jack Valenti, quoted in Gartlan, "Barbara Ward," p. 118.
6. Liz Carpenter OH 2 (II).
7. LBJ, "Remarks at the University of Michigan."
8. WHD, June 28, 1964.
9. WHD, April 15, 1964; Press release, "Remarks of Mrs. Lyndon B. Johnson, YWCA National Convention," Cleveland, Ohio, "Mrs. Johnson—Speeches," Reference File, LBJL.
10. *Berman v. Parker,* 348 U.S. 26 (1954); Howard Gillette, Jr., *Between Justice and Beauty: Race, Planning, and the Failure of Urban Policy in Washington, D.C.* (Philadelphia: University of Pennsylvania Press, 2006), p. 157.
11. Benjamin Grant, correspondence with author, October–November 2019; WHD, April 15, 1964.
12. "River Park High-Rise Opens Soon," *Washington Post, Times Herald,* November 3, 1962; John B. Willmann, "A Walk in Southwest Will Refresh Tired Eyes," *Washington Post, Times Herald,* February 16, 1963; Hugh Wells, "New Breed Moves into Southwest," *Sunday Star,* September 16, 1962; John B. Willmann, "People Divorced from Cars in River Park Cooperatives," *Washington Post, Times Herald,* December 23, 1961; "Social Work Professor Became Activist for Southwest Washington Neighborhood," *Washington Post,* November 24, 2009.
13. Andrew Small, "The Wastelands of Urban Renewal," CityLab, February 13, 2017, https://www.citylab.com/equity/2017/02/urban-renewal-wastelands/516378/; Herbert J. Gans, "The Failure of Urban Renewal," *Commentary,* April 1965, https://www.commentarymagazine.com/articles/the-failure-of-urban-renewal/.
14. Elizabeth Meyer, "Historical Context: Elizabeth Meyer Presents at the 2016 LAF Summit," June 10, 2016, Philadelphia, YouTube, https://www.youtube.com/watch?v=_XcjnKgsjxE.
15. Jane Jacobs, quoted in Robert Kanigel, *Eyes on the Street: The Life of Jane Jacobs* (New York: Vintage Books, 2017), p. 250.
16. Susan Brownmiller, "Jane Jacobs," *Vogue,* May 1969, reproduced in Max Allen, ed. *Ideas That Matter: The Worlds of Jane Jacobs* (Owens Sound, Ontario: Ginger Press, 1997), pp. 22–23.
17. WHD, June 16, 1964.

18. Susan Brownmiller, "Jane Jacobs," *Vogue,* May 1969, reproduced in Max Allen, ed., *Ideas That Matter: The Worlds of Jane Jacobs* (Owens Sound, Ontario: Ginger Press, 1997), pp. 22–23.
19. Jane Jacobs, "A Great Unbalance," speech, Washington, D.C., June 16, 1964, Project for Public Spaces, https://www.pps.org/blog/a-great-unbalance/.
20. WHD, June 16, 1964.
21. Barbara Ward, "The City May Be as Lethal as the Bomb," *NYT,* April 19, 1964.
22. Jacobs, "A Great Unbalance."
23. Kanigel, *Eyes on the Street,* p. 250; Grant, correspondence with author, October–November 2019.
24. LBJ, "Remarks at the University of Michigan."
25. Memo, Stewart Udall to LBJ, "Memorandum for the President: The Administration and Conservation—a Look at Programs and Priorities," November 27, 1963, EX LE/NR WHCF Box 142, "11/22/63–10/20/64," LBJL.
26. WHD, June 14, 1964.
27. Senator Tom Udall, author interview, Washington, D.C., September 28, 2013.
28. Stewart Udall, *The Quiet Crisis* (New York: Avon Books, 1964), p. 160.

Chapter 6: "We Might Have a Small War on Our Hands"

1. WHD, January 28, 1964.
2. Brian VanDeMark, *Road to Disaster: A New History of America's Descent into Vietnam* (New York: Custom House/William Morrow, 2018), p. 226.
3. WHD, March 22, 1964.
4. "Memorandum Prepared by the Directorate of Intelligence, Central Intelligence Agency," Document 159 in *FRUS: Vietnam,* https://history.state.gov/historicaldocuments/frus1964-68v01/d159.
5. Michael Beschloss, ed., *Reaching for Glory: Lyndon Johnson's Secret White House Tapes, 1964–1965* (New York: Touchstone, 2002).
6. Dallek, *Lyndon B. Johnson,* p. 175.
7. "Notes Prepared by the Secretary of Defense (McNamara)."
8. WHD, May 17, 1964.
9. Letter, Lady Bird Johnson to LBJ, "Mrs. Johnson 1964 Campaign (letters to LBJ)," Reference File, May 14, 1964, LBJL.
10. Robert Dallek, *Camelot's Court: Inside the Kennedy White House* (New York: HarperCollins, 2013), p. 429.

11. Ibid., pp. 429–30.
12. WHD, August 1, 1964.
13. WHD, May 17, 1964.
14. "Memorandum from the Board of National Estimates to the Director of Central Intelligence (McCone)," Document 209 in *FRUS: Vietnam*, https://history.state.gov/historicaldocuments/frus1964-68v01/d209.
15. WHD, June 5, 1964.
16. WHD, June 16, 1964.
17. Dallek, *Flawed Giant*, p. 136.
18. LBJ, quoted in Eric Frederick Goldman, *The Tragedy of Lyndon Johnson* (London: Macdonald, 1969), p. 79.
19. Ibid.
20. WHD, July 12, 1964.
21. WHD, July 2, 1964.
22. Ibid.
23. Ibid.
24. WHD, July 12, 1964; "William Butler Yeats, Apocalyptic Writings," *The Norton Anthology of English Literature—Norton Topics Online*, https://www.wwnorton.com/college/english/nael/20century/topic_3/wbyeats.htm.
25. OH transcript, Walter Jenkins, interview by Emmette S. Redford and Richard McCulley, Austin, TX, November 12, 1980, LBJL.
26. Barry Goldwater, "Transcript of Goldwater's Speech Accepting Republican Presidential Nomination," *NYT*, July 17, 1964.
27. Dallek, *Flawed Giant*, pp. 147–49.
28. WHD, August 4, 1964.
29. Ibid.
30. LBJ, "Special Message to the Congress on U.S. Policy in Southeast Asia," Washington, D.C., August 5, 1964, American Presidency Project, https://www.presidency.ucsb.edu/documents/special-message-the-congress-us-policy-southeast-asia.
31. WHD, August 4, 1964.
32. LBJ, quoted in WHD, August 4, 1964; LBJ, "Radio and Television Report to the American People Following Renewed Aggression in the Gulf of Tonkin," Washington, D.C., August 4, 1964, American Presidency Project, https://www.presidency.ucsb.edu/documents/radio-and-television-report-the-american-people-following-renewed-aggression-the-gulf.
33. WHD, August 4, 1964.

34. "Memorandum of a Conversation, White House," Document 298 in *FRUS: Vietnam,* https://history.state.gov/historicaldocuments/frus1964-68v01/d298.
35. WHD, August 6, 1964.
36. WHD, August 5, 1964.
37. WHD, August 6, 1964.
38. Ibid.
39. Peter Yarrow, author interview, June 13, 2017.
40. Ibid.
41. WHD, August 6, 1964.

Chapter 7: The Strategist: The 1964 Campaign

1. WHD, July 14, 1964.
2. Letter, Katie Louchheim, August 31, 1964, Papers of Katie Louchheim, Box 79, Library of Congress, Washington, D.C.
3. Tom Wicker, "Mississippi Delegates Withdraw, Rejecting a Seating Compromise; Convention Then Approves Plan," *NYT,* August 26, 1964.
4. Lady Bird Johnson and Jack Valenti, "Draft Statement," August 31, 1964, WHCF, "Lady Bird, July 16, 1964–October 1, 1964," LBJL.
5. Ibid.
6. Theodore White, *The Making of the President, 1964* (New York: Harper Perennial Political Classics, 2010), p. 289.
7. PDD, August 24, 1964, President's Daily Diary Collection, LBJL.
8. LBJ, *Vantage Point,* p. 95.
9. Ibid., pp. 96–97.
10. Ibid., p. 97; Telephone conversation recording, LBJ and Walter Jenkins, August 25, 1964, Miller Center, University of Virginia, https://millercenter.org/the-presidency/secret-white-house-tapes/conversation-walter-jenkins-august-25-1964.
11. Letter, Lady Bird Johnson to LBJ, August 25, 1964, "Love Letters," Reference File, LBJL; reproduced in LBJ, *Vantage Point,* pp. 97–98.
12. Ibid., p. 98.
13. RFK, "Tribute to John F. Kennedy at the Democratic National Convention," speech, Atlantic City, NJ, August 27, 1964, JFKL, https://www.jfklibrary.org/Research/Research-Aids/Ready-Reference/RFK-Speeches/Tribute-to-John-F-Kennedy-at-the-Democratic-National-Convention.aspx.

14. "Democratic National Convention," Convention Hall, Atlantic City, NJ, August 27, 1964, Barbra Streisand Archives, http://barbra-archives.com/live/60s/democratic_convention_64_nj.html; Peter Yarrow, author interview, July 13, 2017.
15. WHD, August 2, 1964.
16. Letter, Pierre Salinger to E. C. Chamberlin, EX PP 5, WHCF, Box 64: "Johnson, Lady Bird," LBJL.
17. Memo, LBJ to Warren Harding, August 29, 1964, EX PP 5, WHCF, Box 62: "Johnson, Lady Bird," LBJL.
18. Letter, Stewart Udall to Lady Bird Johnson, July 29, 1964, Stewart L. Udall Papers (AZ 372), Box 145, "Correspondence (S.L.U. and Mrs. Johnson, 1964–1965)," Special Collections, University of Arizona Libraries.
19. Letter, LBJ to Warren Harding, August 15, 1964, EX PP 5, WHCF, Box 62: "Johnson, Lady Bird, 7/15/64–10/1/64," LBJL.
20. WHD, August 1, 1964.
21. Memo, Stewart Udall to LBJ, August 17, 1964, EX PP 5, WHCF, Box 62: "Johnson, Lady Bird," LBJL.
22. Memo, DNC, Series II, Lady Bird Special, Box 49, LBJL; "Mrs. Boggs and Mrs. Russell Names Co-Chairman of 'Lady Bird Special,'" October 5, 1964, WHSF Alpha, Box 295, LBJL.
23. WHD, August 1, 1964.
24. Carpenter, *Ruffles and Flourishes*, p. 145.
25. Doris Fleeson, "Mrs. Johnson Draws Names," (Washington, D.C.) *Evening Star*, October 8, 1964; OH transcript, Virginia Foster Durr, interview 1 (I), October 17, 1967, by Mary Walton Livingston, LBJL.
26. Carpenter, *Ruffles and Flourishes*, p. 145.
27. Ted Gittinger and Allen Fisher, "LBJ Champions the Civil Rights Act of 1964, Part 2," *Prologue Magazine*, Summer 2004; LBJ, "July 2, 1964: Remarks upon Signing the Civil Rights Bill," Presidential Speeches: Lyndon B. Johnson Presidency, Miller Center, University of Virginia, https://millercenter.org/the-presidency/presidential-speeches/july-2-1964-remarks-upon-signing-civil-rights-bill.
28. Bill Moyers, quoted in Mark Updegrove, *Indomitable Will: LBJ in the Presidency* (New York: Skyhorse Publishing, 2012), pp. 56–57.
29. Transcription, "Meeting for WST Advance Coordinators," p. 1, Lady Bird Special, Whistle Stop Tour, Personal Papers of Lindy Boggs, LBJL.
30. "Eleanor Roosevelt Biography," Franklin D. Roosevelt Presidential Library and Museum, https://www.fdrlibrary.org/er-biography.

31. Myra Greenberg Gutin, "The President's Partner: The First Lady as Public Communicator, 1920–1976," vols. 1 and 2 (unpublished PhD diss., University of Michigan, 1983), p. 406.
32. OH transcript, Elizabeth (Liz) Carpenter, interview 1 (1), December 3, 1968, by Joe B. Frantz, LBJL.
33. "Planning Memorandum: Support for Mrs. Johnson's Whistle-Stop, Week of October 6–10," October 5, 1964, EX PL 2, WHCF, Box 84: "West Wing Organization of Publicity," LBJL.
34. Ibid.
35. Carpenter, *Ruffles and Flourishes,* p. 143.
36. OH transcript, Bess Abell, interview 1 (I), May 28, 1968, by T. H. Baker, LBJL.
37. OH transcript, Elizabeth (Liz) Carpenter, interview 1 (I), 12/3/1968, by Joe Frantz, LBJL.
38. For example, see: WHD, May 2, 1964; WHD, June 24, 1964; WHD, September 9, 1965; WHD, March 26, 1966.
39. Carpenter, *Ruffles and Flourishes,* p. 146.
40. Memo, "Operation Skyhook for the Lady Bird Special," Personal Papers of Lindy Boggs, Box 1-01: "Lady Bird Special—Whistle Stop Tour [1 of 2]," LBJL.
41. Ambassador Jim Jones, author interview, Washington, D.C., February 2015.
42. Transcription, "Meeting for WST Advance Coordinators," Personal Papers of Lindy Boggs 1, Lady Bird Special—Whistle Stop Tour [1 of 2], LBJL.
43. Carpenter, *Ruffles and Flourishes,* p. 152.
44. WHD, September 11, 1964.
45. Memo, Steve Alex to Bess Abell, "Campaign Materials for Lady Bird Special," Personal Papers of Lindy Boggs, Lady Bird Special—Whistle Stop Tour [1 of 2], LBJL.
46. Press release, "Remarks by Mrs. Lyndon B. Johnson, Petersburg, Virginia," October 6, 1964, "Mrs. Johnson—Speeches," Reference File, LBJL.
47. Carpenter, *Ruffles and Flourishes,* pp. 149–50.
48. Press release, "Remarks by Mrs. Lyndon B. Johnson, Mobile, Alabama," October 9, 1964, "Mrs. Johnson—Speeches," Reference File, LBJL.
49. "The Whistle-Stop Tour," PBS, http://www.pbs.org/ladybird/epicenter/epicenter_report_train.html.
50. Carpenter, *Ruffles and Flourishes,* p. 148.

51. Ibid., p. 161.
52. Nan Robertson, "First Lady Booed in South Carolina," *NYT,* October 8, 1964.
53. Letter, Lady Bird to John Bailey, October 1964, "Whistle Stop Tour," WHSF Alpha, Box 124, "Whistle Stop Tour (Only), 09/28–10/16/64 Misc," LBJL.
54. Ibid.
55. Letter, Lady Bird Johnson to Bailey, October 1964.
56. "Lady Bird Johnson: At the Epicenter: November 1963–January 1965," PBS, https://www.pbs.org/ladybird/epicenter/epicenter_index.html.
57. "Remarks of President and Mrs. Johnson, and Lucy upon Arrival of 'Lady Bird Special' at Union Station," DNC, Series I, Johnson, Pres.: Campaign Speech, October 9, 1964, New Orleans, Box 177, LBJL.
58. *AWHD,* p. 198.
59. Memorandum, Walter Jenkins, "Résumé of Garth's Evaluation for Campaign Efforts," October 5, 1964, Office Files of Bill Moyers 30—Pre-Election Material, LBJL.
60. OH transcript, Elizabeth (Liz) Carpenter Interview IV, August 27, 1969, by Joe B. Frantz, LBJL.
61. Telephone conversation #5895, sound recording, LBJ and Lady Bird Johnson, October 15, 1964, 9:12AM, Recordings and Transcripts of Telephone Conversations and Meetings, LBJL; Kate Andersen Brower, "Lady Bird Wielded Power with a Delicate Touch," *Smithsonian Magazine,* July 6, 2016, https://www.smithsonianmag.com/history/lady-bird-johnson-wielded-power-delicate-touch-180959696/.
62. Ibid.
63. Caroli, *Lady Bird and Lyndon,* p. 259.
64. Alan Duke, "New Tapes Show LBJ Struggles with Aide's Sex Scandal," CNN, last modified September 18, 1998; "Conversation with Billy Graham and Office Conversation, October 20, 1964," audio file, Miller Center, University of Virginia.
65. "Jenkins Defended by Mental Group," *NYT,* October 22, 1964.
66. "The Issue Is Subtle, the Debate Still On: The APA Ruling on Homosexuality," *NYT,* December 23, 1973; Neel Burton, "When Homosexuality Stopped Being a Mental Disorder," *Psychology Today,* September 18, 2015.
67. Al Weisel, "LBJ's Gay Sex Scandal." *Out,* December 1999, pp. 76–83.
68. WHD, November 17, 1964.
69. Weisel, "LBJ's Gay Sex Scandal."

Chapter 8: "Our Presidency"

1. "Gender Differences in Voter Turnout," September 16, 2019, Center for American Women and Politics, Eagleton Institute of Politics, Rutgers University, New Brunswick, NJ, http://cawp.rutgers.edu/sites/default/files/resources/genderdiff.pdf; Jo Freeman, "Gender Gaps in Presidential Elections," letter to the editor, *P.S.: Political Science and Politics* 32, no. 2 (June 1999): 191–92; Jill Lepore, *These Truths: A History of the United States* (New York: W. W. Norton, 2018), p. 616.
2. Alan Flippen, "Black Turnout in 1964, and Beyond," *NYT*, October 16, 2014.
3. Memo, Libby Rowe to Lady Bird Johnson, "Spanish Language Tapes," October 27, 1964, WHSF Alpha, Box 1792, "Rowe, Mr. & Mrs. James (Libby)," LBJL.
4. Memo, Pedro Sanjuan to Craig Raupe, "Use of Mrs. Johnson's Tape in Spanish," October 27, 1964, WHSF Alpha, Box 1792, "Rowe, Mr. & Mrs. James (Libby)," LBJL.
5. WHD, November 11, 1964.
6. WHD, November 14, 1964.
7. WHD, November 15, 1964.
8. WHD, November 17, 1964.
9. Ibid.
10. Ibid.
11. WHD, January 7, 1965.
12. Ibid.
13. WHD, January 18, 1965.
14. Ibid.
15. Ibid. For a transcript of the moose joke routine, see Michele Norris, "Woody Allen Routine on Moose Hunting Recalled," *All Things Considered*, NPR, September 17, 2008.
16. "Looking Back—January 20, 1965," January 11, 2013, LBJL, http://www.lbjlibrary.org/press/lbj-in-the-news/looking-back-january-20-1965.
17. Letter, Katie Louchheim, January 25, 1965, Papers of Katie Louchheim, Box 79, Library of Congress, Washington, D.C.
18. WHD, January 22, 1965.
19. Ibid. The "courtship letters" were released by the LBJL in 2015.
20. Letter, LBJ to Lady Bird Taylor, October 24, 1934, Personal Papers of Lyndon and Lady Bird Johnson, 1934–1968, LBJL; Rebecca Onion, "Fastest Courtship in the West: How LBJ Won Lady Bird," *Slate*, February 14, 2013,

http://www.slate.com/blogs/the_vault/2013/02/14/lbj_lady_bird_johnson_love_letters_from_their_whirlwind_courtship.html.

21. WHD, January 22, 1965.
22. WHD, January 13, 1965.
23. WHD, November 19, 1965.
24. WHD, January 23, 1965.
25. WHD, January 24, 1965.

ACT II: February 1965–December 1967

Chapter 9: Beautification, Euphemism by Design

1. WHD, January 29, 1965.
2. Lady Bird Johnson, October 9, 1967, Yale University, quoted in Terry Tempest Williams, *The Hour of Land: A Personal Topography of America's National Parks* (New York: Picador, 2017).
3. WHD, November 20, 1964.
4. LBJ, "Presidential Policy Paper No. 3: Conservation of Natural Resources," November 1, 1964, American Presidency Project, https://www.presidency.ucsb.edu/documents/presidential-policy-paper-no-3-conservation-natural-resources.
5. WHD, February 4, 1965; letter, Katie Louchheim, February 4, 1965, Papers of Katie Louchheim, Box 79, Library of Congress,Washington, D.C.
6. WHD, February 10, 1965.
7. WHD, May 15, 1965; OH transcript, Sharon Francis interview 1 (I), May 20, 1969, by Dorothy Pierce (McSweeny), LBJL.
8. Lady Bird Johnson, quoted in Williams, *The Hour of Land,* pp. 263–65.
9. Pierre Charles L'Enfant, "To Thomas Jefferson from Pierre Charles L'Enfant, 26 February, 1792," Founders Online, National Archives, https://founders.archives.gov/documents/Jefferson/01-23-02-0148.
10. Wolf Von Eckardt, "Washington's Chance for Splendor," *Harper's Magazine,* September 1963.
11. LBJ, "Special Message to the Congress on Conservation and Restoration of Natural Beauty," February 8, 1965, American Presidency Project, https://www.presidency.ucsb.edu/documents/special-message-the-congress-conservation-and-restoration-natural-beauty; LBJ, "Special Message to the Congress on the Needs of the Nation's Capital," February 15, 1965, American Presidency Project, https://www.presidency.ucsb.edu/documents/special-message-the-congress-the-needs-the-nations-capital; LBJ, "Letter

to the Secretary of Commerce on the Need for Making the Highways More Attractive," January 21, 1965, American Presidency Project, https://www.presidency.ucsb.edu/documents/letter-the-secretary-commerce-the-need-for-making-the-highways-more-attractive.

12. LBJ, "Special Message to the Congress on Home Rule for the District of Columbia," February 2, 1965, American Presidency Project, https://www.presidency.ucsb.edu/documents/special-message-the-congress-home-rule-for-the-district-columbia.

13. LBJ, "Special Message to the Congress on the Needs of the Nation's Capital," Washington, D.C., February 15, 1965, American Presidency Project.

14. "Mark Twain's City of Washington," excerpted from Mark Twain and Charles Dudley Warner, *The Gilded Age* (1873), in *Washington Post,* December 9, 1979, https://www.washingtonpost.com/archive/opinions/1979/12/09/mark-twains-city-of-washington/f6683987-72d4-4749-8f3d-9fcfd7bcc476/?utm_term=.72ad177d9048.

15. WHD, February 3, 1965.

16. Victor Gruen, *The Heart of Our Cities: The Urban Crisis; Diagnosis and Cure* (New York: Simon & Schuster, 1964); "Kirkus Review: The Heart of Our Cities by Victor Gruen," *Kirkus Reviews,* https://www.kirkusreviews.com/book-reviews/victor-gruen/the-heart-of-our-cities/.

17. WHD, March 9, 1965; "Beautification Summary: The Committee for a More Beautiful Capital, 1965–68," WHSF, Beautification, Box 22, LBJL.

18. Chris Myers Asch and George Derek Musgrove, *Chocolate City: A History of Race and Democracy in the Nation's Capital* (Chapel Hill: University of North Carolina Press, 2017), p. 324.

19. Robin W. Winks, *Laurance S. Rockefeller, Catalyst for Conservation* (Washington, D.C.: Island Press, 1997), p. 147.

20. WHD, April 8, 1965.

21. Taylor Branch, *At Canaan's Edge: America in the King Years, 1965–68* (New York: Simon & Schuster, 2007), p. 23.

22. Ibid., p. 29.

23. PDD, March 5, 1965.

24. Dallek, *Flawed Giant,* pp. 213–15.

25. WHD, March 7, 1965.

26. WHD, March 13, 1965.

27. Branch, *At Canaan's Edge,* pp. 95–96; Dallek, *Flawed Giant,* p. 217.

28. WHD, March 14, 1965.

29. Ibid.

30. Branch, *At Canaan's Edge*, p. 111; WHD, March 15, 1965.
31. LBJ, "Special Message to the Congress: The American Promise," March 15, 1965, American Presidency Project, https://www.presidency.ucsb.edu/documents/special-message-the-congress-the-american-promise.
32. Branch, *At Canaan's Edge*, p. 111.
33. WHD, March 15, 1965.
34. WHD, April 21, 1965.
35. Dror Yuravlivker, "'Peace Without Conquest': Lyndon Johnson's Speech of April 7, 1965," *Presidential Studies Quarterly* 36, no. 3 (September 2006): 457–81.
36. WHD, April 7, 1965.
37. WHD, April 18, 1965.
38. WHD, April 17, 1965.
39. WHD, April 28, 1965.
40. *Beauty for America: Proceedings of the White House Conference on Natural Beauty*, Washington: US Government Print Office, 1965.
41. Mumford, the president of the American Academy of Arts and Letters, addressed an audience gathered for the opening of the Academy's annual festival. Mumford said: "We have a special duty to speak out openly in protest on every occasion when human beings are threatened by arbitrary power: not only as with the oppressed Negroes in Alabama and Mississippi, but the peoples of both North and South Viet Nam who must now confront our government's cold-blooded blackmail and calculated violence"; Sanka Knox, "Mumford Speech Rankles Benton: Attack on Policy in Vietnam at Honors Fete Irks Artist," *NYT*, May 20, 1965; AP, "Artist Benton Sizzles at Mumford Viet View," *Boston Globe*, May 20, 1965.
42. Press release, "Remarks by Mrs. Lyndon B. Johnson, White House Conference on Natural Beauty," May 24, 1965, "Mrs. Johnson—Speeches," Reference File, LBJL.
43. Lewis L. Gould, *Lady Bird Johnson: Our Environmental First Lady* (Lawrence: University Press of Kansas, 1999), pp. 91–93.
44. Ibid.

Chapter 10: "We Could Fall Flat on Our Faces"

1. Robert S. McNamara, with Brian VanDeMark, *In Retrospect: The Tragedy and Lessons of Vietnam* (New York: Times Books/Random House, 1995), pp. 187–88.
2. Bernstein, *Guns or Butter*, p. 446.

3. "National Foundation on the Arts and the Humanities Act Media Kit," LBJL, http://www.lbjlibrary.org/mediakits/neaneh/.
4. Bernstein, *Guns or Butter,* p. 446.
5. Goldman, *The Tragedy of Lyndon Johnson,* p. 419.
6. WHD, May 21, 1965.
7. Letter, Joseph H. Hirshhorn to LBJ and CTJ, May 17, 1965, WHSF, Alpha Files, Box 957, "Hirshhorn, Mr. & Mrs. Joseph H. (only)," LBJL.
8. WHD, May 21, 1965.
9. Ibid.
10. Memo for Jack Valenti, Program for the White House Festival of the Arts, June 9, 1965, WHCF EX AR 2, Box 3, LBJL; Howard Taubman, "White House Annual?," *NYT,* June 20, 1965.
11. It was the first time the White House had ever promoted photography as an American art form.
12. Goldman, *The Tragedy of Lyndon Johnson,* p. 422; memo, Barbaralee D. Diamonstein to Eric F. Goldman, "Some Recollections of the White House Festival of the Arts," May 11, 1966, WHCF EX, SF AR 2-AR-MC, Box 3, LBJL.
13. Memo for Jack Valenti.
14. Richard F. Shepard, "Robert Lowell Rebuffs Johnson as Protest over Foreign Policy: Poet Refuses to Attend Arts Festival—Voices Distrust of US Actions Abroad," *NYT,* June 3, 1965; Dwight Macdonald, "A Day at the White House," *New York Review of Books,* July 15, 1965.
15. Shepard, "Robert Lowell Rebuffs Johnson."
16. Ibid.
17. Letter, John Hersey to Eric Goldman with attached excerpts, June 5, 1965, WHCF, Subject File AR, Box 2, "EX AR/MC, 6/5/65–6/12/65," LBJL.
18. WHD, June 8, 1965.
19. Goldman, *The Tragedy of Lyndon Johnson,* pp. 455–60.
20. WHD, June 8, 1965.
21. Memo for Jack Valenti.
22. WHD, June 13, 1965.
23. Ibid.
24. Excerpt provided by Hersey to Goldman from John Hersey, "Hiroshima," *New Yorker,* August 24, 1946, p. 91: "This was the first chance she had had to look at the ruins of Hiroshima; the last time she had been carried through the city's streets, she had been hovering on the edge of unconsciousness. Even though the wreckage had been described to her, and though she was

still in pain, the sight horrified and amazed her. . . . Over everything—up through the wreckage of the city, in gutters, along the riverbanks, tangled among tiles and tin roofing, climbing on charred tree trunks—was a blanket of fresh, vivid, lush, optimistic green; the verdancy even from the foundations of ruined houses. Weeds already hid the ashes, and wild flowers were in bloom among the city's bones. The bomb had not only left the underground organs of plants intact; it had stimulated them. Everywhere were bluets and Spanish bayonets, goosefoot, morning glories and day lilies, the hairy-fruited bean, purslane and clotbur and sesame and panic grass and feverfew. Especially in a circle at the center, sickle senna grew in extraordinary regeneration, not only standing among the charred remnants of the same plant but pushing up in new places, among bricks and through cracks in the asphalt." WHCF, SF AR, Box 2, "EX AR/MC, 6/5/65–6/12/65," "letter from John Hersey to Eric Goldman with attached excerpts," June 5, 1965, LBJL. See also Muriel Dobbin, "Foreign Policy Critics Stir White House Arts Festival," *NYT*, June 15, 1965.

25. Muriel Dobbin, "Foreign Policy Critics Stir White House Arts Festival," *NYT*, June 15, 1965.
26. LBJ, "Remarks at the White House Festival of the Arts," Washington, D.C., June 14, 1965, American Presidency Project, http://www.presidency.ucsb.edu/ws/index.php?pid=27035.
27. WHD, June 15, 1965.
28. WHD, June 15, 1965; Memorandum, Eric Goldman to Jack Valenti, WHCF AR 2, AR MC, 6/5/65 [Executive], LBJL.
29. "Only a tiny grouplet agreed to sign: Goldman says seven, Macdonald nine." John Rodden and John Rossi, "Kultur Clash at the White House: Dwight Macdonald and the 1965 Festival of the Arts," *Kenyon Review* 29, no. 4 (Fall 2007): 179; WHD, June 15, 1965.
30. WHD, June 15, 1965.
31. Mary McGrory, "Art with Anguish: Dilemma at the White House," (Washington, D.C.) *Evening Star*, June 15, 1965.
32. WHD, June 15, 1965.
33. WHD, June 16, 1965.
34. WHD, July 8, 1965.
35. Ibid.
36. WHD, July 2, 1965. Bird notes LBJ's mention of this planned sequence one week earlier, on the plane up to New York City for a speech at Madison Square Garden.
37. WHD, July 22, 1965.

38. Ibid.
39. WHD, July 23, 1965.
40. WHD, July 24, 1965.
41. WHD, July 25, 1965.
42. WHD, July 16, 1965.
43. Dallek, *Flawed Giant*, pp. 270–71.
44. Ibid., pp. 270–77.
45. Clark Clifford and Richard C. Holbrooke, *Counsel to the President: A Memoir* (New York: Doubleday, 1991), pp. 416–22; McNamara, *In Retrospect*, pp. 194–204.
46. WHD, July 25, 1965.
47. LBJ, "The President's News Conference," Washington, D.C., July 28, 1965, American Presidency Project, http://www.presidency.ucsb.edu/ws/index.php?pid=27116.
48. Dallek, *Flawed Giant*, p. 276.

Chapter 11: "Impeach Lady Bird"

1. Carol Anderson, *One Person, No Vote: How Voter Suppression Is Destroying Democracy* (New York: Bloomsbury, 2018), pp. 22–23.
2. WHD, August 6, 1965.
3. CTJ DD entry, August 4 and 5, 1965, Lady Bird Johnson's White House Diary Collection, LBJL; WHD, August 6, 1965.
4. WHD, August 6, 1965.
5. Ibid.
6. OH transcript, Sidney Dillon Ripley II, interview 1 (I), undated, by T. H. Baker, LBJL.
7. Lady Bird Johnson, "Lady Bird Johnson Writes Her Own Picture Story," *Life*, August 13, 1965.
8. WHD, August 10, 1965; WHD, September 15, 1965.
9. WHD, August 17, 1965.
10. Jackie Kennedy won an Emmy for her 1962 television special, *A Tour of the White House with Mrs. John F. Kennedy*, and Lady Bird flew to Los Angeles to accept it on her behalf. Lady Bird won a Peabody Award in 1966 for her documentary, *A Visit to Washington with Mrs. Lyndon B. Johnson on Behalf of a More Beautiful America*, and accepted the award in person.
11. LBJ, "Remarks on Project Head Start," Washington, D.C., May 18, 1965, American Presidency Project, https://www.presidency.ucsb.edu/documents/remarks-project-head-start.

12. WHD, January 14, 1965.
13. Letter, Miss Yvonne K. Wilson to Mrs. Johnson, July 20, 1966, "Project Head Start W (2 of 2)," WHSF, Alpha, Box 1709, LBJL.
14. Letter, Pauline Tait to Hugh Hardyman Center, April 12, 1966, "Project Head Start H (1 of 2)," WHSF, Alpha, Box 1706, LBJL.
15. WHD, February 3, 1965.
16. WHD, August 17, 1965.
17. Memorandum, Liz Carpenter to Marvin Watson, August 4, 1965, WHSF LC 17, "Jackson, WY 9/7–10/65 [1 of 2]," LBJL.
18. WHD, August 23, 1965.
19. Ibid.
20. WHD, September 5, 1965.
21. Press release, "Mrs. Lyndon B. Johnson's Remarks," Jackson, WY, August 14, 1964, "Mrs. Johnson—Speeches," Reference File, LBJL.
22. Press release,"Remarks by Mrs. Lyndon B. Johnson to the National Council of State Garden Clubs and American Forestry Association," Jackson Hole, WY, September 7, 1965, "Mrs. Johnson—Speeches," Reference File, LBJL.
23. Prior to 1979, when President Jimmy Carter created the Federal Emergency Management Agency (FEMA), the federal government provided disaster relief through a piecemeal approach, with a large responsibility for rebuilding going to the U.S. Army Corps of Engineers.
24. LBJ, "Statement by the President Making Public a Joint Report on Natural Beauty in America," October 2, 1965, American Presidency Project, https://www.presidency.ucsb.edu/documents/statement-the-president-making-public-joint-report-natural-beauty-america.
25. "In 1965, a Conservative Tried to Keep America White. His Plan Backfired," *Weekend Edition Saturday*, NPR, October 3, 2015, https://www.npr.org/2015/10/03/445339838/the-unintended-consequences-of-the-1965-immigration-act.
26. LBJ, "Remarks at the Signing of the Immigration Bill," speech, Liberty Island, New York, October 3, 1965, American Presidency Project, https://www.presidency.ucsb.edu/documents/remarks-the-signing-the-immigration-bill-liberty-island-new-york.
27. WHD, October 5, 1965.
28. Ibid.
29. LBJ, "Remarks at the Signing of the Heart Disease, Cancer, and Stroke Amendments of 1965," Washington, D.C., October 6, 1965, American Presidency Project, https://www.presidency.ucsb.edu/node/241288.

30. PDD, October 6, 1965; Joseph A. Califano, *The Triumph and Tragedy of Lyndon Johnson: The White House Years.* (New York: Atria Books, 2015), p. 84.
31. Mrs. Johnson did not publish this entry in the 1970 partial collection of her diaries. The LBJL released the unredacted entry in 2012; PDD, October 12, 1965; WHD, October 12, 1965.
32. WHD, October 12, 1965.

Chapter 12: "Little Flames of Fear"

1. "This is the most fun of any party, and I am glad we have begun having special friends spend the night at the White House, although I think I shall not talk about it from the day I leave." WHD, December 14, 1965.
2. Drew Pearson, "Johnson Problems: Vietnam, Luci: Luci Arranged Things," *Washington Post, Times Herald,* January 20, 1966.
3. WHD, January 7, 1966.
4. WHD, January 10, 1966.
5. WHD, January 12, 1966.
6. WHD, January 2, 1965; WHD, January 4, 1965.
7. Ibid.
8. Press release, "Remarks by Mrs. Lyndon B. Johnson, University of Alabama and American Association of University Women Leadership Conference," Tuscaloosa, February 22, 1966, "Mrs. Johnson—Speeches," Reference File, LBJL.
9. Nan Robertson, "Unwed to Receive Birth Control Aid," *NYT,* April 2, 1966, p. 1; Jane E. Brody, "The Pill: Revolution in Birth Control," *NYT,* May 31, 1966.
10. Dan T. Carter, *The Politics of Rage: George Wallace, the Origins of the New Conservatism, and the Transformation of American Politics,* 2nd Edition (Baton Rouge: Louisiana State University Press, 2000), p. 278.
11. Jefferson Walker, "Public Servant and Southern Lady: Public and Private Tensions in Lurleen Wallace's Battle with Cancer," *Alabama Review,* April 2, 2014, p. 167.
12. Peggy Wallace Kennedy's memoir suggests that her mother's decision to enter the race reflected a measure of autonomy and ambition. Peggy Wallace Kennedy, *The Broken Road: George Wallace and a Daughter's Journey to Reconciliation* (New York: Bloomsbury, 2019), pp. 135–42.
13. Nan Robertson, "U.S. Doing More on Birth Control," *NYT,* April 10, 1966.
14. LBJ, "Annual Message to the Congress on the State of the Union," Washington, D.C., January 12, 1966, American Presidency Project, http://www.presidency.ucsb.edu/ws/index.php?pid=28015.

15. Ibid.
16. WHD, January 18, 1966.
17. Ibid.
18. Robert Weaver, "A Cabinet First," *Chicago Defender,* February 19, 1966, p. 5; Adolph Slaughter, "The Slaughter Pen: Cabinet Gets Negro, Little Else," *Chicago Defender,* January 22, 1966, p. 2.; Wendell E. Pritchett, *Robert Clifton Weaver and the American City: The Life and Times of an Urban Reformer* (Chicago: University of Chicago Press, 2008).
19. WHD, January 23, 1966.
20. Letter, Lady Bird Johnson to Polly Shackleton, January 26, 1966, "Beautification Committee/Committee Outreach," WHSF Alpha, Box 1846, LBJL.
21. "Biographies of Nominees for New D.C. City Council," (Washington, D.C.) *Evening Star,* September 28, 1967.
22. Letter, Polly Shackleton to Lady Bird Johnson, January 21, 1966, "Beautification Committee/Committee Outreach," WHSF Alpha, Box 1846, LBJL.
23. Paul Richard, "Slum Area Beautifying Considered: Selected Targets Would Benefit by Expected U.S. Funds," *Washington Post, Times Herald,* March 6, 1966.
24. Marion Barry as quoted in Harry Jaffe and Tom Sherwood, *Dream City: Race, Power, and the Decline of Washington, D.C.,* 20th anniv. ed. (New York: Argo-Navis Author Services, 2014), p. 39.
25. WHD, February 20, 1966.
26. Between January 28, 1966, and February 6, 1966, the forty-two-day operation in South Vietnam left 228 Americans dead, 788 wounded, and 1,342 NVA losses.
27. E. W. Kenworthy, "Senators Reluctantly Back President on Air Strikes," *NYT,* February 1, 1966.
28. WHD, February 22, 1966.
29. WHD, February 6, 1966.
30. WHD, March 13, 1966.
31. Jean Stafford, "Birdbath," *New York Review of Books,* December 3, 1970.
32. LBJ as quote in John A. Farrell, *Richard Nixon: The Life* (New York: Vintage/Penguin Random House, 2018), pp. 342–43; Peter Baker, "Nixon Tried to Spoil Johnson's Vietnam Peace Talks in '68, Notes Show," *NYT,* January 2, 2017.
33. WHD, March 16, 1966.

Chapter 13: At Home

1. George Hamilton as quoted in The Reliable Source, "Lynda Johnson Robb and George Hamilton: When a President's Daughter Dated a Movie Star," *Washington Post,* February 13, 2012.
2. WHD, February 6, 1966.
3. WHD, June 4, 1966.
4. WHD, June 5, 1966.
5. WHD, June 13, 1966.
6. WHD, June 13, 1966; "Luci and Pat Make Court Appearance," *Washington Post, Times Herald,* June 15, 1966.
7. Dallek, *Flawed Giant,* p. 486.
8. LBJ, "Remarks at the Woodrow Wilson School for Public and International Affairs, Princeton University," Princeton, NJ, May 11, 1966, American Presidency Project, https://www.presidency.ucsb.edu/documents/remarks-the-woodrow-wilson-school-for-public-and-international-affairs-princeton.
9. "Galbraith Urges U.S. to Reduce Military Action in Vietnam War," *NYT,* June 12, 1966.
10. WHD, June 23, 1966.
11. WHD, July 14, 1966.
12. Ibid.; Drew Pearson, "LBJ Is Unable to Shake 3 Irritations," *Washington Post, Times Herald,* July 14, 1966.
13. WHD, August 2, 1966.
14. "The White House: Three-Ring Wedding," *Time,* August 5, 1966.
15. Caroli, *Lady Bird and Lyndon,* p. 11.
16. WHD, August 1, 1966.
17. Pamela Coloff, "The Reckoning," *Texas Monthly,* March 2016; Pamela Colloff, "96 Minutes," *Texas Monthly,* August 2006; UPI, "Sniper in Texas U. Tower Kills 12, Hits 33," *NYT,* August 2, 1966; Robert B. Semple, Jr., "President Asserts Texas Shooting Points Up Need for a Law: President Calls on Congress to Prevent Another 'Tragedy,'" *NYT,* August 3, 1966.
18. "The White House: Three-Ring Wedding."
19. WHD, August 6, 1968.
20. Edward C. Burks, "Negroes Assail SNCC Protest," *NYT,* August 5, 1966.
21. Douglas Robinson, "5,000 in Times Square: Thousands March to Protest War," *NYT,* August 7, 1966.
22. WHD, August 6, 1968.

23. Drew Middleton, "President Seeks Any Sign of Move in Hanoi for Talk," *NYT,* August 12, 1966.
24. WHD, August 8, 1966; WHD, August 15, 1966.

Chapter 14: Protest and the Urban Crisis

1. Nan Robertson, "Johnsons Unite in a Beauty Plea," *NYT,* June 28, 1966.
2. "Beautification Summary: The Committee for a More Beautiful Capital, 1965–68," WHSF, Beautification Files, Box 22, pp. 31–32, LBJL; Ralph Waldo Emerson, "Self-Reliance," in *Essays: First Series* (1841), https://emersoncentral.com/ebook/Self-Reliance.pdf.
3. "Beautification Summary: The Committee for a More Beautiful Capital, 1965–68" WHSF, Beautification, Box 22, LBJL, pp. 32–33.
4. Charles W. Eagles, ed., *The Civil Rights Movement in America* (Jackson: University Press of Mississippi, 1986), p. 42.
5. "Taconic Foundation Records (FA407)," Biographical/Historical Note, Rockefeller Archive Center, http://dimes.rockarch.org/FA407/biohist.
6. Asch and Musgrove, *Chocolate City,* p. 347.
7. Gillette, *Between Justice and Beauty,* p. 174.
8. Asch and Musgrove, *Chocolate City,* p. 349; Wolf Von Eckardt, "Shaw Area Will Launch New-Style City Renewal," *Washington Post,* April 8, 1966; Jim Hoagland, *Washington Post,* "Shaw Area Told to Aid in Renewal," December 4, 1966.
9. Polly Shackelton, "Project Pride: Report to the First Lady's Committee for a More Beautiful Capital," October 5, 1966, WHSF Beautification, Box 7, "Project Pride," LBJL.
10. Wolf Von Eckardt, "Highway Agreement Ignores Social Impact," *Washington Post, Times Herald,* May 29, 1966; "In the City and Out, No Place for Our Children to Romp or Splash," *Washington Post, Times Herald,* July 10, 1966.
11. Wolf Von Eckardt, "City Planning Here Is Defined as an Endless Mess: A Critique," *Washington Post, Times Herald,* July 4, 1966; Wolf Von Eckardt, "Residents Launch Shaw Area Cleanup of Trash and Rats: Backed by First Lady," *Washington Post, Times Herald,* July 20, 1966.
12. Letter, Stephen R. Currier, Andrew Heiskell, and August Heckscher to Nathaniel Owings, June 16, 1966, Papers of Nathaniel Owings, Box 20, Library of Congress, Washington, D.C.
13. Press release, "Remarks of Mrs. Lyndon B. Johnson, Reception for Delegates to Urban America Conference," September 12, 1966, "Mrs. Johnson—Speeches," Reference File, LBJL.

14. Benjamin Grant, author interview, November 2019.
15. Nathan Heller, "Private Dreams and Public Ideals in San Francisco," *New Yorker,* August 6 and 13, 2018.
16. Lawrence Halprin, notes from telephone calls with Victor Weingarten and Sharon Francis, September 14, 1966, Lawrence Halprin Collection, Architectural Archives, University of Pennsylvania.
17. Ibid.

Chapter 15: "This Is a Stepchild City"

1. Sam Farr, author interview, September 27, 2013.
2. Press release, "Remarks of Mrs. Lyndon B. Johnson upon Arrival at Hamilton Air Force Base," California, September 20, 1966, "Mrs. Johnson—Speeches," Reference File, LBJL. The quote is from the title of a poem by George Sterling, "Cool Grey City of Love," 1921, http://www.alangullette.com/lit/sterling/coolgrey.htm.
3. "Draft of Proposed Remarks by Mrs. Johnson Point Reyes National Seashore," WHSF LC 27: Faces of the West (CA, AZ, NM) 9/20–23/66, Folder 3 of 6, "Speeches—California," LBJL; press release, "Remarks of Mrs. Lyndon B. Johnson at the Dedication of Point Reyes National Seashore," California, September 20, 1966, "Mrs. Johnson—Speeches," Reference File, LBJL.
4. WHD, September 20, 1966; UPI, "Bomb Threat, Pickets for Mrs. Johnson," (San Mateo, California) *The Times,* September 21, 1966.
5. Wolf Von Eckardt, "What San Francisco Achieved, We Could Do with Powerhouse," *Washington Post, Times Herald,* June 13, 1965.
6. WHD, September 21, 1966.
7. Ibid.
8. Although the ice plant had been present in California for centuries, after the initial success on a few California highways, it soon could be found up and down the coast of California, on roads, highways, and Pacific cliffs, regarded by some as an invasive menace, others as a necessary and, when in bloom, radiant norm of the state's coastline.
9. Gary Kamiya, "Officer's '66 Killing of Black Teen Sparked Hunters Point Riots," *San Francisco Chronicle,* September 16, 2016.
10. Laurie Olin, foreword to Lawrence Halprin, *A Life Spent Changing Places* (Philadelphia: University of Pennsylvania Press, 2011).
11. Walter Thompson, "How Urban Renewal Destroyed the Fillmore in Order to Save It," *Hoodline,* January 3, 2016, https://hoodline.com/2016/01/how-urban-renewal-destroyed-the-fillmore-in-order-to-save-it; Walter Thomp-

son, "How Urban Renewal Tried to Rebuild the Fillmore," *Hoodline,* January 10, 2016, https://hoodline.com/2016/01/how-urban-renewal-tried-to-rebuild-the-fillmore?utm_source=story&utm_medium=web&utm_campaign=stories; Todd Whitney, "A Brief History of Black San Francisco," *KALW,* February 24, 2016, https://www.kalw.org/post/brief-history-black-san-francisco#stream/0; Thomas Fuller, "The Loneliness of Being Black in San Francisco," *NYT,* July 20, 2016, https://www.nytimes.com/2016/07/21/us/black-exodus-from-san-francisco.html; *Take This Hammer* (the Director's Cut), directed by Richard O. Moore, produced for National Educational Television, featuring James Baldwin and Orville Luster, aired February 4, 1964, in the Bay Area on Ch. 9 KQED, https://diva.sfsu.edu/collections/sfbatv/bundles/216518; Dan Kopf, "Data Prove the Truth of 'The Last Black Man in San Fransisco,'" *Quartz,* June 10, 2019, https://qz.com/quartzy/1638972/the-data-behind-the-last-black-man-in-san-francisco/; Benjamin Grant, correspondence with author, February 10, 2020; Peter Cole, "St. Francis Square: How a Union Built Integrated, Affordable Housing in San Francisco," *JSTOR Daily,* January 2, 2016, https://daily.jstor.org/st-francis-square-affordable-housing-san-francisco/.

12. For correspondence and memos about freeway construction, see WHSF, Beautification Files, Box 10: "Freeways—Routing and Design," LBJL.

13. Halprin, *A Life Spent Changing Places,* p. 152.

14. Lawrence Halprin, handwritten notes in notebook, "Notes on class and living conditions," December 9, 1965, Lawrence Halprin Collection, Architectural Archives, University of Pennsylvania.

15. For details on freeway routing being monitored by the White House, see the papers in WHSF Beautification, Box 10, "Freeways—Routing and Design," LBJL.

16. Sharon Francis, correspondence with author, April 26, 2018; OH transcript, Sharon Francis, interview 1 (I), May 20, 1969, by Dorothy Pierce (McSweeny); Lawrence Halprin, handwritten notes in notebook, December 9, 1965, Lawrence Halprin Collection, Architectural Archives, University of Pennsylvania.

17. Emergency Recreation Council for Capitol East, "The Capitol's Background: A Citizen's Survey of Recreation Problems and Possibilities in Capitol East," October 31, 1965.

18. WHD, September 5, 1965.

19. Emergency Recreation Council for Capitol East, "The Capitol's Background: A Citizen's Survey of Recreation Problems and Possibilities in Capitol East," October 31, 1965, p. 28.

20. "White House Joins in Area Improvement," *Capitol East Gazette,* February 1967.
21. OH transcript, Sharon Francis, interview 1 (I), May 20, 1969, by Dorothy Pierce (McSweeny), LBJL, pp. 15–17, 22.
22. Sharon Francis, correspondence with author, April 26, 2018; Sharon Francis OH, I, pp. 14–30; WHD, December 13, 1966.
23. Sharon Francis, correspondence with author, April 26, 2018.
24. OH transcript, Sharon Francis Interview 1 (I), May 20, 1969, by Dorothy Pierce (McSweeny), LBJL, p. 17.
25. Halprin, *A Life Spent Changing Places,* p. 137.
26. Lawrence Halprin, handwritten notes and drawings in notebook, December 1966–February 1967, Lawrence Halprin Collection, Architectural Archives, University of Pennsylvania.
27. Ibid.
28. WHD, December 28, 1966.
29. "13 Youths Visit Johnson's Ranch: President and Wife Salute Young Conservationists," *NYT,* December 29, 1966.

Chapter 16: "Not a Luxury . . . but a Necessity"

1. Roberta Hornig, "Stress on Neighborhood Slated for Beautification," (Washington, D.C.) *Evening Star,* January 12, 1967.
2. Asch and Musgrove, *Chocolate City,* pp. 346–47.
3. Transcript, Meeting of the First Lady's Committee for a More Beautiful Capital, January 13, 1967, p. 8, LBJL.
4. Transcript, Meeting of the First Lady's Committee for a More Beautiful Capital, January 13, 1967, LBJL.
5. Press release, "Meeting of the First Lady's Committee for a More Beautiful Capital," January 12, 1967, WHSF Beautification, Box 6, "Halprin Report," LBJL; Wolf Von Eckardt, "Plazas, Gardens, Parks Proposed in Bold, New Beautification Plan," *Washington Post, Times Herald,* January 13, 1967; Roberta Hornig, "Beauty Planned for Capitol East," (Washington, D.C.) *Evening Star,* January 13, 1967.
6. Ibid., pp. 44–48.
7. Ibid., p. 48.
8. Memo, March 17, 1967, Folder 1343, Box 136, Taconic Foundation Records, Society for a More Beautiful National Capital, Rockefeller Archive Center.
9. Wolf Von Eckardt, "Proposed New Parks Are Badly Needed: A Critique," *Washington Post,* January 13, 1967.

10. "13 Youths Visit Johnson's Ranch."
11. Letter, Sharon Francis to John Simon, June 23, 1967, Folder 1343, Box 136, Taconic Foundation Records, Society for a More Beautiful National Capital, Rockefeller Archive Center.
12. Letter, Gerald Rubin to Lawrence Halprin, "Taconic—Scope of Work and Fees," January 17, 1967, WHSF Beautification, Box 6, LBJL.
13. Loudon Wainwright, "The Resonance of Charity," *Life*, February 24, 1967, p. 21; "Stephen Curriers Missing on Flight," *NYT*, January 19, 1967; "Search Is Pressed for Currier Couple," *NYT*, January 20, 1967.

Chapter 17: Chaos or Community

1. Letter, Audrey and Stephen Currier to Lady Bird Johnson, December 25, 1966, WHSF Alpha, Box 0632, "Currier, Mr. & Mrs. Stephen (Audrey)," LBJL.
2. Cermetrius Lynell Bohannon, "The Urban Catalyst Concept" (master's thesis, Virginia Tech, Invent the Future, April 27, 2004), https://vtechworks.lib.vt.edu/handle/10919/9954.
3. Letter, Lady Bird Johnson to Audrey and Stephen Currier, January 9, 1967, WHSF, Alpha File, Box 632, "Currier, Mr. & Mrs. Stephen (Audrey)," LBJL.
4. WHD, January 10, 1967.
5. Roberta Hornig, "$14.3 Million for Recreation," (Washington, D.C.) *Evening Star*, January 21, 1967; Wolf Von Eckardt, "Danish Pastry for Our Island Park," *Washington Post, Times Herald*, January 29, 1967.
6. "White House Joins in Area Improvement Push," *Capitol East Gazette*, February 1967.
7. Marie Smith, "Woman on the Go," (Louisville, KY) *Courier-Journal*, January 15, 1967.
8. OH transcript, Sharon Francis, interview 1 (I), May 20, 1969, by Dorothy Pierce (McSweeny), LBJL, p. 42; Interview with author, Sharon Francis, March 15, 2017.
9. Jesse Locke, "The Other Voice," letter to the editor, (Washington, D.C.) *Evening Star*, February 28, 1967.
10. Letter, Sharon Francis to John Simon, June 23, 1967, WHSF Beautification, Box 5, "Capital East—Inner Blocks," LBJL.
11. The editor of the *Capitol East Gazette* wrote in his feedback on the Halprin plan: "It should be made clear to government planners that our community will not be satisfied with mere prettification of the area. Capitol East has been badly neglected in recreation matters. Completion of the Halprin Plan should not be regarded as a kind gift, but rather as partial payment of

a long overdue debt." Letter, Sam Smith, January 28, 1967, WHSF Beautification, Box 5, "Capitol East—Inner Blocks," LBJL. For community input, see "67/01/28-05/10 Community Response to Halprin Report," WHSF Beautification, Box 5, "Capitol East—Inner Blocks," LBJL.

12. Asch and Musgrove, *Chocolate City*, p. 349.
13. "Dr. King Rallies Shaw Renewal Forces to 'Revive a Dream,'" (Washington, D.C.) *Evening Star*, March 13, 1967; John Carmody, "Dr. King Pushes Shaw-Area Renewal," *Washington Post, Times Herald*, March 13, 1967; "A Right to the City," exhibition, Anacostia Community Museum, Washington, D.C., April 21, 2018–April 20, 2020.
14. LBJ, "Remarks at a Ceremony Marking the 100th Anniversary of Howard University," Washington, D.C., March 2, 1967, American Presidency Project, https://www.presidency.ucsb.edu/node/237648.
15. Sharon Francis, "Progress Report—Halprin Proposals," April 1, 1967, WHSF Beautification, Box 6, "Halprin Report," LBJL.
16. Marie Smith, "Big Things Ahead in Beautification," *Washington Post, Times Herald*, December 28, 1966; Meryle Secrest, "He Puts Green into City Gray," *Washington Post, Times Herald*, November 8, 1967.
17. Letter, Lawrence Halprin to William Slayton, May 29, 1967, Folder 1343, Box 136, Taconic Foundation Records, Society for a More Beautiful National Capital, Rockefeller Archive Center.

Chapter 18: "Without the Momentum of Success"

1. WHD, March 26, 1967; WHD, January 17, 1967.
2. WHD, February 20, 1967.
3. WHD, March 9, 1967; LBJ, "The President's News Conference," Washington, D.C., March 9, 1967, American Presidency Project, https://www.presidency.ucsb.edu/documents/the-presidents-news-conference-1188.
4. WHD, March 9, 1967.
5. Dwight Macdonald, "Birds of America," *New York Review of Books*, December 1, 1966, https://www.nybooks.com/articles/1966/12/01/birds-of-america/; Barbara Garson, *MacBird!* (New York: Grove Press, 1967). In subsequent correspondence, Barbara Garson indicated she felt, even at the time of writing the play, that she had done Lady Bird a disservice by depicting her as having ambitions akin to those of Shakespeare's Lady Macbeth. More interesting is Ms. Garson's explanation, lost at the time on a White House convinced the play was pure satire, of her awareness of LBJ's failure to garner recognition for his positive contributions. "I knew when I wrote it (not just retrospect) that I wasn't accurate about Lady

Bird. As in MacBeth, she's pictured as the ambitious one who eggs her mate on then falls behind as his ambition oe'r leaps the bounds of her invention. In other words, I simply went with Shakespeare's Lady MacBeth and that wasn't fair to Lady Bird Johnson. But anyone who says I wasn't fair to Lyndon hasn't read or seen the play. My *MacBird* is a colossus tormented by the fact that Kennedy, who did so little, looks so princely while he who does so much for so many is still sneered at." Barbara Garson, correspondence with Robert Kanigel, May 23, 2017, and Robert Kanigel, correspondence with author, May 23, 2017.

6. WHD, June 5, 1964; WHD, February 14, 1964; Susan Shillinglaw, *Carol and John Steinbeck: Portrait of a Marriage* (Reno: University of Nevada Press, 2013).
7. John Steinbeck, "A President—Not a Candidate," 1964 DNC convention pamphlet; WHD, June 5, 1964.
8. WHD, March 10, 1967.
9. Gregory Daddis, "Johnson, Westmoreland, and the Selling of Vietnam," *NYT,* May 9, 2017.
10. Paul Beston, "The Truth About Muhammad Ali and the Draft," *Wall Street Journal,* April 27, 2017.
11. WHD, July 31, 1967.
12. Ibid.
13. WHD, May 13, 1967.
14. Ibid.
15. Ibid.
16. WHD, September 5, 1967.
17. WHD, September 8, 1967.
18. For more on LBJ's dreams, see Doris Kearns Goodwin, *Lyndon Johnson and the American Dream* (New York: St. Martin's Press, 1991), p. 342.
19. WHD, September 8, 1967. See also Dallek, *Flawed Giant,* pp. 513–24; James Reston, *The Lone Star: The Life of John Connally* (New York: Harper and Row, 1989), p. 325; LBJ, *Vantage Point,* p. 425.
20. WHD, September 25, 1967.
21. Press release, "To the Guests and Friends of the Citizens Committee for Children," WHSF LC, Box 36, "Citizens for NY Children Dinner (2 of 2), LBJL; Speech, "Remarks of the Honorable Thurgood Marshall, Solicitor General of the United States," May 10, 1967, WHSF LC, Box 26, "Citizens for NY Children Dinner (2 of 2)," LBJL; WHD, May 10, 1967.
22. Califano, *The Triumph and Tragedy of Lyndon Johnson,* p. 218.

23. "Johnson Signs Bill for Women Generals and Pins Medals on 2 Nurses," *NYT,* November 9, 1967.
24. WHD, November 8, 1967.
25. WHD, November 8, 1967; LBJ, "Remarks upon Signing Bill Providing Equal Opportunity in Promotions for Women in the Armed Forces," Washington, D.C., November 8, 1967, American Presidency Project, https://www.presidency.ucsb.edu/documents/remarks-upon-signing-bill-providing-equal-opportunity-promotions-for-women-the-armed.

Chapter 19: The Generation Gap

1. Paul Vitello, "Robert Stein, Who Led 'McCall's' and 'Redbook' for Decades, Dies at 90," *NYT,* July 17, 2014.
2. For example, Clare Boothe Luce, "Without Portfolio: Birth Control and the Catholic Church," *McCall's,* February 1967, p. 48; James Baldwin, "Tell Me How Long the Train's Been Gone," *McCall's,* February 1967, p. 118; Gloria Steinem, "A Woman for All Seasons: Margot Fonteyn," *McCall's,* May 1967, pp. 86–87, 130–32; Gloria Steinem, "An Interview with Truman Capote," *McCall's,* November 1967, pp. 76, 148–54; Alice Lake, "The Pill," *McCall's,* November 1967, pp. 96–97, 166–74.
3. For example: Susan Sheehan, "Letter from Abroad: A Vietnamese Woman," *McCall's,* March 1967, p. 48; Clare Boothe Luce, "Without Portfolio: The 1968 Campaign for President," *McCall's,* March 1967, p. 42.
4. Lynda Bird Johnson, "They Act As If We'd Invented Sin," *McCall's,* June 1967, pp. 32, 135–37.
5. WHD, October 20, 1967.
6. LBJ, *Vantage Point,* p. 428.
7. WHD, October 4, 1967.
8. Ibid.
9. Ibid.
10. Nan Robertson, "Beautification: US Is Helping Cities Attack Blight," *NYT,* July 3, 1967; Nan Robertson, "Beautification: Planners Fear Vietnam Will Drain Urban Grants," *NYT,* July 4, 1967; Nan Robertson, "Key to Beautification: Money, Power and Imagination Found Vital to Successful Urban Programs," *NYT,* July 5, 1967.
11. Letter, John E. Sawyer to Liz Carpenter, October 3, 1967, WHSF LC 42, "Visit to Yale and Williams [3 of 5]," LBJL.
12. "Fall Convocation: Center for Environmental Studies Is Opened at Convocation," *Williams Newsletter,* Fall 1967, WHSF LC 42, "Visit to Yale and Williams [1 of 5]," LBJL.

13. WHD, October 8, 1967.
14. Ibid.
15. Ibid.
16. "Lady Bird Visits University Today," *Yale Daily News,* October 9, 1967, http://digital.library.yale.edu/cdm/compoundobject/collection/yale-ydn/id/23052/rec/1.
17. Jeffrey Rosen, Yale College Class of 1969, author interview, June 30, 2018.
18. WHD, October 9, 1967.
19. Letter, John O'Leary to Lady Bird Johnson, July 27, 1967, WHSF LC, Box 42, "Visit to Yale and Williams [4 of 5]," LBJL
20. "Lady Bird Visits University Today," *Yale Daily News,* October 9, 1967.
21. WHD, October 9, 1967.
22. Ibid.
23. Ibid.
24. Press release, "Address of Mrs. Lyndon B. Johnson at Yale Political Union, New Haven, Connecticut," October 9, 1967, "Mrs. Johnson—Speeches," Reference File, LBJL; WHD October 9, 1967.
25. WHD, October 20, 1967.
26. WHD, November 5, 1967.
27. WHD, December 3, 1967.
28. WHD, December 4, 1967.
29. Susan S. Daily, "For the Robbs, Wedding Is Also a Homecoming," *NYT,* December 1, 1967; Marie Smith, "Anatomy of a Guest List," *Washington Post, Times Herald,* December 3, 1967; Nan Robertson, "Lynda's Wedding Will Be Different," *NYT,* December 3, 1967; Elinor Lee, "Chef's Summit Is Six Feet High," *Washington Post, Times Herald,* December 7, 1967.
30. Peter Manseau, "Fifty Years Ago, a Rag-Tag Group of Acid-Dropping Activists Tried to 'Levitate' the Pentagon," *Smithsonian Magazine,* October 20, 2017.
31. LBJ, *Vantage Point,* p. 429.
32. These conversations took place between Thanksgiving 1967 and New Year's Day 1968. According to Krim, it was on New Year's Day 1968 that LBJ gave the green light for Krim to put together political and financing task forces, with the caveat that Krim not raise too much money too quickly, as the plans might well be aborted. At the time, it was not required that all candidates for presidential elections put themselves into statewide primary contests: LBJ opted to skip the first ten in the country other than the Wisconsin primary, which was scheduled to take place on April 2,

1968. He did, however, face a deadline of March 31, 1968, after which the law required him to appear on primary ballots. OH transcript, Arthur Krim interview 5 (V), April 7, 1983, by Michael L. Gillette, LBJL; Dallek, *Flawed Giant*, pp. 524–28; LBJ, *Vantage Point*, pp. 428–29.

33. See McNamara, *In Retrospect*, chap. 10, "Estrangement and Departure," pp. 273–317, for his account of his exit from the Johnson administration. See also WHD, November 29, 1967.
34. WHD, January 4, 1968.
35. Ibid.

ACT III: January 1968–August 1968

Chapter 20: "Maggots of Doubt"

1. WHD, January 4, 1968; WHD, January 15, 1968.
2. Carroll Kilpatrick, "LBJ Blueprint for Re-election: State of the Union to Open Race," *Washington Post, Times Herald*, January 15, 1968.
3. WHD, January 17, 1968.
4. Ibid.
5. Following the last line of her draft, Lady Bird tacked on the final sentence ("I also know the weight of . . .") on a separate page. The draft is dated January 15, but her diary entry on January 17 indicates she wrote this statement on the seventeenth. Lady Bird Johnson, draft statement announcing LBJ decision not to run, January 15, 1968, "Decision Not to Run in '68," Reference File, LBJL; WHD, January 17, 1968.
6. WHD, January 17, 1968.
7. Ibid.; CTJ DD, January 17, 1968.
8. PDD, January 17, 1968.
9. The Fish Room is now called the Roosevelt Room.
10. WHD, January 17, 1968; PDD, January 17, 1968; CTJ DD, January 17, 1968.
11. WHD, January 17, 1968.
12. LBJ, "Annual Message to the Congress on the State of the Union," Washington, D.C., January 17, 1968, American Presidency Project, https://www.presidency.ucsb.edu/node/237325.
13. WHD, January 17, 1968.
14. Ibid.
15. LBJ, *Vantage Point*, pp. 428–30; Dallek, *Flawed Giant*, pp. 513–19.
16. PDD, January 17, 1968; WHD, January 17, 1968.

Chapter 21: "Somewhere . . . Between the Words Gut and Pot"

1. WHD, January 18, 1968; John Herbers, "Decline of Rights Issue: Neither Johnson nor Congress Shows Past Enthusiasm for a New Measure," *NYT*, January 19, 1968.
2. Marjorie Hunter, "5,000 Women Rally in Capital Against War," *NYT*, January 16, 1968; Richard Harwood and Elizabeth Shelton, "Antiwar Women March on Capitol," *Washington Post, Times Herald*, January 16, 1968; Barry Kalb, "'Rankin Brigade' Ponders Results of March," (Washington, D.C.) *Evening Star*, January 16, 1968; Judith Martin, "Portrait of the Rankin File: Peace in Policy, Manner," *Washington Post, Times Herald*, January 16, 1968.
3. Sy Ramsey, "If She Wins, She'll Dream of Running for President," (Owensboro, KY) *Messenger-Inquirer*, August 4, 1968; Gay Pauley, "Congress Next? Katherine Peden Hopes to Stay in the Limelight," (Louisville, KY) *Courier-Journal*, August 16, 1967; "Obituary: Katherine Peden, 80; Broadcaster Served on Panel Studying Riots," *LA Times*, January 12, 2006.
4. John L. Williams, *America's Mistress: The Life and Times of Eartha Kitt* (New York: Quercus, 2014); memo, Liz Carpenter to CTJ, January 19, 1968, re: The Eartha Kitt Invitation, WHSF LC 45: WDL 1/18/68, LBJL.
5. Williams, *America's Mistress*.
6. Nan Robertson, "First Lady Asks Race Tolerance," *NYT*, February 25, 1966, p. 43.
7. Winzola McLendon, "Mrs. LBJ Talks Tolerance," *Washington Post, Times Herald*, February 24, 1966; Isabelle Shelton, "Hate Signs Missing in Alabama: First Lady Given Southern Greeting on Tuscaloosa Visit," (Washington, D.C.) *Evening Star*, February 26, 1966.
8. CTJ DD, January 18, 1968; WHD, January 18, 1968.
9. Transcript, Doers Luncheon, January 18, 1968, WHSF LC, Box 45, "WDL 1/18/68 [1 of 2]," LBJL.
10. WHD, January 18, 1968.
11. Ibid.
12. Transcript, Doers Luncheon, January 18, 1968.
13. WHD, January 18, 1968.
14. Transcript, Doers Luncheon, January 18, 1968.
15. WHD, January 18, 1968.
16. Ibid.
17. WHD, January 18, 1968; UPI, "'Kitt Denounces War Policy to Mrs. Johnson," *NYT*, January 19, 1968; DeNeen L. Brown, "'Sex Kitten' vs. Lady Bird: The Day Eartha Kitt Attacked the Vietnam War at the White House," *Wash-*

ington Post, January 19, 2018; Ethel L. Payne, "The Inside Story of the 'Pussycat,'" *Chicago Daily Defender,* January 22, 1968; Liz Carpenter OH, Interview II, April 4, 1969.

18. Carolyn Lewis, "'Shrill Voice' Jars First Lady: First Lady Berates Singer as 'Shrill Voice of Discord,'" *Washington Post, Times Herald,* January 20, 1968; AP, "Mrs. Johnson Sorry Furor Obscured Other Ideas," *NYT,* January 20, 1968; Isabelle Shelton, "Country Rallies with Rage as Kitt Blast Backfires," (Washington, D.C.) *Sunday Star,* January 21, 1968; Isabelle Shelton, "Lady Bird Cut to the Bone: Hears Sympathy from Country," (Washington, D.C.) *Evening Star,* January 20, 1968.
19. AP, "Kitt Continues the Tempest," (Washington, D.C.) *Evening Star,* January 23, 1968.
20. "Singer Feels Justified for Outburst," *Chicago Daily Defender,* January 22, 1968.
21. Memo, Liz Carpenter to LBJ, January 22, 1968, WHSF LC, Box 45, "WDL 1/18/68 [2 of 2]," LBJL.
22. Liz Carpenter OH, Interview II; Janet Mezzack, "'Without Manners You Are Nothing': Lady Bird Johnson, Eartha Kitt, and the Women Doers' Luncheon of January 18, 1968," *Presidential Studies Quarterly* 20, no. 4 (Fall 1990); UPI, "Eartha Was Right, Dr. King Contends," *Chicago Daily Defender,* January 22, 1968; "Dr. King Calls Outburst a 'Very Proper Gesture,'" *Baltimore Afro-American,* January 27, 1968.
23. "Singer Feels Justified for Outburst."
24. Lewis, "'Shrill Voice' Jars First Lady."
25. Letter, Gregory Peck to Lady Bird Johnson, January 31, 1968, EX PP 5 WHCF 62, 1/30/68–3/22/68, LBJL.
26. "Report of the National Advisory Commission on Civil Disorders," February 29, 1968, http://www.eisenhowerfoundation.org/docs/kerner.pdf.
27. Seymour Hersh, "CIA in '68 Gave Secret Service a Report Containing Gossip About Eartha Kitt," *NYT,* January 2, 1975.
28. WHD, January 18, 1968. Other than her diary entry, she left no indication of how she felt about the impact of White House pressure on Eartha Kitt's career.

Chapter 22: "Standing Still When I Should Be Running"

1. Memo, Liz Carpenter to Marvin Watson, "Photographic Coverage of Mrs. Johnson by White House Photographers," March 2, 1968, EX PP 5 WHCF 63, "1/30/68–3/22/68," LBJL.

2. Liz Carpenter provided LBJ with seven talking points, among them Lady Bird's understanding of how government operates, her clarity and objective counsel, her availability, her "large political following," and, finally, "I love her—she gives me strength." The *Look* interview was never published. Memo, Liz Carpenter to the president, "Off-Record Interview—Warren Rogers, LOOK," March 22, 1968, EX PP 5 WHCF 63, 1/30/68–3/22/68, LBJL.
3. "Final Words: Cronkite's Vietnam Commentary," *All Things Considered,* NPR, July 18, 2009, https://www.npr.org/templates/story/story.php?storyId=106775685.
4. Dallek, *Flawed Giant,* p. 506.
5. Charles Kaiser, *1968 in America: Music, Politics, Chaos, Counterculture,* 30th anniv. ed. (New York: Grove Press, 2018), p. 102.
6. Ibid.
7. LBJ, "Letter to the Speaker of the House Urging Prompt Action on the Civil Rights Bill," dated March 11, 1968, released March 12, 1968, American Presidency Project, https://www.presidency.ucsb.edu/node/237345.
8. Ibid.
9. Jeff Shesol, *Mutual Contempt: Lyndon Johnson, Robert Kennedy, and the Feud That Defined a Decade* (New York: W. W. Norton and Company, 1997), p. 422.
10. Ian Shapira, "'It Was Insanity': At My Lai, U.S. Soldiers Slaughtered Hundreds of Vietnamese Women and Kids," *Washington Post,* March 16, 2018.
11. WHD, March 21, 1968.
12. OH transcript, "Special Interview," Robert Dallek interview of Lady Bird Johnson (with Michael L. Gillette present), Mrs. Johnson's office, December 15, 1986, LBJL (hereafter cited as Dallek, "Special Interview").
13. WHD, March 21, 1968.
14. WHD, February 7, 1968.
15. Betty Beale, "LBJ Camp Worried; First Lady Relaxed," (Washington, D.C.) *Evening Star,* March 29, 1968.
16. Ibid.
17. WHD, March 27, 1968.
18. WHD, February 28, 1968; WHD, April 13, 1968.
19. Kyle Longley, *LBJ's 1968: Power, Politics, and the Presidency in America's Year of Upheaval* (Cambridge, UK: Cambridge University Press, 2018), p. 8. See also pp. 54–83 for background.
20. WHD, March, 10, 1968.
21. Ibid.
22. WHD, March 16, 1968.

23. Ted Conover, "The Strike That Brought MLK to Memphis," *Smithsonian Magazine*, January 2018; "Memphis Sanitation Workers' Strike," MLK Research and Education Institute, Stanford University, https://kinginstitute.stanford.edu/encyclopedia/memphis-sanitation-workers-strike; Branch, *At Canaan's Edge*, pp. 697–700.
24. DeNeen L. Brown, "'I Am a Man': The Ugly Memphis Sanitation Workers' Strike That Led to MLK's Assassination," *Washington Post*, February 12, 2018.
25. Ibid.
26. WHD, March 22, 1968.
27. "Report of the National Advisory Commission on Civil Disorders"; Alice George, "The 1968 Kerner Commission Got It Right, but Nobody Listened," *Smithsonian Magazine*, March 1, 2018; "The Kerner Commission," *The Great Society*, National Museum of African American History and Culture, https://nmaahc.si.edu/blog-post/kerner-commission.
28. Branch, *At Canaan's Edge*, p. 746; WHD, March 31, 1968; LBJ, *Vantage Point*, p. 431.
29. Nash Castro, author interview, Williamsburg, VA, May 25, 2014.
30. Ibid.; WHD, March 31, 1968.
31. LBJ, "The President's News Conference," Washington, D.C., March 30, 1968, American Presidency Project, https://www.presidency.ucsb.edu/node/238067.
32. Ibid.

Chapter 23: March 31, 1968

1. WHD, March 31, 1968; PDD, March 31, 1968, CTJ DD, March 31, 1968.
2. Charles Mohr, "Johnson's Health Cited in Quitting," *NYT*, July 9, 1968; Drew Pearson, "The Ghosts That Haunted LBJ," *Look*, July 23, 1968.
3. LBJ, *Vantage Point*, p. 431.
4. WHD, March 31, 1968; LBJ, *Vantage Point*, p. 431; Pearson, "The Ghosts That Haunted LBJ."
5. WHD, March 31, 1968.
6. PDD, March 31, 1968.
7. LBJ, *Vantage Point*, p. 432.
8. Ibid.
9. Arnold A. Offner, *Hubert Humphrey: The Conscience of the Country* (New Haven, CT: Yale University Press, 2018), pp. 273–74; James R. Jones, "Behind LBJ's

Decision Not to Run in '68," *NYT,* April 16, 1968; Pearson, "The Ghosts That Haunted LBJ"; Ambassador Jim Jones, author interview, July 9, 2019.

10. MLK, "Remaining Awake Through a Great Revolution," Sermon, March 31, 1968, https://kinginstitute.stanford.edu/king-papers/documents/remaining-awake-through-great-revolution.
11. Bernadette Carey, "4,000 Hear Dr. King at Cathedral," *Washington Post, Times Herald,* April 1, 1968.
12. MLK, "Remaining Awake Through a Great Revolution"; Carey, "4,000 Hear Dr. King at Cathedral."
13. Isabelle Shelton, "First Lady Tours," (Washington, D.C.) *Sunday Star,* March 31, 1968; Joy Miller, "Campaign Spirit of '52 in the Air, Says Pat Nixon of This Year's Try," (Washington, D.C.) *Sunday Star,* March 31, 1968.
14. Richard Nixon, *RN: The Memoirs of Richard Nixon* (New York: Simon & Schuster, 2013), "1968 Campaign and Election," e-book.
15. PDD, March 31, 1968; WHD, March 31, 1968.
16. PDD, March 31, 1968; LBJ, *Vantage Point,* p. 434; WHD, March 31, 1968.
17. WHD, March 31, 1968.
18. LBJ, *Vantage Point,* p. 434.
19. WHD, March 31, 1968.
20. Goodwin, *Lyndon Johnson and the American Dream,* p. 344.
21. WHD, March 31, 1968.
22. Ibid.
23. Ibid.
24. Ibid.; Beschloss, "Lyndon Johnson on the Record."
25. WHD, March 31, 1968.
26. Anatoly Dobrynin, *In Confidence: Moscow's Ambassador to Six Cold War Presidents* (New York: Henry Holt and Co., 1995), pp. 172–73.
27. "Memorandum for the Record," FRUS, 1964–1968, Volume VI, Vietnam, January–August 1968, eds. David C. Humphrey and Charles S. Sampson, Document 268, https://history.state.gov/historicaldocuments/frus1964-68v06/d168; Dobrynin, *In Confidence,* pp. 170–173; Robert Dallek, author interview, September 29, 2018; WHD, March 31, 1968.
28. WHD, March 31, 1968.
29. LBJ, *Vantage Point,* p. 435.
30. WHD, March 31, 1968.
31. LBJ, "The President's Address to the Nation Announcing Steps to Limit the War in Vietnam and Reporting His Decision Not to Seek Reelection,"

Washington, D.C., March 31, 1968, American Presidency Project, https://www.presidency.ucsb.edu/node/238065.

32. WHD, March 31, 1968.
33. LBJ, *Vantage Point*, p. 435.
34. Ibid.; PDD, March 31, 1968.
35. WHD, March 31, 1968.
36. Ibid.
37. LBJ, "The President's News Conference," Washington, D.C., March 31, 1968, American Presidency Project https://www.presidency.ucsb.edu/node/238047.
38. Special to *The New York Times*, "Move Called 'Completely Irrevocable,'" *NYT*, April 1, 1968.
39. WHD, March 31, 1968.
40. Ibid.

Chapter 24: Assassination

1. LBJ as recounted in Goodwin, *Leadership in Turbulent Times*, pp. 308–9.
2. WHD, March 31, 1968.
3. WHD, April 4, 1968; CTJ DD, April 4, 1968.
4. Clay Risen, *A Nation on Fire: America in the Wake of the King Assassination* (Hoboken, NJ: John Wiley and Sons, 2009), p. 42; PDD, April 5, 1968.
5. LBJ, "Statement by the President on the Assassination of Dr. Martin Luther King, Jr.," Washington, D.C., April 4, 1968, American Presidency Project, https://www.presidency.ucsb.edu/documents/statement-the-president-the-assassination-dr-martin-luther-king-jr.
6. PDD, April 5, 1968; Longley, *LBJ's 1968*, p. 110.
7. Shirley Elder, "Few Hear Kennedy, but Thousands Cheer," (Washington, D.C.) *Evening Star*, April 4, 1968.
8. WHD, April 4, 1968.
9. Larry Tye, *Bobby Kennedy: The Making of a Liberal Icon* (New York: Random House, 2016), p. 411.
10. Dallek, "Special Interview," 1997.
11. WHD, April 5, 1968.
12. PDD, April 5, 1968; LBJ, *Vantage Point*, p. 176; Longley, *LBJ's 1968*, p. 113; Risen, *A Nation on Fire*, pp. 54–55; Califano, *Triumph and Tragedy*, p. 276.
13. Califano, *Triumph and Tragedy*, p. 276.

14. Longley, *LBJ's 1968,* p. 113; Risen, *A Nation on Fire,* p. 86; LBJ, *Vantage Point,* p. 176.
15. Leontyne Price sang this song at LBJ's funeral.
16. Longley, *LBJ's 1968,* p. 116.
17. WHD, April 5, 1968.
18. Ibid.; "Status Report Washington, D.C., U.S. Secret Service Command Post," April 5, 1968, WHCF Human Rights, Box 20, "Hu 2/FG 216 Situation Reports," LBJL.
19. WHD, April 5, 1968.
20. CTJ DD, April 6, 1968.
21. Press release, "Remarks of Mrs. Lyndon B. Johnson at the Opening of Hemisfair," San Antonio, TX, April 6, 1968, "Mrs. Johnson—Speeches," Reference File, LBJL.
22. Terence McArdle, "MLK Was Dead. Cities Were Burning. Could James Brown Keep Boston from Erupting, Too?," *Washington Post,* April 5, 2018.
23. PDD, April 6, 1968.
24. "Status Report Washington, D.C., U.S. Secret Service Command Post," April 6, 1968, WHCF Human Rights, Box 20, "Hu 2/FG 216 Situation Reports," LBJL.
25. "Sen. Kennedy Tours Areas Torn by Riots," *Washington Post, Times Herald,* April 8, 1968.
26. Thurston Clarke, *The Last Campaign: Robert F. Kennedy and 82 Days That Inspired America* (New York: Henry Holt and Co., 2008), p. 114.
27. LBJ, "Remarks to the Press with General Westmoreland Following the General's Report on the Situation in Vietnam," Washington, D.C., April 7, 1968, American Presidency Project, https://www.presidency.ucsb.edu/documents/remarks-the-press-with-general-westmoreland-following-the-generals-report-the-situation.
28. "Status Report Washington, D.C., U.S. Secret Service Command Post," April 7, 1968, WHCF Human Rights, Box 20, "Hu 2/FG 216 Situation Reports," LBJL.
29. PDD, April 7, 1968; WHD, April 7, 1968.
30. WHD, April 9, 1968.
31. Ibid.
32. Califano, *Triumph and Tragedy,* p. 283.
33. WHD, April 8, 1968; Status Report Washington, D.C., U.S. Secret Service Command Post," April 8, 1968, WHCF Human Rights, Box 20, "Hu 2/FG 216 Situation Reports," LBJL. For a visual mapping of the riots and destruc-

tion in Washington, D.C., see "The Four Days in 1968 That Reshaped D.C.," *Washington Post,* March 27, 2018, https://www.washingtonpost.com/graphics/2018/local/dc-riots-1968/?noredirect=on.

34. Memo, "Your Humble Servants Nash, Rex, Elmer Atkins, Sharon, Cynthia, Bess and Liz" to Lady Bird Johnson and Mary Lasker, WHSF LC 49: Beautification Lunch, LBJL.
35. WHD, April 11, 1968.
36. William F. Zeman, "Today in D.C. History: Rioting Spreads Following MLK's Assassination," *Washington City Paper,* April 5, 2011, https://www.washingtoncitypaper.com/news/city-desk/blog/13063287/today-in-d-c-history-rioting-spreads-following-mlks-assassination.
37. Letter, Henry L. Kimelman to Lawrence Halprin, April 8, 1968, WHSF Beautification, Box 4, "Anacostia–Kingman Lake," LBJL.
38. Memo, Sharon Francis, "Notes on Kingman Lake Contract," WHSF Beautification, Box 4, "Anacostia–Kingman Lake," LBJL. Halprin presented Hartzog with a fourteen-page detailed manifesto setting forth a maximalist vision for converting the Anacostia riverfront into not just a version of a Danish amusement park but an entire Scandinavian-like empire. From A to V, Halprin proposed more than 150 suggestions for recreational, cultural, and community spaces within the District. His proposal included a "Federal Building Complex" replete with an esplanade along the riverfront, an interior pedestrian mall, and a marina for tour boats; the revitalization of marinas with updated dry docks and designated small-boat repair areas; six acres of neighborhood "passive" recreation center with strolling areas, viewpoints, and free play and picnic areas; and ninety acres of citywide recreation facilities that would include: four lighted tennis courts, four basketball courts, one baseball field, two softball fields (one lighted), two Little League fields, and two soccer/football fields; an outdoor pool that would convert to a skating rink in winter; picnic and barbecue areas; a pavilion to rent rowboats, paddleboats, canoes, and hydroscooters; a model boat sailing pond. Also listed: an updated Spingarn School and Recreation Center Complex with a stadium for track meets, football games, and soccer matches and a range of other practice fields and courts, an indoor gymnasium, an indoor/outdoor pool facility, and free play areas with wading pools; a forty-seven-acre beach and amusement center, featuring an amusement park, boat rides, a sky tram, a boardwalk with arcade games, a bandstand, children's rides, specialty food shops, and a major recreation building whose facilities would include an indoor swimming pool; a gymnasium for court games, gymnastics, and wrestling; space for ceramics, painting, photography, and sculpture; rooms for boat testing, model racing, and woodworking; a "teen island"; boat rentals (limited); waterskiing;

a dance pavilion and an amphitheater; a fish-catching farm; beach and swim facilities; and walking and bike trails. Also: a four-year-college at Fort Lincoln; an additional smaller, neighborhood recreation center with a softball and Little League field and a one-and-a-quarter-mile track surrounding a field and two tennis courts; 156 acres for allotment-demonstration gardens, where the public can tend to vegetable garden plots and have access to free fruit; display gardens and rose and specialty gardens; an even smaller neighborhood recreation center, with one softball field, one football/soccer field, and space for picnicking; a 100-acre Camping Center with facilities for day camps, Boy Scouts, and the YMCA to use; group picnic and cabin facilities; a conference center; a canoe center with space to drydock and repair boats; a 2-acre community recreation center with softball fields, Little League fields, tennis courts, basketball courts, picnic space, and an outdoor pool; a "semi-active/semi-passive" community recreation center with all the usual fields, courts, and play areas, but also 10 acres developed "naturally" and a woodland and passive area for nature study and hikes, as well as bike, horse, and pedestrian trails; a small, 25-acre golf course that can be reached by the continuation of the trail system along the river; an "intensive 'mod' cultural community center," where the public can race go-carts and build and test model airplanes and model boats, as well as a dance pavilion, commercial and amusement facilities, and space for "experimental sound, photography, and metal labs"; an "intensive" community recreation facility with an outdoor/indoor swim complex adaptable for winter skating, tennis courts, ten fields, a public sailing dock, and bike rental; a four-year liberal arts college known as the Anacostia Uptown Center, with physical education facilities and a combined college-marine recreation development, including enough space for shell racing and a small marina with boat dockage, yacht club facilities, and launch ramps; a river park known as the Anacostia-Bolling Development, with boat-docking facilities, vistas, promenades, a cultural/recreation center including space for dancing and an amphitheater, and neighborhood recreation centers with space for field sports, court games, gym facilities, and picnics; and finally, a 150-acre eighteen-hole golf course in the Oxon Cove Area, with a large-scale marina with a public yacht club, a children's farm, and a tree nursery.

39. WHD, April 17, 1968; CTJ, in transcript, Beautification Committee Meeting, April 17, 1968, LBJL.

40. Walter Washington, "Remarks of Mayor Walter Washington at the First Lady's Beautification Luncheon in the East Room," Washington, D.C., April 17, 1968, WHSF Beautification, Box 6, "Mayor's Remarks [on LB's legacy]," LBJL.

41. Ibid.
42. WHD, April 17, 1968.

Chapter 25: Resurrection

1. WHD, May 2, 1968.
2. Coretta Scott King and Rev. Dr. Barbara Reynolds, *My Life, My Love, My Legacy* (New York: Henry Holt and Co., 2017), p. 180.
3. Elsie Carper, "Mother's Day Parade Opens Drive by Poor," *Washington Post, Times Herald,* May 13, 1968; Charles Conoci, "King's Widow to Open March with Mother's Day Parade," (Washington, D.C.) *Sunday Star,* May 12, 1968.
4. Ben A. Franklin, "5,000 Open Poor People's Campaign in Washington," *NYT,* May 13, 1968.
5. Califano, *Triumph and Tragedy,* p. 289.
6. Ben A. Franklin, "Capital Prepares for Poor's March," *NYT,* May 12, 1968.
7. Carolyn Lewis, "Resurrection City Women Confront D.C. Counterparts," *Washington Post, Times Herald,* May 26, 1968.
8. Lauren Pearlman, "More Than a March: The Poor People's Campaign in the District," *Washington History* 26, no. 2 (Fall 2014): 29; Nash Castro, author interview, May 25, 2014.
9. Ben A. Franklin, "City of the Poor Begun in Capital," *NYT,* May 12, 1968.
10. Paul W. Valentine, "Marshals Picked from Gangs," *Washington Post, Times Herald,* May 17, 1968; John Wiebenson, "Planning and Using Resurrection City," *Journal of the American Institute of Planners* 35, no. 6 (November 1969): 410–11; Gloria Billings, "Health Care in Resurrection City," *American Journal of Nursing* 68, no. 8 (August 1968): 1695–98.
11. Gertrude Wilson, "An Inside Look in Resurrection City," *New York Amsterdam News,* June 8, 1968; Gertrude Wilson, "Explaining Resurrection City," *New York Amsterdam News,* July 13, 1968; Justine Priestley, *By Gertrude Wilson: Dispatches of the 1960s, from a White Writer in a Black World* (Edgartown, MA: Vineyard Stories, 2005). In 1974, Priestley moved permanently to Oak Bluffs, on Martha's Vineyard, where her editor, James Hicks, and the paper's publisher, C. B. Powell, also had homes.
12. "Obituary: S. Dillon Ripley Dies at 87; Led the Smithsonian Institution During Its Greatest Growth," *NYT,* March 31, 2001; Wolf Von Eckardt, "The Capital's Dashing Suitor of Culture," *Washington Post, Times Herald,* October 23, 1966.
13. Nan Robertson, "City of the Poor Develops Style All Its Own," *NYT,* May 24, 1968.

14. Gertrude Wilson, "Poor and Non-Poor March in D.C.," *New York Amsterdam News,* June 22, 1968; Lillian Wiggins, "'Woman Power' Major Factor in Solidarity Day Activities," *Baltimore Afro-American,* June 22, 1968; Faith Berry, "The Anger and Problems and Sickness of the Poor of the Whole Nation Were in This One Shantytown," *NYT Magazine,* July 7, 1968; Leonard Downie, Jr., and Robert G. Kaiser, reported by Irma Moore and Bernadette Carey, "Mrs. King Lifts Spirits of Poor," *Washington Post, Times Herald,* May 31, 1968; Judith Martin,"Rosa Parks Lives in Detroit and Doesn't Mind a Back Seat," *Washington Post, Times Herald,* June 3, 1968.
15. WHD, May 1, 1968.
16. Ibid.

Chapter 26: "Claudia All of My Life"

1. Tye, *Bobby Kennedy,* p. 431.
2. "Transcript of Kennedy Primary Victory Speech," *NYT,* June 6, 1968.
3. WHD, June 4, 1968.
4. WHD, June 5, 1968; CTJ DD, June 5, 1968; PDD, June 5, 1968.
5. Ibid.
6. Califano, *Triumph and Tragedy,* p. 298.
7. Longley, *LBJ's 1968,* p. 141.
8. WHD, June 5, 1968.
9. Clifford and Holbrooke, *Counsel to the President,* p. 544.
10. WHD, June 5, 1968.
11. LBJ, "Address to the Nation Following the Attack on Senator Kennedy," Washington, D.C., June 5, 1968, American Presidency Project, https://www.presidency.ucsb.edu/node/237145.
12. Ibid.
13. Ibid.
14. Richard Pearson, "Former Ala. Gov. George C. Wallace Dies," *Washington Post,* September 14, 1998; James T. Patterson, *Brown v. Board of Education: A Civil Rights Milestone and Its Troubled Legacy* (Oxford: Oxford University Press, 2001), p. 154.
15. Longley, *LBJ's 1968,* p. 143; LBJ, "Address to the Nation Following the Attack on Senator Kennedy."
16. LBJ, "Letter to the President of the Senate and to the Speaker of the House Urging Passage of an Effective Gun Control Law," June 6, 1968, American Presidency Project, https://www.presidency.ucsb.edu/documents/letter-the

-president-the-senate-and-the-speaker-the-house-urging-passage-effective-gun.

17. James Jeffrey, "How Robert Kennedy's Assassination Emboldened the NRA for 50 years," *Guardian*, June 5, 2018.
18. PDD, June 7, 1968; WHD, June 7, 1968; photograph contact sheet, June 7, 1968, 1968-06-07-D452, White House Photo Office Collection, LBJL.
19. WHD, June 8, 1968.
20. WHD, June 8, 1968; Bernstein's rendition prompted Jackie Kennedy to write the conductor a thank-you note, stating, "When your Mahler started to fill (but that is the wrong word—because it was more this sensitive trembling) the Cathedral today—I thought it the most beautiful music I had ever heard. I am so glad I didn't know it—it was this strange music of all the gods who were crying. And then—if only you could have seen it—it was the time when Ethel had thought of the most touching thing—having the littlest nephews and nieces, small children, before that terrifying array of Cardinals and gold and Gothic vaults, carry all the little vessels for Communion up to the high altar, so that they could have some part in the farewell to the uncle they all loved so much. They were so vulnerable—and your music was everything in my heart, of peace and pain and such drowning beauty. You could just close your eyes and be lost in it forever." "June 6 and 8, 1968: Bernstein, Mahler, and Remembering Robert F. 'Bobby' Kennedy," The Bernstein Experience, June 5, 2018, https://bernstein.classical.org/features/june-1968-remembering-robert-f-kennedy/.
21. WHD, June 8, 1968; George Bernard Shaw, *Back to Methuselah*, act 1, in *Selected Plays with Prefaces*, vol. 2 (New York: Dodd, Mead and Co., 1948).
22. WHD, June 8, 1968.
23. Ibid.
24. Mary McGrory, "A Gifted Man Is Gone," June 9, 1968, in Phil Gailey, ed., *The Best of Mary McGrory: A Half Century of Washington Commentary*.
25. WHD, June 8, 1968.
26. Francis X. Clines, "Is Everybody All Right?," *NYT*, June 22, 2009.
27. WHD, June 8, 1968.
28. WHD, April 8, 1964.
29. Califano, *Triumph and Tragedy*, p. 303.
30. WHD, June 8, 1968.
31. Eve Edstrom, "Funeral in NY, Burial Here Today," *Washington Post, Times Herald*, June 8, 1968.
32. WHD, June 8, 1968.
33. Joseph A. Califano, Jr., quoted in WHD, June 8, 1968.

34. Max Frankel, "Johnson and Kennedy," *NYT*, June 9, 1968.
35. WHD, June 8, 1968.
36. Robert F. Levey, "Bulldozers Level Tent City," *Washington Post, Times Herald*, June 26, 1968.
37. OH transcript, Sharon Francis interview 3 (III), by Dorothy Pierce McSweeny, June 27, 1969, pp. 16–17, LBJL (hereafter cited as Francis OH 3).
38. Whitney Young, "Full Remarks of Whitney M. Young Jr. AIA Annual Convention in Portland, Oregon June 1968," American Institute of Architects (AIA), http://content.aia.org/sites/default/files/2018-04/WhitneyYoungJr_1968AIAContention_FullSpeech.pdf; "Commemorating 50 Years: Whitney M. Young Jr.'s 1968 AIA Convention Speech," AIA, https://www.aia.org/resources/189666-commemorating-50-years.
39. Young, "Full Remarks."
40. Press release, "The 'B.Y. Morrison Memorial Lecture,' by Mrs. Lyndon B. Johnson at the Convention of the American Institute of Architects, Portland, Oregon," June 26, 1968, "Mrs. Johnson—Speeches," Reference File, LBJL.
41. Ibid.
42. See, for example, Sarah Williams Goldhagen, *Welcome to Your World: How the Built Environment Shapes Our Lives* (New York: HarperCollins, 2017).
43. "The 'B.Y. Morrison Memorial Lecture' "; "Mrs. Johnson Asks 'New Conservation' on a Human Scale," *Washington Post, Times Herald*, June 27, 1968.
44. "The 'B.Y. Morrison Memorial Lecture.' "
45. WHD, June 26, 1968.

Chapter 27: "Over by Choice"

1. WHD, August 10, 1968.
2. LBJ, *Vantage Point*, pp. 547–48.
3. WHD, August 1, 1968.
4. Arthur M. Schlesinger, Jr., *Robert Kennedy and His Times*, 40th Anniversary Edition (Boston: Mariner Books, 2002), p. 234.
5. WHD, August 9, 1968; "Alabama Gov. George Wallace on Meet the Press—June 30, 1968 (audio only)," YouTube, https://www.youtube.com/watch?v=7VXPxJzUzqU.
6. WHD, August 9, 1968.
7. Notes, Sharon Francis, "re Highway Program," August 2, 1968, WHSF Beautification, Box 6, "DC Freeways, 12/67–08/19/68 SF memo & notes," LBJL. The explanation for Washington's non-action remains unclear.

8. Francis OH.
9. LBJ, "Statement by the President upon Signing the Federal-Aid Highway Act of 1968," Austin, TX, August 24, 1968, American Presidency Project, https://www.presidency.ucsb.edu/node/237643.
10. Lewis L. Gould, *Lady Bird Johnson and the Environment* (Lawrence: University Press of Kansas, 1988), pp. 194–95; memo, Sharon Francis to Lady Bird Johnson, August 22, 1968, WHSF Alpha, Box 151, "Beautification (Memos)," LBJL; LBJ, "Statement by the President upon Signing the Federal-Aid Highway Act of 1968."
11. Sylvan Fox, "Guard Told to Shoot If Defied in Chicago," *NYT,* August 24, 1968.
12. Timothy Burke, "When Aretha Franklin's Star-Spangled Banner Drew a Torrent of Racial Abuse," *Daily Beast,* August 17, 2018, https://www.thedailybeast.com/when-aretha-franklins-star-spangled-banner-drew-a-torrent-of-racial-abuse.
13. CTJ DD, August 26, 1968; Longley, *LBJ's 1968,* p. 216.
14. Dallek, *Flawed Giant,* p. 572; Longley, *LBJ's 1968,* p. 204; Judith A. Nelson, "Drafting Lyndon Johnson: The President's Secret Role in the 1968 Democratic Convention," *Presidential Studies Quarterly* 30, no. 4 (December 2000): 688–713.
15. WHD, August 27, 1968.
16. "Johnson Says He's Not Running for Anything but Rocking Chair," *NYT,* August 25, 1968.
17. WHD, August 27, 1968.
18. Ibid.; "The President's News Conference Held on His 60th Birthday at Austin, Texas," August 27, 1968, American Presidency Project, https://www.presidency.ucsb.edu/documents/the-presidents-news-conference-held-his-60th-birthday-austin-texas.
19. "Johnson Mocked as a 'Freak' at 'Unbirthday Party,'" *NYT,* August 27, 1968.
20. "CBS News' Dan Rather gets roughed up while trying to interview a Georgia delegate," *CBS News,* July 25, 2016, https://www.cbsnews.com/video/1968-cbs-news-dan-rather-gets-roughed-up-while-trying-to-interview-a-georgia-delegate/.
21. WHD, August 27, 1968.
22. Michael Lind, "Buckley vs. Vidal: The Real Story," *Politico,* August 24, 2015, https://www.politico.com/magazine/story/2015/08/buckley-vs-vidal-the-real-story-121673; Hendrik Hertzberg, "Buckley, Vidal, and the 'Queer' Question," *New Yorker,* July 31, 2015, https://www.newyorker.com/news/daily-comment/buckley-vidal-and-the-queer-question.

23. Califano, *Triumph and Tragedy*, p. 322; Goodwin, *Lyndon Johnson and the American Dream*, pp. 350–51; Dallek, *Flawed Giant*, p. 572.
24. PDD, August 28, 1968.
25. Photograph contact sheet, August 28, 1968, 1968-08-28-A6700, White House Photo Collection, LBJL.

Epilogue: To Survive All Assaults, January 1969–July 2007

1. WHD, January 20, 1969.
2. WHD, December 18, 1968.
3. Ibid.
4. Julie Nixon Eisenhower, *Pat Nixon: The Untold Story* (New York: Simon & Schuster, 1986), p. 251.
5. WHD, January 20, 1969.
6. Ibid.; "Gloomy Day Casts a Pall over Inauguration Mood," *NYT*, January 21, 1969.
7. WHD, January 20, 1969.
8. John A. Farrell, "Nixon's Vietnam Treachery," *NYT*, December 31, 2016; Farrell, *Nixon*, pp. 342–43.
9. LBJ, *Vantage Point*, pp. 566–67.
10. Ibid., p. 565.
11. The president also awarded the Medal of Freedom to Gregory Peck, Ralph Ellison, Roy Wilkins, and Whitney Young, Jr.
12. It may be apocryphal, but lore has it that when the plane took off for Texas, LBJ lit his first cigarette since his heart attack in 1955.
13. WHD, January 20, 1968.
14. Robert Semple, Jr., "Nixon Hails Johnson Birthday and Dedicates a Park," *NYT*, August 28, 1969.
15. Ibid.
16. Ronald Reagan, while speaking before the Western Wood Products Association in San Francisco, March 12, 1966, said, "We've got to recognize that where the preservation of a natural resource like the redwoods is concerned, that there is a common sense limit. I mean, if you've looked at a hundred thousand acres or so of trees—you know, a tree is a tree, how many more do you need to look at?" Subsequently, a campaign staffer to Governor Pat Brown summarized the quote as "If you've seen one redwood, you've seen them all." Lou Cannon, *Governor Reagan: His Rise to Power* (New York: PublicAffairs, 2003), pp. 299–300; Thomas H. Harris, "How Many Trees Do You Need to See? Said the Governor," *NYT*, June 24, 1973.

17. Semple, "Nixon Hails Johnson Birthday and Dedicates a Park."

18. Richard Nixon, "Annual Message to the Congress on the State of the Union," January 22, 1970, American Presidency Project, https://www.presidency.ucsb.edu/node/241063.

19. "Opinion: Bill Ruckelshaus, Conservationist Who Also Protected the Rule of Law," NPR, November 30, 2019, https://www.npr.org/2019/11/30/783752250/opinion-bill-ruckelshaus-conservationist-who-also-protected-the-rule-of-law.

20. David R. Jones, "Ceremony in Capital Led by President as 400 Attend," *NYT,* January 9, 1969; Grace Glueck, "Hirshhorn Museum Unveiled in Capital," *NYT,* October 2, 1974; Henry Mitchell, "The Hirshhorn's Grand Opening," *Washington Post,* October 2, 1974; Sally Quinn, "Hirshhorn II: Night of the 'Important Ones,'" *Washington Post,* October 3, 1974.

21. Crucial leadership for passage of the 1973 District of Columbia Home Rule Act was provided by the new District Committee chair, Congressman Charles Diggs, the first African American from Michigan elected to the House and a champion of home rule. Asch and Musgrove, *Chocolate City,* p. 379.

22. Asch and Musgrove, *Chocolate City,* pp. 379–81.

23. Bob Levey and Jane Freundel Levey, "End of the Roads," *Washington Post Magazine,* November 26, 2000; Harry Jaffe, "The Insane Highway Plan That Would Have Bulldozed DC's Most Charming Neighborhoods," *Washingtonian,* October 21, 2015.

24. Halprin's single most material imprint on the nation's capital would come in precisely the area he and Lady Bird had once cast aside, monumental Washington. In the 1970s, he began competing to design a monument to another president. Completed three decades later, under the patronage of another First Lady and her husband, Hillary and Bill Clinton, Halprin designed a monument on the National Mall to honor Franklin Delano Roosevelt, the very president whose New Deal legacy Lady Bird and Lyndon had so consciously felt themselves put on this earth to expand. The only monument to Lyndon Johnson near Washington, D.C., is not on the National Mall but on the way to an airport, one now named after another president, Ronald Reagan. Adjacent to the area of Southeast that was razed in the 1950s, the Navy Yard now comprises an array of sports facilities, restaurants, businesses, and public recreation spaces, including a large public fountain designed by the New York firm founded by Paul Freiberg, one of the two designers of the Buchanan School's play space championed by Lady Bird Johnson. Lawrence Halprin Collection, "014.II.A.004 Anacos-

tia Park; project files, 6735," Architectural Archives, University of Pennsylvania; Paul Hodge, "Congress Votes for $26 Million FDR Memorial," *Washington Post,* July 15, 1982; Benjamin Forgey, "Commission Approves FDR Memorial, $47 Million Design to Be 'Gardenesque,'" *Washington Post,* June 22, 1990; Benjamin Forgey, "A Natural Choice to Honor FDR: Landscape Architect Lawrence Halprin Planted an Idea That Blossomed," *Washington Post,* April 30, 1997; Kriston Capps, "D.C.'s Vacant Stadium Dilemma," *City Lab,* November 7, 2019, https://www.citylab.com/equity/2019/11/rfk-stadium-dc-housing-development-sports-arena-demolition/601552/.

25. Lady Bird Johnson, speech at 1977 National Women's Conference, Sam Houston Coliseum, Houston, TX, Texas Archive of the Moving Image, 15:54, https://texasarchive.org/2013_02597.

26. Garrett Epps, "The Equal Rights Amendment Strikes Again," *Atlantic,* January 20, 2019, https://www.theatlantic.com/ideas/archive/2019/01/will-congress-ever-ratify-equal-rights-amendment/580849/.

27. The citation for Lady Bird's Presidential Medal of Freedom read, "One of America's great First Ladies, she claimed her own place in the hearts and history of the American people. In councils of power or in homes of the poor, she made government human with her unique compassion and her grace, warmth and wisdom. Her leadership transformed the American landscape and preserved its natural beauty as a national treasure." Mrs. Johnson was honored with more than fifty awards over her lifetime and more than fifteen honorary degrees. *First Lady: Lady Bird Johnson, 1912–2007, Memorial Tributes in the One Hundred Tenth Congress of the United States* (Washington, D.C.: U.S. Government Printing Office, 2008), pp. 36–37; "Awards Presented to Lady Bird Johnson," LBJL, http://www.lbjlibrary.org/lyndon-baines-johnson/lady-bird-johnson/awards.

28. Adrian Higgins, "The Value of Beautification," *Washington Post,* October 21, 2012; Kathleen A. Bergeron, "The Environmental First Lady," *Public Roads,* March/April 2008, pp. 16–23; Margaret Biser, "Lady Bird Johnson's Floral Legacy," White House Historical Association, https://www.whitehousehistory.org/lady-bird-johnsons-floral-legacy.

29. "Lady Bird Johnson Forever Stamp Sheet Dedicated Today," U.S. Postal Service, November 30, 2012, https://about.usps.com/news/national-releases/2012/pr12_141.htm; Sonia Smith, "Lady Bird Johnson Forever," *Texas Monthly,* January 21, 2013.

30. Harry Middleton, author interview, March 6, 2014; Caroli, *Lady Bird and Lyndon,* pp. 395–96.

31. CTJ as quoted in Williams, *The Hour of Land,* pp. 263–65.

32. Ibid.
33. Enid Nemy, "Obituary: Lady Bird Johnson, 94, Former U.S. First Lady," *NYT*, July 12, 2007; Liz Carpenter, "In Tribute," in *First Lady: Lady Bird Johnson*, pp. xxxv–xxxvi.
34. Lucinda Robb, in *First Lady: Lady Bird Johnson*, pp. liii–lv.

Bibliography

Archives and Libraries Consulted

Significant Archival Holdings
Consulted at the LBJ Presidential Library, Austin, Texas

Post-presidential Papers
  Name File
  Reference Files

Pre-presidential Confidential File

Presidential Papers

Diaries and Appointment Logs

National Security File

Office of the President File

Special File on the Assassination of John F. Kennedy

Statements of LBJ

White House Central Files 11/22/1963–1/20/1969
  Subject Files
  White House Names Files
  Confidential Files

White House Social Files

Pentagon Papers

White House Naval Photographic Center Films, 12/22/1963–1/20/1969

Mrs. Johnson's Home Movies, 1940–ca. 1969

White House Photo Office Collection, 11/22/1963–1/20/1969

Sound Recordings of President Lyndon B. Johnson, 11/22/1963–1/17/1969

Personal Papers of Lyndon and Lady Bird Johnson, 1934–1968

Lady Bird Johnson's White House Diary, 1963–1970

Personal Papers
  Bess Abell Papers

Lindy Boggs
Joseph A. Califano
Elizabeth S. Carpenter
Leslie Carpenter
John B. Connally
Walter Jenkins
Lady Bird Johnson

Other Archives and Libraries Consulted

John F. Kennedy Presidential Library and Museum, Boston, Massachusetts

Library of Congress
Papers of Katie Louchheim
McCall's magazine

University of Arizona Libraries, Special Collections, Tucson, Arizona
Papers of Stewart L. Udall

The Architectural Archives of the University of Pennsylvania, Philadelphia, Pennsylvania
Lawrence Halprin Collection

Manuscripts and Archives, Yale University Library, New Haven, Connecticut
Abe Fortas Papers

The Arthur and Elizabeth Schlesinger Library on the History of Women in America, Radcliffe Institute for Advanced Study, Harvard University, Cambridge, Massachusetts
Papers of Mary Ingraham Bunting-Smith
Papers of Virginia Foster Durr
Papers of Catherine Atwater Galbraith
Papers of Nan Robertson

Records of the Radcliffe College Office of Public Information, 1923–2005

The Historical Society of Washington, D.C.

New York Public Library, Manuscripts and Archives Division, New York, New York
Papers of Arthur M. Schlesinger, Jr.

Richard Nixon Presidential Library and Museum, Yorba Linda, California

Special Collections Research Center, The George Washington University, Washington, D.C.
Papers of Walter E. Fauntroy
Papers of Polly Shackleton

Miller Center, University of Virginia, Charlottesville, Virginia
Johnson Secret White House Recordings Collection

American Presidency Project, University of California, Santa Barbara

Rockefeller Archive Center, Sleepy Hollow, New York
 Laurance Rockefeller Collection
 Taconic Foundation Records

Dolph Briscoe Center for American History, University of Texas at Austin, Austin, Texas

Smithsonian Institution Archives

Personal Papers of Nash Castro, Dallas, Texas

Interviews and Correspondence with Author

Bess Abell

Tyler Abell

Charles A. Birbaum

Joseph A. Califano, Jr.

Nash Castro

Antonia Chayes

Barbara Cline

Robert Dallek

Samuel Farr

Sharon Francis

Michael Gillette

Benjamin Grant

Dalia Halprin

Tom Hayden

Shirley James

Tom Johnson

James R. "Jim" Jones

Bennetta Jules-Rosette

Robert Kanigel

Jon Meacham

Elizabeth K. Meyer

Harry Middleton

Ann Rachlin

Jeffrey Rosen

Clarissa Rowe

James H. Rowe III

Jeff Shesol
Larry Temple
Luanne Temple
Betty Tilson
Thomas Stewart Udall
Darren Walker
Peter Yarrow

Oral Histories

Bess Abell
Stewart Alsop
Hale Boggs
Lindy Boggs
Pat Brown
Gordon Bunshaft
Horace Busby
Elizabeth Carpenter
Leslie Carpenter
Clifton C. Carter
Nash Castro
Douglass Cater
Marie Fehmer Chiarodo
George Christian
Ramsey Clark
Clark M. Clifford
John Connally
C. Douglas Dillon
Virginia Foster Durr
Fred Farr
Abe Fortas
Sharon Francis
Joe B. Frantz
Orville L. Freeman
Ashton G. Gonella
Katharine Graham

George B. Hartzog
John W. Hechinger
Hubert H. Humphrey, Jr.
Walter Jenkins
Claudia "Lady Bird" Johnson
Luci Baines Johnson
Jim Jones
Barbara Jordan
Nicholas Katzenbach
Edward Kennedy
James R. Ketchum
Arthur B. Krim
Erich Leinsdorf
Katie Louchheim
Thurgood Marshall
Robert S. McNamara
Harry C. McPherson
Kenneth P. O'Donnell
Jacqueline Kennedy Onassis
Nathaniel Owings
Drew Pearson
Katherine Peden
J. J. (Jake) Pickle
Devier Pierson
George E. Reedy
S. Dillon Ripley
Lynda Johnson Robb
Laurance Rockefeller
Nelson Rockefeller
Walt W. Rostow
Elizabeth Rowe
Dean Rusk
Arthur M. Schlesinger, Jr.
Larry Temple
Helen Thomas

Stewart L. Udall

Cyrus R. Vance

Earl Warren

Walter and Bennetta Washington

Robert C. Weaver

Roy Wilkins

Books Consulted

Anderson, Carol. *One Person, No Vote: How Voter Suppression Is Destroying Our Democracy*. New York: Bloomsbury Publishing, 2018.

Asch, Chris Myers, and George Derek Musgrove. *Chocolate City: A History of Race and Democracy in the Nation's Capital*. Chapel Hill: University of North Carolina Press, 2017.

Barker-Benfield, G. J., and Catherine Clinton. *Portraits of American Women: From Settlement to the Present*. New York: Oxford University Press, 1998.

Barnet, Andrea. *Visionary Women: How Rachel Carson, Jane Jacobs, Jane Goodall, and Alice Waters Changed Our World*. New York: Ecco/HarperCollins, 2018.

Beard, Mary. *Women and Power: A Manifesto*. New York: Liveright Publishing Corporation, 2017.

Bernstein, Irving. *Guns or Butter: The Presidency of Lyndon Johnson*. New York: Oxford University Press, 1996.

Beschloss, Michael R., ed. *Reaching for Glory: Lyndon Johnson's Secret White House Tapes, 1964–1965*. New York: Touchstone, 2002.

Bird, Kai, and Martin J. Sherwin. *American Prometheus: The Triumph and Tragedy of J. Robert Oppenheimer*. New York: Vintage Books, 2005.

Boggs, Lindy, and Katherine Hatch. *Washington Through a Purple Veil: Memoirs of a Southern Woman*. New York: Harcourt Brace, 1994.

Brammer, Billy Lee. *The Gay Place*. Austin: University of Texas Press, 1961.

Branch, Taylor. *At Canaan's Edge: America in the King Years, 1965–68*. New York: Simon & Schuster, 2007.

———. *Pillar of Fire: America in the King Years, 1963–65*. New York: Simon & Schuster, 1999.

Brownmiller, Susan. "Jane Jacobs." In *Ideas That Matter: The Worlds of Jane Jacobs*, edited by Max Allen, pp. 22–23. Owens Sound, Ontario: Ginger Press, 1997. Previously published in *Vogue*, May 1969.

Bugliosi, Vincent. *Reclaiming History: The Assassination of President John F. Kennedy*. New York: W. W. Norton and Company, 2007.

Califano, Joseph A. *The Triumph and Tragedy of Lyndon Johnson: The White House Years.* New York: Atria Books, 2015.

Cannon, Lou. *Governor Reagan: His Rise to Power.* New York: PublicAffairs, 2003.

Caro, Robert A. *Master of the Senate.* Vol. 3 of *The Years of Lyndon Johnson.* New York: Alfred A. Knopf, 2002.

———. *Means of Ascent.* Vol. 2 of *The Years of Lyndon Johnson.* New York: Alfred A. Knopf, 1990.

———. *The Passage of Power.* Vol. 4 of *The Years of Lyndon Johnson.* New York: Alfred A. Knopf, 2012.

———. *The Path to Power.* Vol. 1 of *The Years of Lyndon Johnson.* New York. Vintage, 1990.

Caroli, Betty Boyd. *Lady Bird and Lyndon: The Hidden Story of a Marriage That Made a President.* New York: Simon & Schuster, 2015.

Carpenter, Liz. *Ruffles and Flourishes: The Warm and Tender Story of a Simple Girl Who Found Adventure in the White House.* College Station: Texas A&M University Press, c. 1970, 1993.

Carson, Rachel. *Silent Spring.* Boston: Houghton Mifflin, 1962.

Carter, Dan T. *The Politics of Rage: George Wallace, the Origins of the New Conservatism, and the Transformation of American Politics,* 2nd Edition. Baton Rouge: Louisiana State University Press, 2000.

Charters, Ann, ed. *The Portable Sixties Reader.* New York: Penguin Books, 2002.

Clarke, Thurston. *The Last Campaign: Robert F. Kennedy and 82 Days That Inspired America.* New York: Henry Holt and Co., 2008.

Clifford, Clark M., and Richard C. Holbrooke. *Counsel to the President: A Memoir.* New York: Doubleday, 1991.

Collins, Gail. *America's Women: 400 Years of Dolls, Drudges, Helpmates, and Heroines.* New York: HarperCollins, 2003.

———. *When Everything Changed: The Amazing Journey of American Women from 1960 to the Present.* New York: Little, Brown, 2009.

Cook, Blanche Wiesen. *Eleanor Roosevelt.* Vol. 2, *The Defining Years, 1933–1938.* New York: Penguin Books, 2000.

Coontz, Stephanie. *A Strange Stirring: "The Feminine Mystique" and American Women at the Dawn of the 1960s.* New York: Basic Books, 2011.

Cross, James U., Denise Gamino, and Gary Rice. *Around the World with LBJ: My Wild Ride as Air Force One Pilot, White House Aide, and Personal Confidant.* Austin: University of Texas Press, 2008.

Dallek, Robert. *Camelot's Court: Inside the Kennedy White House.* New York: HarperCollins, 2013.

———. *Flawed Giant: Lyndon Johnson and His Times, 1961–1973.* New York: Oxford University Press, 1998.

———. *Franklin D. Roosevelt: A Political Life.* New York: Viking/Penguin Random House, 2017.

———. *Lone Star Rising: Lyndon Johnson and His Times, 1908–60.* New York: Oxford University Press, 2006.

———. *Lyndon B. Johnson: Portrait of a President.* New York: Oxford University Press, 2012.

———. *Nixon and Kissinger: Partners in Power.* New York: HarperCollins, 2007.

DeFerrari, John. *Lost Washington, D.C.* Charleston, SC: History Press, 2011.

Dickerson, John. *On Her Trail: My Mother, Nancy Dickerson, TV News' First Woman Star.* New York: Simon & Schuster, 2006.

Dickerson, Nancy. *Among Those Present: A Reporter's View of Twenty-five Years in Washington.* New York: Random House, 1976.

Didion, Joan. *Slouching Towards Bethlehem: Essays.* New York: Open Road Integrated, 2017.

Dobrynin, Anatoly. *In Confidence: Moscow's Ambassador to Six Cold War Presidents.* Seattle: University of Washington Press, 1995.

Durr, Virginia Foster, and Hollinger F. Barnard. *Outside the Magic Circle: The Autobiography of Virginia Foster Durr.* Tuscaloosa: Alabama University Press, 1990.

Eagles, Charles W., ed. *The Civil Rights Movement in America.* Jackson: University Press of Mississippi, 1986.

Einberger, Scott. *With Distance in His Eyes: The Environmental Life and Legacy of Stewart Udall.* Reno: University of Nevada Press, 2018.

Eisenhower, Julie Nixon. *Pat Nixon: The Untold Story.* New York: Simon & Schuster, 1986.

Farrell, John A. *Richard Nixon: The Life.* New York: Vintage/Penguin Random House, 2018.

Friedan, Betty. *The Feminine Mystique.* New York: W. W. Norton and Company, 2013.

Garson, Barbara. *MacBird!* New York: Grove Press, 1967.

Gibbs, Nancy, and Michael Duffy. *The Preacher and the Presidents: Billy Graham in the White House.* New York: Center Street, 2007.

Gillette, Howard, Jr. *Between Justice and Beauty: Race, Planning, and the Failure of Urban Policy in Washington, D.C.* Philadelphia: University of Pennsylvania Press, 2006.

Gillette, Michael L. *Lady Bird Johnson: An Oral History.* New York: Oxford University Press, 2012.

Goldberg, Dorothy Kurgans. *A Private View of a Public Life.* New York: Charterhouse, 1975.

Goldhagen, Sarah Williams. *Welcome to Your World: How the Built Environment Shapes Our Lives.* New York: HarperCollins, 2017.

Goldman, Eric Frederick. *The Tragedy of Lyndon Johnson.* London: Macdonald, 1969.

Goodwin, Doris Kearns. *Leadership in Turbulent Times.* New York: Simon & Schuster, 2018.

———. *Lyndon Johnson and the American Dream.* New York: St. Martin's Press, 1991.

———. *No Ordinary Time: Franklin and Eleanor Roosevelt; The Home Front in World War II.* Various editions. New York: Simon & Schuster, 2013.

Gould, Lewis L. *Lady Bird Johnson and the Environment.* Lawrence: University Press of Kansas, 1988.

———. *Lady Bird Johnson: Our Environmental First Lady.* Lawrence: University Press of Kansas, 1999.

Graham, Wade. *Dream Cities: Seven Urban Ideas That Shape the World.* New York: HarperCollins, 2016.

Greek, Mark S. *Washington, D.C., Protests: Scenes from Home Rule to the Civil Rights Movement.* Charleston, SC: History Press, 2009.

Gruen, Victor. *The Heart of Our Cities: The Urban Crisis; Diagnosis and Cure.* New York: Simon & Schuster, 1964.

Halberstam, David. *The Best and the Brightest.* New York: Random House, 1972.

———. *The Powers That Be.* New York: Alfred A. Knopf, 1979.

Halprin, Lawrence. *Cities.* New York: Reinhold Publishing Corporation, 1963.

———. *A Life Spent Changing Places.* Philadelphia: University of Pennsylvania Press, 2011.

Harvey, Brett. *The Fifties: A Women's Oral History.* New York: ASJA Press, 1993.

Hayden, Tom. *The Long Sixties: From 1960 to Barack Obama.* London: Routledge, 2015.

Heymann, C. David. *The Georgetown Ladies' Social Club: Power, Passion, and Politics in the Nation's Capital.* New York: Atria Books, 2003.

Hill, Clint, and Lisa McCubbin. *Mrs. Kennedy and Me.* New York: Gallery Books, 2012.

Hyra, Derek S. *Race, Class, and Politics in the Cappuccino City.* Chicago: University of Chicago Press, 2017.

Isenberg, Alison. *Designing San Francisco: Art, Land, and Urban Renewal in the City by the Bay.* Princeton, NJ: Princeton University Press, 2017.

Isserman, Maurice, and Michael Kazin. *America Divided: The Civil War of the 1960s*. 5th ed. New York: Oxford University Press, 2015.

Jaffe, Harry, and Tom Sherwood. *Dream City: Race, Power, and the Decline of Washington, D.C.* 20th anniv. ed. New York: Argo-Navis Author Services, 2014.

Janeway, Elizabeth. *Between Myth and Morning: Women Awakening*. New York: Morrow, 1974.

———. *Man's World, Woman's Place: A Study in Social Mythology*. London: M. Joseph, 1972.

———. *Women: Their Changing Roles*. New York: New York Times Books, 1973.

Johnson, Lady Bird. *A White House Diary*. New York: Holt, Rinehart and Winston, 1970.

Johnson, Lyndon B. *The Vantage Point: Perspectives of the Presidency, 1963–1969*. New York: Holt, Rinehart and Winston, 1971.

Kaiser, Charles. *1968 in America: Music, Politics, Chaos, Counterculture*. 30th anniv. ed. New York: Grove Press, 2018.

Kanigel, Robert. *Eyes on the Street: The Life of Jane Jacobs*. New York: Vintage Books, 2017.

Keefer, Edward C., and Charles S. Sampson. *Foreign Relations of the United States, 1964–1968*. Vol. 1, *Vietnam, 1964*. Washington, D.C.: U.S. Government Printing Office, 2010.

Kennedy, Jacqueline. Interview by Arthur M. Schlesinger, Jr. In *Jacqueline Kennedy: Historic Conversations on Life with John F. Kennedy*. New York: Hyperion, 1964.

Kennedy, Peggy Wallace. *The Broken Road: George Wallace and a Daughter's Journey to Reconciliation*. New York: Bloomsbury Publishing, 2019.

King, Coretta Scott, and Rev. Dr. Barbara Reynolds. *My Life, My Love, My Legacy*. New York: Henry Holt and Co., 2017.

Kurlansky, Mark. *1968: The Year That Rocked the World*. New York: Random House Trade Paperbacks, 2005.

Lawson, Laura J. *City Bountiful: A Century of Community Gardening in America*. Berkeley: University of California Press, 2005.

LePere, Gene Hirshhorn. *Little Man in a Big Hurry: The Life of Joseph H. Hirshhorn, Uranium King and Art Collector*. New York: Vantage Press, 2009.

Lepore, Jill. *These Truths: A History of the United States*. New York: W. W. Norton and Company, 2018.

Leslie, Warren. *Dallas, Public and Private*. New York: Grossman Publishers, 1964.

Liebow, Elliot. *Tally's Corner: A Study of Negro Streetcorner Men*. Lanham, MD: Rowman and Littlefield, 2003.

Longley, Kyle. *LBJ's 1968: Power, Politics, and the Presidency in America's Year of Upheaval.* Cambridge, UK: Cambridge University Press, 2018.

Mailer, Norman. *Miami and the Siege of Chicago: An Informal History of the Republican and Democratic Conventions of 1968.* New York: Random House Trade Paperbacks, 2016.

Manchester, William. *The Death of a President: November 20–November 25, 1963.* New York: Little, Brown/Back Bay, 2013.

Mannes, Marya. *Out of My Time.* London: V. Gollancz, 1972.

Marton, Kati. *Hidden Power: Presidential Marriages That Shaped Our History.* New York, NY: Pantheon Books, 2001.

McDowell, Marta. *All the Presidents' Gardens: Madison's Cabbages to Kennedy's Roses; How the White House Grounds Have Grown with America.* Portland, OR: Timber Press, 2016.

McGrory, Mary. *The Best of Mary McGrory: A Half Century of Washington Commentary.* Edited by Phil Gailey. Kansas City, MO: Andrews McMeel, 2006.

McNamara, Robert S., with Brian VanDeMark. *In Retrospect: The Tragedy and Lessons of Vietnam.* New York: Times Books/Random House, 1995.

McPherson, Harry. *A Political Education: A Washington Memoir.* Austin: University of Texas Press, 1995.

McWhorter, Diane. *Carry Me Home: Birmingham, Alabama; The Climactic Battle of the Civil Rights Revolution.* New York: Simon & Schuster Paperbacks, 2013.

Meacham, Jon. *Destiny and Power: The American Odyssey of George Herbert Walker Bush.* New York: Random House, 2015.

Morris, Sylvia Jukes. *Price of Fame: The Honorable Clare Boothe Luce.* New York: Random House Trade Paperbacks, 2015.

Motley, Constance Baker. *Equal Justice Under Law: An Autobiography.* New York: Farrar, Straus and Giroux, 1998.

Mumford, Lewis. *The City in History: Its Origins, Its Transformations, and Its Prospects.* New York: Harcourt, Brace and World, 1961.

Nixon, Richard. *RN: The Memoirs of Richard Nixon.* New York: Simon & Schuster, 1990.

Norris, John. *Mary McGrory: The Trailblazing Columnist Who Stood Washington on Its Head.* New York: Penguin Books, 2016.

Offner, Arnold. *Hubert Humphrey: The Conscience of the Country.* New Haven, CT: Yale University Press, 2018.

Onassis, Jacqueline Kennedy, Arthur M. Schlesinger, and Michael R. Beschloss. *Jacqueline Kennedy: Historic Conversations on Life with John F. Kennedy.* New York: Hyperion, 2011.

Packer, George. *Blood of the Liberals.* New York: Farrar, Straus and Giroux, 2001.

Patterson, James T. *Brown v. Board of Education: A Civil Rights Milestone and Its Troubled Legacy.* Oxford: Oxford University Press, 2001.

Perlstein, Rick. *Before the Storm: Barry Goldwater and the Unmaking of the American Consensus.* New York: Nation Books, 2009.

Priestley, Justine. *By Gertrude Wilson: Dispatches of the 1960s, from a White Writer in a Black World.* Edgartown, MA: Vineyard Stories, 2005.

Pritchett, Wendell E. *Robert Clifton Weaver and the American City: The Life and Times of an Urban Reformer.* Chicago: University of Chicago Press, 2008.

Reston, James. *The Lone Star: The Life of John Connally.* New York: Harper and Row, 1989.

Risen, Clay. *A Nation on Fire: America in the Wake of the King Assassination.* Hoboken, NJ: John Wiley and Sons, 2009.

Rockefeller, Laurance. *Catalyst for Conservation.* Washington, D.C.: Island Press, 1997.

Rodota, Joseph. *The Watergate: Inside America's Most Infamous Address.* New York: William Morrow, 2018.

Rosen, Ruth. *The World Split Open: How the Modern Women's Movement Changed America.* New York: Penguin Books, 2006.

Rothman, Hal K. *LBJ's Texas White House: "Our Heart's Home."* College Station: Texas A&M University Press, 2001.

Rowley, Hazel. *Franklin and Eleanor: An Extraordinary Marriage.* New York: Farrar, Straus and Giroux, 2010.

Russell, Jan Jarboe. *Lady Bird: A Biography of Mrs. Johnson.* New York: Scribner, 2016.

Schlesinger, Arthur M., Jr. *Journals, 1952–2000.* New York: Penguin Press, 2007. Edited by Andrew Schlesinger and Stephen C. Schlesinger.

———. *Robert Kennedy and His Times.* Boston: Mariner Books, 2002.

Scobie, Ingrid Winther. *Center Stage: Helen Gahagan Douglas; A Life.* New Brunswick, NJ: Rutgers University Press, 1995.

Shaw, George Bernard. *Back to Methuselah,* act 1. In *Selected Plays with Prefaces.* Vol. 2. New York: Dodd, Mead and Company, 1948.

Shesol, Jeff. *Mutual Contempt: Lyndon Johnson, Robert Kennedy, and the Feud That Defined a Decade.* New York: W. W. Norton and Company, 1997.

Shillinglaw, Susan. *Carol and John Steinbeck: Portrait of a Marriage.* Reno: University of Nevada Press, 2013.

Shreve, David, and Robert David Johnson, eds. *The Presidential Recordings. Toward the Great Society.* Vol. 5. New York: W. W. Norton and Company, 2007.

Slevin, Peter. *Michelle Obama: A Life*. New York: Alfred A. Knopf, 2015.

Smith, Marie. *The President's Lady: An Intimate Biography of Mrs. Lyndon B. Johnson*. New York: Random House, 1964.

Smith, Sally Bedell. *Grace and Power: The Private World of the Kennedy White House*. New York: Random House, 2004.

Smith, Thomas G. *Stewart L. Udall: Steward of the Land*. Albuquerque: University of New Mexico Press, 2017.

Souder, William. *On a Farther Shore: The Life and Legacy of Rachel Carson*. New York: Crown Publishing Group, 2012.

Srodes, James. *On Dupont Circle: Franklin and Eleanor Roosevelt and the Progressives Who Shaped Our World*. New York: Counterpoint, 2012.

Stossel, Scott. *Sarge: The Life and Times of Sargent Shriver*. Washington, D.C.: Smithsonian Books, 2004.

Thomas, Helen. *Front Row at the White House: My Life and Times*. New York: Scribner, 2014.

Tye, Larry. *Bobby Kennedy: The Making of a Liberal Icon*. New York: Random House, 2016.

Udall, Stewart L. *The Quiet Crisis*. 14th ed. New York: Avon Books, 1964.

Unger, Irwin, and Debi Unger. *LBJ: A Life*. New York: John Wiley and Sons, 1999.

Updegrove, Mark. *Indomitable Will: LBJ in the Presidency*. New York: Skyhorse Publishing, 2012.

VanDeMark, Brian. *Road to Disaster: A New History of America's Descent into Vietnam*. New York: Custom House, 2018.

Ward, Barbara. *The Rich Nations and the Poor Nations*. New York: W. W. Norton and Company, 1961.

West, J. B., and Mary Lynn Kotz. *Upstairs at the White House*. New York: Warner Books, 1973.

White, Theodore. *The Making of the President, 1964*. New York: Harper Perennial Political Classics, 2010.

Williams, John. *America's Mistress: The Life and Times of Eartha Kitt*. New York: Quercus, 2014.

Williams, Terry Tempest. *The Hour of Land: A Personal Topography of America's National Parks*. New York: Picador, 2017.

Wilson, Robert H., Norman J. Glickman, and Laurence E. Lynn, Jr., eds. *LBJ's Neglected Legacy: How Lyndon Johnson Reshaped Domestic Policy and Government*. Austin: University of Texas Press, 2015.

Wiltse, Jeff. *Contested Waters: A Social History of Swimming Pools in America*. Chapel Hill: University of North Carolina Press, 2007.

Winks, Robin W. *Laurance S. Rockefeller: Catalyst for Conservation.* Washington, D.C.: Island Press, 1997.

Wright, Lawrence. *In the New World: Growing Up with America from the Sixties to the Eighties.* 2nd ed. New York: Vintage Books/Random House, 2013.

Yarrow, Peter, Noel Paul Stookey, and Mary Travers. *Peter Paul and Mary: Fifty Years in Music and Life.* Watertown, NY: Imagine, 2014.

Zelizer, Julian E. *The Fierce Urgency of Now: Lyndon Johnson, Congress, and the Battle for the Great Society.* New York: Penguin Books, 2015.

Zelman, Patricia G. *Women, Work, and National Policy: The Kennedy-Johnson Years.* Ann Arbor, MI: UMI Research Press, 1982.

Photo Credits

FRONTISPIECE: LBJ Library photo by Robert Knudsen

INSERT Page 1: (top) LBJ Library photo by Unknown, (middle) LBJ Library photo by Frank Muto, (bottom) Bettmann via Getty Images; page 2: (top) Bettmann via Getty Images, (middle) PhotoQuest via Getty Images, (bottom) LBJ Library photo by Yoichi Okamoto; page 3: (top) LBJ Library photo by White House Photo Office, (bottom) Hulton Archive via Getty Images; page 4: (top) Stan Wayman via Getty Images, (middle) Stan Wayman via Getty Images, (bottom) AP/Shutterstock; page 5: (top) Bettmann via Getty Images, (bottom) LBJ Library photo by Yoichi Okamoto; page 6: (top) LBJ Library photo by White House Photo Office, (bottom) LBJ Library photo by Yoichi Okamoto; page 7: (top) Jack Mitchel via Getty Images, (bottom) LBJ Library photo by Yoichi Okamoto; page 8: (top left) LBJ Library photo by Robert Knudsen, (top right and middle) LBJ Library photo by White House Photo Office, (bottom) LBJ Library photo by Yoichi Okamoto; page 9: (top) Bob Gomel via Getty Images, (bottom) Hechinger Company records, Historical Society of Washington, D.C.; page 10: (top) LBJ Library photo by Robert Knudsen, (middle) Lawrence Halprin Collection, The Architectural Archives, University of Pennsylvania, (bottom) LBJ Library photo by Yoichi Okamoto; page 11: (top) LBJ Library photo by Yoichi Okamoto, (middle) Bettmann via Getty Images, (bottom) LBJ Library photo by Robert Knudsen; page 12: (top, middle, and bottom right) LBJ Library photo by Yoichi Okamoto, (bottom left) LBJ Library photo by Robert Knudsen; page 13: (top) LBJ Library photo by White House Photo Office, (middle and bottom) LBJ Library photo by Yoichi Okamoto; page 14: (top) LBJ Library photo by Mike Geissinger, (bottom) LBJ Library photo by Yoichi Okamoto; page 15: (top) LBJ Library photo by Robert Knudsen, (bottom) LBJ Library photo by Frank Wolfe; page 16: (top) LBJ Library photo by Frank Wolfe, (middle) Warren K. Leffler, U.S. News & World Report magazine photograph collection, Library of Congress, LC-DIG-ppmsca-54478, (bottom) Greg Smith/AP/Shutterstock

Index

D

H

I

J

K

M

O

S

T

About the Author

Julia Sweig is an award-winning author of books on Cuba, Latin America, and American foreign policy. Her writing has appeared in *The New York Times, The Atlantic, The Washington Post, Financial Times, Los Angeles Times, Foreign Affairs, The Nation, The National Interest,* and Brazil's *Folha de São Paulo,* among other outlets. Her book *Inside the Cuban Revolution* won the American Historical Association's 2003 Herbert Feis Award for best book of the year by an independent scholar. She served as senior fellow at the Council on Foreign Relations for fifteen years and concurrently led the Aspen Institute's congressional seminar on Latin America for ten years. She holds a doctorate and master's degree from Johns Hopkins University and an undergraduate degree from the University of California, Santa Cruz. She is a nonresident senior research fellow at the LBJ School of Public Affairs at the University of Texas at Austin and lives with her family outside of Washington, D.C.